ABRAHAM KUYPER

A Centennial Reader

ABRAHAM KUYPER

A Centennial Reader

Edited by

James D. Bratt

William B. Eerdmans Publishing Company
Grand Rapids, Michigan / Cambridge, U.K.

The Paternoster Press
Carlisle

255 Jefferson Ave. S.E., Grand Rapids, Michigan 49503 /
P.O. Box 163, Cambridge CB3 9PU U.K.

First published 1998 jointly
in the United States by
Wm. B. Eerdmans Publishing Company
and in the U.K. by
The Paternoster Press,
P.O. Box 300, Carlisle, Cumbria CA3 0QS

Printed in the United States of America

03 02 01 00 99 98 7 6 5 4 3 2 1

Library of Congress Cataloging-in-Publication Data

Kuyper, Abraham, 1837-1920.
Abraham Kuyper : a centennial reader / edited by James D. Bratt.
p. cm.
Includes bibliographical references.
ISBN 0-8028-4321-2 (pbk. : alk. paper)
1. Calvinism. 2. Christian life. 3. Conduct of life.
I. Bratt, James D., 1949- . II. Title.
BX9422.5.K89 1998
284'.2 — dc21 97-45850
CIP

Paternoster Press ISBN 0-85364-922-7

Reproductions on pages 22, 49, 50, 52, 60, 68, 70, 128, 132, 157, 168, 229 (below), 307, 316, 345, 365 (above), 406, 443, 446, and 465 appear by permission and with the cooperation of the Historisch Documentatiecentrum voor het Nederlands Protestantisme (1800-heden), Vrije Universiteit, Amsterdam.

Reproductions on pages 25, 95, 207, 208, 229 (above), 272, 365 (below), and 407 are from *Dr. Kuyper in de Caricatuur* (Amsterdam: Van Holkema & Warendorf, 1909).

To my children

Peter, Suzanne, David, and Eric

Their heritage, my legacy

Contents

Culture and Education

Foreword

This book is a product of the Calvin Center for Christian Scholarship (CCCS), which was established at Calvin College in 1977. The purpose of the CCCS is to promote creative, articulate, and rigorous Christian scholarship that addresses important theoretical and practical issues.

The present volume results from the collaboration of James D. Bratt, Calvin College, and Dirk Th. Kuiper, Vrije Universiteit, Amsterdam, who received a grant from the CCCS to pursue this project. It was they who conceived of an anthology of Abraham Kuyper's writings, selecting from that great corpus those pieces most illuminating of his time and for our own. The year 1998 marks the centennial of Kuyper's delivering the Stone Lectures at Princeton Theological Seminary. It is fitting that an anthology of Kuyper's other work be presented in English for the first time at the centennial celebration.

As James Bratt writes in the Introduction, in his 1898 Stone Lectures at Princeton Kuyper was every inch the statesmanlike scholar. The genius of this volume is its broad coverage of the rest of Kuyper's diverse callings, interests, and — importantly — moods. These pieces "show a remarkable mind wrestling with an uncertain world," as Bratt says. The pieces selected are fully set in Kuyper's Dutch context, but they also address the timeless issues that concern all Christians in the modern world. Because Kuyper was both "part of his age and apart from it," his contribution to his own time can be historically admired, and his relevance for our time can be profitably engaged.

Grand Rapids
July 1997

Ronald A. Wells
Director, CCCS

Editor's Note on the Selections

Abraham Kuyper's bibliography runs to 223 items, including some multi-volume works and *not* including many of the columns he wrote as a political journalist. Gathering a representative selection from such a corpus is no easy task, especially since Kuyper's career spanned five decades and a dozen fields. I have aimed for a balanced sample from his early, late, and middle periods (using 1880 and 1895 as approximate divides) and across his entire range of interests, clustering these in three broad categories: Church and Theology, Politics and Society, and Culture and Education. I have favored shorter pieces that could be reproduced almost completely over extracts from longer works, not least because such allow a glimpse of Kuyper's whole meaning in compressed form. I have bypassed important works available in English translation at bookstores or major libraries: these include his Princeton *Lectures on Calvinism* (1898), the *Principles* [originally *Encyclopedia*] *of Sacred Theology* (1894), *The Work of the Holy Spirit* (1888-89), and his 1891 address "Christianity and the Social Question" (*The Problem of Poverty,* 1991). More of Kuyper's devotional writing has been translated into English than any other genre, so I have excluded such with two brief exceptions.

A few of the pieces included were translated into English a century ago but languish in obscure places; with the exception of *The South African Crisis,* they have all been translated anew for this volume. Whether this is their second or first appearance in English, I have edited all the scripts to produce texts that are as accessible as possible to a current readership while scrupulously respecting Kuyper's original meaning and without losing the variations in style that Kuyper played so well before different audiences. In particular I worked to eliminate some of the wordiness, run-on sentences, pronoun series, passive verbs, *it* and *there* expletives, and like afflictions native to Kuyper's Teutonic tongue. Similarly, I have introduced a number of paragraph breaks to comport with American standards. Without employing all the apparatus of critical editions, I have generally replicated the capitalization and subheads of the original texts and have placed any editorial additions of my own [in brackets]. I have occasionally bracketed a bit of Kuyper's Dutch as well to show a nuance or pun in the original. Ellipses indicate that some original material has been eliminated, usually a few words to avoid repetition, occasionally a substantial passage [duly summarized within brackets] not germane to the central argument.

Readers interested in exploring the context or implications of any of the selections should consult the Suggested Readings at the end of this volume.

Acknowledgments

It is a pleasure to salute the many people who have been important to the successful completion of this volume. Jon Pott and Charles Van Hof of Eerdmans Publishing Company pledged their support to this project years ago and have made good on their promise by expediting publication for the 1998 Kuyper-American centennial. Ronald Wells of the Calvin Center for Christian Scholarship gave timely suggestions for getting the work underway and showed patient trust en route, and Donna Romanowski of the Center office was generous with her counsel and hospitality. It is particularly appropriate that the CCCS fund a Kuyper volume, for the Center (and, behind it, Calvin College) carries on his legacy in a unique way. The Center deserves not only this formal acknowledgment but the gratitude of all the people it has supported in the cause of intentionally Christian scholarship. I am happy as well to repay an older debt to the Fulbright program for a grant that enabled on-site research on the Kuyper papers in Amsterdam.

As the headnotes to the various selections indicate, most of the original translations for this volume were executed by Reinder Bruinsma and John Vriend; I am grateful for their prompt and reliable work, and in addition for John Vriend's insights on Kuyper's use of Scripture. I also drew upon the labors of Walter Lagerwey, George Kamp, Hans van de Hel, and a noble British anti-imperialist from a hundred years ago, the Rev. A. E. Fletcher. My thanks to John Bolt of Calvin Theological Seminary and the *Calvin Theological Journal* and Wayne Bornholdt of Ex Libris Books for their permission to use material in *Evolution* and *Common Grace in Science,* respectively, that was originally published under their aegis. Several colleagues at Calvin College lent me expert aid: Kenneth Bratt, as good a brother as a scholar, on Greek and Roman references; Arie Leegwater and Clarence Menninga on scientific terms and context; David

Diephouse on all things German. Jan de Bruijn and Hans Seijlhouwer of the Historisch Documentatiecentrum voor het Nederlands Protestantisme at the Vrije Universiteit of Amsterdam have repeatedly helped this stumbling American around the Kuyper archives, while James McGoldrick of Cedarville College generously shared his Kuyper bibliography. All of this assistance went into a mix for which I bear final responsibility.

My final acknowledgment is the most important. Dirk Th. Kuiper of the Vrije Universiteit collaborated on this project from the start, giving good advice on selections and sparing me many errors of fact and interpretation. But he started my real education on Kuyper-in-context long before that. As a professor, scholar, practicing politician, and university administrator he is a latter-day model of Kuyper's many roles; happily for me, Dirk has much more patience and a better sense of humor. It is a pleasure to salute his knowledge, hospitality, and friendship.

Christmas 1997 James D. Bratt

Abraham Kuyper: His World and Work

Abraham Kuyper is a significant figure in the history of the Netherlands, an intriguing study in nineteenth-century cultural dynamics, and one of the most remarkable figures in the annals of Calvinism. He celebrated the Reformed founders, subscribed heart and soul to their teachings, and worked ceaselessly to restore their authority in an age that had either forgotten them or contradicted their word. From their theology, moreover, he extruded a whole worldview, and by that worldview he hoped to refashion the politics, scholarship, art, and social arrangements of his time. "Calvinism" was his soul and his system, the purest form of Christianity, the treasure of the past, the hope of the future. Thus, when Princeton University awarded him an honorary doctorate in 1898, Kuyper returned the favor by delivering his *Lectures on Calvinism,*[1] putting his whole vision in brief compass.

This anthology marks the centennial of that occasion by presenting some of Kuyper's other classic pieces in a mode and language comprehensible to an English-speaking audience of a significantly different era. That requires translation in more than the ordinary sense of the term. To begin with, Kuyper was a man of many voices. His preferred public sound was that of a baroque Dutch master evoking the Netherlands' golden age in support of his own program — and unintentionally making his meaning obscure to people not of his tongue or memory. He was multivocal too in the number of fields in which he spoke: church and theology, politics and society, culture and education, international affairs

1. The *Lectures* have gone through any number of editions; the one currently in print is that of William B. Eerdmans Publishing Co. (Grand Rapids, 1931).

and village life, the home, the self, the cosmos. Moreover, Kuyper was one of those rare intellectuals who actually led a popular movement. He thought it not enough to articulate a worldview but built the organizations needed to implement it — a newspaper, a complete school system, his country's first mass political party. He was at once a national-class scholar and stump-speaker extraordinaire, a writer of pious devotions and of ruthless polemics, conversant with Protestant scholastics, Parisian *philosophes,* German poets, and contemporary science.

In his Princeton lectures Kuyper played the role of the statesmanlike scholar. This anthology aims to recover the rest of him. The documents here represent all his genres: newspaper columns, sermons, party speeches, academic addresses. While they never lack apodictic note of the *Lectures,* they catch more of his nuances of thought, his pragmatic applications of principle, the contexts of his thinking, the sources off which he drew, the tensions and mixed-mindedness behind his professed consistency. They show a remarkable mind wrestling with an uncertain world, perhaps too hungry for security, yet (or therefore?) innovative with questions and daring in solutions — thus providing Christian believers of later times an example for their own cultural engagements.

Kuyper may be most pertinent on this score because of his deep ambivalence toward modernity. Early on he rejected the theological liberalism by which some leading lights in the Dutch Reformed Church tried to adjust the traditional confessions to a scientific-rational age. Instead, he championed the old doctrines all the more. He marked the dawn of deleterious time from 1789, denouncing the spirit of the French Revolution and much of its work. His first major address as cultural critic mourned the symptoms of social modernization and the future they betokened (see "Uniformity: The Curse of Modern Life"). His writings from the 1890s are often thick with *fin de siècle* fever; they complain of Europe's "atrophy," of the eclipse of the heroic, of technical sophistication and moral fecklessness. For his Calvinist religion and Dutch nationality, the seventeenth century was the golden age.

Yet Kuyper also steadfastly favored democratization, used new techniques to spread his message, had a keen eye for the latest possibilities in social organization, and told his followers again and again that their Calvinism needed to be updated, overhauled, translated out of its original idiom to address modern times. Reflex conservatives he liked even less than forthright modernists, and mere time-servers, the timid observers of precedent, he liked least of all. His ultimate purpose in the *Lectures,* to expand Calvinism from a dogmatic theology into a comprehensive worldview, was a thoroughly end-of-the-century project, as modern as the modernism he hoped to pit that Calvinism against. Against yearnings for a return to an integral society, for the preservation of the national church, for a single school system teaching everyone off the same page, he championed pluralism, diversification, and free choice. He loved the anonymity of the modern metropolis, to walk about London or Paris for hours on end. He affirmed all this of the modern world — yet feared for the demise of real personality, community, and traditional Christianity.

Kuyper thus was and was not a Protestant "fundamentalist."[2] He *was* in manner: a militant in all things, including his anti-Modernism; as adaptable in means as traditionalistic in message. In substance, however, he was *not*. He did not hold to Scriptural inerrancy as Fundamentalists today understand that term; he thought dispensational premillennialism (to the extent that he thought about it at all) a bizarre surrender of Christian responsibility; and he had a short, disastrous engagement with the Holiness movement at the birth of its Keswick phase (see *Perfectionism*). He was philosophically informed beyond an American fundamentalist's imagination, and furthermore drew off continental, particularly Romantic, writings rather than the Scots Common Sense Realism which shaped that fundamentalism's assumptions. He was deeply rooted in classic Reformation theology and tried to convey its full riches to his readers, a far cry from the short-list reductions of the American sort. He did not try to eradicate history but to grow from it. His review of Evolution (see below) achieved a scale of information and critique quite beyond that, say, of William Jennings Bryan (Kuyper's favored candidate, by the way, in the 1900 American presidential election).

Kuyper was an evangelical Christian, but with a difference.[3] He underwent a born-again experience that he was happy to share with others (see *Confidentially*), two signs of the evangelical spirit. He had no end of moral earnestness, promoted missions and evangelism, thought people drank too much alcohol, and used his terms in political office to curtail the practice. Every week for nearly fifty years he wrote a devotional column, and its contents were replete with the Bible-Christ-Cross triad of true evangelical piety. Yet Kuyper had a respect for institutions that the genuine evangelical, at least the twentieth-century American sort, does not share. Stranger still would be his systematic thinking, his archi-

2. The best treatment of the American movement is George M. Marsden, *Fundamentalism and American Culture* (New York: Oxford University Press, 1980). For comparative global accounts, see R. Scott Appleby and Martin E. Marty, eds., *Fundamentalisms Observed* (Chicago: University of Chicago Press, 1991).

3. For comparison, see Mark A. Noll et al., *Evangelicalism: Comparative Studies of Popular Protestantism in North America, the British Isles, and Beyond, 1700-1900* (New York: Oxford University Press, 1994); and David W. Bebbington, *Evangelicalism in Modern Great Britain: A History from the 1730s to the 1980s* (London: Unwin Hyman, 1989).

tectonic habit, his insistence on a consistent logic rooted in first principles and carried out until it comprehended every domain in life. Theology by the week, single-issue politics, this being religious but that not, Christ here but country there — Kuyper would have none of it. If his theory could sometimes be too wooden to practice, and if his practice built the theory more often than he might admit, the very inclination toward theory makes him distinct among the Evangelicals of his time and useful for Evangelical, and other, Christians today.

Finally, Kuyper could — and would — not have been a postmodernist, but he anticipated some varieties of that position in a striking way. He insisted (see *Common Grace in Science*) that the human subject be restored to the center of scholarship, that value-free knowledge did not amount to much, that particularity and pluralism be celebrated in society and encouraged by the state. He could join this piece of the sixteenth century to that bit of the nineteenth in a manner strange to original context but admirable for contemporary imagination. Yet through all this he insisted on the absolute truth of Christianity and the hard reality of the world as given. He anticipated that Western civilization would come to its apex in Berkeley, California, but most definitely did not have in mind the San Francisco of Michel Foucault.[4]

Kuyper may speak profitably to our time, in short, because he stands astride some of our basic categories. He certainly defied many terms of his own age, too, and tried to fashion new ones to fit his vision. That struggle, however, was steeped at every point by his time and place. We can best grasp his vision if we see how it emerged.

Kuyper's Inheritance

Kuyper was born in 1837 to a place that had seen better days.[5] This was true of his hometown of Maassluis, seaport to a merchant marine shrunken from its glory days and about to drop lower still. It was true of the Netherlands, which just seven years before had lost what was to become Belgium and, with that, its stab at restored political glory. It was

4. Unless, of course, the polymorphous sexuality of Foucaultian postmodernism is "the higher development" for which Kuyper saw "the shores of the Pacific reverently await[ing]"! See Kuyper, *Lectures on Calvinism,* p. 34, in the context of Jan Willem Schulte Nordholt, *The Myth of the West: America as the Last Empire* (Grand Rapids: Eerdmans, 1995).

5. The standard biography is P. Kasteel, *Abraham Kuyper* (Kampen: Kok, 1938). For additional references on his life and various domains of interest, see the appropriate sections of the bibliography in this volume.

true of the Dutch economy and society, which everyone perceived to have dipped slowly, steadily, and by now gravely from its power and verve of the seventeenth century. It was also true, some said, of the Dutch Reformed Church (*Nederlandse Hervormde Kerk* [NHK]) in which Kuyper's father, Jan Frederik, served as minister. This body still enjoyed the privileges of law and public funding, but the Restoration regime of King William I (reigned 1813-40), taking a page from Napoleon, had reorganized its governance in 1816 to subject church affairs to direct state regulation. The move aroused dissent in its own right; when, besides, it prescribed new liturgical standards and tolerated theological liberalism in podium and pulpit, the dissension increased until it gave birth in 1834 to a separate free church.[6] Kuyper was born under a secessionist sign.

Kuyper's father was not troubled by this departure nor, much, by the issues that gave rise to it. The NHK had been good to him. It gave him a career quite above his father's broom shop and a status he enjoyed. His vocation was genuine, too, for Jan Frederik early on showed interest in religious matters and got work translating tracts for an English evangelist, who in turn arranged for the lad's theological studies. Thus the Kuyper family came into touch with the *Réveil,* a Continental revival of Protestantism initiated by British and Swiss-French Evangelicals, spread through the old Reformed territories along the Rhine, and linked at least in concept with the Lutheran resurgence in Germany. The *Réveil* was fit for a Romantic and Restorationist age: full of feeling for the experience of Christ, stretching hands across old doctrinal divisions, morally earnest, conservative in politics, yet concerned for the suffering and afflicted. It made Christianity plausible again, even popular, among the young and cultivated who a generation before might have gone rationalist or revolutionary but now found in inward fulfillment, in spiritual depth, in charity and fellow-feeling a better option than the gods who had failed.[7]

Yet the *Réveil* also set off some serious thinking about what Christianity meant in a post-Revolutionary age shaped, willy nilly, by the Enlightenment. In Dutch circles the answer was threefold. As some pious youths matured, they decided that so affective a faith had little salience for public or intellectual issues which should therefore be measured by rational standards. This was the Modernist option. Others tried mediation, interweaving Christian spirit and modern fact to create a meaningful

6. The standard history on the NHK as a whole is A. J. Rasker, *De Nederlandse Hervormde Kerk vanaf 1795* (Kampen: Kok, 1974); see also its bibliographical references. The Secession of 1834 is covered in chapter 5.

7. Rasker, *NHK,* chapter 6; M. Elizabeth Kluit, *Het Protestantse Réveil in Nederland en daarbuiten, 1815-1865* (Amsterdam: Paris, 1970).

inward and moral outward world. In the Netherlands these comprised the "Ethical" school. A third party were strict Confessionalists who judged modern times by classic Reformation standards, not vice versa, and who abhorred the Revolution and all its works.[8] Such were the options Abraham Kuyper faced in his formative years as university student and new pastor. He would take up each in turn before settling upon the third.

Kuyper's youth reached beyond church and school, however. His childhood play on the wharves of Middelburg, port of the old Dutch East Indies Company, gave him his global eye and zest for travel — not to mention a nostalgia for Dutch mastery of the seas. His undergraduate passion was literature, manifest later in his rhetorical command, experienced then, it would seem, by deep immersion in Shakespeare and the German *Sturm und Drang*. His third passion was politics, even though it had little luster at the time.[9] The new monarchy of 1813 notwithstanding, power in Dutch society remained with the commercial elite that had been running things for two hundred years. Some were sanctified by old-enough money to count as regents, others were just smug or hungry, but none had a real vision of government, much less an innovative sociopolitical imagination. They suffered the loss of Belgium in 1830. They did little with the colonial Indies but tap the bottom line. They did nothing to promote industrialization, despite the ambitions of the "merchant-king" William I. Their sloth might have kept the country immune to the Revolutions of 1848, but King William II, whether from fear or opportunism, took the occasion to call upon a group that could see a different future.

These were the Liberals, "doctrinaires" as the regents called them by virtue of their book-learning, but supple enough to weave the chastened commitments of 1789 with strands from British Whiggery into a garment tailor-made for the Netherlands. Such was the inspiration of Johan R. Thorbecke in the new Constitution of 1848.[10] It created a genuine constitutional monarchy, spreading sovereignty between the monarch and the States-General. It divided the latter's legislative functions between the First or Upper Chamber, representing the provinces, and the Second or Lower Chamber, which was directly elected by the

8. Rasker treats the first two schools in, respectively, chapters 9 and 10-12 of *NHK*, the third in chapters 6-7.

9. I have relied on E. H. Kossmann, *The Low Countries, 1780-1940* (Oxford: Clarendon, 1978) for a general narrative of Dutch history. On the circumstances in this paragraph, see pp. 179-95.

10. Kossmann, *Low Countries*, pp. 190-95, 208-10.

people. The effective agent of government would be a Cabinet formally commissioned by the monarch but after 1868 in practice responsible to the Second Chamber. Of particular moment for Kuyper's career, the new system made education a matter of national, not local, policy.

The Constitution was careful enough not to offend too many, although some objected to it in principle. Orthodox Protestant or "Antirevolutionary" leaders like Guillaume Groen van Prinsterer and Isaac da Costa protested its neglect of religious foundations and transcendent authority, a weakness they thought would accelerate a parliamentary system's inevitable derogation of genuine right to factional interest. Their voice was not much heard. The real protest came against Thorbecke's next moves. First, the franchise was so restricted by property qualifications that fewer participated under the new regime than under the old. Second, in April 1853 he proposed allowing the Roman Catholics to reintroduce their hierarchy.[11] The Protestant populace exploded with bishop-baiting and paeans to ancestral liberties; the archbishop came back to Utrecht anyway; the Thorbecke government fell; the Conservatives got a decade to run the government, though they did not change Thorbecke's church policy. Of greatest long-term consequence, the "April movement" put religion — from concrete questions of church and state to identity issues of faith and nation — back on the political agenda. Kuyper was part of its frenzy by heritage. His genius would be to break with that reflex, to reshuffle confessional loyalties, to link the religious question to that of the franchise, and in that way to turn the Liberals' Constitution to transliberal ends.

Education and Conversion

Kuyper entered university at Leiden in 1855, two years after the April movement; he published his first pamphlet in 1867.[12] The twelve years in between were definitive for his faith and career. As an undergraduate Kuyper worked exceedingly hard, bemoaned boring lectures, and chafed at the short string, financial and patriarchal, that forced him to live at home. On the other hand, the professors he liked, he adored. The one he liked best in graduate school was J. H. Scholten, the best systematic theologian in the country and the foremost Modernist. Kuyper later

11. Kossmann, *Low Countries*, pp. 194 (franchise), 275-83 (April movement).

12. Two contrasting pictures of Kuyper's early life are given in George Puchinger, *Abraham Kuyper: De jonge Kuyper, 1837-1867* (Franeker: Wever, 1987); and Johan Stellingwerff, *Kuyper en de VU* (Kampen: Kok, 1987), chapters 1 and 2.

recalled applauding a lecture that denied the physical resurrection of Christ, but it is not clear that he ever subscribed fully to the Modernist gospel. He certainly did absorb Scholten's example of bold undertakings and his method of principial consistency — that is, of assuming a fixed starting point and building upon it logically and fearlessly. He also followed Scholten back to the founding documents of the Reformed tradition in search of its first principles and in admiration of its iron spirit. All these qualities — the energy, the ambition, the Reformation zeal — came together in the prize-winning paper he wrote for a competition sponsored by the University of Groningen in 1859. Kuyper completed the project, which became the core of his doctoral dissertation, in less than a year at age twenty-two, while simultaneously wooing by mail and rail the seventeen-year-old daughter of a Rotterdam stockbroker, Johanna Schaay. When he tried, besides, to complete his comprehensive exams on the pre-essay schedule and with honors, he broke down and had to go on vacation for six months. The episode was a preview of things to come.

Clearly, Kuyper had significant scholarly potential, but he also faced a future of parish ministry. He felt the rub and said so in his voluminous correspondence with Jo, now his fiancée. She responded by giving him a novel that cut through to both of his afflictions: his ambition and his religious uncertainty. As he recalled some ten years later (in *Confidentially*), *The Heir of Redclyffe* (1853) leveled so piercing a "judgment on my own ambitions and character" as to leave his heart "devastated." At the same time, the hero's funeral rites in the Church of England conveyed the comforts available from a pure "mother-church" that was there to guide each step of her pilgrims' way. The church did not have to be a second-rate career; it could be the road to salvation.

Charlotte Yonge, author of *The Heir of Redclyffe*, came right out of John Henry Newman's Oxford Movement and wrote her book in its sacramental, high-church light. Kuyper's ecclesiology would take a different form, though no less intensity or import, during his 1863-67 pastorate in the country town of Beesd. Kuyper believed again in Scripture and the supernatural, so Modernism was no longer an option. The mediating Ethical school was more plausible since its esteem for religious experience certainly reverberated with the awakening the new pastor had just undergone. So Kuyper reapplied himself to the theologians he had heard about at Leiden: Dutch Ethicals like J. H. Gunning; their Swiss guide, Alexandre Vinet; their German paragon, Karl Immanuel Nitzsch. But none of them satisfied, Kuyper recalled, because none of them had an adequate doctrine of the church. Yet the voices who did win him had no such doctrine either. These were the "pious malcontents" of Beesd, the fringe dissenters so enamored of the Calvinist classics and so insulted by the contrast they heard at church that they forsook Sunday services and gathered with each other in small groups instead.

This old conventicle mode of Dutch pietism was a strangely sectarian path for someone searching for "mother church." The pietists' theology held part of the answer. Theirs was predestinarian Calvinism of the purest water, "sovereign grace" communicated by unconditional election, absolutely sealed if not transparently certain. For Kuyper, it turns out, their psychology was equally to the point. It was in the rock of divine decree, rather than the high-church rock of St. Peter, where he found the "shelter . . . which, being founded on the rock and being hewn from the rock of thought, laughs at every storm. . . . [H]ere I discovered the foundations which, banning all doubt, permitted the edifice of faith to be constructed in a completely logical style. . . ." Scholten's Modernist consistency found fulfillment in confessional orthodoxy, and Kuyper had the absolute certainty he always craved. So he said. So he repeated, often enough to betray some lingering anxiety. Kuyper's love of system and consistency thus came partly from his cultural milieu but partly from his own personality. His love of intellectual combat, the militant tone and imagery that saturate his pages, reflected to his last days the war of the spirits fought in his own soul during its formative years.

Church Affairs

Kuyper happened to begin his career in the decade that was the most decisive of modern Dutch history, the 1860s.[13] Politically, "the half-way solutions, the policy of adaptation, evasion, and delay practised by the 'higher classes,' the blurring of issues by the moderates, these were no longer acceptable." Internationally, colonial questions regarding the Netherlands Indies spelled trouble at a distance; the unification of Germany and Italy raised threats nearby. Industrialization would finally begin at the end of the decade and with it a rapid process of differentiation that multiplied the number of interest groups and voluntary associations in society. Custom and local hierarchy broke down as the orbit of life and mode of control, inviting new grids to replace them. The signals of these tides went up as Kuyper left Beesd for his next pastorate (1867-70) in

13. Kossmann so characterizes the decade in *Low Countries,* p. 283, the source also of the quotation in the next sentence. For the period in general see pp. 210, 287-309, and Dirk Th. Kuiper, "Het Nederlandse protestantisme in ontwikkelingsperspectief (1860-1940)," in Jan de Bruijn, ed., *Een land nog niet in kaart gebracht* (Amsterdam: Passage, 1987), pp. 1-10.

Utrecht. In 1867 regulations for church elections were altered so that consistories (congregational boards) would no longer be self-perpetuating but subject to congregational vote. In 1868 the long-standing parliamentary coalition between Liberals and Catholics broke up, the latter's gratitude for 1853 no longer compensating for the former's secular agenda. In 1869 the first Radical-Liberal was elected to the Second Chamber and the Conservative caucus entered its years of dissolution. If things were pliable in church and state, the reduction of statutory and economic restrictions on voluntary associations and the popular press supplied new tools for the right sculptor.

Kuyper entered the lists in 1867 with a brochure urging the laity to use the new church law on behalf of orthodoxy.[14] This combination of new measures with old commitments was typical, and his broader insight about democratization proved true: the commons was more orthodox than the elite. Dutch Modernism never recovered from this loss of privilege; besides, some of its leading ministers now began to leave the church for the reasons of intellectual honesty that had turned them liberal in the first place (see *Modernism*). But Kuyper's church battles were just beginning. His Utrecht pastorate went badly because he insisted on pushing the orthodox offensive hard and by new methods; the conservatives-by-custom, not conviction, that he saw in power there resisted (see *Conservatism and Orthodoxy*). He quickly moved on to Amsterdam (1870-74), where a working-class/shopkeeper audience gave him a better reception. At the same time he switched his attack from theological deviation to the church's administrative system. Indeed, this received his most intense invective. The Synodical Bureaus of the NHK were at once the symbol of state intrusion into church affairs, the open channel by which errors came into its midst, and the irresponsible time-servers who avoided decisions when possible and made them, when necessary, in their own interests. Quite simply, if the church had been prostituted, the Bureaus were the pimps.

Though Kuyper did not use that language himself, the imagery is not too strong. It also recalls the link between his church politics and his conversion dream of a pure "mother." The church question for Kuyper involved salvation — the proper nurture of each child of God and the maximum possible redemption of the broader world. Yet this did not fit smoothly with his decretal theology. For Kuyper God saved the elect from eternity, publicly manifested that fact at their baptism, and began the regeneration of each individual privately, by the direct, unmediated operation of the Holy Spirit. All those so redeemed constituted the "church

14. *Wat moeten wij doen . . . ?* (Culemborg: Blom, 1867).

organic," the church Kuyper truly valued, the body of believers at work every day, in all their capacities, as testaments of God's glory in the world. The "church institute," on the other hand — all the public assemblies, buildings, officers, and necessary instruments — was not the high-church channel of salvation but a means to those larger ends. Kuyper regarded it as a crucial means nonetheless. Only if the church-institute's word was pure and strong, its ministry undefiled by error or half-heartedness, could the church organic be made vital for its mission in society and culture. The church was Jesus' light to the world (see *Common Grace*); neither saint nor sinner had a chance if its windows were clouded by synodical soot.

In 1874 Kuyper took emeritation from the formal ministry to go into politics, but he retained a seat as elder on the Amsterdam consistory. From there he helped organize a national network to build up the ranks of the orthodox in pulpit and council room. The jockeying continued until 1885, when the Amsterdam consistory took the step that brought the issue to a crisis. They passed a statute assigning church properties to the orthodox majority in case of schism and were immediately suspended from office. Kuyper's followers seized key church properties; polemical brochures fired the ecclesiastical skies; hearings were called, charges exchanged, appeals made, and the suspensions formally upheld. (See *"It Shall Not Be So Among You."*) Kuyper found himself outside the NHK "in Doleantie," "mourning" and "aggrieved" by its faithlessness. Some 10 percent of its members, parts of several hundred congregations, had come with him. This was not the reformation of the church he had hoped for, but it was all the reformation he would get. In 1892 his movement joined the churches descendent from the secession of 1834 to form the *Gereformeerde Kerken in Nederland* (GKN).[15]

Politics

Meanwhile, Kuyper had been giving more attention to politics. His election to the Second Chamber in 1874 came at an opportune time for realignment.[16] The Catholics were floating free, the Conservatives were bankrupt, and the Liberals were splitting into three factions in the wake of Thorbecke's death (1872). Industrialization was forcing all parties to rethink their notions of individual rights, social well-being, and the

15. On the Doleantie and its background, see Rasker, *NHK*, chapters 12 and 13.

16. For Dutch society and politics in the 1880s and '90s, see Kossmann, *Low Countries*, pp. 310-61.

government's obligations toward each. Then the religious question took a new and intimate turn with the Liberals' attempt to drive religious schools out of the market so as to put their stamp on culture and society as they already had on politics. Kuyper entered this melee eagerly. He began publishing a daily paper, *De Standaard,* in 1872, organized a national Anti-School Law League in 1873, took to the floor of the Second Chamber with facts and fancy oratory about every question before it — and stayed up late at night to prepare for the next day. In 1875 he sought relief from his assorted strains by repairing to Brighton, England, to attend meetings organized by American evangelist Robert Pearsall Smith, an entrepreneur — as his wife, Hannah Whitall, was a theoretician — of the "higher life" of Christian holiness (see *Perfectionism*). Kuyper caught the spirit of the occasion. He served communion to once-warring French and Prussian soldiers. He experienced the inward warmth of "consecration." He dashed home with yet another cause to organize. By February 1876 he had collapsed into the second breakdown of his life; this time it took fifteen months to recuperate, at Nice and Lago di Como.

Kuyper returned more modest in his spiritual claims and more focused as to the roles he would play. He gave up political office to work, most successfully, as a journalist and organizer. He mounted a petition campaign in 1878 against the Liberals' education bill, collecting 305,000 signatures in three months in an unprecedented example of popular mobilization. (The voting population was some 160,000 at the time.) When the king signed the bill into law anyway, Kuyper knit the petitioners into a permanent organization dedicated to building a separate system of Christian elementary schools; used the same lists to create an association for Reformed higher education; and in the same year, 1879, brought the names and the causes together in the Antirevolutionary Party (ARP), the country's first truly modern, mass-based political organization. It knit local and regional clubs into a national federation coordinated by a central committee, chaired by Kuyper and committed to a common platform, which he wrote in several hundred pages. All this took but two years and gave his movement a lasting foundation.

Ten years later the ARP was in the Cabinet presenting a bill to subsidize religious schools with one-third of their costs; step by step that share increased to the point of full equity in 1917.[17] But Kuyper's was no single-cause politics. He also pushed for franchise extension, which proceeded right along with school-financing reform to reach universal male (1917) and female (1919) standards. The synchrony between the

17. Kossmann, *Low Countries,* pp. 301-2, 354. On franchise extension, see pp. 350-51, 359-61, 510, 555.

two causes confirmed the insights Kuyper originally had about class sympathies in the church: the more the "little people" could vote, the better the orthodox cause fared (see *Our Instinctive Life*). But his commitment was principled too. Kuyper's support for franchise extension in the 1890s, together with his ardent words for a social democracy at the Christian Social Congress of 1891, caused a split in the ARP that took out almost half its leadership and some of its rank-and-file. The division brought Kuyper back into office as a member of the Second Chamber in 1894, whence he rose to prime minister in the second Antirevolutionary-Catholic Cabinet (1901-5). Even though his term was no great success, designing the coalition that turned Calvinism's age-old enemy into its long-range partner was a strategic masterstroke and a recognition of changed times. Kuyper knew confessors of Christ when he saw them, knew that Catholics qualified and that liberal humanists did not, their Protestant pedigree notwithstanding.

This reversal of a historic enmity, if admirable, seems strange in a man who reiterated a commitment to "Christian-historical" principles. So do the democratic proclivities of one who ever insisted upon being "Antirevolutionary." Since the disjunction might pose as great a barrier to understanding today as it did for political success back then, Kuyper's particular objections need to be heard. He disliked three things about 1789: that it displaced divine transcendent with human rational authority; that it substituted ideological schemes for patterns of historical development; and that it shattered social bonds by valorizing the individual and the ethics of self-interest. The first two Kuyper had inherited as the special emphases of his political godfather, Groen van Prinsterer; over time he diminished the second note, perhaps because his own cause was so ideological, and played up the third. Respect for history did not mean locking on to everything that had come into being; it meant adapting long patterns of historical character and conduct to the signs of the times. Thus, the "Liberalism" Kuyper fought does not necessarily equal "liberalism" now; in fact, with its devotion to free-market individualism it shared much with what passed for "Conservatism" in the age of Reagan and Thatcher. Further, the Conservatism he saw was less a well-wrought alternative to the Liberal program than a habit of those accustomed to power and status. As Kuyper predicted, the Conservatives of the 1870 breakup who lacked religious conviction sidled over to the Liberals, their objection being not to humanism but to the class of the humans in charge (see *Maranatha*).

Kuyper's positive commitments can be better read in his own words below than summarized here, but a few interpretive keys may aid understanding. First, Kuyper was always corporately minded. He did not begin his thinking from individual rights but from social righteousness, from mutual obligation for the hearty functioning of the whole. He was a fulsome admirer of the Puritan commonwealth (see *Calvinism: Source and Stronghold of Our Constitutional Liberties*), radically though it played with history, revolutionary (it was not "Revolutionary" because it believed in God) as it worked in government. The rise of the centralized state in his own time bothered him less by its threat to property than by its clogging of the social arteries; the rights he upheld against it were those of social bodies, not of individuals. Kuyper could take an interesting view on the "social question" of his day, therefore, by insisting that labor be as well organized as capital, with compulsory arbitration used to resolve their differences (see *Manual Labor*). If this required the expansion of state powers, so be it; justice and order might require bold command.

Most of the time, however, Kuyper took an adverse view of the state. Government was to see to structural balances but otherwise let the free play of society proceed. And he was quite willing to use state power to maintain order, as he demonstrated while prime minister by calling up troops to suppress a railroad strike in 1903. That decision probably would have been duplicated by every party except the Socialists, but the energy and moralisms with which Kuyper pursued the case left bitter resentment. Gender issues troubled him as well. Much as he supported men's, he opposed women's suffrage for its "individualistic" premises. More exactly, he advocated a universal household franchise on the view that the home, not the individual, was the foundational unit of society. Those (likely widowed) women who were heads of households might vote, therefore, but females not so afflicted would have virtual representation in their male head. Kuyper's progressiveness did not cross the color line either, for he shared the late nineteenth-century assumption that European hegemony was inevitable, benevolent, and racially endowed. His polemics on *The South African Crisis* are most striking for the few — terrified, and terrifying — words he gives to the black majority.

But even a duly reeducated Kuyper might argue that these were not the issues of his time, that white male political equality and a postconfessional state were. Kuyper wanted to reduce not only class but religious privilege in formal public institutions, and he argued such from a Christian social perspective. Not, therefore, on the view that religion is a private individual matter; nor in hopes that a civil religion would absorb particular faith traditions. Just the opposite: precisely because Christianity had so much to contribute to public life, not least as a corrective to the idols of the tribe, it should make its way as a vital faith instead of as a tool of the state. Kuyper did not want a naked public square but a crowded one, each confessional grouping taking its portion of public space but none of them having an official advantage. This was pluralism under secularization but not secularism, positive conviction without imposed belief.

Culture

Kuyper opened his career in the church and closed it in government; in between (1880-1901) he taught theology at a university he helped to found. He had real ability in his discipline but also had to speak to higher education as a whole and liked to speak to the state of European culture. Several of those addresses are included in this collection, requiring only a few comments here.

First, many traits of Kuyper's politics apply to his cultural commentary too: the love of free development, the contempt for Reaction and Revolution, the pluralistic structures, the passion for first principles. This last was a consequence of the very assumption of principialism — that actions are ideas in the flesh and social systems the precipitate of collective convictions. For Kuyper, then, the real Revolution behind the French one came in the Enlightenment's turn to autonomous reason and self-sufficient natural law. The course of nineteenth-century thought was a poignant attempt to recover human feeling on the one hand and human dignity on the other, an effort that failed because it failed to break with the root assumption of its predecessor. Kuyper was therefore a critic of cultural liberalism in every form; at the same time he applauded the unfolding and refinement of the possibilites inherent in the created order. This being a created order, its proper development required a proper recognition of God's authority over human thought, of God's glory as the object of human effort, of God's prescribed limits for human action. But such "proper development" lay close to God's own heart; better, it was a tracing of his very mind (see *Common Grace in Science*). For reasons positive and negative, in sum, Kuyper saw cultural work, particularly first-order reflection upon the assumptions and parameters of that work, as the most pressing and promising calling the church faced.

Two theological points were crucial to this task. The first was the antithesis, the antagonism that must obtain between Christian and non-Christian views of the world owing to the contrary commitments that inspired them. Kuyper recognized that all people live in a common creation, and he repeatedly listed the common procedures all parties follow in the scholarly enterprise. But his emphasis fell on the different directions such procedures would serve, the *un*common worlds people build by their distinct assumptions. For Kuyper the key differences were religious; hence the stakes were ultimate and conduct had to be militant.

Yet the war was to proceed by words only and was to be scrupulously respectful of public space; that is, Christians might not try to drive out or absorb all other voices but might only profess their own knowledge from their own institutional base. Such was the lesson of history but also the consequence of common grace, the other hinge of Kuyper's theology. By God's bountiful good pleasure non-Christians excelled in certain fields, and all their efforts had excellent points. None of this might be squelched, out of respect for God's providence in the world. All of it had to be appreciated, so that the pious might come to respect real learning. Common grace gave the saints incentive and the sinner safe passage.

Weaving these themes together shows how Kuyper was part of his age and apart from it. His cultural commentary works by constant wrestling with German Idealism, borrowing its procedures, denying its claims. From beginning to end, Kuyper insisted on God's real world while fully allowing for variable human constructions within it. His attacks on evolutionary Monism came from and helped build an equally comprehensive, consistent Christian system. His thrill and alarms at the conquest of nature, at imperial forays into Africa, at the spread of popular initiative and the explosion of knowledge — these he shared with his century. His effort to orient all of them by the Word of God he shared with his Calvinist forebears. Kuyper's examples thus come to us in the same way that he suggested Calvin's examples had come to him in the nineteenth century: not for slavish imitation, far less as binding revelation, but for instruction, warning, and inspiration in our own efforts to view the world whole and to address it with a creative faith.[18]

18. *Lectures on Calvinism,* p. 171.

BEGINNINGS

Uniformity: The Curse of Modern Life

When Kuyper delivered this speech on 22 April 1869, he was known to a few scholars for his work on the Polish Reformer Jan Laski [à Lasco] and had caused something of a stir with his first pamphlets on church reform. Now he staked a wider claim as a cultural commentator. *Uniformity* was something of an inaugural address, then, and was delivered, appropriately, from the stage of the Odeon theater in Amsterdam.

Kuyper's speech on this occasion was the fourth and final in a series of lectures sponsored by a Christian young men's club during the winter of 1868-69. The people in his audience he could therefore expect to be fairly cultivated, heirs to the nation's Christian past — more particularly to the evangelical *Réveil* that had given rise to the society in 1851. Their political affiliation was generically Christian Historical, and Kuyper appealed to the same, but he was just as concerned with spelling out issues for the future as reaffirming loyalties from the past. Thus he closes on the causes that would last him a lifetime: the free church, sphere sovereignty ("a distinct form for a distinct life"), and Christian schools.

Uniformity is virtually unique in Kuyper's corpus for its display of the whole man in brief compass. The habits of mind it shows are a virtual catalogue of Romanticism. Kuyper extols the wild over the tamed, the unplanned over the calculated, the free-forming over the manufactured, the unique individual over the standardized type, and above all, the organic over the mechanical. His celebration of variety, diversity, and multiformity echoes the medieval — and anticipates the postmodern. On other occasions Kuyper could sound scholastic, and he always showed a passion for order, but the Romantic authors of his youth and the philosophical Idealism with which he long wrestled obviously left a deep imprint.

In that spirit Kuyper takes on two spectres. The one he addresses at length would later be labeled modernization: the course of technical innovation in production and communication that would make the world urban, industrial, and calculated. Given the affirmations Kuyper could make of such "progress," it is good to remember that antimodernists have often indicted the process precisely in the terms Kuyper used, for spreading the "curse of uniformity." The present piece thus shows the side of Kuyper haunted by the "iron train" (p. 33) of modernity, but its last pages also foreshadow how he would construct and run a Calvinistic car on its tracks — the project to which he devoted most of his career and which made him complicit, perhaps, in the forces he decried.

Kuyper's other fear does not get explicit treatment here but looms over the whole speech — the national unification of Germany and Italy that dominated and dramatically altered European politics in the 1860s. The German venture was more menacing for being closer by and for breathing an unapologetic spirit of "blood and iron"; but the Italian case was promoted by France, the Netherlands' other neighbor and most recent (1795) invader. The drive toward unification would climax in the Franco-Prussian War a year after Kuyper's address; but to him, the question of which country would win was less important than the ruthlessness of their means and the consolidated power that was their end. His concluding paean to Dutch distinctiveness must be understood in this light. So also his hope in the unity that God, and God only, was working over time.

The text, reprinted here virtually entire, was originally published by H. de Hoogh, Amsterdam, 1869, and was translated by John Vriend.

LADIES AND GENTLEMEN, I believe I am within the scope of this lecture series if this evening I ask you to consider with me, from a Christian-historical viewpoint, the false uniformity of our age. This phenomenon is of great interest precisely because the sustained drive of our age toward uniformity is such a dubious feature — I dare say, the *curse* — of modern life. To persuade you of this conviction I will obviously have to start with the rather abstract question: what do I mean by false uniformity? Then I will have to demonstrate from experience and the observable facts of life that it really dominates our time. And after I have stated the reasons why I dare call it a curse, I will finally speak to the practical question of what our policy as Christians should be in fighting that phenomenon in church and state. . . .

I

First, then, the rather abstract question. What do I mean by "false uniformity?" In this connection, ladies and gentlemen, I ask you to grant me this one thesis: that unity is the ultimate goal of all the ways of God. Yes, life rustles and glitters all around us in an endless profusion of new forms and configurations, and the immense number of phenomena floating by on the stream of life are all intrinsically different. Life often presents itself to us as an enormous muddle, a vast multicolored miscellany of things in which we look in vain for unity. But the deep meaning of the whole of divine revelation is that the ways of God lead from all this diversity toward unity, out of this chaos toward order. It tells us that one day by his will all dissonances will dissolve into harmony. This comes across every time Revelation speaks to us of a unified kingdom established by our King, a kingdom of heaven all-encompassing in glory. All the movements of Revelation culminate in that unity as their ultimate goal. For eighteen centuries now the Christian mind has worked to establish that imperial unity by breaking down every dividing wall. And that divine ideal will only be reached when Christ's prayer on the eve of his death is fulfilled for all of earth and heaven: "So that they may be one as we are one, Father, as you are in me and I am in you, so may they become completely one!" [cf. John 17:22, 23].

You do not expect me to defend the statement that unity, the only ideal in which our thinking can find rest, is the ultimate goal of the ways of our God. Rather, I ask your full attention for this, which takes us immediately into the heart of our subject: the world in its sinful endeavor has arrogated this same ideal for itself. The world, too, strives for unity. You understand what I mean by that sinful striving of the world. You, with me, recognize sin not just as a developmental phase in an otherwise healthy human life but as the degeneration of that life. You, with me, recognize that as a result of sin not only the life of the individual but the life of humanity as a whole has taken an abnormal direction. Thus we are not just dealing with isolated sinful facts but with a power of sin that controls sinful life in all its expressions. All sin has a common face, bears the stamp of a common origin, shows a well-ordered coherence in its manifestations and a regular development in its progress. In a word, there is a *history* of sin. All through the centuries the family of sinners weaves at the self-same garment for which no one of us has strung the loom.

Kuyper as a 35-year-old minister in Amsterdam (1872), beginning his rise to national fame.

We here and those on the other side of the earth are together building the same unholy temple but do so according to specifications we do not know, following a plan that is not our own. Either you must leave that momentous phenomenon completely unexplained or yield to what Scripture has taught you concerning Satan: that there is a thinking mind, a personal being, whose unity of plan and conception is manifest in that life of sin and whose mighty but disastrous endeavor is served by all humanity in its pursuit of sin.

To me, then, that dynamic drive of sin is no rhetorical phrase but hard reality. And as its ideal, I say, that hard reality has opted for the same unity we always find as the ultimate idea in the revelation of Scripture. Sin always acts so: it puts the stamp of God's image on its counterfeit currency and misuses its God-given powers to imitate God's activity. Itself powerless, without creative ideas of its own, sin lives solely by plagiarizing the ideas of God. Having estranged the nations from God, it can hold out to them no other dream than the vision unveiled by God's prophets . . . a kingdom modeled on the kingdom of our Lord, an imperial unity on the model of the unity that God wills. . . .

All history bears witness to this fact and supports my assertion. Was not that striving for unity, that hankering to be one people and to have one language, majestically put down in the collapse and rubble of the tower of Babel? What is the history of Eastern antiquity but a series of restless, bloody attempts to rebuild by the power of the sword the unity shattered on the plain of Shinar? Have the mighty pharaohs of Egypt or the rulers of Lydia, has Nebuchadnezzar or Cyrus ever followed any other design than one aiming to establish a world empire? And when history's center of gravity shifted from Asia to Europe, the same political agenda moved to our continent and came to self-conscious, energetic manifestation in the careers of Alexander the Great of Macedonia and the Caesars of Rome. Nor was it otherwise in the Middle Ages. The governing dream of its whole history was of *one* holy Roman Empire, with all Europe's rulers gathered as vassals around the throne of Germany's emperor. Later, both in Madrid and Vienna the ambition of the Hapsburgs opened a new age with a drive toward the same end. France's great king [Louis XIV] revived the plan a century later. Possessed by the same maniacal dream Napoleon, too, sought to complete his world empire. Indeed, in our day the same spirit of Caesarism has revived now that the man of "blood and iron" has seen his master plan succeed and the emperor of France openly ventures to say: "only the mightiest states can still maintain themselves; the time of small nations is over."[1]

The similarity between God's plan and that of the world is therefore undeniable. . . . But as with counterfeit currency, the similarity is only in name. In God's plan vital unity develops by internal strength precisely from the diversity of nations and races; but sin, by a reckless leveling and the elimination of all diversity, seeks a false, deceptive unity, the uniformity of death. The unity of God is written in the blueprint of the foundations; the unity of the world is merely painted on the walls. The Lord's unity is like the organic strength which holds together the fibers of the oak tree; the world's unity is like the spider web which upholds tenuous

1. The first reference is to Otto von Bismarck (1815-98), the "iron chancellor" of Prussia who orchestrated the process of German unification. At the time of Kuyper's address, this had not yet reached its final act of war with France, whose emperor, Napoleon III, deemed himself Bismarck's equal at international affairs and showed no greater respect for small states, as the quotation by Kuyper indicates.

tissue in between. Organically one or an aggregate, a natural growth or a synthetic formation, become or made, nature or art — there, in a word, lies the profound difference distinguishing the spurious unity of the world from the life-unity designed by God.

I spoke with good reason of the yearning for false unity that dominates the course of world history. But since the end of the eighteenth century a most notable change has occurred in that drive. I would point to the French Revolution, the birth year of modern life, as the beginning of that new direction. The striving for imperial unity was not abandoned by the revolution; on the contrary, the goal has remained the same. But here's the difference. Whereas in the past that unity would be imposed upon the life of nations externally — by the sword — today it would be insinuated into the very heart of the peoples by its own fermentation. The bare *political* unity of the past was metamorphosed by the catastrophe of 1789 into a *social* unity. Just read what history tells you of Nebuchadnezzar or Alexander, of Cyrus or Caesar, of Charlemagne or Charles V, and you will find in each case the immediate goal of founding an empire. That unity was effected by the sword. Violence shackled together peoples whose mutual aversion was virtually inborn. Only when that imperial unity had been achieved by a mighty military arm did the vain attempt begin to melt that diversity into a single unity. But what does experience teach? That the unity shattered and the peoples broke apart over and over because the necessary unity and homogeneity of social life was missing. It was precisely national differences, the peoples' diversity of character, the ineradicable uniqueness of their ethnicity, that time and again broke up imperial unity at almost the moment it was created.

Since the direct pursuit of this goal had brought nothing but disappointment, with the French Revolution people opted for another strategy. They prepared to take a longer road, one that would lead them all the more surely, even infallibly, to the great goal. If imperial unity kept foundering on the national diversity of ethnic groups, eliminating that diversity was the goal inherent in the French Revolution. "Liberty, equality, fraternity" is therefore the basic principle it seeks to inscribe in the constitutions of the peoples. For once the peoples have been robbed of their characteristic genius and rendered homogeneous, the triumph of imperial unity is assured. Hence the slogan of false unity today has become: through uniformity to unification, by centralization toward Caesarism. Should that effort succeed, the victory of that false unity will be celebrated on the ruins of what land and folk, race and nation, had that was peculiarly their own.

. . . The cries for brotherhood and love of fellow-man are but a

A cartoon published in 1908 upon Kuyper's last great cultural oration, some 40 years after he had made his debut. Start to finish, he was a master of the form, as the crowd's reaction shows.

slogan. Not fraternity but a false uniformity is the goal toward which its glittering images drive us. . . . If multiformity is the undeniable mark of fresh and vigorous life, our age seeks to realize its curse in its quest for uniformity. Its attempts to blend all shades into the blank darkness of the grave are becoming ever more obvious. Ever more shrilly it cries out that in our modern society, everything, however distinctive in nature, must be shaped by one model, cut to a single pattern, or poured into one fixed mold. It is like the ancient outlaw [Procrustes] who, myth tells us, compelled every traveler he could catch to lie on an iron bed, cutting off their legs by as many inches as they were too long and stretching those who were too short until each completely and precisely fit its dimensions. Blind to the rich profusion of the different shades of life, it crushes everything fresh and natural by its thirst for the conventional. Unable to appreciate the distinctive features of the face of humanity, it grinds away with a coarse hand all the divinely engraved markings on the copper plate of life. By filing away all that is uneven and buffing up the natural ore it aims at the mirrorlike smoothness in which no semblance of uniqueness can ever be found again. Indeed, it hacks away at the green wood of the tree of life until neither sprig or twig can ever sprout from the skeletal trunk again.

II

You rightly demand proof for this thesis, ladies and gentlemen, so now I must show you from the facts that this spurious uniformity really does dominate the life of our age and demonstrate how the diversity of life is increasingly vanishing from around us.

Let me start then by elaborating on what the new editor of the *Javabode*[2] recently bemoaned about our newly constructed streets. What is it in the architectural styles of our old Dutch cities that so charms the visiting stranger? What else but the infinite variety in width or narrowness, the looseness of twists and curves, the pointed and obtuse angles of even our most elegant canals that tell you they were not *made* but *grew*. It is as if a mysterious history speaks to you from every curve and narrows. You can immediately tell that no shoddy, money-hungry developer threw up that line of houses but that every dwelling is the fulfillment of a personal dream, the precious product of quiet thrift, based on a personal plan and built slowly from the ground up. Those tufted, tiered, triangular, and shuttered gables were not symmetrically measured with a level but reflected, every one of them, the thinking of a human being, the whimsicality of a somewhat overconfident human heart. This motley collection of houses bespeaks a city full of architects, and precisely in that teeming variety you sense the vigor of folk life as in earlier centuries it throbbed only in the heart of Holland's free citizens.

Compare that with America's new cities or, if you prefer to stay closer to home, one of the modern suburbs that have been added on to our cities. Imagine yourself in Berlin (if you are familiar with it) and consider the irreproachable straightness of the lines which run southward from Unter-den-Linden to the Leipzigerstrasse to be transsected at regular intervals by other lines of equally unimpeachable straightness. Even the ash-colored plaster that coats house after house in the new sections of our cities is virtually identical. There is not a gable to be seen which in any way violates the absolute symmetry to which door and window, cornice and roof window, have been fitted. Precisely those straight streets and rectangular corners, those utterly level gables and standardized houses make the modern outgrowths of our cities fatally exhausting and

2. A Conservative party journal published in the Dutch East Indies. The paragraphs that follow comment on the geographical expansion of Amsterdam that began around 1850. Until then the city still lay within boundaries dating from 1660 (roughly the Singelgracht and Stadhouderskade). As part of the expansion some of the radial canals in the old city were filled in (a process stopped by the 1890s preservation movement) and new residential districts were constructed in the style that Kuyper here laments.

boring. You have to number the streets and count them out so as not to get lost in so featureless a collection of houses. Better: not houses but blocks of tenements that make you think of institutions of mercy or army barracks rather than of the homes of free citizens. Unfortunately, in Berlin and Wiesbaden as well as in Paris, it is the modern spirit of Haussman[3] which violates even the consecrated soil of Montmartre to run a straight line through the circular pattern of its boulevards. Whatever Paris invents Brussels imitates and, via Brussels, comes to haunt Holland's cities as well. All the poetry of our cities vanishes, all the quaint gables disappear. The plasterer's trowel covers up in grey the white panes around the red bricks, and before long all diversity has been removed from Holland's cities. Conclusion: the cause of uniformity has won the day in the field of architecture.

The same thing is happening with *age* differences. In the past a young man's heart beat in a young man's body; he wore young man's clothing and around him was a young man's world. Short-tempered, informal, rash and full of spirit: that was his portrait. The opposite was true for the old man, and also natural: his seriousness, his confident laugh, his cautious and deliberate movements. In short, the young man acted his age and so did the old man. But how things have changed! How obvious the attempts of our young men to play at being old, and of our old men to play at being "boys." Perhaps you have seen that witty cartoon in *Punch:* a clownish peddlar of bric-a-brac faces a boy of fourteen over his display table. With a pince-nez buried deeply over his nose the young fellow asks to see some toys. "For you or for your sister?" asks the eager salesman, but the young gentleman, blushing deeply, snaps back at him: "No, for the old man to play with!" Perhaps a bit of overkill but what the cartoonist was panning is not an illusion but sad reality. Our children are no longer children. What they read are not fairy tales or fables but manuals on natural science and mathematics. They have their own newspaper, their own cigars; they play at chaperoning a dance, at being deacons in their children's worship; they sometimes look ludicrous dressing like little lords or ladies. A little later their skin turns pale, their hair falls out, and all their animation and enthusiasm are gone. Stoical formality mixed with epicurean license soon robs them of young manhood. And

3. Georges Eugene Haussmann (1809-91), as prefect of the *department* of the Seine 1853-70, supervised modernization projects in Paris that included cutting broad straight boulevards across the old warren of side streets. This provided more rapid traffic flow, also for security forces against Parisian crowds. Haussmann was the picture of a modern administrator in service to an autocratic regime for purposes of order and efficiency.

old age — is not the *Punch* cartoon on target there? Is it not often childish? Does it not have its own toys? Does it not frequently dress in the bright colors of kindergartners, bleach out its grey hair, and by insipid buffoonery and affected rashness play at enjoying a second youth? When we see these decrepit youth and those pseudo-youthful graybeards, don't we have a right to complain that the old-fashioned difference between young and old is fading away and that here, too, uniformity is gaining the day?

Not to the same extent but just as undeniably, an attempt is being made to transform the two sexes, masculine and feminine, into a neutral hybrid of the two. Also in our country, prophetesses have arisen who insist — as though they were part of an antislavery league — on the emancipation of women and demand that they too be entitled to wear a liberty cap on their heads. In modern America a woman has recently taken a professor's chair at one of the colleges, and in England a Ph.D. adorns more than one woman's name. In Germany and Belgium women's skirts swirl around office stools. The bluestockings of earlier days were ignoramuses compared to the female polymaths that our normal schools graduate in multitudes today. Still, this is only the beginning. Total equalization of men and women is the demand being broached at the moment in Great Britain's House of Commons. The ancient fable of the Amazons is fast turning into a prophecy that is rushing with impetuous urgency to its fulfillment. Something heroic, something manly, something high-spirited had better emanate from our young beauties if they are not to be dismissed as household drudges or staid old crones. The modesty and diffidence that formerly adorned our young maidens no longer fit the robust woman of our age.

As for the male? Ulrici states in his psychology: "the masculine woman is possible only where the effeminate man is already a reality."[4] That is true also in our days. Visit our fraternities, wander around in our salons, take a stroll along our main streets. If you can, take along a Durgerdam fisherman to have a lively image of the male form in its untrimmed dimensions.[5] Then tell me whether many an alleged masculine entity you see sauntering along does not testify to a softening, an emasculation, a feminization in our men. Or when you see one of our modern pedestrian amazons with a spirited look and a relaxed bearing walking briskly down the street in sturdy laced-up boots, her arm joined to a diminutive male figure shuffling along on lacquered bottines, more than half eclipsed by the dashing garments of his escort — tell me, does

4. Hermann Ulrici (a German professor of philosophy at Halle), *Leib und Seele* (Leipzig: T. O. Weigel, 1866).

5. Durgerdam was a small fishing village across the River IJ from Amsterdam.

the suspicion ever cross your mind that a woman in men's clothing has been taken by the arm by a man in the guise of a woman? . . . [Kuyper alludes to a poem "He and She"/"Hij en Zij," by seventeenth-century Dutch poet Jacob Cats.]

In the matter of dress we see the same phenomenon. Look how, when Minerva's young manhood[6] hold their masquerades, thousands upon thousands of people travel from villages and cities, by barge and boat, road or rail, to our university towns to feast upon the endless variety of colors and shapes. Compare this magnificent attire from times past with the stiff uniformity of the clothing worn by the thronging spectators and you will agree that here too a deadly uniformity has doused the sparkle of life. What an enormous array of forms in the days when every difference in rank or status was openly displayed in people's dress. What a profuse diversity of styles and costumes, of fabrics and colors, when everyone, from whatever district or region, guild or group, office or occupation he might be, remained recognizable by his clothing and everyone felt the urge to show in fabric and color, in the shape and elegance of their traditional costumes, who they were.

Oh, I know as well as you that there was often something tasteless or even gaudy about that finery. Still, in my opinion, there was also an element of straightforwardness in wearing your own colors so that human society in those days had an immediate warm, sociable look to it. Today, unfortunately, little of that splendor of forms has remained. By comparison with the luxuriant dress of the past, male attire in our day is flat and undistinguished. There is no fanciful form which has not been trimmed, no color combination which has not been dulled, no widening which has not been taken in, no collar which has not been shrunk, no pleat which has not been ironed out. All that is called male, of whatever vocation or title, rank or status, is clothed in the same ill-fitting, undistinguished garments. The gap left open by the gleaming white of piping or collar may be alternately wider or narrower, the rim of our hats flatter or more curved — but the pattern remains the same for all, the vacuous idea behind it occasionally broken not by people's own ideas but by something fantastic.

The situation seems to be better in women's clothing because it tends to err more by excessive fickleness than by a wooden sameness, but even here the deadly uniformity of our age asserts itself, though in

6. Male university students. Minerva had long been honored at universities as the goddess of learning, invention, and the arts. Kuyper's description anticipates the similar observations, and tone, taken by the great Dutch historian of a subsequent generation, Johan Huizenga, in *The Autumn of the Middle Ages* (1921).

another way. Changes in fashion are dizzying indeed, but in fact that fashion is the same for all. A designer's whim in the capital of France, one hint from Paris — and before long every woman in Europe wears the same style of dress, has the same hairstyle, is shod with the same style of boot, is painted the same fashionable color. Year after year — better, every new season — an increasingly fitful industry diversifies its creations frivolously and without principle, and regardless of geographical region or climate, figure or color, social status or financial resources, every female believes she is the most beautiful of all by slavishly following its cues. Only the silks or cottons, the heavier or lighter silk, the real or artificial lace, distinguishes the clothing of the higher from that of the lower classes. Soon the costumes of our maids will surpass those of their mistresses, and if you watch our country women at the farmers' market you can tell that our "Aglaia" or "Gracieuse"[7] is not spurned even by the dairy stalls. Only in outlying areas does the traditional costume of our Frisian farming community still — agonizingly — maintain itself. The army is the only sector of our nation which, precisely by its uniform, breaks with the general uniformity. And as though to scare us away forever from returning to the profusion of bygone days, life in our cities evidences no exception to the uniform than the grotesque garments in which the orphanage wraps its charges and the Home of the Aged dresses its crones.

The pulse of a nation beats in its *language*. No wonder, then, that the same demon rages here as well. Certainly, there is much resistance, for a language is deeply rooted in the heart of a people. Yet here too the mindless drive toward uniformity has tried its stunts. After all, though no hydraulic jack can wrench the entire building of a language out of joint, one can still burn the glossy paint off the door frames and split the stone stoop. That's what is happening in the attempt to replace Europe's vernacular tongues with an international language brewed out of all of them together. Much even seems to favor the attempt. In the past, language was almost exclusively oral, and any person who wanted to write had to listen to the vernacular as it was spoken by the people. But nowadays people don't have the time constantly to look up that living lexicon. Who could demand this from the swarming army of word-mongers who day after day make the presses groan with reams of writing? They have to make do with their bare vocabularies; if that proves impossible, then without the least compunction they seek emergency help from the three foreign languages they have picked up. With such clumsy hands they abuse our language, crumpling its marvelous attire and be-

7. These were brand names of the time.

smirching the purity of its face with their foreign forms. Not that Holland's language should be prim and prissy and ward off every word that grew on foreign soil. When you speak of foreign things you have to call them by their foreign names or no one will understand you. Who, in any case, would wish to be so inhospitable and rude as to indiscriminately block all that comes from foreign lands at our borders? On the contrary. But what we may demand from foreigners is that they conform their conduct to our laws. There's the rub. From the South, the East, and the West they flood our borders and attempt to force their way into our home uninvited. Once inside the door, they forget all forms of courtesy and boldly boss us around so as to throw the household of our language into disarray with their foreign whims.

I must say, that vandalism has already gone a long way toward ruining the beauty of our language. Just read once the advertisements at the lower levels of our business world — that hodgepodge of private lingo laced with a supply of double-crossed mongrel words they alone are privy to. Not to fall behind their competitors for lack of advertising, the owners of small newspapers then swallow their regrets by following — at some distance — this newfangled mutilation in their "lead articles." Next come the translators — by whole or by half — of rarely sought-after novels. In many devotional pieces the authors send samples of that demented Dutch into our back streets. And many a learned work, frequently even government documents, offers all too vivid proof of how this language corruption is spreading ever wider and higher. Spoken language is admittedly more durable because it is alive, but anyone who has ever listened to the fractured lingo of our "gentlemen travelers," the hopeless gobbledygook of our store clerks, the droll babblings of our globetrotters, need not be told by anyone how far the indulgence in barbarisms has gone in corrupting our language.

The same thing is happening outside our borders. Year after year France's vocabulary is overloaded with foreign words made up of forced combinations of Greek roots. Our German friends, with their endless "-iren," increasingly "extinguiren" the Germanic glow of their muscular mother tongue. In England, French influence increasingly pushes back the Anglo-Saxon component of its language. Thus slowly but noticeably, especially in the circles of our traveling public, the languages of nations run together. The sharpness or mellifluousness, the smoothness or fullness with which every language had to be pronounced is increasingly dissolved in a flat unaccented lisp. And though we know beforehand that in this expression of human life such mindlessness will never totally succeed because a language simply does not tolerate such toying with it, still the trend toward uniformity is undeniably present here as well.

So here we are. Everything has to be equalized and leveled; all diversity must be whittled down. Differences in architectural style must go. Age differences must go. Gender differences must go. Differences in dress must go. Differences in language must go. Indeed, what doesn't have to go if this drive toward uniformity succeeds? For what I have said so far is barely a beginning of the indictment against uniformity. Are we not equally witnessing the disappearance of every difference in form of government? Is not the whole country being overlaid with a web of uniformity all the threads of which are pulled by a power-hungry centralizing monster? Does not just this model state call for a modern educational establishment that pays no attention to differences in religion, character, or aptitude but loses itself in filling up brains with content administered to all in the same way and as much as possible in the same measure? Indeed, are not people themselves gradually becoming more uniform by virtue of sheer mediocrity? Who doesn't notice that the grand figures, the solid characters of our ancestors, are being reproduced in ever smaller dimensions, or how, for lack of great men among the living, people are erecting statue after statue for the giants of the past? It is no longer the willpower of a man but a dumb ballot box which today decides the destiny of state and church. One is no longer his own person but a member of a party, condemned to follow its line, speak its language, and fit its mold.

Thus every difference disappears. An iron steam engine is eliminating the rich diversity that used to confer on every enterprise its own charm, on every branch of industry its own character. The power of capital, in ever more enormous accumulations, drains away the life blood from our retail trade. A single gigantic wholesaler swallows up the patronage that formerly enabled any number of stores to flourish. The well-to-do middle class sees its ranks reduced every day by social forces that consistently tend to level all ranks and classes, finally to leave behind nothing but the pitifully shrill contrast between poverty and wealth. Under the motto of brotherhood even holy ground has to be made common for the purpose of dissolving all religious differences into a "Christianity" above confessional division, to "comfort" all persons equally with the faith that one must strive for virtue and wait to see what comes of it! So must everything become uniform, level, flat, homogeneous, monotonous. No longer should each baby drink warm milk from the breast of its own mother; we should have some tepid mixture prepared for all babies collectively. No longer should each child have a place to play at home by its mother; all should go to a common nursery school. No longer should every man spend his evening hours at home with his own wife and children, but all should meet around the card tables of our clubs or in the taprooms of the local bars. No longer does personal courage prompt a bluejacket to jump into the rigging of the enemy, grappling-iron in hand. What passes for a sea battle today is a ramming and jolting against an iron behemoth in which men sit hidden away. No longer an intrepid mind and a chivalrous heart but the reliability of a gun and the caliber of the weapon decides the battle. In all this what you see is the disappearance of the human personality. It is finally machines, not people, that you see in motion, their cogs locking into each other: machines all put together the same way, operating by the same drill, and all showing the same motions through the all-compelling, all-regulating, and all-leveling power of society.

And now, to my final point, don't you sense how such a striving spells the death of national feeling and patriotism? After all, why still be attached to the country of one's birth, "when" — to speak with Paulin, the consummate Communist — "when all peoples seem to have been cast in the same mold, when all the cultural differences between countries, all usages, customs, and traditions disappear more and more, crushed under the wheels of locomotives."[8] If within our own borders and those of our neighbors all citizens increasingly resemble each other, to what end do we still speak of "our own" people, "our own" national character, "our own" mother country? No: if the iron train not only unites people with people but prompts the peoples to abandon their own unique character, if the rails do not facilitate the lively exchange of our own thoughts but have to serve the monotonous exchange of standardized ideas, then the soul of a people is lost. To still speak of a fatherland would then be no more than a vestige of an earlier narrow-mindedness. To still feel a love for folk and fatherland is then nothing but self-deception and false excitement. If we would be the perfect children of our age, we should all seek to become world citizens, not the citizens of our own country. It is not enough, then, for the nations to lift the barriers and demolish the walls that separate them; no, the very borders between them must be abolished. Indeed, everything should become one, indivisibly one, to the point that no longer should river or mountain range, lake or strait, divide; and every difference in age and sex, of rank or class, of aptitude or character, of language and national genius must be planed away and hollowed out until on the surface of the whole earth there would be just one people and one language — one vast cosmopolis in which there would no longer be any east or west, north or south, but all of human life would be the same because it would collectively bear the uniform features of death.

8. Kuyper transposed the first for the second name of Paulin Poulin (b. 1810), a follower of Belgian utopian socialist Baron Jean Guillaume Hippolyte de Colins and author of *Religion et Socialisme* (Paris, 1867).

III

Ladies and gentleman, do I need to argue the point that all such striving for a false uniformity, the leveling principle of modern life, the demand for one people and one language, run counter to the ordinances of God? You well know the divine word, full of holy energy, that Scripture opposes to that striving: "Else nothing they plan to do will be impossible for them" [Gen. 11:6b]. That all life should multiply "after its kind," after its own, unique, given character is the royal law of creation which applies to more than seed-bearing herbs. That everyone who has been born from above will someday receive from the Lord a white tablet on which will be written a new name that no one knows except the one who receives it [Rev. 2:17]: what else is this but a most forceful protest against all the conformity into which the world tends to pressure us? Or — if in this hall you resent an exclusive appeal to Scripture — look about you in the theater of nature and tell me: where does creation, which bears the signature of God, exhibit that uniform sameness of death to which people are nowadays trying to condemn all human life? Raise your eyes, look up at the starry heavens, and you will see not just a single beam of light but an undulating, scintillating sea of light coming from myriads of bright-shining stars, each of which the Lord calls "by name" for the simple reason that each has a name, a nature, and a substance of its own. They all differ in the speed of the light they emit and each of them sparkles along its own path. Uniformity in God's creation! No, rather infinite diversity, an inexhaustible profusion of variations that strikes and fascinates you in every domain of nature, in the ever-varying shape of a snowflake as well as in the endlessly differentiated form of flower and leaf. Where in God's entire creation do you encounter life that does not display the unmistakable hallmark of life precisely in the multiplicity of its colors and dimensions, in the capriciousness of its ever-changing forms?

Should it be any different in the realm of spirits? Unless an impenetrable curtain still blocks your view of that world, you have learned that there are seven spirits before God's throne who are different from the seraphs, that there are cherubs who are set over the archangels, and that these again rule over the angels. In the human world you can find nought else. Again, the same infinite diversity undulates and teems about you, the same generous God who from the riches of his glory distributed gifts, powers, aptitude, and talents to each according to his divine will.

But that artful embroidery of infinitely varying colors and shades does not lack unity of conception, nor has the statement "you are all brothers" lost its validity for us. On the contrary, the drive toward unity in God's revelation is so powerful that every false theory of political unity has hung its banner from the standard of Christianity. Even the theme song of the communists and the revolutionary slogan of "equality, liberty, and fraternity" were taken from Scripture with seeming legitimacy. But people have failed to see that the unity of the human family may only be looked for in its origin and destiny, never in the developmental phases it passes through on its way. All humanity stems from one ancestor, but from its very beginning it was destined to be sent forth in a variety of directions along different roads. If humanity at Babel's tower tries to unite itself to be a single people forever, the Lord disturbs that undertaking and scatters the peoples over the ends of the earth. The founding of empires, however frequently attempted thereafter, is just as frequently frustrated, and humanity's division into nations and peoples, tribes and races, clans and families goes on its age-old way. Yet just as it was one in origin, so for all its diversity and dispersion its ideal unity for the future still holds in the promised Messiah, the head of humanity, who is coming. That unity, however, is not based on the sameness of a *model* but on the oneness of a *body* in which every member retains its own place. Not like a drop of water in a stream or piece of gravel in a pit but like branches grafted into the one vine, the members of the human race must find their unity in Christ. In the unity of the kingdom of God diversity is not lost but all the more sharply defined. On the great day of Pentecost the Holy Spirit did not speak in one uniform language; instead, everyone heard the Spirit proclaiming the mighty works of God in his own tongue. Though the wall of *separation* has been demolished by Christ, the lines of *distinction* have not been abolished. Someday, before the throne of the Lamb, doxologies will be sung to him who conquered, not by a uniform mass of people but by a humanity diversified in peoples and tribes, in nations and tongues [Rev. 5:9].

For this reason I do not shrink from calling false uniformity the *curse* of modern life: it disregards the ordinances of God revealed not only in Scripture but throughout his entire creation. What is a "curse" in the sense in which we are now using the word? A curse — I'm sure you have the same sense of it — is every tendency which, often unwittingly but by a fatal impulse, propels us on a road that leads to the destruction of life. Just that I see happening here. In that idea of uniformity there lies a quiet charm, an apparent source of order, a prophecy of peace that seduces the peoples. Once articulated and accepted as a life principle, it is irresistible in its urgency, a powerful leaven that runs through all the arteries of life and never rests until all that lives and moves has been distorted by its fatal standards. It extinguishes the glow of life, cripples its vitality, and must end by injuring the very root of life precisely because it is in multiform diversity, not in uniformity, that the finest fiber and deepest principle of natural life is found.

Humanity fashions for itself an iron fence made up of identical stiles. That is its unity. But if you wish to see the unity of God, go out into a wild forest, observe there the crooked trunks, the twisted branches, the mingling colors, the endless variety of shades, and note how it is precisely in the whimsical interplay of colors and lines that unity is revealed in its finest expression. But what is our age doing? On the model of that iron fence, it trims frolicsome shrubbery into a smooth hedge and prunes those wild trunks to the very top to create a forced unity in the tangled mass by an artificial uniformity. It confuses monotony with harmony and fancies that the full accord of life has been found when every instrument is properly attuned and no dissonances are heard. . . . The *average* is the standard to which it artificially elevates the one and forcibly flattens others, which explains the mediocrity of modern life. In fact, the flourishing of the arts is the true measure of the vitality of an era. Art is born out of a zest for the beauty of true unity, out of an impulse toward a fuller life. The curse of uniformity is thus manifest in the fact that our modern life is almost totally devoid of artistic talent of any kind, poverty-stricken in aesthetic vitality, and totally destitute of great artistic creations. Let no one think that this deficiency is accidental. It is rather the necessary consequence of the drive toward uniformity. When that drive gains ground, no revival of the arts is to be expected and there is nothing left for us but to cry out with one of the apostles of the modern world: "Art is dead, thoroughly dead. Our efforts to resuscitate it only amount to an attempt to revive a corpse. The true poetry of our century must be not to have any."[9]

IV

If I have persuaded you, ladies and gentlemen, that modern life is geared to the pursuit of uniformity and that such uniformity is to be considered a curse, we must finally ask the practical question: what line of conduct does this phenomenon require of us in our struggle in church and state?

Allow me to begin with the former, with the *church,* and at the very outset to state the opinion — however hazardous it may seem — that it

9. This unattributed quotation is perhaps from Baudelaire. It was also a sentiment shared by Impressionist painters, just now emerging, over against the prevailing salon or academic art of the times.

was the church more than any other agency which prepared the ground for the dominance of uniformity. Naturally, the problem of *unity in diversity* surfaced much earlier and much more sharply for the church of Christ than for the life of society in general, both because personal identity and diversity tend to stand out much more sharply among the regenerate and because in Christ, its head, the unity of the church is felt much more powerfully. So from the beginning of its history the church was confronted by the difficult problem of how the unity which in principle it already possessed in Christ could emerge from the rich diversity of powerful Spirit-shaped personalities. It is that question which dominates its entire history and which also explains the conflict of our day.

It hardly needs saying that the Roman phase of the church was nothing but the burial of that great question in the coffin of uniformity. Since the fifth century the church has simply done in the spiritual arena what Nebuchadnezzar did in his day in the political domain when, ignoring all national diversity, he imposed an external unity on the peoples by force. The church fatally opted not for a unity that would develop organically but for one that had been preconceived and simply demanded conformity. Every free expression of life was silenced by the sword or funeral pyre, and every person who would not bend his neck under this yoke was cut off as a sectarian or thrust out as a heretic. The oneness of the grave in which Loyola sought to bury every spirit "as though it were a corpse" was but the shrillest expression of the same drive. And how was that unity obtained? By no other method than the same wretched uniformity that poisons the life of society today. Its belief system had to be uniform, its government uniform, its liturgy uniform, its message to all regions of the world carried in *one* language, and life everywhere shaped by one model. Hence the natural understanding between the leaders of the church and the champions of imperial unity: though often embroiled in conflict with each other, basically the two groups were pursuing the same goal.

The Reformation broke up that false unity in two ways. Its *national* Germanic character asserted its claims in the matter of religion, and the *personal* power of a reborn heart sought to break the bonds by which it was shackled. The Reformation, that is, contained both *national* and *individual* resistance, which resulted in the uniformity of the Christian church being localized. Please note: I say that ecclesiastical *unity* was broken while ecclesiastical *uniformity* had only been tempered. For what have the churches of the Reformation done but restore the uniformity of Rome in their own bosom and in a different way? The *national* opposition worked its way through; in place of a uniform church from all nations came the national church in a multiple forms. But *individual* resistance, the right of personality and with it liberty of life, was smothered in our Reformed churches as well. Also among us, taking each nation by itself, you see uniformity in confession, uniformity in type of piety, uniformity in liturgy and government. Also among us Reformed people the stream of life was all too quickly frozen over by the frigid air of a formalistic uniformity. Here again, as in Rome before, unity did not develop organically but was imposed by force.

Is it so hard to understand that the experiment had to fail? Was it not a gamble to take over Rome's error of uniformity without maintaining the mighty hierarchy by which Rome held that uniformity together? To proclaim individual liberty, as the Reformation did, and still to impose the yoke of uniformity upon all spiritual life — did it not have to end in pitiful disappointment? Was it not natural for the ground swell of the stream to constantly push up against that layer of ice until it broke? First, while the organism was still being held together, a part of the church had to be thrown out; later, when the church lost its power to maintain uniformity, a host of malcontents assembled, producing an unhealthy ferment. Ordinary unbridled life, not bothering about that uniformity, went its own way; and now, when in our church we witness a motley mixture of the most divergent opinions, what are we facing but the logical consequence of that monstrous alliance between freedom and false uniformity with which we embarked?

So now what are we to do? Espouse doctrinal liberty and turn the church into an auditorium like this Odeon, where people will argue by turns for and against the sacred? That means the destruction of the church. Freedom of thought in state and society I understand, but one who speaks of doctrinal liberty in a church contradicts himself and nullifies the church's essence. Then what? Shall we recall the days of old and, as confessionalists in the worst sense of the word, press the people of our generation into a form that has not arisen from their own convictions? But that is to try the impossible! The past does not return; all repristination is nonsensical; every attempt at reaction is condemned to fail inasmuch as it denies the claims of the present. That way one becomes a confessionalist, zealous for the form but without the courage of the confession. That does not help us move forward but takes us back to a failed uniformity. But suppose we simply abandon every concept of church, drop the idea of being a confessional church, and decide to be nothing but a confessing church without restrictions or definitions of any kind? That ideal too, I know, has its respectable advocates. But I ask: how do people conceive of this? A community without sacraments? Of course not! But if not, do not the sacraments require some visible organization? Then, whatever you call that organism, you have re-created an ecclesiastical form. A life without form would certainly eliminate uniformity, but does not such formlessness block all expression of the life?

No, ladies and gentlemen: if ecclesiastical uniformity is not merely localized by *national* resistance as in the days of the Reformation but totally eliminated by the full strength of a personal spiritual life, I know of no other solution than to accept — freely and candidly, without any reservations — a free multiformity. A church such as ours today is in a worse state than that of dissolution; it is rotting away while still alive. Now then, those who want the church to recover should not seek to restore an ecclesiastical form that has already proven unfit. Any new church formation, no matter what, should first of all completely purge away the curse of uniformity, which is the mother of lies. Nothing should be forced and nothing united which is not organically one. If there are people of good will who are one in mind and spirit, let them join together and courageously confess the faith of their hearts, but let them not claim any greater unity than that which is really their common possession. Thus, with complete autonomy let groups and circles unite who know what they want, know what they confess, and possess an actual, not merely a nominal, unity. If here and there such circles exist which share a common life-trait, let them become conscious of their unity and display it before the eyes of the world, but let it be only that feature and no other bond that unites them.

I do not mean by this to espouse congregationalism. Those who do so fail to appreciate the living bond between human spirits and nullify the community of people that has grown out of the root of Christ. No, but only by a voluntarily chosen kinship can the true connections between souls manifest themselves. The inherited sickness of an earlier error can only be driven out by that heroic medicine, and a communal life can only develop by a route which neither steals the claims of freedom nor entertains a false unity. People have sometimes suspected me of clericalistic tendencies because of a plea I made under the still prevailing order. I therefore feel compelled to say with all the power I can muster that I detest all clericalism. All clericalism is the same, all confessionalism is the same. The life of a free church community can manifest itself only where that life finds its own form. A *confederative system* is what I have in mind as being most consistent with the character of our people. It seems to me the only way to combine freedom and unity without violating the truth and to lay the groundwork for a future in which the form is not artificially created but grows by the power of the Spirit from one's own corporate life.

Barely touching upon this idea, ladies and gentlemen, let us take a quick glance at the struggle to be waged in the *political* arena. There, too, the uniformity of modern life is raging. A uniform constitution has to be adopted in all European states, a uniform structure of government in every region and every city. Uniform the model by which the life of Javanese and Hollander has to be tailored; uniform the pattern on which all education must be organized. Uniformity, in a word, is the shibboleth that recurs in the debates on all the burning issues of our time. Well then, right here everyone belonging to the Christian-Historical school rises in principial opposition, for this school strives toward the unity that is in *Christ* precisely through the free unfolding of *historically* developed life. Far from wanting to inject the virus of reaction into the bloodstream of our national life, this school's opposition to the existing state of affairs aims only to maintain the unique life-form of our people against the lethal uniformity of our age. It loves "Freedom and Development."[10] "Progress and Refinement" is its watchword when it girds itself for battle against the tyrannies sanctioned by a false uniformity that buries freedom in voluntary slavery and, by severing the root, renders all developmental growth impossible. Accordingly, it is weak when, repristinating, it would substitute the forms of the past for the uniformity of the modern state, but irresistible when it argues the case for the rights of its own form against the blandishments of a false uniformity. It therefore has the right but also the obligation to defend the vital national components still present in our constitution against Anglomania and against every attempt to impose a uniform model-constitution on the Netherlands.[11] It has the obligation to maintain not an arbitrary but a historical autonomy — an autonomy bound to the laws of life itself — for persons, cities, and regions against an all-homogenizing centralism. It has the calling to oppose with vigor the attempts to structure our colonies by the standards of life at home, should there be people who would introduce the experiments of revolution also among the Javanese and Madurese people. Its slogan has to be: by Javanese or European, a distinct form of government for a distinct way of life. Nor must it anxiously cling to the existing system of culture if it is evident that life's vitalities have totally outgrown that form. On the contrary, following Sinai's laws and practicing justice with integrity, I should not exact the treasure from but rather introduce the Gospel to

10. These are Liberal party slogans which Kuyper wished to co-opt, also to secure them on their proper foundations.

11. The Dutch Liberalism of the time emulated both English and French ("uniform model-constitution") proposals, which Kuyper here repudiates.

the peoples of the Indonesian archipelago, not to make them "Dutch" but to make them Javanese Christians in whose domestic and social life a spiritual life will flow according to its own character and form.

No less persistent should be the struggle against the uniform mold in which the state attempts to cast all education — again, not to oppose the mixed form of education for those who want it, but to challenge the supremacy, the monopoly, of the mixed school and to demand alongside of it equal and generous legal space for every life-expression that desires its own form of education.[12] Indeed, our unremitting intent should be to demand justice for all, to do justice to every life-expression. If electoral law as we now know it makes it impossible for a minority to manifest itself, then another electoral method based not on arbitrary local precincts but on the precincts of the spirit should be a plank in our platform. Above all, "a form of its own for whatever has a life of its own"[13] is the energetic demand with which it confronts the uniformity of the modern state. It should shun every fusion or merger with those who are otherwise-minded, whoever they may be. It should consistently be itself and wear its own colors, proudly and freely.

Since in the discussion of every political issue the same argument over uniformity returns, it is the cancer of that uniformity which we must remove as we finally face the question of the state as a whole, the question of our national independence. The uniformity of Caesarism is our external enemy, the uniformity of Cosmopolitanism our internal enemy; these two in a fateful alliance now jointly threaten our national existence. No, it was not Napoleon nor Bismarck but solely the uniformity of modern life that posed the "question Hollandaise."[14] It is this dynamic that raises the physical, impersonal power of violence "through blood and iron" to such appalling heights that it threatens to overwhelm and crush all independent national existence. It is the same uniformity which so enervates our national life that it sometimes seems as if, without being asked, we slip into enemy hands the evidence that Holland has outlived itself.

12. "Mixed" education refers to the system of nonsectarian public schools that had a monopoly of state funding.

13. A motto of the day in the Christian-Historical and Antirevolutionary political movement.

14. "Caesarism" refers to Germany/Bismarck; "Cosmopolitanism" at the time connoted a spirit spread by France, thus Napoleon. The "question Hollandaise" troubled European diplomacy in the wake of the Congress of Vienna (1815) and the Belgian Revolution of 1830. Kuyper saw the same issues being raised again in his own time, given German unification and French imperialism. In particular, King William III of the Netherlands was also archduke of Luxemburg, which a unified German Empire might claim by historical precedents.

When the foreigner asks: "is such a one fit to govern?" we ourselves supply the answer of Macduff:

> Fit to govern?
> No, not to live, O miserable nation![15]

To fight against that uniformity, accordingly, is to fight for our fatherland. To undermine that drive implies laying a solid foundation on which all national life can rest. To that end we can all work together, each in his own family, each of us in his own heart. For the national spirit does not descend from the air but arises from the spirit of the home, and the spirit of the home is shaped by nothing else than the hearts of those who live together under the same roof. Without a Dutch heart there is no Dutch family, and without the latter there is no Dutch fatherland — who can deny it? Therefore, if you wish to remain a nation, if the prophecy is to be fulfilled that old Holland will "grow again and flourish," indeed, if your heart bursts to answer "à la Hollandaise" if ever that "question Hollandaise" should be posed again, then may your chosen motto be: "A form of our own for a life of our own!" Hold the Dutch national character in honor. Drive out our national sins but still love our national ways. Be true to your nature as Hollanders, ladies and gentlemen! Remove from your midst the spineless tendency to bestow extravagant accolades on everything that comes from abroad, and in your appraisals give preference to the things that are made at home. Uphold Holland's fame in learning foreign languages but let there be no language you would rather speak, and especially write, than that splendid, rich mother tongue in which alone Dutch people can express what a Dutch heart feels. Do not just feed your mind with what has been thought and sung abroad but drink of the vital stream of Holland's life also from your own poets. Daughters of the Netherlands, do not make yourselves ridiculous by being old-fashioned but also have the good taste and modesty never to present yourselves in a foreign outfit conceived in the capital of France by women who no longer understand the honor and dignity of being a woman. If there are among you people who often travel abroad, let it not be from shame of your national character but rather to journey as Hollanders, to show yourselves to be Hollanders, and, upon your return, to greet the borders of your dear fatherland with a heart that beats proudly for this country.

15. Quotation from William Shakespeare, *Macbeth,* Act IV, Scene 3. Shakespeare was Kuyper's most frequently quoted author, and *Hamlet* the single most common source.

May the illustrious history of your ancestors be more to you than a monument to the past; let it be for you the current of national life that you feel pulsating in your own veins. Yes, just let us be who we are: Hollanders! — in every circle and sector of life. Though our flag no longer dominates the seven seas, still we shall regain the rightful influence by which the legacy entrusted to our people may be made a blessing for all humanity. Let the Dutch people, standing on the blood-soaked soil of our fathers, rise again from its grave. Then, although another Spain attempt to annihilate our national life, another band of soldiers give our sons to the death, another despot put his knee upon Holland's chest, the Maccabean courage of our fathers will revive in us, and our people, again taking as their watchword the much abused motto of the House of Orange, will sound a forceful "nous maintiendrons" ["We shall maintain"] wherever people are bent on our extinction.

Would that God gave us such a national will — but then a will anchored in his will. While every nation is subject to the deep truth that it strikes itself from the roster of nations by devaluing its piety, this applies all the more to the national existence of the Netherlands which owes its origin to a religious movement. The sayings of the Moabite woman, "my people are your people" but also "my God is your God" [Ruth 1:16], should continue to be paired in the heart of every one of us. Without religion there can be no patriotism; where religion is most intense, there the love of country and people is most robust: so history teaches us on every page. If solidity of character shapes the soul of a nation and if religion is the primary sculptor of true human personality, then it is not in false enthusiasm but in the cultivation of genuine piety that we must find the power that fosters, reinforces, and ennobles our patriotism. So then, people of the Netherlands, if you want to remain a people, let godliness be your primary weapon in the struggle for independence and only secondarily artillery and sidearms. If you love your country, know your calling to become ever more devout, more religious, and believe that the larger the number of children of God who inhabit the land of our fathers, the higher will be the wall which protects its liberty. Even aside from being extinguished, if you do not wish to die out, if Holland's glory is not to expire for want of manliness on your part but our illustrious fathers will have descendants from your loins, then find your help where your fathers found it and, as free men, bow your heads before no one but bow even your knees and teach your children to bend them before the God of your fathers.

Religion alone can stand for life against the death of uniformity. Therefore let the patroness of Dutch cities be the image you take along as you leave this place. You know her from our old coins.[16] She is shown hemmed in, for if the boundary walls collapse and our Holland is incorporated in some other state, Old Holland can no longer exist. She has a javelin in her hand, for our sons must be armed when they go to battle if they are not to be murdered as cowards but conquered as heroes. Besides this, she is also leaning on Scripture, on the Bible, for no slender figure, no high enclosure, no javelin of steel will save her if she cannot draw from that Scripture the strength to live and the courage to die. But then, *with* that Scripture, she proudly waves the liberty cap high in the air because *from* that Scripture she has learned that those can live who are prepared to die and that where God is with us no bully can make us crawl.

16. This was "the maid in the garden," a symbol of Leiden's resistance to the Spanish in the Eighty Years' War and later retooled by Kuyper in the image of Minerva as a symbol of the Free University. My thanks to Robert Sweetman for this reference.

Confidentially

That Kuyper's first practical application in *Uniformity* involved the church can be explained from the remarkable autobiographical account that follows. Kuyper began his career troubled by the same question current in the circle around John Henry Newman in England, among Lutherans all across Germany, and in Lutheran, Reformed, and Episcopal circles in the United States: how was the church to maintain its autonomy and integrity in the face of rising state power and the rationalist critiques of the Enlightenment?[1] For Kuyper this was at once a deeply personal and a commanding public question.

High-church partisans like Newman saw the church as nothing less than the continuing presence of the divine and supernatural on earth. This conviction, it turns out, animated the book that triggered the second stage of Kuyper's conversion process. If the third and final step took him to strict Reformed confessionalism, that resting-place was never separable from its corporate, churchly context, as Kuyper himself here insists. Kuyper was passionate about things ecclesiastical, in short, because they involved salvation.

But they also involved the personal — more specifically, family experiences central to Kuyper's identity formation. He does not articulate this so much as give it away, nor should we make too much of his words by way of psychohistorical speculation. But given the confessional tone of his memoir and the intensity of his church polemics, it is not too much to say that the contempt he shows for his father's situation in Leiden and the longing he expresses for a pure mother-church bespeak some unpleasant family dynamics and a rebel-hero in quest of himself. On both counts it is notable that the first phase of his conversion process hangs from Hamlet's most famous saying.

1. Walter H. Conser, Jr., *Church and Confession: Conservative Theologians in Germany, England, and America* (Mercer, Georgia: Mercer University Press, 1984), gives a fine overview of this phenomenon.

This does not impugn the authenticity of Kuyper's conversion, nor should it distract our attention from the piece as a conversion narrative. So it registered among thousands of Kuyper's followers, all the more since the hero turns out to require absolute certainty beyond himself and finds it where they had, in "the shelter of the rock" of Christ. By their Reformed standards, however, the story had a most unusual pivot: Kuyper came to repentance by reading not the Bible but a novel! Religion could hardly be more closely associated with culture. Nor was the third, political partner any secret given the memoir's circumstances of publication. Kuyper penned his narrative in "confidential" guise to permit personal disclosures, then broadcast it in a brochure aimed at exerting public pressure on the church council of Amsterdam, where at this time, in 1873, he was the leading pastor of the orthodox party.

Kuyper's entire treatise, published as *Confidentie: Schrijven aan den Weled. Heer J. H. van der Linden* (Amsterdam: Höveker & Zoon, 1873), runs to 114 pages. The portion included here is one-seventh (pp. 34-49) of the whole and was translated by Reinder Bruinsma. In the original it follows on Kuyper's review of recent ecclesiastical controversies and leads on to the legal grounds and substantive proposals of his position. But first, "I would like to tell you where my passion for the Church question comes from."

PARTICULARLY IN ANSWERING this first question, your fraternal sense will pardon a rather intimate recollection. Our way of thinking is inevitably rooted in our own life-course, in what we each have experienced in our heart and life. How then could I explain my profound interest in the Church question if I were only allowed to touch upon the things that I share with many others?

In the years of my youth the Church aroused my aversion more than my affection. Having grown up in the Church, I knew it inside out, and particularly through the way that church life manifested itself in Leiden, I felt repulsed rather than attracted. In Leiden, under the liberal regime of the time, a most pitiful situation prevailed, and the deceit, the hypocrisy, the unspiritual routine that sap the lifeblood of our whole ecclesiastical fellowship were most lamentably prevalent in the old university town. In particular, the arguments about the Huiszittenhuis and city council[2] made it plain as day that neither side acted from a higher principle, from a more noble spiritual interest. The church there was not really a church. The spirit was absent, and my heart could feel no sympathy either for a church that so blatantly dishonored itself or for a religion that was represented by such a church. For that reason I postponed my profession of faith until the last possible moment, just before the [ministerial] candidate's exam. And it will hardly surprise you that, upon entering the academic world, I stood without defense or weapon against the powers of negation, which robbed me of my inherited faith before I knew what was happening. My faith was not deeply rooted in my unconverted, self-centered soul and was bound to wither once exposed to the scorching heat of the spirit of doubt. Not that I ever completely fell for positivism or atheism, but of the old treasure I retained nothing!

You can tell, therefore, that my later conversion to Christ was not a gradual shift from childlike piety to a sweet sense of salvation, but rather demanded a total change of my personality — heart, mind, and will. You can tell, further, that the special circumstances which collaborated in this process impressed me profoundly and, together with my conversion, determined the direction for my spiritual life on this new terrain. Careful self-examination, coupled with the memory of momentous days, leaves me not the slightest doubt that my heart's intimate bond to the Church question must be explained by the remarkable impressions from that intense epoch in my life.

Considering the delicate nature of this subject, I will touch on only three incidents even in this intimate account. I am sure you will not consider this a lack of full trust in your friendship. Not everything is proper. We should be especially reticent when it comes to sacred things. So I will only mention those facts that can be proclaimed in the courtyard without removing the veil behind which my soul retreats for its hidden encounters with God.

My first memory is fixed fast to the man whose name it is a pleasure once again to mention with respect and gratitude, my loyal counselor and inspiring teacher, Professor de Vries.[3] Towards the end of '58 he called me in and told me about the contest organized by the

2. The Huiszittenhuis was the meeting place of the directors of a charitable agency that provided for the city's homebound poor. Kuyper apparently is referring to a dispute between church and civil authorities over the supervision of poor relief.

3. Matthias de Vries (1820-92) was professor of Dutch literature at the University of Leiden, 1853-91. Both professor and subject were Kuyper's favorites as an undergraduate.

theological department of the University of Groningen. Its subject was the Church question! — the Church question as it had been resolved in the days of the Reformation by Calvin and à Lasco![4] I got interested and set to work. With the gracious assistance of the amanuensis at the Leiden library the works of Calvin were soon in my room — but how to get what à Lasco had written? The great university library offered almost nothing. The libraries at The Hague, Utrecht, and Groningen were just as poor. Even the catalogues of the Paris, St. Petersburg, and London libraries contained only a few items under à Lasco's name. However intensely I searched, not one of the major libraries of Europe held a significant collection of à Lasco's writings. The list of his known works, which is now at twenty-four, then already numbered sixteen. But none of the richest, most opulent libraries of Europe most famous for their completeness had a collection of more than three or four works.[5] You understand what this meant for me. When even one of the theology professors assured me that à Lasco's works were not to be found, and when I further reflected that the library at Groningen — probably the best furnished in this respect — was naturally closed to me, I decided to give up and went to tell Professor de Vries of my decision.

But he did not concur. He thought it was worth a try, since the other contestants would not have access to better resources. Furthermore, things were not as hopeless as they appeared. There were private book collections in our dear Holland which might have a few items to be gleaned. I should begin with a visit to his father, at the time still a minister in Haarlem.[6] He had a lot on church history. And even if he had nothing of à Lasco, he might be able to put me on the right track. His urging was too well-intended to resist, so I went to Haarlem. There I found the worthy old graybeard, who has since gone to the grave — so pleasantly disposed, most interested in my plans, most willing to help. But he couldn't disguise it: to the best of his recollection he had nothing on his

4. Jan Laski (Kuyper uses the then-customary Latinate form), 1499-1560, was a Polish convert to Protestantism and superindendent of the Reformed churches in East Frisia during the 1540s. There he showed remarkable talent for organization and controversialism, in both of which he upheld the Zwinglian/Zurich as opposed to the (strictly speaking) Calvinist/Genevan position. The church-polity dimension of that debate was the subject of the Groningen contest.

5. Kuyper's recollections on this point are not altogether accurate, since the Utrecht university library had at least seven Laski titles at the time. Further, the evidence from his surviving letters does not jibe with the account the next paragraph gives of his travels back and forth to Haarlem. See J. Stellingwerff, *Dr. Abraham Kuyper en de Vrije Universiteit* (Kampen: Kok, 1987), pp. 26-28.

6. Abraham de Vries was pastor of a Mennonite congregation in Haarlem.

Kuyper as a newly minted doctor of theology in 1862; his dissertation was a revised form of the essay he wrote for the Groningen prize.

shelves of what I was looking for. Yes, a small book by Menno Simons *to* à Lasco, but *by* à Lasco — he didn't think so. He was willing to give it a closer look, though, and he invited me to come back a week later. I was hardly disappointed by this outcome. I had expected it. And so, more to enjoy another beautiful afternoon in the Haarlem woods than with any hope for a better result, a week later I got back on the train to hear how his search had turned out.

You can imagine my feelings when, upon entering the old preacher's home and having been welcomed in a most friendly manner, I heard him say as if it were the simplest thing in the world: "Here's what I've found," pointing to an ample pile of duodecimos waiting for me on a table. Truly, I could hardly believe my eyes. How could this be? To have rummaged through all the libraries in our country. To have gone through the catalogues of the major libraries of Europe. To have found nowhere, not even in some forgotten corner (and what I learned then is still so today) the slightest collection of à Lasco's works. In all the anthologies, in all the guides to rare works, in all the literary

The model ship Kuyper built while recovering from overwork during his graduate studies (1861).

compendia I had read time and again that people had simply recopied the titles of à Lasco's works without ever seeing the actual volumes; that his works were considered extremely rare; that most were probably lost for good; and that, except for two or three individuals, no one in the last two centuries had actually held them in his hands! Then suddenly, as if by a divine miracle, to see before me a collection of Lasciana more complete than was — and is — to be found in any library in all of Europe. To find this treasure — for me, the "to be or not to be" of the contest — with a man to whom I had been referred by a good friend, who had no idea that it was to be found, indeed, who just a week earlier barely remembered the name of à Lasco and could not say whether there was anything among his precious books written by the Polish reformer. In all honesty you must personally experience such a surprise in your own life-struggle to know what it is to encounter a miracle of God on life's journey.

Now I say this with an infinitely greater sense of gratitude, but even then it touched me. It touched me so mightily that I renewed my prayers of thanksgiving, which I had neglected. Nor could I deny that it was no old wife's tale to speak of "the finger of God!" . . . Yes, I know: such an experience is not to be equated with a conversion. But it is an encounter with the living, acting, sovereign God on life's way. And the impression this almost unbelievable experience made on my heart was so deep and permanent that, by whatever route I go back in memory to recall the searching love of my God, I always return to this miraculous event of the Lasciana. Do I need to say that my work for the contest acquired a sacred and hallowed character that so far had been missing from my studies? Do I need to say that, when I won the prize, even my self-righteous heart was willing to give part of the honor and gratitude to another power than my own mind? Naturally, then, a year with such impressions, solely dedicated to the study of the Church question, gave my mind a lasting shape that remained even when the Groningen contest had been long forgotten.

My second recollection concerns an English novel that, though not in value, stands next to the Bible in its meaning for my life.[7] You know it well. It was written by Miss Yonge: not her *Trial,* nor her *Daisy Chain,* and neither her *Heart's Disease,* but the solemn scene set partly in Hollywell House, partly in Recoara, that she sketched under the title *The Heir of Redclyffe.*[8] This masterpiece was the instrument that broke my smug, rebellious heart! How? Let me recall a few incidents from this fascinating story and you will understand. The deft touch of this tale lies in its bringing together two diametrically opposed characters. These two torment each other, collide with each other, repel each other, and stubbornly fight through all the complexities of a most interesting family life. At last they are reconciled through the defeat of the stronger and the complete triumph of the seemingly weaker.

Philip de Morville is the first character, the rather unattractive Sir Guy is the second. Philip is a man of the world, sharp of mind, glib of

7. Kuyper's extant correspondence supports the authenticity of this episode; see George Puchinger, *Abraham Kuyper: de jonge Kuyper, 1837-1867* (Franeker: Wever, 1987), pp. 176-95.

8. Charlotte Mary Yonge (1823-1901) was a prolific writer of Victorian edifying literature, popular Bible and church histories, and romances. A resident of John Keble's parish of Otterbourne, Hampshire, Yonge was deeply taken with the Oxford Movement and wrote *The Heir of Redclyffe* as a "tract for the times" in fictional dress. It was her first great success, the most popular book of the year (1853) and particularly attractive to young men, whether junior military officers or esthetes like Dante Gabriel Rossetti and William Morris. (Margaret Mare and Alicia C. Percival, *Victorian Best-seller: The World of Charlotte M. Yonge* [London: Harrap, 1948], ch. 6, especially p. 136.) The other titles Kuyper mentions are *The Daisy Chain* (1856), *The Trial* (1864), and *Heartsease* (1854; Kuyper mistakes the title). Kuyper also consistently misspelled Philip de Morville as "Philipp"; I have corrected the error.

The young Johanna Schaay, who, as Kuyper's fiancée, gave him the novel that triggered his conversion.

tongue, moving gracefully in all circles. But he is wrapped up in his own self-confidence. He makes God do his bidding. He is blind to subtleties, convinced he can do whatever he wants, and takes pleasure in impressing others with his recklessness. Guy, on the other hand — such a different spirit. Tender and sensitive, gentle, not deft or well endowed with courage; a youth who prefers that others act rather than taking the lead himself; but strong in his faith by a power that flows in him from above; abundant in the life of the heart; possibly too focused on himself, yet also directed towards others with all the tenderness of a quick-tempered, sympathetic disposition. These two come into confrontation. Philip has to be first, while Guy resigns himself to the minor role. But even this submissiveness is not enough for Philip. He provokes Guy to resist so he can defeat him time and again in a new struggle. In the eyes of the world there is no more courageous, strong-willed, reliable young man in the whole region than Philip de Morville, while poor, tormented, inhibited, rather hot-headed Guy makes a fairly weak impression.

I shared that opinion. I was fascinated by Philip's character; it captivated me and pulled me along. I merely smiled when I thought of poor Guy. Philip was my hero, Philip I admired. That sort was great in my eyes and became greater as Guy's pathetic personality withdrew more and more into the shadows. But what happens? The climax of the story removes to Italy where Guy, on his way to Venice, learns that an English lord by the name of Morville has been involved in an accident and lies sick in Recoara. The two meet again under totally different circumstances. Philip is now bereft of his world of glittering success, while the sick room is precisely where Guy can unlock the greatness of his soul. All the more so when, after Philip's recovery, Guy himself is afflicted by what the Italian doctor alarmingly calls "una febbre molto grave" and sees his end approaching. Then, almost imperceptibly, automatically, the roles are reversed so that the once so extraordinary Philip is disclosed in all his vanity and inner emptiness while Guy excels in a true greatness and inner strength.

This fascinated and touched me, even before I realized what was happening. At first it was purely esthetic. But then the author skillfully diminished Philip even in his own estimation, led him step by step to recognize his own limitations and Guy's moral superiority, and gradually awakened in him a sense of discontent with his own character. He felt remorse for his early derision, he repented of his improper self-confidence, until at last the haughty Philip fell to his knees before the poor Guy. Oh, at that moment it seemed as if in the crushed Philip my own heart was devastated, as if each of his words of self-condemnation cut through my soul as a judgment on my own ambitions and character. I envied the fortunate repentant as I read: "His confession of guilt brought him restoration. His repentance was genuine, to the extent that he realized his sins. And once he had come to the point where he could speak of it, he no longer found anything in Guy to criticize or condemn but only a warm friend with a good and noble heart who was anxious not to hurt him by even the slightest word!"[9]

I read on until I reached the day of Guy's death. The Anglican

9. In the J. M. Dent/E. P. Hutton edition (1909), this episode comes at p. 408, ch. 32. Kuyper's Dutch paraphrases rather than exactly translates the English.

clergyman of the coastal resort met with the family members to celebrate the Lord's Supper together with the weak sufferer. But Philip was afraid to enter; this was not for him! "I cannot, I cannot come, I am not worthy!" he told Amabel, who persistently urged him. But when the devout and noble woman whispered to him: "A broken and contrite heart, O God, you will not despise," the story continues with these words: "This was a drop of balm for his soul, a drop of balm that soothed his pain! Philip got up, went, and knelt next to Amabel at Guy's deathbed."[10] At that moment — I was by myself — I felt the scene overwhelm me. I read how Philip wept, and, dear brother, tears welled up in my eyes too. I read that Philip knelt and before I knew it, I was kneeling in front of my chair with folded hands. Oh, what my soul experienced at that moment I fully understood only later. Yet, from that moment on I despised what I used to admire and I sought what I had dared to despise!

Enough. My friend, you understand how unforgettable is the impression of so intense an experience, how this internal struggle of soul belongs to the realm of the eternal, how even after so many days it stands out in the mind fresh and powerful as something that just happened. Now if you're wondering what this has to do with the Church question, I'll answer: read *The Heir of Redclyffe* and you will understand. That same evening I read on, read how the blessed Guy died peacefully, read how he was brought to Recoara's cemetery, and then came upon this sentence: "The word of peace rustled over the graves with the melodious sounds of the English Liturgy as his remains were laid to rest below the foliage of a beautiful chestnut tree, rendered a home by those words of his Mother church — the mother who had guided each of his steps in his orphaned life."[11] That was what I wanted. Such a church I never saw or knew. Oh, to have such a church, a "mother who guides our steps from our youth!" That was my homesickness, the thirst of my whole being. That I had missed. That had to be my means of salvation. And so my ideal for churchly life came to me in this fleeting word. When I thumbed through this delightful book again, mindful of the care of the Church; when I realized how Guy had been touched by what we seem to have lost, by the lofty significance of the Sacrament, by the prescribed forms of private and public worship, by the impressive liturgy and the blessed "Prayer-book," which he bequeathed to Philip just before his death: at that moment the predilection for prescribed ritual, the high estimation of the Sacrament, the appreciation for the Liturgy became rooted in me for all

10. *The Heir of Redclyffe,* p. 448, ch. 35.

11. *The Heir of Redclyffe,* p. 458, ch. 36. Kuyper quotes the text beginning with "rendered a home" exactly in English.

time. From then on I have longed with all my soul for a sanctified Church wherein my soul and those of my loved ones can enjoy the quiet refreshment of peace, far from all confusion, under its firm, lasting, and authoritative guidance.

I now come to my third recollection — no longer from my student years but from the time of my ministry.[12] I was entrusted with a congregation to which I came not primarily to give out of what I possessed but with the quiet prayer that my empty heart would be quickened and fed by the life of the church. For many days that hope was disappointed. The circles in which I moved were (with some exceptions) characterized by a rigid conservatism, orthodox in appearance but without the genuine glow of spiritual vitality. No voice from the depths, no word from distant history spoke in the daily life of the church. Everybody was content with the way things went. They were willing to accept from me but preferred not to give anything back. I heard that there was a small group of malcontents in the flock, but the rumors about these know-it-alls were more for ill than good. They were a bunch of cantankerous, proud eccentrics who "make life miserable for every minister." Besides, most of them were of such low social status that it was deemed best not to worry about them but to ignore them, just as previous ministers had done.

But I found it impossible to do so. Thus, with a trembling heart that befits a young minister who has to face such fires, I knocked in the course of my visitations on the doors of these "fanatics" too. The reception that awaited me was far from cordial. Rumors had reached them that my orthodoxy was yet in its infancy, and discerning in me rather a representative of the church they disliked than an individual human being, they set themselves against me. Nonetheless these simple, if somewhat irritated, souls did not repel me. For here, I realized, was more than mere routine. Here was conviction. Here the topics of conversation went beyond the nice weather and who happened to be ill and who had dismissed his workman. Here was interest in spiritual matters. Moreover, here was knowledge. With the meager Bible knowledge I had picked up at the university I could not measure up to these simple folk. And not just knowledge of the Bible but also of a well-ordered worldview, be it of the old Reformed type. At times it seemed as if I were back in the classroom hearing my talented professor Scholten lecture about the "doctrine of the Reformed Church," though with reversed sympathies. Furthermore — and for me this was the greatest attraction — here spoke a heart that had

12. This refers to Kuyper's pastorate at Beesd, July 1863-November 1867.

a history and life-experience, its own observations and emotions, and that not only had them but knew them. All this made me come back, and that in turn won their welcome. And so the debate began.

It was soon over. Of course I did my best to maintain my ministerial honor but despite myself I felt more inclined to listen than to speak during these encounters. And somehow I noticed that, after such a meeting, the preaching on Sunday went better. Yet it annoyed me that these people were so inflexible. Having shown so much sensitivity myself, I felt I could rightfully claim a more flexible response. But no, never even a hint of budging. I observed that they were not intent on winning my sympathy but on the triumph of their cause. They knew of no compromise or concession, and more and more I found myself confronted with a painful choice: either sharply resist them or unconditionally join them in a principled recognition of "full sovereign grace" — as they called it — without leaving room for even the tiniest safety valves in which I sought refuge. Well, dear brother, I did not oppose them and I still thank God that I made that choice. Their unremitting perseverance has become the blessing of my heart, the rise of the morning star for my life. I had been convicted but had not yet found the Word of reconciliation. That they brought me, with their imperfect language, in that absolute form which alone can give rest to my soul: in the worship and adoration of a God who works all things, both the willing and the working, according to his good pleasure!

Yet, you can see they didn't give me enough. The thinking of our era differs from that of Gomarus,[13] and their world of thought was literally still rooted in the days immediately following the Reformation. Where could I find help? Orthodox books I neither had nor knew. So it was in those days among the theological students at Leiden. The orthodox faith was presented to us in such a ludicrous, caricatured way that it seemed a luxury and waste of money for students of modest means to spend anything on such misbegotten writings. I had become acquainted with Calvin and à Lasco, but in reading them it never occurred to me that this might be the truth. My heart still stood against this. I read and studied them when dealing with some historical problem or theoretical question but simply severed their ecclesiological views from their taproot. My thesis in the essay-contest was thus to thoroughly contest the Calvinist and advance toward the Groninger position. At the time the tenderness

13. Franciscus Gomarus (1563-1641), long professor of theology at Leiden and Groningen, led the attack on Jacobus Arminius and his followers that ended with the Dutch Reformed Church's strong assertion of predestination at the Synod of Dort (1618-19).

of this school attracted my soul, which had experienced an inner change but had not yet been illuminated by the light of the Word.

But now I could no longer do without books. Once a ray of light had fallen upon the eye of my soul from this humble abode I simply had to acquire more knowledge. At first Gunning interested me. I had heard about him in Leiden, through the Berch van Heemstede family. Gunning led me to Dr. de la Saussaye's writings.[14] I had met him twice in Leiden but without any real spiritual connection. The works of both greatly fascinated me; they were a link in the chain of my development that I can never overestimate. And yet, despite all my efforts to that end, they did not satisfy me. Our friend and brother Bronsveld unwittingly made me aware of this. At a regional meeting we asked each other about what we liked to read. When I mentioned Saussaye and Gunning, he commented with his unique drollery: "Really! I need more than that!" I had to admit, I did too. Inspiring, fascinating, captivating, but too relative, too uncertain of definition, too fluid and accommodating, too bubbling and drifting to give my spirit stability. Gunning gave substance for my soul and pulled it from its cocoon, but the framework for my thinking depended more on my simple malcontents.

Could the precision missing in our country perhaps be found abroad? Who knew? It was worth trying, so I summoned Martensen, Nitzsch, Lange, Vinet, etc. and devoured them with rare pleasure.[15] But even here I did not find that shelter in the rocks which, being founded on the rock and being hewn from the rock of thought, laughs at every

14. Johannes Hermanus Gunning, Jr. (1829-1905) and Daniel Chantepie de la Saussaye (1818-74) were leading proponents of the "Ethical" school of theology that attempted to mediate between traditional orthodoxy and rationalist critiques of Christianity by amplifying pious experience and ethical concerns (hence the name of their school). Andries Willem Bronsveld (1839-1924) was a contemporary and (at this juncture) associate of Kuyper but later became one of his harshest and most persistent critics. He too belonged to the Ethical party, was a devout defender of the national church, and took an elitist stance on sociopolitical matters.

15. Hans Lassen Martensen (1808-84) was a Danish Lutheran bishop and theologian enamored of comprehensive systems, his own being built upon a reconciliation of Schleiermacher and Hegel via Franz Baader. His dogmatics was published in 1849; his three-volume ethics in 1871-78. Karl Immanuel Nitzsch (1787-1868) taught theology at Bonn and Berlin and was the foremost German mediating theologian of his time. He defended the plan to unite the Reformed and Lutheran churches and was most noted for his three-volume practical theology (which centered on church life), published 1847-67. Johann Peter Lange (1802-84) was a student of Nitzsch, a professor of dogmatics at Zurich and Bonn, a poetic and fanciful spirit, and author of a five-volume rejoinder to David W. Strauss on the historical Jesus. Alexandre Rodolfe Vinet (1797-1847) was a Swiss-French Reformed pastor and professor of theology at Lausanne, a tireless champion of freedom of conscience, a consummate mediating theologian, and an individualist-voluntarist in ecclesiology.

The "stubborn fanatic" Kuyper remembered best from his first pastorate at Beesd was the young woman Pietje Baltus. Upon her death, some fifty years after their first encounter, Kuyper published this tribute.

Pietje Baltus

Our paper too must include a brief word of recollection upon the death of Pietje Baltus.

As the reader knows, Dr. Kuyper became acquainted with this humble soul when he was a preacher in the village of Beesd, an event not without consequence for the subsequent course of his life.

The thing that marked this woman, who was still young at the time, was *her decisiveness.* In Beesd no modern preacher had yet occupied its pulpit and the principal of the public school in this Betuwe village was a dear old believer, Mr. Kievits. But though "orthodoxy" more or less continued to set the tone in Beesd, Pietje Baltus wanted no part of this kind of church life. It was a poor halfway thing to her, a lot of tomfoolery that simply led to further decline. The church of God could not live on it, let alone flourish. So she attended no church and did not even want to receive such a half-baked preacher into her home. She insisted on a *full* confession of the faith for which our martyrs had died. In all those compromises and accommodations and concessions she had seen the face of death.

So when Dr. Kuyper became the preacher, she wanted no part of him. Presumably he was just another one of those half-grown,

storm. It was Calvin himself (with the help of Kohlbrugge's[16] vigorous, deep-delving words) who first disclosed to me those solid, unwavering lines that only need to be traced to inspire full confidence. I saw at once that we had to advance exegetically, psychologically, and historically beyond him, but nonetheless here I found the foundations which, banning

16. Herman Friedrich Kohlbrügge (1803-75) was a theologian and long-time pastor of an independent Reformed congregation in Elberfeld, Germany. He was deeply informed by the thought of Calvin and widely read by laity, but at odds with church establishments, the modernizing state, and academic theology. Although the two did not always agree, Kuyper took inspiration from him, particularly with respect to his valorization of the local congregation as a new organic community radiating benefits to the broader society.

half-committed, half-baked, half-winged church wreckers. And this was understandable. When he arrived at Beesd, though he was what was then called "conservative," he leaned strongly toward the "ethical" wing of the church and therefore tended to be anti-Reformed.

Still a meeting did take place and that encounter brought about a change in Dr. K.'s conviction. He suddenly grasped *the power of the absolute* in this woman and broke with all halfheartedness. Then he got acquainted with the spiritual legacy of the fathers. Dordt, which had first repelled him, from that time on became attractive to him. Also from Calvin he absorbed rays of light.

That simple woman had bent the line of his life from a halfway position to a whole one, and it has consistently remained Dr. K.'s grateful confession that only when he made her acquaintance did he get to where he now felt he had to be.

On the occasion of her death the *Telegraaf* commented on the remarkable influence this Pietje Baltus had on our church history the past half century. That comment is correct. And so by her graveside we may be permitted to pray that the "simple in the land," in line with the noble example given by this devout woman, may persevere in the *absoluteness* of their faith!

One child of God, however insignificant by the world's standards, can be like the morning star, again bringing radiance into the night of the church's life.

De Standaard, 30 March 1914

all doubt, permitted the edifice of faith to be constructed in a completely logical style — and with the surprising result that the most consistent ethic ruled in its inner chambers. And what else became clear? Simply that these laborers, tucked away in a corner, had uttered in their coarse dialect the same thing that Calvin gave me to read in his precise Latin. Calvin was still present, however gnarled, in these simple peasants who hardly knew his name. And Calvin had so taught that, centuries after his death, in a foreign land, in an obscure village, in a room with a stone floor, people with a common laborer's brain could still *understand* him.

That mystery allowed of only one solution: Calvin had *founded a church,* and through his *fixed church form* he succeeded in spreading blessings and peace to receptive hearts among all the nations of Europe and across the

A later photo of Pietje Baltus in the classic pose of resolute rural Calvinism.

sea, in town and village, even among the poor and the lowly. And precisely on the doctrine of the church the systems of Gunning, Saussaye, Martensen, and Lange were the weakest. They touched this topic only superficially. Their word, marvelous in all other respects, was indecisive here; it failed to give direction and left you in your fix! And so the old memories revived and the impressions of earlier experiences went to work. I remembered what Calvin had so beautifully stated in the fourth book of his *Institutes* about God as our Father and "the church as our Mother."[17] I pondered anew on

17. Kuyper is referring to Calvin's *Institutes,* IV/1/1, which concludes, quoting Mark 10:9: "'Therefore, what God has joined together, let not man put asunder,' so that for those to whom he is Father the Church may also be Mother."

the touching words of Miss Yonge: "The Mother church, the mother who had guided each step in his orphaned life." And now I saw in actual persons, in very fact, what miraculous, unutterable, almost unbelievable power a spiritually organized church may yet reveal, silently and unobtrusively, even amid the disintegration we had suffered, so long as she knows what she wants and allows her word to be the form of her essential thought. I couldn't help it. The lack of a solid church concept had become, in spite of myself, the "Carthago delenda" of my personality. And so, taking my own thirst as a measure of the inner needs of others, and longing with all my heart that they might also receive that supreme, calm commitment: for my own sake and for others', the restoration of "a church that could be our Mother" had to become the goal of my life.

Here then, dear friend and brother, an intimate glimpse into my past to explain my great interest in the Church question. I realize that many an unspiritual person will ridicule these reminiscences. But that ought not deter you from helping others to praise and worship Him who as the faithful Shepherd has ever shown forth his searching Compassion. Moreover, since people have preferred to attribute my feeling for the Church question to sinful and unholy motives, I do not wish continued silence about the truth to provide these false rumors with a semblance of justification. One more thing. I am often told: "We agree in our beliefs; we just differ on the church," thereby suggesting that my general beliefs and my particular views on the church are unrelated, without a connecting spiritual bond, that they can be combined or separated at will. My whole soul rises up against that notion. I cannot, I must not, allow it to persist. My view of the church is indeed a matter of conviction. And provided that people open their hearts sufficiently, I believe that in many cases I can point to a deviation in the very first phase of their spiritual life which leads to a divergent concept on the "locus de ecclesia."

CHURCH AND THEOLOGY

Conservatism and Orthodoxy: False and True Preservation[1]

A farewell sermon preached in the Domkerk at Utrecht, 31 July 1870

". . . hold fast to what you have . . ." (Rev. 3:11b)

With the issues of personal faith resolved, Kuyper returned to the "church question" that had been troubling him all along. His move from the village of Beesd to the university city of Utrecht gave him an eminent stage on which to take it up. A friendly one, too, for Utrecht was the Jerusalem of conservative Dutch Calvinism, and some of its most eminent representatives had engineered his appointment to its venerable church on the city square in 1867.

Kuyper soon discovered his differences with these patrons, however. He insisted that their conservative sentiments were not enough but required firm doctrinal definition. He chafed at their reactive strategy and yearned to seize the initiative. And he did not stay on church ground but began agitating about public education as well. The Utrecht establishment was not pleased. For purposes of moral control they were committed to a unified national church, only under more conservative auspices than those currently prevailing, and to a

1. The last word in the Dutch title, *behoudzucht,* literally means "a craving to preserve or maintain" and is usually translated as "conservatism." The text follows this convention but the title is rendered differently, since Kuyper there uses two different Dutch terms for "conservatism." Beyond that, the entire sermon is built on a pun. *Behoudenis* means "salvation," and for Kuyper the proper solution to the church question has direct import for the church's proclamation of the gospel. "True" *behoudzucht,* that is, entails true *behoudenis.*

modestly Christian common school. Kuyper, on the other hand, wanted well-defined bodies of disciplined commitment, even at the cost of institutional fragmentation. Within three years of his arrival he departed for Amsterdam, delivering the sermon that follows as a farewell.

Kuyper used the occasion to conduct a postmortem not only on his three years in Utrecht but on a whole generation of conservative Protestant history in the Netherlands. Dutch Calvinism Utrecht-style was in a sleep verging on coma, he insisted, because its formulas were adapted to an age that had passed. This sermon spells out what the new era required: a more radical spirit in the service of a renewed tradition, and a sharp eye to distinguish the heart of that tradition from mere custom, the stolid usages fit only for the dustbin.

That prescription rested on a key philosophical assumption that Kuyper conveys with color and verve. Form and spirit need each other absolutely; if authentic, they would give rise to each other naturally; once corrupted, they would pervert each other and the church inevitably. Yet Kuyper thought reform was ever possible, and in leaving for the national capital he testified eloquently to his faith that vital conviction cannot be withstood and that the most venerable theology can be the wedge of a dynamic future.

The sermon, published as *Conservatisme en Orthodoxie: Valsche en Ware Behoudzucht. Afscheidsrede uitgesproken in de Domkerk te Utrecht, 31 Juli 1870* (Amsterdam: H. de Hoogh, 1870), is reproduced here virtually entire and was translated by John Vriend.

THERE IS A TIME for coming, my Congregation, and a time for leaving. Although the first moment occurred for me less than three years ago, the second has already arrived. So in taking my leave from you, how could I forget my coming to you, and at this moment of departure ignore that other moment when from this same pulpit I brought you my first message? Given the brief time that has elapsed and given the turning point at which I now find myself, you will be prepared, I trust, to tolerate a reminder of that first sermon.

I do not intend by this reminder to plead for your interest in the things that have befallen me personally. My choice of text has already signaled how little I am disposed to misuse this occasion of divine worship for the purpose of human self-worship. Nor do I intend to work on your emotions. In my opinion, a Christian rather should be averse to the whipped-up emotionality that regales itself on weak nerves and sneaks in sadness from an imaginary world. . . . [Kuyper differentiates between his personal friends in the assembly, for whom emotional expression would be appropriate, and the congregation as a whole, for whom a calm sensibility ought to be preserved.]

No, it is the content, not the occasion, of that first sermon that prompts me to recall it.[2] As some of you remember it concerned the problem of the church. I spoke of that as being, in my opinion, the primary problem of the day. I argued against the view that this problem does not touch your faith. I ventured the opinion that the time had come to solve that problem and did not hide my intent to strive to do my duty in this connection. What has happened to us since then seems to me ill-suited to weaken that conviction. These have been stormy years that we have lived through; many a brick has come crashing down from the crumbling ruins. The absence of a church worthy of the name swelled the demand for its reconstruction. Gradually recovering from a befuddled spirituality that vaporizes everything, people have ever more insistently called for the appearance of a Christianity with firm forms, and through a threefold struggle involving church *elections,* church *property,* and churchly *baptism,* the demand has been put with mounting urgency to our ecclesiastical apparatus either to give us back a church of Christ or to dissolve and so to disappear from the scene.[3]

Outside the sphere of the institutional church this problem had powerful repercussions all around. Top-level politicians and the shapers of the popular mind increasingly realized that with the revival of the faith the church again had to be reckoned with. After all, the barren years behind us, however badly they reflected on the influence of a vacuous denomination, decided nothing with respect to the influence of a vital *church.* Too soon had people sounded the death knell over the age-old conflict between church and world, as they realized when the "free church" emerged as a new phenomenon, and no one dares guess the importance that this reborn power might well achieve in the future. Rome forged a double bond: of the human conscience to the church and of the

2. Kuyper's Utrecht inaugural sermon, *De Menschwording Gods het levensbeginsel der Kerk* (God become man: the life-principle of the church), showed his high-church proclivities and, according to his critics, a Hegelian-Idealist streak. His work at Utrecht was to take the new slant of refining the true from out of the nominal membership and investing church autonomy and purity in that band.

3. In his pastorate Kuyper had worked against synodical officials to enhance the role of the congregation in the election of church officers and the control of church properties, and wanted to have the official formulary followed exactly at baptism.

Johan Rudolf Thorbecke,
the great leader of mid-century Dutch liberalism
who set the model Kuyper vowed to match
and the agenda he would combat.

church to the state. That double bond had to snap if the human spirit was to be free again. The Reformation yielded freedom of conscience but did not relax the ties that bound the church to the state. For this reason the church of the Reformation soon saw the stream of its life freeze over, could not finish building its organization, and in the end drove the free life of the spirit from its premises. Thus its soul was separated from its body. A lifeless church had to do without the Christian spirit and no longer embodied the mind of Christ, so both lost their influence. But now, now that the second bond has increasingly relaxed and almost snapped, now that the Christian spirit has reawakened, wed again to the newly liberated church, now those who are for Christ hope for, and those who are against Christ dread, the development of that new power. Now people on either side no longer deny the decisive weight that the church can bring to bear in the struggle over the schools, society, and the life of the people. Now people more readily believe the truth that the problem of the church is none other than the problem of Christianity itself.

The clarification of a once-so-confused situation, Congregation, has been an incalculable boon. One feels driven to shout a Hallelujah to Christ at seeing this surprising turn in fortune as the battle lines are drawn more sharply. After all, what were our chances like a quarter of a century ago and what are they now? Consider: those who hid their heads then can now be seen venturing out into the open field. Today those are putting on laurels who were then scourged by abuse and insult. Those who were oppressed yesterday are today called to rule over their oppressors. The sounds of lament have died away and songs of rejoicing are in the air.

Yes, in this I rejoice with you, but I want to add: precisely in this unprecedented prosperity lies a danger. Sometimes overconfidence is more to be feared than despondency. As long as the cross presses hard, that which is false automatically separates itself; but when we start waving palm leaves, we had better be unsparingly critical of our own hearts, check our own weapons with sharper scrutiny, and examine our ranks with a penetrating eye. In the absence of this kind of vigilance — who knows? — the day of our victory could some day be the day of our defeat! Therefore let everyone listen to what the Spirit says to the church: "Hold fast to what you have." Hold on to what you have gained, hold on to what you have been given. Hold on to it, but not in the spirit of a killing conservatism which, under the motto of "safe and sound," causes life to wither. This fallacious preservation has nothing in common with the true sort. *Conservatism* and *orthodoxy,* terms which are often confused, need to be most sharply distinguished today. And so, before I leave you, the prosperity of the moment prompts me to warn you against the *false* and to rouse you to the *true conservatism*.

* * *

Far from being hostile to Christianity, conservatism lies in its blood. Christianity came to save. Salvation is the hope-giving word that it unfurls on its banner. Precisely as a power of salvation it militates against destruction. True: Christianity aims at a new creation, but the new from the old, a new-fashioned from the old fallen world that already exists. It produces children of God not by calling them forth from the stones of the wilderness but by regenerating human beings. Every stanza of the

Guillaume Groen van Prinsterer, the Antirevolutionary (confessional-Calvinist) political leader whom Kuyper took as a mentor during his Utrecht years.

psalm of grace is rooted in the unchanging refrain: "And calls sinners to be children of God" [1 John 3:1]. Unlike the revolution which it opposes, it lives not by hollow ideas but by real power; it does not conjure up castles in the air but builds a solid home on the *given* foundation from the materials at hand. Revolution demolishes and destroys, willfully overturning all existing structures to rave about a better world, a world that appears in its dreams and disappears along with them. It is — to quote Isaiah — like one "who flees upon horses and has no confidence in quietness" [Isa. 30:15-16]. Restlessly, ever onward, it trots up its highway in the sky until the world sinks away at its feet, leaving not a whisper of compassion for that broken creation down below. Thus it finds conservatism repugnant; both the false type and the true fall under its judgment.

Not so Christianity. While it uncovers the curse and points out the decay in the root of life, nevertheless it seizes that cancerous root to revitalize its fibers and says: "Let what is broken be bound up; may what is injured be healed; what has gone astray I will bring back." With Ezekiel's oracle it says to that which is flailing about in its blood: "As you lie in your blood, I say: Live!" [Ezek. 16:6]. Conservatism is so integral to the core of its being that it even refuses to abandon the human body to death but in the article concerning the "resurrection of the body" prophesies complete salvation.

Precisely because it seeks to save, Christianity detests a false conservatism that adorns itself with the name of Christianity but is devoid of its power. Who would save the sick by keeping the patient in the status quo? He will die before your eyes, with your false conservatism responsible for his death. To be conservative in that sense, to preserve in that sense, is to block Christianity from pursuing its goal. In a world of sin, that which is cannot remain as it is. It will not be saved in its present state, for there it remains a certain prey to destruction. Therefore, to the person who after the fall still wants to eat of the tree of life, Christianity is like the cherub with the flaming sword who drives him out of his now-lethal paradise [Gen. 3:24]. For the plant of this world sin is not just a scorching wind that withers the top of its leaves but a deadly toxin which, once absorbed into the root, attacks its very life, seeps through its fibers, and causes leaf and blossom to wilt and die. What is there, what can you name, that has escaped its infection? It is all sick, devoid of freshness and vitality, a ruin in your own heart and, by virtue of the curse, no less a ruin in the world around you. How then, I ask you, could Christianity refrain from fulminating against a conservatism which, looking around in such a world, affirms even of the fallen creation "that it is good"? How could it refrain from raging against a false conservatism which seeks to dam up the stream of life, swears by the status quo, and resists the surgery needed to save the sick? Of course, if you do not know the corrosive power of sin and death, then that explains why you believe you could combine Christianity with such a conservatism. But in reality the two are sworn enemies. In reality Christianity is like the arm of God by which he would lift that world out of its decline, and that conservatism is like the sinister arm from below which seeks to frustrate God's work, pulling that world down so that it may continue to languish in its sunken state.

Sin: there is the gulf that forever separates Christianity from that conservatism, a gulf no one can cross. Whereas this conservatism wants to keep the sin-sick life as it is, Christianity intends to save the sin-sickened life by driving out the sickness. While *it* swears by *the temple as it stands,* Christianity would tear it down and build it anew by its spirit. Whereas it walks by *sight,* Christianity walks by *faith.* While it would freeze the eternal in the form of things, Christianity seeks to reanimate that dead form with the eternal breath. That is why it clings tightly to a world which Christianity teaches us to hate, and settles down to rest there while Christianity remains a leaven that leaves nothing unaffected by its continuing ferment.

However sharply delineated the difference may be, there is a very serious danger that this conservatism will creep into the church, if for no other reason than that a tenacious attachment to tradition has been a demonstrable feature of religion in every age and among every people. In part this is because a sense of guilt keeps whispering in our ear of a paradise that lies behind us and makes us timid in the face of progress. Even more because the soul that seeks the eternal reaches out not only to what lies ahead but also to what lies behind. It not only turns to God but has its origin in God. Though the everlasting behind us is not more pure, it is certainly more tangible than the everlasting which lies ahead. Without being aware of it, fascinated by what lies behind, we close our eyes to what lies ahead. Quenching life, we find our peace solely in the past. Besides, this same conservatism exists outside the church of Christ as a beneficent school of thought necessarily required by the nature of things. There, in every sphere of life, it constitutes a real power whose support one does not easily spurn, especially since it has consistently proved inclined to protect a firm religious outlook against skepticism. In the face of intense religious struggles and the fierce harassment of Christianity, what could be more natural than to court this school of thought as an ally?

Now then, put those two together: conservatism in the life of society and the attachment to tradition which religion never abandons. In the process do not overlook our national character which is loath to rouse itself from its slumbers. Note too the fierce conflict in which Christianity is involved today. Then you will no longer deny that the vitality of our faith is once again threatened with enervation by false conservatism and that many are joining our ranks whose goal is not, as is ours, the victory of Christianity but merely the triumph of conservatism.

* * *

This sickness, Congregation, usually manifests itself in three forms. It either wants to restore what our ancestors built up, to preserve what has been saved thus far, or to be content with the ever-diminishing influence still left to us.

The first group, those who want to recall the old, compel respect even when one opposes their efforts.[4] As a rule they are men of integrity, and what they want they want utterly. They cannot imagine for themselves a principle that does not control life in all its expressions. And therefore, averse to the aimless meandering to which our age has accustomed its children, they search for a life-concept that can give firm direction to their conduct and, by the magical power of unity, strengthen the muscles of their life. But alas, all their searching is in vain. They do not see this life-concept around them, and the kind of religion that dared present itself in this vein, while not marred by halfheartedness, so rudely breaks the tenderest cords in the human heart that, far from being an explanation of life, it proved to be its destruction. And yet, they themselves can't create it. For such heroic labor they lack the intellectual strength and moral courage.

Is it any wonder, then, that the past gradually begins to attract them so powerfully, that their imagination is increasingly fascinated by the manly strength so brilliantly displayed by the heroes of the Reformation? There they see what they are looking for: an unbroken unity encompassing the whole of life, a single-minded devotion to the cause that possessed their soul, a total poise resulting from an unassailable faith. In those lives was character, and hence not a hint of halfheartedness. Every field of life was controlled by one idea which bound their soul to the eternal. If only they could have lived then! If their lot had fallen in that age, how they would have expanded their lungs to inhale all that fresh and vital air! Why did it vanish, that wondrous age of power whose ripples can still be faintly felt in the motives of our century? O yes, there were dark shadows, but with such a bright shining of the light, how could it have been otherwise? No, the lighter shadows of today cannot reconcile them to the twilight of our time. They try again for that fullness of light even if the shadows have to be painted all the darker for it. "Return! Return!" they cry to the age of our ancestors. Matching the deed to their cry they gird themselves for imitation and set out to reconstruct what the hands of their ancestors had fashioned.

But why was it that they never succeeded in keeping one stone permanently on another? It was because they wanted to *repristinate* and because *repristination* is an undertaking that is self-condemned. "Always

4. Kuyper refers here to such groups as the Seceders of 1834 and the followers of Philip J. Hoedemaker (1839-1910), who were devoted to the letter as well as to the spirit of classic Reformed theology and church polity. Hoedemaker cooperated with Kuyper in founding the Free University and, at first, in the Doleantie, but finally broke with him in favor of national church ideals. Significantly, Utrecht was his native city.

flow and never reverse yourself" is the high decree that the Creator himself laid down for the stream of time. No place can be found today for what existed yesterday, so their cries ever come back to them without effect. "Hold fast" not what your fathers had but "what you yourselves have" is the word of life that renders sterile from the start whatever ventures to violate that law of life. And so they squander their energies in building something they will never finish. They force themselves outside of their own time at the cost of having any influence on the life that surrounds them. In the end they turn against their own brothers, fragmenting even more the little power that remains. Worst of all, their own spiritual life has to suffer, and as a result of continual disappointment, the grave of their dearest wishes must become the grave of their faith itself.

No, you men who honor the fathers: first seek to have for yourself the life your fathers had and then hold fast what you have. Then articulate that life in your own language as they did in theirs. Struggle as they did to pump that life into the arteries of the life of our church and society. Then not being a dead form but a living fellowship will unite you with them, faith will be a power in your own life, and your building project will reach complete success.

* * *

Another group is more suited for life but less resilient, Congregation: those who do not want to have for themselves all that their ancestors had but only wish to keep that which is still left of the legacy.[5] Even in the saddest times of spiritual decline something of the sacred still remained available to the church; since then, this century's revival of faith brought back to us many a precious heirloom. To save that, not to ask for more; to take a firm stand for that, not to reach for more, became the slogan of these folks. They venture not to create anything new; the old they cannot call back; what else can they do, then, but devote all their love to what has been preserved, firmly resolved to strike back every hand reaching out to rob them of that jewel.

Still, such striving can only satisfy people for a time. Naturally, those once robbed of nearly everything jump for joy when a part of their treasure returns to them. For that reason, among our orthodox folks the first revival ruled out every notion but gratitude and prompted every one to

5. This section is Kuyper's critique of the *Réveil*'s course of development and inherent weaknesses, especially as they were manifest in Utrecht. The "first revival" in the next paragraph refers to the birth of the movement some fifty years previous.

unite with his brother on the standard of spiritual affinity alone. This flexibility was entirely understandable where greater rigor would have quenched the dimly burning wick, the newly generated life. If opinions were divided on many issues, there was a common basis, however limited, on which they could stand united. Oh, those first days of new life were beautiful indeed when in childlike innocence people let themselves float down the stream, not yet fearing any storms or thinking of the demands of life.

Nevertheless, those demands came, and then it became clear that to live together requires more than a common basis. One soon gets accustomed to shared beliefs, but the question of the next step could no longer be suppressed. The more people tried to ignore their differences the more they were drawn to them — and then the problems burst into full view. For then everyone began to apply his own measures and there was no standard that could decide. Then everyone began to swear by his own slogans and wander down his own paths, and all too cruelly the carefree circle of brothers had to pay the penalty for opting to be *a circle of friends* rather than a *church.* People now discovered that for public life spiritual affinity is not enough; one needs the bond of a confession.

Timidly they asked each other: "what confession should it be?" The ties with the past had been broken; to demand too much would offend too many. And so the fumbling search was on. Arbitrariness became the rule; a boundary was roughed out; a standard was set based on guesses about majority opinion to henceforth decide what could rightfully claim the honor of being called "orthodox." "Hold fast to what you have" was still the rallying cry, but *what* people had in Christ remained uncertain for the heart and undecided for the mind. Afraid of the driving force of principles, people shrank from thinking through the implications of truth, and an unprincipled "approximately" was chosen over the absoluteness of our fathers as the article of highest wisdom. From that moment on a nervous scrupulosity hindered every step; mutual distrust blocked every demonstration of power. People were doomed to inaction. They kept gliding over the surface, fearing that if they immersed themselves more deeply they would drown. And so, internally divided, now swinging one way, now another, they could not stand firm, much less show a character that compelled respect from the enemy. That road, too, failed to lead to victory. Neither was there any power in it. The once frozen stream burst loose; for a moment we heard the ripple of its waves. Are we now already to slow it down so that it will soon stagnate for ever? No, beloved, it is not the frozen waters but the foaming streams which carry life and bring salvation!

* * *

The third form of the disease gradually evolves from the former: I mean the desire only to preserve what the enemy has left to us.[6] Naturally the uncertainty into which we have fallen had to come to the point where people accepted *any* circumstance. When the boundary that defines your sacred turf is sharply drawn and visible to all, a line you will not allow to be crossed, a line whose violation makes you reach for your sword, then, at that location, it is a matter of "now or never." But if your boundary has become uncertain, vague, even invisible, the fear of drawing your sword soon keeps your hand from the hilt and no one fears any blame for taking one step backward after another. This process continues until finally the sacred domain is totally lost and no courage remains for a struggle that is now useless. It is precisely that uncertainty which cuts the lines of our power, that lack of firmness which makes us hesitant, that hesitancy which causes us to hang back and procrastinate, and with that procrastination the fire of our enthusiasm dies out before we realize it.

Yet, my Congregation, that is what has happened to us. We said we were prepared to leave *this* alone but if *that* were violated we would absolutely take a stand! First it was the attempt to uphold the *Confession.* When that was lost, people were prepared to hold the line on *Scripture.* When that was lost, some six *fundamental truths* would serve as our shibboleths. When that too proved untenable, people were prepared at least to stand by the *miracles.* In the end they also surrendered those forward trenches and made the *Resurrection of Christ* the breastwork of Christianity, but that too was lost. Today the adversary has already laid hands on our *Baptism* — but people get used to everything and they still have not found "the formula for resistance."

Thus the line of defense was shrunk again and again. Where people still took a position, it was no more than a sham. Hardly had the battle begun than one could hear retreat being sounded from afar; "peace, peace" was the sweet refrain with which people comforted themselves in the face of so much indignity. Who has not grieved over these inglorious retreats? But there was no swimming against the current. We are paying for the false starting point we chose, and never-ending disappointment is the inevitable fruit of our indecision. A lack of firmness prevented discussion, the absence of discussion wrought a lack of policy, and in the

6. Kuyper here is attacking the apologetics orientation of his erstwhile Utrecht patron, Nicolaas Beets (1814-1903). Beets was pastor at Utrecht 1854-74 and professor there 1874-84, in both of which posts he held great prestige from the poetry he had written earlier in his career.

course of retreat those who had thought of another possibility were soon persuaded of the opposite. As such things go, that which appeared unnecessary for all devolved into the peculiar habit of the few, and the mere preservation of what we were left with began to be the policy and system. To preserve that which *is,* not as it is but as from day to day it turns worse — *that* is the level to which the waters of conservatism sank. From that moment on the possibility of taking a stand ("so far and no further") had become inconceivable. At first the boundary was indefinite; now it is to be determined by the enemy. The "approximately" that governed the temporary definition of the boundary was quickly turned by inner necessity into "nowhere."

* * *

So now, beloved Congregation, judge for yourself whether there is reason to scrutinize that false conservatism in all its ways. It has still not shown its true face. Up until now it has still been mixed with and tempered by the sacred. Yet consider the damage it has done! What then will happen when, dropping its disguises, it shows its colors openly and tears the emblem of life from the brow of the church of Christ to replace it with the mark of death! The times are serious. How intense the battle of supernatural forces must be to produce such horrendous aftershocks on this earth. It is as if the powers of destruction are doing their utmost to undo the blessing with which the Lord had surprised us. For indeed: the Lord, he who is mighty, our Savior, has done wonders. There it lay — the once-flourishing valley of the Christian life seemingly turned into a desert plain. The church of Christ had become a valley of dry bones rather than a field teeming with life. But look: the Lord had mercy on us. Those bones have begun to live [Ezek. 37:1ff.]; it is as if a radiant reflection of the Pentecost miracle has shone over our generation. We again hear the rustle of life and the raising of songs of praise. People are again calling on the name of the Lord. His outstretched arm is again being revealed to his own!

But now there are signs we may forfeit that blessing — the blessing which has been given us and for which we are therefore responsible. Forfeit it by our unbelief. Forfeit it by the rejection of development. Forfeit it by our halfheartedness. We are again divorcing the form from the essence so that the essence runs on without form and the form, being devoid of the essence, becomes hard as rock. We are again absorbing the poison in our veins, splitting up into countless sects, eliminating precious and powerful elements of life. We yearn for support which God has not raised up for us. Despising the power of Gideon's band we are broadly extending our ranks, which will soon disperse when the hour of separation arrives for those who were not of us. True: there is still a semblance of unity but it will last only as long as it pleases the enemy to unite us by his opposition. There will come a day when the props of our unity will vanish along with that opposition; then there will be weeping and mourning in Israel's tents. Then it will become evident that one can never with impunity desecrate the holy war waged for the glory of God by freebooting in favor of earthly rest. Then our last state will be worse than the first and the demon which we drove out will return into the empty temple, accompanied by seven other spirits more evil than itself [Luke 11:24-26].

Still, beloved Congregation, we must not despair. That danger threatens, I admit, but it is not inevitable provided we realize it is there. An eruption of a thunderstorm may clear the air. The arm of the Lord can still make those who are always looking back face forward, confirm the unstable, and drive the lovers of an inglorious peace from their mistaken sense of security. Only you must break with false conservatism in your own heart, in your church, in life. Hold fast not what you have but what you *yourselves* have, and glory not in a crown you put on each other's heads but in a crown, an invisible crown, which has been prepared for you by God [2 Tim. 4:8; James 1:12; 1 Pet. 5:4].

II

Is every kind of conservatism really so damaging? Far be it from us to think so, provided we drive out the false variety and opt for the true. I've pointed out how a tenacious hold on tradition is synonymous with religion and how "salvation by resurrection" is the theme song of the Christian. For this reason alone Christianity and conservatism are closely related; now let me add another which makes the two inseparable.

Christianity does not live solely by the grace of beautiful ideas but strikes its roots into existing reality by a series of mighty facts. It is, after all, a *historical phenomenon.* Being a revelation of the unseen in what is *visible,* a revelation of the eternal *in time* is precisely its incomparable superiority over every other religion on earth. In those facts is found the hallmark of its authenticity; by those facts it was created; from those facts flows the stream of its life. Now, those facts have been fitted like stones in the solid foundation on which we stand; they occupied a place of their own in the past, but with the willful negation of the past they too disappeared from the scene. Therefore, if our minds reach out, no, not to an ideal Christ who is a product of our own invention but to the Christ

Kuyper complained about Conservatives not only in Church but also in State. In a *Standaard* "three-star" editorial, 28 May 1873, he mocked their wobbly compass.

The Conservatives

The *Dagblad,* official organ of the Conservative Party, is playing its last card. It is mindlessly and in full view tossing overboard the last vestiges of fidelity to principle. In its desperation it is offering its hand to — guess whom?

To the *Catholics?* You know better!

To the worn-out *Liberals?* Isn't that marrying within the family?

To *our* side? We know that our vote totals inspire a love that tolerates "rust" ["*de roest*"].

No, you'll never guess. The Hague's *Dagblad* is coolly offering its hand to our *Radicals!* De Roo and Jonckbloet [Progressive-Liberal leaders] have found favor in its eyes.

Note well: this is no longer a party. It's just a passel of *malcontents,* so any *malcontent* will do.

of the Scriptures, to him whose life has historically manifested itself in the life of this world, then the searching mind cannot be spared the journey through that past. For it is solely to the incarnation of the Son of God that Christianity owes its existence. That fact alone is the source of its power. From that alone can it derive its beauty. To the church the past, including that miracle of his birth within it, is the coarse shell in which, by a divine act, the precious pearl has been enclosed. "Preservation," therefore, must remain its rallying cry, since without that drive to preserve it would also lose the precious pearl.

Indeed, not only must the power of that past be protected from deliberate neglect but for the sake of the past the present must also rouse the Christian mind to a posture of defense. For the past lives on in the present. The centuries are not juxtaposed to each other as airtight compartments; what was then works on now. The miraculous historical facts by which Christianity was begun have impregnated succeeding centuries with their power. A part of that power is still present all around us in the very fabric of human relations. The aftereffects of those facts have been woven into our present existence. An unconditional rejection of the life that now environs us would thus entail the deliberate destruction of that sacred power as well. Christianity must save that imperfect soil since even now it has its roots there.

Perhaps you ask: "if conservatism is warranted, even required, for Christianity, then wherein does true conservatism differ from the false?" Dear Congregation, the conservatism we must condemn wants to hold on to what is *as it is*. True conservatism seeks to preserve what is in terms of what it will become in Christ, that is, resurrected from the dead.

True conservatism exerts itself not for the shell but for the pearl within the shell. It loves not the appearance of things but the hidden germ of life with which Christ has impregnated it. Through the curtain of visible form it reaches for the pure image of things that unfolds from that new germ of life. It looks at what is, not as it now exhibits itself, but as it will one day in eternity unfold its true glory. Therefore it hates the world as it is now and nevertheless loves the world for the sake of the life-producing Word of God that lies hidden in its depths. It knows the present form of this world will pass away, indeed heaven and earth will pass away, but the Word of God remains for ever, and in that Word lies a new heaven and a new earth, a new life-form for every creature that escapes destruction. Therefore all its love is focused on that Word of God, the Word not only as it is spoken in sound but also as it became flesh in Christ, and from Him entered the joints of this world as the unique life-force in which all things rest.

Two forms of life are therefore currently interwoven, and true conservatism aims only to preserve the second, the new life. Hence, if orthodoxy fails to make a sharp distinction between the two forms of life, it must gradually disappear. Should that distinction be unclear, it will blindly grope around the question of what must and must not be preserved, unable to escape the danger of — on the one hand — maintaining a life it ought to oppose and — on the other — giving up things that are indispensable and integral to the whole of its life. A confession of sin does not help if it views sin outside of its connection with life and does not explain the indispensability of a new creation of life precisely in terms of that sin. The defense of miracle imparts no power if it views miracle as something incidental and does not insist on that counter-natural invasion into the existing world as the foundation of the new life. Above all, upholding *grace,* as opposed to the fruit of human work, cannot guarantee its own future if it does not extend the line of grace to the ultimate and again make God's sovereign election the starting point of its life. To put it more succinctly: its battle for the Bible must necessarily end in suicide if it does not unconditionally yield to the Word of God and open its eyes to the totally unprecedented, totally other new life of which that Word shows us the beginning, the substance, and the final goal, the life whose typical patterns and movements it portrays for us, and for whose recognition it offers the only genuine touchstone.

Christ posits an all-embracing and absolute *principle [beginsel]:* that is, from him a whole new life derives its *beginning.* Up till now we have seen only a very small part of the eternal life-treasure that lies in that *principle.* A part of what that principle bears has emerged, but by far the larger part is still concealed. One can aim at preserving either that which has so far emerged from that principle or the principle itself. Conservatism does the former; genuine orthodoxy must do the latter. It must be concerned to keep not just a few blossoms that have budded on the plant but the plant itself — that plant, along with the formative power present in its roots, that plant along with its promise of the innumerable blossoms its life brings us.

The plant must be preserved not on the assumption that our hands must create the ripe fruit and then tie it to the branches but in the firm belief that the plant already contains that fullness of fruit within. It must hold on to the Christ not merely to maintain a distinct life, not only as the absolute principle of that life, but equally as the Eternal One in whom the fullness of that life is already present, also for yourselves. Orthodoxy is unfaithful to that eternal principle if it shrinks from saying, as our fathers did, that in Christ we already *have* everything and need not first acquire it.

One who still wishes by himself to bring the Lord even a single stone for the construction of his eternal home, or thinks that he must still complete what Christ has merely begun, cannot preserve what he himself acknowledges he does not yet have and is still looking for. Only the eternal is worth keeping — but then the eternal not empty but in its fullness, not in part but the whole. That eternal, though you do not yet possess it, is nonetheless *yours;* it is the inheritance purchased for you. You *have* it, that fullness of eternal life, but you have it by *faith.*

That life which you have in Christ, that life in its *uniqueness,* in its sharply delineated *principle,* and in its eternal *fullness* — to have and to hold that life is our sacred calling. Friends, do you believe that this world lies in death and that life is present only in Christ? At the very least this is what you confess. But then all doubt has to make way for this truth. For only that Christianity has in it the germ of life which can regenerate the world, and you are the ones called to bring that life to the world. Then you have in your hands the fiery medicine which, when every other remedy has proved useless, bears the only power that can heal the fatally sick world. Don't you hear the unconscious cry of pain with which the world is calling out to you: "Hold on to what you have, Congregation of the Son of God! Do not throw it away or destroy its power to heal." For its sake and for your own, it is as if Supreme Wisdom joins the world in begging you: "My children, be attentive to my instruction; do not let it escape from you, but keep it within your heart!" [Prov. 4:21].

* * *

Hold on to that eternal but also free yourself from the delusion that "attitude" and "effort" are sufficient to the task. Real life creates itself a form. A life without a firmly defined form cannot exist in this finite world. Accordingly, you can only hold on to the eternal in the form that real life manifests it in and around you. Naturally that form must be taken from this life and so must change with the alterations through which life passes. Certainly, it must have continuity with the form it had for our fathers, for we know no other life than that in which they rejoiced and which has been passed on to us in their forms. Still it is our calling to hold fast what we have in Christ *in our own time,* not in theirs, and so it is from our own time that we must take the material with which to prepare that form today. That labor is enormous, Congregation, especially where so much of it has been neglected. No, you cannot cobble it together on the basis of a plan you yourself have dreamed up. The form has to emerge from life itself and conduct itself by the laws of that life. The skin of a snake does not change artificially but only as a result of the vitality of the life which manifests itself at every point on its surface. It is the same vitality, the same life-force, which detaches the old skin and covers the writhing body with a new one. So you too will never bring about that new form unless you bring the whole of our existence, in all its relations, in touch with the vitality of that life — with the energy of that eternal.

Hold fast that eternal, then, first of all in the center of your heart. Neither your emotions nor your intellect alone have been chosen to be the exclusive carrier of that eternal life. Be clear about this: what you have will escape if you try to hold on to it with anything less than your whole person. Hold on to it, further, in your personal life. The Christian spirit is not an oil that floats on the surface of the water but a caustic fluid that has to permeate every drop of your stream of life. One who is not a Christian in small things cannot be a Christian in big things either. Your Christianity demands not only what you are prepared to set aside for it but the whole of your life. But your calling does not even end there. Almost all of us have families; we are all members of a society and the sons and daughters of a nation. Those connections too are indispensable and must also be bound to the reality of the eternal to keep that eternal life. Christ does not tolerate our living a double life: our lives must be one, controlled by one principle, wherever it may express itself. Life forms in all its rich ramifications one high and holy temple in which the fragrance of the eternal must rise, and whoever wishes to serve at the altar of his soul but not at the altar of life's temple has perhaps been consecrated a priest by himself or by others but certainly not by Christ.

* * *

Therefore, let us not complain if in church life too the old forms become ever less useful. Let us rather recognize our duty to search for new ones. You are all members of that church; in that church everyone has a place. Show in that church only the eternal that *you* have. Never suppress it but bring it into touch with all your activities and every act of duty. Believe me: the dead in the old forms will not be able to resist you. Whether you pray or raise your songs of praise, whether the Word is preached or the Sacrament served, whether you exercise your rights of membership or ask to be admitted as a member, whether you make only your own offering or direct the gifts of the entire congregation — wherever you act as a member of the church, there be true, banish falsehood, stop being mindless, be serious, drive out humdrum routine. To everything bring the eternal you have received in your soul, and you will be invincible. The future will be ours, and if the powers of eternity then begin to flow again through the arteries of our church, do not worry. Before you know it, the old form automatically lets go and what you have is preserved in a new form.

It is not the least of your calling to lead others in this renewal. You are the church of Utrecht, the church whose name has been linked for many long years to the struggle for orthodoxy and faith in our denomination. Though you are grateful that the times are past in which you stood alone in that struggle among the larger congregations of our country, the most ancient privileges still belong to you, and so also the most solemn obligations. People still have their eyes on Utrecht; Utrecht is still for many a city situated on a hill. Even today the honor of the believers is bound up with Utrecht's vitality and Utrecht's spiritual growth.

And not without reason, Congregation, for the Lord has done great things in your midst. From your midst first emerged the men who enthusiastically joined the battle against unbelief, continued the struggle with perseverance, and conducted it with wisdom. Your Congregation was chosen by the Lord to be a center of spiritual activity from which a stream of blessing flowed over a large region. In your midst the burning issue of the schools was first adequately resolved, and for a long time this insured the preservation of the Christian school. Here the Christian life had free rein and was able to penetrate into every sphere of life. What talent was concentrated here! Your Congregation's abundance of gifts made the spiritual poverty elsewhere all the more conspicuous.

That talent is something you have, and of that too I say: Hold on to it! If people elsewhere envy you, then let it be on account of something more than your orthodox *name*. Let it rather be the vitality flowing from your orthodoxy that arouses others to jealousy. Elsewhere people complain of the obstacles that stand in the way; here you are free. Elsewhere people still struggle to drive back the preaching of unbelief; here that struggle has already been won. So please, do not rest on your laurels; banish the illusion that with these first skirmishes the big battle has been fought. For the really fearful struggle is only beginning now. Now everything depends on demonstrating the fruits of the first struggle by persuading everyone that the reign of orthodoxy builds up the church of Utrecht, awakens its life, heightens its resilience, and causes the leaven of Christianity to ferment in the life of the city. Now it becomes your calling to decide, not just for yourself but also as a church, whether you still have the option of obeying human ordinances if they hold back the power of the Word of God. Now comes the difficult task of giving firm guidance to newly awakened church life and of enjoining that all which is called spiritual truly be so. Especially now awaits the enormous task of bringing the power of the gospel to bear again on the nonbelieving part of the Congregation — people who until now have not been of much concern to us — and to break with that false state of affairs in which you have so far found yourself, I want to believe, against your will.

And though I will not be here to participate with you in that struggle, I do in all seriousness call upon you to engage in it, Congregation. Though the struggle already behind you now awaits me in another congregation, that second struggle will have to be waged there as well, and it will be a great joy to me to be able to say to others: "Consider Utrecht and see what orthodoxy has accomplished there!"

It is not appropriate for me to recall what I myself have tried to accomplish along those lines in your midst. All the more because I have been here too briefly to do more than sow a few seeds. Now that work has come to an early halt. I offer it to Him whom I had the honor of serving as minister. May He forgive the sinful elements my heart brought to that task and bless that which was done in accordance with his will.

If in the performance of my work as a minister I was involved in conflict from time to time, it was because I could not always think as others thought and considered glossing over the difference inconsistent with my duty. Perhaps I had a different view of many things because I was raised in different circles, but I had to act in accordance with that view as long as no one convinced me of being wrong. In this connection I have consistently sought to speak openly and to use honest weapons, and even in the case of differences of opinion, to give honor to those to whom honor was due. Please forgive the ways in which I fell short in this. Forgive me on account of the delicacy of the struggle in which I was involved. Forgive me above all on account of the often oppressive isolation in which I found myself with my views.

So I am leaving you, Congregation, with a grateful heart, for I have gained a lot from my short stay in your midst. Now that through "ill repute and good repute" [2 Cor. 6:8] I have arrived at this juncture on my life's journey, I greatly value the blessing of spending almost three years in your midst. I was not spared affliction but neither did I lack consolation, and my God always proved for me a Hearer of prayers. You have given me and my family much love and generously lightened my burdens. I know: you are not expecting my thanks for these things, but *I* feel the need to bear witness to the magnitude, the discriminating delicacy, and the tenderness of your love. *What it means to have brothers and sisters who are spiritual kin is something I have only fully learned at Utrecht!*

The fact that, for all this, I did not stay here — no, really, it was not because life in your midst was painful to me. The charm of your beautiful city, the attraction of your theological school, above all the strong ties by which I was bound to so many people inclined me to make a very different choice. Still, you believe that I acted from a sense of duty in accepting a call elsewhere, and that belief gives me peace today.

Congregation, for my part I will never be able to forget you. For your part please continue to remember me. Let us each in our own way seek to finish our course. We do not know what things will come over our country and our church. But whatever storms erupt, beware of false conservatism. Do not bury our splendid *orthodoxy* in the treacherous pit of false *conservatism.* Hold fast to what you have in Christ, and may the day of days make clear that many people, brought forth in your midst, not only finished the race but also have kept the faith and received the crown from their Lord [2 Tim. 4:7-8].

And now, Congregation, before I pronounce the Amen, receive my final "Farewell." May the Lord never take away the candlestick He so marvelously gave you, but may His light shine from it ever more brightly. I came to you with an open heart; with a much enriched heart I take my leave. And if I succeeded in contributing only the odd stone to the building of your spiritual temple, Congregation, to Him be the glory whose alone is the power. Henceforth may He spread over you here, and over me over there, the wings of His eternal compassion. Amen.

Modernism: A Fata Morgana in the Christian Domain

Kuyper's farewell gibes at Utrecht were more than counterbalanced in an oration he delivered the next year against theological liberalism. If conservatives were objects of his disappointed affection, Modernism was a youthful passion that lived on, warm and fearful, in his memory. Kuyper may have never accepted the substance of that school, but its intellectual scope, courage, and consistency deeply impressed him and set a standard he wanted orthodoxy to match. Kuyper's speech throughout bespeaks his personal involvement with the issues and especially with the pioneer of Modernism, his Leiden professor J. H. Scholten.

Classic theological liberalism has so faded from the scene that it may be difficult to recall how compelling its proposals once seemed to be, and how certain its eventual triumph. In its time, therefore, Kuyper's was a bold and startling statement. It challenged the seemingly inevitable with the bravado of a graveyard whistler. It took some cultivated figures to the theological woodshed. It faulted advanced, prestigious thinkers for being sentimentalists playing out of their depth. Kuyper's critique was also original, perhaps being the very first to use "modernism" in what would become the common sense of the term.[1] If some of his arguments seem worn or predictable, then, the fault lies less in Kuyper than in the (often inadvertent) copying a century of anti-Modernist polemics would make of his work.

Yet Kuyper's piece also differed from many of these. For instance, the most famous American critique, J. Gresham Machen's *Christianity and Liberalism,*[2] worked by close textual analysis to show the propositional divergences be-

1. This is the contention of Malcolm Bull, "Who Was the First to Make a Pact with the Devil?" *London Review of Books,* 14 May 1992, pp. 22-23.

2. New York: Macmillan, 1923.

tween Scripture and Modernist statements. Others mounted a philosophical or theological defense of the supernatural and miraculous. Kuyper certainly shared these commitments, yet brackets them here. Instead he spends half his time giving a historical interpretation of Modernism's ascent, half a phenomenological critique of its limitations. Little Bible, little dogma, much religious experience: Kuyper meets Modernism on its own grounds.

They are his own grounds too. Kuyper's youthful wrestling with Romantic poets and his lifelong concern for religion and culture are much in evidence here, from the title evoking Arthurian legend to the pivotal proof-texts taken from Shakespeare, Beethoven, Bürger, and Goethe. The piece as a whole is suffused with his quests for an integral epistemology and the integrity of the church. On both scores he demands the real, the genuine. On 14 April 1871, he returned to the stage of the Odeon theater in Amsterdam to expose a counterfeit.

Kuyper's lecture was not published for four months after delivery to allow him time to add extensive notes to the text: some sixty in all, covering twenty pages in tiny type. Therein he answered critics, responded to recent literature, added personal commentary, and elaborated philosophical and theological positions. I have included those which add to an understanding of Kuyper's sources, context, or implications.

I have also hewn closely to Kuyper's own scheme of capitalization with respect to M/modernism; i.e., the inconsistencies in the text are his. This translation, by John Vriend, has dropped about one-sixth of the original text (*Het Modernisme, een Fata Morgana op christelijk gebied* [Amsterdam: H. de Hoogh, 1871]), mostly to avoid repetitions and immaterial local references. Some of these are retained in a translation by John H. de Vries which appeared in *The Methodist Review* 88/1-2 (March and May 1906): 185-203, 355-78.

WERE IT POSSIBLE to pull aside the curtain that hides the world of spirits from our view, I am convinced a conflict so intense, so volcanic, so sweeping in its reach would present itself to our mind's eye that the bitterest war ever waged on earth would look, by comparison, like child's play. The collision of forces that really matter is occurring not here but up there, above us. In our struggles here below we experience only the after-shocks of that massive collision.

Still, to our feebler minds even these after-shocks can be alarming. Look around: from all directions the battle of the spirits rushes in upon you. Underneath and around you everything is seething and in ferment. The most firmly laid foundations are being battered, our deepest and dearest principles uprooted. It almost seems as if the shrieks of the French Revolution in 1793 were but the prelude to the mighty battle march now being played in our hearing.

At the present juncture one might imagine it better to refrain from participating in that battle than by our participation to inflame it. Does not resistance steel the courage of the adversary, and self-defense stoke the fire of contention? So one might ask, and wait to see if, thanks to our quietness, the fire of contention would not gradually die out. . . . Yet with undiminished respect for those who cling to this opinion from a sense of duty, I wish to state as my conviction that this tactic of looking on *may not* any longer be ours. . . . [Kuyper here cites Burke's confrontation with Fox in Parliament 6 May 1791.[3]] As soon as principles gain ground that are contrary to your deepest convictions, then resistance is your duty and acquiescence a sin. Then, at the price of the finest peace, you must attack those principles, stigmatizing them before the eyes of friend and foe alike with all the ardor of your faith.

In that sense, then, I believe that we can no longer avoid the struggle against Modernism — the theory in which the polemic against Christianity has created its most coherent system. Admittedly this is painful, for our religion loses some of its attraction when we must argue its cause before enjoying its benefits. But in spite of this aversion it is fitting for us in this respect to confess with Burke that "Such is now the misfortune of our age that everything is to be discussed as if the truth of religion were to be always a subject rather of altercation than enjoyment."[4] You cannot walk away from your own time but must take it as it is, and the

3. Kuyper, note 1, shows acquaintance with Burke through James Prior's 1854 biography. Burke's denunciation of the French Revolution caused a strain with his old friend and fellow Whig leader Charles James Fox (1749-1806) that culminated with a full break of relations in the episode Kuyper cites. For an exposition that shows the intertwining of personal and ideological differences in the case, see Conor Cruise O'Brien, *The Great Melody: A Thematic Biography and Commented Anthology of Edmund Burke* (Chicago: University of Chicago Press, 1992), pp. 381-84, 394-400, 414-31. Burke's dramatics and pose of lonely, principled suffering in the showdown on the Commons floor clearly foreshadowed Kuyper's own behavior during his 1874-76 term in the Second Chamber.

4. Kuyper, note 2, cites *Reflections on the Revolution in France* in the Thomas McLean 1823 edition of Burke's collected works, vol. V, p. 174. Kuyper notes that he had substituted "the truth of religion" for Burke's original reference to "the Constitution of our country" as the subject of chronic altercation.

times demand that we either accept the unsettling of our faith or enter the fray. Given this choice, the committed person does not hesitate.

So speaks faith, and so insists the spirit of our time which goads anyone who is serious to self-defense. Granted, the dealers in varnish and plaster have worked long and bravely to cover over every crack and tear in our society, but to no avail; in the end even the least serious of them had enough of this tinkering. Today this hush-hush strategy is no longer wanted. The honeymoon of spiritual impassivity is over. We have finally learned that conventional form is a gravestone, not a shield. Courage has returned to our blood and luster to the pallid eye. We again dare to consider it natural to engage the opponent in unsparing combat. Indeed, we have already advanced to the point where pretending to confess Christ according to the Scriptures while avoiding the battle with Modernism would forfeit the sympathy of sharper minds.

But precisely because it is serious, our battle may not go forward by belittling the enemy or resorting to vilification. Whoever disrespects the enemy is not combating him but the specter of his own imagination. From that mode of combat I wish to abstain. It is, above all, appreciation for Modernism that gives me the grounds for opposing it. I cannot state more succinctly and accurately both what I appreciate and what I oppose in Modernism than by presenting it to you as a "Fata Morgana in the Christian domain."

* * *

Let me explain the strange metaphor by which I wish to characterize my opponent. "Una fata" is Italian for what we would call a fairy. Among these figments of the imagination there was one to which Italy's peasantry gave the name "Morgana," and from this fairy the inhabitants of Reggio derived the name "fata Morgana" for a splendid aerial phenomenon which, they imagined, her scepter painted on Reggio's horizon.[5] . . . [Kuyper insists that this phenomenon be distinguished from a "mirage" and gives illustrations from the folklore of England and Greenland before returning to Reggio to view the phenomenon in its "full splendor."] Let Minasi's own words convey the marvelous vista which he observed no less than three times.

> Scarcely had the morning sun reached the halfway point between the horizon and the zenith when, in a moment in which neither wind nor

5. Kuyper, note 3, traces the term back via south Italy's Norman links to English Arthurian legend, where the original specter appeared in the person of Morgan le Fay, Arthur's sorceress sister.

> current occasioned the slightest ripple on the face of the waters, there arose suddenly from the blue surface a majestic and glorious scene which, multiplying itself in endless series, broadened and widened before my astonished eyes. First there appeared in blinding splendor long rows of marble pillars, adorned with the most artistic capitals and supporting the most perfect arches. These gradually passed from sight, but only to give way to other colonnades of heavier mold and, if possible, of richer form. And now from the depths arose stateliest palaces of gigantic size and imposing splendor of towers and pinnacles, all brilliantly illumined by sunlight pouring through every window. But these beautiful appearances also soon dissolved in light, and now I saw sweet rural scenes of fields and trees, grassy meadows, and green hillsides, richly dotted with vast multitudes of grazing cattle and sheep. And these presently disappearing were followed in turn by great armies of infantry and cavalry of splendid accoutrements and rhythm of motion and color. All this passed on before me in panoramic style, so vividly near that I could almost touch them, clear in outline, sharply defined, brilliant in color, exact in proportion, with rapid, yet stately, paces gliding along the blue-green level of the sea.[6]

Tell me, ladies and gentlemen, with such a majestic phenomenon before us, am I not right to identify *fabulous beauty* as its primary characteristic? But there is more: the Morgana *follows a fixed law* of refraction; it creates nothing new but only reflects things that exist. For on the island of Sicily or the west coast of Italy those palaces do stand, those green parks flourish, those flocks and herds graze and those armies move which, enlarged and multiplied, mirror themselves on Reggio's horizon.

Finally, the Morgana *lacks all reality.* Granted, those who have seen it vie with each other in protesting that it was almost impossible to call what they saw unreal. But . . . "scarcely had the sun advanced a few degrees in its circuit and a morning breeze played upon the waves, when the last traces of Morgan's magnificent creation vanished."[7]

Thus the Morgan-phenomenon was fabulously beautiful. It had to come. But it is devoid of all reality! That is why I called Modernism a Fata Morgana in the Christian domain. For Modernism, too, is a phenomenon that fascinates us by its deceptive beauty, that was born not by a quirk of fate but in accordance with a fixed law, and that — for all its

6. Kuyper, note 4, references the 1773 *Dissertazione . . . Fata Morgana* by Minasi as the source of the quotation. He also offers a detailed meteorological comparison of the morgana and mirages, supported by descriptive accounts in travel literature.

7. This seems to be the conclusion (unattributed) of the previous quotation from Minasi.

splendor — loses itself in unreal forms. . . . To these three traits I wish to direct your attention. And since I would not make one part of the argument needlessly long and another overly brief for the sake of some artificial symmetry, I will ask only a moment for the first point of similarity, a somewhat longer period for the second, in order finally to consider at greatest length the third trait which settles everything — the charge, namely, that it is devoid of all reality.

I

First of all, then, Modernism like the Morgana is beautiful. If perchance you feel inclined to question the sincerity of this tribute, then allow me another brief historical recollection. At its beginning some fifteen years ago, when Modernism, still rarely called by that name, offered the first-fruits of its mind, a singular phenomenon occurred in many a little town: the most rigorously Reformed of the old school believed that in the preacher of Modernism they had found *their* man. You know what had become of these hyper-conservatives! For a long time they had avoided the church: ah, they could not stomach that shallow, saccharine sermonizing. Their Reformed roots had accustomed them to living in the depths, to incisive seriousness. Neither the old liberals nor the Groningers nor the quasi-confessionals could satisfy them.[8] Though people laughed at them, they maintained that they could not live on such food and so in quiet solitude or in a circle of the like-minded they sought spiritual nourishment in the stern old books that had fed the church in its heyday with stronger meat. But behold: suddenly something happened which no one expected. A young new preacher began his ministry, and now that intractable, incorrigible hairsplitter showed his face in the little parish church again, Sunday after Sunday. More than that: he was so caught up in what he heard that the sparkle in his eyes, the surprised smile that played around his lips, then again the frowning brow that spelled disappointment, told you even from a distance that the man was responding to the message.

How could that be? He didn't get it. The new preacher alternately fascinated and repelled him. But he kept hoping, and that hope revived

8. Kuyper in note 5 claims to have witnessed such an episode firsthand and was sure that others from both sides had as well. Old-liberals, Groningers, and quasi-confessionalists were Dutch theological parties in the first half of the nineteenth century that tried to mediate ("compromise," Kuyper would prefer) between traditional Reformed orthodoxy and either rationalist or Romantic religious constructions.

his heart. Certainly this was more than the usual burying of the deep things of life beneath a blanket of flowers. They came and went, those deeply engraved lines of a holier view of life, but still our conservative friend had once again seen them glint. Who knows? The new preacher has not quite gotten there, he said, but gave evidence of a start — would not greater maturity follow? Our good man was already having the sweet dream that the truth of God would again break through in the church of his fathers! It took a long time, a very long time, before he heard something so crass, so offensive, that he had to admit to his wiser friends: "You were right; I was misled." Now, embittered by fresh disappointment and more fiercely conservative than ever, he again buried himself in his ancient tomes.[9]

What explains this piquant phenomenon, you ask? Let me first remind you — for things change fast — that the virginal Modernism of that day still wrapped itself completely in the folds of the old biblical dress. Without this disguise the illusion would have been unthinkable. But there was more. Remember how our fathers used to speak of the bondage of the will and of divine predestination? They used to give prominence to God's sovereign grace and located the essence of religion precisely in humanity's deep dependency. But in their infinite wisdom the theological dwarves who arose later had judged all this to be empty chitchat and got the church out of the habit of believing it. Then lo and behold, the moderns appeared on the scene as a new phenomenon and, in their early deterministic phase, said virtually the same as what had been taught of old. Don't you understand that the old-Reformed pinched themselves for joy when free will was again chased out the church door and God's predestination was glorified? Nor did it stop there. Regeneration came back as well. Sometimes the irresistibility of grace struck a responsive modern cord. Of the perseverance of the saints they said some penetrating things. Even when they began to give some hints of their hazardous project on sin, it was as if the winged specter of the Supralapsarians circled over them in benediction. Was it so surprising, then, that for a moment people thought it was their own colors they saw flying in the breeze? Was it so strange that the advent of the new preacher was deemed a gain rather than a loss?

But let us move on. Modernism's real beauty to the mind is most evident from how it enchanted the choicest minds among us, men of intellectual power and seriousness of life. Just consider the people of high repute in every sector of our public life (excepting only the poets) who, as the most prominent, spring to mind first. You have to admit, despite

9. Dutch, *kwartijnen,* books composed of quarto-sized pages.

yourself, that almost all of them gave Modernism their sympathetic support and that not a little of its glory derives from the splendor of their names. And do you ask again why this should be so? Ladies and gentlemen, do you know what people in modernist circles think of one who remains true to the old traditions, yet is not stupid? They consider him a monomaniac, three-quarters insane, and openly declare to everyone within earshot that they cannot understand such a weird product of nature. From this it is apparent that in modernist circles a caricature of Christianity is taken to be the real thing and that this distortion is confidently declared to be incompatible with a serious reading of life, unfit for the children of this age. And they are absolutely right! There is no age in all the hoary past where this caricature would fit! No human mind, no human heart could possibly live by that broken-down, watered-down Christianity which, under all sorts of labels, announced itself as "positive." Had Athanasius or Augustine, Calvin or Luther, à Marck or à Brakel, been told: choose *this* Christianity or settle for Modernism, I am sure they would have opted for the latter unless by the grace of God they had been spared the horror of this dilemma.[10]

Let us not forget: the thinking world has not sought out orthodoxy in its own camp but knows it solely from the form in which it is registered on the retina of public opinion. And how has "positive" Christianity appeared there? Just compare the skeletal little primers of our age with the Heidelberg or Westminster Catechism, and the answer is clear: they are rootless little fungi next to those oak trees. They sum up what appears above ground — on the one hand, a series of singular facts, and next to them a series of singular moral claims — but they show nothing of the ingenious organism which, hidden under the surface of things, unites those facts and claims. Naturally, no one could live on that. The human heart is too deep, the riddles of life are too dreadful, to be stupidly ignored. Therefore the thinking world had long ago abandoned this Sunday-school Christianity. And when Modernism came, once again displaying the splendor of the ideal, again analyzing the human heart, tracing the causes, principles, and interconnectedness of things, and making its fingers play upon the vibrant strings of life, it was bound to fascinate and win people over. Even the reflection of a weeping willow on the surface of a stream

10. Johannes à Marck (1656-1731) codifed the anti-Cartesian theology of Gijsbert Voetius into *the* system of orthodoxy as recognized in conservative Dutch Calvinist circles. Wilhelmus à Brakel (1635-1711) gave Voetius's theology a more pietist/experiential turn and was widely read by orthodox common folk. "Positive" Christianity was that content of the faith said to have survived the tests of reason, so labeled by theologians sympathetic to the Enlightenment.

Kuyper's address on *Modernism* won him lasting fame.
A cartoon published 30 years later, during the campaign that would make him prime minister, cited the speech's title while implying that Kuyper had always had political ends in view. "Land Ho!", cries Kuyper, pointing toward the shores of Rule. "That's what you're always saying," replies his Catholic collaborator Herman Schaepman, "but this one's no Fata Morgana."

is a thousand times more beautiful than the chopped-off trunk of an oak tree which lies contemptibly by the side of the road.

Besides, from the start Modernism was bathed in the soft glow of a tragic sadness. O yes, they would much rather have remained in the old camp [of orthodoxy], but you were told, dear church, that this was not permitted them. For the truth stands above all, and that truth was too much for them. So they preferred to live with the truth in the wilderness than in an Eden where the truth was maligned. Of course! This lent their whole public conduct an aura that commanded respect. Something of a martyr's crown clung to their brows. A tone of melancholy about their conduct left the impression of a powerful faith that enabled them, in the face of so much shipwreck, still to believe in a deliverance and from the depths of their melancholy still to speak jubilantly of the love of God. In brief, their manly break with the anemic Christianity of those days brought out their native Dutch candor, while their search for basic principles allied them to the thought of our age. By their tragic bearing they won the tenderhearted; by their wistful sadness the hearts of women were swept away; and if their preaching is measured by the standard: "all types of preaching are good except the boring," then certainly the initial rush it attracted is readily explained.

Finally, real Christianity is a fact of life wholly adapted to the human heart, aiming to fill the depths of that heart with its sacred content. That Christianity, therefore, is essentially human — humanistic — to the core. But alas! Genuine Christianity of that kind had been left as trash in the marketplace of life. Something that people called Christianity was still available, but the tender roots by which it must attach itself to our heart had been severed and the consciousness in our heart which must lead to an appreciation for Christianity had grown callous. You remember! Almost spiritless we were sitting in the sand dunes and, as before Reggio's horizon, nothing presented itself to the mind's eye but the flat colorless surface of the sea. But look — there looming up before us are the modern figures who in humanistic style again take seriously the demands of the heart and tolerate no Christianity unless it offer comfort and acclaim to human beings as human beings. Now all at once the deathlike pallor of the sea is swept away, fresh images arise, a sparkling life unfolds, and a glittering palace seems to beckon from the distance. Tell me: was it any wonder that just as the inhabitants of Reggio greeted the *Morgana,* so thinking minds welcomed *Modernism* with applause and enthusiasm, indeed with the joyful acclaim of admiration?

II

Thus, like the Morgana, the impression made by Modernism was enchanting. But to the second point of similarity: Modernism *had* to appear in the spiritual atmosphere by a fixed law of necessity. Only an unwary simplicity that reduces history to a game of chance can still believe that whim or willfulness gave rise to Modernism, that if only Pierson had not spoken or Opzoomer had remained silent it would never have arisen among us.[11] The simple observation that it manifested itself almost simultaneously north and south, here and far away, renders such an opinion untenable; and the equally undeniable fact that in almost the

11. Allard Pierson (1831-96) was reared in a *Réveil* evangelical family but converted to Modernism under J. H. Scholten's teaching at Leiden. He was among the first Dutch Reformed preachers to bring Modernist views to the public. Cornelis Willem Opzoomer (1821-92), professor of philosophy at Utrecht, was the leading Dutch intellectual of his generation. A philosophical empiricist and a doctrinaire liberal in religion and politics, he generated endless publicity and polemics for his views.

same decade it summoned its apostles everywhere — in Germany its Strauss, in the Alps its Baur, its Renan in Paris, its Parker in America, and in the Cape its Colenso — points too imperiously to an inner necessity to let one imagine that mere whim or willfulness could ever account for the heresy of Modernism.[12]

Heresy! It sounds, perhaps, too harsh in your ears? Does it smell too much of the stake for me to use the word so boldly? But you all know Schleiermacher, of course, and you know how the big stars of Modernism (this time in league with the orthodox) have outdone each other in singing his praises. Well then, it is not I but Schleiermacher who restored the word "heretic" to a position of honor and included it as an indispensable concept in Christian theology.[13] . . . [Kuyper attributes the opprobrium of the word to the medieval Church's having made heresy a capital offense.] There are and there *must be* heresies inasmuch as they arise in the Christian domain in accordance with a fixed law, like the Morgana in the atmosphere. Let the sun but rise halfway to its zenith, let there be objects that can be reflected, let the atmospheric conditions be right, and the Morgana *must* appear on the bosom of the Mamertine Sea. In the same way, following an age of darkness, when the light of knowledge has risen only halfway and Christianity falls under this glow and the spiritual atmosphere has the right kind of ferment, then heresy is *bound* to appear; it *cannot* stay outside the circle of the church of Jesus Christ. For just as the Morgana is nothing but the refraction of the sun's

12. David Friedrich Strauss (1808-74) was a German theologian whose *Leben Jesu* (1835) launched modern biblical criticism and whose left-Hegelian history of Christian doctrine denied the reality of the supernatural. Ferdinand Christian Baur (1792-1860), theologian and church historian at Tübingen (in Württemberg), was Strauss's teacher and the head of a critical but less radical school of biblical studies. Ernest Renan (1823-74) wrote Strauss-like lives of Jesus, Paul, and the apostles in the 1860s and tried to reconcile the conflict of science and faith in a religion of humanity. Theodore Parker (1810-60) did more than any other American to popularize higher-critical and German Idealist approaches to Scripture and faith, leaving behind his native Unitarianism in the process. John Colenso (1814-83), liberal Anglican bishop of Natal, was deposed from office in 1869 for his critical views of the Pentateuch.

13. Kuyper (note 7) references Schleiermacher's *Der Christliche Glaube*, 3rd edition (1835), vol. I, pp. 122-24. In note 8 he comments on the phenomenon more generally: "Heresy is not a difference of scholarly insight but a taking by theft of what in truth belongs to Christ alone: founding a church. Heresy is powerless outside the church. Therefore it nestles itself in her curves, seeks to dominate her, and, when thrown out, builds a replica outside her door. Its appeal to scholarship is feigned. It springs from much deeper and spreads much farther than that domain. Its root lies in the heart."

rays in the atmosphere, so heresy is but a necessary refraction of the beams of Christianity in the spiritual atmosphere of a given age.

So long as such a false theory does not cross over from the scholarly arena, no one may condemn it as a heresy. It only becomes a heresy when, contrary to the church's confession, it asserts itself within the church's domain, seeks to bind the conscience to its recognition, and aspires to a position of authority in the church. Then will follow the attempt to reconstruct history, to date back the credentials of its nobility, as though they had been sealed by Christ himself. Then heresy, despite itself, must force its way from the schools of the learned to the pulpit and the prayer room. In the end it wields it own death-blow by asserting, as the only way of salvation, that what the church confesses is not only less than correct but immoral and pernicious, and that there is no salvation outside of itself.

In that sense every vigorous and resilient age must give rise to its own brand of heresy in the church of Jesus; yet since that heresy can be overcome only by spiritual combat, it must serve precisely to heighten the church's moral power. Understand me well. While I contend that heresies are integrally related to the spirit of the times, I do not mean that any heresy was ever generated by the age alone or ever completely eradicated by its suppression. On the contrary: the root of every heretical phenomenon lies in the human heart; each one of us carries the germ of it within. For this reason each and every heresy that has ever been known has always existed and will ever remain. Still, in every age of awakening there is one particular heresy that finds an ideal breeding ground in the mindset of that age and is nurtured by its dominant concepts. Such an error then achieves central significance. Then, far from spreading under cover as before, it openly takes a position against the church of Jesus. That is the zenith of its power. Thus being the offspring of the age, it must be explained as the refraction of Christianity in the spirit of that age.

And so we come back to Modernism. This, too, is a heresy in the true sense of the word. In fact, in this trend the fundamental nature of heresy has perhaps uttered its deepest thought. Remember that all heresy aims to rob Christianity of its absolute character and to shift the fact of atonement ever farther from the center of life to the periphery of ideas, disposition, and will. To put it as gently as possible, Modernism exhibits the same ground-traits as every other heresy, only these are modified in line with the character of the age. Modernism is not even new. All through the centuries it has brought about sorrow in the church of Jesus and it will continue to ferment till the Day of the Lord. Yet it has never *ruled* as now, never achieved the central importance it has today. Only in our age could it become what it really is. Today it stands at the zenith of its power. But this will last only until an equally inexorable shift of the dominant concepts to a new center makes it suddenly descend from its lofty height to disappear almost completely below the horizon of life.

But it is not enough just to say this. I must demonstrate how Modernism really satisfies the three above-mentioned claims of all heresy.

In the first place, the Morgana cannot come until, following the night, the sun has reached the halfway point between the horizon and the zenith. I have tried to apply this to our subject by saying that whenever the light of knowledge again begins to shine after centuries of spiritual torpor, then heresy can — no, *must* — show its face. History, I believe, demonstrates this law. I will not argue the point but merely observe as a fact that, in the course of the Christian era, the fourth, the ninth, and the sixteenth centuries form the great turning points in European history. It may similarly be stated without argument that the sixth to the eighth, the tenth to the sixteenth, and no less the centuries from that time to our own have been times of spiritual aridity in which no fresh breezes could blow through the heart of the nations. And what do we see? We see that precisely those great centuries were the centuries that generated great heresies. The fourth century gave us the conflict over the Trinity and free will; in the ninth the issues were the *Filioque* and the sacrament; and precisely in and as a result of the Reformation the heresy of Socinus germinated, while after John of Leyden Remonstrantism arose in the person of our own Arminius.[14]

If no one will gainsay that our own nineteenth century must also be accorded a place of honor in human history, if one can even now predict that, as in the days of the Reformation, we have come to such a pivotal point in the life of the nations that the next several centuries will be completely dominated by this one, then it follows in accordance with the law of history that a resounding heresy was bound to surface in our time as well. With the present century a new day has dawned over our continent. The light of knowledge has once again risen. Still it has only reached its halfway point and will attain its zenith when it concentrates all its rays in the incomparable name of our God. This, all signs indicate, has not yet occurred. The sun of our century has not yet moved to the center

14. Fausto Sozzini (1539-1604; Kuyper uses the conventional latinized Socinus) was an Italian convert to Protestantism who developed an anti-Trinitarian position owing to his disagreement with traditional concepts of Jesus' divinity. John of Leyden (Jan Beukelszoon) was proclaimed king of the radical Anabaptist commune in Münster after the death in 1534 of its visionary, Jan Matthyszoon. Kuyper links that episode somewhat dubiously with the rather refined, anti-predestinarian Remonstrant party that claimed the mantle of Leiden theologian Jan Harmenszoon (Jacobus Arminius, 1560-1609) and was reproved by the Synod of Dort (1618-19). The two were connected chiefly as the *bêtes noires* of orthodox Dutch Calvinism.

of truth and hence is not yet manifest in the church's confession but only in a heretical refraction: Modernism.

But this is not enough; a second condition must be met. Were Sicily and Italy deserted, wild, and uninhabited, no images of the Morgana would appear on Reggio's horizon. If stately colonnades are to be seen on the quiet surface of the sea, then those colonnades must exist in the vicinity. Thus also in the case of Modernism the question arises whence it derives the content of its images, and what reality it mirrors in its reflections.

Without a moment's hesitation I reply that the reality is nothing less than Christianity itself. Modernists have often been subjected to the charge that they stand on a pagan foundation, and certainly they of all people have the least right to take offense at this reproach, since their study of the science of religion openly professes to be looking for a common basis with paganism. The reproach goes too far, however, if it is taken to mean that Modernism might have come equally well had there never been a Christian church. On the contrary: as little as the reflection of a beech tree could quiver on the surface of a stream if that tree had not actually struck its roots in the bank, so Modernism would never have conjured up its images had there been no Christian church in our age. Granted that it never brought its light to bear on real Christianity and only caught its image in the camera obscura of its own pagan premises. Nevertheless also in its transparencies you can discern the main outline of the Christian faith, however faint and shadowy it may be. In their song your ear picks up untrue and often quite distorted echoes of the music of Christianity. Every current it takes account of has its source in the pages of the gospel, and every color with which it charms has its pure rays only from Scripture. It is therefore safe to say that, however far it has wandered down pagan roads, Modernism still belongs to the sphere of Christianity, for shadows cannot be separated from the trees which cast them. Certainly, along with paganism it builds up the truth from within the human mind, but by the light of Christ it has discovered human depths that were never discerned by the pagan eye. Hence the kinship between the two, hence also the difference.

And now the last question: what was there in the spiritual atmosphere of our century that gave rise to this phenomenon? Why did the particular heresy of our century have to be a strident Modernism? The fundamental feature of our century is its realism, its thirst for actuality. People have left off raving over hollow ideals and want above all to see and handle — and, I may add, freely enjoy — things. Four impulses irresistibly drove the people of our age onto this track: the bankruptcy of philosophy, the impotence of revolution, the enormous expansion of the study of nature, and the somnolence of the church. . . . [Kuyper gives a thumbnail sketch of how nineteenth-century developments in each of these fields worked toward a common rejection of speculative schemes in favor of the concrete and practical.[15]]

These four factors worked together to impress a very realistic stamp on the life of our age. In this realism, accordingly, we must look for its strength but also its weakness. "Its weakness," I say, because, as anyone who is spiritually alive senses, that realism also threatens us with a real danger. The distance from its base to the fatal abyss of materialism is easily measured, and we are well on our way toward it. You yourselves see how in political life might is increasingly gaining on right. At a recent conference of jurists at Liège it was openly stated that no other legal ground exists than the right of the most powerful. The dream of communism which is ever more widely shared (think of delirious Paris!) aims at nothing less than violence. All human thought is reduced to secretions of the brain, all feeling to a discharge of the glands. It takes no close acquaintance with the youth of our modern society to sense at a distance the depths which yawn at the feet of all spiritual and intellectual life in so bottomless a materialism.[16]

Against this Modernism tried to react. It owes its birth to a most serious attempt to defend faith in an ideal world against the coarseness of materialism. Speaking now not of deviations and excesses but of Modernism as a general phenomenon, I assert that it *tried to mediate between the things that are above and the realism that marks our age* so that if at all possible, while sharing its realism, the radiance of the ideal life might again shine from its [our age's] increasingly lusterless features.[17]

15. This sketch would be much more fully elaborated in Kuyper's rectorial addresses, *The Blurring of the Boundaries* and *Evolution* (see below), especially with respect to the practical consequences of materialist thought as adumbrated in the next paragraph of the text.

16. With respect to "delirious Paris" Kuyper notes (note 19) that the Commune uprising, which had occurred subsequent to his lecture, bore out his position: "Little could I suspect . . . in March that factual proof for my thesis was so imminent in Paris."

17. Kuyper adds in his note 20: "Modernism can only be explained as a reaction against the materialist tenor of our time. It does not attack our spiritual treasure but would defend it. . . . Modernism deplores our age's want of religion and would supply one. Hence its impressive debut. But this only prepares Modernism for a deeper fall. Because it lacks every means of defense, it must at last be driven by the Spirit of the Age to the deplorable conclusion of abandoning, as a hallucination, its hopes of making that Spirit pious. Or to the dreadful alternative of taking the road of Comte or Proudhon, i.e., developing a religion against God, an anti-Christian fanaticism . . . ," for which he cites Paul Poulin, *Religion et Socialisme* (Paris, 1867).

Kuyper kept up a steady critique of Liberalism in politics, too. This "three-star" editorial comes from *De Standaard*, 25 February 1888, when the Liberals were licking their wounds from an electoral loss.

The Cat's Paw

These days the Liberals have been playing "cat's paw" again. Not a nail is visible; no claw can be seen. They just stroke you with their velvet paw.

To listen to them you'd say: What utterly decent, devout folks these Dutch Liberals are. So respectful of everyone's rights! So earnest! So ready to stand up for the *church of the fathers!* If only genuine religion and quiet virtue prevail in the land, how delighted they are! How grateful and content!

Let the simpleton who's falling for this beware. Once that pussycat gets set securely again, you'll see how it arches its back and flicks out its paw. You'll see those nails sharp and clear. And every stroke of that stinging claw will aim at things sacred to you.

How grandly that effort might have been rewarded if people had only let themselves be led to the realism of Scripture, taking as their motto Baader's own statement that "corporeality is the end of the road of God."[18] Our dull world would have been refreshed by the divine realism that is expressed in the incarnation of the Word, that sets the heart on fire precisely by miracle, that displays its luster so gloriously in the bodily

18. In note 21 Kuyper's enthusiasm for the mystic-Romantic theologian Franz von Baader (1765-1841), professor at the (Roman Catholic) University of Munich, affords an interesting glimpse into his state of mind at this juncture. He acknowledges the debt he owes the Ethical theologians J. H. Gunning and Daniel Chantepie de la Saussaye for drawing Baader to his attention, commends Baader's spiritual realism for fending off both spiritualism and its "twin-brother," dualism, and then delivers this enconium: "He is a mighty personality from whose mind flows a unique current of thought that has already watered every field of learning with its nurturing stream. His school is not theological but global . . . [and] cosmological. . . . [T]here is no better counterweight to the thinness of Modernism." The primary source he cites is Franz Hoffmann, *Die Weltalter: Lichtstrahlen aus F. von Baader's Werke* (Erlangen, 1868). Kuyper's connection with the Ethical theologians is also evident from Gunning's having earlier used the Fata Morgana metaphor for, and various arguments regarding, Modernism that Kuyper here adapted. See Rullmann, *Kuyper-Bibliografie*, vol. I, p. 127.

resurrection of Christ from the tomb! But alas, from the very beginning people broke down that realism and wound up, paradoxically, in a most unreal position. Instead of confidently and courageously castigating our guilty age and so securing a moral advantage over its sinful endeavors, Modernism bowed before its majesty and sought salvation in compromise. . . . It admitted that one must not live too much for heaven but first of all for this earth. It granted that the study of nature is still to lead the way into the Kingdom of the Spirit. It conceded that this world should never yield in a conflict with the other, and that hence there can be no such thing as miracle. It allowed that to still speak of supernaturalism implied a criticism of the present state of affairs, a criticism no true son of our age should tolerate. Indeed, in the end it agreed that if there were to be knowledge of God, it had to be explained in terms of humanity as it is, and if there were to be Christianity, it must renounce its claim to being "the only true religion" so as to live henceforth on the same level with the other religions which it had previously shunned as idolatry.

At first the impossible seemed to succeed. Modernism spun out a worldview so ingenious, so subtle, and so marvelous that every sacred interest seemed secured. The ideal seemed to be preserved without violating the hard choice extorted from it by the realism of our age. But this was an illusion. It soon became apparent that by the most generous calculation not even half the bottom of our spiritual treasury could be covered.[19] As you know, Modernists are most eager to claim the honorable name of Protestant and would love to make people believe that Modernism and Protestantism are branches of the same tree distinguished only by the earlier or later appearance of their first sprouts. But nothing is less true. In matters of faith Modernism chooses human authority as its starting point, the very thing against which Protestantism raised its mighty protest. It forfeits the right to adorn itself with the honor of the Reformation if for no other reason than that it never knew the desperation, brokenheartedness, and mental anxiety from which Luther cried out to his God. The Reformation sought *redemption* for the troubled heart, Modernism only the *solution* to an ingenious problem. This is why Modernism only knows the reality of visible things and misses the reality of the other kind, which is much higher and much more firmly established, which speaks to us of the "immovable" kingdom of God even in the fact

19. Kuyper, note 24, cites "rich in books but poor in cash" as descriptive of Modernism itself but not of modern life in general. The latter is "poor in books too, wants to be so, and tosses overboard its spiritual treasure in the quest for materialism. Not so Modernism. . . . Its spiritual inventory is splendid, which makes its moral powerlessness not a conscious, willed sobriety but a painful bankruptcy."

of sin. Here Modernism erred. It spoke, as though we were still in Eden, of a *natural* connectedness between the visible and the invisible and did not understand that if we still lived in Eden, there would never have been a real salvation or any Christianity.

Do you recall the illusion of the alchemists? From base ore they tried to make precious metal, since they did not yet know what we have more recently learned from chemistry, viz., that by a fixed law of nature there is a fixed line of distinction between the base and the precious. In the alchemists' illusion you see the picture of the self-delusion to which Modernism succumbed. Modernists too erased the boundary line which, being engraved in life itself, can never be violated with impunity, the line separating the sacred from the profane. They too, by a process of mixing and melting, sought to prepare the precious nature of the holy from the base nature of the sinful. Like the alchemists who praised their Hermes Tresmegistos,[20] they lauded their good genius when not a single grain of real gold had yet been won but a mere yellowish reflection shone from their deceptive creation.

III

. . . It is not enough for us to have marveled at the *beauty* and to have understood the *necessity* of Modernism and the Morgana. We must continue the comparison by saying that in both cases *the images they present are devoid of reality*.

"Modernism, devoid of reality?" I think its swift development over a few brief years seems to validate that judgment. Who, upon seeing Modernism in its voyage careening along the curves of its stream, does not recall the line in Bürger's "Lenore":

Hurrah! The swift ride of the dead,
But does it not fill you, my dear, with dread?[21]

20. The Greek name for the Egytian god Thoth, associated with alchemy, astrology, and the occult sciences generally.

21. The original lines: "Hurrah! die Todten reiten schnell,/graut Liebchen auch fuer Todten?" occur at stanza 20, line 6. Gottfried August Bürger (1747-94) was a German poet of the *Sturm und Drang* who wrote popular ballads in folk style and influenced such German Romantics as Novalis and A. W. Schlegel. "Lenore" (1773) was his first great success and, as Kuyper notes (in his note 28), worked themes of illusion and reality apropos a returning military hero and his alienated love. The English pre-Raphaelite Dante Gabriel Rossetti executed this poem as his first English translation in 1844 at age sixteen.

After all, in speaking of "the dead" Bürger's Lenore has in mind the false idealism that is consumed by its inner strife with brute reality. "Hurrah! The swift ride of the dead" therefore characterizes the macabre music to which the ethereal in all ages speeds to its dissolution. Shadows are proverbially swift compared to the sluggish motion of what is truly lasting. . . . [Kuyper explicates Schiller's "Die Ideale" in support of his point.] Leaving the architect of the Crystal Palace[22] far behind, our Modernists have erected in the twinkling of an eye a splendid temple for which the building blocks still had to be prepared and whose vaulted domes, covering every area of life, were to provide shelter for all the peoples of the world. Consider that it got a name no more than fifteen years ago; yet one already hears from every side not that the building is nearly finished but that the completed and since antiquated edifice demands alteration and renovation. A mere fifteen years — what does this say for a spiritual movement? . . . Already Modernism has turned ecclesiastically conservative. This does not put me in mind of the growth of an oak but of a wild grapevine. The course of life does not run so fast for people who really have their feet on the ground.

Nor does it convey a sense of real substance when already in its first years we see the standard-bearers of the movement abandon it. The cradle of a really deep religious conviction, possessed of moral vitality, cannot produce such renegades. . . . Barely was the baby weaned when the ominous signs began to appear. Modernism had not yet been around ten years when men of enthusiasm and rare talent who had brought its message to our nation with ravishing eloquence themselves lost faith in what they had preached to others and doffed their official robes. . . .[23]

But we must also take account of its success. For success has real weight, provided it is not measured by the standard of cheap applause but by the gauge of the enthusiasm engendered and the power exerted. And certainly, Modernism has not lacked acclaim, at least not when it championed its negations. . . . It was another matter, however, when it issued its own summons to seriousness. And that is precisely the issue when it comes to judging its success. What, after all, was its purpose? What did it presume to do? Was it to give to people who were already earnest a channel for their

22. The Crystal Palace was the central hall of London's Great Exhibition of 1851, the prototype of subsequent World's Fairs with their celebration of modern progress and civilization. The Palace itself, though of monumental size, was quickly erected, then taken apart and relocated after the Exhibition was over.

23. Kuyper names such leading Dutch Modernists as Conrad Busken Huet (1826-86) and Allard Pierson, both of whom, after having taken up the Modernist cause in the 1850s, quit the ministry in the 1860s for reasons of intellectual honesty. Busken Huet went into elite journalism, Pierson into academia.

seriousness? No, it was — remember? — to throw up a dam against materialism and thereby to win back that sensual, willful, ever-bantering crowd to the ideal. And now I ask, have they reached that goal or even come close? You have your experience and I have mine, but to me it is not evident that they have. On the contrary. Among people of consecrated mental power in their midst I nearly always discovered the afterglow of a genuinely orthodox upbringing. The learned in other fields who echoed them were mostly content with that echo. Lay members of the church whom they fired with enthusiasm had spent their time in more serious circles before they climbed aboard this bandwagon. The success of their preaching is already on the wane. . . . If you mingle in the company of theatergoers and club members and gadabouts, you will discover them to be as averse to earnest thinking as ever, with this difference — that now they can also use Modernism to forge a weapon by which to banish the earnestness of life with more relaxed conscience. Do not misunderstand me. I am not saying that Modernists condone this, much less that this was their aim. I even realize that this must grieve them. I only refer to it as a standard by which to measure the reality of their power.

Similarly, a lack of formative power does little to demonstrate Modernism's inner vitality. A spiritual movement solidly rooted in reality will evidence its fresh vitality above all in the form it creates. Though that form may long be marred by the roughness of the newly wrought, you cannot deny that the life of the mind in its glory days is known more by a lavishness than by a paucity of creative power. But one sees nothing of this in the case of Modernism. What one does see in it is a singular phenomenon — that signs of decay and death are already appearing before its buds have set. Make no mistake about it: while Modernism certainly wants to do battle with modern scientific weapons, it also seeks to be a practical direction for religion in society. Hence, having a distinctive life-form in which to present itself would be no luxury! But what have we witnessed so far? That it continued to wear the old garments, however ill-fitting they might be; that it continued to disapprove of the old church but failed to find something better. For the time being it continued to carry the new wine in the old wineskins, but when it discovered that it is hard to maintain a church exclusively with the cultured, when the once-despised plebs regained their importance, well then Modernism swallowed its own scorn and openly confessed its lack of creativity by watching how we knit our fishnets and doing it the same way.[24] How

24. Kuyper is referring to amendments in the church order in the 1860s that gave the laity more power in church affairs. He describes the Modernists' imitations of orthodox practices as "plowing with a calf" (note 35).

they had once ridiculed those little tracts! How droll they had found those Sunday Schools! How often had they made our Young Men's Societies the butt of their jokes! What fun they had at the expense of those "piety factories"! But now, as a last resort, the Modernists distribute their own little tracts, even the wives of their professors are opening Sunday Schools, and — *mirabile dictu* — Young Men's Societies are being launched under modernist patronage! Once they expected to celebrate our funeral; now we see them robed in what they thought were our winding-sheets.

Now then, ladies and gentlemen, that early success, puny strength, and admitted paucity of creative power by themselves make for a low estimate of the reality at Modernism's disposal. But at this point we want to take the next step and examine the actual data on which they base their conclusions. Then you can judge for yourselves whether the facts and figures are solid. Since they take account of religion, morality, theology, and the church, we will briefly consider each of these in turn.

First then their "religion" — or rather, to use their idiom, their "religious standpoint." . . . [Kuyper treats the Modernist use of the imported *"religieux"* instead of the Dutch *"godsdienstig"* as a token of its inauthenticity.] Against it I wish to lodge a threefold objection: that their God is an abstraction, that their prayers are lacking in petition, and that to be consistent they must deny the reality of divine government.

1. *Their God is an abstraction* and has no actual existence. I say this in all seriousness. I know that Modernists are not conscious of it for they venerate, worship, love, and adore something they not infrequently call "God." By the process of personification they confer both reality and personhood on that something. To the object of their adoration they attribute power to affect their moral life. Summed up in their idea of God is the noblest and purest essence they can imagine. They lose themselves totally in that self-generated God and devote to him the sighings of their heart. Indeed, in their inner contemplations that God-idea is so much their all that from him as the sum of all good they sooner or later expect the triumph of all good. But does it follow that there really is a living God corresponding to the God-idea they have created for themselves?

Ladies and gentlemen, the memory of a feature from the poet's life casts a special light on this question. Above all else the poet's heart yearns for a pure idyllic love; yet their lives in many cases offer a most singular contrast. They sang the finest hymns to their Beatrice or Laura, their Molly or Adelaide, but often entered such impossible marriages that divorce is anything but a rare occurrence in their world. Upon the death of his wife one of them did not even shrink from singing:

As one escaped from night's dark lair
I feel myself newly risen
To the light and Spring's fresh air.[25]

Whence this contrast? Check the early writings of Europe's great poets and you will find that not only do they rave over the ideal unfolding of an all-consuming love but also — inferring the reality from the idea — worship Love itself in the imagined person of a pure maiden resplendent in form and beauty. Yet every sober mind that stays outside their illusions knows that such an image only reflects their own stirrings of soul and simply misses reality. . . . [Kuyper gives an extended example from the case of Schiller, quotes lines from Matthison's "Adelaide," and mentions Dante, Byron, and Bürger as well.]

There you have the picture of the Modernists' idea of God. Urged on by the need to worship, they create for themselves an image of an eternally beautiful Love that lacks the power of existence — in this instance, "holiness." They may refer to this image by the borrowed sound of "God" or "the All" or, following the latest fashion, the eternal Cosmos. The name itself does not matter: they believe they have a "God." What they love is no more than the reflected image of their own soul; still they rave and adore. They will not grant that their idea of God is unreal. The state of illusion is powerless to distinguish appearance from reality, and their mind's eye would only be able to see this if the living God revealed himself to them, melting their illusory image before the splendor of his majesty.

Perhaps you ask, how in our worship of God can we tell the true from the false? In a more robust age the catechist of the Palatinate would have curtly replied to that question with an answer that cuts our conscience to the quick: that "to devise another God than the one who has revealed himself in his Word is idolatry."[26] But I know that today people would much rather listen to Shakespeare. To me too he is a great poet who will not die as long as human hearts are alive since the claims of the human heart

25. The women named were the loves of, respectively, Dante, Schiller, Bürger, and Friedrich von Matthison (1761-1831). The original lines are from Bürger's "Das hohe Lied von der Einzige:" "Wie aus Nacht und Moderduft/Fühl ich froh mich auferstanden/Zu des Frühlings Licht und Luft." Bürger was referring to his own escape from marriage to his first wife, Dorette, to marry her sister, his lover, Molly. She, in turn, died a year later in childbirth.

26. Heidelberg Catechism, Q & A 95.

emerge in his creations more fully than it itself realizes. You all know his "Hamlet." In that play too a battle is being fought between appearance and reality. At midnight a ghost is seen moving in front of the walls of Elsinore. It seems to be the newly deceased king, but there are doubts. Horatio, Hamlet, everyone present refuses to believe it at first. And what test automatically suggests itself to everyone's mind? Listen. The ghost appears and Bernardo says: "See, it stalks away." But Horatio cries out: "Stay, ghost! Speak, speak, I charge thee, speak!" And when Hamlet finally sees through the specter, what gives him hope that the apparition is not a reality? At first he too cries out: "O! answer me! Let me not burst in ignorance, but speak." Only when there is no answer does he cry: "It will not speak, then I will follow it."[27] That test applies here as well. "O God, my God, if you exist, then speak to me" voices the deepest yearning of the human heart, and it only finds peace when the oppressive silence is broken and the living Word proclaims to us a God who has spoken to his human children by the mouth of the prophets and by his Son.

2. Look at *prayer* and ask whether the unreality of the modern idea of God is not confirmed precisely here, in the most sublime expression of human life. Until now people prayed in all parts of the world, in every age and in every nation, in the quiet, childlike confidence that the praying heart was heard by listening ears above and believing that the truth of the Eternal was most fully shown in answers to prayer. Even now, as you mingle with believers, you are refreshed by their stories of answers to prayer; in fact, you cannot find a believer whose soul has not known the mystery of faith at work precisely in God's responses there. But behold, contrary to the testimony of every age and nation, Modernism announces that no one has ever understood the true nature of prayer since it is not a petitioning to be heard but merely an outpouring of the soul. I am well aware that sometimes in speaking of prayer they will so define it that the differences are blurred and their idea of prayer blends almost imperceptibly with yours. But whenever that threatens, I pose this question or one like it: "Suppose there is a mother whose son, having sailed overseas, seems to have gone badly astray, and she falls on her knees here to beg God to rescue her child. Can that mother's prayer, which ascends to God here, bring down from above a blessing over there where her son is out wandering alone?"[28] "Of course

27. *Hamlet,* Act I, Scene 4.

28. Kuyper would have occasion to live out this example with his own son Fred (Jan Hendrik Frederik, named after Kuyper's father), who left the Netherlands in 1886 at age twenty to study dentistry at the University of Michigan. Fred's subsequent career in the Netherlands Indies, where he became a theosophist and, apparently, quite familiar with local women, would test Kuyper's theory of prayer.

not," comes the answer. For me that fixes the breach between modern prayer and the religious consciousness. So I would simply ask, stop using the word "prayer." What you call prayer is an uninhibited self-elevation of the spirit, an outpouring of the heart, a dialogue with your own soul, a process of self-discovery in sacred silence. All that is good, it is indispensable, even something in which we would join you. But the point at which all this ends for you is precisely the point where, for us, prayer just begins.

3. Finally, if they wish to be consistent, they must deny the reality of *divine government*. They confess that they draw their knowledge of an Eternal Love from both nature and history, while the idea of a curse resting on both seems to them insane. But this is self-contradictory. Yes, one can hear the language of love in nature, but from its depths one also hears the voice of wrath which speaks in still mightier tones of cruelty, of death agony, and of mindless destruction. Not only the hen with her chicks but also the fly in the spider's web discloses its terrible secret. As in nature, so in history. There too justice at times prevails, but just as often the poor are oppressed, the righteous tormented, and those who dare to honor God trampled underfoot. O cross of Calvary! The very mention of it is enough to seal for us the law that never denies itself. Seriously, in the face of so much grief, so much appalling injustice, so many bitter tears, one must be as superficial as a butterfly to say of nature or history that it teaches the eternal Love of my God. If Modernism would think these things through, it could not continue to deny these facts but come to a choice: either abandon the idea of love in God or abandon God's government in history. If, denying the curse, it persists in maintaining that its God reveals himself in nature, the eternal Love in its God must grow dim. But if it continues in its God-concept of eternal Love, it must slip toward the fearful acknowledgment: I see nothing of divine government.

We now come to the sphere of *morality*, where again we want to ask whether human nature as Modernism pictures it, the sin it militates against, and the moral ideal it pursues can stand the test of reality.

We first inquire concerning the nature of man, for he is a moral being. But is that still true for Modernism? You have probably seen the lithograph on the title page of Darwin's *Descent of Man:* a man walking in the same forest in which his more agile ancestors swing exuberantly from branch to branch. People have laughed at it but it really is no joke. It implicitly denies the reality of a special creation of man, a denial in which Modernism follows the new zoology. "No miracle, and consequently no special creation in an already-existing world," they say. Which leaves us with a choice: either man ceases to be moral or he ceases to be one whole being. For if one derives his moral nature from animal nature, the distinction between the two has been discarded and the absolute, and hence unique, character of the moral life collapses. The alternative is to say that in the hour of his humanization, by a new effusion, moral life flowed into the most noble quadruped in existence. Then I would say that you have miracle back despite yourself and thereby cease to be a Modernist. But you still do not have a real being, only an apparition that is divided and cobbled together like the old Docetic Jesus and thus lacks the unity of origin which is the indispensable characteristic of all being. In the modernist sphere no choice remains but to be an occasionalist like Geulinx or a materialist along with Moleschot.[29] Either the moral life is the sublimate of physical forces, or what only the wildest kind of Docetic dared to dream about Jesus has to be attributed to every human being. To that fork your path is leading; both directions take you to the abolition of man.

Even less does Modernism know anything of real sin. What we have thus far called "immoral" it has ingeniously translated into "not yet moral," thereby destroying the whole concept of sin. It's no secret how people can argue that black is white, the two being distinguished only by a relative difference. You only have to picture the endless variations — charcoal, slate, dove, pearl, and the like — that mark the transition from ebony black to arctic white, and ask in which shade of gray lies the boundary that separates white and black. Starting with black, you continually go on to the next shade until, having run the gamut, you have reached the brightest kind of white without discovering the slightest tint among them that could serve as a boundary. By a similar route Modernism has arrived at the immoral thesis that sin has always been misunderstood. For here, too, the firm line of distinction that separates light from darkness has been abandoned, which had to lead on to the lamentable assertion that — as Opzoomer put it — though sin and holiness are distinct to us, they are not so to God; the difference is only relative. You ask whether they do not have a sense of sin? Oh, certainly! Just as an artist is obsessed by the beautiful image that has taken shape in his imagination

29. Arnold Geulinx (1624-69) was professor of philosophy at Leiden, a convert from Catholicism to Calvinism, and a vigorous exponent of Descartes. He was a strong body-soul dualist and inclined toward a denial of the empirical, asserting God's counsel as that which kept the material and mental universes in perfect conjunction. Jacobus Moleschot (1822-93) was an eminent Dutch physiologist devoted to proving the materialist theories of Ludwig Feuerbach and George Foster.

and allows him no rest until it is reflected on canvas, so they know an inner restlessness, a never slumbering self-reproach, a sense of being relentlessly pursued by the moral ideal. I grant that this makes sense so long as we move in the company of the more cultured, where the finer forms of life prevail or where people seclude themselves in their study or studio far removed from the marketplace of life. But go into the real world and see there the fury of sin which ruins everything it touches. Consider the miserliness, the self-indulgence, the animosity, the voluptuousness. Think of the hyenas on the battlefield, strangling the wounded, devilishly violating even the bodies of the dead. Think of the tigresses of Belleville or the murder scene of Place Vendôme,[30] and then tell me whether the modernist's cry "not yet holy; an indispensable phase in a person's moral development" does not make the blood rush to your face and demonstrate to you that he no longer believes in the reality of sin.

Their *moral ideal* is even less real, for it is not fullness itself, only the demand that fullness be realized. They are underway; they pursue it; they strive with all their might to inch their way toward the goal. Yet this will always remain a fumbling, they confess, for by their lights an ideal attained is an ideal no more. Just this I deny. My ideal is that which in a higher and holier sense makes me blessed and happy, fills and permeates my whole being. But then the ideal may not be an empty demand but the full treasury from which one, as John puts it, receives grace upon grace [John 1:16]. Then you do not rise to your ideal but the ideal comes down upon you. Then it is not the demand of the good and the true but eternal goodness, truth, and beauty itself that spreads out its wings over you in benediction, that gives you pure harmony in place of passionate, restless pursuit, a peace unfathomably profound and a calm which never ends.

Mark this in the world of music which is most distant from intellection and therefore furnishes the strongest possible proof. Listen as Mozart himself testifies that the chords he reproduces are waiting for him, that they merely use him as their medium, and that through his heart they break into the world with a fullness and depth he himself can barely understand. Consider how, in Beethoven's *Busslied,* the entire gospel of the atonement — profound contrition suddenly succeeded by the purest, holiest rejoicing — washes over you in waves of glorious sound, though the composer himself was not aware of this when he put

30. Belleville is a city in West Cape province, South Africa. Place Vendôme is a Parisian square that was the site of fervid gatherings of the *sans-culottes* during the Revolution and (very recently for Kuyper's readers) of a Commune riot that toppled the statue of Napoleon that had been erected there.

Gellert's poem to music.[31] Such is the case in every sphere of life. It is not we who pursue the ideal but the ideal which pursues us, apprehends us, masters us, drenches the depths of our being with its fullness, and molds our empty form increasingly to itself. Not "*become* perfect" but "*be* perfect" [Matt. 5:48], not "*become* holy" but "*be* holy" [1 Pet. 1:16] is the summons of the eternal ideal to the person who has heard the divine cry "it is finished" on Mt. Golgotha. Bethlehem's cradle and the open sepulcher behind Golgotha are the holy realities in which alone that ideal can be known. Not until I know and confess a Word become flesh do my groanings turn into joy. Only then can you who thirst for the ideal join Goethe's Faust in singing:

> Here I find my footing, here are realities;
> Standing here the spirit may give spirits battle.
> Here the great double realm begins.[32]

And now, to cast a cursory glance at their *theology* to see whether more reality can be found there, we will inquire into their *historical* sense, their *critical* touchstone, and their *dogmatic* foundation.

The Modernists work hard at history; indeed their unflagging zeal in this discipline is most commendable. But do they work at it with historical sense? You must have seen the Catholic pictures of sacred history in which Joseph the carpenter is shown wearing a priestly robe

31. Kuyper, in his note 49, gives this extensive comment: "The pagan idea of reconciliation is a matter of gradual purification. The Christian is one of a sudden salvation that is cast down by an act of God into the depths of our deadness. This is undeniably expressed in Beethoven's musical composition. First dull and solemn tones plunge into the depths to mourn the soul's pain more deeply than the soul itself can do; then, suddenly, a soaring into the highest, finest tones, like a stream of holy sounds rolling over each other, reverberating with a hallelujah of deliverance. Gellert's 'Busslied,' on which Beethoven based this composition, means something entirely different. Beethoven thus unconsciously took over from the world of music the Christian idea of reconciliation which he did not seek but found there and, unbeknownst to himself, glorified in his music." Christian Fürchtgott Gellert (1715-69) was a popular German hymn-writer of natural-religious inclinations, infusing Enlightenment rationalism with religious feeling.

32. The lines are from *Faust,* Part II, Act 1:

> Hier fass ich Fuss, hier sind es Wirklichkeiten
> Von hier aus darf der Geist mit Geistern streiten,
> Das Doppelreich, das grosse, sich bereiten!

Kuyper acknowledges changing the last line is his quotation, which reads: "Das Doppelreich hier fangt es an."

and the apostles are crowned with mitres. Our century has ventured a similar anachronism when it presented Jesus of Nazareth to us in the garments of a modern theologian. This has now been acknowledged as untenable. Yet the domain of Catholicism offers another method, the method of Father Brouwers, and that was chosen here.[33] Rather, it *had* to be chosen here, for every view of life that has been spun from thought and not derived from reality has to collide with the facts until they have been reshaped according to demand. So it is with our Catholic country-men. The two — their view of life and our national history — cannot both be true. And so they pour the nation's history into a new casing, not intentionally but impelled by their viewpoint and to maintain their view of life. Not merely the object perceived but also the seeing eye determines the image on one's retina, and Rome actually sees our nation's history as it depicts it to us.

In the same way I do not question the good faith of the modernists' historiography; it is just the flawed lens they have chosen that makes a better view impossible. Modernism is the imprint in religion of what became of the [French] Revolution in the state; it tries to squeeze every-thing into the mold of its idea. That idea, not derived from reality but born from an illicit union between the sacred and the unholy, must clash with the *present* as it asserts itself in heart and conscience and with the *past* as it speaks in history. One or the other has to yield — either Mod-ernism to the facts, or the facts to the modernist idea. If I do not want the former, if the life of my mind has become too closely bound up with Modernism and I therefore believe that above all else that modernist principle is sacred, then of course what history says cannot be valid, nor can what Scripture says of Jesus be true. The whole of the past simply *has to* be modified, tinted, and transposed until that history, in spite of itself, supports my Modernism. But then, understandably, there can be no talk of the historical sense, for the nerve of that sense has been deadened by my apriorism. Though such historical research can tell me what nineteenth-century Modernism has up its sleeve, it cannot teach me what happened eighteen centuries ago.

Their criticism was powerless to do that because, fancying itself to be objective, it broke all connection with life. If I am to test the genuine-ness of gold, then the stone I plan to use must first be examined to see if it is a real touchstone. The precious metal only conveys its gold streak when touched with a stone that suits it. There has to be a natural affinity between the object you choose and the touchstone you employ or the

33. Jan Willem Brouwers, a Roman Catholic historian, wrote essays contesting Groen van Prinsterer's Calvinistic interpretation of Dutch history.

test will fail. But Modernism denies this. It calls this prejudice and partiality and wants you instead to assess the world of colors even though your eyes have no affinity for color. So in this case. A Christian world presents itself to our observation with a spirit, a language, a life all its own. A sensible critic would say: You cannot rightly judge this phenomenon unless you have the intellectual affinity that enables you to enter into its life. But no, says Modernism, the object here must be everything, the subject nothing, and by a savage criticism bent on inspecting everything but itself, it proceeds to destroy your Christianity.

Thus and only thus could it happen that, as late as 1858, an eminent professor argued with sweeping enthusiasm and captivating glow that the genuineness of the Gospel of John (a few verses excepted) was as clear as day — so historical were the characters, so profound the coherence, so natural the stamp on its brow. Then in 1861 this self-same professor published an article that said everything had changed. The same persons and words and traits that once gave indubitable proof for authenticity now made inauthenticity so obvious that this whole Gospel contained not a single word of John. Naturally I do not object to better insights; anyone of conviction will honor that. But we must dispel the sacred haze in which a critique dares to hide while it remains alien to the essence of things and, demanding the subordination of all, toys with the *corpus vile* according to the whim of its apriori.[34]

Their *dogmatics* is no different. Their "dogmatics" I say, for however much they rage against dogmas, they are themselves the most stubborn dogmatists. A dogma, after all, is a proposition that you want others to accept on pain of being proven wrong. "We confess," says the church,

34. This was the existential crossing for Kuyper, as he states in his note 52: "It scarcely needs to be said that this refers to the *Gospel of John* [Leiden, 1864] by Professor Scholten. I bring this up, first, because Professor Scholten himself states in his foreword that his transit in these years from a Platonic toward a more Aristotelian worldview is the chief cause of his divergent conclusion, thereby himself acknowledging the apriori as the guiding star of his critique; but also because reading this book, in conjunction with the memory of the enthusiastic delivery of his lectures, made such a deep impression that from that hour on the authority of modern criticism for me was finished." In an earlier note (31) to his own description of the fleeting nature of Modernists' proposals and personal faith, Kuyper said apropos of Scholten: "This is not to retract any of the warm regard that I have for my professor and friend. You have to have been a student of his yourself to appreciate how a personality like his electrifies his disciples. But this piety may not tempt us to misjudge the truth or misconstrue the facts. Scholten has been pushed out of his own life-sphere by Modernism. Modernism offers a spirit such as his no ground for the development of his characteristic power. A *facile princeps* on his own terrain, precisely the spiritual power wherein lies the secret of his mastery is thereby doomed to idleness."

"and you who confess otherwise, depart from us." Similarly Modernism: "We believe, and those who think otherwise forfeit their right to be considered cultured and well-educated." Tell me, with what else but unproven premises and therefore (from their own viewpoint) cheap dogmas does Modernism start in all its preaching? Its confession can be broadly sketched as follows: "I, a modernist, believe in a God who is the Father of all humankind, and in Jesus, not the Christ, but the rabbi from Nazareth. I believe in a humanity which is by nature good but needs to strive after improvement. I believe that sin is only relative and hence that forgiveness is merely something of human invention. I believe in the hope of a better life and, without judgment, the salvation of every soul."[35] Naturally they are free to confess those dogmas and so are we to demonstrate their lack of substance. It is a characteristic of dogma, after all, that independently of the shifting sands of opinion it articulates the indisputable ground-lines along which the sacred truth advances in every age. Their dogmas, by contrast, are merely the transcript of ideas currently in vogue, transferred from the marketplace of unexamined life into the church of Jesus and sanctioned by present-day authority. Notice how often in just a few years they have already recast their dogmas. Tell me if you can believe in the substance of a dogma that leans on what it should itself be supporting, and that is ashamed of its own character.[36]

Finally, their *church* lacks every essential attribute of the church. Their motto, "we shall maintain," is their pretension but no proof and settles nothing. If they are to be accorded the right to use that motto, we must first examine the argument they use to support their pretension. One of their leaders recently undertook to do so as follows: "The church of Jesus is an association of all who live for the ideal; we modernists belong to that category; therefore the church also belongs to us." Why not say: "The French nation is an association of people who fight for idea x; you fight for idea x; therefore you are a Frenchman"? The very rules of syllogism knock this argument out cold. But listen to this: "The Reformers revolted against Rome, demanding the right of 'free inquiry.' That inquiry, which they barely began let alone completed, is the hallmark

35. This anticipates H. Richard Niebuhr's famous indictment: Liberals believed that "a God without wrath brought men without sin into a kingdom without judgment through the ministrations of a Christ without a Cross" (*The Kingdom of God in America* [Chicago, 1937], p. 193).

36. In his note 53 Kuyper adds: "For Modernism public opinion has taken the place that the Church has awarded to the witness of the Holy Spirit in the congregation. . . . Rejection of dogma thus no longer places one outside 'the fellowship of the saints' but outside the aristocracy of enlightened humanity. Dogma, once at its core eternal as the Spirit that stamped it, has now become a child of the day. . . ."

of the Reformation, its vital principle, its boast and glory. This principle lost its vitality among us long ago, and the church reconciled itself to the still unexamined legacy bequeathed to us by Rome. We, the real sons of the Reformation, now resume that stalled inquiry. By virtue of principle, therefore, we must be given not only rights of membership in the church but a place of prominence!"[37] This syllogism, though less transparent, suffers from the same defect. "Free inquiry" is used in both cases but each time in a different sense. A child can be very free in examining its toys by breaking them to pieces; a merchant in pearls freely examines his collection as well but does so to discern the true from the false. Modernism has acted like that child, the Reformation like the merchant. Up until now we have not seen much family resemblance between the two. Do you want to know, perhaps, how men like Luther and Calvin thought about that untrammeled inquiry? Then read how they chastised Carlstadt and Servetus, the "Schwärmer" and the Unitarians, and guess with what fatherly tenderness they would have said "bone of my bone" in the case of a Strauss and a Renan![38]

But do not the Remonstrants and, before them, the Erasmians show undeniably that side-by-side with the stream of orthodoxy a heterodox current has run through the life of our church? Who denies this, provided you add that it has always been censured by the church as incompatible with its nature and the source of its life? There are people who ask: "But what is the church? Have not we been born in the church as well, and along with us thousands of people whose aversion to Modernism is equalled only by their aversion to your orthodoxy? Though an earlier time had a different opinion, how can an earlier generation tie us down? The church is the generation now living. It has the right to make of its church what it pleases!" Even to make it into its opposite, like an association of teetotalers that eventually undertakes to run a distillery? Undoubtedly, the generation now living *can* do this. But that is not the question. The question is whether it can do this and at the same time *remain the church of Christ*. Naturally, this is not decided by the will of one generation but by a fixed law of logical thinking, a law which demands that you first of all track down the marks of the church as such and then decide whether these marks are consistent with your demands. Only history can show

37. Kuyper was also staking claims to the legacy of the Reformation against prevailing custom in the church. He would change the polity and keep the doctrine; the Modernists, just the opposite.

38. Andreas Bodenstein of Karlstadt (1480-1541), an early supporter of Luther, took the Reformation imperative to a far more radical conclusion, earning Luther's denunciation. Michael Servetus (1511-53) was executed in Calvin's Geneva for his rejection of the doctrine of the Trinity.

you what these marks are. Your view or our view is immaterial here. If history teaches that one of the most undeniable marks of the church is the calling to ban the very thing that seems to you the only truth, then judge for yourself whether your school of thought is compatible with the essential nature of the church.

"But the church has accepted me and ordained me as its minister!" What of it? Not even a church can morally perform what militates against its nature as a church. If it did, it did so wrongfully, and it can never again become conscious of itself without immediately feeling the goad of its calling to right the wrong and to undo that which, if allowed to continue, would render it guilty of suicide. Tell me, what is the "church" to Modernism? It surely has to be something which something else is not. It must therefore be defined by some kind of boundary that determines where it starts, where it ends, what will and what will not belong to it. That boundary or limitation may not be determined arbitrarily but must flow from its very nature. It therefore may not remain what it is now: an association held together by accident, in which qualification for membership is only a given of the past or of inertia. It may neither lose its identity by melting into society nor pursue the same goal as some local humanitarian society. It may not be something one may also find among the followers of Buddha or Confucius but must have a distinguishing character of its own. How will Modernism settle this issue? If it says: "an ethical-religious association," then what of the humanitarians? "A society for divine worship," then what of our Jews? "A society for those who venerate Jesus as the ideal man," but watch out! Not everybody believes that. Besides, many an Israelite, even the odd Brahmin, does this too! What then? Already Modernism is ashamed of its own hollow phrases. Conscious of its own poverty, it joins with us in calling for a "Confession." A "Confession," no less! Of course, it had to come to this, but by returning to what it had once rejected, Modernism has demonstrated its powerlessness — at least its powerlessness to give us a church. Everyone senses that the idea of a "confessional church" can never be the product of Modernism because that violates its own principle and so was taken not from its own stockroom but from the well-filled treasury of orthodox ideas.

And so we have found it, ladies and gentlemen. Wherever we threw out the plumbline, the bottom of reality sank away beneath us. No real God, no real prayer, no real divine government, the reality of human life under threat, no real sin, no real ideal, no genuine history, no true criticism, no dogma that could withstand scrutiny, nor a real church. We found the names and shadows of all these but no rootedness in real being. Still, I want to repeat what I said at the beginning: I would not for that reason wish Modernism away. I stand by my earlier assertion. In a church such as ours was, situated in a century like the one in which we were born, Modernism not only had to come but has tended to be a blessing as well. Principles had been trifled with and behold: Modernism's bold negations called them back from their grave! We had ceased to develop, but Modernism's unsparing assault has forced us again to our intellectual chores. The church had no apparent connection with our age; Modernism has prompted us to look for it. Precisely because it ignored the claims of reality, it was able in the twinkling of an eye to run through all the passages of the mind and has shown us countless bypaths and sideroads that we had never ventured down and that the church had not yet imbued with its Christian spirit. In short, when I say that without the Modernists we would still be groaning under the leaden weight of an all-killing Conservatism, you will understand in what sense I dare state openly that, both in reality and morally, Modernism has saved orthodoxy in the church of Jesus!

"Saved" indeed, but only as cutting a cankerous tree down to the trunk sometimes causes it to produce new shoots again. "Saved" as at times a sick person is saved by an injection of poison or, if you please, as a crushing enemy assault alone can sometimes revive a nation's will to live. Thus a "salvation" that I well understand strikes terror into your heart. You call Modernism a blessing — it may be retorted — but what if the axe cut too deeply, what if the poison was too strong, what if that assault turned into an annihilation and the waters of Modernism totally inundated our ancient faith? Look how powerful it has already become! What a brain trust it has at its disposal! What enormous influence it exerts! Above all, consider how the whole intellectual climate of the day favors the Modernist party and contradicts our faith!

I do not deny these facts. Still, when the popularity of Modernism threatens to rob you of courage, there is comfort in history. We will be safe if we focus on the future with knowledge of the past in mind. . . . On that basis, I say with total conviction: Church of Christ, have no fear of Modernism! This is not the first time such an all-corrupting heresy has broken out in the church of Jesus. Go back to the early centuries of Christianity and you will find there the Arian heresy which no less than Modernism shook the Christian edifice to its foundations, and whose history you cannot browse through without being surprised at its resemblance to Modernism. Not only are the two alike in that, following in the footsteps of Arius, Modernism denies the deity of Christ. The deeper motive of the two is also identical. Lest anyone think that I am carried away by my subject and looking for resemblance where there is none, I will appeal to an apostle of Modernism himself, Ferdinand Christian Baur. He highlights the essence of Arianism in these two features: first, by its lack of affinity for the religious life, and second, by its refusal to recognize Christianity as the absolute revelation of God.[39]

But there is still more that warrants drawing a parallel between the two heresies. Let me tell you of Arianism and judge for yourself whether you are not reminded of Modernism. According to Dr. Réville's testimony,[40] Arianism won its strongest support among the cultured classes and was acclaimed by academia. It was unable to strike root in the church and was only maintained there, with difficulty, by the support of the state. In Alexandria the people totally turned their backs on the Arians and deserted their houses of worship. In some places everything was Arian, while in other provinces not a trace of it was to be found. They held meetings and gave lectures and tried to reach the masses by their popular writings. In a book of popular songs called "Thaleia" ["The Banquet"] Arius sang the praises of his own theology. Philostorg, the Baur of the Arians, wrote a history to demonstrate that his view was that of the church from the beginning. Like Modernism today, the parties were divided into numerous subgroups, and Conservatism was the brake that held back the wheels of the church's movement. And history shows — unfortunately by a trail of blood — that then too the conflict was waged with vehemence. In short, the resemblance is so strong that one would almost say: insert other names and dates into the history of the Arian heresy (taken very broadly) and you have before you the story of Modernism.

Now then, you fear the power of Modernism, but I tell you that in its day Arianism was more powerful than Modernism today! While among us there has been some discussion whether it would not be better to ban the orthodox, in Arius's day people acted on that impulse. For a while Arianism was so much in control that it sent the leaders of the orthodox movement into exile, condemned its confession, and scattered its adherents. Indeed: it was very powerful and highly esteemed. But what has become of all that greatness and those bold expectations? Like the stars of the night they paled before the dawn; now you have to look

39. Kuyper in his note 56 references Baur's 1859 *Die Christliche Kirche vom Anfang des vierten bis zum Ende des sechsten Jahrhunderts,* pp. 97-100.

40. Albert Réville (1826-1906) was a preacher of pronounced Modernist convictions in the Walloon Church in Rotterdam. A sympathetic commentator on Theodore Parker and Ernest Renan, he had just published *Histoire du dogma de la divinité de Jésus Christ* (Paris, 1869).

up ancient histories to discover that there ever was a movement called Arianism. Please understand: by saying this I do not mean that Modernism will be gone by tomorrow, or even in this century. But don't forget either that Modernism has been around only for fifteen years and that it took four centuries before Arianism completely disappeared. So let's not be impatient! The sickness cannot go away until its virulence has been spent.

Still — I will not deny it — still it is my heart's prayer that the church of Christ may be spared a long sickbed. It is my heart's prayer because I love the church and once myself dreamed the dream of Modernism. Along with others I called slanderous the assertion that what I saw was unreal. I only discovered the enchantress's hand of Morgan le Fay and saw her splendid creation sink away into nothingness before my eyes when a gentle breeze from higher realms caused the horizon of my life to quiver and the truth appeared to me in the glory of my Lord and King.

Oh, there is a poisonous snake which seeks to enter the hearts of us all and, upon getting in, sucks the last drop of lifeblood from our veins. We too indulgently call this vampire "Addiction to doubt." I have seen its victims, have seen the enervated souls, the weak of heart who float along with the crowd, powerless to resist the tide, people who know only the momentary flush of excitement but are inwardly dying so that only a dissembling life can, for the moment, conceal their spiritual death.

Well now, that monster has wrapped itself around our age and crept into its breast. Look at those pale faces, those lusterless eyes, and ask whether that poisonous snake has not already struck at its heart. And you who would save it from death, Apostles of the new school! I do not doubt your good intentions but what, I ask, will your mirage produce but a momentary flickering that is soon sunk in total despair? You tell me you would restore faith. Praise God! But where, I pray, is the basis on which this faith, this highly commended faith, can rest? Your answer of course is "in man," inasmuch as "I believe in man" is the indispensable overture to your whole oratorio and the closing refrain of all your songs. You thereby judge yourselves, for either your faith is an illusion or, if you want to believe in truth, you must cling to the object of your faith and not, conversely, base it on yourselves.

Oh, I know: "Truth, truth!" Even as I say it many of you ask: "Who will tell us what the truth is?" Just here lies an enormous danger. For once you give a foothold to the tendency to doubt, it will take over and carry you along until you will find yourself doubting even the certainty of your own sense perception. Jouffroy's recent assertion "that man believes by instinct and doubts by reason" is false, as if skepticism can be limited to the intellect by an act of the will. On the contrary, as Royer Collard so powerfully stated in the French Academy, "Do not split man, for as soon as skepticism enters the understanding, it inhabits the whole person."[41] It forces its way from his intellect to his conscience, from his conscience to his self-consciousness, and undoes all sense of solidity. Once you begin to slide down this slope, there is no stopping; caught up in this process of questioning and doubting you may finally get to where, with the Eleatics of old and Berkeley more recently, you call into question the entire visible world and insanely say: "I indeed see this house but it does not follow that that house exists!" Indeed, you can be drawn so deeply into this vortex that finally, as one deprived of his senses, you become a phantom in your own eyes and with your head in your hands cry out in agony: "Am I real or am I not?" That is the point toward which you are drifting and toward which you are taking all who have come aboard with you, driven by the winds of your elusive idealism. Well might you say: "How wonderfully the fresh sea breeze cools my tired head; its play upon the rolling waves is just enchanting!" But for all that, we are human, we are people of flesh and blood, and now that Eden is behind us, the ideal must prove its reality to us also in the visible and tangible or its dancing haziness will evaporate even the consciousness of our mind and heart.

Ladies and gentlemen, even for a poet like Goethe, a man who never inhaled the unadulterated fragrance of Christianity, the craving

41. In his note 58 Kuyper references (Achille de) Jouffroy (1785-1859), *Essai sur le scepticisme* (1830). Pierre P. Royer Collard (1763-1845), a French philosopher, was a moderate during the Revolution and a liberal legitimist during the Restoration. His epistemology emulated Thomas Reid's, arguing the existence of an external world known to consciousness beyond the senses. Kuyper references the quotation in the text to Royer Collard's opening lecture of the year 1813, as recorded in Jouffroy's translation, *Oeuvres de Reid*, p. 426. He then gives a lengthy comment to the effect that the denial of miracles is linked to a supposition of man's "divided composition" and thus also to skepticism. "I do not deny in the least that there are 'honest skeptics,' but what people mean by this banal plea is difficult to tell. That the road to knowledge has to pass through the dimness of skepticism I utterly reject. If in a given era the certainty of ruling convictions is so weak that fear of doubt should rob all courage to investigate, then the guilt of the individual is lesser but the responsibility of the sick spirit of the age is greater. The right of Skepticism hangs entirely on the question: who doubts, your thinking or you yourself? If only the unreflective can give the first answer, then it is clear that Skepticism is not an intellectual but a moral disease which, in full course, must end in madness." Kuyper concludes with references to current literature, including Allard Pierson's, to portray Nihilism and Idealism as twin types of "unhealthy" or "abnormal" thinking, attributable to the "sick spiritual constitution" of the times.

for that "manifestation in the flesh" was sometimes irresistible. You know how, in his Torquato Tasso, he brings on the scene the laurel-crowned singer of Italy's age of art as one consumed by love for Leonore von Este, the illustrious daughter of his king, whom he met at Belriguardo. Gently and with great dignity the princess repulses him, as though this poetic heart could pursue only vain ideals. And how does Tasso respond? "No; whatever may resound in my song, I owe everything to one person and to one alone!" It is not hollow ideals he is chasing.

> There is no spectral mental image
> hovering before my face,
> blinding me by its brightness one moment
> and withdrawing from me the next.

And what is his evidence? Listen as he puts it in his own words:

> With my own eyes have I seen it:
> the archetype of all virtue, all beauty.

Thus Tasso too asks for "a manifestation of his ideal in the flesh" so that he may believe in its reality. He finds it in Leonore. That is nonsense — idolatry even. Yet Goethe's creation shows us that the shadows clear up only when one can say with full conviction: "With my own eyes have I seen it. I know they are eternal, for they are."[42]

Still Goethe is merely fantasizing. Let me show you another poet, endowed with an infinitely richer mind. Listen to him, John, the son of

42. The quoted lines are from Goethe's *Torquato Tasso,* Act II, Scene 1, lines 1094-98, 1104.

> Es schwebt kein geistig unbestimmtes Bild
> Vor meiner Stirne, das der Seele
> Bald sich überglänzend nahte, bald entzöge.
> Mit meinen Augen hab ich es gesehen,
> Das Urbild jeder Tugend, jeder Schöne.
> . . .
> Ich weisse es, sie sind ewig, denn sie sind.

Tasso (1544-95) was the preeminent poet of the late Italian Renaissance. His star-crossed love, political imprisonment, restless travels, mental suffering, and self-absorption made his, to Romantics, the epitome of the poet's life. Goethe's 1790 play was the most famous of their many treatments of the subject. Kuyper adds with respect to the lines quoted from Goethe (note 59): "I should almost have supposed that Goethe had the words of John's epistle [see the next paragraph in the text] in mind, so strong is the similarity of expression in the two thoughts."

Zebedee, witness to you not in play but with a supreme degree of holy earnestness and clear-eyed sobriety.

> What we have seen with our eyes,
> what we have looked at and touched with our hands,
> concerning the Word of life —
> therein, and therein alone, lies our power. (1 John 1:1)

John sang of the Word of life, a Word of God that was "in the beginning" and is eternal (John 1:1, 2). That, and that alone, is the ideal for therein alone we see sparkling before our eyes what is eternally true and good and beautiful.

Is it not so? This jubilant music sounds not only from our lips; you Modernists sing it with us! So far then we walk together, but here we also part company, never to meet again. For while you have the ideal but no more than the ideal, the church of Christ confesses an ideal that was reality from all eternity and has been manifested in the flesh.

Or, if you please, here yawns the bottomless abyss which makes you other than the church of Christ. You indeed have the Word but you let it shine only in fascinating Morganas, while the church of Christ enters into a real sanctuary on whose threshold God Triune has engraved with a diamond pen this quiet word of Eternal love: "The Word became flesh and dwelt among us" (John 1:14).[43]

43. Kuyper's last note (60) sounds once more the incarnational theme that was so important to his own conversion, ecclesiology, and epistemology in these years: "Here too the person of Christ is our touchstone. The deeper minds among the moderns will readily grant that the ancient concept of the 'word become flesh, reconciling and risen again,' which the Church has linked to the name of Christ, is not only beautiful but true and indispensable. They will deplore with you the low, small-minded mockery of this idea of ideas and attribute it to the wandering superficiality of a less noble nature that does not grasp how the taint which it sees in the holy comes not from the holy but from its own unwashed hands. Taken in the ideal sense they are thus ready to give the church's teaching their applause. They would only deny that the true and beautiful idea became a reality in Jesus of Nazareth. Here too, then, the 'division' of man. Their thinking but not their whole being has need of such a Christ. In their own being their power of thought is abstracted from the reality of their existence, and then the shadow of the division in their soul falls across the Christ. . . ."

"It Shall Not Be So Among You"

If Kuyper disagreed with Modernist theology, he detested church hierarchy. With liberals one could honestly disagree; with bureaucrats one could not even have a meaningful discussion, since they recognized no principle but their own power. Their toleration of all opinions corrupted the church and demeaned theology by indifference.

So Kuyper fumed from his first brochure of 1867 into the 1880s. By 1883 he was part of a shadow organization dedicated to overturning the Church Order of 1816 and enforcing strict confessional subscription upon prospective ministers. The issue came to a head in December 1885 when, in the face of a dispute over the latter provision, eighty members of the Amsterdam church council (a 75 percent majority) approved a revision in the by-laws that would award church properties to those loyal to the traditional confessions in case of depositions or schism. They were promptly suspended from office by the regional (classis) board of the Dutch Reformed Church.

This opened a drama by turns tragic and absurd. The classical commission botched due process. On January 6 some of Kuyper's followers sawed their way into the archives of the New Church to commandeer records, while others set (and for a year maintained) a watch by night with lanterns and cudgels to keep the building out of enemy hands. Finally, on July 1 the provincial church board upheld the suspensions and deposed the defendants from office.[1]

The sermon that follows was the first Kuyper preached after this action. It is a striking piece of applied theology, bringing abstract principles down to a very concrete situation. It is a vivid example as well of rhetorical method. Saturating his audience with biblical language and dear historical references, Kuyper inscribes his listeners into a story of a faithful remnant. Their predeces-

1. See A. J. Rasker, *De Nederlandse Hervormde Kerk vanaf 1795* (Kampen: Kok, 1974), pp. 182-86.

sors had successfully stood the tests of time, so their own prospects were noble, present hardships notwithstanding. Most remarkable is the empathy — along with the rage — that Kuyper extended to his opponents and the call to repentance that he issued to his followers at this, of all junctures.

As an Antirevolutionary in rebellion, Kuyper had to carefully define due authority and legitimate resistance; as a charismatic leader convinced of total depravity, he had to wrestle with issues of power. His answer was classic Calvinism: walk obediently to God "and you will experience how precisely from this obedience is born the power of spirited resistance to the false domination that would force your submission." It was patriarchical populism, too: the right to self-rule requires firm governance of wives and children.

The text for Kuyper's sermon was Matthew 20:25-26. The first half of the address, not reprinted here, recognizes the ways of the world according to verse 25: Gentile rulers (i.e., the state) exercise power smartly. The second half takes off from verse 26 to explore why and how things had to be different in the church.

Kuyper delivered this sermon in the Frascati auditorium in Amsterdam on Sunday evening, 11 July 1886. (His deposition barred him from churches and forced him to call this a "Bible lecture" instead of a sermon.) It was published in *Uit de Diepte: Bijbellezingen door de Afgezette Leeraren en hun Trouwe Medebroeders* [From the Depths: Bible-Lectures by the Deposed Ministers and Their True Brethren] (Amsterdam: J. A. Wormser, 1886). The translation is by John Vriend.

. . . ALAS, MY FRIENDS, how the splendid ideal of Holy Scripture clashes with the reality we see around us! There should be a contrast: this is how it goes in the world, but among you, that is, in the church, let it not be *so*. But behold: having betrayed its holy calling, the church has been conformed to the world by lust for power and haughtiness. It should be: "Not like the world but like the Son of man." It became: "Not like the Son of man but like the world!"

O, world-conformity: is not that the whole sin of the church? There is only one sin: *unbelief,* and what is unbelief but turning one's face away from the Son and toward the visible world? Conversely, what is faith but courageously turning one's eyes away from the world and toward Immanuel, to contemplate him so that his image becomes imprinted on our mind?

So it is with the church of God, in its inner state and in its government. In the latter respect, too. Just consider what has become of our once glorious Reformed churches in the hands of the Powers of our age. There need be "lordships" in the world, in the state, but not in the church, nor did these exist until early in this century. Precisely such "lordships" were established in our churches in 1816.[2] In the world there was "dominion" and so from that time on there would be "dominion" in the church of God on earth. In the world there was a Power to which, the apostle declares, we should be subject; similar "Powers" were introduced into the church, Powers that demanded obedience from every soul over which they exercised authority.

Thus three levels of "lordship" were introduced. One called "Classical Government," set up over a small group of local churches. A "lordship" called "Provincial Church Government," set up over the churches of an entire region. And over all the churches together an "overlordship" bearing the name "Synodical Government." Three "lordships" in the church of Christ in the place of one. There were governors among the nations exercising lordship over them, so now there had to be governors in the church exercising lordship over it. Result: a hierarchy of power in both church and state.

Still the work of 1816 does not deserve the least credit for originality. For King William I, who endowed our churches with this gift of "world conformity," merely copied what he had seen among the Episcopalians and the national churches,[3] a system that in turn was no more than a faded copy of the Catholic original. Indeed, to Rome and not to our potentates belongs the credit of having so ingeniously conceived this worldly system of church government with its "lordships" and "powers," and it is this Roman model that our Synodical organization has copied. If the organizers had been more honest, they would simply have reintroduced bishops like the Episcopalians and national churches: a bishop over a smaller area, an archbishop over a region, and a kind of papal government over the entire country. But they did not have the nerve; that would have stirred up suspicion and produced reaction. We must have the thing, not the name. Our people would have staged an enormous protest at the name of bishop, and so they adorned their exquisite imitation with an innocuous label. Not a bishop but a *Classical* Government, something that

2. The year the Dutch Reformed Church was reorganized under King William I.

3. Kuyper's term "Territorialen" might refer to the established Lutheran churches on the continent or to Anglican churches in the British colonies.

Kuyper with his family in 1886, the year of the Doleantie.
Front row, l to r: Henrietta (age 16), Catharina (10), Johanna (11), Jan Frederik (20); *back row:* Guillaume (8), Herman (22), Willy (4), Kuyper (49), Johanna Kuyper-Schaay (44), Abraham, Jr. (14).

hardly sounded different from our old classis! Not an archbishop but a *Provincial* Government, something reminiscent of our old provincial synods! Not a papal government but a *General Synod,* evoking the memory of our Synod of Dordt!

And so it was accepted. So our people were misled. So they willingly put their neck under the yoke. Of course I do not mean to say that King William I intentionally misled us. That never occurred to our good prince. More likely he thanked God for this scheme. But despite himself he became an instrument of the wily Counselor against whose assaults on the church of Christ our people had — unfortunately — forgotten how to pray.

What inevitably followed on the heels of this imitation of a worldly *form of government* was the imitation of worldly *social* conditions. Because the state had "lordships," "lordships" were also established in the church of Christ; but then, because the higher classes stood out conspicuously from the lower ones, so also in the church of Christ "the smaller congregation" was slighted while the people of prominence were held in greater esteem. This evil even crept in to some extent in our better days, as the "distinguished pews" in our church buildings demonstrate. What was it that the Lord's holy apostle said of the fellowship of rich and poor in the church of Christ? Just read again the stirring words of James in chapter 2 of his epistle:

> My brethren, show no partiality as you hold the faith of our Lord Jesus Christ, the Lord of glory. For if a man with gold rings and in fine clothing comes into your assembly, and a poor man in shabby clothing also comes in, and you pay attention to the one who wears the fine clothing and say, "Have a seat here, please" while you say to the poor man, "Stand there," or "Sit at my feet," have you not made distinctions among yourselves, and become judges with evil thoughts? [James 2:1-4]

That is how it should be. Scripture demands it and our heart says Amen to it. But what have we and our ancestors done by our sinful covetousness? All sorts of *distinctions* have been reintroduced in the church. To anyone with a little status we offered a pew of his own; to another, a better one; to a third, a better one still. And the poor of the church — O it cries to high heaven but it has to be confessed — for centuries now the poor of the church here in Amsterdam were virtually excluded, crowded out, sent packing. Church pews were rented out for money, and more money bought better places. So it was always the man with the golden ring who had priority, and the poor man in shabby clothes was turned out into the street. All this happened while on the pulpit lay the apostolic word: "Listen, my beloved brothers: has not God chosen the poor in the world?" [James 2:5]. Do you imagine that God the Lord will not avenge this abomination? And are you not struck by the idea that in the perplexity now descending on our church this discrimination against the Lord's poor, this introduction of class distinction, is punishing itself?

O, the snide comments you hear over and over from the mouths of preachers: "The people of the islands tag along but we're the ones who count: the people from de *Heeren-* and the *Keizersgrachten!*"[4] They reveal in a dreadful way how our ancestors' worldly sin has caused the evil of clericalism to strike root here. They show how far we have drifted from the only good state in the churches, where ministers lovingly serve the people for the Lord's sake, where "not many mighty," "not many noble" [1 Cor. 1:26] are titles of honor in the sight of God!

"It shall not be so among you!" is the soul-searching command of our Lord, but against it the ministers cry out: "It *shall* be so among us.

4. Two of the canals in central Amsterdam that are lined by the elegant houses of the merchant class.

We too shall have lordships; among us too the powerful will predominate." And of course where lordship enters, the desire to dominate comes along. If we go over to "many noble" and "many powerful," then the mighty ones will want to have power.

Precisely by this world conformity our Synodical Organization has fostered sin in the hearts of the powerful. The sin of passion, the sin of power lust, the sin of class prejudice lurked in their hearts as it does in every human heart, though it could have lain dormant without being aroused. But the Synodical Organization began to stimulate that sin in the men who sat in the seats of power. The high dignitary gradually changed in character. The box office clerk became his model, the civil servant his example, and maintaining status his passion.

Once upon this sinful way, people who imitated the world fell into worse habits than does the world itself. The rulers of the world might trample on the people in their lust for power, but certainly the political arena always has restraints on these lusts. A sense of accountability. Constitutional safeguards keeping watch over our civil liberties. Above all, an independent judiciary which did not ask what was pleasing to the ruler or shrink from defending the rights of the poor against the people in power. But in the church these guarantees were totally lacking. Unmindful of any calling by the grace of God, church personnel lapsed into mindless bureaucratic patchwork. The church members' right to vote hangs by the fragile thread of the arbitrary will of the higher-ups. As to the church's administration of justice, after our current era in church history is over it will be self-evident that it is devoid of any holy drive to do justice.

This should not surprise you, my friends. Inasmuch as "lordship" belongs in the state, the apparatus that dispenses justice is integral to it. God has bestowed upon the state and nations a powerful sense of justice and a generous dose of legal talent. The pagan nations excelled here and still are the leaders in this sacred domain. But the Lord God did not bestow this talent on the church. Thus, although the church wanted to practice and dispense justice, it did not have the gift or intuition for it. It simply abused legal forms as tools for domination. In the church we see not the judge who watches over the persecuted and tormented but party warring against party to trample on the wretched from the seat of judgment. We see a striving that does not accord with the heavenly hosts but seeks support in the worldly newspapers that are hostile to the Lord and his anointed. The good are not supported so that evildoers may tremble, but the deniers of the deity of the Lord occupy the seats of honor. Drunkards and fornicators go scot-free, while the faithful witnesses of the Lord are being threatened with ecclesiastical death.

Thus the deeply sinful, unspiritual, worldly striving runs its course to its own shame. And what is most appalling of all, the unholy business wraps itself in the robes of piety. For a military commander, naturally, can sentence a man to death with a curse on his lips; a police officer can drag along a recalcitrant while abusing the name of the Lord. But an ecclesiastical agency can sentence a person to death only by involving the name of the Lord, and so, in the end, they hem the robe of ungodly, accursed "lordship" with a Pharisaic memorandum.

It is my prayer that they may wake up from the unspiritual self-inflicted blindness in which they are racing forward headlong. Certainly we are called to rule as kings but, in the classic words of the Catechism, this royal rule manifests itself on earth only in that "we may fight against sin, the devil and his whole dominion."[5] Certainly there is lordship in the church of Christ, but among all those born of a woman there is only one of whom the prophet sang: "But you, O Bethlehem Ephrathah, who are little among the clans of Judah, from you shall come forth for me one who is to be ruler in Israel, whose origin is from of old, from ancient days!" [Micah 5:2]. *All* power in the church of Christ must forever be traced back to Christ. He and He alone is our King. To Him alone is given all power in heaven and on earth. And just as the sun has been set in the sky above as the greater light to rule the day, so the Sun of righteousness shines out from above to exercise lordship over the church militant on earth. He is the Immanuel, beside Him there is no other. He is the Ruler in Israel, but only after letting Himself be trampled to give his life as a ransom for many.

. . . [Kuyper summarizes his presentation to this point.] But I may not stop here. We also need admonition and consolation in the face of so great an affliction. Therefore I want to remind you in the first place of what Jesus said to Pilate: "You would not have power over me unless it were given you from above" [John 19:11]. A dog bites the stone thrown at it and ignores the hand from which it came. Let it *not* be so among you. No evil befalls a city, and so no evil befalls a church, unless the Lord has done it [Amos 3:6]. Even the Holy One in Israel was delivered up and counted among malefactors "according to the definite plan and foreknowledge of God" [Acts 2:23].

So now too we stand by the proven confession of our Reformed

5. Although Kuyper attributes these words to the Heidelberg Catechism, they actually occur in the prayer of thanksgiving that concludes the Form of Infant Baptism used in his day.

The door to the consistory room of the New Church in Amsterdam, showing the broken panel by which Kuyper's followers gained entry during the Doleantie.

fathers, that "all creatures" (and thus also the powers in the newly created ecclesiastical "lordships") "are so in his hands that without his will they cannot so much as move" [Heidelberg Catechism, Q/A 28]. Also this suspension and deposition have befallen us subject to his permission and in accordance with his ever holy rule! So don't make it personal; banish all bitterness from your soul.

I, too, feel within me the deep, very deep indignation that prompted Judah to cry out to heaven when Ephraim its brother made a league with the Syrians against the people of God [2 Kings 15:37; Isa. 7:1ff.]. Far from asking you to restrain this feeling of indignation, I am greatly delighted to see that this stimulus is still alive in you. A people who can no longer be scandalized becomes shallow and soon slips away in impotence. In no way, then, do I wish to detract from it. Rather, I myself have openly vented this feeling of indignation and outlined the prime features of the scandalous conduct that offends and grieves us.

But precisely because I have not hidden anything, the One who sends me urges me to warn you all the more seriously to keep your indignation *holy* and *not to sin* in your wrath. Hence I urge you to refrain from all bitterness against *persons.* Those who drive are themselves driven, and the sin of domination and world-conformity which they contracted in an evil hour propels them on and on, much farther than they themselves wanted.

This dynamic is familiar from your own soul's experience, is it not? In whatever form, the stimulus of sin has also operated in our minds. Who of us has not felt: "I may not!", did not say to himself: "I will not!", and still the power of sin overcame him, drove him on, and made him do what he himself soon began to loathe and confess as sin before God. So it is with these men. Their mistake was to get on the wrong train. Once aboard they found that no complaining helped, no willing otherwise was of any use. On and on they have to go, as far as the steam-horse — over which they have lost all control — pulls them. Precisely for that reason none of us may despise them as *persons.*

We do not despise Peter either, the man who with his cursing and swearing thrice disowned his Master. He had not intended this development either but, contrary to his own will, was driven from bad to worse by the sentries, and that charcoal fire, and the servant girl, and the bystanders. Our souls do not despise Peter since the Lord did not despise him either but drew him back with the cords of love and had regard for his heart-breaking repentance. And when the words resounded in his soul: "Simon, son of Jonas, do you love me?" [John 21:15], the truth was that for all his denial and all his oaths, he remained at bottom united in faith and love to his Savior.

Could it not be the same here as well? Could it not be that those who do persecute not *us* but the *Lord* in us, who carry on wildly, unable to stop, driven by the goad of their own sin, will later weep bitter tears of repentance? Could it not be that already now they sense an impulse toward better things in their conscience? Could it not be that some day they will come to the shamefaced but still genuine confession: "O Lord, although partly out of cowardice I have persecuted your church and trampled on the brothers, You, who know all things, know that I loved you!" [John 21:17].

My friends, turn your eyes away from man and look at what the Lord is doing. Note how even now, in the midst of our sorrows, the Lord's work shines out.

Answer me: amid all the insults we must endure, all the power that is turned against us, all the violence aimed at us, is there not also the cry of Zechariah: "Fear not, Zerubbabel, before those who inflict violence on you, for not by might, nor by violence, but by my Spirit it will come to pass!" [Zech. 4:6; Hag. 1:2]. That very word has been used against us. We have been slandered as though we were practitioners of violence and would resort to brute strength. Now it has become clear that it is our adversaries who cling to power, coerce through their "lordships," and resort to violence.

Therefore I appeal to you, people of the Lord, you other Zerubbabel son of Shealtiel, fear not, for it is already happening by the Spirit of the Lord. All their power is being shamed and all their strength is disarmed. Judge for yourself: Does not what lies behind us and around us bear splendid witness to the triumphant power with which the Spirit of the Lord is advancing?

For many years did not the Arminian have the upper hand so that the confessor of the free sovereignty of the Lord was almost completely marginalized? Did not the Arminian glory in the fact that the old fable of Dordt had been done to death by the speech of some and the silence of the rest? Were not their voices crying throughout the land: "Though the Lord is powerful, I am the master of my own soul!" How the tide has turned in just a few short years! How the old confession has revived! How the theme that "God the Lord is almighty *also* in the work of grace" has again become like the voice of many waters!

Others spoke against the Word of God. The authority of that Word just *had* to be broken. The high and holy Word of the Lord *had* to yield to the human word of criticism. Indeed, it seemed as if the defense of that Word would be silenced. But how the tide has turned here as well!

How spiritedly the confessors of that Word of our Lord have risen up again! How resplendent is its glory! How thousands upon thousands again ecstatically speak about Holy Scripture!

How it was declared that your attachment to church buildings, your dependence on the existing organization [of the church] had become a weight that would render you incapable of free movement. You were bound, so they said, to your money and church properties and could never get loose. But behold: the Spirit of the Lord came and blew and in less than a month freed you from this false attachment. You generously opened your wallet to give gold and silver. The steeples and galleries of your church buildings with their worldly embellishments became a source of loathing that stung you and now makes you thrill in the freedom you have regained and the grace you received.

"In the grace received," I add, for at the start of this year Satan planned to break the power of the Lord in the church. How differently things turned out! Tell us yourself: have you ever experienced so much tenderness in your soul, so much loveliness and peace in your circles, felt such a oneness of Spirit in our meetings as you did since the fourth day of January of this year?[6] Satan thought to strike Jesus in his royal rule, but behold: the royal power of Jesus has not for years shone so brightly in our hearts as it does just in these days. Not Jesus but Satan had to yield in the end.

Do you remember the all-important fine point on which everything depended, my friends? Was not the pivotal question whether your ministers would knuckle under and for a brief moment bow before the Synod instead of before Jesus their Lord? After all, the Synod alone and no other body had the mandate to exercise lordship in the church. It let anything go and all the waters of unrighteousness flow *if only people would submit to it.* One only had to acknowledge, even reluctantly, some part of its power to be immediately received with acclaim and restored — as they said — "in full honor." The monk with his crucifix stood by the martyr on the pyre! Just touch the crucifix with your lips and you are saved. After that, if necessary, you can again pollute your lips with lies. So here: bow for a second; for a second admit that the Synodical Organization can rightfully claim your submission, also where Jesus forbids it, and you will receive the mark, honor will attend you, and all the dignitaries of the world will walk with you.

Especially preachers were targeted. What did they care about elders or those who took care of the poor? But the preachers! All power was

6. The day on which the Classical Committee of the Dutch Reformed Church suspended the eighty members of the Amsterdam church council.

concentrated in their hands. They had become the rulers in Jesus' church but were on that account also obligated, out of gratitude for the authority granted them, at all times to kiss the image of their copycat power. That *ought* to happen. That *had* to happen. Strong provision had been made for it. A layman was powerless before a preacher, but a preacher, if uncooperative, was subject to the absolute discretion of the potentates. A death sentence awaited him. Woe to you, reckless fool, who dares to disagree. Your office, your vocation, your position in life, your livelihood, even your pension — everything could be taken from you at a single stroke. You were simply pronounced ecclesiastically dead without ado. And that, people said, no preacher ever risked. For that they were too powerfully attached to their position and too keen on their money. They were so beautifully tethered to their silver chain.

True enough, my friends! It is an appalling thing for a husband and a father to be suddenly confronted with such a dilemma: a quick momentary genuflection or lose everything! For years the results have shown how brutal the pressure was. How many ministers succumbed; how many, after being a man for a moment, collapsed like a wall of plaster.

Indeed, had not the Spirit of the Lord intervened, we would have witnessed the same humiliating spectacle again this time. Remember, brothers and sisters, your ministers who today are being driven into ecclesiastical death are people of like nature with the others who succumbed. The voice of the tempter is heard whispering in their hearts too. They too dearly love their office and their position. But look: we have already reached the point where five — I do not say *just* five but five, and soon it will be six — ministers have been found in the church of Amsterdam alone who have not kissed the image of the Synodical Organization, who have not given one hour of submission. Rather than momentarily betraying the honor of their king, they have made an offering of all the fruit of their earlier labor. *That* is from the Lord, *that* is a marvel in our eyes, and *in that fact* not our adversary but Jesus our mighty Ruler triumphed.

That, more than anyone dares believe, shatters the lofty position of the Synodical hierarchy! People have again seen that there were still confessors of our Lord who did not buckle under. A power has again manifested itself to the minds of men against which the entire show of strength staged by the Synodical dignitaries proved powerless. Clericalism has been handed a lethal blow! And for Immanuel there was triumph!

Just here was the marvel: over against the ungodly power that invaded the church, the *power of the Spirit that belongs in the church* reawakened. At this point I no longer distinguish your deposed ministers and elders from yourselves. The same holy calling beckons us all, both to confess the unholy power of our own sin and to reach as one for that holy power which causes things to grow and flourish in the courts of the Lord.

What is confession of sin but to dissociate yourselves from joint responsibility for this sin of oppression? I am not saying, of course, that the rod which comes over God's children could ever be *punishment* for sin in the true sense of the word. Those who say that fail to do justice to the all-atoning power of the blood of Golgotha. *There* all sin and guilt has been atoned for. He who died there bore *all* the wrath of God and hence *all* our punishment. The child of God no longer knows punishment in that sense. But there is a dissociation from sin by chastisement, a judgment which separates God's children from complicity in sin.

Brothers and sisters, every one of us is jointly responsible for the emergence of alien "lordships" and "powers" in the church of God. If the people of the Lord in this city had consistently held high the power of the Lord, had honored all power and government only for the Lord's sake, had strictly maintained the power entrusted to them and not arrogated power that did not belong to them, there would everywhere have been a clear sense of the difference between a false invasive power and the powers instituted by God.

But it was not so. How seldom did you bother yourselves about the omnipotence of the Lord! How often we obeyed the government, not for conscience' sake, but solely from fear of its sword. How slack we often left the bonds of discipline in our own home and circle! How each of us sinned by our lust for power; how we loved the front-row seats! How eagerly did we not savor the strong drink of presumption and usurped power in our own circles, even among our own children! Thus has the sense of right and wrong become perverted in our blessed land. Thus has each of us individually added to the flood of the arrogant assumption of power that is now washing up against the foundations of our church. Our own exhalations have so helped to befoul the atmosphere that the power to resist is lacking. Therefore, please do not speak of the common sins of everyone but now, above all, confess this particular sin of the abuse of power as your own sin before the Lord your God. Then pull yourselves up in his power and return, giving God the glory; and sin no more in matters of power and domination.

Abstain from willfulness in hearth and home and act justly. Give up all power you have wrongfully assumed and again honor the divinely ordained influences and powers. Be again subject to the government for God's sake, to your employers and the men and women who are your teachers. Let honor and respect and awe return in our midst. Further, uphold your own authority, i.e., the part of the Lord's authority that has been delegated to you in your own home and circle. Husbands, rule your wives. Parents, rule your children.

Obedience, where divinely willed, is morally powerful, spiritually noble, heavenly in its beauty — beauty like that of angels, those ministering spirits who obey the high command that comes from the mouth of God. Take that road yourselves and persuade your children to take it, and you will experience how precisely from this obedience is born the power of spirited resistance to the false domination that would force your submission. In such a situation the hireling tends to run away, but the person called of God courageously remains at his post and by his firm refusal to obey falsely constructed powers practices the highest obedience to his Lord and King.

Then, automatically, imperceptibly, there comes over the church that better, nobler, holier power which does not seek its strength in force but finds its watchword in the apostolic saying: "When I am weak, then am I strong" [2 Cor. 12:10]. For the Lord does not doom us to impotence but calls His own to power, a power against which violence is powerless and no rule on earth can prevail. Then from His place on high He looks upon the children of the church and sees among them those who have strayed and did not claim their eternal inheritance, and to them too He gives power, power to become children of God by believing in His name. And if you have already become one of His children, even then He gives you power, a power that comes from the Tree of Life called Immanuel, whose blossom is the merit of the cross and whose fruit is grace. That fruit returns twelve times a year and is fresh with every new moon [Rev. 22:2]. Not a stream that flows one moment and dries up the next, but a fountain of life that is always available and from which those who know salvation drink all day and all night.

So He gives power. To those who are still afar, the power to come to Him. To those who have come, the power to stay by Him. But this grant of power and dominion goes further yet, for He also gives power to cast out unclean spirits and to unfetter the captive souls of others. That divine power of the Spirit paves its golden trail on all the pathways of life. It is powerful to save; powerful in compassion; powerful in wiping away tears; powerful in easing pain; powerful to banish Satan from afar; powerful in controlling one's own tongue and triumphing over one's own flesh! Then that divine, holy, and heavenly power goes on further. Having called back the children, raised up the backslidden, released those who were bound, comforted those who mourned, it finally spreads over our enemies and *you receive power even to pray for them*.

O God: may that holiest of all powers be generously manifest in your people also these days! For, brothers and sisters, to battle is good; to be consumed by zeal for the house of the Lord is excellent; not to bow before a powerful intruder honors the spirited wrestler. But more regal than all these is the hero of the Lord who can bless those who curse him and pray for those who violate or persecute him. Oh, it's nothing to praise such things in days of peace or to parade them as proof of piety against fits of anger. But now that the fat is in the fire, now that real oppressors and persecutors and violators of our rights have come on the scene, now it becomes a most serious question for every tender child of God: "Have I, I myself, reached the point where, in all sincerity before the Lord, I can pray for those who are persecuting me?"

Sometimes these days we have heard the menacing tone of those who spoke of "taking by force," who said "they could gather thousands of people on the Dam or in front of our church doors."[7] That sounded very powerful but, really, was it not spiritually powerless and weak? In such a show of force, everything would depend on the muscle of your arm or the force of your fist, and so a ruffian from a back alley would probably outdo you. But if you have acquired spiritual power, the power also *to pray for your enemies,* then, brothers and sisters, there is at work within you a holy urgency that no one in the world can imitate and by which you overcome all opposition.

Certainly, Scripture never takes exception to *power,* but only to the wrong *kind* of power. The child of God does not want to be weak for the purpose of being weak but, to the contrary, just because it makes him powerful. Similarly, the Son of man became weaker than all the rest and threw Himself in self-abandonment under the weaknesses of all, not because powerlessness appealed to Him but because that weakness was for Him the road leading to the highest and most glorious power.

Do you ask for a place of honor in the palace of the King who rose from the depths of weakness? I assure you, that place of honor exists, but only on one condition: to be thought worthy of being close to Him, you also travel the road on which He preceded you. "Through suffering to glory!" [Rom. 8:17]. "By weakness to power!" [2 Cor. 12:10].

There, finally, *there* lies all our hope of victory in the struggle that has broken out. For this, brothers, I tell you in the name of the Lord: If it cannot be said that there is more *of Christ* to be seen among us than among our oppressors, a blasting wind will blow through our ranks and our enthusiasm will go up in smoke. Conversely, if He who knows our hearts and tries our inmost thoughts knows and sees that on us more

7. The Dam is the principal square in Amsterdam, next to the New Church where Kuyper's young followers were standing guard.

than on them the Image of the Son stands out, that Christ is present not only on our banners but also in our ranks, then the outcome of our struggle will be liberation and triumph for the people of the Lord.

A band of believers in whose midst the Image of Christ is truly seen has never yet been overcome and will not succumb now either. Amen.

Perfectionism

Kuyper made his name by fighting church hierarchy and theological liberalism, but he did not necessarily approve of everything on the other side of the street. That was most poignantly demonstrated by his encounter with Anglo-American evangelicalism at a crucial moment in its history, the renewed debate over Christian perfection in the 1870s that gave birth to the Keswick school of Holiness theology.[1]

Sanctification became part of the European evangelical agenda in consequence of the 1872 Moody-Sankey revival in Great Britain and the follow-up campaign of Robert Pearsall and Hannah Whitall Smith. When the Smiths called an international gathering at the English resort of Brighton in the first week of June 1875, Kuyper was among the eight thousand who came — and certainly among the most enthusiastic who left. "Brighton was a Bethel for me," he told Dutch sympathizers; there he had realized the special "consecration" of dying to the works of the flesh and rising with new power for complete service to the Lord. Kuyper had entered upon the "higher life."

Back home he set out to promote Holiness meetings and teachings through *De Standaard*'s Sunday edition *(De Zondagsblad)*. He ran a series on the "sealing" of the Spirit (largely taken from Hannah Whitall Smith), another on fasting, and in early 1876 began a third on consecration. Just then he suffered

1. On the Holiness movement see Melvin E. Dieter, *The Holiness Revival of the Nineteenth Century* (Metuchen, N.J.: Scarecrow Press, 1980); more briefly, George M. Marsden, *Fundamentalism and American Culture* (New York: Oxford University Press, 1980), pp. 72-80. On Kuyper's connection therewith, see E. J. C. Verbeek, "De Brighton Beweging en Nederland," *Polemios* 9/4 (9 January 1954): 21-24; Hans Krabbendam, "Zielenverbrijzelaars en zondelozen: Reacties in de Nederlandse pers op Moody, Sankey en Pearsall Smith, 1874-1878," *Documentieblad voor de Nederlandse kerkgeschiedenis na 1800* 34 (May 1991): 39-55; and J. C. Rullmann, *Kuyper-Bibliografie,* vol. I (The Hague: J. Bootsma, 1923), pp. 180-93, 205-9.

a nervous collapse that took him out of the country and out of commission for fifteen months.

The most obvious cause of the breakdown was overwork. Besides editing a newspaper, Kuyper at the time was a member of the States-General and deeply involved in church polemics and politicking. But an inner turbulence plagued him as well, and there Brighton was part of his undoing. Brighton had promised him peace instead of squabbling, a quick path to purity that would resolve the church question, a new source of energy equal to his vocational overload. In fact it left him in a self-righteous dudgeon. He recited "Dare to be a Daniel" in the Second Chamber; his opponents quoted Christ on whited sepulchres. Nor did it help that Pearsall Smith had fallen into scandal over his doctrine and an episode with a female convert.

One of Kuyper's first projects after resuming full activity was to publish an eighteen-part series on "Perfectionism" in his Sunday paper (renamed *De Heraut*). Four of those articles are reprinted below. Kuyper's approach throughout was that of biblical and historical theology, since a large part of Holiness's problem, in his eyes, was its absorption in the present moment with too little attention to its hidden assumptions and their dangerous consequences, as could be gleaned from studying comparative cases in the past. "By their precedents ye shall know them." His opening warning and closing apology, however, make his target unmistakable, while his recurrent contrasts disclose the Dutch Calvinist piety he upheld against the Holiness sort: theocentric, deep and solemn, cultivated by organic nurture. That this, too, gave "power for service" Kuyper went on to demonstrate over the next two years by organizing the university, school system, and political party that became the institutional bedrock of his movement.

The series was originally published as *Volmaakbaarheid* in *De Heraut*, 17 March–4 August 1878. It appeared in book form under the same title as Part II (pp. 61-163) of *Uit het Woord: Stichtelijke Bijbelstudien* [From the Word: Edifying Bible Studies], 3rd series, 2nd edition (Amsterdam: Höveker & Wormser, 1879). These excerpts have been translated by John Vriend.

I. In What Company?

"Be perfect, therefore, as your heavenly Father is perfect."
(Matt. 5:48)

For many long years, at least in the Reformed churches, the doctrine of human perfection[2] has lain dormant. True, it was practiced by some under cover, it crept into people's thoughts and reflections, but as doctrine it did not come out into the open nor was it propagated as a system.

The Reformed church had impressed the message of profound sinfulness and misery so deeply into the hearts and minds of our people that even to hear a person say: "I am free from sin; I've gotten past it; for months, even years now, I have not committed any sin!" would have struck our entire churchgoing public as blasphemous conceit and earned condemnation as the height of willful self-deception. The unspiritual in the church would not buy it because their dealings with the "sanctified" had certainly taught them otherwise. Searching souls shrank from it because such a doctrine would rob them of all courage. And the "meek" whom the Lord had led out of their prison lived too close to the Word, stuck too faithfully to their church, and scrutinized their own heart too carefully ever to feel anything but the deepest aversion to such a monstrous error.

Gradually, however, this began to change. In the absence of a church that could keep poison away from her children and prepare them bread, like the tenderhearted mother that Calvin wanted it to be; in the absence from the church of a sound, penetrating, and coherent knowledge of the sacred truths of God; as a result also of the lack in many a pulpit of the solid footing and well-developed muscles that alone can give power to the nervous system; and not least as the result of the importation into these lands of miscellaneous uninspected spiritual wares of most dubious origin, the confession of man's deep sinfulness — also after his conversion — has in fact been given a formidable blow in the minds of many. For the same reasons a group of ill-equipped and ill-grounded minds have been sidetracked into the paths of the old perfectionists. Ensnared in their own ideas, a number of them even believe they are rendering God

2. This translation does not distinguish between the two different words Kuyper uses for "perfection" in this series: *volmaakbaarheid* and *perfectisme*. As a foreign import the latter had a pejorative connotation for someone with Kuyper's linguistic principles. Kuyper also makes frequent use of *"Geestdrijvers,"* which can be rendered as "spiritualists," "enthusiasts," or "fanatics." The present translation takes the kinder options except when the context clearly warrants otherwise.

a service by again advocating, with the zealotry of the renegade, the doctrine of human perfectibility which has so often been rejected in the past.

This development lays on us the duty to repeat what our fathers already accomplished four times over, that is, to demonstrate the untenability of the grounds on which this erroneous opinion is based.

Our fathers successfully and persuasively defended their confession on this point, first against the Roman Catholics, then against the Socinians, after that against the Spiritualists, and finally against the Arminians.[3] That struggle is lost on the present generation. The weapons then stockpiled in our ecclesiastical arsenal for combatting Perfectionism have gradually been forgotten as so much excess luxury by preacher and pew-sitter alike. As a result the church now stands unarmed in the face of an attack on its faith and confession. Nothing is more reasonable, therefore, than for the organs of the press that seek to support the church in its struggle for right and truth to bring out those eminent weapons again. If possible, we could reforge and augment them in keeping with the demands of the time, and then redistribute them to those who wish to stand firm with us against any attempt — also by the born-again sinner — to re-erect a throne for humanity instead of casting them down with a crushed heart before the throne of almighty God.

Let it be said that we feel no bitterness toward those who have gone astray in this direction or are luring others into it. If the saying of our Lord is applicable anywhere, certainly it is here: "Let anyone among you who is without sin cast the first stone" [John 8:7]. How I wish that people could see that as the churches of the Reformation lie in ruins, so our theology lies powerless on its sickbed. The confession of the church as well as the preaching that should buttress it have been lacking,

3. Socinians were a radical movement that emerged within later sixteenth-century Protestantism, denying the deity of Christ (hence the Trinity) and putting central focus on the moral life of the believer. Arminians were a party in Dutch Protestantism named after theologian Jacob Harmenszoon (Jacobus Arminius, 1560-1609). As the "Remonstrants" they had a momentous argument with the staunchly orthodox Calvinists whom Kuyper favored, climaxing in the condemnation of their position at the Synod of Dort (1618-19). They emphasized human initiative and ability in the salvation process, and their later representatives were associated with a pronounced ethical piety of a sometimes humanistic tinge. In the section of citations and commentary deleted below, Kuyper under "Spiritualists" *(Geestdrijvers)* refers primarily to the Dutch Anabaptists of the sixteenth century, but he extends the operational principle to "Enthusiasts" such as Kaspar Schwenkfeld, to assorted "Quietists," and to Dutch Labadists, German pietists, and Quakers.

not just for ten but for fifty, even eighty, years now: the spiritual energy and depth and sturdy cohesiveness that are indispensable for producing solid, single-minded people. So it is not at all surprising that in the midst of this chaotic confusion, after almost every heresy and error has successively reappeared on the scene, finally the pale specter of Perfectionism should also return from the grave to mislead people. If we must confess — frankly, honestly, and with heartfelt regret — that hardly anyone today displays his wares in the market of ideas without mixing worm-eaten fruit along with the good, and if we can by no means escape that confession with reference to ourselves, why should we be bitter against a person going his own way solely because he is straying differently than we are?

No, what is required in arguing a position before the bar of sacred truth is the kind of seriousness in which everyone senses that the plaintiff means business. The kind of holy enthusiasm which evinces a joy that one has been counted worthy to take part in such a weighty discussion. Even the presence of unfeigned anger against everything that fails to do justice to the glory and truth of God. But to be empowered with such seriousness, to be filled with that enthusiasm, and to be entitled to that anger one must speak from the *depths* and not from a *pedestal*. Especially in the battle against the theory of human perfection one is well-advised to remain conscious of his own imperfection.

The issue presented for discussion here can be defined by the following question: "Is it or is it not possible for the born-again person to achieve already in this life a degree of holiness such that he no longer violates the perfect law of the Lord either in thought, word, or deed?" For our part we prefer the shorter version: "Does a child of God completely shed his sinful nature already before or only in death?" But because our opponents (owing to the shallowness of their position) rarely focus their argumentation on human *nature* but almost exclusively on the sinful or holy *expressions* of that nature, the first formulation seems preferable.

To that question the Christian church in these lands — and let me unreservedly add: in accordance with the Word of God — has always answered: "No; we cannot. For in this life even the holiest have only a *small beginning* of this obedience. Yet with earnest purpose they begin to live not only according to some but according to all the commandments of God" (Heidelberg Catechism, Q/A 114) in order only "after this life to arrive at the goal of perfection" (Q/A 115). . . .

[Kuyper concludes this article with several paragraphs of citations from sixteenth- and seventeenth-century Reformed authorities against various perfectionist movements of the times. I have interpolated here instead the summary that he put in the last article of the entire series, laying out its program of argument.[4]]

We [will] thus successively demonstrate how the error of perfectionism has been defended in the course of the centuries by almost all heretics, while it was unanimously and resolutely rejected by the churches of the Reformation (Art. 1); always arose out of self-deception (Art. 2); could creep in only as a result of ignorance concerning the basic conception of God's Word (Art. 3); runs counter to the spiritual experience of God's children (Art. 4); is condemned by sound psychology (Art. 5); lowers the ideal of the moral life (Art. 6); is not favored in Scripture by the honorific titles of God's saints (Art. 7); cannot stand before the "perfection in the parts" that God's Word teaches (Art. 8); is contradicted by the ongoing struggle between flesh and Spirit that Scripture presupposes also in the case of the saints (Art. 9); is completely overthrown by Romans 7 (Arts. 10, 11, and 12); finds no support whatever in the power of faith (Art. 13); may never be confused with the cessation of the dominion of sin (Art. 14); is refuted rather than confirmed by the lightness of the yoke of Christ (Art. 15); is incompatible with both the command to be holy and the prayer to become holy (Art. 16); and, finally, is condemned rather than commended by the false distinction between conscious and unconscious sin (Art. 18). [The material that follows comes from Articles 2, 6, and 18.]

II. Misled by What?

"To keep me from becoming conceited because of these surpassingly great revelations. . . ." (2 Cor. 2:7a KJV)

The profoundly sinful error of the "perfectibility of God's saints already here on earth" results from two forms of superficiality: a superficial view of what God's holiness demands and an equally superficial notion of what the

4. The following paragraph appears on pp. 159-60 in the original text. The list fails to record Article 17 in the series, a summary of the biblical materials that Kuyper treats throughout. He organizes this review in the mode of the Apostles' Creed, exegeting twelve verses from Scripture and entitling the whole "De Twaalf Artikelen der Schrift" (The Twelve Articles of Scripture). As the present selection passes over the extended biblical argumentation that his series as a whole contains, and as Kuyper ends the entire work with an erroneous quotation from Scripture (see note 5), it is only fair to record here the twelve verses he cites in support of his position: Ecclesiastes 7:20, 1 Kings 8:46, Proverbs 20:9, Job 15:14-15, 1 John 1:8, James 3:2, Psalm 130:3, Psalm 143:2, Isaiah 64:6, Daniel 9:5, Philippians 3:12, and 1 Corinthians 13:9-10.

corruption of sin produces. Perfectionists tend to underestimate both. Of the holiness of God they have much too low, and of the corruption of sin much too light, a view. And so they imagine as actually present a holiness whose purity they underestimate in a sinner whose powers they overestimate. All one needs to ward off this heretical disease is a knowledge "of God and his attributes" and, in consequence, a knowledge "of ourselves and our unholiness" [the opening words of Calvin's *Institutes*]. This is ever the core, the fruit, and the power of all good theology, provided this twofold knowledge is not the fruit of imagination and impressionability but is drawn exclusively and purely from the Word of God.

A person who bases his opinions on impressions and turns his fancies into foundations is lost here. For how do things really stand? The level on which most of God's children today pass their time on earth is incredibly low. There is almost no uplift in their spiritual lives. Over and over you encounter an alarming weakness of will. Every moment you have to rage against a painful addiction to sin. Conscience is not scrupulous. The pulse of the soul can scarcely be felt. There is such a vagueness of conviction, so weak a self-denial, so flaccid a communion with the Lord! No zeal for the name of the Lord, no overflow of love, no standing firm, no perseverance, no vital prayer! We see this dismal level not just for a moment but always. It is true for all regions of our country, and by all reports the situation is equally sad in most other Christian countries. It is your own personal and deeply painful experience, and every brother who opens his heart to you pours out his soul in the same complaint. Alas, it seems to have become the permanent and persistent condition of the church.

But you have no peace with that situation. You struggle against the general decline in grace when you make your plea to God. Indeed, you thirst with all your soul for an escape from that enervating, oppressively tepid atmosphere. Every day with mounting urgency your captive spirit cries out: "Sanctify us, O God of all holiness!"

In such a circumstance one of four things can happen. Either you meet a *person* holier than yourself, or you come into contact with a *circle* of people who are on a higher spiritual plane than your own. Or as a reader of history you project yourself into an *era* when the church had not yet fallen so far. Or you yourself are graced with a *spiritual awakening*. Unfortunately, in each of these four cases you so easily make the same mistake as the poor man who becomes acquainted with the rich — the mistake of imagining that the wealthier man has no worries, that his bank account never dips, that his treasure is immeasurable. Suppose someone on the same pathetically low level as most meets a godly person who, thanks to God's good pleasure, has managed quite remarkably to

From February 1876 to May 1877, Kuyper lingered out of the country, mostly in the Alps, recovering from his breakdown. Ever after, mountain hiking remained a passion, a way to restore the body and an apt time for reflection too. In a meditation he later published in *De Heraut*, Kuyper clearly spoke of what he had learned from his illness — and of his perceived role as another David, bringing the peak revelations of God back to the plains of daily life.

In the Roar of Your Waterfalls

"Deep calls to deep in the roar of your waterfalls; all your waves and billows have swept over me." [Ps. 42:7]

God the Lord did not give us His revelation in a land of plains but in a land with mountains. Only in these highlands does a person learn to understand many a saying in Scripture.

David, too, roamed the mountains when he fled from Saul. There in the mountain caves, amidst cliffs and rocks, he heard an

wrestle free from the common — actually epidemic — lukewarmness of spirit. The distance between that exceptionally blessed person and our own heart seems so immense, so far-reaching, virtually immeasurable, that we almost begin to think ourselves in touch with a heavenly person. We whisper: "If only I could get to where he is, I would have arrived!" This utterance of soul, you notice, differs little from the opinion that the other person had reached perfection.

Here lies the psychological explanation for how Rome arrived at the veneration of the saints precisely in the days of its deepest corruption. In the Swiss Alps where everything is high and every hill a mountain one sometimes passes a peak six or seven thousand feet high without noticing it, whereas in the Low Countries even a mound of dirt of a few hundred feet is proudly pointed out from every side as a mountain. This happens in the spiritual world as well. In the highlands of Apostolic times and of the Reformation, giant peaks stood next to each other shoulder-to-shoulder, but no one found this to be remarkable or extraordinary, and everyone was quite aware that even the most giant peaks were far from the highest heaven. But in the time between, in the era of the church's corruption under Rome, when the terrain measured low to very low, the exhausted deer cry out for streams of water. In that cry he heard echoed the cry of his own soul for his God.

From mountain heights the world looks majestic, elevated, divinely great. On the plains and in the valleys man is everything. There he builds his cities and towns and fills them with his worldly possessions. There he accumulates his wealth, creates his pleasures, and covers the earth with the works of his hands.

But on mountain heights the picture is very different. There man is the creator of nothing and God alone is the majestic master craftsman. There every peak, every cliff, every gorge is an eloquent witness to His divine greatness. There one sees lightning and thunder clouds working in concert, not above himself but below and all around. There God the Lord has His eternal snow and never-melting icefields. There the only witness of His royal splendor is the eagle and only the gemsbok prances before His face.

Silence, a sacred silence, fills the air over those mysterious highlands. There the pounding of hoofbeats, the rattle of implements, the buzz of human voices is never heard but everything lies wrapped in solemn and divine quiet. Now and then an avalanche of

few figures who were nobler and better than the rest raised their crown to the clouds and made so imposing and enchanting an impression that everyone mistook the clouds for the sky and thought that, reasonably speaking, no distance remained anymore between their crown and the precincts of heaven.

Naturally we are subject to the same optical illusion when we make a quick visit to spiritual circles that have not sunk so low as our own. For example, in our country when we time after time run into massive greed as a form of bondage in which God's people lie fettered and then observe that in American circles, where distributive generosity is habitual, that particular form of bondage has been almost completely overcome, we easily make the mistake of grossly overestimating the spiritual condition of such an unfamiliar environment. It is the mistake of imagining at a great distance that all the other snares of sin have been broken along with that form of bondage; the mistake as well, in light of the short distance they are ahead of us, of overlooking the much greater distance that still separates them from the holy perfections of God.

The same self-deception occurs in the pages of history. There is no doubt that in the days of the apostles and of the Reformation the opera-

snow comes thundering down the mountainside; otherwise there reigns a holy calm. One hears only a muffled, regular, heavenly roar, a voice of God, the roar of the waterfalls of the Almighty.

For David, the servant of God, the voice of God in those plunging waters was full of holy poetry: they mediated to him the sacred presence of God. God created those waters. He caused them to roar down His mountains. And when those waters plunged down those steep heights, cascade upon cascade; when he heard the thunder of the falling waters in the gorge to his left and, as if in antiphony, the thunder of another waterfall in a gorge to his right, he felt as if God were enclosing him, that all God's waves and billows were slamming over and around him.

God's power on those mountains became to him a revelation of His wrath. As on those mountains, so were things in his own soul. There, too, deep gorges yawned. There, too, the waters of the Lord came down with a dull roar. And when in nature, full of majesty, deep called to deep, David felt how in his own soul one

tions of the Holy Spirit were more forceful and less restrained than they are today, and so the Church's level of holiness was notably higher. When now, amidst our own lamentably lackluster situation, we again read of the scintillating work of the Lord on the pages of history, it is only natural that our souls should leap up, that something in us should long powerfully for the return of such a state among ourselves. And as we gaze from our darkness into a brilliance so much brighter than we know, we quickly begin to think that scarcely any distance remains between that brilliance and the splendors of heaven.

The same thing, finally, may happen in our own personal situation. It may happen as a result of a marvelous inworking of God's sovereign grace which came over us suddenly when we hardly expected it any more. Not finding a listening ear anyway we had ceased to pray, only to experience such a release from the bonds of Satan, such an untying of the snares of sin, such showers of blessing on the dried-out garden of the self, such an anointing with fresh oil, such an awakening of our deadened listless soul, that it seemed we had all of a sudden made the leap of our life from a barren pit to the shores of the river of God and could not imagine any state of bliss more blessed than this one. Going still deeper, still higher? Never!

As a rule one becomes the victim of this fourfold illusion all at once.

abyss called to another with an enormous groan, ever calling out to the God of his life in whom alone was his help.

Still, it is not in the mountains but on the plains that God provided a home for humanity. Though a person might roam on mountain heights, he could not live there, and after years of being tested David, too, returned to the plain of the Jordan. But the memory of his God as he received it in God's mountains remained indelibly imprinted on his soul.

He had seen God there — God in His majesty, God the Lord in His omnipotence. And when on the plain thousands upon thousands mocked: "There is no God," David would stand up against them as a witness to the God of glory he had touched by hand on the mountains and carried down with him in the depth of his soul.

Moses had similarly seen the Invisible One in the faces of Sinai's cliffs. Likewise Elijah saw the majesty of the Eternal One on Mt. Horeb. So too David carried the memory of the Unfathomable One down from God's mountains to be a witness to the living God, first in Israel, later,

We come into contact with a more godly person, through whom we hear of people whose spiritual life is on a higher plane, wherein we again see welcome signs of the powerful working of the Spirit that marked the best times of the church. By all of these we are so powerfully affected by the Spirit that we awaken from our own slumbers.

Just then looms a danger. The danger that, with respect to that certain pillar of grace, we have eyes for his godliness but not for his repellent sins; of that pious circle, for the light but not the shadow side; of that wonderful period of the church's Reformation, for the glory but not the shame. Similarly in our own spiritual life, we sense the quickening of fresh spiritual gifts but are not alert to the new temptation that came along with them.

So it is that our holiest high points are paired with the deepest abysses. Satan is still at his post to stretch our own guile around our soul like a noose. He tempts you to adopt those impressions, those experiences of the soul as your spiritual foundation in place of the certainties of the Word of God. He talks you into being oh so diligent not to sink back into your earlier stupor but to push ever forward as quickly as possible, if not today or tomorrow then certainly soon, ever nearer to the holiness of God. Most dangerous of all he will teach you the habit of boasting — before those who do and do not agree with you — of ever greater bless-

by his psalm, among a thousand generations. . . . Having come down from the mountains, seeing his God also in the lives of the children of men, there ever came to him the voice of God saying that people should worship Him, giving Him honor and glory.

Sometimes the scene on those mountains becomes especially impressive. The sky grows dark and the clouds stack up and the rains come down in torrents that you never see on the plains. Everything is shrouded in a haze. Wrapped in a somber grey one's view is entirely cut off. But in the midst of that darkness the voice of the waters swells in power and majesty. One no longer sees anything but instead hears all the more dreadfully the majesty of the tumbling, roaring waters. Every trickle becomes a river; all the streams double the power of their cataracts. Now the thunder of God's waterfalls becomes truly gripping. In the plunging roar on every side it sounds as if God the Lord has turned up the volume of His majestic voice tenfold.

David carried down a memory from these awful moments for us, too. For in our life too a fearful somberness often overcomes us. Everything becomes dark and cloudy; the last rays of the sun sink over the mountain's rim. It may come from suffering and

ings, ever more powerful grace, still more marvelous overflowings of love, in ever more surprising and mounting doses, so that one would think himself failing to give God's power its proper praise and to be losing stock in the eyes of his brothers, if sometimes he boasted less than the other. This will go on in such a way that a person who at first was truly drawn up by the Lord now gradually works himself up and imperceptibly (except that the devils rejoice and God's angels weep) begins to float high above the masses languishing below, "holier than the common run of believers."

This is the way the doctrine of human perfectibility originates not among Socinians and Arminians but among Enthusiasts of all stripes. Pelagius *always* lurks in the shadows of this heresy. Among the Arminians and Socinians that spirit nestles in the unrepentant heart or in the self-sufficient intellect; sooner or later it becomes a matter of cool calculation and, after a lingering illness, degenerates into public apostasy. But among those who have a genuine desire for the holy, the evil makes itself at home in the life of piety, turns into self-elevation, and from the very start, before one is aware of it, degenerates into dangerous fanaticism.

misfortune. It may come from deep anxiety and inner distress. But whatever the cause, a child of God, listening amidst that somberness, also hears the mounting sound of the voice of God. The Lord Himself is in that darkness. And consequently the child of God, sitting amidst those dark clouds, does not collapse but instead is comforted and again rises to his feet in God.

However deep may call to deep, he does not feel abandoned. Just listen: it is the waterfalls of the Lord that roar down over him. And above the clouds, whence the waters are poured, God still has His sun that He keeps in readiness to pour out its rays and break those mountain mists and clouds.

Indeed, above the sun the Lord is in His sanctuary, presiding there in majesty. To that sanctuary the child of God, pouring out his soul in trusting, childlike supplication, directs his eyes. Why are you downcast, O my soul, and why are you disquieted within me? Soon enough, at the royal command of Him who sent them, those clouds will break and disappear from His heavens without a trace.

Put your hope in God, for I will yet praise Him. He is my ever-present Savior and *my* God!

Dangerous in two respects. In the first place, because it lures pious, unstable, tender souls into its web and injures their spiritual growth by too rapid a development — an injury that is not easily overcome. But dangerous as well because, after stimulating a sense of dissatisfaction with the existing state of the church, it dulls and deadens this sense at an evil hour, before it can bear fruit.

The church knows that things are not well. It knows that, aside from having to carry the burden of our sinful nature which is with us till we die, its moral tone, the public opinion of piety, the common spiritual state of the children of God should be more disciplined and noble. So sometimes there occurs in its midst a revival of the dry bones, splendidly manifest in a deeper confession of sin, a life lived in closer conformity to the Word, a more decisive renunciation of the world, of carnal indulgence, of earthly treasures of the self. That could have a marvelous effect! But if at some evil hour the Enthusiasts make their presence known and "perfectibility" again becomes a popular spiritual play-thing, the church promptly closes its eyes to its disgrace, pulls in its spiritual feelers, and with righteous disdain at this unholy "perfectionism," considers itself entitled to make peace again with its own deathly state, to mistrust every call to rise from the dead as the unholy tune sung by the fowler seeking to ensnare them.

That's the way it is, and a good thing too. The church will not hear of a higher and holier life unless you can show them "the way up through the depths." By a sound and vigorous instinct it rejects any elevation of the self on the part of the saints as detrimental to those saints. Accordingly, we must resist the doctrine of perfectionism not to give license to slumber on in unspiritual barrenness but precisely to deprive arid traditionalists of that license. Resist it not faintly or by halves, but energetically and totally. Resist it if at all possible from the invincible standpoint that our forefathers always chose: the confession that *even the best deeds of the saintliest persons are imperfect in this life and polluted by sin. . . .*

VI. Lowering the Ideal of Holiness

"Holy, holy, holy is the Lord of hosts." (Isa. 6:3)

The all-controlling and all-sufficient reason why the advocates of perfectibility have to be stopped in their tracks is that they pull down the ideal of holiness to the level of their own moral life. All the power, all the marvelous energy that the Christian religion has thus far displayed it owes precisely to the glorious, divine, unsearchable height to which, borne on the wings of revelation, it was able to raise the ideal of the moral life and hence of holiness. The higher this ideal stands, the deeper the roots of moral earnestness and the more ample the holy powers that arise from the hidden recesses of the grace-gifted heart to prevent human society from deeper decline. To the degree that a church pitched that ideal to a higher key it released a flood of blessings upon its members.

Accordingly, if one should press for the hidden reason why Protestantism is on a higher plane than Rome and why in the Protestant sphere the influence of Calvinist peoples has markedly overshadowed that of sister churches, in both cases you will find no better explanation than this — that the ideal of holiness was more securely established in Wittenberg than in Rome and was possibly raised even higher, be it with something of a one-sided gravity, by the hero of Geneva.

Your ideal of holiness, after all, is nothing other and nothing less than the holiness of your God. Anyone who detracts from the former thereby detracts from the glory of the thrice-holy God. Then, from a moral viewpoint, you either worship "another God" or worship the same God but no longer take the fullness of his glorious attributes as the standard for the moral life. . . . [Kuyper illustrates this point from non-Christian religions.] God's absolute holiness and the impossibility for human beings to be satisfied with *anything* less than a corresponding holiness is the foundation for all preaching of the law. Conversely, the whole secret of godliness lies in the love-driven impossibility of God's debasing that holiness in any way, joined to the mystery of his nevertheless being able to transform an accursed sinner into a child of the thrice-holy God. Therefore, whenever, wherever, and by whomever one of these two certainties is tampered with, any compromise is sin and resistance is imperative. . . .

[Kuyper proceeds to draw a lengthy comparison between the perfectionistic teachings of the Enthusiasts and those of Rome, concluding as follows.] So with Rome there at least remained the significant guarantee that the saints did not canonize themselves but were canonized — and then usually after a person's death and only after an investigation which at least assumed the appearance of seriousness and took well-known facts into account. But this guarantee falls entirely by the wayside in the case of these Enthusiasts. For they are not declared but declare themselves to be saints or allow their friends to do so. Not after their death but in their own lifetime. Not after careful investigation but upon most superficial impressions. Not based on well-known facts but, despite certain well-known facts, on the image of their own good qualities which they have seen in the mirror of their own imagination.

One senses the danger inherent in this mindset, a danger against which Rome at least is on its guard but which these Enthusiasts walk into blind: the deadly danger of spiritual self-elevation, pride, and arrogance. Since all Enthusiasts find the final ground of their faith in their desire to believe, that is, in themselves, it has only been a special grace that has kept some of God's children who have lapsed into these erroneous ways from falling into this pit of pride. When you consider in addition that to maintain their system and to maintain themselves at the top of their system, these fanatics finally have to ignore the reality of moral responsibility, you can understand without another word how a pride that has been separated from the certainties of conscience so often begins in the spirit but ends up in the flesh. For it is self-evident that to make good their talk of "perfection already here on earth," these Enthusiasts must covertly shrug off responsibility for the things that well up from their own flesh. They will assume responsibility for the things they do, also for the things they intend to do, even for the things they have harbored and approved of. But if despite all this something unholy, unclean, flares up from "flesh and blood," or from that other flesh that

Reflecting on his recuperation in the French Alps, Kuyper later wrote:

In the quiet solitude of the suffering that I went through in Nice my soul was ferried over to the resolution of the well defined, energetic religion of our fathers. Previously my heart had proceeded thence but at Nice I committed to this definitely for the first time.

Bedoeld noch gezegd (1885), p. 26.

I was sick and *my soul* needed healing too. The Higher mercy that was my saving medicine could only be mixed from that field of strong herbs where our fathers, for all their wounds, could still sing.

"Strikt genomen" (1880), p. 140.

dwells in our evil heart, or from that yet more evil flesh in our brains, and that which is sinful still makes its presence felt in us, then, provided they have not consented to it, they do not deem their sacred person encumbered by it.

"Thou shalt not covet!" The divine word from Sinai which mortifies everyone who denies his responsibility for the root of sin has to be rendered null and void by a most tempting distinction between "conscious" and "unconscious" sins. Consequently, the deeply hidden inner stirring of sin, thus severed from the bond of God's law, will undertake an adulterous marriage with the conceit of a proud mind. If not in the first generation then in the second, it will bear offspring that is scandalous and impure.

Let no one regard this statement as a personal insinuation against the teachers of the Reformed church who felt they had to unleash this demon of enthusiasm. Our struggle is not against persons. We are rather inclined to embrace these teachers and the awakened souls who are carried along by their doctrine with all the tenderness and love with which only one who regularly errs himself can love the erring. But this sentiment does not exempt us from doing our duty. If we see how today, as in the past, some of the most tender souls are seduced by these far-fetched ideas solely from lack of knowledge, may we be required to suppress the truth for the sake of the persons involved? Are we to be censured because we call things by their name?

No, by God, too much depends on it. Too much for these brothers

A studio shot of Kuyper as mountain climber during his recuperation in the Alps in 1876.

themselves and for the souls who follow them. Too much for people's peace of mind and the power of their godliness. Too much, above all, for the glory of God's holy name! . . .

XVIII. Unconscious Sin Is Also Sin!

"Create in me a clean heart, O God." (Ps. 51:10)

To say that a sin of which we ourselves are not conscious does not count in the appraisal of our spiritual state is an idea that already as such, as a *new* sin, defiles the person who holds and advocates it. Accordingly, let

Kuyper's organicism defined his psychology and ethics and accounted for one of his principal disagreements with Anglo-American Holiness currents.

As concerns the fourth and final difference — between *perfection in the parts,* which a child of God possesses in every sense, and *perfection in the steps,* which he will never attain on earth — here too the seal of Scripture and of spiritual experience is unmistakable.

A grain of mustard seed, however small, contains in itself the germ not only of the stem and trunk and root system but just as much of the branches and twigs, of the buds and leaves, of the blossoms and fruit that in a mild climate adorn the mustard tree at its maturity. . . . This is a sacred and unalterable characteristic of all that God does. When we human beings make something, we must first prepare it piece by piece, part by part, and then attach these to each other and set them fast in glue. But in everything God does *all parts alike* are foreordained and, so far as the seed is concerned, brought into existence by developing in order, one after another. Our *human* work in process is never, *God's* work always, *perfect in the parts.*

This is true of the plant. It holds for man and animal. But no Perfectionist ever whisper into your ear "that there is a sharp distinction between conscious and unconscious sins; that of course we can neither fight against nor prevent unconscious sins; that these, accordingly, do not count; that things are already well with you if only you have once and for all left behind the stage of falling into conscious sins." We know this old tune of the tempter! It sounds so sweet and enchanting in your ear. It seems so true! What can be said against it? Before you know it, talking to yourself along those lines and resonating to that sweet music, you yourself have joined in this deeply immoral error.

O, it is certainly true: a sin you are not conscious of is one you cannot fight, much less overcome in the power of God. A failure to see this is simply a failure to think straight. Conscious knowledge — i.e., a personal knowledge — of your enemy is absolutely imperative in every moral struggle. But *that* you are not conscious of it, is that not the consequence of your *sinful state?* If for the rotten tree it is still winter so that the sickly twig has not yet budded and the corrupt fruit has not yet

it holds more strongly still for a person's spiritual development after rebirth. If a man's sanctification is *his own work,* then here too he tries to prepare it piece by piece and then attach these all to each other. Accordingly, he will show a tendency to fight one specific sin while at the same time another, no less detestable sin has free play. He will, e.g., practice at making his prayers and supplications perfect or to be emptied in humility and mortification, all the while his avarice runs free, his irritability increases, and his fellow-feeling diminishes. Strong development of one thing and the shriveling of another is part of our nature. A growth imperfect in the parts.

But if you're dealing instead with genuine rebirth, with thoroughgoing conversion, with upright faith, i.e., with a *work of God,* then a hatred for *all* sins and a love for *all* virtues arise together. Even if it is not yet outwardly manifest, the germ of all loveliness is planted. . . . We must love God not only "with the heart but also with the soul, the mind, and all the strengths with which our being has been endowed." In short, sanctification must proceed in us through Christ but in such a way that He sanctifies us not in a particular piece of our being but *"all in all."*

Volmaakbaarheid, pp. 105-6

appeared on the branches, does that make the tree healthy? Is your sinful *state* less sinful, unholy, and abhorrent than your sinful *deed?* Do you only *work* before the eyes of God or do you also *exist* before Him? And if the latter, if you also have to answer to the Holy One for your existence, for your way of being, for the root of your essence as God knows it, then, my dear brother, what advantage is it to you that you can say "I have cleansed my heart" if the deep wellspring of impurities continues to gurgle up even during the sleep of your spiritual consciousness and therefore without your notice?

The idea of measuring sin by your consciousness of it, by what you know and note of it — that is precisely the shallow and utterly unholy view of Pelagius that you find in all his intellectual children, synergists or not. Scripture has revealed, taught, and instilled just the opposite in all the devout of the Old and the New Covenant, who without this higher light would never have known anything other than Pelagius. Sin is not what you but what God sees and knows and detests as sin. . . . [Kuyper quotes Psalms 19:12 and 130:3.] We neither may nor can abandon that standard. Let God remain God! His and his alone is the high and holy prerogative to judge what is contrary to his will, to decide what does or does not grieve his eternal love. That is not for us to decide, seeing who we are.

And so to say to each other or ourselves what sometimes is so confidently declared: "My conduct has been blameless, I have kept my conscience clear before God and man and I am not conscious of any evil thing" — this says absolutely nothing about our holiness. For at the bottom of our heart, in the tissue of our thoughts, in the webs we have woven with our words, in the network of our deeds, right down to our prayers, our piety, and our finest acts there may lurk something so detestable, self-centered, and arrogant before the eyes of the Holy One on his throne that we would be objects of bitter ridicule before God, his Christ, and his holy angels if we imagined ourselves on a higher and holier plane than others. God, not your brother, not your own imagination, not even your own consciousness will one day be your judge; and therefore that crafty distinction between conscious and unconscious sin must be intolerable to anyone who calls on the name of Jesus.

Certainly, there is growth in Christ, an increasing holiness. There is a daily process of self-crucifixion, of mortification, and of burying the lusts and desires of the flesh. Undoubtedly, after the lamentable cooling down of our first love comes a moment of nameless contrition from which is born a sacrifice of our whole being, fuller than ever, before Him who purchased us with his blood. Indeed, there are those blessed of the Lord who, having been led through deep waters and chosen as instruments of God's good pleasure, have almost reached the point where they no longer feel the goads of the flesh. Of them a spiritually blind multitude would cry out: "A holy man!" But the "holy men" themselves know better, and differently. Their God had taught them to look not only at the rash on the skin but, more urgently, into the infection in the blood. And so the rule prevails that allows for no exceptions and is regularly confirmed: precisely those who are most advanced in the killing, denial, and control of external evil have also entered most deeply into contrition and persevered most powerfully in calling out for the forgiveness of their guilt! They no longer cling to the external but have been taught by their God to press deeper. And just there, in the depth of their existence, they discovered the loathsome essence, the scandalous root of sin and became acquainted with the demon who stirs up these ungodly realities from the depths of Satan! . . . [Kuyper here gives the series summary that we relocated above.]

* * *

In conclusion, if people ask us whether we are deliberately helping to break down what we earlier helped to build up, we feel obligated not to avoid the question but to answer it forthrightly, albeit with some intense pain in our heart.

Strictly speaking, the answer is no! By itself our fundamental opposition to the doctrine of perfectionism says nothing that can be used against the spiritual revival associated with the name of Pearsall Smith insofar as we commended it. In fact immediately upon his return from England the author of these articles submitted to the brothers who came back with him a declaration that included, among other things, the following statement: "this movement does not intend to promote the theory of perfectionism and, as to the doctrine of sin, restores rather than overthrows classic Reformed principles." In addition, each of the brothers who heard the declaration or read the *Zondagsblad* of that time can now be our witness that the author of these articles consistently condemned Perfectionism and never whitewashed it. Nor do we have to apologize for less-than-Reformed sympathies which were attributed to us when we stood in the current of this movement. What we said and wrote to this point at the time demonstrates that we explained the theology of this movement in no other sense than as a return to a genuinely Calvinistic purgation of all Arminianism, overt or implicit. On top of all this and perhaps unnecessarily, let me repeat that our identification with Mr. Smith only occurred following a firm declaration on his part that the relevant answers of the Heidelberg Catechism were for him the correct expression of his opinions.

Yet, however true all this may be, we do not wish to conceal from friend or foe alike that, in retrospect, the Arminians were in control of the field at Brighton. Nor would we conceal that our judgment would in all likelihood have been different from the very beginning had we been as familiar with the history of Perfectionism, the theological articulation of Perfectionism, and the historical polemics against Perfectionism as we are now. Indeed, we wish to state openly, with deep sorrow before God and men, that our understanding of this entire revival was partly in error and, being in error, sinful! Not as if a "spiritual revival" is less than a glorious good toward which the prayers of the church should be directed and for which everyone who loves God yearns. But an awakening, when it really comes from the Holy Spirit, always starts with the quietly devout of God, is spontaneous in its expressions, and shuns human exhibitionism, external boisterousness, and artificiality in its organizations.

Nor would we in any way retract our judgment that the standard of holiness among the Christians of our age has sunk far too low, that separation from the world, the focus on things sacred, the maintenance of discipline and order, and the avoidance of unrighteousness were better in the past and should be better now. But we failed to see that this elevation of the Christian life can come only by the opposite road: by awe before God's majesty, by bowing before his law, hence by mortification, by the confession of sin, by repentance and conversion.

Nor, finally, do we adhere any less firmly to the conviction that a quiet seclusion among those who thirst for a holy good, seeking the face of our God in fasting and prayers, can effectively move the soul to the breaking of one's own ego. In fact, in the past, under the impact of the workings of the Holy Spirit, many people have been thus deeply humbled, broken before God, and reborn. But this seclusion may not imply feasting at a spiritual delicatessen to which all the fleetfooted among the devout will flock. Rather it is born out of need among close relatives or friends, emerges very gradually into the light of day, and then must remain on ecclesiastical tracks.

This mixture of truth and untruth prompted groups of the most tender and God-fearing folks to join the spiritual feast in England. And it produced glorious and blessed moments of spiritual ecstasy. As in all countries, so in ours, it awakened a thirst in many a heart to make this glory constant. There was something bewitching in this mighty event, so glorious a contrast, it seemed, with the materialistic and ungodly driving forces of our age. Clothe all this in the marvelous form to which English Christians are accustomed, wrap it more thickly still in the guise of the stranger which tends to hide many a wound from the eyes of others, and the deception was complete.

Still, here as always, the unreal was winnowed from the real by the facts which, presently interpreted by the Holy Spirit, brought about a division of souls. What happened to Smith himself is well known. It is also known how the godliest folk in England soon turned away and how rumors of false teaching gradually surfaced which had earlier been suppressed. People also know how in our own country someone sinful like each of us forgot himself so badly as to publicly ask his audience: "Which of you convicts me of sin!" Naturally, that was the end of it.

What we saw at home then occurred almost everywhere. The unstable spirits, the synergistic types, the Arminian fanatics and the enemies of a deeper life increasingly took control of this movement, proved themselves at home in it, and indulged in ever grosser spiritual extravagances. Then the light of truth could not but dawn over this sad spectacle, and those true sons of our Dutch-Calvinistic — i.e., deeply serious — spiritual life who had drifted away on these waters could not help coming to the shameful confession that intellectually and, worse, spiritually they had erred in their appraisal of this phenomenon. Far from being innocent, that error had to lead to self-appraisal and a straightforward confession of guilt.

Herewith the author of these articles also acquits himself of this painful task, all the more readily and candidly inasmuch as he raised the hope among a wide circle that with this rustling of the wind of a day the breeze of the Spirit was bound to come. Whether the nervous exhaustion which shortly thereafter broke out in such serious illness may help explain this misappraisal I leave to the judgment of the spiritually minded among God's children, above all to the judgment of Him who knows our bodies as well as our souls. Perhaps I may add that the one-sidedness of our theological training, which makes us more at home in the byways of criticism than in the labyrinth of the spiritual life, leaves us open to such misappraisal.

But whatever may be said in mitigation does not alter the fact that fuel was added to a fire that was ignited in part by ungodly sparks. To confess responsibility for this is something the present writer regards to be not only his duty but also sweet. He may declare before God and man that at the time he was not conscious of any error and spoke sincerely and with unfeigned enthusiasm with the knowledge then available to him. But here, too, one must abide by the truth that "if my heart does not condemn me, this does not excuse me, for God is greater than my heart and he knows all things!" [1 John 3:19-20].[5]

So then let me write *"dixi et salvavi animam"* [I have spoken and thereby saved my soul] to indicate that this series of articles was meant not only as a word from my mouth but also as an act of my heart.

5. Kuyper misquotes and misconstrues this passage, which speaks of God's greatness and omniscience affording believers reassurance particularly when their hearts *do* condemn them.

Common Grace

The year after his series on perfectionism Kuyper set out on a long explication of divine election and the covenants, the hard iron in the Reformed bedrock to which he had re-anchored himself.[1] Such projects showed his passion to write constructive theology for a common lay audience. Kuyper would go on to write a three-year series on the work of the Holy Spirit — published under that title in three volumes, 1888-89 — and an eight-year commentary on the Heidelberg Catechism that appeared as *E Voto Dordraceno* (four volumes, 1892-95).

Kuyper's farthest-reaching work in this vein was doubtless his elaboration of the Reformed doctrine of common grace. His conservative opponents complained that this was more "invention" than elaboration, for Kuyper by his own admission greatly expanded and systematized what earlier Reformed theologians had left as hints and pieces. This was consistent with his stated purpose of updating the tradition, of making it speak to the demands of the times and the needs of the faithful. At the moment he began this work (the series ran from September 1895 through July 1901) these demands were new. Around 1880, when his work on particular grace appeared, Kuyper had been concerned with raising Reformed consciousness among a strictly Reformed people. Now he wanted to bring that group back in touch with the larger society and culture — also for immediate political purposes. He completed the series simultaneously with his election as prime minister.

Common grace was thus a theology of public responsibility, of Christians' shared humanity with the rest of the world. It was also, in the words of one historian, "the valve through which Kuyper pumped fresh air into his people....

1. These articles ran in *De Heraut* in two series — 20 April 1879–13 June 1880 and 29 August 1880–23 October 1881 — and were published in book form as, respectively, "Grace is Particular" and "The Doctrine of the Covenants" (*Uit het Woord: Stichtelijke Bijbelstudien*, 2nd series, vols. I and II [Amsterdam: J. H. Kruyt, 1884/1885]).

Through common grace he not only made his own group acceptable to 'the thinking part of the nation'. . . but at the same time opened the world of science and art for his fellow-believers."[2] Kuyper's ire for world-flight and nay-sayers jumps off these pages and forms an intriguing counterpoint to his own *fin de siècle* anxieties as manifest in *The Blurring of the Boundaries* and *Evolution* (see below). His praise of technical achievement and his valorization of bourgeois civilization reached unwonted heights in *Common Grace,* perhaps to the bemusement of conservative critics who saw in common grace a license for world conformity.

The contest over its implications can mask how closely *Common Grace* follows a classic Calvinistic agenda. As Kuyper declared in his foreword to the trilogy: ". . . the doctrine of common grace proceeds directly from the Sovereignty of the Lord which is ever the root conviction of all Reformed thinking. If God is sovereign, then his Lordship *must* remain over *all* life and cannot be closed up within church walls or Christian circles. The extra-Christian world has not been given over to satan or to fallen humanity or to chance. God's Sovereignty is great and all-ruling also in unbaptized realms, and therefore neither Christ's work in the world nor that of God's child can be pulled back out of life. If his God works in the world, then there he must put his hand to the plow so that there too the Name of the Lord is glorified."[3]

Common Grace also recalls Kuyper's particular emphases, and the excerpts that follow are arranged to show the linkages. The work begins with creation and proceeds through the mixed qualities of human history, braiding a double helix of nature and grace. Along the way it must define the church and the relationship of Christ and culture. It hums throughout with Kuyper's alternating currents of polarity and unity.

The material that appeared in the six-year series in *De Heraut* was collected and published as *De Gemeene Gratie* in three volumes — 1902, 1903, and 1904, respectively — by Höveker & Wormser in Amsterdam. Kuyper's usage of "particuliere genade" has been rendered here as "special grace," meaning first of all "specific" (as the Dutch has it) to particular persons, but inevitably conveying, whether Kuyper agreed or not (and he was ambivalent on the point), a higher rank or worth as well. The translation is by John Vriend.

2. Jan Romein, "Abraham Kuyper: De Klokkenist van de Kleine Luyden," in Jan and Annie Romein, *Erflaters van onze Beschaving* (Amsterdam: Queridos, 1971), p. 754.

3. Abraham Kuyper, "Voorwoord," *De Gemeene Gratie,* vol. I.

A. Creation and History

[The first volume of *Common Grace* Kuyper designated "Historical," studying mostly the very beginnings of human history as recorded in early Genesis. He comes to the heart of the issue in chapter 30, "Forms of Grace," after the fall and before the flood.[4]]

There is neither doubt nor uncertainty about the situation that followed the fall. On the one hand, Scripture vividly pictures it to us; on the other, it continues in part to this day and can therefore be read from what we see and hear all around us. We have noted before that this newly inaugurated situation did not correspond to what had been predicted as the consequence of sin. Death, in its full effect, did not set in on that day, and Reformed theologians have consistently pointed out how in this non-arrival of what was prophesied for ill we see the emergence of a saving and long-suffering grace. Nor was this the first manifestation of grace, for human life in Paradise was inconceivable without an environing and invasive grace. To every rational creature grace is the air he breathes. But now for the first time this divine grace assumes its character as *saving* grace in which, inasmuch as we are sinners, we first and most naturally recognize the grace of God.

Let no one construe this saving grace as a form of indulgence, a certain weakness on the part of God, as if God should have persisted in demanding his full pound of justice but was deflected from his purpose only by the impulse of pity. Such shrinking from the demands of justice is simply inconceivable in the case of the Holy One and would be a projection upon God of what may be to the credit of us humans but would be dishonoring to God. Accordingly, we may never picture this manifestation of God's grace as though it helped and saved us but did so at the expense of the integrity of his majesty. Indeed, one of our objections to the Infralapsarian[5] position (whose relative validity we readily grant) is precisely that it cannot escape this misguided view. Without further pursuing this point here, we do want

4. This section is from vol. I, pp. 217-24.

5. Infralapsarianism was a rival to (Kuyper's preferred) Supralapsarianism as an interpretation of God's decrees. "Infras" put election-to-salvation after creation and fall; Supras, before. The dispute was particularly acute at the time of Kuyper's writing since the two currents that had merged into the Gereformeerde Kerken differed on this point, the Seceder tradition generally taking the Infra position and Kuyper's Doleantie the Supra. The debate was resolved at the GKN Synod of 1905 with Infra being deemed the preferred and Supra a tolerable position. Kuyper's point in the text — that Supras put highest emphasis on the majesty or glory of God while Infras focused more on the particular people elected — is historically warranted.

Common grace provided the theological basis for Kuyper's educational and political ventures. *Left:* The staff of the Free University featuring the ancient goddess of wisdom, Minerva. *Right:* The recently defeated prime minister of the Netherlands around 1905, the year after *Common Grace* appeared in book form.

to observe that also this manifestation of grace served ultimately not to save us but to bring out the glory of the Divine Being, and only in the second place, as the consequence of this end, to snatch us from our self-sought ruin. This manifestation of grace consisted in restraining, blocking, or redirecting the consequences that would otherwise have resulted from sin. It intercepts the natural outworking of the poison of sin and either diverts and alters it or opposes and destroys it. For that reason we must distinguish two dimensions in this manifestation of grace: 1. a *saving* grace, which in the end abolishes sin and completely undoes its consequences; and 2. a *temporal restraining* grace, which holds back and blocks the effect of sin. The former, that is saving grace, is in the nature of the case *special* and restricted to God's elect. The second, *common* grace, is extended to the whole of our human life. The question then arises whether these two forms of grace, this *special* and this *common* grace, exist independently side-by-side or operate in connection with each other, and if so, how.

That there is in fact a connection between the *saving* grace which is *special* and the *restraining* grace which is *common* cannot be doubted. This is immediately evident from the undeniable fact that, without common grace, the elect would not have been born, would not have seen the light of day. Had Adam and Eve died the day they sinned, Seth would not have been born from them, nor Enoch from Seth, and no widely ramified race of peoples and nations would ever have originated on earth. On that basis alone all special grace assumes *common grace*. But there is more. Even if you assumed that their temporal death had been postponed so that the human race could have made a start, but that for the rest sin in all its horror had broken out unhindered, you would still be nowhere. For then life on earth would immediately have turned into a hell and under such hellish conditions the church of God would not have had a place to strike root anywhere. Sometimes people speak — quite erroneously in fact — of a hell on earth and do this with reference to a few frightening outbreaks of human depravity which, in some families and circles, assume such a diabolical character that they end in general bestialization, murder, and insanity. But such conditions are so outrageous, so gruesome, and so hideous that the church simply could not continue to exist in a world composed solely of such social relations. It would be massacred in less than no time. From whatever angle one looks at this issue, then, special grace presupposes *common grace*. Without the latter the former cannot function.

The connection is therefore undeniable, but how are we to construe it? There's no point in disguising it: this connection is frequently pictured as though common grace served solely to make it possible for the elect to come to salvation. Though there is undoubtedly an element of truth in this thesis, it is sometimes exaggerated to the point where it becomes offensive and makes you shudder. We are not making things up when we say that now and then there have been people in our country who, believing in their own election while viewing their parents as total reprobates, did not shrink from harshly stating: "O my parents — they're outside of the whole thing and served only to make my existence possible." Fortunately such statements are exceedingly rare but they are not unheard of, so we must pause here to call attention to the right relation between special and common grace. The error lies solely in that, in defining this connection, people focus on *their own salvation* instead of on the *glory of God*. This is the nuance by which you can always tell whether you are dealing with the genuine Reformed confession or with a faulty *imitation* of it.

Certainly, there is nothing wrong in saying that everything happens for Christ's sake, that therefore the *body of Christ* is the all-controlling and central element in history, and that on this basis the church of Christ is the pivot on which the life of humanity hinges. Those who overlook or deny this reality will never find any unity in the course of history. For them century follows century, and in the process development follows decline and regression progression, but the stream of life as a whole is not going anywhere, has no goal. This life lacks a center, a pivot on which it turns. Should this go on for all eternity, history would consist in boredom without end. Should it be terminated at some point because the elements of fire and water got the better of earth, the termination would be completely arbitrary; no goal would have been reached, nor any advantage gained. The Reformed confession — which maintains that all things, also in this world, aim at the Christ, that his *Body* is the key component, and that in this sense one can say the church of Christ forms the center of world history — offers a basis for a view of history far superior to the common one. So we will think twice before we will detract in any way from this confession. Not *common* grace but the order of *special grace* prevails.

But this thesis leads to a purer confession only if you respect the *order.* All things exist *for the sake of Christ* and only as a corollary for his *Body* and the *Church* — hence not for *you* and then for the *Church* and so also for the *Body* of Christ and finally for the *Christ.* No: Christ, by whom all things exist including ourselves, is before all things. He is the reflection of God's glory and bears the very stamp of his nature. We confess that all things are created by him — whether visible or invisible, in heaven and on earth — in whom all things now hold together. That is the Christ around whom all things revolve, since in him the fullness of God dwells bodily and before him every knee shall bow and every tongue confess that Christ is *Lord* to the glory of God the Father [Col. 1:16-19, Phil. 2:10-11]. Certainly the *Body* also shares in that honor. Something of his radiance is reflected by his church on earth, and every *elect* person catches some part of it. But surely that is very different from starting with myself as an elect person, putting myself in the foreground, and only from there ending up with Christ. In the only true system everything else is second, Christ is at the head and is made central not insofar as he became our brother but because he is the Son of God the Father, and because the Father loves the Son and glorifies him with everlasting honor. When we are speaking of the Son of God, *our concern is with God himself,* and our soul ultimately finds peace only when it sums up under one heading the entire course of history from paradise to the Second Coming. In that sense, then, we must acknowledge that common grace is only an emanation of special grace and that all its fruit flows into special grace — provided it is understood that special grace is by no means exhausted in the salvation of the elect but has its ultimate end only in the Son's glorification of the Father's love, and so in the aggrandizement of the perfections of our God.

That this is the only correct position must be further illumined by reference to a point of the greatest moment for the right view of common grace: *the relation between nature and grace.* We will revisit this weighty issue later, but we need here to point out a particular element. Is Christ exclusively the *Expiator of sin?*

For many otherwise warm Christians the answer almost has to be *yes,* but for Holy Scripture that certainly cannot be the answer. The idea that Christ has no significance but as the Lamb of God who died for our sin cannot be maintained by those who read Scripture seriously. Do not misunderstand me. We are not now talking about the speculative question whether the Word would have become flesh even if Adam had not fallen into sin; insofar as the question is legitimate, we would answer in the negative. No, our concern can be summed up as follows: shall we say that Christ has been given us only for our justification and sanctification, or shall we continue to confess with the apostle in 1 Corinthians 1:30 that Christ was also made to be our *wisdom* and our full *redemption?* Shall we say that in him we possess only the atonement for our sin or shall we maintain that he will some day also change our humiliated body to be like his glorified body by the working of the power by which he subjects all things to himself [Phil. 3:21]? Shall we consider the work Christ finished on Golgotha to be settled and closed or, with Scripture and the entire church of the first centuries, continue to look for our Lord to come down from heaven to end the present scheme of things and to bring out a new earth and a new heaven? To put it in a nutshell, shall we imagine that all we need is a Reconciler of our soul or continue to confess that the Christ of God is the Savior of both soul and *body* and is the Re-creator not only of things in the invisible world but also of things that are visible and before our eyes? Does Christ have significance only for the *spiritual* realm or also for the *natural and visible* domain? Does the fact that he has overcome the world [John 16:33] mean that he will one day toss the world back into nothingness in order to keep alive only the souls of the elect, or does it mean that the world too will be his conquest, the trophy of his glory?

We have no desire to exaggerate this point and to close our eyes to the danger of pushing the forgiveness of our sins into the background. Undeniably that danger exists. In some circles people so restlessly immerse themselves in questions relating to our Lord's Second Coming that the more basic questions pertaining to the knowledge of our sin and the justification of the sinner hardly get discussed anymore. For the past eighteen centuries the Church of Christ has prudently and consistently placed the psychological issues in the foreground and somewhat downplayed the issues relating to the last things. The sects on the other hand have consistently attempted to change this healthy balance by diverting attention from the deeper questions of justification to drive us toward Chiliasm or the Millennial Kingdom by speaking much about the manner of our physical resurrection, about a prior second coming of our Lord, about whether, according to Paul, the Jews will return to Jerusalem, and the like. One can thus have a stimulating religious conversation without being troubled in conscience or convinced of one's wretched state before God. Therefore we cannot warn often enough against the danger of shifting conversations in Christian circles away from the salvation of the soul to such external but sensational topics. In truly Reformed circles that danger is avoided when the substance of conversation is not Chiliasm or the Jewish question but the question of how God is honored and our soul is justified.

. . . [W]e have no right to conceptualize the image of the Mediator in ways other than Scripture presents it. People fall into one-sidedness in the opposite direction if, reflecting on the Christ, they think exclusively of the blood shed in atonement and refuse to take account of the significance of Christ for the body, for the visible world, and for the outcome of world history. Consider carefully: by taking this tack you run the danger of isolating Christ for your soul and you view life in and for the world as something that exists *alongside* your Christian religion, not controlled by it. Then the word "Christian" seems appropriate to you only when it concerns certain matters of faith or things directly connected with the faith — your church, your school, missions and the like — but all the remaining spheres of life fall for you *outside the Christ*. In the world you conduct yourself as others do; that is less holy, almost unholy, territory which must somehow take care of itself. You only have to take a small step more before landing in the Anabaptist position which concentrated all sanctity in the human soul and dug a deep chasm between this inward-looking spirituality and life all around. Then scholarship becomes unholy; the development of art, trade, and business becomes unholy; unholy also the functions of government; in short, all that is not directly spiritual and aimed at the soul. This way of thinking results in your living in two distinct circles of thought: in the very circumscribed circle of your soul's salvation on the one hand, and in the spacious, life-encompassing sphere of the world on the other. Your Christ is at home in the former but not in the latter. From that opposition and false proportionality springs all narrow-mindedness, all inner unreality, if not all sanctimoniousness and powerlessness.

. . . Obviously, this touches at once upon the connection between *nature* and *grace.* For if grace exclusively concerned atonement for sin and salvation of souls, one could view grace as something located and operating outside of nature. One could picture it as oil poured on turbulent waters, floating on those waters while remaining *separate* from them, solely so that the drowning person can save his life by grabbing the life buoy thrown out to him. But if it is true that Christ our Savior has to do not only with our soul but also with our body, that all things in the world belong to Christ and are claimed by him, that one day he will triumph over every enemy in that world, and that in the end Christ will not gather a few separated souls around him, as is the case now, but will rule as king on a new earth under a new heaven — then, of course, everything is different. We see immediately that *grace* is inseparably connected with *nature,* that grace and nature belong together. You cannot see grace in all its riches if you do not perceive how its tiny roots and fibers everywhere penetrate into the joints and cracks of the life of nature. And you cannot validate that connectedness if, with respect to grace, you first look at the salvation of your soul and not primarily on the *Christ of God.*

For that reason Scripture continually points out that the *Savior* of the world is also the *Creator* of the world, indeed that he could become its Savior only *because* he already was its *Creator.* Of course, it was not the *Son of man,* not the *incarnate Word,* who created the world. All that was human in the Mediator was itself created, creaturely as it is creaturely in us. Still, Scripture repeatedly points out that he, the first-born of the dead, is also the first-born of creation, that the Word Incarnate nevertheless always was and remained the same eternal Word who was with God and was God, of whom it is written that without that Word nothing was made that is made [John 1:1-3]. Christ then is connected with *nature* because he is its Creator, and at the same time connected to *grace* because, as Re-creator, he manifested the riches of grace in the midst of that nature.

[Kuyper returns to these themes toward the end of his second, "theological" volume when he takes up eschatology and, with that, considerations of history.[6]]

. . . Obviously, one misunderstanding naturally leads to another in this connection. For if we set *nature* and *grace* against each other as two mutually exclusive concepts, we get the impression that nature now persists *apart from* all grace and that grace is and has been extended exclusively to God's elect. This inference is absolutely untenable. *Common*

6. This section is from vol. II, ch. 81: "The Eternal Course," pp. 609-12.

grace has been shown to nature and *special grace* to God's elect; only under this proviso can the contrast be maintained. Much clearer and sounder, therefore, is the contrast between *Creation* and *Re-creation* [*Schepping* and *Herschepping*] to which people today are becoming more accustomed. What we call *nature* is everything that has its origin and law in the original *creation*. Though all this suffered under the curse which began to work after the fall, common grace averted the lethal consequences of the curse and made possible and certain the continued, be it afflicted, existence of all that came from the original creation. By contrast, what came about from *re-creation* belongs altogether to the terrain of special grace. Special grace not only restrains things but *creates new things*. The saved person is "a *new creature* in Christ"; he is "the *new* human being." So is the whole of sacred revelation. So is the Christ; so are all the regenerate; so is the church; so is the body of Christ. It is altogether a *new Creation* which, though linked with the original (for it is *Re-creation*), in its newness cannot be explained from the old. The inaccurate antithesis between *nature* and *grace* that has come down to us from medieval theology can be used only if qualified by the addition that nature, cursed as it is by itself, can endure only by the action of common grace. The Reformed principle produces a much purer distinction between the things that originate from the Creation and the things that originate from the Re-creation. That far-reaching distinction is this: in common grace there is never anything new, never anything but what can be explained from the original creation; on the other hand, in special grace nothing arises from the creation but everything is *new* and can only be explained from the new Creation or Re-creation.

. . . [Second,] *common grace* opens a history, unlocks an enormous space of time, triggers a vast and long-lasting stream of events, in a word, precipitates a series of successive centuries. If that series of centuries is not directed toward an endless, unvarying repetition of the same things, then over the course of those centuries there has to be constant change, modification, transformation in human life. Though it pass through periods of deepening darkness, this change has to ignite ever more light, consistently enrich human life, and so bear the character of perpetual development from less to more, a progressively fuller unfolding of life. If one pictures the distance that exists even now between the life of a Hottentot in his kraal and the life of a highly refined family in European society, one can measure that process in the blink of an eye. And though people imagine at the end of every century that its progress has been so astonishing that further progress can hardly be imagined, every century nevertheless teaches us that the new things added each time surpass all that has been imagined before. How has the nineteenth century not changed and enriched our human life and blessed it with new conveniences!

The tendency in devout circles to oppose that progress and perpetual development of human life was therefore quite misguided. It must undoubtedly be acknowledged that Christians, by refusing to participate in that development, were the reason why morally and religiously that development often took a wrong turn. Those who are in Christ must not oppose such development and progress, must not even distance themselves from it. Their calling also in this cultural realm is rather to be in the vanguard. Calvinism in the sixteenth and seventeenth centuries was in the forefront and so set the tone and tempo of life. That we in our age under a variety of Anabaptist and Methodist influences abandoned the field to the forces of unbelief is a fault of our fathers, the bitter consequences whereof we are now experiencing.

Therefore, we must emphatically state that the interval of centuries that have passed since the fall is not a blank space in the plan of God. The ages lying behind us, by God's decree, must have a purpose and goal, and that purpose can be understood only if we understand that the ongoing development of humanity is *contained in the plan of God.* It follows that the history of our race resulting from this development is not from Satan nor from man *but from God* and that all those who reject and fail to appreciate this development deny the work of God in history. Scripture speaks of the "consummation of the ages" [Matt. 13:39-40], a term that does not mean the centuries will terminate at some point but that they are directed toward a final goal and that everything contained in those centuries is linked to that final goal.

God goads people toward that development by distress, by suffering, and by the experience of misery. Thus we are thoroughly misguided to see in that suffering only judgment under which we must groan. We must rather recognize that suffering is *the enemy* against which God calls us to do battle. However — and here the shoe pinches — God does not reveal all at once what he alone can show us: the means by which we may protect ourselves from and resist that suffering. Successively, in the course of centuries, God has over and over inspired us to discover something new, giving us a clearer glimpse of those means. In this respect Noah was farther along than Adam, Moses than Noah, Solomon than Moses, and, continuing in that line, we are farther along than our ancestors. It is not as if something totally new were created. All that God has disclosed to us already lay stored up in the creation from the beginning. But we did not know it and did not see it, and God has used the centuries, step-by-step, to help us discover ever more, ever new things by which our human life could be enriched. . . . *That* has been the development of our race; therein alone lay the real component of progress. . . .

* * *

So then, we arrive at this clear insight.[7] The ages must continue not solely for the sake of the elect, nor solely for God to disclose means to us in our struggle against suffering, but in the interest of developing the world itself to its consummation — for as long as is needed to take the world from its beginning and the earliest germination of our human life to the point where the whole process is complete and God has truly reached the final goal he had in mind for it. Thus not a half century, not even a quarter century, will be wasted. There is neither vacuity nor stagnation here. The things that do not yet grow above ground already grow underground in the germination of the seed or the strengthening of the root-system. Not a year, not a day, not an hour can be spared. For all those centuries God has restlessly continued his work in our human race, in the totality of the life of this world. Nothing in it is purposeless or redundant. Things had to go as they did, there was no other way, and the sign of the Son of man will appear in the clouds only when the whole magnificent work of God is complete and the consummation of the world has been inaugurated.

Therefore every view that would confine God's work to the small sector we might label "church life" must be set aside. There is beside the great work of God in *special* grace also that totally other work of God in the realm of *common* grace. That work encompasses the whole life of the world, the life of Kaffirs in Africa, of Mongols in China and Japan, and of the Indians south of the Himalayas. In all previous centuries there was nothing among Egyptians and Greeks, in Babylon and Rome, nor is there anything today among the peoples of whatever continent that was or is not necessary. All of it was an indispensable part of the great work that God is doing to consummate the world's development. And though a great deal in all this *we* cannot connect with the Kingdom or the content of our faith, nevertheless it all has meaning. None of it can be spared because it pleases God, despite Satan's devices and human sin, to actualize everything he had put into this world at the time of creation, to insist on its realization, to develop it so completely that the full sum of its vital energies may enter the light of day at the consummation of the world.

7. The next two paragraphs are from vol. II, ch. 82: "The End of the Age," pp. 618-19.

[Kuyper next moves to the imprint of God's image on the human race. This truth, he says, every believer affirms but usually applies almost exclusively to individuals, and at that to spiritual attributes that have been largely lost in the Fall. Kuyper offers a different suggestion for how that image has survived.[8]]

For good reason, therefore, we pose the question whether the creation of man in God's image does not have a significance vastly greater than what has been acknowledged up until now in individual terms. The answer lies in the simple observation that the image of God is certainly much too rich a concept to be realized *in one single person.* In looking at parents and children we can sometimes see the facial features and character traits of the parents to be spread out over the several children in varying proportions but always in such a way that none displays them in their fullness. How much more do we not have to confess that the image of Eternal Being, if we may so put it, is much too full and rich to be reproduced in *one* individual. Do we not come closer to the truth by saying that the bearer of the full multifaceted image of God is not the individual person but *our entire human race?* Christ is *the* image of the invisible God since in him all the treasures of wisdom have been hidden, but can that be said in the same sense of any one of us? It can be said that the whole image of God was germinally concentrated in Adam as head of our entire race, but only in the sense that he carried the whole human race in his loins. Is it not true then that, not individually but socially, the image of God can be understood in all its dimensions only if we look at what the immensely rich development of our entire race permits us to see of it?

In saying these things we are by no means denying or even weakening the truth of our individual creation in the likeness of God's image. Just as Peter says of the temple of God that it is made of "living stones" which are each of them individually a temple in miniature [1 Peter 2:4-5], so also here it remains true that all the constituent parts of the human race are carriers of the human type and that human type can be understood only as the imprint of the divine image. Our existence as human beings in soul and body and similarly our entire humanity as such is controlled in the most absolute sense by the image of God. Just as every tiny part of the root, stem, bark, bloom, and fruit exists organically in the whole of a tree, so it has to be that in the great organism of our human race which mirrors the image of God, every individual, every separate human specimen has to be created in conformity to that type of

8. This section is from vol. II, ch. 83: "The Display of the Image of God," pp. 623-27.

God's image and even in its sinful degradation has to exhibit the inverted outline of that image.

So we leave intact and completely unabridged the truth of our individual creation after the image of God. We would rather enhance it than detract from it by the demand that our entire human nature, in soul *and body,* in both the state of rectitude and *the state of sin,* be explained in terms of the typology of the divine image. We would insist only that people also apply the typology of the divine image to the *plurality* of humans, to our entire *race,* to *humanity as such,* to the emergence and development of the life of humanity in its *entirety.* Only in this manner do you get an impression of that endless mass of the children of men which, though composed of individual drops of water like the sea, still causes you to forget those drops in order to dazzle you with the mighty surges of an endless ocean. Thus alone arises before your mind's eye the immeasurable fullness of human life that presents the wide stream in which the image of God can mirror itself in its *entirety.* . . .

The social side of man's creation in God's image has nothing to do with salvation nor in any way with each person's state before God. This social element tells us only that in creating human beings in his likeness God deposited an infinite number of nuclei for high human development in our nature and that these nuclei cannot develop except *through the social bond between people.* From this viewpoint the highly ramified development of humanity acquires a significance of its own, an independent goal, a reason for being aside from the issue of salvation. If it has pleased God to mirror the richness of his image in the social multiplicity and fullness of our human race, and if he himself has deposited the nuclei of that development in human nature, *then* the brilliance of his image *has to* appear. Then that richness *may not* remain concealed, those nuclei *may not* dry up and wither, and humanity will *have* to remain on earth for as long as it takes to unfold as fully and richly as necessary those nuclei of human potential. Then will have occurred that full development of humanity in which all the glory of God's image can mirror itself.

Though people may pluck the enjoyment and profit of that development, its realization is in fact not for the sake of humanity but for God. The supreme Artisan and Architect will want all that has gone into his design to be realized and stand before him in a splendid edifice. God will take delight in that high human development. He himself will bring it about and into view. Then he will seek in it his own glorification. The control and harnessing of nature by civilization, enlightenment, and progress, by science and art, by a variety of enterprises and industry will be entirely separate from the totally other development in holiness and integrity; indeed, that *exterior* development may even clash openly with an *interior* development in holiness and become a temptation to the believer. Still, that exterior development has to continue and be completed to bring the *work of God* in our race to full visible realization. Whether or not this will subsequently be consumed in the coming cosmic conflagration does not matter. Its very completion will have sparkled before God's eye, and Satan will not have succeeded in preventing its culmination. And after the cosmic conflagration, that same God will once again reveal the reflection of his image in the kingdom of his glory, but then in a totally different way, that is, in complete harmony with our interior development.

At the same time "common grace" will thereby achieve a purpose of its own. It will not only serve to bring about the emergence of the human race, to bring to birth the full number of the elect, and to arm us increasingly and more effectively against human suffering, but also independently to bring about in all its dimensions and in defiance of Satanic opposition and human sin the full emergence of what God had in mind when he planted those nuclei of higher development in our race. Without the fall this magnificent development would undoubtedly have been different. It would have unfolded much more swiftly and not have borne the fearful character of conflict and struggle that is now inseparable from the history of our race. Eve would have given birth apart from a fall but without pain. Humanity would have reached its acme of development without the distress and grief that have given such a somber cast to the history of the ages. Nevertheless, humanity arrives at its goal, it lifts itself up from its sunken state, it gradually reaches a higher level. The fundamental creation ordinance given before the fall, that humans would achieve dominion over all of nature thanks to "common grace," is still realized *after* the fall. Only in this way, in the light of the Word of God, can the history of our race, the long unfolding of the centuries as well as the high significance of the world's development, make substantial sense to us.

Common grace not only allowed the human flourishing that Kuyper so fulsomely praised; it also made possible the development, the *full* development, of human evil. Put another way, it kept the human game going for good and ill. Kuyper spelled out the terms of his ambivalence with rare explicitness toward the end of *Common Grace,* vol. I, in commentary about the last days of human history as forecast in the Revelation of St. John. That epoch will feature Antichrist, the "man of sin"

> in whom all the powers, gifts, and talents inherent in humanity are concentrated and whom Satan could not put on the stage of history apart from its full development under common grace.

Sheer malevolence, pure hostility against God, is not sufficient here. The powers, means, and instruments also have to be available to make possible the full, cumulative effectiveness of that malevolence. This was not the case in paradise or in Noah's days. The development of human power could only occur gradually and can only unfold its full potential in the end. What was human power three centuries ago compared to the power of humanity at the end of the nineteenth century? Science is already predicting quite a different set of powers for the century ahead of us. So it continues and so it will continue until the very end when at last development can go no further, when all hidden powers have been discovered, released, subjected to human control, and fully harnessed. Only then can the dreadful person arise who, uniting all the threads of these various powers in a single hand, will want to possess them apart from God, direct them against God, and apply them as though he were God. Erase the factor of "common grace" and that development of human power would never have taken place; its basis would have been lacking, and everything would have returned to chaos. For that reason the closing scene in the drama of common grace can be enacted only through the appearance on stage of the man of sin.

If you ask whether the term "common grace" is not self-contradictory since, though called "grace," it leads to the most powerful manifestation of sin in history, I must insist on sharp distinctions. The Cross of Golgotha remains the absolute apogee of special grace; still, on Golgotha human evil manifests itself in its most appalling form. Is this a contradiction? You know better. It is no different here. God is glorified in the total development toward which human life and power over nature gradually march on under the guardianship of "common grace." It is his created order, his work, that unfolds here. It was he who seeded the field of humanity with all these powers. Without common grace the seed which lay hidden in that field would never have come up and blossomed. Thanks to common grace it germinated, burgeoned, shot up high and will one day be in full flower, to reward not man but the heavenly Farmer. The ingenious work of God that Satan sought to destroy will then be completed, in spite of everything. A finished world will glorify God as Builder and supreme Craftsman. What Paradise was in bud will then be in full bloom. Only, just as man by his sin misused Paradise and therefore had to be expelled from it, so also the "man of sin" will try to turn this whole system against God and on that account will be blown away by the breath of God's mouth. . . . At the moment of its destruction Babylon — that is, the world power which evolved from human life — will exhibit not the image of a barbarous horde nor the image of coarse bestiality but, on the contrary, a picture of the highest development of which human life is capable. It will display the most refined forms, the most magnificent unfolding of wealth and splendor, the fullest brilliance of all that makes life dazzling and glorious. From this we know that "common grace" will continue to function to the end. Only when common grace has spurred the full emergence of all the powers inherent in human life will "the man of sin" find the level terrain needed to expand this power. Only then will the end be near and judgment come over him suddenly, on a single day, in the span of a single hour.

Naturally here too we have to distinguish between the two very distinct operations of common grace. Though "common grace" impacts the whole of our human life, it does not impact all aspects of this life in the same way. One common grace aims at the *interior*, another at the *exterior* part of our existence. The former is operative wherever civic virtue, a sense of domesticity, natural love, the practice of human virtue, the improvement of the public conscience, integrity, mutual loyalty among people, and a feeling for piety leaven life. The latter is in evidence when human power over nature increases, when invention upon invention enriches life, when international communication is improved, the arts flourish, the sciences increase our understanding, the conveniences and joys of life multiply, all expressions of life become more vital and radiant, forms become more refined, and the general image of life becomes more winsome.

But in the end it will not be these *two* operations which flourish to perfection in "Babylon the great." The glory of the world power which collapses in the time of judgment will consist solely in the second kind of development. Enrichment of the *exterior* life will go hand-in-hand with the impoverishment of the *interior*. The common grace that affects the human heart, human relations, and public practices will ever diminish, and only the other operation, the one that enriches and gratifies the human mind and senses, will proceed to its culmination. A splendid white mausoleum full of reeking skeletons, brilliant on the outside, dead on the inside — that is the Babylon which is becoming ripe for judgment. Whoever compares the glitter of human life today with the dullness of a century ago knows where things are headed. That judgment he must even now render over the unprecedented developments of our *external* human life.

Common Grace, vol. I, ch. 61:
"The Final Decision" (pp. 447-48, 451-52)

[At this point in what might have seemed new and troubling territory for some of his readers, Kuyper turns back to two classic hard themes of Calvinism, special grace and election.[9]]

. . . The cross of Christ has with good reason been called the center of world history. It is the point on which all the lines of the past converge and from which all the lines for the future receive their direction. This is implied when Scripture calls the Christ of God the *Alpha* and *Omega* . . . indicating that the entire series of developmental stages through which human history has passed is governed by the Christ of God. It means that this series proceeds from him and culminates in him.

But this general confession cannot stand on its own. For Christ as the center of world history not only *can* but often *is* confessed in a sense that does not get us anywhere. Formerly people took it that Christ embodies himself in the Christian church, that the result of all previous history is the appearance of the church on the scene, and that the history of Europe these nineteen centuries is then completely dominated by the history of the church. For the sake of the small part of the human race that lived in Europe and that for centuries was not much over a hundred million people, people lose sight of the much greater part of humanity that lived and struggled in Asia and Africa. In the European context they regard the entire collective life of our ancestors as little more than a secondary expression of the life of the

9. This section is from vol. II, ch. 84, "The Two Life Spheres Intermingled," pp. 631-34.

church. As a result, the independent goal of the life of common grace hardly comes into its own.

But Holy Scripture has by no means taught us this. Holy Scripture repeatedly tells us of the intertwinement of the life of special grace with that of common grace but simultaneously discloses that the point at which the two come together is not Christ's birth in Bethlehem but his eternal existence as the *Eternal Word*. Granted, the Gospels of Matthew, Mark, and Luke give only a few allusions to this, as for example in Matthew 13[:35] where we read that what Jesus disclosed in his parables were mysteries *hidden from before the foundation of the world*. But John's Gospel sharply highlights this truth at the very outset. John begins not with the Mediator of redemption but with the Mediator of creation. He starts out from the position of "common grace" and from there arrives at the position of "special grace." This linkage is picked up later in the Epistles where, in the person of the Redeemer of sinners, we are shown the Mediator of creation by whom all things were created and in whom all things even now hold together, indeed, in whom the wisdom of God dwells bodily [Col. 1:16-19]. And this by no means occurs in the New Testament as something brand-new but clearly harks back to what was revealed in the days of the Old Covenant in Proverbs 8 and elsewhere about the personal Wisdom who had been anointed from eternity.

The un-Reformed, half-hearted orthodoxy of the latter part of the eighteenth and beginning of the nineteenth century, without denying this part of God's revelation, did not know what to do with it and so distorted it. It did not push from Bethlehem back to Creation but focused the divine powers of the Eternal Logos on the "holy child Jesus" in his human manifestation. In reference to the cradle of Bethlehem it delighted to exhaust itself in high-flown rhetorical linkages that applied the attributes of the Creator to that which is creaturely in the Savior. That "Infant in the cradle" had created the world; that "Infant in the cradle" upheld the world; and before long, in its view, the God who carried the world died in Jesus on the cross. Of course this kind of theologizing deteriorated into a magic show that left people unable to make any sense of it or to feel any meaningful response to it. In the end it ran the danger, standing by the cradle, of lapsing into creature-worship, that abomination to every Reformed heart.

We are well acquainted with the transfer of the Second Person's attributes to the Mediator after his incarnation. We know very well how Scripture contains any number of expressions that attribute to the Christ — i.e., to the Anointed, therefore to the Mediator of redemption — holy qualities that essentially apply only to the Eternal Word. But this only asserts the truth that the *I* of the Mediator is and always remains the *I* of the eternal Word, a truth our ancestors allowed to come into its own by the express confession that the eternal Word, the second Person, at the time of his incarnation assumed not a human person with its own human "I" but *our human nature*. Therefore nothing is further from our mind than to say anything against the perfect identity of the *I* of Mary's Son with the *I* of the eternal Word. But this semi-orthodox theology deteriorated into something very different. It reversed the order. It did not proceed from the eternal Word to then see his revelation also in the infant of Bethlehem, but it proceeded from the cradle as such, from the human being Jesus Christ, and said things of that human being that do not rightly belong to what is creaturely, nor to the human being Jesus, but only to God — to whom above all be praise in all eternity.

As a result, utterly false notions have come into the church, magical combinations of the divine with the human that could be held as true by unreflective sentimental people but that aroused revulsion in those who reflected on things and sought clarity. These notions inevitably drew out the Ethical side and finally led to the Jesus of Schleiermacher and his school:[10] a Jesus who in fact *is nothing more than a human being*, hence a human being in whom not God but only *the divine* is embodied — and after further development, only the sense, the feeling, the *consciousness* of the divine. By that process we lost the God-man and were left in Jesus with the perfectly religious person until finally, under Modernist influences, that perfect religiosity was questioned too. Jesus was certainly very godly for his time, but the freely devout person of our time is again more godly than Jesus.

For that reason a well-considered protest must be issued, not just against this Modernist idea and Ethical dilution but also against the original error of semi-orthodoxy that was the mother of all that followed. It must again get through to the Reformed mind that the work of creation and the work of redemption — and to that extent also the work of common and of

10. The German theologian Friedrich Schleiermacher (1768-1834) founded a new direction in Christian thought that answered Enlightenment-rationalist critiques by grounding religion in human feeling and experience. Consequently, his theology strongly emphasized the human nature of Jesus, a feature also in the work of theologians Daniel Chantepie de la Saussaye (1818-74) and Johannes H. Gunning, Jr. (1829-1905), who drew some inspiration from Schleiermachian sources and led the "Ethical" school in Dutch Reformed circles. Kuyper's implication that Ethical theologians thought Jesus to be human without remainder is disputable.

special grace — find a higher unity in Christ only because the eternal Son of God is behind both starting points, and that the Father together with the Son and the Holy Spirit as the triune God has himself posed this starting point and the point at which the two operations diverge. Not "the human being Jesus Christ" has created the world, but He who created the world and still maintains it entered into his clearest and highest mystical self-revelation for the sinful human heart *in* "the human being Jesus Christ." Jesus Christ did not come into the divine plan from without as a strange element enlisted as a result of our fall. Rather, the Son of God with the Father and the Holy Spirit himself determines the plan of the world. He is not enlisted *by* the Decree and *for* the execution of that Decree, but that Decree is *His.* In what people call the "eternal counsel of peace" He incorporates himself in that Decree and obligates himself to bring about its fulfillment. But just as truly as He obligates himself in the decree of redemption to be the Mediator of sinners, so in the same decree He is the Mediator of creation. Not first the Mediator of redemption and now, to achieve that role, also admitted as the Mediator of creation. But rather, first the original Mediator of creation and after that also the Mediator of redemption to make possible the enforcement and fulfillment of the decree of creation and everything entailed in it. He does not first come into being as a result of the decree but, in the order of time and thought, precedes it. He is present in its establishment. In that decree, as it pertains to all things and to himself, He determines all things so as to make their origin, development, and outcome answer to the ultimate goal of all things, that is, to his own self-glorification, along with that of the Father and the Holy Spirit.

And since the Eternal Word exists *before* the decree, is *in* the decree, and in that decree maintains the unity of creation and redemption in *his own person,* the work of redemption accomplished by special grace cannot stand isolated from the life of the world. The two, proceeding as they do from a single decree and from the self-same person in the triune Godhead, are and remain basically one. It is the same *I* of whom it is written that by him all things are created and exist, and elsewhere that by him every soul must be saved, as many as are called to [eternal] life. So also it is one and the same person who enjoys God's "common grace" in the life of society and enjoys God's "special grace" on holy ground. It is one and the same *I* who is a citizen of the country and a member of the church. It is one and the same world in which God causes his common grace to sparkle and glorifies his divine compassion in bringing people to salvation.

Therefore, common grace must have a formative impact on special grace and vice versa. All separation of the two must be vigorously opposed. Temporal and eternal life, our life in the world and our life in the church, religion and civil life, church and state, and so much more must go hand in hand. They may not be separated. To avoid such separation we must consistently make a sharp distinction between them, for it is on the correctness of this *distinction* that the progress of life depends. One senses this immediately, for example, in connection with the dispute about Article 36 [The Belgic Confession, art. XXXVI, on "Civil Government"]. You may not *separate* church and state as the Liberals demand; you may not collapse them into a single entity as the fanatics wish. Both must exist interwoven. And precisely on that account one must examine the peculiar nature and calling of each to find the correct *distinction* that determines the particular sphere of each and their interrelationship.

[Kuyper summarizes that relationship by recourse to the Scriptural *locus classicus* of his position.[11]]

. . . If, then, there is contact between the two spheres, we need to see what sort of contact it is. Arrows bound together in the same bundle touch each other only externally; this is always the case . . . with every mixture, intertwinement, and interweaving of heterogeneous things. In each of these modes of contact we are dealing with materials that have been brought together externally and only for that reason. It could be, therefore, that the spheres of common and special grace approached each other from two very different directions and finally touched each other without having any antecedent commonality between them. The case is different, however, when two branches *of the same tree* are intertwined. For then the two branches have a common origin. They share the same root-system. Before they branched out they enjoyed life in one and the same trunk.

If we consult Scripture we will find it clearly spelled out that the latter comparison applies here. Does not the apostle write to the church of Colosse that the self-same Christ is simultaneously two things: the root of the life of creation as well as the root of the life of the new creation? First we read that Christ is "the first-born of all creation, for in him all things were created, in heaven and on earth," so that he is "before all things and in him all things hold together" [Col. 1:15-17]. It could hardly be stated more plainly and clearly that Christ is the root of creation and therefore of common grace, for it is common grace that prevents things from sinking into nothingness. (Does not the text say that all things *hold together* in him?) But we immediately note in the

11. These two paragraphs are from vol. II, ch. 85: "The Contact of Sphere and Sphere," pp. 640-41.

second place that the same Christ is "the *Head of the Body* and the first-born from the dead" [Col. 1:18], hence also the root of the life of the new creation or of special grace. The two things are even stated in parallel terms: he is the root of common grace for he is *the first-born of all creation* [v. 15], and simultaneously the root of special grace, for he is the *first-born from the dead* [v. 18]. There is thus no doubt whatever that common grace and special grace come most intimately connected from their origin, and this connection lies in Christ.

B. Church and Culture

[Kuyper returns to his old church question in the ecclesiological section of volume II. His term "De Volkskerk" has been rendered here "the national church," though it should be understood in the social as well as the political sense of the original. The discussion begins in chapter 33, "The Church as Institute and as Organism," a concept of long standing in Kuyper's thought, one crucial for his church reforms in particular and emblematic of his social thought in general.[12]]

. . . *Institute* is related to *organism* as that which has been *built* to that which has *grown*. All that has been *constructed* of parts and pieces or *established* by force from without is an *institute;* an *organism,* on the other hand, is anything which its vital parts have produced on their own and which, subject to changes in its form, perpetuates and enlarges its own life.

Applying this terminology to the church of Christ, that church is an *organism* insofar as we view it in its hidden unity as the mystical body of Christ existing partly in heaven, partly on earth, and partly unborn, having penetrated all peoples and nations, possessing Christ as its natural and glorious head, and living by the Holy Spirit who as a life-engendering and life-maintaining force animates both head and members. Viewed as *institute,* on the other hand, the church is an *apparatus,* a local and temporally constructed *institution* grounded in human choices, decisions, and acts of the will, consisting of members, offices, and useful supplies. As such it is a phenomenon in the external, visible, and perceptible world, something you can see with your eyes, hear with your ears, and touch with your hands but having real substance only insofar as the mystical

12. Kuyper spelled out the concept already in his inaugural sermon in Amsterdam, *"Geworteld en gegrond"* ("Rooted and Grounded"; 1870). The material in this section comes from vol. II, pp. 249-50 and 255-56.

body of Christ lies behind it and manifests itself through it, however imperfectly. When that ceases to be the case, the institute is no longer a church except in appearance, a false church.

. . . The mystical body of Christ no more originates by gathering together a few converted persons than a plant comes into being by our wiring together some root fibers, a stem, a few leaves, and a flower. In the visible realm there is most certainly a gathering of individuals, which our Catechism has in mind when it says that "the Son of God, from the beginning of the world, gathers, defends, and preserves for himself, by his Spirit and Word, a church chosen to everlasting life" [Heidelberg Catechism Q/A 54]. But behind this act of gathering lies the *incorporation into Christ* which our Baptismal Form says already exists before our infant children are converted. This *incorporation into Christ* is directly connected with their birth in *the Covenant of Grace* which is not composed of individuals but runs genealogically through generations of men and women. Finally, the apostle Paul points to the *counsel* of God behind that *incorporation* in the *Covenant of Grace* as that by which all believers are elect in Christ *before* the foundation of the world [Eph. 1:4]. Unity and connectedness, therefore, do not come into being because individuals enter into a relationship with each other, but individuals enter into both a unity and an organic connectedness which precedes their personal existence and for which they were made and designed. We are *eternally in Christ* in accordance with the counsel of God; we are *included in the Covenant* by being in the seed of previous generations; we are in the process of being *incorporated into Christ* by the working of the Holy Spirit which precedes this process; and, finally, we are *personally drawing near to Christ* with all his saints. . . .

[Kuyper illustrates the close interconnection between the spiritual and the material from the example of human language. He concludes with a broader application of the point.]

. . . [A]ny number of *combinations* and *organic connections* unite human life into a single whole, in keeping with the original creation ordinance. The Christian religion has seized upon this to promote mutual growth into one entity as well as to advance the glory of God in that connected whole. The same is true of our life together in the home, of our life together in society, of the common world of thought, of customary practices in business, art, and science, and many more. All these are examples of life-connectedness in the human race, connections which we have not made but *find*. They exist outside of us and they exert pressure on us; we influence them but they exert a much greater influence on us. These connections are all thoroughly human at bottom and therefore cannot be denied, sloughed off, or ignored by us Christians either. The Christian spirit has put its stamp on all these connections and combinations. It has entered, modified, and transformed them, making them serviceable to its purpose. . . .

We are thoroughly misguided, therefore, if in speaking of the church of Christ (not as *institute* but as *organism*) we have our eyes fixed almost exclusively on elect persons or initiates and deliberately close them to the rich and many-sided combinations which, in the final analysis, unite the multiplicity of members into the unity of the Body. This exclusive interest in persons is the curse of nominalism that still lingers on in present-day Liberalism. Christianity is more than anything *social* in nature. Paul has pointed graphically and repeatedly to these three: *body, members,* and *connective tissue.* The church as organism has its center in Christ; it is extended in his mystical body; it individualizes itself in the members. But it no less finds its unity in those original "joints," those organic connections, which unite us human beings into one single human race, and it is on those joints that the spirit of Christ puts its stamp. Though it is true that these Christianized connections serve in common grace to restrain sin and to advance general development, their Christianization is rooted in special grace and they find their original and primary goal in the propagation of special grace.

[Kuyper next returns to his long-standing critique of the national church but underscores as well the inadequacy of the sectarian alternative, which exerted an influence, Kuyper believed, on too many of his readers.[13]]

This is the place to examine the idea and assess the phenomenon of the *national church,* because what the national church's advocates have always intended relates directly to the impact that the church and its means of grace exert upon *common grace.* These spokesmen have consistently contended that the church of Christ cannot and may not consist solely of "believers and their seed" (plus the hypocrites who have crept in) but should, if possible, include all the sons and daughters of the land. And they want this not because they are blind to the unbelief that thereby enters the church but because only by this inclusiveness can the church bless ordinary life in its wider circles and have a nurturing impact on the masses. Hence, we and they agree that Christ's church and its means of grace cover a broader field than that of special grace alone. Both sides

13. This section is from vol. II, ch. 34, "The National Church," pp. 256-57, 259-62.

acknowledge that the church does two things: (1) it works *directly* for the well-being of the elect, lures them to conversion, comforts, edifies, unites, and sanctifies them; but (2) it works *indirectly* for the well-being of the whole of civil society, constraining it to civic virtue. We differ in how to reach that good goal: *they* include civil society in the church, whereas *we* place the church as a city on a hill amid civil society.

Let us not stumble over words: our interest is in the issue. It is certain that the national church system aims to absorb the entire population of a country into the church as quickly and comprehensively as this can be done. The system we advocate aims to distinguish the church from civil society, to admit to the church only "believers and their offspring," and to tolerate hypocrites only insofar as they cannot be unmasked, with the expectation that the comparatively small circle of the church will radiate influence upon civil life outside the church. We trust this clearly states the contrast in a way that avoids misunderstanding, does full justice to the sentiments of our opponents, . . . and makes clear how the idea of the national church pertains directly to the present discussion of one part of "common grace." . . .

[Kuyper gives a historical review of the national church's predominance since the Emperor Constantine, then takes up the sectarian alternative.]

The more deliberate and persistent opposition to the idea of the national church has, unfortunately, come almost exclusively from the side of spiritualistic sects. Over and over in history we see small separatistic groups who want nothing to do with the national church but who, in opposing it, fall into the opposite extreme of denying the covenant of God, abolishing infant baptism, tearing apart nature and spirit, and letting the church be solely oriented to heaven — meanwhile, turning their back on ordinary human life in spiritual one-sidedness and presumptuous pride.

The last feature defines the very essence of sectarianism. For though the word "sect" has been applied to any group that separated itself from the national church, such separation is not its true distinguishing mark. If it were, there would always be but one *real* church and all other Christian denominations would be sectarian. But this cannot be the position of a Protestant. Never have Lutherans and Reformed, Episcopalians and Nonconformists, Methodists and Presbyterians seriously contended that a person cannot be saved in one of the other Christian denominations. From the beginning the Protestant creed — which is directly opposed to the idea of one salvific church institution — carried the multiplicity of churches in its bosom and acknowledged differences which, though they may not be ignored, do not decide a person's eternal weal or woe. No, a group is a *sect* only when it puts itself outside the context of *human life.* It becomes a sect when a certain number of individuals locate their fellowship outside the life of humanity and view themselves as a tiny holy circle that has remained on earth by mistake and really has nothing to do with the life that is lived down here. That circle is a sect only when it ceases to confess Jesus as *the Son of man.* And since it cannot be denied that precisely the sects have most firmly opposed both the idea and the phenomenon of the national church, the national church has derived no small advantage from being able to pose the choice: "either stay with us or become a sect." In our country too, since 1834 and 1886 the spokesmen of the national church have consistently charged us with the Labadist intent of forming a sectarian circle composed solely of saints. When in 1886 the Synod of The Hague condemned and expelled Dr. Kuyper, the main indictment against him was taken from a phrase in his *Confidentie* in which he pleaded for a "little flock" [Luke 12:32] in the midst of the world, distorting his idea as though he had advocated sectarianism.[14]

Although the struggle against the national church has to be waged under most unfavorable circumstances, we may not desist from it. But conducting that struggle strictly on a spiritual basis offers a weak case. It is perfectly true that the church is the "gathering of believers" and that, however broadly this term is applied, it has no room for *un*believers or *non*-believers. But the *confession of the Covenant,* which in turn is bound up with the *organic bond between generations,* gives rise to tangible difficulty here. If one adopts a Pelagian posture, holds exclusively to the existence of individual persons, and posits that only those who personally profess Christ as their Savior belong in the church, one indeed has the means of determining who does and who does not belong to the church — but one also comes into immediate conflict with the Covenant, with the bond between generations, and hence with the practice of child baptism. If, on the other hand, one is convinced on the basis of Scripture (1) that the covenant idea may not be abandoned, (2) that the bond between believers

14. "Labadist" refers to the teachings of Jean de Labadie (1610-74), an eminent figure in seventeenth-century Dutch pietism. His drive to fashion a spotless community of the "reborn" made him controversial at the time and made his name a lasting epithet with which strict reformers in the Dutch National Church were often branded, as Kuyper's reference to the Secession of 1834 and Doleantie of 1886 indicates. Notice as well that by this point in his career Kuyper is referring to himself in print in the third person.

and their offspring is a holy organic connection which must be strictly honored, and (3) that, consequently, a church which holds exclusively to adult baptism proceeds from a false principle, this individualistic position simply proves untenable. The same path also loses the Scriptural teaching that the church has significance *for the world,* for the development of human life, for civil society and its natural life potential.

A narrow mutual-appraisal society, existing in isolation from its own generation, eventually loses all connection with the life of the world and locks itself into a box of spiritual one-sidedness. History has confirmed this phenomenon over and over; given the principle involved, it cannot be otherwise. Those who under various names have isolated themselves as *Plymouth Brethren,* for example, have vigorously and sharply opposed the national church as a disgusting falsification of the true church idea, a falsification that had led to Satanic aberrations. But in the process they confused the idea of the "church" with that of the "national church," turned in principle against the idea of "church" in any form, and now only want to form "dear, devout fellowships." Precisely by this mistaken course of action they placed themselves outside the flow of history. While intent upon a lovely peace for their own soul, they otherwise exist in isolation in all countries and have deprived themselves of any influence on the course of events.

The struggle against the national church can be undertaken fruitfully and in hope of better results only when one opposes the idea of the national church with a better, purer, more Scriptural church concept. In formulating such, one attempts to do justice to the idea of covenant, notes not only individuals but also the organic bond between generations, and clearly indicates in what way the church of Christ, by accepting its proper boundaries, can nevertheless be a blessing to the ordinary life of humanity. This is possible only on a Calvinistic basis because only the Reformed have clearly perceived the distinction between "special grace" and "common grace." As long as one remains blind to this distinction, one can know no other grace than that existing within the circle of the church. One is therefore virtually *obligated* to incorporate, if possible, all one's fellow citizens if one does not wish to abandon civil society to demonic powers. This last point is no exaggeration. Sin brings a curse, and where a curse predominates demonic powers have free rein. Now if only *grace* can avert a curse and block the superior power of the demonic, then one of two things must happen: either grace must be at work outside the church, or all that lies outside and cannot be absorbed in the church remains bereft of grace and so helplessly in bondage to the curse. "Exorcism" is then the natural means applied by the church to break this power, to withdraw a part of the world from bondage to the curse and bring it under grace. Even the plot of ground at stake must then be consecrated, for there too the world is divided in two parts: one *consecrated*, the other *not;* and all that is not consecrated remains outside the sphere of grace. All this ends, however, the moment one sees that there definitely *is* a *grace* operating outside the church, that there is *grace* even where it does not lead to eternal salvation, and that we are therefore duty-bound to honor an operation of divine grace in human civic life by which the curse of sin, and sin itself, is restrained even though the link with salvation is lacking.

[Kuyper now proceeds to the heart of the dilemma: how to keep the church reasonably pure but also publicly influential.[15]]

"National church" and "church as organism" (as distinct from institute) stand in much greater an antithesis than is usually perceived.

The national church preaches the principle that an entire people, an entire nation, must be incorporated into the church by baptism, not because the whole population believes or may be supposed to believe, even though brazen unbelief has broken out not only among the members but among the officebearers and boards, and even though everybody knows that the real believers comprise no more than a painfully small number among the large masses of people. National church proponents defend this public lie in two ways. First, they say in antinomian fashion that the modification of sinful conditions is not a task to which the transgressors themselves are entitled but must wait until God himself directly intervenes to remove the sin. Secondly, they point to the many good things that accrue from continuing such a mixture, perhaps not to the church but certainly to the nation and the life of its society. The latter is apparently the goal and the essential thing, while the former is nothing but an excuse to justify acquiescence in this false synthesis before the bar of conscience.

They would dearly love — in the idiom of the national church — to "sanitize" the situation, but alas! that is impossible. So it has always been and so it always will be. They groan under a fatal law which dictates that *everything fermenting in the fatherland must have its effect in the church.* Therefore the church of Christ or the Gospel does not act as a yeast in the life of the world but, contrariwise, the principle of the world must ferment in Christ's church. Before that fearful law people are powerless. Christ's church no longer has any guiding principle or controlling spirit, not even a center from which action can proceed. The church as a body

15. This section comes from vol. II, ch. 35: "The Church's Radiancy in the World," pp. 264-65, 267-68.

is frozen into one inert mass simply because its composition militates against the absolute ABC of church principle. On the other hand, civil society — "the world," if you please — definitely remains in its element and is not the least bit hampered in its action, so its principle is at full strength. And where such action surges up from the life of the people, often directly counter to the gospel, a dull anemic church has no choice but to let it wash over its own premises. The sooty fog of this process, coating everything it touches, robs the church of its color and glow. . . .

This, then, is the system of the *national church.* Directly opposed to it is the system of the *church as organism.* . . . It maintains that the blessing of Christianity can only be truly effective in the wider circle [of human life] if the institutional church organizes itself in accordance with the demand of Scripture, if Baptism as an ecclesiastical sacrament is administered only to believers and their offspring, and if church discipline is consistently exercised to purify the church. Accordingly, they distinguish between the church as *organism* and the church as *institute* in order that *both* may come into their own: both the sanctity of the covenant among those who confess Christ *and* the influence that should impinge upon the world outside this circle.

This is impossible from the national-church standpoint, which recognizes only one circle, the circle of the church as institute. . . . But we believe there are two circles. First the circle of confessors, the objective church, the circle of the covenant. According to the Heidelberg Catechism, Baptism is extended solely to this first circle — that baptized children may be *"distinguished from the children of unbelievers"* (Q/A 74). The Lord's Supper is administered only within that circle, and solely within that circle can a "gathering of believers" be honored. Only the church that coincides with this circle can therefore possess the marks of the "true church" which are "the pure preaching of the gospel, the pure administration of the sacraments, and the exercise of church discipline both as to confession and the conduct of life" (Belgic Confession, art. XXIX).

But we cannot stop here. This institute does not cover everything that is Christian. Though the lamp of the Christian religion only burns within that institute's walls, its light shines out through its windows to areas far beyond, illumining all the sectors and associations that appear across the wide range of human life and activity. Justice, law, the home and family, business, vocation, public opinion and literature, art and science, and so much more are all illuminated by that light, and that illumination will be stronger and more penetrating as the lamp of the gospel is allowed to shine more brightly and clearly in the church institute.

Aside from this first circle of the institute and in necessary connection with it, we thus recognize another circle whose circumference is determined by the length of the ray that shines out from the church institute over the life of people and nation. Since this second circle is not attached to particular persons, is not circumscribed by a certain number of people listed in church directories, and does not have its own office-bearers but is interwoven with the very fabric of national life, this extra-institutional influence at work in society points us to the *church as organism*. That church, after all, exists before the institute; it lies behind the institute; it alone gives substance and value to that institute. The church as organism has its center in heaven, in Christ; it encompasses all ages from the beginning of the world to the end so as to fulfill all the ages coming after us. The church as organism may even manifest itself where all personal faith is missing but where nevertheless some of the golden glow of eternal life is reflected on the ordinary façades of the great edifice of human life. . . .

[The broad influence of a disciplined church is not only theoretically possible, Kuyper argues, but practically auspicious. Notably, the title he gives this chapter (vol. II, no. 36), "A City on a Hill," is resonant in the history of the United States, to which Kuyper appeals at the end of this chapter — the end as well of his treatment of ecclesiology.[16]]

Precisely because the church, in Jesus's words, is a city set on a hill, its light must extend over a wide area. To put it in plain prose, a sanctifying and purifying influence must proceed from the church of the Lord to impact the whole society amid which it operates. That influence must begin by arousing a certain admiration for the heroic courage with which it has borne persecution and oppression. Next it must inspire respect for the earnestness and purity of life lived in church circles. It must further excite feelings of sympathy by the warm glow of love and compassion in the community of faith. And finally, as a result of all this, it must purify and ennoble the ideas in general circulation, elevate public opinion, introduce more solid principles, and so raise the view of life prevailing in state, society, and the family. In fact this has historically been the case. The church of Christ has almost nowhere established a lasting presence without also modifying the general outlook on life beyond its institutional walls. This certainly did not happen overnight for, as a rule, the church initially had to endure a period of persecution. But once that phase had been splendidly surmounted, its public and private conduct usually —

16. This material comes from vol. II, pp. 271-75.

one can say: almost without exception — led to the elevation of the standards of life. The result was twofold: (1) the establishment of the church as a "city set on a hill"; and (2) a process by which civic life outside the church was gradually elevated and purified. And in that twofold outcome we behold the natural fruit of a twofold grace: the fruit of *special grace* in that "city set on a hill" and the fruit of *common grace* in that ennobled society.

Granted: one can apply the demands of the highest ideal here and break into complaints about the spiritual wretchedness of the churches and the rapid degradation of society. We will be the last to deny that there is often reason for such complaints. But the love of your ideal may not tempt you to yield to a morbid and demoralizing pessimism. Undoubtedly, even the most properly instituted church, at home or abroad, leaves much to be desired; but by comparison with so many other churches, especially compared to many other religious corporations, it still ranks very high and is a source of profound gratitude. Again, we have every reason to complain about an accumulation of abuses, crimes, and horrors without number in our civil society, but if you place it alongside a pagan or Muslim society you immediately sense our superiority, sometimes at every point. Take marriage, for instance. Compare the position of the married woman under paganism and Islam with what exists among us, and you are immediately struck by a big difference. . . . And so it is in every area. With the appearance of the church of Christ a leaven was hidden in three measures of meal [Matt. 13:33], a leaven which keeps working and affects all relationships of life. This influence is absolutely not restricted to the confessors of Christ but extends to the whole of society, so that Jews as well as unbelievers among us undergo this effect without reflecting on it. Precisely this proves the error of viewing it as a manifestation of special grace. Special grace always leads to eternal life, but what is at work here is completely bound up in time and is therefore to be considered under the rubric of common grace.

. . . [By contrast, the broad Christianity of the national church collaborates with its apparent opposite, militant secularism.] Today new attempts are being made to nullify the church's influence on civil society. This is evident from the efforts being made to substitute free love for marriage or at least to undermine the marriage bond. It is evident as well from attempts to weaken parental authority, to put the upbringing of children under state control, and so forth. This development must be laid at the doorstep of the church. By acting as national church almost everywhere, it has had to admit deception into its own bosom, has thereby fallen into all sorts of false relationships, and can no longer exert the natural influence it once had. Today, it will even ally itself with the opponents of Christianity to frustrate those who argue in favor of Christian influence. As a result those who work for the Christian character of state and society labor under a severe disadvantage in the performance of their duty, all the more so since many still cannot conceive of any other Christianization than to gather everybody into one church and to "baptize" society institutionally.

We can exert power for good, therefore, only if we are prepared to drum it into our heads that the church of Christ can never exert influence on civil society directly, only indirectly. Therefore its goal must remain (1) to assure the church full freedom of action and full authority to maintain its own unique character; (2) to avert any attempt to introduce pagan concepts and ideas into the country's laws, public institutions, and public opinion in place of Christian ones; and (3) to continually expand the dominance of nobler and purer ideas in civil society by the courageous action of its members in every area of life. In a nutshell: what we want is a strong confessional church but *not* a confessional civil society *nor* a confessional state.

This secularization of state and society is one of the most basic ideas of Calvinism, though it did not succeed in immediately and completely working out this idea in pure form. Acting on a scene which for centuries cherished the exact opposite, Calvinism had no choice but to develop its basic idea step by painful step. Nevertheless, this idea is gaining ground at every step, and the progressive development in the life of the nations increasingly allows the secularization of state and society to come into its own. It cannot be gainsaid that the false idea of the French Revolution temporarily interrupted this process, thwarting the further impact of the Calvinist idea. But this does not alter the fact that Calvinism from its own roots produced the conviction that the church of Christ cannot be a national church because it had to be rigorously confessional and maintain Christian discipline, and that the Christian character of society therefore cannot be secured by the baptism of the whole citizenry but is to be found in the influence that the church of Christ exerts upon the whole organization of national life. By its influence on the state and civil society the church of Christ aims only at a *moral triumph,* not at the imposition of confessional bonds nor at the exercise of authoritarian control. The example of the United States of America, accordingly, demonstrates how the various divisions of the Christian church, the moment they unitedly adopt this position, not only give up fighting among themselves in order to contend together peacefully in matters of faith, but also that precisely these good mutual relations enable them to exert a much greater influence on civil and national conditions than the most powerful national church ever could.

. . . Generally speaking, the religion of a given nation has always and everywhere put its own unique stamp on the mores and customs, on the laws and controlling ideas of that nation. This being the case, there is nothing strange about the fact that wherever the Christian religion asserts itself, it exerts a similar influence. Religion is and will always be the expression of what is central in our lives. However degenerate and obscured a people's religion may be, you will always find expressed in it their fundamental ethos. In any given case this ethos will be bound up with a people's character and nature, with its history, even with the conditions of the soil on which it lives and the climate in which it breathes. For that reason alone the liberals' assertion that we must seek our future well-being in the separation of church and state, of religion and nation, of our spiritual life and our civil life is such irritating folly. . . . After all, both parties, humanist and Christian, very well understand religion's great importance for the basic values of the nation and vice versa, but the humanist parties are bent on converting the Christian character of those underlying values into one that fits their humanistic system. Thus one can clearly distinguish two periods in their opposition to the Christian parties: an early period in which they contested the right of religion to exert influence on *public* life; and a second period in which they contended *for* that influence. The two periods differed in that earlier the influence of the old religion was still against them, while in the second period a modernized religion supported them. . . .

Vol. II, ch. 90: "The Perfecting of Common Grace," pp. 671-72

[At the conclusion of vol. II, Kuyper sketches a typology of societies based on different relationships or combinations of special and common grace. But first he warns against a prevalent misunderstanding in this regard.[17]]

. . . Terms such as "a Christian nation," "a Christian country," "a Christian society," "Christian art," and the like, do not mean that such a nation consists mainly of regenerate Christian persons or that such a society has already been transposed into the kingdom of heaven. This was never the

17. This paragraph comes from vol. II, ch. 89: "The Goal of the Church on Earth," pp. 661-62.

case anywhere. Even in Israel the great majority was always apostate and idolatrous and the "faithful" always a rather small minority. No, it means that in such a country special grace in the church and among believers exerted so strong a formative influence on common grace that common grace thereby attained its highest development. The adjective "Christian" therefore says nothing about the spiritual state of the inhabitants of such a country but only witnesses to the fact that public opinion, the general mind-set, the ruling ideas, the moral norms, the laws and customs there clearly betoken the influence of the Christian faith. Though this is attributable to special grace, it is manifested on the terrain of common grace, i.e., in ordinary civil life. This influence leads to the abolition of slavery in the laws and life of a country, to the improved position of women, to the maintenance of public virtue, respect for the Sabbath, compassion for the poor, consistent regard for the ideal over the material, and — even in manners — the elevation of all that is human from its sunken state to a higher standpoint. . . .

[Kuyper proceeds to his typology, concluding on the images from the Sermon on the Mount that have wound through his entire treatment of common grace.[18]]

We must be careful to distinguish four terrains. First, the terrain of common grace that has not yet undergone any influence of special grace. Second, the terrain of the institutional church that as such arises totally and exclusively from special grace. Third, the terrain of common grace that is illumined by the light emitted by the lamp of special grace. Fourth, the terrain of special grace that has utilized the data of common grace.

China is an example of the first terrain. Common grace operates there in no small measure but special grace has not yet influenced that gigantic empire to the extent of changing Chinese life. Or, to look at our own setting, think of the broadly developed terrain of sports which still lives solely from the forces of common grace and pays no attention to any higher standard. The second terrain manifests itself in those instituted churches that avoid all usurpation and limit themselves to fulfilling their own task. Of the third terrain you can find any number of examples in all Christian churches of Europe and America where a wide variety of customs, usages, mores, and laws are current that clearly manifest the influence of divine revelation and are followed by a broad class of people who personally want nothing to do with faith or conversion. Finally, you

18. This material is from vol. II, ch. 90, "The Perfecting of Common Grace," pp. 676-78.

find the fourth terrain wherever the church as organism manifests itself, i.e., where the personal confessors of Jesus in their own circle allow the life of common grace to be controlled by the principles of divine revelation. In that sense we speak of Christian art, a Christian school, a Christian press, Christian scholarship, etc., but there the word "Christian" has a very different and much more specific meaning than where people speak of a Christian nation, a Christian people, Christian states, etc.

So then, juxtapose life in China, life in the institute of a Christian church, the life of non-confessors in a Christian country, and the life of Christ-confessors outside of the church institute. Take this fourfold life not in reference to unconnected individuals but in its social and organic connectedness, and the four distinct terrains lie clearly before you. Of the first Scripture says "that the world lies in the power of the evil one" [1 John 5:19]. The second occurs in Scripture as the church endowed with offices. The third Scripture refers to as the part of the world that is illuminated by the light of believers. And the fourth Jesus calls the "three measures of meal" [Matt. 13:33] which the leaven of the Gospel has leavened through and through.

Still, there is an acute danger of confusing particularly the two last terrains with each other; in fact, that happens all the time. The majority of people do not even grasp the difference between the two images Jesus employed in this regard, that of the light shining out and that of the leaven. Preachers in their Sunday sermons tend to neglect the distinction, . . . yet it is clear. When the kingdom of heaven is compared to a mustard seed which grows into a tree in whose branches all kinds of birds build nests, those birds remain alien to the nature of the tree that has shot up from the soil. On the other hand, when a leaven has permeated the three measures of meal, then that meal has been basically transformed by the leaven. The former is based on merely external contact, the latter on internal kinship. The sower sows the seed which mingles with the minerals of the soil and the chemicals of the air, a process that produces fruit. All salt does is stop decay. So also with the light that shines out into the world. Of that process we read in Matthew 5:14-16: "You are the light of the world. A city set on a hill cannot be hid. Nor do men light a lamp and put it under a bushel, but on a stand, and it gives light to all in the house. Let your light so shine before men, that they may see your good works and give glory to your Father who is in heaven." Hence the world does not climb up to the city, nor does the city descend into the world. The two remain distinct and separate but the light of the city shines out into the world. The candle and the people in the house remain separate but the people in the house receive the candle's light on the retina of their eyes. Similarly, believers emit light upon other human beings, but even so the believers who emit the light and the people who receive the light are two distinct kinds of people. Hence the distinctions we made above are not arbitrary but rooted in Scripture itself.

POLITICS AND SOCIETY

Maranatha

No single statement better captures the themes, the tone, and the purpose of Kuyper's politics than the following address with which he opened the Antirevolutionary Party convention at Utrecht in 1891. This is fitting, for the party at the moment stood at a crossroads, and there was nothing Kuyper liked better than a definitive situation.

First, the pending national elections would be a referendum on the party's first term in power. The constitutional revision of 1887 had doubled the size of the electorate, and the newly enfranchised lower-middle class (males) gave the Roman Catholic and Antirevolutionary forces a majority in the States-General. The coalition moved immediately on key grievances, passing an education act that permitted state aid to religious schools and a labor bill that mandated state protection of vulnerable workers. The cabinet foundered, however, on an Antirevolutionary proposal (opposed by the Catholics) to outlaw the purchase of exemptions from military service. That precipitated the 1891 elections.

Second, the very success of Kuyper's strategy caused some strains in his organization. The church quarrels to which Kuyper twice alludes below involved both National Church loyalists embittered by the Doleantie in 1886 and old Seceders suspicious of his overtures for union with them (effected in 1892). These voices and others, moreover, were strongly averse to his coalition with Catholics, deeming it a sell-out of national history, political freedom, and Protestant principles. Kuyper thus had to pluck several strings two ways at once. The text shows how well he performed.

Finally, and most significantly, the party faced a fundamental choice about future direction. Full-scale industrialization and its concomitant agricultural depression were now twenty years old in the Netherlands, and the pain they bred could be ignored no longer. Hence the coalition's social legislation of 1889, the Christian Social Congress Kuyper was helping to organize for November 1891, and — European-wide — Pope Leo XIII's great social encyclical of the same year, *Rerum Novarum*. In short, social as well as political democratization was on the table. Kuyper's genius in this speech was to free it from its Revolutionary connotations, save it as well from knee-jerk Christian conservatism, and make its realization a duty before God.

Kuyper's rhetorical prowess swept the 700-plus delegates in the hall this May day in 1891, but his coalition lost the summer elections and the Antirevolutionary Party split a few years later over the issue of franchise extension. *Maranatha* is therefore a high-water mark of Antirevolutionary confidence and unity. It evokes the national-Christian memory and old Calvinist heroes that inspired the movement, spells out the political-philosophical assumptions that guided it, and turns all these toward a truly modern future of pluralism and democracy. Kuyper's deft alignment of Conservative, Liberal, and Radical as common kin on a single line is a particularly memorable achievement and should caution the reader from simply equating the "Liberalism" Kuyper denounces with the "liberalism" of today; in fact, Kuyper had in mind some of what currently passes for "conservative" policy.

The text was first published as *Maranatha. Rede ter inleiding van de Deputatenvergadering op 12 Mei 1891* (Amsterdam: J. A. Wormser, 1891), and is reproduced here complete. The translation is by John Vriend. All biblical quotations were italicized in the original.

ONCE AGAIN, men and brothers, in keeping with our custom, I take the liberty as your chairman to open your convention with a brief, fraternal address.

With the day of Jesus' Ascension just behind us, the note I wish to strike in this speech is *Maranatha: our Lord is coming!* For, however divergent our respective church ideals may be, we were all touched a few minutes ago when, before our prayer, we heard of the "bride of the Lamb clothed in fine linen, bright and pure" [Rev. 19:7-8]. For a second we imagined ourselves caught up in that splendid moment at which I trust every one of us will be present, when *he* returns from the heavens on whose head the glorious crown of David will forever rest and on whose thigh is inscribed the name "Lord of lords and King of Kings" [Rev. 19:16]. Sometimes our soul is surprised by a longing for that future in which not a single note of discord will ever divide us again and in which the

Kuyper as political leader: a bold style (and short stature) befitting a new Napoleon, rhetorically armed for combat, yet also the lonely watcher on the walls of Calvinism.

quiet attraction of a love that flows from God will forever unite us with "the Lamb that was slain" [Rev. 5:12] and with all his saints and martyrs. Yes, even now, as we consider that happy prospect, we all honor the divinely anointed king. It is our fidelity to him who is called *"Faithful* and *True"* [Rev. 19:11] that *brings* us and *binds* us together.

The *destination* of a journey always determines the *road* you have to take. If for you and me that destination is wrapped up in the final catastrophe which is scheduled to occur when Jesus returns to this earth, then the cry of *Maranatha* is the crossroads where our road and that of our opponents diverge. To them the return of the Lord is an illusion hardly worth the laughter of ridicule; to us it is the glorious end of history — also the history of our national existence — which we invoke with the laughter of a holy joy. To plunge immediately into the purpose of our convention: To us it is the decisive fact of the future by which not only

Kuyper's critics saw his politics as pure self-interest. Here the prime-ministerial dog with his favorite bone, the "Higher Education Act" that would give equal status to the Free University.

our *spiritual life* but also our *political* course of conduct is utterly controlled. For what does the *Maranatha* cry imply? Just this: that, when the history of nations will have exhausted itself and cannot continue, the king anointed by God will appear to intervene in the life of all nations and therefore also in the life of *our* nation, to strike his sickle also into the harvest of *our* national life, and *to destroy* the anti-Christian world power with the breath of his mouth (2 Thess. 2:8).

Now of this reality the Conservative, the Liberal, the Radical, and the Socialist have no inkling. Although among these groups a few stray individuals seek out the cross of Golgotha for the forgiveness of their sins, even for them the Man of Sorrows has no place whatsoever in the context of our national history. They refuse to acknowledge Jesus' royal authority in the sphere of politics. For them religion and politics are two totally different things. If you ask these fellow citizens — those who

In this "three-star" of 8 March 1882 Kuyper criticized Conservative concepts and tactics.

Fishing in Muddy Waters

The conservative papers in both capitals, real snigglers but without an eel in their well, have suddenly pushed their boat toward our reeds, tossed aside their worms, and are now waiting, trammel in hand, to see if any fish from our bulrushes will dart over to their side.

We cannot promise anything tasty from this approach.

Groen lived too long and *De Standaard* has editorialized too much to let our people so quickly forget that the conservative coterie is nothing but an inconsistent bunch of liberals — liberals disguised or watered-down, rootless and devoid of any meat of their own, and therefore doomed to disappear.

Still, they'll probably catch a thing or two. From time to time a number of unprincipled sorts from their camp have slithered over toward us, but in the long run they tend not to stick it out. Now they'll probably sneak back again, under water.

A good fisherman separates his catch into two batches: one for the market, the other for the cat. Now of these *catfish* the odd little minnow is almost bound to get caught in their net. That's a piece of good luck for the conservative pussycat. We'll just keep the perch.

totally reject the Christ of the Scriptures or those who fail to honor him as the divinely anointed king over all nations and peoples — where things are headed with the world and its history, they will either tell you they haven't the slightest idea or they will drivel on about a never-ending, ever-ongoing evolution by which the human race will ascend to an ever higher state of well-being.

This is *not* the conviction of one who confesses Christ in accordance with the Scriptures. He knows that there will be an *end* just as there was a *beginning,* and that *both* are determined by God. He knows that the nations pass through a history, the turning point of which is the cross of Golgotha. He knows and confesses that the Hope of humanity, who died on that cross, soon arose again, ascended into heaven, and now sits there

In a "three-star" of 7 June 1897, Kuyper mocked the Liberals' use of biblical metaphor against the Catholic-Calvinist coalition. The *Nederlander* belonged to ex-Antirevolutionary dissenters.

Where Is Samson?

The [Liberal Amsterdam] *Handelsblad* is elated over "the jawbone of an ass" to which its editor was alerted by the *Nederlander*.

Catholics and Antirevolutionaries, it cries out in ecstasy, once fought each other like "Philistines" and "men of Judah," but today help each other tie up the *liberal Samson.* They'll be sorry. For this Samson too will soon reach for his "ass's jawbone" and slay them "heap upon heap, more than a thousand men" [Judges 15:15-16].

Reading this we thought: Yes indeed; *if* the Liberals had a Samson, they might still do miracles. But it's just their luck that no Samson has risen up among them; that — to use Bible-language ourselves — they often make one think of the men Nahum 2:4 describes: *"they rush back and forth in the squares; they dart like lightning."*

In other words: they *have* no leader. All that remains is "the jawbone of an ass." Hardly a choice weapon, it would seem, for the noble tourney of the ballot box.

at the right hand of God clothed with authority and power over all peoples and nations. And, persuaded by the Word of God, he also has the unwavering conviction that this divinely anointed king, whose authority and power is still being denied, misjudged, and resisted by the spirit of the age, will return from heaven on a day and hour fixed by God for this purpose, to break all resistance, to do away with those who oppose him, and to give this earth as an inheritance to the meek who have understood and put into practice the summons: "Kiss the Son" (Ps. 2:12).

This conviction determines the course of his conduct also in the politics of this nation. For however fanciful the expectation of the Lord's coming may seem to those on the outside, even the most radical unbeliever, if he is a logical thinker, will have to grant that it would be utterly absurd for a person to take such a confession of Christ on his lips and ignore the consequences that flow directly from it for our national politics. If you confessed a Christ only for the salvation of your soul, it would be different. But now that you speak of a Christ to whom has been given "all power in heaven and on earth," in whose hand lies also the destiny of peoples and states, who compels the nations to choose also as nations for or against him, who will return in person (who knows how soon?) clothed with divine power to intervene in the history of all nations and hence to put an end to their political existence — then obviously it will not do to confess all this of peoples and nations without applying it to *your own nation*, without taking account of it in the Netherlands *even today*.

So what is it we have been *told* by Jesus and *foretold* by his holy apostles concerning the end of history? Does the program they unfurled concerning the history of the nations offer a preview of progressive Christianization so that, when Jesus returns, he will find them as one kneeling under the shadow of his cross? A sacred state of happiness prevailing everywhere on earth? You know better, for you know Jesus' melancholy question: "And when the Son of man comes, will he find faith on earth?" [Luke 18:8]. You are no less familiar with the prophecy of such anxious and appalling trials that "if those days had not been cut short, even the elect would be led astray" [cf. Matt. 24:22, 24]. No, the opposite is true. We are told that a great apostasy awaits us. That "the rulers of the earth will take counsel together against the Lord and his anointed to burst their bonds asunder and cast their cords from them" [cf. Ps. 2:2-3]. That all kinds of unholy spirits will agitate against God's will and law. That in the end this opposition will culminate in the advent of an appalling *anti-Christian* world-power which, if Christ did not break it, would rip this whole world forever out of the hands of its God and away from its own destiny.

It is this knowledge and nothing else that compels Christians in the Netherlands to ask whether also in the history of our nation and in the political policy of our people we cannot already discern the signs and birth-pains heralding this anti-Christian development. It is a question to which Bilderdijk and Da Costa and Groen van Prinsterer[1] gave the per-

1. Kuyper was here invoking the three successive ideological leaders of the confessional Calvinist political movement. William Bilderdijk (1756-1831), an exile during the French occupation of the Netherlands, became the leading Dutch poet of the Restoration upon his return, introducing Romantic themes and styles but also conveying an emphatically monarchial, Calvinist, and antirevolutionary vision of politics and culture. Isaac da Costa (1798-1860), a Portuguese-Jewish convert to Christianity under Bilderdijk's inspiration, did much to define the antirevolutionary cause over the second quarter of the century as a poet, essayist, lecturer, and author of a multivolume biblical commentary. After the 1848 revolutions and Dutch constitutional reform, leadership passed to Guillaume Groen van Prinsterer (1801-76), a

tinent answer: that in the theory and practice of the Revolution which broke out in 1789, this anti-Christian power became principally manifest. Not as if Europe was again being inundated by the paganism of antiquity, for men like Aeschylus and Plato never stood over against the Christ. Much worse, it was the emergence of a spirit that stole into the historical life of nations and fundamentally set their heart against Christ as the God-anointed king. Nor at the end of the previous century did the Netherlands reject this false principle at its borders as contraband but *welcomed* it. The leading class forced it upon our baptized nation, and like a toxic fluid it seeped into nearly all our institutions, laws, and customs. It was a national sin which in *our* case is all the less pardonable because in no other country had the Christian principle gained such command as in the Netherlands.

Since then events have all too clearly confirmed the correctness of the view that Bilderdijk, Da Costa, and Groen van Prinsterer had of the situation both inside and outside our country. The revolution in Paris proved to be not just a change in *regime* but a change of *system,* of political *organization,* of general human *theory.* In place of the worship of the most high God came, courtesy of Humanism, the worship of *man.* Human destiny was shifted from *heaven* to *earth.* The Scriptures were unraveled and the Word of God shamefully repudiated in order to pay homage to the majesty of *Reason.* The institution of the church was twisted into an instrument for undermining the faith and later for destroying it. The public school had to wean the rising generation away from the piety of our fathers. Universities have been refashioned into institutions at which Darwinism violates the spiritual nobility of humanity by denying its creation in the image of God. Hedonism replaced heaven-mindedness. And *emancipation* become the watchword by which people tampered with the bond of marriage, with the respect children owe their parents, with the moral seriousness of our national manners. This went on until first Philosophy, then Socialism raised its voice. The former replaced *certainty* in our hearts with *doubt;* the latter, logically developing upper-class liberal theory, applied to the *money* and *goods* of the owners what the liberal already had the audacity to do against God and his anointed King.

Is then the anti-Christian character of this century already pure and unadulterated? The answer of Scripture and history is uniformly negative. We are told in Scripture that this anti-Christian power will manifest itself in all its naked brutality only *toward the end,* that what precedes that end

---

historian, political theorist, and one-time secretary to King William I. Groen's theoretical contributions were not matched by organizational acumen, which Kuyper supplied by such conventions as he was addressing on this occasion.

will still be veiled. The facts bear this out. Even the dreadful revolution that broke out in Paris undeniably displayed a good side — not in its *principle* but in its *effect.* Nor in our own country would you be entirely fair if you failed to appreciate our Conservatives' *historical bent,* neglected to honor our Liberals' *love of liberty,* overlooked the Radicals' *sense of justice,* and counted as nothing the nobler Socialists' *compassion* with so much indescribable misery. We therefore do not cast any slur on our opponents personally, nor do we stigmatize the *conscious* motive that drives and stimulates them. What we take exception to and resist is solely their disastrous *principle,* which is detached from Christ and which is the same in all these groups. Together they form single spiritual family, bred from a single stock. The father of the *Liberal* is called *Conservative,* the offspring of the *Liberal* presents himself as a *Radical,* and the *Socialist* is the legitimate child in the third generation.

Our opponents do not understand this because they think that there is no Satan and therefore no Satanic influence working in peoples and persons to set them against Christ. But *you* understand this. From the Lord's Prayer you have learned the petition: *"Deliver us from the evil one."* For that reason you have no difficulty firmly denouncing the *unholy principle* operative in the spirit of this age, while at the same time thanking the Lord for much this age has produced, continuing to love your opponents personally as your fellow citizens, indeed, not abandoning all hope for their conversion. Only one thing the cry of *Maranatha* has irrevocably instilled in you: you may not accede to their counsel. You may not join them or connive with them. Nor may you abandon the country to them. Rather, all those who love Christ and await his return from heaven must heartily unite with all sincere believers in the land to resist their philosophy and to rescue the country from their pernicious influence. And this you must do — do you confess it with me? — not by might nor by power but only in a lawful way driven by the Spirit of the Lord alone.

Therefore let everyone ambitious to gain honor or power for himself, to secure a high post or monetary advantage, pack his bags and leave us. The hand that reaches out for personal advantage cannot clasp the banner of the cross. You who would march as a hero in this conflict: your concern must be for Christ and his future, and in light of that future, for the salvation of your country. You must be driven by a quiet passion to throw up a dam against the rising influence of the anti-Christian principle. All your energies must be devoted to strengthening the power for Christ that still resides in our people. What urges you on must be the passionate desire to prepare a people who, at Christ's return, will not strive against him but welcome him with Hallelujahs — here, on this nation's soil which is soaked with the blood of martyrs.

So then, you see the need for the rise of our Antirevolutionary party, and at the same time a sketch of its purpose. If Jesus was just the Savior of our soul and not at the same time the King of Kings to whom also our nation belongs and by whom also our history is governed, there would be no Antirevolutionary party. And if our opponents' motivation were already anti-Christian in an *absolute* sense, we could not legitimately participate in this political struggle; rather, we would have to wait in fear and trembling until the Lord returned. But now we know that in our country too all spiritual conflict must finally culminate in being *for* or *against* Christ. We are persuaded that the anti-Christian principle, though already a smoldering fire in our midst, has not yet scorched shut the conscience of this nation. So then everyone who believes in Christ as the sovereign Ruler also over our country *must*, if he has true patriotic love, rise to the defense of the honor of Christ in our politics. So long as we do this with all resolution, wisdom, and our combined strength, the possibility still remains that the spirit of apostasy can be arrested.

* * *

Men and brothers, to this pitch I had to raise you before the electoral campaigns once more commence, to shield you from immersion in the questions of the day and the small inconveniences of the moment that so easily blur the vision and discourage the heart. For alas, in this political struggle the sacred motives that prod your conscience almost never come to mind pure and clear. They lie hidden behind formal legislation, small measures, and personal cases that finally become concentrated for you in the choice between A and B and in the exhausting drive to the ballot box. But don't forget: the same is true of a mother's love for her darling child. However mechanical it may be when the clothes have to be mended or the stockings darned or the spoonfuls of medicine administered every hour, a real mother knows how to infuse all this technical work with the impulse of a holy love, and because she loves, she does it better. So also for us. What we have to do in our local caucuses and campaigns may be more mechanical than "spiritual"; still in that context too we may experience a holy thrill if our basic drive is love for Christ. Only those who know that they are propelled by that love will be powerful in this campaign.

Whoever lacks that higher impulse cannot look beyond the present. He only wants to put up a candidate who can win. If his goals are a little higher, he wonders whether 50 percent plus one of those elected will be on our side. And if he has a bigger vision still, he asks whether the Ministry will be able to continue. If none of this happens, then so far as he is concerned, the game is up. The battle has been lost and so is his heart for the cause. He thinks that we Antirevolutionaries are through. Petty, right? Just as small-minded as the boy who thinks that no apples will ever again grow on the tree because papa has pruned away a few branches. Yet that's what you fall into if you cannot raise your sights to a higher level, if you fail to take account of the high and holy goal for which we are fighting our battle. When fifteen years ago [i.e., 1876] God took Groen van Prinsterer from us, and in '77 we suffered an electoral setback, and in '78 the Sharp Resolution came, these shortsighted folks figured that we, too, were finished.[2] But just compare the way we've bloomed and grown since then!

No, you *may* not judge a principial spiritual struggle by the incidental level of success it reaches at some particular point. That's what the Jews in Jerusalem used to do, but the prophets of Jehovah certainly taught them otherwise. This sort of struggle goes on for decades and centuries, and the only question is whether the influence of the Name of the Lord is shrinking or gaining over the years.

In that light, who would dare say that in our country the near-miraculous has not occurred? Listen to Bilderdijk and feel in your bones the raw anguish of this solitary struggler who is ready, over and over, to bury himself under the collapsing domes of Ashdod. Hear Da Costa bewailing the plight of a nation whose ears have been stopped. Consider Groen van Prinsterer when his whole little army bolted and only the general stood firm. Recall the enormous efforts made to open the first Christian school in our national capital and how Da Costa's seminary collapsed: the press gave it a few bare inches of space.[3] In the city councils we had no one; no one in the provincial governments; in the Lower House we had all of three individuals; and in the Upper House the Antirevolu-

2. The elections of 1877 instituted a Cabinet under the lead of Johannes Kappeyne van de Coppello (1822-95), who was committed to a liberal-progressive society under state direction and militantly anticlerical. His first proposal, therefore, was the Education Bill of 1878 that would have so improved the quality of common schools and so strictly enforced the new standards as to make substantial central-government subsidies necessary for their operation. Yet such aid would remain forbidden to religious schools, spelling their extinction. This threat prompted Kuyper's clientele to dub the bill the "Scherpe" resolution, i.e., the sharp scalpel, a term originating in the Dutch war for independence as an epithet against the Duke of Alva and so invoking primal religious-political memories. The Kappeyne bill was the single greatest catalyst to Kuyper's organizing efforts — political party, lower-school, and university — in the late 1870s.

3. Da Costa had been the director of a small seminary in Amsterdam affiliated with the Free Church of Scotland and aiming to provide a strict-confessionalist alternative to the theological training available at the national universities. It was founded in 1852 and failed in 1860.

tionary party was unknown. One more thing: in 1871, in this very building, I presided over a convention of delegates in the smallest room the building offered, with only sixteen men around me.

And now: well, I'll not sketch the contrast of today, for it is not appropriate to boast. But if you compare the rich growth of the present with such a painful past and are still not moved to gratitude nor inspired with courage and hope for the future, I would almost be inclined to ask what you expected to do here among this enthusiastic corps — indeed, to ask whether from the depths of your soul you never responded to the cry of "Maranatha" with the words: "yes, come Lord Jesus!" Personally, I spent six unforgettable years very close to Groen van Prinsterer, exchanging letters and having numerous conversations with him, but I tell you: never did Groen van Prinsterer even dream of the possibility that four of our men would sit in the Crown Council at the same time, not, mind you, to doff their Antirevolutionary duds at the door but to stand firm and fight *in the Cabinet* for our sacred principles. For more than thirty years, under Groen's masterful leadership, people struggled for "the School with the Bible," and look, on this point the "Coterie-flag" has come down at last. Though our flag has not yet replaced it, still on top of the old pole we now see our pennant fluttering in the wind with the battle cry: "equality before the law."[4]

In that way God the Lord has proved his promise that *there is reward for our labor.* For though people are complaining — a complaint I myself share — that the gains of this three-year term were fewer than we had hoped for, we may not shut our eyes to the incredible difficulties with which our men in the Cabinet had to contend. Nor must we forget that finally only the man at the rudder can decide the direction in which things must go. Understand as well that in a second term the construction of a superstructure should go much faster, now that the foundation has been laid. Whatever faults we may find, there remains this lasting gain: we have proved ourselves "capable of governing" [*Regierungsfähig*] and, thanks to the unwavering loyalty of our men in the Cabinet, we have been spared any repetition of 1857 and 1866.[5]

4. The Antirevolutionary Party had four members in the Mackay Cabinet of 1888-91, whose own Educational Act (1889) permitted religious schools to pass along one-third of their costs to the state. This represented a lasting defeat for the secularist-Liberal "coterie" behind the Kappeyne bill of 1878.

5. The Education Act of 1857, proposed by Justinus L. L. van der Brugghen (1804-63), among other things deconfessionalized the common schools. A former ally of Groen in the Antirevolutionary movement, van der Brugghen broke with him at this point. Groen was similarly forsaken by erstwhile allies in the 1866-68 disputes over colonial policy and Crown-Parliamentary prerogatives.

If you complain about defections — not in the Cabinet to be sure, but among the voters — and about some who committed treason and deserted to the enemy, so what? For one who knows the cry of *Maranatha* and is familiar with Scriptural prophecy, it is not at all strange that the ranks are constantly broken; in fact, he knows for certain that such defections *must* come. Even David complained about the betrayal of a bosom friend "who ate of my bread and with whom I kept pleasant company" (Ps. 41:9; 55:13, 14). Of the twelve Jesus chose, the man from Iscarioth went out to commit his vile atrocity. There *must* be defections among those who first walked with you, says Paul, "for only so will it become clear who among you are genuine" (1 Cor. 11:19). Thirty years after Jesus' ascension the apostle John was already complaining of these renegades: "They went out from us, but they did not belong to us; for if they had belonged to us, they would have remained with us" (1 John 2:19). With similar conviction the apostle Paul tells us that Maranatha cannot begin "unless the apostasy come first" (2 Thess. 2:3). We all share the fault that, though we read these things in Scripture, when they actually occur in our own surroundings we forget that this is how *it was written* there.

Besides, you must not exaggerate by applying the prophecy of desertion to all who shrink back for a moment. Of how many martyrs do we not read — as a warning to ourselves — that initially, in a moment of fright, they abandoned the cause of the Lord; nevertheless at a later time, having returned with contrition and penitence, they offered themselves up for their Savior in death with the noble bearing of heroes. Of how many wars is it not recorded that a legion or regiment which first turned tail at sight of the enemy ended by courageously holding their position and sharing in the victory. Much, too, must be attributed to our bickering, meddlesome national character. As our country's coat of arms shows, the seven arrows would immediately fly apart if you did not draw them tightly together by a strong organization.

Further, is it any wonder that so many a spirit is bewildered at the repeated shocks in the life of our church? Is it not rather cause for gratitude that a movement in the sphere of the church, which elsewhere would scarcely cause a ripple, in our country still proved capable of stirring the mud up to the surface? This should tell you that the church of the Lord still carries some weight among us, still exerts pressure on people's conscience, still lives among us. No — to disclose my most intimate thoughts — I do not complain about defections; rather I am astonished that so few have left us. In fact I actually consider the little purge that took place in part a healthy thing,[6] and I am delighted that

6. Kuyper refers to defections in the 1880s by three leaders — Lucas Lindeboom

throughout the country, among higher and lower classes alike, it was precisely the men of consequence, of solid study, energy, and character who not only remained unanimously on our side but even strengthened their ties with our people. And therefore, though I regret the withdrawal of people who really do belong among us, I am guided by the words: "They know not what they are do" [Luke 23:34]. Really, they do not understand how by giving their vote to a Liberal in the context of our national struggle they are actually voting against their Lord. So I appeal to them: Come back, men and brothers. Let the Maranatha-cry be decisive for you as well. For whoever will rise from the dead, when the Lord returns, to stand on the mountain of the Lord as one bought by the blood of the Lamb, that person must also now, while he is still among the living, cling in heart and home and *country* to the banner of his Lord: "faithful unto death."

If you reply: then Roman Catholics belong in the same organization with us, I must ask you to beware of such a rash conclusion. Granted: whereas all the parties of the Revolution ignore, if not ridicule, the Second Coming of the Lord, our Roman Catholic countrymen confess with us: "Whence he will come again to judge the living and the dead." The Maranatha-event is certainly alive among them. What is more, the same background of convictions and facts lie behind that Maranatha for them as well. They, like we, acknowledge that all authority and power on earth flows from God and is rooted in the reality of creation. They confess along with us that the Lord God has revealed his will also for the political life of nations in an extraordinary way, and that both the ruler and the ruled are consequently bound to the will of God. They say as do you that this God has sent his only Son into the world and as a reward for his cross has placed on his head the Mediator's crown. And they testify with you that this divinely anointed King now sits at the right hand of God, controls the destiny of peoples and States from the throne of his majesty, and one day, at the end of history, will come again to summon all nations and all humanity before his judgment seat. So you are absolutely right in saying that the cry of Maranatha resounds from their lips as well as from ours and aligns us with them over against all other parties which do not know of any "Hallelujah" sung to "the Lamb that was slain" [Rev. 5:12].

Still, I reject as firmly as I know how the conclusion that we can therefore stand as one with them. This *cannot* be, due to our glorious

---

of the Seceder line, Andries W. Bronsveld and S. H. Buytendijk of the National Church — from the Antirevolutionary Party over its strategic coalition with the Catholics. The latter two also strongly opposed Kuyper's Doleantie and attack on the national-church ideal.

Kuyper's worries about the Catholics were not just old Protestant suspicions but recalled the hostile reception two Catholic newspapers had given the birth of the Antirevolutionary Party. In one of his "three-star" mini-editorials (15 May 1879) Kuyper answered back.

Rather a Liberal than a "Standaard" Man

From the *Maasbode* we learn that a new kind of people seem to have entered our fair land. That paper makes it sound like a dangerous gang, very much worse than a band of gypsies.

They are called *Standaard*-people. Their signature is that they are "hypocrites." As *De Tijd* informs us, one of their ancestral figures named Marnix of St. Aldegonde [a Protestant leader in the uprising against Spain] was an "arch-maligner." In addition they are "papist haters," "underhanded sneaks," and to top it off "worse than the Liberals!"

Those who know what black devils the Liberals are in the mind of the *Maasbode* will be scared silly at the thought of encountering an even worse, more sinister, gang.

So beware! Beware of the danger! For the gang that is "worse than the Liberals" is "us."

history; this *cannot* be, due to the *blood of martyrs* that has been shed; this cannot be *now* or *ever*, due to the shrewd old gentleman at Rome who claims to be the authorized vicar of Christ on earth. . . . I would therefore call it a betrayal of our history and our principles were there ever to be a fusion or even a very close association between our Catholic countrymen and ourselves. What separates us, after all, is the sacred cause of *freedom of conscience* for which we, like our ancestors, would again shed our blood and against which they, however accommodating their practice, remain fundamentally opposed. It is precisely the cry of Maranatha that binds us to the line of *history*. That line demands that, being loyal to our glorious history, we remain *Calvinists*, jealously watching over the inheritance entrusted to us. Indeed, this inheritance must not just be called by the vague term *Christian* but by *Calvinist* in a very definite sense, for you have the Christian name in common with Rome, but only in Calvinism lies your fundamental and historically distinguishing Dutch characteristic.

Freedom of conscience — precisely for that reason we must employ

More typical of Kuyper was his contempt for the national-Protestant prejudices of people like A. W. Bronsveld of Utrecht, once his collaborator, always a keen rival. In a "three-star" of 14 February 1898 he satirized the Rome-baiting of the 1897 summer elections and what had come of it.

A Serious Case

Antipapism triumphed in the June elections.

Oh, those Catholics! In secret warehouses they were stacking up sticks and twigs for the stakes to be erected in the near future. Alva was on the way. But Utrecht turned the tide. Dr. Bronsveld saved the fatherland. And those vicious Catholics skedaddled with their hirelings and fellow travellers.

But behold: an antipapist [Liberal] Cabinet comes into power, and it seems for all the world as if in donning their ministerial tailcoats the new ministers have been infected with a papist germ.

Schaepman and Michiels van Verduynen [Dutch Catholic leaders] at Paris become nominal presidents of all the Netherlands. A Catholic is appointed to the Council of State. During debates in the [Second] Chamber the Catholics hear nothing but friendly words from the ministerial table. And now that we are finally going to have compulsory military service, everything is stacked in favor of the Catholics. Even the men in monk's clothing will get an exemption.

What's going on? ask the members of the Antipapist League. For this we ran our legs off preaching religious hatred around the country? In that case we'd rather have no compulsory military service! cries the *Middelburger.* In Utrecht the pot bubbles and steams.

And so we learn how to tell the distance between the *sincerity* of election-time antipapism and ministerial *conciliation.*

persuasion to the exclusion of all *coercion* in all spiritual matters. Someday there will be coercion, when Christ descends in majesty from the heavens, breaks the anti-Christian powers with a rod of iron, and, in the words of Psalm 2, dashes them in pieces like a potter's vessel [v. 9]. He has a right to this because he knows the hearts of all and will be the judge of all. But we do not. To us it is only given to fight with spiritual weapons and to bear our cross in joyful discipleship. Therefore, without any craftiness or secret intentions we accept the position of equality before the law along with those who disagree with us and, as Groen said, ask for ourselves no other constitutional liberty than that which makes possible the performance of our Christian duty. In the civil state all citizens of the Netherlands must have equal rights before the law. The time *must* come when it will be considered inconceivable, even ridiculous, to discriminate against or offend anyone, whoever it may be, for his convictions as a Seceder or Doleant,[7] as a Catholic or Jew.

This same principle not only determines our formal policy, it also designates the *task* to which we are called. Calvinism does not know the rust of conservatism but attempts to exert active influence on every emerging change in our national fortunes. It never limps along in the rear but always chooses for itself a place of honor in the front ranks. For that reason, at the present juncture in our nation's existence, it also hears itself earnestly called to its duty.

The politics of Europe is undisputably in search of a new configuration. The oligarchy of financially and intellectually advantaged classes is finished. The masses are now in a state of ferment. Interest in social concerns has pushed itself to the foreground. In threatening speech and with even more threatening gestures the oppressed are asking the Liberal why, if "the people are sovereign," that sovereign people should any longer be trampled en masse by the oligarchs. It is not the game of politics that attracts them; they are not interested in power for its own sake. What they want is power as a means of improving their own fortunes. They are crying out for bread and for more than bread. They believe that of the trio "liberty, equality, and fraternity," *liberty* has been too sparsely allocated, *equality* too long delayed, and *fraternity* utterly preempted. Driving the masses onward is the pressure of their pain and misery but without any nobler inspiration — passion and bitterness without higher ideals. They are simply applying the principles of the French revolution — the very principles, therefore, of Liberalism — but with merciless consistency and without any nobler chords. This evil haunts our political parties like a nightmare. They see the avalanche coming and attempt to stop it, to no avail. This avalanche levels everything in its path and drives before it whatever offers resistance. The bandages our Liberals bring out Social Democracy laughs at, and rushes on.

This agitation is not likely to lead on at once to a violent revolution, at least in our country. Our national character is too phlegmatic for that.

7. That is, a member of the Secession of 1834 or of the Doleantie of 1886.

But it does push our politics inevitably in the direction of *democracy*. Our Conservatives are losing all influence on the course of events. The Liberals are putting on their best democratic pose, while the Radicals are already there. So rushes in the tide that will soon base *our* governmental institutions in universal suffrage and put the balance of power in the hands of the less educated masses. Whether the powers that be recognize it or not, we are heading toward a very different revision of our Constitution than Heemskerk cobbled together, by comparison with which the Revision of 1848 will be child's play.[8]

Considering this state of affairs and course of development, what is the Antirevolutionary party to do? Must it just resist what seems to be going too far? Or should it put itself in the vanguard to guide the movement into safer channels? That is the leading question which must determine our national action. And so let it be said here, said with emphasis, said with all the passion of our deepest conviction, that those who believe in Christ and await his return from heaven *may* not sit still and *may* not confine themselves to reinforcing the dikes but are duty-bound in Christ, come what may, to position themselves courageously in the breach of this nation and to prepare for *a Christian-democratic development of our national government*. This can still be done *now*. But if you squander this God-given moment and let it pass unused, you will be to blame for having thrown away the future of your country and you will soon bend under the iron fist which will strike you in your Christian liberty and, unsparingly, also in your wallets and property.

I repeat: A *Christian-democratic shape* must be given to our state institutions precisely to hold back ochlocracy [mob rule] along *anti*-Christian lines. Be sure of this: you no longer have a choice between aristocratic privilege and democratic broadening. That time has long since passed. With or without your participation, you will inevitably see development in a more democratic spirit. That spirit is pushing the waters of our national life into a rising, swelling stream that will break the dikes and inundate the fields. To try to hold it back would be a fool's game. And why should you? Don't you as Christians know from Scripture that also in Israel the whole nation, all its tribes, clans, and

8. The Constitution of 1848 (replacing that of the Restoration of 1813) was written by J. R. Thorbecke along classic liberal lines. It reduced the power of the monarchy, mandated direct election of the lower house, provincial representation in the upper house, with the cabinet responsible to both. At the same time it enfranchised only 75,000 voters (about 13 percent of adult males) in a nation of three million people. (E. H. Kossmann, *The Low Countries, 1780-1940* [Oxford: Clarendon, 1978], p. 194.) The Constitutional revision of 1887 under Jan Heemskerk (1818-97) doubled this proportion to about 28 percent of adult males.

families had a voice even in the election of its kings? (1 Sam. 11:15; 2 Sam. 2:4; 5:3). Is it not inherent in the nature of a constitutional state that popular influence, once it is consulted by the government, *has to* expand in an ever-widening circle and *cannot* rest until it has touched bottom? Do not all the Scriptures preach, and do not history and experience teach, that the moral power of faith tends to reside much more among the "little people" who run short every year than among the affluent who annually increase their net worth? Was it not true in the time of the Spanish occupation and has it not remained true ever since that a small percentage of our more talented aristocracy added to the little folk represented the real power of the Christian religion in our country? Indeed, has not the entire Calvinist movement — in Great Britain, the Netherlands, and America alike — relied precisely on *the extension of popular influence* to strengthen their governments? You know how the grand aristocrat Groen van Prinsterer unceasingly appealed to the "people behind the electors" and in the matter of the census consistently "bid a guilder less" than Thorbecke.[9]

Taking that road, therefore, is not yielding to pressure or a spineless resignation that would disown one of our sacred principles for the illusion of the day. On the contrary: you will deny your principle if you choose otherwise. Even if the *zeitgeist* were *anti*-democratic, *you* should still seek the broadening of popular influence. That should be our direction all the more now that the democratic current has become overpowering and threatens to sink into crude ochlocracy if Christian principle gives it no direction.

Finally, if you ask in what direction we must guide that stream, I will drive in four stakes to mark off the territory: (1) *religion held* in honor; (2) *freedom of conscience* restored; (3) our people set again in their *organic relations;* and (4) *the spirit of compassion* poured out over our entire governmental apparatus.

Religion held in honor, because the current trend threatens authority, lowers the standard of human life, and drives the less-advantaged to despair. No authority or government can stand unless it finds support in *conscience;* lacking that, it will *have to* find its strength in bayonet and

9. That is, the Calvinist Groen would propose a slightly lower property requirement for the franchise than would Liberal party leader J. R. Thorbecke. The issue was debated exactly in these terms in 1874 (although Thorbecke was dead by then), when the Liberals proposed tax payments of 28 guilders, and Kuyper 24, as the standard of qualification for an adult male to vote.

pistol, and history teaches that this kind of power lasts only until someone else finds a longer bayonet and a faster pistol and topples the authority. This is how one restrains animals or savages but not how one governs a nation that has ripened to a higher level of human development from having heard the message of the gospel. Hence our demand that the government shall again acknowledge and confess its responsibility before the Kings of kings and, far from adopting a posture hostile to religion, honor it again, for the benefit of the people. If this is not done, our *standard of human life* will be lowered, for we are God's offspring, created in his image. Government abandons the nobility of our human nature if at its universities it teaches the people that our ancestor was a chimpanzee. As a result in the press and in popular meetings people argue exclusively for *material* well-being as though this were the highest good of humanity. If that trend continues there will no longer be a God or an ideal for the nation. Moral life will degenerate into the pursuit of utility until, in the end, even though people do not descend from the animal world, you will degrade them into brutes. Indeed, without religion you will by irresistible logic drive the disadvantaged to despair, for if a people no longer believe that eternal bliss may await us following this brief and fearful life, they will say: "Life is short and must be enjoyed now! Let us eat and drink, for tomorrow we die!" As soon as this unbelief has been internationally organized and the spirit of revolt has penetrated the armies, a raging fury will turn against the life of our whole society and from the nihilism of despair will arise the triumph of unbridled insanity. Against this tide neither laws can help nor weapons protect us. That demon must be exorcised in the human heart itself. And the only thing that can bind it is the return of the rule of religion to the human heart.

To that end we ask only for one thing: that *freedom of conscience*, both direct and indirect, be completely restored. Positive government action in matters pertaining to our *spiritual* life is something we do not desire but fundamentally oppose. The gospel spurns the crutches of the powerful. All it asks is unlimited freedom to develop in accordance with its own genius in the heart of our national life. We do not want the government to hand over unbelief handcuffed and chained as though for a spiritual execution. We prefer that the power of the gospel overcome that demon in free combat with comparable weapons. Only *this* we do not want: that the government arm unbelief to force us, half-armed and handicapped by an assortment of laws, into an unequal struggle with so powerful an enemy. Yet that *has* happened and is happening *still*. It happens in all areas of popular education, on the higher as well as the lower levels, by means of the power of money, forced examinations, and official hierarchy. For this reason we may never desist from our protest or resistance until the gospel recover its freedom to circulate, until the performance of his Christian duty will again be possible for every Dutch citizen, whether rich or poor.

In the third place I said that our nation must again be *restored in its organic relations.* Naturally, not the organic relations from before 1793. These were too medieval, insufficiently developed under Calvinism, and corrupted by the haughty Regents of unlamented memory. None of us mourns the fall of that rotten structure. But *this* is our grievance: that those tottering walls were demolished and the solid bricks broken up only to be stacked in a heap without any plans for a new building. Liberalism is fundamentally *anti*-social because it is individualistic and sees in a people only a heap of solitary souls on a piece of ground. With that our whole national life goes to corruption and decay. In the end all natural connections are torn up so that the individuals who constitute 50 percent plus one can tyrannize the 50 percent minus one. As long as people persist in this approach there will be no improvement. Only when each part of our national body can carry on its own function will that body be restored to health. Hence we ask for *universal* proportional suffrage but on the basis of the *family,* for a restoration of the old guilds in a new form, for Chambers of Labor and Agriculture. Our desire will obtain only when there is next to the political Chamber in the capital also a Chamber of Interests in which all parts of the national body, hence also the church of Jesus Christ, will be represented in fair proportion.[10]

And finally, must not the *spirit of the Compassionate One* be poured out over our whole government administration? We are not a pagan but a Christian nation, a nation that has to take account of the human heart also in its dread and nameless suffering. For all our thought and effort, suffering will always be a part of this world. Thousands upon thousands of people are commanded by one single drudgery their whole life long: to get bread — if only bread — to eat by the sweat of their brow. Illness ever threatens us. Old age saps our virility. Employment is not available for everyone who wants to work. Death still makes widows and orphans. A severe winter like the one just past is the cause of indescribable misery. All sorts of contention and wrangling embitter life and often violate a person's rights. Sin and temptation prowl night and day to catch the younger generation in its snares and to make the hearts of parents bleed. True, there is still much laughter but, as in the time of Solomon, so also today there are "the tears of the oppressed — with no one to comfort

10. For more on this proposal, see *Manual Labor,* pp. 246-48, 252-55 below.

them. On the side of their oppressors there is power — and no one to comfort *them*" (Eccl. 4:1). This untold misery is not alleviated but worsened when the state seeks its strength in heartless bureaucracy, knows no other power but that of coercion, and follows the model of *mammon* rather than that of the *gospel*. The Antirevolutionary party accordingly asks that a new spirit may control our public administration; that our legislation may show a *heart* and officialdom some sympathy for suffering citizens; that powerless labor may be protected from coolly calculating capital; and that even the poorest citizen may count on the prospect of swift and sound *justice*.

Men of the Antirevolutionary cause, there in outline is the ideal that beckons you in the name of Christ. If you now sit still and do nothing, nothing will come of it. You will be quietly coupled to the slow train of dead-end Conservatism, and democracy *without* you will triumph *over* you in an increasingly demonic form. Owing to your hesitation and hanging back, your lack of courage and resilience, the political development of the Netherlands will increasingly run along anti-Christian lines. And whether it's you or your children who experience it, when Christ returns on the clouds *yours* will be the guilt before God that the wrath of the returning One will erupt also against our country, a country richly blessed by God and steeped in an abundance of grace. Therefore I beg you to abandon all petty calculations. Remove from your midst all that might contribute to dividing God's people at the ballot box. Show yourself to be on the high level of your calling. Know what your goals are and pursue them in tightly closed ranks, not just asking what the results will be on June 9 but what the outcome will be at the time of Maranatha. The question is: what will have been instilled in our national spirit, what will appear embodied in our government when our national history will be wrapped up and the harvest stands ripe and ready for the Judge of the nations to appear?

Never forget: the hallmark of this era is the turnabout in the national mind from individual and intellectual pursuits to a thirst for *social* life. This is to your advantage, for if anything is *social*, it is the Christian religion. How irresponsible would be your spiritual inertia, then, how unpardonable your sin before God and country if you let this God-given moment pass by *unused* and do not diffuse into that social endeavor what you alone can mix into it: the *moral* power of a love that binds because it flows from God. For our ancestors a like moment once dawned when the battle for freedom of conscience had to be fought, and *they* did *not* let it pass by. They did *not* sit still. Rather, under the inspiring leadership of Orange they chose to be ahead of their time, risking their possessions and their lives for the moral uplift of their country so that even today, along with our own nation, all of Europe, even America, is obliged to the vitality and resilience demonstrated in the era of our greatest glory. Truly, if the Lord had then appeared on the clouds, more than any other nation on earth the generation of martyrs which then blossomed in its blood on this soil would have been *his* people, the people *of the Lord.*

Praise be to God: the tree of Orange still stands, covering us with its shade. Therefore, in the struggle that has been unleashed in our day show that you are not devoid of the resilience of your fathers, nor estranged from their courage, nor bereft of their holy seriousness. Prove yourself to be not just the *physical* but also the *spiritual offspring* of those fathers. Keep your horizons wide, your conceptions broad, your energy indomitable. Do not go limping behind others but run ahead of the procession by the light of prophecy and the radiance of *Maranatha.* In the future our people will bow either before the *gods of this age* or before *our God,* so I do not understand you if you have forgotten Da Costa's saying: *"They shall not have us!"*[11] Better: I understand you well, you faithful, honest men who, from high estate or low, feel your hearts tremble with joy when you hear once again the summons to work for the glory of your God and the banner of the cross beckons anew. Though at times you remained behind, *you do wish to advance.* Indeed you are already in motion as the command "Forward in the name of the Lord" again resounds through the ranks. For though you may not be poets, you certainly sing along with me in your own way the words of our Da Costa:

For me, *one* goal drives me onward,
  Just one purpose stirs my soul,
And rather may my life's breath fail me,
  Than I ever lose this goal.

11. This line began the chorus that served as something of an anthem in Dutch Neo-Calvinist circles. It originally occurred in Isaac da Costa, "Aan Nederland in de Lente van 1844"; see J. P. Hasebroek, ed., *Da Costa's Kompleete Dichtwerken,* 3rd ed. (Leiden: Sijthoff, 1876), vol. I, p. 484. The whole verse, with rather literal translation, reads:

Zij zullen het niet hebben,
  ons oude Nederland!
Het bleef bij alle ellenden
  Gods en der Vaadren pand!
Zij zullen het niet hebben,
  de goden van den tijd!
Niet oom hun erf te wezen
  heeft God het ons bevrijd!

They shall not have it,
  our old Netherlands!
It remains through every misery
  To God and Fathers true!
They shall not have it,
  the gods of our time!
Not to leave it to their possession
  Has God made us free!

'Tis this: with holy, joyful heart
To tear all unbelief apart
   And drive oppression from its throne.
He who could crush Goliath's power
Can free this land from evil's hour
   Through one united, heartfelt tone.[12]

12. This is the concluding stanza of Isaac da Costa, "Vrijheid," in Hasebroek, ed., *Da Costa's Kompleete Dichtwerken,* pp. 201-2. The translation is by Henrietta Ten Harmsel.

Voor mij! één doel slechts kent mijn leven,
   Één uitzicht slechts verrukt mijn ziel,
En moog mij de adem eer begeven,
   Dan dat dit uitzicht mij ontviel.
't Is om in heilge geestverrukking
Het Ongeloof en zijn Verdrukking
   Omver te stooten van den Troon.
Hij die de Goliath's kon treffen,
Kan 't land van 't Ongeloof ontheffen,
   Door één uit 't hart gewelden toon.

Kuyper made a few changes from the original appropriate to the political occasion. He also used a free variation on this verse to conclude his speech at the 25th-year celebration of his editorship of *De Standaard.* See J. C. Rullmann, *Kuyper-Bibliografie,* vol. III, p. 5.

„Zoo temt men dieren, zoo bedwingt men wilden, maar zoo regeert men geen volk".

Dr. A. Kuyper in 1891.

As prime minister, Kuyper was criticized for the zeal with which he crushed a nationwide railroad strike in 1903. *Left:* the cartoonist bitterly quotes Kuyper's line from *Maranatha:* "This is how one restrains animals or savages but not how one governs a nation." Kuyper also began to tilt in a more pro-German direction despite previously opposing German social-welfare schemes as paternalistic. *Below:* Kuyper visiting Berlin in 1902.

Manual Labor

In the 1880s the Netherlands suffered some of its hardest economic times in a century. The course of industrialization, which had finally picked up in the 1870s, was jolted by local difficulties and slowed by a general depression. Workers in the cities faced prolonged unemployment without insurance, daily provisions, or sure prospect of improvement, while the ongoing crisis in Dutch agriculture, now bereft of urban outlets for its surplus labor, was exposed for all to see. Although the labor violence that exploded in more industrialized Belgium and northern France at the time never erupted in the Netherlands, no one was sure of that in advance. The worst years of the depression (1882-86) thus mixed real suffering with acute anxiety.[1]

Local authorities and labor associations were overwhelmed by the situation, and the Conservative-dominated Cabinet in The Hague did little until, at the prompting of progressives in the States General, it appointed committees to investigate farm and factory conditions. These *Enquêtes* (Inquests) were comparable to Congressional hearings in the United States, compiling sworn testimony in a formal report with mandates for legislation. That legislation was forthcoming in 1889, courtesy of the Catholic-Antirevolutionary coalition Cabinet headed by Aeneas Mackay.

The entire process received ample, and often acute, commentary across the spectrum of Dutch opinion. Kuyper entered in with the following series of articles in *De Standaard* during February 1889. In them he speaks not only to immediate concerns, though he does that with a fine eye for detail, but to the structural problems, ideological premises, and broader consequences of industrialization as a whole. This is applied political philosophy conveyed at a rapid pace (the seven articles appeared every other day!) to a lay audience who,

1. E. H. Kossmann, *The Low Countries, 1780-1940* (Oxford: Clarendon Press, 1978), pp. 314-19.

the writer intends, would thereby receive a quick education, some calming hope, and a license for appropriate rage.

Some classic Kuyperian motifs run through this piece: sphere sovereignty, the horrors of 1789, the celebration of a free society, the derogation of Liberals and Conservatives as outmoded variations on the same premise. Kuyper's class consciousness is more pronounced than usual, however, and poses a challenge to his usual theme of law and social order. His solution is to unleash full class combat within tight rules — better, within a legally constituted grid of formal institutions. Thus Kuyper comes to some of his most innovative suggestions: to enhance the rights of labor, a modern version of the old guild system; to solve the "social question," labor councils to match corporate cartels; to settle their disputes, binding arbitration; to stabilize the entire system, parliamentary representation by social function as well as by geographical district. These proposals were never enacted, but they show a philosopher with an eye for the concrete, a steadfast man ever willing to experiment, and a devotee equally of order and freedom facing up to new social circumstances.

The series originally appeared in *De Standaard,* 8-22 February 1889, and was issued as a brochure, *Handenarbeid,* in June of the same year by J. A. Wormser, Amsterdam. The text is reproduced here complete except for a few minor deletions of repetitive summaries or commentary on local events. It was translated by Reinder Bruinsma.

I. The Foundations of the Building

A nation lives by labor, but labor takes many forms . . . [physical, mental, precise, unskilled, speculative, etc.]. In contemplating a possible "Code of Labor,"[2] then, it would be more correct to speak of a code of *manual* labor, as this is the type of labor that has been coming into more and more difficulties.

The matter of manual labor is of social importance because the class of citizens who depend on it is so large; in our country the majority have

2. In 1874 Kuyper had proposed a "Wetboek van de Arbeid," a complete code of labor regulations whose equivalence to civil and criminal codes would give labor/economic issues a dramatic new status. Such a code was never passed.

it as their sole means of existence. Thus, the condition in which manual labor finds itself inevitably exerts an influence on the entire social and domestic condition of the greater part of our nation. Naturally, every Netherlander is eager to know whether this majority is doing well, has a reasonable existence and is prospering morally, or whether it is depressed by worries, tending towards discontent, and declining in morals.

In the long run this matter of manual labor is of the greatest importance for the safety of our society too. For however phlegmatic our nature may be, however composed our Dutch way of life, history clearly teaches that a confrontation cannot be avoided if the larger part of the people were to live long years anxious and disgruntled and thus become morally vulnerable. The social question so far has not taken that threatening form in our country only because the spirit of discontent and moral decline has remained confined to a small part of those who work with their hands. In particular agricultural workers have not been affected until now, although it must be feared that before too long the slump in the prices of land and agricultural products will give free play to evil spirits in this domain too. You can already see something of this in the North.

Apart from the question whether the social order is sufficiently armed to deal with a violent eruption, it is beneath the honor of the government and the dignity of our people to ignore such a serious matter until the situation is out of hand. Regardless of necessity and danger, our government and our people must open their eyes to the unsatisfactory situation and ask themselves seriously whether the legislature is entitled and able to help deal with the undeniable need. This is demanded of wise national government — demanded by justice, which elevates the nations; demanded also by tender compassion, which may be expected of a baptized nation.

It is far from certain that the legislature would *be able* to arrest the diminishing regard for manual labor, even if it believed itself entitled to any measure and agreeable to any demand. The very fact that the market of goods is cosmopolitan, and that therefore conditions in other countries influence our situation, makes this improbable. Besides, preventing *all* misery and alleviating *all* poverty is a problem that has always escaped solution. Finally, the course of world history shows that great nations, after a period of glory, tend to enter a period of spiritual exhaustion and, once sunken in this spiritual miasma, become inferior to other nations in every form of life.

Therefore, it is high time that moral forces be considerably strengthened among the common people. To "be content with little" will help to cultivate submissiveness and patience in distress and difficulties, and looking toward a higher ideal will draw the tranquil eye away from the world and its desires. The matter at stake is the happiness of the people. If these moral forces enable you to teach the larger part of our nation to be content with little and in condition also to catch the luster of a higher ideal, you have achieved more than if you artificially raise wages 10 or 15 percent. For if people lack moral fibre, an overriding discontent will result only in another demand that wages be raised another 10 percent.

Yet, for now we will set these moral forces aside. We will stay silent as well about the contribution that the marvelous power of love can make to improve the circumstances of many through graciousness, compassion, and liberality. Here we are concerned only with the Legislature. Thus we face the question: What can the legislature do to eradicate from our society this imbalance which unmistakenly burdens a considerable part of the population and robs it of its happiness? We must courageously and openly acknowledge that the Social Democrats are right when they maintain that the situation calls not only for the *physician* but most certainly for the *architect* as well.

Let us clarify what we mean.

At first, the well-heeled class regarded the social question like a schoolmaster does a couple of rascals in his class. Liberals and Conservatives alike demanded to know what all this bunkum and Jewish hullabulloo was supposed to mean. For their holy doctrine was nonnegotiable: the *laissez faire, laissez passer* philosophy was the bedrock of wisdom. A national system like ours, born from these sagacious depths, *had* to be El Dorado for all. Sure there was inequality, but this was simply the struggle between the stronger and the weaker in which the weaker was — now, for once — "predestined" to succumb. Complaints or resistance were inappropriate. All this grumbling had to stop, the sooner the better. But if it did continue and if the people sooner or later raised their fists, so what? One simply reinforced the police and made sure to have enough troops. That would be the end of it.

Less than twenty years ago this fairly described the general feeling among our ruling powers. But since then, mainly due to the nobler policies of other nations, the terrible pride and selfishness expressed in this cold egoism began to soften a little. No, the complaints were not so totally unfounded. There were indeed abuses. For all kinds of reasons the much-lauded system of liberal wisdom had not been able to realize its ideal in every aspect. The social *organism* was still perfectly in order, but here and there some less desirable phenomena had found their way into its constitution. And thus, it was gradually admitted, the *physician* had to be called and the pharmacist would get some work.

To be sure, not all Liberals want to go to the same length. Listening to the diagnoses of Quack and Levy, we notice that Levy quits with licorice on *aqua pura,* while Quack — a man of more serious study, milder heart, and tenderer mind — would not object to the cost of some iron pills and, if need be, some minor surgery.[3] Even so, this usually separates the Liberals from the Social Democrats in the matter: the Liberals are looking only for a medical solution, while the Social Democrats want to work from an architectural angle. For they argue that society cannot be salvaged by eliminating a few abuses since the evil does not reside in such but in the *entire structure* of our social system.

For the time being we will leave aside the question whether their arguments are correct and in particular whether their new design is practicable. But on this we agree with them: when a house creaks and warps, the notion of making some superficial repairs and applying a coat of paint without first examining the supporting walls, joists, and foundations is not serious. It's not even serious from the point of view of our Liberals, who live by *reason* and know nothing of divine ordinances. For this would imply that the foundations, supporting walls, and joists too have been constructed by human consent and thus ought to be changed if human wisdom so indicates. Here indeed the Liberals and Democrats meet. Both do the building themselves. Neither the Liberals nor the Social Democrats in their politics know anything of a God who built everything. In this respect Jonkheer Six yields nothing to Domela Nieuwenhuis.[4]

The real issue between them comes to this: that the Liberals arrived ahead of the Social Democrats, built the house according to their design,

3. Isaac A. Levy (1838-1920), an Amsterdam lawyer and sometime member of the Second Chamber, and Hendrick P. G. Quack (1834-1917), a professor of economics at Utrecht and Amsterdam, were leaders in the Progressive Liberal wing of Dutch politics. Exact contemporaries of Kuyper, they too were troubled by the social question and dissatisfied with classic liberalism's (lack of) answers thereto. Both sympathized some with Social Democratic views but not with its proposed policies, and generally favored political solutions that would arise out of a broadened franchise. Quack, like Kuyper, admired the medieval guilds (as well as St. Francis and St. Bernard) and sharply criticized the French Revolution for destroying the latter without any replacement but the nostrums of market and individualism.

4. Jonkheer [Sir] Willem Six (1829-1908) was a model of classic liberalism in Kuyper's eyes: a conservative devotee of the National Church, an heir of the Dutch elite, and, as Minister of Domestic Affairs 1879-82, responsible for pushing the Kappeyne school laws that Kuyper's followers found so repellent. Ferdinand Domela Nieuwenhuis (1846-1919) was the foremost Dutch socialist of his generation and the embodiment of political and social radicalism. Trained as a Lutheran minister, a popular charismatic leader in the same mold as Kuyper but less skilled as an organizer, he was a member of the Second Chamber at the time of Kuyper's writing. In late-century intra-socialist debates he opted for the anarchist rather than the dogmatic Marxist wing.

and now demand that the Social Democrats accept the dwelling — though, as landlord, offering them some repairs. For their part the Social Democrats say: *Your whole house is useless. Let's demolish it altogether. Then we will build, at our combined expense, a new house according to my design. You'll be amazed how much better we both like it.*

Liberals have no principial reason to object to this. But Antirevolutionaries do. For we answer: There must be a distinction. The design of the house we already have shows a part that has been ordained by God and that has to be preserved as is in any reconstruction. But we also say loud and clear, the same design has many parts that little attract us, being the product of the Liberals, and that can be reconstructed in a different way *without contravening* God's decrees. Critique of this part of the house must remain free and the suggestions of other architects listened to. The existing situation should not be regarded as perfect as long as it has not honorably withstood the test of criticism.

II. Economic and Political Influences

. . . While these two architects [the Liberal and the Social Democrat] fight it out, we need to pay attention to two equally important matters. First, it's important that the class of people who live by manual labor be able to buy good quality and quantity with the money they earn. Wages will always remain relative. In more than one area a farm laborer who earns five guilders is in fact much richer that a laborer in Amsterdam who gets eight or even ten. The government has all sorts of ways to influence the price of the goods that are for sale. Enclosing a city within narrow walls will make the houses expensive. Building good roads will let people live farther away. Border tariffs have an influence on the price of goods. Everyone pays duty on salt, soap, and sugar. Taxes on land, patents, and real estate are figured into the prices of houses and goods. In brief, our entire fiscal system is like the web of a spider where each vibration is transmitted along all threads from the center to the outer edges.

With regard to agriculture, we recently pointed to our unsuitable inheritance laws whereby the continuity of large farms, which need a lot of manual labor, is endangered again and again. Endless partitioning has led to a higher density of population. A greater number of people must bid too high against each other for the small pieces of land they want to rent. And so it's happened that land owners who at one time received only twelve hundred guilders in rent from a farm got more than two thousand after the land had been partitioned. That means an extra eight hundred guilders which has to be paid by the lower class.

Then too we see how the government through *Freizüglerei* [freedom of movement] may burden each laborer with ten or twelve competitors. "Where there is carrion the eagles will gather." And those eagles arrive just as much from other provinces as from beyond the borders. Large State projects also figure in, for when the government creates extra work of ten years' duration or longer, it attracts a large circle of manual laborers who, on that basis, get married, live, and make plans. Then the work is suddenly finished and the immense crew of laborers is left empty-handed.

We could add much more, but this will suffice to illustrate how the financial system and the government affect the situation of the manual laborer in all sorts of ways. Thus, not only the structure of society but also the manner in which the social household is run is a powerful factor that either works to the advantage of the laboring class or can oppress it. Even if you assume that any kind of household will cost money and that it is fair for all classes to share in this expense, it is obvious that the share a particular class can bear depends on the relative prosperity this class enjoys. Understandably, then, the class of people who live by manual labor demands a better condition since it has come into narrow straits.

It does not at all follow that every change these folk desire is possible or even profitable for them. But that does not remove the urgent necessity for thorough research on this aspect of the social question — not only because the people want it, but because God requires the government to be *fair* in its dealings.

This automatically brings up the third key element in this question: *politics*. In the past, when the government was elevated more highly above the different classes, politics did not get involved in the class struggle. Precisely because of her lofty position the government was conscious of her calling to stand in the breach for the weaker classes and to defend them against the stronger. When the Psalmist extols the King of kings with such words as "O Lord, who is like You? You deliver the weak from those too strong for them!" [Ps. 35:10], he is specifying at the same time the most beautiful pearl in the crown of our rulers: to defend the weak and needy that they may not be too heavily oppressed by the big and powerful.

But sure enough, the Liberals put an end to this noble conception of government too. Liberalism robbed the king of his majesty and gave him some tinsel by way of compensation. A king made of marzipan. The power to rule was no longer with the king but with the majority in the Second Chamber, which explains why Liberalism had no scruples whatsoever in its attempts to acquire that majority. Seeing that the Second Chamber does not in fact represent all classes but only one, namely the *bourgeoisie*, the metamorphosis that occurred came down to this: the king

Kuyper wrote this "three-star" mini-editorial on 11 November 1885, as the Dutch economic depression worsened.

Unemployment

In years past England suffered the fever of unemployment, too, even worse than we do today. That's when Potgieter [E. J., 1808-75] translated Hood's "Lay of the Labourer" for us. And although that translation was a dismal failure, nevertheless by the "Lay of the Laborer" and "Song of the Shirt" Potgieter helped us feel what England's working man was struggling with then and what is still happening in our own cities today.

Back then the unemployed in England suffered in large numbers, suffered hopelessly, suffered horrible deprivation. Only the "poor rates" offered relief.

We cannot let our fellow man die of hunger. To say: "Go and be warm" is not Christian. But also, given the scope of the problem,

remained king in name but the actual power of government was transferred to the well-heeled, the propertied class. At the time it consisted of about 100,000 people, representing a household population of about 400,000 — approximately one tenth of the population.[5]

This has triggered repugnance and disturbed our civil peace. For if it could not be denied that whoever has the power of government can, by rearranging the foundations of society and by its mode of management, exert a predominant influence on the fate and the condition of the various classes in their conflict of interests; and if de facto this governing power now played into the hands of one of these classes — then the evil suspicion *had* to arise that this ruling class would abuse its power to strengthen its own station and to weaken the others'. And so was born the demand for *universal suffrage* — from the liberal viewpoint a very reasonable demand, if only for the all-sufficient reason that any other system is purely

5. Kossmann, *The Low Countries,* p. 194, estimates that the regime of the 1848 Constitution (to which Kuyper is referring) enfranchised 75,000 men out of a population of three million — thus, the same proportions as Kuyper's statistics but on a lower scale. Kuyper could have been citing a later census since the franchise did not increase relative to population until 1887.

help does not come via vague promises. Even less should it seem to be extorted by threats. It is unacceptable that our laboring population sink ever lower morally to the dismal level of demanding money by intimidation.

We are not just facing a *need* but a *situation* that needs to be regulated, a set of circumstances that requires provision.

If back in 1874, when the Antirevolutionary caucus in the [Second] Chamber urged regulation, this demand had been met by the adoption of a Labor Code, our misery today would not be half of what it is. We would have our guilds, and through the guilds a set quota of laborers for every trade, and through that a drop in the marriage and population figures so that the entire imbalance between work and workers would be eliminated.

So in our opinion there should be no further delay. A Labor Code *has to* be passed now. Meanwhile, consider England's "poor rates" the only remedy. A few thousand guilders won't suffice. A few tons should do!

arbitrary. For from this standpoint, requiring voters to have a certain level of prosperity would be an aggravated form of tyranny. But the question concerns precisely those who lack that prosperity. Their fate is mainly in the hands of those who run the regime. This control lies with the majority of the voters, and the vote is given only to the well-to-do, i.e., only to those who in this social controversy *oppose* the less-privileged.

We do not say that the Social Democrats are a whit better in their intentions. On the contrary, they intend the very same thing as the Liberals but to the opposite practical conclusion. Their system also puts the power of government in the hands of the two chambers. These chambers are elected by all the people. Among these people the less privileged are in the majority. Therefore, all power should be in the hands of the less privileged. Then the voters who live by their manual labor will use the power of the law to change the foundations of society, the political system, and above all the tax rates so that the liberal bourgeoisie will be in just as unpleasant a position under the Democrats as the Democratic majority currently is under the press of the Liberals.

Whatever way we find to solve the problem, this much is beyond doubt: it would be childish prattle or worse to see the social question as simply a matter of a few repairs and a layer of paint. The social question in actual fact touches (1) the foundations of society, (2) the entire mode of state management, and (3) not least the principle of authority, *the* political issue par excellence.

III. The Government's Jurisdiction

The jurisdiction of the government has hardly come into play with the three cardinal issues discussed so far. For, returning to our point of departure, this competence is not in dispute so far as the *political* question is concerned. Once the government assumes the right and the duty to seek the will of the nation in its governance, to rule only in close consultation with the Provinces and other Councils on the basis of a mutually agreed upon Constitution and with recognition of the historical rights and liberties of the people, then it is only natural that the suffrage can be extended to all adult citizens if need be. For now we'll not discuss whether this would be desirable, but there is no doubt about the government's right to do so.

The same is true of the fiscal laws. If it were convincingly shown that the present system of taxation imposes an unfair burden and if the government felt it prudent to shift this burden in various ways, she would be allowed to do so, *nemini contradicente*.

Finally, as to the *foundations of our social system,* the government, ruling as she does by the grace of God, would be totally outside her jurisdiction to loosen or move one of the divinely ordained foundations. But where these foundations were laid not by divine command but merely by the magistrates' design, the current magistrate could no doubt change what its predecessors effected, so long as it did not violate historic or individual rights. For instance, should the government feel that communal possession of land would make the Netherlands a happier nation, then there could be no doubt that the government might proceed towards this preference as long as she took adequate measures to reach this goal without violating anyone's acquired right.

Thus, the road is open in a threefold respect. *Politically,* the government may not let the Second Chamber become the sole governing body; *fiscally,* she may not introduce communism; with respect to the *principles* on which communal life rests, she may violate neither God's ordinances nor historical rights. But avoiding this threefold snag, should the government deem it desirable to introduce universal suffrage, shift the tax burden, and improve the social foundations, she would *not* be legally incompetent to do so.

The matter would take on a totally different color, however, if we were to ask more precisely whether the government has the jurisdiction to exercise *direct* influence on manual labor as such. The social conditions of the common people who live by manual labor are only *indirectly* determined by the political, fiscal, and social structure of the community. They depend *directly* on the prospering or languishing of manual labor itself. If there is ample demand and generous reward for that labor and if it can take place under circumstances that elevate the manual laborer, this class of common folk will prosper. But if it is hard to get work, if the pay is meager and has to be done under demeaning conditions, this class as a whole will languish.

The question is whether the government may directly interfere in this area. Or do the authorities overstep their bounds when they create labor or reduce competition, raise wages or shorten the work-week, and in general support manual labor by making it available only under such conditions which ensure that the manual laborer is also respected as a *human being?*

We believe it beyond doubt that the government does *not* have this right, at least not in the absolute sense. State and society are not identical. The government is not the only sovereign in the country. Sovereignty exists in distinct spheres, and in each of these smaller circles this sovereignty is bound to primordial arrangements or ordinances that have been created not by the government but by the Creator of heaven and earth. Only in one instance can these sovereign entities tolerate, or even demand, government intervention: when two or more of these spheres collide at their common borders and a great imbalance between their respective powers makes it likely that the more powerful entity would suffer from *hypertrophy* and the other would be inequitably suppressed. To take an example. The point of contact between the sphere of capital and the sphere of manual labor is always a contract — either formally drawn or presupposed. Because the authorities are involved in court cases about contracts, this is the formal point that lies within the reach of the government.

This poses the question: should the State allow any kind of contract, or do the authorities have the right to stipulate that *every* contract dealing with such matters must presuppose or include certain conditions? Then the next question: is it within the government's power to set a punishment when such contractual conditions as she deems essential have not been followed? For this reason, in criticizing the factory labor bill proposed by Mr. Ruys,[6] we wondered whether the legislature would not have had a better point of departure if it had taken up the matter of form of

6. Jonkheer [Sir] Gustave L. M. H. Ruys van Beerenbroek (1842-1926) was a lawyer from Maastricht, the heir to an eminent Catholic family in Limburg, and a participant in the 1886 Inquest into labor conditions. He was Minister of Justice in the Mackay Cabinet of 1888-91 and chief sponsor of the Labor Act of 1889.

contract. As this proposal attempts to intervene *directly* in a domain that is sovereign *in its own sphere* and governed by law, we think that a first step has been taken on a road that will leave every sphere of society at the mercy of the magistrate. A *principiis obsta!* [withstand beginnings!] was therefore not superfluous.

Let's take it from another vantage point. It is our deepest conviction that the government has no jurisdiction to stipulate how labor matters must be regulated, even when it concerns form of contract. The States-General do not remove this objection. For although the States-General represent the people as one entity, they do not adequately represent the *subentities,* such as capital and labor, which may collide with one another. For that reason we have always insisted that labor be organized on the basis of constitutional law. Capital is of course already strongly represented in the Provincial States and other Councils. It is firmly entrenched in the highest circles of the government and possesses its own organizational network in the Chambers of Commerce. *Labor* stands on the opposite side, unarmed and defenseless. Private labor associations do not constitute a counterbalance, since they must camp in the open field *outside* the constitutional edifice. The least that should be done, we think, is to immediately create Chambers of Labor which the government must consult. But this is not enough. "Chambers of Labor" will remain an odd element as long as they are not rooted in the organization of labor as such. Capital has only *one* form, but labor has *many.* Therefore, if labor is to be organized it must have a structure that accommodates *each of its forms.*

We do not care whether one wants to use the old label of *guilds* for this type of organization. Nobody wants to restore the guilds in their ancient form. But we do demand that the Revolution acknowledge — and we would prefer a confession of sin before the end of *1889* — that it made an enormous mistake when it demolished the traditional organization of labor without replacing it with something new. Society is not served by a *tabula rasa* as we have had now for almost a century.

IV. The Old Guilds

The deterioration of society that resulted from the destruction of the organization of labor has once again focused our attention on the ancient system of guilds. We should take care that this never lead to a movement which intends to restore the ancient guilds in their historic form. It was an unforgivable mistake for the Revolution simply to abandon the existing organization of labor without putting a better one in its place. But it was a laudable act and not an error that in the second half of the past century more than one country in Europe abolished the antiquated guild system as it existed at that time.

The blame lay with the Revolution. Not as if France struck the first blow with other nations simply following after. In Germany the law of 4 September 1731 had already laid the ax at the root of the tree, and Emperor Joseph II through his edicts hacked away mightily at the trunk.[7] What the Revolution accomplished was this. First, long before the storming of the Bastille, a false idea had spread among the nations promising untold earthly happiness, also for the working class, through unbridled freedom. Second, clothed with authority for the first time in France, it suddenly in 1791 (after a futile attempt by Turgot in 1776) brushed aside every organization in the sphere of labor with one stroke of the pen.[8]

The misguided *idea* that boundless liberty would solve everything and the rude *example* of turning everything instantly into a *tabula rasa* eventually inspired most governments to go in a similar direction. And even though in Germany freedom of occupation [*Gewerbefreiheit*] was fully applied only on 21 June 1869, and even though in Germany and Austria (see the law of 15 March 1883) some remnants of the ancient guild system are still honored,[9] we should recognize that the *guild system* has in fact

7. King Frederick William I of Prussia (1688-1740; reigned 1713-40) suppressed the craft guilds as part of his campaign to improve the Prussian army. (Hajo Holborn, *A History of Modern Germany, 1648-1840* [New York: Knopf, 1969], p. 200.) Unfortunately for the political-religious linkages Kuyper proposes elsewhere, this epitome of bureaucratization, state power, and military might was a Calvinist of marked puritan-pietistic leanings. The Hapsburg Joseph II (1741-90; Holy Roman Emperor 1765-90) was guided by Enlightenment ideals in his program of political and economic rationalization, including the elimination of serfdom and guild restrictions.

8. Anne R. J. Turgot (1727-81) was finance minister in the early reign of King Louis XVI of France. One of his famous Six Edicts of 1776 proposed to suppress the guilds and encountered no opposition, but resistance to other measures in the package forced his resignation and brought the plan to nothing. The National Assembly in 1791 did, as Kuyper suggests, implement Turgot's scheme on this and other points: it deregulated the grain trade, used the army to enforce its ban (14 June 1791) on workers' associations, and so left peasants and workers alike to the forces of the market.

9. Freedom of movement and occupation was part of an overall plan of economic integration that Otto von Bismarck instituted in the North German Confederation with the help of the National Liberal party. Otto Planze dates this particular measure to 1867, not 1869 (*Bismarck and the Development of Germany*, vol. I [Princeton: Princeton University Press, 1990], p. 412). The 1880s were the key decade of industrialization in Austria, with concomitant protective regulations being installed under the Edward Taaffe cabinet between 1883 and 1885. (Arthur J. May, *The Hapsburg Monarchy, 1867-1914* [Cambridge: Harvard University Press, 1960], pp. 222-23.)

been replaced by absolute "liberty" and that the languishing remains of the old corporations seem to continue only as curious antiquities without exerting any real influence on the course of affairs.

The old *guild system* was doomed to fail because it was ominously taken over from *Roman* into *Germanic* law and thus inevitably conflicted with the character of the new European way of life. A better way would have been to follow Solon's approach in Athens instead of trying to imitate ancient Rome. Solon gave free rein to private initiative. He did not allow the government to get involved in business but merely stipulated that manual laborers constitute their own class of citizens, that nobody be allowed to have two trades at the same time, that foreigners from the outside be allowed to offer competition only if the local craftsmen agreed. Furthermore he gave industry the right to be sovereign in its own sphere and to make its own rules, the only restriction being that it was not to decide anything contrary to the law of the land.

This was possible in Athens since there the manual laborer was regarded as an honorable citizen. In Rome this was not the case. Most manual laborers in Rome were slaves; for free men to join them was considered a humiliation. Thus their corporations were looked down upon with contempt. . . . Guilds of that kind, transferred on that basis to the towns that Rome built along the Rhine, the Danube, and the Meuse thus contained the seeds of political struggle. The citizenry and the guilds were two. Unavoidably the ambition gradually arose in the heart of the guilds to resist the patricians, to demand equality with the other citizens, and finally to try to acquire power over their fellow-citizens. Well organized, heavily armed, confident of a numerical majority, these guilds waged real war often enough, losing sight of their craft's well-being in their hunt for political power. . . .

Yet it may not be denied that, even in this extremely defective form, the guild system served society well, particularly in areas like Flanders and Holland where it did not rest on such a strong division between two classes of citizens. Thanks to the guild system in the sixteenth and seventeenth century, our craftsmen were not only outwardly prosperous but so able in their trades that the most exquisite and artistic products were made in the Netherlands. The craftsman was a sort of artist in his workshop, and the rest of Europe learned real craftsmanship from us.

But now the struggle is no longer between the craftsmen and the citizens who purchase their products but between the masters and the workmen. That overriding fact makes it wholly unsuitable to resurrect the guilds from their grave in their old form as a solution to the social question. Any new rules should pay attention to two things. First of all, to what the crafts themselves require, taking into consideration what the purchasing public demands so that the crafts will not be destroyed by unrestricted freedom while at the same time the public will not be exploited by overly stringent regulations. But also, secondly — and this is the main issue — no new organization can solve the problem unless it so arranges the reciprocal relationship between the factory owners and bosses on the one hand and those who actually perform the work on the other that the worker gain a renewed sense of the security of human existence.

Today this sense of security is totally lacking, and for four reasons. (1) The managers of all sorts of workplaces now have, in steam and engine, a power at their disposal that makes them largely independent of manual labor. (2) The amassing of great capital makes it possible for industrial enterprises to expand on such a scale that small concerns can barely keep up. (3) The *Freizüglerei* — i.e., the unrestricted movement of workers, even from other countries — allows unacceptable competition with the local craftsmen. (4) All workmen, young and old, are now without long-term contract; they can be dismissed tomorrow as long as the wages due them have been paid.

These are the precious fruits of unbridled liberty, this is the grievous result of the *laissez faire, laissez passer* that our Liberals proclaim as the highest wisdom. Today this confronts us with the bitter misery that divides the lower and higher classes of society in hatred, resentment, and passionate anger. For it could not but make the manual laborer among us, as in imperial Rome, a kind of being to whom no human existence need be guaranteed, a sort of *appendix* to the machine. And once again this numerous class reacts by fighting without restraint to defend its right of existence. It does so, first, by creating its own organization and meeting coercion with coercion in *the strike*. Second, through anger, as in Belgium and the North of France — turning against the machines that compete with them and setting factories on fire.[10] Also, by demanding that society be so organized that it will be saved from the tyranny of capital. And finally, if this should not happen, through the notion of overturning, top to bottom, the entire social order which it perceives as the cause of its misery.

Our authorities thus have a choice. Which do you want? Either put

10. Wildcat strikes had erupted in the mining and manufacturing districts around Liège and Charleroi in March 1886. "The blind, elemental force of discontent and despair" evident in the workers' spontaneous looting of the countryside and destruction of factories "showed itself on a scale never before seen in Belgium." (Kossmann, *The Low Countries*, p. 317.) Émile Zola was electrifying Europe in these years with *Germinal* based on conditions in France.

an end to the tension that undeniably exists between the bosses of the industrial enterprises and the manual laborers — not by putting them off with empty promises but by truly eliminating the abuses and creating the climate for well organized cooperation. *Or,* if you don't want this, then things will stay on a war footing, and the struggle already begun by the manual laborers against the machine, against capital, and against the social order becomes unavoidable.

This being the situation, the Antirevolutionary believes that the false Liberal principle of *laissez faire, laissez passer* which has given rise to all these problems must be abandoned, the sooner the better; that it must not come to a war between citizens; that therefore the government has the duty to ensure that organization take the place of disorganization; and that both parties have the opportunity to furnish the building blocks for this organization freely and independently.

V. Chambers of Labor

The Chambers or Councils of Labor that have been proposed from different sides can never give us the positive elements of the ancient guilds. Furthermore, their efficiency is unthinkable without the prior organization of labor. . . . [Kuyper briefly describes the problems he sees in various proposals.] We do not oppose the idea of a Chamber of Labor but, on the contrary, will support any initiative to have them established, even today, in whatever imperfect form, if it is clearly understood that this would only represent the *first brick* for the House and that *the House* as a whole would still have to follow.

In this respect the events of the Middle Ages show us how to proceed. When people first attempted to organize the guilds around the eleventh century, the authorities saw the need to be involved in establishing some rules for the system. But far from pretending that this had settled the matter, they understood their regulations to be nothing but the *scaffolding* for the guilds, which now would build the actual *House* themselves. Not the government but the guilds themselves developed their own organization and regulations, autonomously and fully "sovereign in their own sphere." As the building of the House progressed the authorities removed its scaffolding bit by bit. Contact with the authorities in the fourteenth and the fifteenth century did not primarily concern the guilds' organization but the *political* privileges they demanded, particularly those touching their share in local government.

This is the route to take today as well. We believe the government would make a definite mistake if it were to initiate too many rules. Even today it can do no more than erect the *scaffolding*. And perhaps it would therefore be better, at least for the time being, to have the "Chambers of Labor" only represent the real *laborers*. Let all laborers who can prove that they have received regular wages in the same place for at least a year elect such a Chamber in each town or group of villages which together count some twenty thousand inhabitants. The role of such a Chamber for the time being would be limited to giving advice. But if it had the freedom to establish sub-organizations in various crafts and groups to gather data on which to base their advice, we would see a grassroots organization with an official character emerge that would help us proceed step by step. Having been initiated by the interested party would in itself guarantee that it would not get too far removed from reality.

The Chambers of Commerce could also gradually be changed and expanded in such a way that they would develop into representative bodies with sub-organizations for the various branches of employment. Then we would be on the right track towards two advisory bodies, each from its own perspective and aware of its own interests, offering advice to the government about the organization of and issues relating to labor. Naturally this would presuppose that the government would get advice from the individual crafts and share such advice from the Chambers of Labor with the Chambers of Commerce, and vice-versa, to hear comments from both sides.

This would be much, much more profitable than the best *inquest*, which by its very nature is incidental and bears no lasting fruit, gathers its data atomistically and does not lead to organization, does not allow its advice to spring from life but itself goes out in search of it. It would also give the opportunity to establish *Councils of Arbitration* composed of appointees from both the Chambers of Commerce and the Chambers of Labor. If sub-organizations for separate branches are established, their boards could, depending on the nature of the conflict, assist in the appointment of the members of these Councils of Arbitration.

If more *general* issues were at stake and the government wanted a more general kind of advice, what objection could there be to having each Chamber of Commerce elect a delegate to a *General Chamber of Commerce* and, likewise, to have a *General Chamber of Labor* consisting of one delegate from each local Chamber? This body could be established within a year and could develop further by itself from this start, on condition that the details of its organization be left to the Chambers of Commerce and Labor themselves. The government would do no more than lay the first brick and determine the general design. This would have the advantage of satisfying the generally felt need for an organization within a legal framework and furnishing the government with much better advice than would be possible through an inquest. Furthermore, whatever is brewing in different parts of the country would be vented, the Councils of Arbitration would have a solid basis, and a foundation would have been laid for further construction.

Another condition would be — and this we stress — that the government not establish such an organization *only* to strive for reconciliation between employers and workers. Two other objectives must be added, and this leads us back to the guilds. In the first place — to mention this only in passing — we should also pay attention to the undeniable and inevitable controversy between *those who buy* and *those who produce* the goods, particularly in reference to foreign imports. Secondly, more care ought to be given to the development of *national craftsmanship*. Precisely this common interest joins the employer and laborer together. Do our institutions fully understand our times? Can we revive the spirit that would *improve* them relative to those in other countries? Can this be accompanied by further educating our working class *head, heart, and hand* so that in knowledge, loyalty, and craftsmanship they might successfully compete with other countries? Then we would reach the point where now-clashing interests would melt together. Then a better day would dawn for employer and laborer alike. Our national ethos would be strengthened, our national identity enhanced, and the wellspring of national prosperity would flow more freely.

Alas, the Liberal School fetish has incalculably damaged our national labor. Our young apprentices have become intimately acquainted with the rivers of Asia but have not learned how to work precisely with their hands.

VI. Church, School, and Police

The Liberal approach to the social question bore its bitterest fruit in the foolish arrangements it made for *Church, School,* and *Police* to interact with our society. The Liberals wrought such immense damage here that it is quite uncertain whether the results of their recklessness can still be undone.

Those with sound political insight have long acknowledged that the best way for the government to care for the Church is to leave her alone as much as possible. What is delicate and tender in nature must be spared and respected, as it tends to lose something of its splendor when handled by secular agents. It would have been much better if our politicians in

1813[11] had moved in a direction which, for instance, would have led to a gradual disappearance of all official ties over a twenty-year period, if the churches had become used to living from free-will offerings, and if by means of some careful temporary measures and compensation for historic privileges even the financial tie between State and Church would have been cut. America demonstrates how this is the safest route politically and financially but also from the religious-moral standpoint. To this noble decision America owes its political stability and exceeds all other countries in the vitality of its religious life. At the same time there is no other country where the ministers of religion are so well respected and paid.

But our Liberals felt they were too clever to take such a solid policy as their rule. Not that they fought against it in theory. Far from it. They inscribed "Separation of Church and State" on their program in extra-bold gilded Gothic. Except they thought: "First we can use the Church in our attempts to liberalize the simple people a little more!" They first tried to do that in Belgium, in the *Collegium Philosophicum,* until this backfired in 1830.[12] When their attack on the Catholic Church had failed and Belgium had been separated from us, they tried to make up for their failure by sneaking into the Dutch Reformed Church. This is what they proposed: (1) all clergy were to be educated at state universities; (2) the professors would mainly be recruited among Liberals; (3) synodical administration was to be completely in Liberal hands; and (4) the regulations of the church were to be gradually transformed into a set of rules governing an ethical-religious association without a common Confession. And so they set to work. The whole country was flooded with liberal clergy. Everywhere the old religion was to be eradicated. The light of the Gospel was to be hidden under the bushel, while *their* light was to be kindled throughout the church. The failure of this policy is already apparent. Too late Liberalism is discovering with regret and shame that it has only managed to alienate two-fifths of our people from *any* religion, while the remaining three-fifths have been driven back toward conservatism. Meanwhile it has been too little noted how, in its presumptuous partisanship, Liberalism's failed experiment unwittingly severed all kinds of *moral* bonds in large sections of our population, wrought up the passion

11. That is, the reorganization of the national Dutch Reformed Church under King William I.

12. This was an institution founded by the Dutch government in Louvain in 1825 for the more "enlightened" education of all prospective Catholic priests in Belgium. The Belgian bishops refused to cooperate for reasons analogous to those advanced by the Reformed dissenters against the reorganization of 1816 in the North. The project had failed even before Belgium gained its independence in 1830.

of discontent in their blood, and robbed them of the only comfort many hard-pressed folk have in their misery.

Everyone is entitled to his own opinion about the moral value of religion, but even the most ardent Liberal will agree to this. Comparing two working-class families who live in equal circumstances, except that in the one religion radiates its friendly light while the other is characterized by moaning and social discontent, we find the first family to be happier. That so many thousands of families have been robbed of *this* happiness — for this the Liberals are to blame. Therefore we cannot accede to the pressure exerted on us from so many sides that we not deal with church matters in our political journal. The social question itself forbids this, and therefore we continue to demand the emancipation of the churches.

To a certain extent the same can be said about *education*. The Liberals were also unwilling to respect the independence of the School. On the contrary, it was to be a tool and its staff a recruiting-cadre for elections. This had a dual effect. In the orthodox villages it neutralized the influence of the minister. For the middle and higher classes of society it offered a cheap school and effective method to train almost all their sons and daughters as free-thinkers. It would alienate the lower classes from any kind of religion and — when the suffrage was extended — would incline them favorably toward the Liberals. Besides, it provided lucrative assignments for thousands of teachers and supervisors.

But in this case, too, evil carried its own punishment. Action provokes reaction. The *Schablon*-theory perverted the quality of education.[13] The people regressed rather than progressed. The moral influence of the School was destroyed. The end result was that academic coryphaeuses disappeared from the scene, leaving us nothing but insignificant epigones. The younger generation, coldly calculating and benumbed by the strong dose, lost all passion for ideals. Last but not least, the balance between the *intellectual* and *moral* aspects of life was destroyed, while our laborers, though capable in intellectual matters, rapidly lost much of the *skill* needed in their crafts and industry.

This process served the Liberal masters well for a time but at the expense of the poor, whom the heavy emphasis on book knowledge has left ill-prepared for the intense struggle of life. For we should never forget that the labor question is an *international* issue. You cannot isolate your

13. Probably a corruption of the German *Schablone*, meaning model, stereotype, or "cookie-cutter."

country. If politicians elsewhere deal more prudently with their schools, your people fall behind their neighbors — which is to say, working people here lack money while laborers elsewhere earn well.

A foolish partisanship in the domain of *Church and School* resulted in such an obsession with that issue as to leave no heart or head for the political and social interests of the people. And so our colonial management deteriorated, Atjeh turned into a disaster,[14] market after market closed, Hamburg and Antwerp overtook us in giant leaps, foreign producers pushed our own products aside, leaving our poor laboring class victim to this fanaticism.

Finally, we add a word about the *Police,* for the social question is such a central matter that every part of the political machinery is linked to it. A good police force must be respected by 99 percent of the population as the guardian of peace and should be feared by no more than the 1 percent who are difficult and obstinate. All classes and segments of society should know that they can count on the police. Its appearance on the scene should induce order and calm among the people and disturb only rascals and trouble-makers, whether old or young. "A fright for the wicked and a favor for the rest."

But our police today are nothing like this. One could almost say that in an evil hour they have developed into a sort of Praetorian gang with a military organization that creates unrest in the spirits of the citizens, stimulating — even provoking — them to rebellion. In particular the class from which most of our workers come appear to the police as an inferior lot who need to be kept under the masters' thumb. Whence, of course, the sad fact that the majority of this class often allies itself with the rascals and trouble-makers against the police.[15]

This has a very destructive effect. People begin to see the govern-

14. Atjeh, or Achin, is the region at the northern tip of the island of Sumatra. It had long evaded Dutch hegemony in the East Indies and harbored raiders on European shipping in the Malaccan Straits. With British consent, the Dutch launched a war to subdue the territory in 1873 but met mixed success until they finally negotiated an end to hostilities in 1903. The war was very controversial back home and prompted a general reconsideration of colonial policy.

15. A signal instance of police aggravation was the infamous "eel revolt" of July 1886, when Amsterdam police tried to stop the cruel but popular working-class pastime of eel-stripping. Hard economic times and social frustration were doubtless behind the crowd's fierce resistance, to which the police responded by killing 26 civilians, wounding 100, and imprisoning several hundred more. See Kossmann, *The Low Countries,* p. 316.

ment as an exacting, annoying, more or less hostile power. They have to yield to superior force but would oh, so gladly file through this iron bond. Resistance breeds a feeling of satisfaction and honor to one's class. Punishment creates martyrs. And so the foolish way in which the police are allowed to act threatens rather than protects law and order and keeps rebellious sentiments alive. . . .

VII. Inquest or Organization

Inquest and *Organization* are contradictory concepts. *Inquest* is based on the idea: (1) that the working class remains in tutelage under the guardianship of the high and mighty; (2) that the high and mighty now have begun to realize they may not have been the kind of guardians they should have been; (3) that they hold an inquest to find out whether this suspicion is true; (4) that once the inquest has taken place, they will take adequate measures as good guardians are supposed to do.

Organization, which we support, works from a totally different presupposition. It assumes that the realm of labor is a world of its own and best suited to determine its own interests. When these interests impinge on those of other groups, it will be to the advantage of the laborers to fight this fight themselves. It assumes that the government should come to their aid only when, through no fault of their own, the balance between the social powers has been disturbed. Thus there is no question of guardianship, only of a helping hand for the working-class to get to their feet and stay there. In order to realize this in accord with the nature of life and not contrary to it, there must be organization on both sides. The government should get its information through such a permanent organization rather than a one-time Inquest.

Yet, we will not condemn the present Inquest and will not resist any measure the Minister of Justice might take to go through with it. "Anything that brings to light is light." But we do hope that, once the inquiry has been concluded, the Minister will not be tempted to save the situation by measures from the top down. Any Inquest should have a single purpose: to achieve an efficient organization, the sooner the better. And once advice from this organization has reached the Cabinet, the Minister should do on behalf of the State only what proves to be necessary.

Thus, we have no fundamental objection against the emergency act that has already been proposed. Luther once said that children should get *"Apfel und Birnen"* [apples and berries], and if the Minister feels that public opinion demands this *hors d'oeuvre* to whet the appetite for the main course, we have no problem with that. But those who believe that this type of legislation will silence the storm are totally mistaken. That would be like the concessions of the *Girondins,* which merely betray weakness and increase discontent.[16]

No, organization is the important thing. Not a pseudo-organization as proposed by Mr. Kerdijk,[17] who wants Chambers of Industry alongside the Chambers of Commerce with the kind-hearted admission of a couple workers. In the present struggle Commerce and Industry represent a common, not an opposite, interest.[18] No, we must depend on independent organization of both *Capital* and *Labor.* Only when our legal system has instituted such will order come out of chaos and each interest have its natural advocate.

We should not be led astray by the German example.[19] The German people are accustomed to being under the guardianship of the authorities and receive any mitigation of their fate as a gift from the government. But the Dutch people have a different nature. We are keen on personal initiative. Our strength lies in the spontaneous resilience of the citizens. The air we need is called *civic freedom.* So let the Inquest be pursued a little further and shed some more light on the situation; let some emergency legislation stop a certain abuse. Yet this will not yield any substantial results.

Besides, creating such an organization can be done very quickly since the government needs only to call a very *simple* body into life. From then on it would organize itself and could submit some pertinent proposals if such assistance from the government were needed. . . . [Kuyper recalls the scheme of Labor, Commerce, and Arbitration councils detailed above.]

Only when such an organization exists will no single group among the workers any longer be dominant but the entire working class will find peace and quietly help to build a better house. All the issues that will eventually have to be part of a Labor Code — such as the relationships between apprentices, supervisors, and bosses, the decommissioning of

16. The Girondins were rivals to the Jacobins in the Legislative Assembly of revolutionary France, 1791-93. Their pro-commerce, pro-war (against Austria) policy soon fell into disfavor among the Parisian crowds, to whom they responded, futilely, with small compromises and symbolic gestures. They were killed or exiled in the Terror.

17. Arnold Kerdijk (1846-1905) was a Progressive Liberal and something of a "podium socialist" who as lawyer, member of the Second Chamber (1887-1901), writer, and editor advanced popular education, tax reform, and labor cooperatives as solutions to the social question.

18. Kuyper in a footnote here quotes a statute of 9 November 1851 defining "Chambers of Commerce and *Factories*" as open to merchants and factory owners with both having full voting rights.

19. Bismarck instituted major social-welfare legislation (medical, accident, and old-age insurance) in Germany 1881-84, partly in hopes of preempting Social Democrats' appeal, but also in keeping with his vision of state paternalism.

soldiers, wage scales, working hours, safety provisions, sickness and old age insurance, the care of widows and orphans, strikes, etc. — will be solved in the wrong way if they are imposed on the working class from on high. They will come to good only if they are the fruit of cooperation between the bosses on the one side and the workers on the other.

This also bypasses the legal problem of whether it is within the government's competence to intervene in these matters. In this scenario the State regulates only what it is indisputably allowed, i.e., to enable these social interests to organize themselves on a *constitutional basis* and thus to make their wishes known. It will subsequently give *legal endorsement* to additional regulations only insofar as both parties desire.

We intentionally refrain from discussing more specific problems. Whether it will someday be necessary to change our laws apropos of marriage, property, and inheritance; whether some changes in our fiscal system are in order; whether, owing to the social question, church and school will have to function in a more practical way; whether, in the light of this question, the State will demand to extend the right to vote to all heads of households; and whether the government, in providing for the organization of labor, will follow the German example — we have our opinions on all these matters but feel we ought not to give any final answers as long as *organization* has not come into being.

The very understandable ferment among our laborers, which currently voices its opposition against the State through the creation of all sorts of alliances and associations, should first receive a *legal* basis. Only then can we make progress. We would like to see this organization formed as soon as possible for another reason as well. The controversy that re-erupted over the Provincial States showed once again how foolish it is to have the Upper Chamber elected by them. This is to mix political and provincial interests to the detriment of *both*. For this reason, already in 1878, we suggested transforming the First Chamber into a *Chambers of Interests* and to have its members elected not by the Provincial States but by the various social bodies so that the universities, the large cities, commerce, industry, agriculture, and labor — and why not also church, school, and philanthropy? — would be represented in this chamber.[20]

We come a step closer to this ideal as soon as the Chambers of Commerce, Industry, and Agriculture on the one hand, and the Chambers of Labor on the other, have a solid organization, each with their own roots.

20. Kuyper's 1878 proposal is *Ons Program*, his commentary on the Antirevolutionary platform. The relationship of provincial and national parliaments was a chronic question, particularly bruited at times of potential constitutional reform, as around 1887.

Our Instinctive Life

Kuyper's agitation of the social question and democratic politics helped split the Antirevolutionary Party in 1894. Such reform schemes as he laid out in *Manual Labor* and the ideological duels he favored as prime minister (1901-5) struck some within, not to mention without, the party as an otherworldliness typical of theologians. His domineering style and need for adulation did not diminish with age nor endear him to younger leaders eager for a chance at the top. By 1908, then, when the Catholic-Calvinist coalition had another chance to rule, under Theo Heemskerk, Kuyper faced sufficient dissent to keep him out of the Cabinet.

The following piece was Kuyper's response to his critics. Originally published in *De Standaard* during the first months of the new government, it is a shrewd appeal to "the people" via a flattering description of that people by the wounded veteran who had led them so long. It carries out a polemic within the broader antirevolutionary movement: against elites to the Right (the foes of 1894) and intellectuals to the Left (the young men behind the new Cabinet). It presents a genuine anthropology informed by close observation and the latest social science. Finally it is a précis of political organization, Kuyper's memoir of how he galvanized an amorphous population into his country's first modern party.

If Kuyper appeals to memory here, to Antirevolutionary lore and the Wisdom literature of ancient Israel, he also draws close to modernist intellectuals. Fascination with the instinctive and intuitional was everywhere in the young century, from the philosophies of William James and Henri Bergson to the psychology of Freud and the politics of Georges Sorel. Kuyper invokes Gustav Le Bon's psychology of the crowd in this piece; the pioneering sociology of Émile Durkheim would have worked too. Thus he himself is an intellectual, of the sort that the new vitalists either forgave or deeply feared: a charismatic intellectual, the professor as populist who used his mind to serve — or to twist

— the masses. In that connection these articles are valuable for the self-portrait Kuyper left: ". . . the really eloquent man, the born public speaker . . . feels the contact between his spirit and that of his audience and opens the tap. Almost automatically the words begin to flow, the thoughts leap out, the images frolic — psychological art in action."

Kuyper originally published this material as a three-part series in *De Standaard;* the book form used the title of the first part for the whole: *Ons Instinctieve Leven* (Amsterdam: W. Kirchner, 1908). The translation, by John Vriend, has reproduced the original headings as well as the subdivisions that mark off the original newspaper articles. The first two parts — "Our Instinctive Life" and "Within the Boundaries" — are reproduced almost entire. Slightly more than half of the third rubric, "Party Organization," has been deleted since it involves intramural polemics not necessary for understanding the larger argument. As becomes clear from Kuyper's usage, the Dutch *instinctieve* connotes intuitional as well as physical impulse.

Our Instinctive Life

I

The instinctive life of animals often reaches a level that defies all human explanation. The ancient Hebrew prophet refers to the migration of the crane and the stork [Jer. 8:7], and Proverbs admires the industry of the ant [Prov. 6:6-8]. In olden times the labor of a beehive piqued the curiosity of all. The spider especially offers an exquisite example of this instinctive life in its fabrication of a web. When weaving its first web the spiderling has never had any training, nor does it work from a pattern. Still, with a back leg it grabs the sticky liquid silk which is secreted by a gland, draws it out and stretches it into fine threads. Between the diagonals it fashions cross lines, short in the middle and long at the periphery. And so it produces a gossamer-thin work of art that in its overall dimensions and distances is precise to one-tenth of a millimeter. The result is so nearly flawless a masterpiece that one wonders if even the most skillful female hand, after long training and with the utmost exertion, would ever succeed in creating such a web. Yet there can be no talk here of experience.

This was its first web. Nor can one speak of learning, training, or of any device or tool adapted to web-making. The spider presses the sticky silk from its own body and its mindless leg does the artistic work.

In the case of animals and especially finely endowed animals, we are dealing with knowledge and skill that are completely inborn. Their gifts are present from the moment of birth, perfected from the start. The swallow that, for the first time, builds her nest against some high rafter does the job in precisely the same way her parents did, with the same care and precaution and from the same materials. The instinctive life of animals does not show first a beginning and then a process of development and completion. From the beginning, automatically, it is as it is supposed to be. . . . [Some animals can be trained, Kuyper adds, and "evolution undoubtedly occurs here as well." But these do not nullify the role of instinct.] Instinct even shapes the social life of animals. Ants, bees, and any number of other creatures live in an animal community that demands, and so witnesses, common activity. A certain amount of order is required for this; we would even say, a certain amount of leadership. And, in fact, these are all present but completely spontaneously, and they manifest themselves again as often as new groups are formed.

Now whether, as the disciples of Darwin think, these instinctive gifts were the end result of mechanical adaptation to environment over an almost endless series of generations is a question that can be left unanswered here. . . . [Whether] by immediate creation or by evolutionary creation . . . whether receiving [instinct] from God or acquiring it under his providential order, the newborn animal is not a little machine of some sort, unconsciously propelled by the Supreme Mechanic when it runs or pressured when it squirms; in animals too there is a self-acting principle at work.[1] . . . Further, by virtue of the animals' instinct something of divine perfection lies within them. God's wisdom is no more acquired by reflection than is instinct. Divine wisdom is given with the very being and existence of God, subject neither to decrease nor increase. It is always complete and ready, functioning with unfathomable purity. To that degree, in contrast to the knowledge and skill we gain by learning or practice, the instinctive life of animals is comparable to the wisdom of God. Of course the two are not the same. In God everything is original; in animals instinct is derivative, increated. But . . . in both there is a quality of spontaneity, readiness, and immediacy.

Human knowledge, by contrast, is of a totally different kind, acquired in a completely different way, subject to expansion and shrinkage,

1. In the sentence deleted Kuyper cites Sir John Lubbock (Baron Avebury, 1834-1913), probably his *Ants, Bees, and Wasps* (London, 1892).

and manifest under a wholly different character. A kitten of three months is biologically as complete and functionally as fit as its mother, while a child of three months is still totally helpless. We have a capacity that animals lack. But our capacity for achieving knowledge and skill is developed little by little, not by itself but only by effort, not all at once in a single leap, but in an extremely slow progression from one level to the next. We have to perceive, observe, note, analyze, compare, and combine. And it is far from true that every person possesses that capacity in equal measure or can develop it at the same speed; in fact, only a very few have it developed to a very high degree. Most people learn it from those few and imitate them. And whereas four thousand years ago bees gathered and prepared honey exactly as bees do today, among human beings all knowledge and skill accumulates gradually from century to century. All generations labor at enlarging the slowly growing body of science. No one has ever by personal initiative or by dint of extreme effort magically leaped to the level achieved by our present generation. Human knowledge and skill is the common possession of all people collectively, a possession gradually won by the effort of succeeding generations and guided in its development by an invisible power. The result is what we call *progress* in every area of human endeavor, and that result, thus gained, far exceeds the knowledge and skill of animals. . . .

In this connection it is most remarkable that our way of cultivating knowledge and science by analysis and research has no *enduring* character. "We know in part," says the holy apostle, "but when the perfect comes all that we have gained in knowledge in our way will disappear." "When the perfect comes, the imperfect will be put away" [1 Cor. 13:9]. Not "it will then be *perfected*," but "it will then *be put away*." Probably because we shall then have a totally different, an immediate way of apprehending things. Now our mode is to see things in a mirror so that we can see an object only vaguely, as in half-darkness. This the apostle calls "seeing in a glass darkly." Some day that mode of perception will make way for an entirely different way of knowing. "Now I know in part, then I shall know in the manner in which I am known by God" [1 Cor. 13:12]. No longer via a mirror but "face to face." Now a gradual, partial, never completed knowing; then, spontaneous, immediate, and completed at once.

If one asks which kind of knowledge — human *reflection* or animal *instinct* — the perfect knowledge of the future will resemble most, it is immediately obvious that *instinct* furnishes the much stronger analogy. . . . [I]n divine wisdom, animal instinct, and the instinctive life of the angels, the immediately available is most pronounced. Our reflection enables us to make much more progress *in this dispensation* than instinctive life would allow us; hence its enormous importance. But this knowledge does not last. Some day the instinctive will triumph also in us — nothing but the instinctive, but enriched with full awareness.

II

. . . Among tribes that still live in the state of nature this instinctive life is much more vigorous than among the more developed nations. In the former case, as among many animals, the senses function with exceptional acuteness. People empathize with nature; they *feel* a thunderstorm coming and need neither barometer nor thermometer to know what atmospheric conditions to expect. They are familiar with the animal world and possess something of the animal tamer's ability in contending with an attacking beast. Instinctively, without a prescription, the Eskimo drinks his cup of cod-liver oil, while many an ulcer-sufferer reaches for a piece of chalk or soil. In many places a rather significant medical art has sprung up of itself. . . . The prophet Isaiah said of such human activity, specifically that of the farmer and dairyman: *"his God teaches him"* [Isa. 28:26].

But it doesn't end there. What we call *tact* and *skill* have become instinctive by habituation; we do things automatically, without reflection, almost unconsciously. A nimble twelve-year-old who comes zipping down the stairs doesn't give a moment's thought to how many inches the steps are apart and therefore how far to put his feet down at each of them. He doesn't think of the stairs at all but whizzes down, barely touching the steps beneath him. A Scheveningen woman[2] who knits away as she walks down the road chatting to herself doesn't for a moment consider the motions she has to make. She is on automatic and does everything mechanically without worrying. It is the same in a much broader context with everything that has to do with *tact* or *discretion.* You cannot teach it to the inept. It is a given, something that automatically comes with the person expressing himself. You either have it or you don't; it functions inconspicuously as a quiet skill. Though such a habit can be enriched and reinforced by use and experience, the basic trait that comes to expression in all this cannot be taught or instilled but is elicited by life itself from the nature of the person who has it.

Wider still, in the circle of the *artistic* life the spontaneous element is the impulse for all expression. Here too training and experience afford the artist a higher and richer level of development; the art school undoubtedly has its place. Still, whoever goes looking for this talent at school

2. Scheveningen was a typical South Holland fishing village of the time near The Hague where Kuyper had been residing since 1901.

will never get it. All genuine artistic expression arises spontaneously from the soul of the artist. The impulse is born and imparted in the hidden center of his being and, though he may meditate and ponder under great strain while composing poems, painting, sculpting, or building, the artistic image as such arises from his hidden self and automatically seeks expression by its own inner drive. Art can be ennobled by reflection, but art born of reflection is a monstrosity.

One can take a further step and say that all true *talent,* and especially all *genius,* shines with a special sparkle rooted in the instinctive, the automatic, the spontaneous. Simply compare the genuinely gifted public speaker with one who publicly reads what he has to say from a manuscript. The latter, after quiet reflection, has entrusted his thoughts to paper, line by line, and now communicates line upon line to the ears of his listeners, as if by telephone. But the really eloquent man, the born public speaker, takes up his position before the gathering, feels the contact between his spirit and that of his audience, and opens the tap. Almost automatically the words begin to flow, the thoughts leap out, the images frolic — psychological art in action. This is even more true of the *genius.* He does not plod and pick away at things; he does not split hairs or prime the pump, but senses within himself a fountain ready to flow. By spiritual X-ray vision he sees through doors and walls and virtually without effort grasps the pearl for which others grope in vain.

Nor does this exhaust the human realm of the instinctive. The *social, moral,* and *religious* life as well owes much less than people think to the impressions of reflection but actually derives its power from the instinctive life. Love of country may be capable of development, but the seed from which it springs is not the fruit of study but of a spontaneous movement in the psyche of a people. Similarly a sense of honor or pride is basically innate. The case of the love of truth is no different. A sense of justice is rooted in the life of our soul. The same is true for a sense of shame, a sense of honesty, for fidelity and friendship. The seeds of all these social and moral factors germinate spontaneously in the human heart. Nor is it different with religion. Faith, hope, and love are the three pillars of the holy temple, each of them implanted in us by a higher power. No school can produce them in you. Even faith in Scripture comes not from study nor as the fruit of learning but arises, as Guido de Bres confessed, from the immediate witness of the Holy Spirit.[3] A human life constructed solely by study from books would be bitterly cold, unreal, hollow, and vacuous. It is only the spontaneous, the instinctive, the automatic that gives us inspiration, warmth, and enthusiasm.

3. *Belgic Confession,* Article V. De Bres was the chief author of the confession.

Not that we can therefore restrict ourselves to the spontaneous. Reflection is the noble gift given humanity to enrich its life, deepen its awareness, and multiply its powers. Learning is our glory, provided it is not detached from the instinctive foundation of our existence, thus to degenerate into abstraction. Right here, alas, lies the dark side: to the degree that reflective life expands, the instinctive life tends to lose its vigor and tenderness. Look at how love of country diminishes in vigor the further you remove yourself from the spontaneous life of the people and enter the cultural refinement of our cities. It is the same with religion. What Calvin called "the seed of religion," i.e., the spontaneous need to worship, is still alive in wide circles where reflection has not made life artificial; but in the circles of study, erudition, and second-hand science the need for religious expression is increasingly silenced. As a rule, nowhere do we find a more distressing impoverishment of faith than at the university.

This is not intentional; it is simply the natural consequence of the competition between the instinctive and the reflective life. The man of reflection alone, the man of book learning, tends increasingly to view his cognitive activity as the only means of achieving knowledge and skill until the rich, broad field of instinctive life virtually ceases to exist for him.

III

The phenomena of clairvoyance, hypnotism, somnambulism, and the like are related to our instinctive life in the sense that these, too, point to a mental capacity that finds its strength in something totally other than reflection. They cannot be completely separated from our consciousness, but because consciousness manifests itself in a very different way in these phenomena there is a tendency — currently on the increase — to assume the existence of a twofold awareness in human beings. First of all, our ordinary consciousness; secondly, underneath and deeper, a less lucid but richer consciousness in which all sorts of things are cooking that do not get through to our ordinary awareness. Myers called this our subliminal, others our nighttime, consciousness.[4] For our present argument it is

4. Kuyper's allusion here is not clear. The most likely reference is to the pioneering experimental psychologist Charles Samuel Myers (1873-1946), who cofounded the *British Journal of Psychology* in 1904, participated in the first Cambridge expedition to the Torres straits (1898), and published papers on the psychology of aboriginal peoples there. Other possibilities are Adolph Meyer (1866-1950), a Swiss-American specialist in the treatment of schizophrenia and advocate of holistic psychotherapy, and (least likely) Max F. Meyer (1873-1967), a pioneer of behaviorism.

sufficient to see that our minds can harbor significant content which, though not passed on to our lucid consciousness, still exerts great influence on our way of being and our overall development.

Also connected with our instinctive life is the *Wisdom* to which the book of Proverbs above all bears witness. In speaking of "Wisdom" Scripture does not mean "science" or "philosophy." Admittedly, in our national version of the Bible the concept of wisdom is now and then interchanged with the notion of science [*wetenschap:* formal learning], which often causes confusion. Yet there can be no doubt about what Scripture understands by "wisdom." It is recognized so universally that people frequently refer to this "wisdom" by the Hebrew word *Chokmah* in order to make very clear that it means something very different from what in ordinary life is called wisdom or science. In fact, the two are more like opposites. "The wisdom of the world is called folly on the part of God," says the apostle. That wisdom has to be destroyed and replaced by the gospel which brings "the power and wisdom of God," because "Christ has become in us the wisdom of God."[5]

Of course, this does not apply to natural-scientific or technical knowledge. The difference surfaces only when we get around to the spiritual dimension of humanity, hence to the difference between spirit and spirit which accounts for two people viewing the same subject in different ways. *Chokmah,* or sacred Wisdom, operates not in the material but in the spiritual realm, the fear of the Lord being the principle from which it arises. The principle, the source of this wisdom lies not in observation nor in abstract thought nor in reflection but in the fear of God. Thence it proceeds and there it is ever again nurtured. Hence this wisdom has nothing to do with erudition or book learning. The pious fear of God, however genuine it may be, can never by itself produce erudition. To a certain extent, therefore, this wisdom too belongs to the domain of the instinctive life. Often it flourishes more vigorously among the simple and unlearned than in the most acute thinker or the best informed scholar.

This "wisdom," after all, is the reflection in man of the Wisdom of God. The Wisdom of God expresses itself throughout the entire universe, in the component parts thereof, and in the laws that govern it. Ultimately, therefore, Proverbs personifies that Wisdom in the Son of God, and the New Testament shows how the personified Wisdom of God has appeared in Jesus Christ. But among man the Wisdom of God is reflected only in those people who fear God, making the fear of the Lord also the beginning of the possession of this Wisdom. It is the fear of God that makes the

5. Kuyper cites 1 Cor. 1:30 but also uses vv. 18-20.

heart receptive to this Wisdom. It is this fear of God that affords people fellowship with the Eternal One. And it is thanks to this fellowship, grounded in our creation in the image of God and strengthened by the fear of God, that human beings experience the emergence of practical wisdom in their life. That wisdom, attuned to the wisdom of God, enables them to find their way, to go straight and not get lost in the byways of fools. Practical life-wisdom operates in the sphere of religion and morality, in the home and in society. It gives rise to tact and skill. It does not lose itself in abstractions but speaks out of the context of life to that life. Far more than all erudition, it is the actual power that maintains the higher order of life among humanity. Surely Scripture refers to the animal world and its instinctive capacities to help us see clearly that it is hidden spiritual powers which bring out and maintain this practical life-wisdom. Here too it is God himself who causes this wisdom to arise in people, just as it is God himself who causes instinct to function in ants and bees, cranes and swallows.

But this wisdom is not the private possession of the individual. It is propagated across generations from parents to children. Hence the constant admonition to submit to the discipline of parents. While this wisdom is instinctive in nature and origin, it is enriched and reinforced by experience and understanding. Nor is it just propagated from parents to children by "discipline." It operates simultaneously across many families, providing rules for everyday living. These rules are then collected by wise men and reproduced as proverbial sayings. The book of Wisdom is thus called the book of Proverbs.

Genuine learning is the possession of a very few. The half-knowledge of those who parrot the learned is devoid of real worth. Barely ten in a thousand are really learned. Since a person of average ability still needs practical wisdom he gets it not from scholars or books but from *Chokmah;* precisely because it functions among millions while book learning remains the prerogative of the few, this instinctive life-wisdom exerts such boundless influence on human life. The rearing of children continues quietly and without much notice even though not ten mothers in a thousand have ever read a manual on pedagogy. People sailed the seven seas for centuries before the first handbook on navigation appeared. People lived and traded with each other long before the first manual on human society saw the light of day. Food was prepared and served for centuries before the first school of culinary arts opened its doors. Diseases were healed before the rise of medical science. All principles arise from practical life and from the practical life-wisdom that arose from life itself, and though study and research have pondered upon and enriched these considerably, for untold millions living on this planet the instinctive connection with reality still remains the starting point and nerve center of their power. The better the fear of God connects us with the Wisdom of God, which is manifest in the whole of life, the purer this connection will be. Conversely, the more people distance themselves from that instinctive adherence to the Wisdom of God, the more alienated they will be from life as a whole and the less able they will be to act practically, with tact, skill, and wisdom.

IV

To conclude, let me refer with some emphasis to what people have lately begun to call *the psychology of the crowd,* better known by the French title of an important book: *La psychologie de la foule.*[6] Everybody knows that far and away the majority of people feel, act, and express themselves differently when they are with a group of the like-minded than when they are by themselves. This is particularly evident with youth. At that stage a group dares to do anything, while as a rule a certain caution restrains the boys and a certain bashfulness the girls as long as they act as individuals, by themselves. From this viewpoint the study of youth roaming the streets is highly significant. But while the distinction between "the person by himself" and "the person in a group" is most pronounced in early youth, it is also visible in adults. A gathering mob, a mass meeting, sailors in mutiny, rioters in a slum, a peasant revolt spreading from village to village, or a religious movement of the revivalist sort: they all bring out things in people you would not see when they are by themselves. Something of the difference can even be observed in groups of animals. And what emerges in everyday life as an urge for conviviality, what lends charm to a party, to an outing with lots of company, or to a cruise with hundreds of passengers is all closely associated with the change we experience the moment we can lose ourselves in a crowd.

. . . [The changes that occur when we join a group have been given far too little scholarly attention. But that they occur cannot be doubted.] We were not created to be loners [*Einspänneren*]. The normal person feels

6. Gustave Le Bon, *La psychologie de foule* (1895; E.T. *The Crowd: A Study of the Popular Mind*). A near contemporary of Kuyper, Le Bon (1841-1931) began as a medical doctor but turned toward anthropology owing to his travels in Africa and became a widely recognized, if controversial, pioneer in the field of social psychology. He not only argued, as Kuyper recapitulates here, that individual consciousness can be submerged in the collective mind of the crowd, but in an earlier book (*Les lois psychologiques de l'évolution,* 1894) theorized that history is the product of racial/national character, with emotion, not rationality, being the key to social evolution.

solitariness as a punishment, even abandonment. The lighthouse keeper leads an unnatural life. So unnatural even that it is increasingly a question whether solitary confinement, a punishment once so highly praised, is not counterproductive. As human beings we have been created in organic connection with other people. We belong together. And although it enhances our personality to retreat into privacy to meditate, to enrich our minds, or to pray, the person who overdoes this and fails to alternate solitude with companionship is bound to be impoverished. Ten people working together can exert more than ten times the power of a lone individual. The power of cooperation is exponential; it gives each individual more courage and daring. Hidden forces surface when people join forces. Being together animates people, elevates the mind, arouses enthusiasm. It can also spur the desire to do evil, if people are so minded. Sometimes a group acting in concert commits atrocities that none of the individuals involved could have done by himself. A mass mob can commit follies that, in calmer moments, astonish even the actors themselves. For good or ill, the moment a crowd has formed, it acts from a common impulse. But in whatever direction it may go, the action that arises in the communal mind whenever many people are together displays a unique sort of psychological phenomenon that has enormous impact on our whole society.

These phenomena belong to the instinctive life too, insofar as they are not subject to the reflection of the thinking intellect. The peculiar thing about them is how they work at a distance as though the person affected was himself part of the crowd that produced the enthusiasm. When in 1878 the people's petition was signed by hundreds of thousands of people, all Christians in the Netherlands felt greatly encouraged, even though everyone had signed the petition in solitude. The enthusiasm often generated by our political conventions tends to communicate itself to our sympathizers in the most remote corners of the country, even among those who had not themselves attended. All such phenomena are the natural effect of our organic unity. Anything organized by that very fact comes under "the psychology of the crowd," and it is almost exclusively the instinctive factors of life that explain the psychology of the "man in the mass."

Liberalism therefore committed an incomprehensible error when, in ill-considered lopsidedness, it sought refuge in *intellectualism*. Intellectuality, however good in its own sphere, hurts itself the moment it claims to be *the* power that will control human life. Intellectualism may be able to prevail in a small group of highly educated gentlemen, but the moment you approach the rank-and-file it leaves you in the lurch. The attempt to raise the masses to the level of these gentlemen by a one-sided intellectual education must end in painful failure. The common people live, feel, and breathe otherwise, being guided in the main not by reflection but by the impulses of the instinctive life. If after a hard and anxious struggle the Christian [sector of the] Netherlands has succeeded in pushing back the intellectuals' drive and regained freedom for the development of the popular mind, it is due solely to our success as good Antirevolutionaries in understanding the people in terms of its instinctive life — that we have not despised but valued it, have sought to ennoble and consecrate it, to make it burn in the cause of a high ideal. To return the care of children to their parents, to bring these children to Jesus, and to steep the whole of our life in Christian principles: that is what the Christian people of this country have grasped. By forging a bond with that instinctive life, Groen van Prinsterer's position at last became invincibly strong in the face of Thorbecke's intellectualism.[7]

Within the Boundaries

I

. . . Intellectualism is the peculiar mentality of those who deny the organic character of life and let every individual live by his own wisdom. Over against this individualistic intellectualism we therefore oppose the organic character of life which is inseparable from the instinctive. What is frequently dismissed as "common sense" is something very different from what the French call *sens commun. Sens* is above all the expression of the instinctive life and the word *commun* calls for an organic society. *Sens commun* is the sensibility that the interested parties have in common.

Still, we may never conclude that the instinctive life alone has value to us, as though reflection could safely be neglected if not eliminated. We have always had a different view of the matter, as is evident from the founding of the Free University. We have consistently stressed that a higher and more certain development of our conscious life calls for reflection, and that a political-social-religious group that neglects to arm itself with learning runs the risk of degenerating into a merely emotional undertaking. Against this Anabaptistic trend Calvinism has always asserted the need for sound scholarship. Nor did its theology bog down in sentimental mysticism. It has always insisted on serious theological study, and a very rich practice of theological reflection is far from rare among our "laity."

7. Kuyper is referring to the Calvinist (Groen) and Liberal (Thorbecke) leaders of the previous generation in Dutch politics.

Accordingly, the instinctive life must always remain within the boundaries inherent to its nature. Only when it does this faithfully does it have the right to defend these borders against the disproportionate expansion of authority that learning so often arrogates to itself. If all scholarship were of the same sort as the so-called *exact sciences,* or what we call the natural and mathematical sciences, there would be no danger of the true boundaries shifting. To chemistry, physics, etc., the instinctive life has nothing to offer. Although errors in calculation or observation may occur in this kind of science, once these have been spotted and corrected, the conclusion is generally solid. To the extent that medical science operates from the same sort of data, it too in part yields solid results.

On the other hand, the moment *people themselves* are included in the object of research, things stand quite differently. This is already the case in medicine but much more so in those disciplines that operate in the field of conscious human life, such as history, theology, ethics, philosophy and no less jurisprudence, political science, etc. For in all these fields we are dealing with humanity, and since the instinctive life differs substantially from person to person, everyone tends to view the information, data, and situations through a different lens. Consequently, almost no scholarly finding is ever presented in the area of these disciplines whose correctness is not immediately challenged. . . . [Kuyper adduces examples from theology, philosophy, history, and law, referring not only to disagreements between Christians and non-Christians but also to rival schools among the latter: "Plato and Aristotle, Kant and Schelling, von Hartmann and Marx. . . ."]

Nevertheless these studies too must be unremittingly pursued and gratefully appreciated by the whole nation. Not — let me remind you — that the uninitiated would be able to second-guess the conclusions. One who is not himself a person of study is and remains incapable of such judgment. But the people as a whole benefit from these studies by getting from them the elaboration of what they themselves instinctively felt in essence. The light this process sheds is invaluable. But if the non-learned public has to make a choice on one issue or another, it has no choice but to use its own instinctive life as touchstone and for the rest to rely on its leaders.

II

The course of history shows that the further nations develop intellectually, the more impoverished they become in the area of instinctive life, the more lopsidedly they build on the foundation of so-called "science." In the Middle Ages, which are a mere five centuries behind us, how much richer a poetry lived in the people — right down to the language used! Memories of Reformation times are still alive in conversation and stories: how vigorous the instinctive life of the people in this country still was in the sixteenth and seventeenth centuries! Since then we have indeed become more philosophical, statistically better informed, more acute in our planning, technically much improved, and comprehending much more. But this kind of "knowing" virtually exhausts our popular wisdom. It is all calculated. Everything has become pedestrian and prosaic, measured and formal. The free surge and countersurge of life is blocked and quashed.

In our circles we are still relatively fortunate in that the voice of faith has not let itself be silenced but has consistently opposed the absolute supremacy of "science." The pressure we have long suffered has forced us to seek our strength in other factors of human life. Yet among us, too, life is far less instinctively animated than it was in former times. We too see signs of a trend toward a more intellectual outlook. It could hardly be otherwise. Everyone willy nilly is to some extent a child of his time, and the spirit of the times blows in the hearts of us all. The intellect vies for supremacy; learning seeks recognition and influence. If we do not courageously guard the source of the instinctive life, we too will be threatened by spiritual decline and emotional impoverishment.

The mass of people is usually split into three groups. A broad group of men and women who know nothing of "learning" live on the air of the instinctive life and let themselves be guided by their practical good. At the other end of the spectrum stands a tiny group of "scholars," people who can devote almost all their time and best energies to study. From morning to evening, sometimes deep into the night, the wheels of reflection keep revolving in their heads. Between the broad group of people unaccustomed to reflection and the tiny band who know little else you encounter the intermediate group that lives not by its own study but by others'. It feeds on manuals of second-hand scholarship, peddles this as absolute truth, and to the extent that it retains any feeling for the instinctive life at all, puts it *unmediated* next to its knowledge and learning. Sometimes in senior high school classes you can already hear these amphibians proclaim their superior wisdom. Notably, you are most likely to find those who have managed to escape this amphibious phase and brought the instinctive and the reflective life into a higher synthesis among ministers of religion. In recent years we have also begun to discover a number of nobler types among doctors, linguists, physicists, and jurists whose advanced learning does not crowd out but reconciles itself with the inner life of the spirit and especially the life of faith. Just a few short years ago, however, intellectual top-heaviness still ruled among most of these. Idealism is again on the rise, but the years of materialistic oppression have been many and long.

In those arid days, by reason of both their study and their position in life, only preachers avoided extreme spiritual impoverishment. Not all of them but the best. And as history taught in earlier years, our own days have proved anew that preachers had greater influence among the common people than do other university graduates. Of course, our intellectuals didn't like this. They could not stomach it. Hence their incessant sneering against the "dominee." Indeed, hasn't it happened even in our own circles that people played off jurist against theologian and made it appear as if, yes, the theologian could put in his two cents' worth, but basically the lawyer was the only one who counted? This phenomenon deserves our attention all the more because it is precisely in the best of our preachers that the two are united: in the first place, they are men of study and, second, they have some feeling for the instinctive life of our people. . . .

We can also glimpse here the pathway to harmony in the life of our people. People of all ranks must give fresh and forceful expression to their own instinctive life and not go leaning on mechanically copied pseudo-learning that is devoid of all inner worth. Precisely for that reason our people should not wish to reach beyond their grasp and try to solve problems that are far beyond them. Principle can stand firm, and the people can instinctively grasp the immediate application of that principle to life in all its rich variegations. But they should leave its elaboration and specification to the men of learning and study who have the intellectual expertise and the necessary comparative and historical knowledge for the task.

Conversely, the men of study must see to it that they do not neglect to stay in touch with the instinctive life of the people. They must not expect their study and learning to make the vital decisions that only the instinctive life can make. By not guarding themselves at this point learned theologians have killed religion and scholars-at-politics have robbed the people of their enthusiasm and vitality. So let every group stay within its own natural boundaries. . . . There can be a happy linkage, profound cooperation, and undisturbed harmony between the two groups . . . only if both bow their knees before Him who, by using the two in conjunction, causes the life of the people to flourish.

Party Organization

I

The contrast between *instinctive life* and *reflection* also controls party organization. It is well worth our time and effort to consider this in some detail in the present context.

. . . [Kuyper briefly reviews the history of the Antirevolutionary Party under the thesis that support for his leadership and position have always been strong, with a minor flurry of dissent in the *Rotterdammer* since 1903. Even "the split of 1894 really was no split. In all our local voter associations we lost fewer than three hundred members altogether. And although at that time . . . a few men of high repute left us, the resulting Christian-Historical party was not in the main constituted by disaffected Antirevolutionaries. Rather, it gathered under its banner a group of Christian-minded citizens who had never joined our ranks and would not easily have come to us. In that respect the split even bore desirable fruit and strengthened rather than weakened the position of the parties on the Right."[8]]

To the extent that in the currently emerging criticism a certain reaction against our party structure is rearing its head, it can be entirely explained in terms of the changes the critics wish to introduce in the relation between the influence of the instinctive life and that of study and reflection. Some have insisted that our members be allowed to enter upon the study of high-level issues, and they seek to clear the way for this study by a variety of in-depth presentations and assorted quotations, also from foreign authors. Others have called for annual conventions to

8. *De Rotterdammer* was an independently owned Antirevolutionary paper, thus free of formal party controls. Its circulation was second only to *De Standaard*'s. At this juncture it was publishing the critiques of Dammes P. D. Fabius (1851-1931), professor of law at the Free University and Kuyper's foremost critic on the Right within the party. In a few years it would be the organ of the party's Left. Among the "few men of prominence" who had bolted in 1894, Kuyper mentions Alexander F. de Savornin-Lohman (1837-1924), probably his closest associate and political equal in the party prior to the split, and Barthold J. de Geer van Jutphaas, Baron Lintelo (1816-1903), one of his early rivals for the mantle of Groen van Prinsterer. These two led the formation of the Free Antirevolutionary Party which in turn merged with nationalist-Protestant groups in 1903 into the Christian Historical Party. Though more conservative politically and socially, the CHP usually coalesced with the ARP in elections and Cabinet formation. Polemical tone aside, Kuyper's assessment of the shape and consequences of the 1894 split is generally accurate: ARP elites bolted far more than the rank-and-file, and the CHP did bring into harness people that would never have joined the ARP.

create opportunity to debate such issues among ourselves. Still others have called for the involvement of outstanding jurists to correct the "gaffes" which "bungling theologians" have committed. Even the personal reaction against the founder of our organized party arose from this demand. He, after all, is a theologian too, a theologian who has even ventured, like a fortune teller, to predict the future, thus bewitching credulous villagers and countryfolk.

All this criticism comes down to one question: Do you want a party organization that gets its inspiration and power from instinctive life, or do you want one that rests on the props of study and reflection? If the latter, then our whole party organization should be scrapped as totally useless, not even reparable. Then we should also organize a party along the lines of the old Liberals — and be prepared to sink back into our former political insignificance. . . . [Kuyper briefly analyzes the other Dutch political parties as single-class organizations. The three varieties of Liberals are elitist, the Socialists are proletarian, but all are under the lead of abstract theoreticians.] It is therefore safe to say that in [the rest of] our Dutch party system the instinctive does not come into its own. Virtually all leadership is in the hands of men of reflection; there is not one party in which the whole nation, in all its ranks and classes, is vitally involved and has a voice. We have purposely said nothing about the Christian-Historical Party because its signature and persuasion is no secret to anyone. Only the organization of the Roman Catholics is coming to resemble our own. Here too all social classes are getting a better chance to speak out and to become part of the action.

II

[Kuyper spends two pages describing the discouraging history of the Antirevolutionary cause under the leadership of Groen van Prinsterer.] The scattering of opponents and critics currently raising their voices have almost completely lost sight of this history. They have no clear eye for the incredible change that has occurred, especially since 1878. They take no account of the factors that held back our rise on the political scene, nor the new factors that since 1874 — and especially after 1878 — produced our political prosperity.[9] Being blind to all this, they haven't an

9. Kuyper entered politics in 1874 simultaneously with the formation of a Calvinist league to challenge the regnant educational system. In 1878 he (1) galvanized the school petition drive that (2) led to the formation of the Antirevolutionaries as the Netherlands's first organized, popular party and (3) composed its platform.

Above: "Pardon me! It was instinctive!" A caricature of Kuyper's retort to the "elite intellectuals" of the Antirevolutionary Party in *Our Instinctive Life*. *Right:* The younger generation's picture of Kuyper as a scolding father, here lecturing new ARP prime minister Theodore Heemskerk.

inkling of how everything would fall apart if our party, following their advice, should abandon the instinctive life of our people and return to the sphere of reflection and study where only a few have a part. . . .

The resilience needed to regain our popular liberties had to arise from faith. And although Groen van Prinsterer was himself a man of profound study and serious reflection — and by that token one who challenges all the university-educated members of our party to undertake a learned study of the problem we face — he never shrank from declaring that precisely the simplest people had a deeper sense of, a clearer insight into, what was at stake than did the lawyers. For him the words "not many wise, not many of noble birth" [1 Cor. 1:26] also applied to our national circumstances. Groen was great because he, though easily the first among the men of study, intimately shared in the instinctive life of his simplest followers without ever showing condescension. He understood the importance of the practical wisdom inherent in the instinctive life and he identified with it. Accordingly, the nature and character of our Antirevolutionary action were never more derisively misjudged than when, a few weeks ago, the daily *Rotterdammer* responded to our reference to this "practical wisdom" in our instinctive folk-life with the insulting exclamation: "You flatter our people to pull the wool over their eyes." . . .

III

The character of party organizations is always determined to large degree by the nature of their membership. Here too one can spin fine theories and offer ingenious suggestions on how the inner works of a party should be put together for it to run well. But the moment you have to deal with the realities of the membership, your theoretical inventions fall flat and life itself sets the rules.

When Thorbecke helped us get rid of the old rigged system and managed on 7 July 1856 to get the first direct suffrage bill into the statute book, he chiefly had in mind *one* kind of voter, viz., the upper middle class. Thorbecke knew the country like the back of his hand. He was well aware that in the countryside, among the lower classes and the higher nobility, Christian political sympathies predominated, and that you could count on the factory workers for a revolutionary riot and a victory march from Leiden to The Hague but not in the cause of unadulterated Liberalism. Support for *his* ideas was to be found most widely among the contented bourgeoisie [*bourgeoisie satisfaite*]. Also among scholars, some civil servants, and part of the nobility, but these did not constitute his main force. That came from the men of commerce and industry and the rest of the well-fed bourgeoisie. This explains his magic of a high but declining *census*[10] to restrict suffrage as much as possible to *this* favorably disposed class in order later, once his political ideas had gained ground, to lower the *census* from time to time as the higher level of the people's political development allowed.

This historical course of events put its own stamp on the first political party-organization to emerge here. The group of citizens to be organized was not sought out but marked out. It was the well-to-do merchants, the energetic big storeowners, the scholars, a few elite civil servants and aristocrats who, especially in the big cities, could all be found together in the local voter clubs. After first agreeing on matters there, they could set the direction at the public meetings. The countryside simply had to follow the cities. Noord-Brabant came automatically and some of the northern districts as well.[11] Thus, all informally there emerged the gentlemen's organization that later realigned itself into a liberal and a conservative organization, both of them entirely the same alloy.

Things were very different with the rise of the Antirevolutionary Party. Sympathy for Christian principles was strongest by far in the other part of the population, that which the high *census* was designed to keep away from the ballot box. Among scholars a convinced confessor of Christ was already then an "outsider." In the stock exchange, at the office, in factories, and in the big warehouses, in every circle that could be counted as the turf of the "satisfied bourgeoisie," an arid and sober rationalism increasingly held sway. To find true adherence to the religion of the fathers you had to descend to the petty bourgeoisie, to the wide range of people in the countryside, and to the laboring class. You might discover, later, closer to the top — among a very thin slice of the nobility and people of independent means, and in the odd scholar — a more or less fervent love for Christian political principles. In short, a broad group of "little people" at the bottom and a tiny group of notables at the top: the same set of conditions, in fact, that William the Silent had to contend with. . . .

It obviously followed that the party organization of the Christian part of the nation had to be very different from that of "the gentlemen." Since folks had seen no other model of party organization than that of the mandarins, however, they began by copying that — without success. The model fit neither us nor our circumstances. David could not fight Goliath wearing Saul's armor. Only the sling and the stone from the creek

10. The level of taxes one had to pay in order to qualify for the franchise.

11. These were predominantly Roman Catholic districts, loyal to Thorbecke for his 1853 measure to give the church full rights.

suited him. And only when this truth sank in did a party organization of our own kind arise among us, one that gave us a chance of mobilizing our forces and leading them to victory. . . . [Kuyper recalls the fear of the unwashed that characterized Protestant as well as Liberal elites at mid-century.]

IV

Before the Antirevolutionary party could be organized, it first had to be formed. It did not exist. The people were there but they lived outside of the world of politics. They did not take part in politics, had barely heard of it. They knew Groen's name but his political activity and struggle never reached the majority of them. Rather our Calvinistic circles were marked by a certain aversion to everything political; in several, Anabaptist [world-]flight had even found acceptance. Politics was left to the gentlemen; the people themselves did not bother with it. In all politics there is something that smudges; people examined that tarnish through a magnifying glass and turned away. Toward the end of the eighteenth century some Calvinists had gotten involved in the disturbances of the day, to bad effect. Ever since, not only in the villages but also in our cities, Reformed folks had gone on as if there were no such thing as politics.

The first thing needed was to arouse this slumbering life and to do so throughout the country. Obviously the best tool to this end was the struggle for the Christian school. But it had to go beyond that. The goal could not be just to engage in politics for a time, only to go back to sleep once the Christian school had been saved. When a Calvinist has had his political awakening he immediately starts to survey the whole field of politics. . . . Barely had the alarm clock rung, therefore, than throughout the land a political interest sprang up that of itself generated full-scale political action. The difference between 1870 and the beginning of this century is striking. Until 1870 a large majority of our Calvinistic people drifted along with conservative currents; since then we've seen them put out to sea under their own flag. The faithful host have become political enthusiasts, politically self-educated, and politically mature. Today you can hardly find a village so small but it has a leadership cadre, while our press is keeping political life at a high pitch in all the provinces.

It was especially our 1878 program of principles that pushed the expansion of our political life. In that program our people found their deepest convictions articulated in the political sphere. There they acquired a banner they could march behind. From then on the organization developed almost automatically. It was not imposed but grew from life itself. Everyone became eager to take part in the action. You can now find voting associations everywhere, not only in the cities and big towns but throughout the country — almost seven hundred of them — and these have been linked in district or central associations. In every province a committee gives leadership.

But even this would not have yielded the indispensable unity of action if from the very beginning there had not been a Central Committee providing leadership for the country as a whole, and if the leadership of this committee had not met the demands of the situation. A primary guideline for that leadership has always been that no rank or class should dominate another, but that our party should extend one hand downward and the other upward to insure that our people's varied ranks would also be manifest in our party organization. The second principle of leadership was to strictly respect the local independence of each voting association and never to let power play into the hands of a few potentates in the district capital. The third principle was that we would always maintain a united front at the States General and the Provincial States. The party as party had to know what it wanted to accomplish. Its ultimate goal, the focus of the action of the whole party nationwide, was not to delegate a few "trusted men" but to elect to Parliament "strongly committed men of our own persuasion." That this did not entail a binding mandate was understood; once elected, every member of the Chamber was bound only by his own conscience and conviction. But during the election campaign that conviction had to be made very clear; it had to be evident that candidate and party were in agreement.

Even thus we would have gotten no more than a smoothly functioning voting machine. For a party to be able to carry its platform forward energetically, it needs above all to be powerfully conscious of its unity. It must have the means — as *the psychology of the crowd* demands — to convert sober realism into enthusiasm, cool calculation into holy passion. That is the purpose served by our local meetings and especially our party convention. . . . Someone who joins the battle in an isolated village, with only a couple of sympathizers, easily feels weak, dejected, and abandoned. But bring the solitaries out of their hideouts and to a great gathering. Unite not just the fashionable and high class but representatives of all ranks, the notables along with the simple, the wise alongside the learned, the small and the great, and set them all aglow with the sense that they are *in fact* a mirror image of the whole country. Then faint-heartedness gives way to a sense of power. Good cheer, real animation, and high spirits arise. And if the circle swells (as among us) into a group of two thousand, their gathering amidst the tensions of an election will leave so fundamental and overwhelming an impression that the delegates return home not just encouraged but prepared to make any sacrifice, and exuding their enthusiasm to all who stayed at home.

It is by virtue of the power and animation that radiates from these national conventions that we have become who we are. After every convention new voter clubs apply for membership, our press increases its circulation, local efforts become more valiant, and new volunteers offer their services in the campaign. This action is so effective because the unity that took rise at the convention, thanks to the enthusiasm ignited there, worked with a multiplier effect throughout the country.

Saul was a man of technical *reflection*. He advised young David to put on his, Saul's, armor lest he be unable to defend himself against the mail-fisted, armor-clad Goliath. But David took off all that armor and went out to meet Goliath in the name of the Lord. That was the *instinctive* life coming out. And so not by following Saul's reflection but by following David's example has our Antirevolutionary Party found its strength.

Calvinism: Source and Stronghold of Our Constitutional Liberties

Kuyper always insisted that his politics were philosophically consistent, rooted in and circling back to fixed principles. But one of those principles was respect for historical development, and his inaugural statement on Calvinist political theory, which follows, shows how historically oriented Kuyper's thinking could be. Sometimes he found his principles where he found his co-religionists achieving, or only associated with, ends he approved. To cluster these desiderata into a system attributable to first principles did not make for the soundest history (see his rendition of the American case) nor for tight political philosophy. But it did make for a powerful argument on behalf of Calvinism's progressive potential, which was his intention all along.

Kuyper delivered this lecture to student groups at several Dutch universities on the 25th anniversary of the Constitution of 1848. That was a difficult assignment since orthodox Calvinists had hardly been enthusiastic for the document in the first place. In addition, Kuyper hoped by this speech to make some recruits for the Antirevolutionary cause and to stake his own claim to its leadership. Thus he *had* to show Calvinism's currency with modern aspirations. He *chose* to make a virtue of Calvinism's particularity, its doctrine of election, over against those in the party who wished to take more generic Protestant ground.

Kuyper begins by invoking the two contemporary threats through which his cause had to thread its way — the (German) centralizing state and the (French) excess of liberty. Then he revisits Calvinists in history, sometimes at rule, mostly in resistance, but animated by a consistent set of convictions. If his argument suffers some logical and evidentiary flaws, it is worth noting that more dispassionate accounts in the twentieth century have covered the same ground with congruent results.[1]

Two other features deserve special mention. Principial thinking aside, Kuyper subscribed to a lot of contemporary assumptions about national character — and the characteristics commonly assigned to different nations. If he abhorred the French Revolution, he also had doubts about French Calvinism, raising the possibility that philosophy was not so much the issue as Frenchness. If the Germans look (to put it awkwardly but, in this case, accurately) less unattractive, it is only because their threat is prospective and not a painful memory. The English and Americans are Kuyper's favorites here and would remain so until the Boer War changed his mind (see *The South African Crisis*), but they had to be permanently and uniformly Puritanized to qualify for the role.

Second, the Puritans shine for their ecclesiology as much as for their theology. Kuyper's passion on the church question informed his discussions of state more than we might expect. On that score his confusion of the Pilgrims of Plymouth with the Puritans of Massachusetts Bay and of both with the founders of Rhode Island whom they cordially despised, if understandable from a Dutch distance, was telling nonetheless. Kuyper had to walk a precarious tightrope between liberty and order. In this he caught Calvinism, and much constitutionalism, square.

Kuyper's lecture was published as *Het Calvinisme, oorsprong en waarborg onzer constitutioneele vrijheden* (Amsterdam: B. van der Land, 1874). This translation, by Reinder Bruinsma, represents approximately 80 percent of the original, deleting some repetitive or summary sentences and long historical disquisitions on the Puritans and Huguenots. Some of that material may be found in an older translation by J. Hendrik de Vries, published in *Bibliotheca Sacra* 52 (July and October 1895): 385-410 and 646-75. Kuyper appended 120 notes to his text; I have combined many of these and fleshed out his references.

1. Michael Walzer, *The Revolution of the Saints* (Cambridge: Harvard University Press, 1965); Quentin Skinner, *The Foundations of Modern Political Thought* (New York: Cambridge University Press, 1978).

LADIES AND GENTLEMEN:

It is still generally assumed that we as Western nations, and our nation above all, enjoy the broadest freedom possible and need not worry about the undisturbed possession of the same in the future. I do not share that opinion but rather tend to fear that our civil liberties, though not likely to be lost, may well be restricted. I speak of "freedom," not of "free rein for arbitrariness." I speak of the kind of freedom Winthrop described as early as 1650 when addressing an American gathering:

> Not a perverted freedom, that cheapens a person, that demands free rein for every whim, pays no attention to authority, tolerates no order, and is irreconcilably opposed to truth and justice. No, ours is a genuine, civil, and also moral freedom that does not disrupt but unites, that derives its support precisely from legitimate authority, that offers and guarantees justice so that we may without fear consecrate heart, head and hand to what is good and beautiful, noble and just. This type of freedom alone, (Winthrop declared) is my holy bond, to be defended at any price, and, if necessary, worth the sacrifice of our body and blood.[2]

Of the undisturbed security of this kind of freedom I am far from sure. No one can deny that much good has been achieved. The privileged position of the higher classes has been abolished. Many instruments of tyranny can no longer be employed. There is equality before the law and, more than in the past, the people can be involved in public affairs. This is very laudable. Nonetheless, the sharp criticism by the liberal de Tocqueville remains justified: "These citizens, who appear to be so interested in their freedom, year upon year relinquish almost unnoticeably part of their individual independence to the administrative arm. The very people who have brought down thrones and put the kings of the earth beneath their feet bow before the whims of an ordinary civil servant without any protest."[3]

Can it be denied that the centralizing State grows more and more into a gigantic monster over against which every citizen is finally power-

2. Kuyper (note 1) cites Cotton Mather ("Mathiew"!), *Magnalia Christi Americana*, vol. II, p. 13, and cross-references Tocqueville's *La Démocratie en Amérique*, vol. I, p. 66. He was probably using the Hartford, 1820 edition of Mather; there were any number of three- and four-volume French editions of Tocqueville available from Paris or Brussels.

3. Kuyper (note 2) cites Tocqueville, *La Démocratie*,vol. III, p. 513. Kuyper could refer to Tocqueville as a "liberal," even though the Frenchman was a Bourbon legitimist and wrote negatively of the Revolution, because Tocqueville did not ground state authority in divine sovereignty. Tocqueville thus qualified as a liberal qua secularist, though of conservative stripe.

less? Have not all independent institutions, whose sovereignty in their own sphere made them a base for resistance, yielded to the magic formula of the single, unitary state? Once there was autonomy in the regions and towns, autonomy for families and different social ranks, autonomy for the courts as well as for the universities, corporations, and guilds. And now? The State has annexed all these rights from the provinces, one after the other. Then it tells the towns what to do, comes in your front door, expropriates your property, commandeers the law, makes trustees and professors its servants, and tolerates no corporation but as its own dependent. By inventing administrative jurisdiction, it acts as both party and judge in the conflict whenever citizens launch a complaint against it. People have rightly cursed the violence of the "ancien régime," but let us not forget that the sector of our life over which the State spread its net back then had hardly one tenth the reach of our present government. Just look at Europe's budgets: then, hundreds of thousands; now, in the billions. Not to meddle would seem to the State a sign of weakness, a dereliction of duty, and the best minister is thought to be he who, omnipresent with his cherub-like eyes, does not leave a single place in the old domain outside the reach of his dutiful servants, his laws and decrees.

You're right: in the past corporate bodies oppressed the individual and for the sake of individual freedom they have been pulled down. That was necessary. But is the individual freer now or rather defenseless and helpless when faced with the all-devouring super-corporation of the State? Where will we end if the recent craving for centralization runs its course? How will you resist if the deification of the State continues to brand every form of protest a sacrilege from the start? What will remain of your personal freedom if a form of Caesarism eventually develops out of the modern state? If a modern Imperialism, converting its "panes et circenses" into an economic regime of material well-being, acts as it pleases since no one is able to resist? I realize, until now this danger has been fended off from our realm at our eastern borders. But that could change, and then what? Do you believe that the noble civic spirit, so keen for ancient liberties, will be your shield and breastplate still today, will still flourish the liberty cap on the well-sharpened spear? Ask Opzoomer, who recently and rightly complained how the indifference of the people can barely muster a cold smile, a "little chuckle," since they no longer want to get involved.[4] They have forgotten how, because of what the Greeks

4. Cornelis Willem Opzoomer (1821-92), a professor of philosophy at Utrecht, was the foremost Dutch intellectual of the day and a doctrinaire liberal in theology and politics.

called ακηδια [*akedia*: heedlessness, sloth] — because they have become totally blasé and are no longer enthused for an idea, a right, a particular freedom. That numbing of our sense of justice, this "laissez aller," this political indifference of the citizenry toward a government that constantly grows in power, size, and influence — that is the "bowing down before the whims of a common civil servant" about which de Tocqueville was so concerned. Freedom is in danger precisely when citizens lack pride and the state lacks bounds.

The goal of the Antirevolutionary party is to avert this danger. And I know it may count on your support in this even if the means the party chooses to reach its goal may strike one as impractical, another as doubtful, or many as downright unacceptable. I ask only one thing of you: do not judge our party if you do not know it. And since not all have this knowledge, allow me to sketch our ideals for saving our freedom.

One principle must be accepted as basic. The guarantee of a plant's viability lies in the root from which it grows. Therefore, so our party asserts, those who would guarantee our liberty must first know its origin, must tell us whence it springs. This requires a knowledge of history; therefore the question I submit to you is of a purely scholarly nature.

Some generally known facts define the terrain for our enquiry. We need not argue that, by comparison with Europe, there is no freedom in Asia and Africa. And within Europe few will look for the birthplace of freedom in Russia or Turkey, in Spain or Austria. There is room for doubt concerning Italy, the Nordic countries, Germany, and France. But praise of England, Holland, Switzerland, and America as countries of political freedom wins immediate and universal consensus. This geographical evidence coincides with the chronological. After the Reformation but before the French Revolution political freedom was restricted to England, Holland, Switzerland, and America; and since the revolution of '89, efforts to promote even greater liberties outside the domain of these four have so far remained fruitless. Thus, there is good reason to honor those four nations with a special certificate of suitability for political freedom. Outside their borders you will look in vain for the origin of our freedom.

Why this positive exception?

Bancroft, the famous chronicler of American history, tells you: "My nation's enthusiasm for freedom was born from its enthusiasm for Calvinism." De Tocqueville concurs: "America's freedom regards religion as the guardian angel of its struggle and victory, as the cradle of her early days, the divine source of her law."[5] . . . Precisely in the four countries just mentioned the Reformation bore a decidedly Calvinistic stamp, being controlled from Geneva. That is true for Switzerland and England and can be argued for Holland and America. Yet we shouldn't rely on this premonition. The *propter hoc* ought to be distinguished here from the *post hoc*. Our suspicion will be proven only if the development of Calvinism through its three stages — the French wars of religion, the English Revolution, and the founding of the American union — actually demonstrates the expansion of those civic liberties we are so proud of. Let us proceed with that enquiry.

But first a twofold remark.

The first one is this: Our Calvinists often call themselves Antirevolutionaries. How must this term be understood? Is it right to identify this group with Stahl's Prussian Party or the Ultramontanist world party?[6] Certainly, in one respect. If the question is whether the state can flourish without the root of faith, our answer totally agrees with theirs. We are one over against the French Revolution's basic premise of emancipating the creature from the Creator. But if it is suggested that this common principle leads to the same constitutional law, I must claim for the Calvinistic view the uniqueness to which the Reformed community is entitled. Rome established its own political system on its own confession. In keeping with its hierarchical structure, this was preponderantly monarchic. She succeeded in making this system a reality. All medieval states were based on the theory of the two swords. We should not withhold from Rome the honor she is due: her constitutional law proved to be the germ of creative thought. That was not true for the Lutheran Reformation, which remodeled but did not build anew. After the Reformation the political system of the Middle Ages was simply continued in Germany and the Nordic empires except that Caesaropapism replaced the hierarchy, moving spiritual authority from the Roman Curia to the prince's cabinet.

Calvinism, however, has proved to possess the power that the

5. Kuyper cites (notes 3 and 4) George Bancroft, *History of the United States from the Discovery of the American Continent*, 15th ed. (Boston, 1853), vol. I, p. 464; and Tocqueville, *La Démocratie*, vol. I, p. 69. In the deleted material that follows, he cites Dutch and French authorities to the same effect.

6. Friedrich Julius Stahl (1802-61) was a German Lutheran political theorist of the Restoration, defending throne and altar on the principles of the Gospel and history. His proximity to Dutch Antirevolutionary thought made him an ally that yet needed to be kept distant. Ultramontanism was a postrevolutionary assertion of the powers and leadership of the papacy in the Roman Catholic Church and as a guide to European society as a whole. It was associated in France with such political theorists as de Maistre and Lamennais.

Lutheran Reformation lacked. Like Rome, Calvinism has developed, from its unique principles, its own political philosophy which can be recognized by its republican character even when it takes monarchic form. Calvin accomplished what Luther could not: establish nationalities. Our Union, the England of the "Glorious Revolution," the Scotland of the Covenant, and America in its northern union of states were inspired by him. Do not misunderstand me: I realize that, when expedient, the Catholic Church can adapt to any form of government. I also know that prior to the Reformation the inhabitants of these countries treasured their liberties. And I know that the learned Jesuits even promoted democratic ideas. But leaving exceptions aside and focusing on core principles, I can only characterize Rome's basic thinking as monarchical. Over against this stands Calvin's clear statement: "The republican form of government, whether it be solely aristocratic or a mixture of aristocratic and democratic elements, seems to me much to be preferred." This belief was not rooted in some idea of human greatness but rather in his profound sense of sin. For he adds: "Because of sinful human nature, it is safer and better to let several people together steer the ship of state so that one may restrain the other when the lust for power might degenerate into tyranny."[7]

. . . [The Dutch Antirevolutionaries break with Stahl, Kuyper comments, by rooting monarchy in constitution while his school does the opposite, a difference, moreover, that issues from their respective Reformed and Lutheran confessional commitments.[8]]

To this I add my second, much shorter remark. To guard against misunderstanding, I must strongly emphasize my claim that *not* the French Revolution but rather our political liberty has been born of the Calvinistic faith. Otherwise, I could safely refrain from further argumentation without fear of opposition, for it has been loudly argued from all sides that our present-day revolution is a blood relative of Calvinism. Catholic historians are inclined to name Calvin himself the spiritual father of the French Revolution. Says Professor Alzog of Freiburg: "The consequences of the Reformation became utterly clear when they spilled over from religious to political affairs." And that people in the liberal camp reckon just as reliably with the Reformation factor is clear enough from Cousin's famous remark: "The sixteenth century commenced the philosophical revolution; the eighteenth generalized and spread it." To this Stahl answered: "In essence Puritanism and Revolution are not related

7. Kuyper (note 7) cites Calvin's *Institutes* at IV/20/8.

8. Kuyper (note 8) cites Stahl's *Die Lutherische Kirche und die Union* (Berlin, 1859), p. 62, over against G. Groen van Prinsterer, *Ongeloof en Revolutie,* 2nd ed. (Amsterdam, 1868), p. 138.

but opposed."[9] Why? Do not both seek the fruit of liberty? Undoubtedly, but they grow it from a very different root. "Freedom based on the philosophical idea" is the Encyclopedists' slogan. "Freedom rooted in faith" is the magic word of the Reformation. Our claim is simply that the revolution failed in realizing this freedom, and the Reformation succeeded. . . .

And now my historical argument, taking up the successive stages of Calvinism in reverse order. I will begin with America, then move to England, and guide you via the French wars of religion through Beza to Calvin.

I

I begin with America, since someone who accepts American liberties will certainly escape suspicion of being reactionary. Not that I find America without spot or wrinkle. On the contrary, I have strong reservations about the Yankee spirit in the seaports and among the money barons. But those who would judge should not be unjust, should not forget that America is still very young; that, more than any other nation, it has had to accept depraved elements from other countries; that the vastness of its territory (nearly as large as Russia, Germany, and France together) rendered its national character easily corruptible. Enough. There is no argument that America's Union lacks any of the freedoms for which people are fighting in Europe. There is complete freedom of conscience, freedom to start an enterprise and to engage in commerce, freedom for citizens to participate in public affairs. There is a duly responsible government, a small army, low taxation, freedom of organization, a free press, freedom of worship, and freedom of opinion. The judicial system is quick and cheap. Privileged elites are unknown. All, without exception, are equal before the law. No doubt, then, modern liberties flourish in America without restriction. Some may complain about too much freedom, but to complain about too little freedom in America would be absurd.

To decide whether this generous civic freedom has its origin in the French Revolution or in the Reformation of Geneva we must inquire into the attitude the American Union assumed towards revolutionary France in the latter part of the previous century. If it showed France undisguised

9. Kuyper (notes 9-11) cites Johannes Alzog, *Handbuch der Universal Kirchengeschichte*, 8th ed. (Mainz, 1866-67), vol. II, p. 542; Victor Cousin, *Histoire de la philosophie du 18ème siècle* (Brussels, 1840), vol. I, p. 61; and Stahl, *Die gegenwartigen Parteien in Staat und Kirche* (Berlin, 1863), p. 53.

sympathy and hastened to adopt the innovations of the National Convention, the case for Calvinism would be lost. Should we find, on the other hand, that the Federal government, supported by the core of the nation and fully aware of its actions, rejected with horror the France of the Mirabeaus, then any idea of linkage between free America and the France of '89 falls flat.

For the sake of argument, I am prepared to go to extremes to credit the view that the American and French Revolutions are twin shoots from the same stem. I do not deny that there were strong surface similarities between the demands of the New York riff-raff and the Parisian proletariat. I admit that for a moment the American press raved with hollow sounds and abstract generalizations like the French pamphleteers. I am even prepared to acknowledge that there was a momentary danger that the Jacobinism of the Mountain would spread to the clubs of Charleston and Baltimore. No doubt some aftershocks of the French Revolution were felt in the recently established Union. But what does that prove? Would French assistance in the war of liberation against England be so quickly forgotten or Lafayette's name already have lost its charm? Isn't it obvious that people would fail at first glance to see the difference between Calvinist liberty and French slogans?

. . . Yet the Federal government and the core of the nation fully and firmly supported Washington and Hamilton — who were politically hostile to France — against Jefferson, the Francophile populist with his supporters from the slave states. We hardly need remind you that the core of the American States lay in New England and not the South. The Southern states with their aristocratic stamp and the slave element in their economy have never, even up to the present, been completely amalgamated by the true people of the Union. From the beginning they posed an antithesis to the real Union, followed a different policy, and lived by another spirit. With respect to our present concern this political antagonism first erupted in [17]93 when the South, at Jefferson's instigation, opted for the French, while the true Union, under Washington, embarked on a life and death struggle to disarm Jefferson and his French sympathizers. That fight was fierce and brutal. . . . People understood it to be a struggle over fundamental principles. Which to choose: the *historical* government of Great Britain or the *revolutionary* regime of France? That was the question. And Hamilton candidly answered, as Jefferson himself reported, "that he considered the British Constitution, for all the corruption of its administration, as the most perfect model of Government." The federal government realized, so Professor Holst of Strassburg writes in his recently published study, how useless were the empty abstractions from Paris. Their policies "were based on the real situation, not on abstractions, and they knew that they had to deal with people, not with lifeless numbers or logical concepts."[10] Strengthened by that conviction, they took a firm line. Jay was dispatched to London to ensure the peace with England. They turned their backs on the Paris Convention and stuck unwaveringly to their position, even when France broke off diplomatic relations. . . .

Whether the nation approved of this policy would become clear, as always in America, in their choice of a new president. The elections were held in 1796; Adams and Jefferson were the opposing candidates. Jefferson's candidacy stood for the triumph of the pro-French South, while Adams's meant the endorsement of the government's policies and a break with France. Behold — Adams won, the foreign element had to lower its flag, the core of the nation chose against the French Revolution. That New England in particular — the heart of the Union — was solidly behind Washington is abundantly clear from what Dwight wrote to Wolcott: "Our good people from New England will never tolerate a war with Great Britain. Sooner would ninety-nine out of a hundred of our inhabitants separate at once from the Union!"[11]

Should you ask whether the American Constitution of March '89 was copied from the writings of Rousseau, let Holst answer: "It would be foolish to say that Rousseau's writings have exerted any influence on developments in America." I presume you would agree with that view upon hearing that at a critical moment Franklin rose in the Committee that was charged with writing the Constitution and suggested that they first offer a prayer to the Almighty as he saw no other way out; upon hearing that in the Congress of '97 the debates over the slavery question were based not just on generally religious but on Scriptural arguments; and that one of the most popular journals in America printed this ac-

10. Kuyper leans very heavily on Hermann Eduard von Holst, *Verfassung und Démocratie der Vereinigten Staten von Amerika* (Dusseldorf, 1873), for his quotations. In note 13 he cites therefrom a letter of Jefferson to Van Buren, 29 June 1824; Holst's own statement per note 14 is from vol. I, p. 96. Kuyper adds: "In consulting Holst we should keep in mind that this German scholar himself holds to revolutionary [i.e., Continental-liberal] politics, thus reinforcing the strength of his observations."

11. Kuyper (note 17) quotes Timothy Dwight, arch-Federalist and president of Yale, writing to Oliver Wolcott, a devotee of Alexander Hamilton and Secretary of the Treasury under John Adams, as cited in Holst, vol. I, p. 109. Of course, in the next presidential election (1800) Jefferson defeated Adams and his party retained control of the office for most of the next 60 years. War with England came in 1812, and New England, true to Dwight's word, made secessionist sounds at the Hartford Convention in 1814. This proved to be the demise of the Federalist Party and reinforced the great suspicions which the South, but also many in the mid-Atlantic region, had of the Yankee self-appointed "core of the nation."

knowledgment about the Constitution of the Union: "Such a form of government was not solely the product of intelligence and statesmanship. Rather, it bore a stamp of providence on its forehead. It was the saving gift of God to the endangered and distressed Union!"[12]

Do you still hesitate and wonder whether the war for independence against England was perhaps the prelude of the demolition of the Bastille, the premature fruit of the Encyclopedists' thought? If so, perhaps it would suffice to mention the name of Burke, an excellent Antirevolutionary who nonetheless defended America's uprising in the strongest terms. But preferring that America speak for itself, I would rather point you to Greene's description of the colonists' attachment to the mother land. "They loved England," he writes, "with the love of a child who is forced to leave home, yet as soon as the first bitterness has receded, remembers it with self-recriminations rather than with spite."[13] . . . No, America's uprising, like our revolt against Spain and England's "Glorious Revolution," was not a turning upside down in the sense of the French Revolution. America's uprising did not result in any destruction, it did not mean that an "ancien régime" was replaced by a new order. Everything remained as it was except that a Congress took the place of the royal commissioner. Nor did America's uprising signify an emancipation from the Creator. Rather, it was realized by leaning on his help. We read in the Constitution of New York: "With immense gratitude for God's mercies, we, the citizens of New York, adopt this Constitution."[14]

There might still be one way out. One could argue with Holst that America was not affected by the French Revolution but that the adder of unbelief was already hidden in the grass when the New England colonies were established. But the Christian character that the American nation still shows and the indisputable process whereby its states were founded testify against such a view.

Even today the people of the Union bear a clear-cut Christian stamp more than any other nation on earth. This is an undeniable fact. With few exceptions the population of the United States — not only its lower

12. Kuyper (note 18) quotes Holst at vol. I, p. 26; takes the Franklin story from Jonathan Elliott, *Diplomatic Code of the United States of America* (Washington, D.C.: 1827), as cited in Holst at p. 45; and quotes a fire-breathing Unionist article in *North American Quarterly Review*, 1862, via Holst, p. 160. These data are today the civil religious lore of the Christian Right. In Kuyper's time they were mainline Protestant sentiment.

13. Kuyper (note 19) cites George Washington Greene, *Historical View of the American Revolution* (Boston, 1865), p. 5.

14. Kuyper (note 20) cites Tocqueville, *La Démocratie*, vol. I, p. 341, as the source of this quotation.

By the time of World War I Kuyper had a very different view of the United States, largely because of its support of England in the Boer War. That war he saw motivated by British materialism. In a "neutral" America's commercial support of just one side in World War I, he saw the Yankee equivalent, as he states in this "three-star" editorial of 9 March 1916.

America Has the Power to Make Peace

The most recent reports from Washington reinforce our conviction that, if he acts with vigor, President Wilson can bring about the return of world peace.

As things now stand on the killing field, none of the belligerent states can by itself guarantee a continued supply of the necessary ammunition. Had not the nearly 100 million people of the United States of America shipped masses of articles for death and destruction across the sea to Liverpool and Le Havre, the supply would by now be almost exhausted and peace would return. In this endless production of artillery and ammunition America has no other interest than to make money — loads of it — and to see that its deliveries are paid for at a high price.

and middle classes but also its scholars and politicians — is decidedly religious. It is Christian in a way we tend to call orthodox. And this is so notwithstanding that being a Christian in Europe costs virtually nothing and in America, plenty. A single pew can cost as much as $1500. Orthodoxy is so powerful and dominant that most of the immigrants who arrive as unbelievers and unchurched take over America's supernatural life-concept in very short order. Just the opposite of what we see in Europe! Here it may seem that democratic freedoms are to be bought at the price of faith; there, Calvinism seems to all the best guarantee for their lasting possession.[15] It would thus be wrong to perceive the separation of church and state as does Cavour. This separation is far stricter

15. Kuyper (notes 21 and 22) references Tocqueville, *La Démocratie,* vol. I, pp. 65, 69. The pew rental figure he attributes to Joseph P. Thompson, *Kirche und Staat in den Vereinigten Staaten von Amerika* (Berlin, 1873), p. 102. This is a German translation of Thompson's English edition (Boston) the same year.

Everyone in America — women included — is now at work to insure that bombs and howitzers can be sent by the shipload across the ocean, and to get rich by this trade. And this despite knowing that soon a human life will hang by such a bomb or shell.

It is therefore fully understandable that more than one statesman in America itself is protesting this inhuman practice.

People are getting rich with blood money, and that will brutalize the spirit in America itself. More: the responsibility that America has before God is growing by the day. America has world peace in its hands but refrains to bring it about from its love of lucre. And without America the other neutral states are not capable of forceful action.

And so the mighty country that consistently called for pacification and arbitration not only, by its production, fuels and perpetuates the war but by its vacillation nullifies the potential for neutrals to intervene.

America has everyone's fate in its hand. America *can* end the misery. America *can* organize a force for peace against the power of war. But it stays home. People of all lands look up to America, but how bitterly are they disappointed!

And all this for the love of money.

than in Europe but proceeds from a different principle — not from the desire to be liberated from the church but from the realization that the well-being of the church and the progress of Christianity demand it. This separation does not prevent sessions of Congress, political conventions and meetings from being opened with prayer. The Sabbath rest is totally respected in America, days of prayer and thanksgiving are declared by the cabinet in Washington, and every important state document makes mention of the almighty God in plain English with the reverence and devotion due from the creature to the Creator. Likewise, it would be a mistake to confuse the American "common-school" system with our theory of a neutral school. Read the extensive report Dr. Fraser submitted to the English Parliament and you will be aware of this dual fact: the public school in America is a school "with the Bible," the demise of which is being predicted in light of the Irish protest against it. In America a public school without the Bible would be simply unthinkable; Christianity is just too influential for that to happen. Just listen to the testimony of the man who truly knew this freest of lands: "Domestic morals are much stronger there than in Europe; Christianity rules in America without obstacle, to the benefit of all."[16]

This threefold constellation of unlimited political freedom, strict morality, and the faithful confession of Christianity points directly to the Union's Puritan origins, to the indomitable spirit of the Pilgrim fathers, and to the spiritual legacy of Calvin. For New England put its stamp on the entire Union, and the New England states were founded by martyrs for the Reformed faith. As they themselves testified, the followers of Robinson did not go to Rhode Island to establish a model state but to find a place where they could worship God after the dictates of their hearts.[17] They were no impoverished fortune hunters but properly educated members of the best class of English society. They were no deluded zealots but wise men with practical skills, led by one principle: "the glory of the most High," enthused by one thought: "religious liberty for all the Union." . . . In freedom of conscience lay the secret of their power. A Puritan is the born enemy of every form of clericalism, and "clerical dominion," Bancroft rightly affirms, "is the least tolerable of all tyrannies, for it breaks resilience, extinguishes enthusiasm, and shatters courage." Puritanism, however, is a life-giving principle that gives birth to industry, resilience, and knowledge. As to courage, a Puritan and a coward are natural antipodes. Whoever fears God fears no creature. "My soldiers who pray best are the bravest fighters," Cromwell wrote. And Cromwell was the greatest general of his age.[18]

II

The founders of the American colonies were exiles from Great Britain. Thus, we follow the course of Calvinism step by step if we now focus on its historical development in England. Of course, there it had to assume

16. On Sabbath and prayers Kuyper cites Thompson, *Kirche und Staat*, p. iii (note 23); on public schools, James Fraser, *Report . . . on the Common School System of the United States and . . . of Upper and Lower Canada* (London, 1867), p. 160 and, apropos of the Irish, p. 180 (note 24).

17. Kuyper (note 25) cites Tocqueville, *La Démocratie*, p. 50. Kuyper's mistake respecting the destination of John Robinson's followers was very telling. These, the Pilgrims, did not go to Rhode Island and there establish religious liberty but settled at Plymouth where they soon dwelt in the shadows of Winthrop's Massachusetts Bay colony, *not* a religiously tolerant crew.

18. Kuyper (notes 26-28) cites Bancroft, *History of the United States*, vol. I, pp. 309, 322, 462, 464.

a different form. In America it could unfold the essence of its philosophy unimpeded, but in the British Isles it had to reckon with history and existing circumstances. Calvinism is not a rigid, unalterable power that had reached its final conclusions, its definitive shape, already in Calvin's time. On the contrary, it is a principle that only gradually reveals its power, that has a unique insight for every age, that assumes a form suitable for every country. Precisely in this restless metamorphosis its development continues. A most important phase in that process is the history of the English disturbances in the seventeenth century. . . .[19]

Not the sixteenth but the seventeenth century saw the vigorous Reformation of the English people. Only then did much the larger part of the nation, under the influence of Scotland and Holland, join the Reformation heart and soul. *Hinc illae lacrymae!* "Hence all the misery poured out over England!" Inevitably, this double reformation — of the throne and of the people, of the sixteenth and of the seventeenth century — had to come to a collision. In the cities and in the North of England the reformed nation rose against the Episcopalian Church. They were Calvinists and wanted their church organization to be Calvinistic too. This form of church governance had taken shape in Geneva, France, and Holland. As with the Reformed Church in those countries and in Scotland, so should it be in England! They wanted the Presbyterian system. Calvinism was a petrifaction, they maintained, bound to the form it had assumed, take it or leave it.

This Robinson resisted. Against this system Milton hurled his fervent eloquence. The deepest zeal of the Independents was directed at that misunderstanding. And rightly so. They were fighting with Calvin at their side — Calvin, who had unambiguously rejected the idea that one should be bound to an established form. In so doing they saved the future of the Calvinist Reformation. They gave voice to the heart of the English people, who could not abide the form of French church governance. The

19. At this point Kuyper undertakes a three-page discussion of the injustice done to the English Independents by Catholic and Protestant historians alike. Anticipating the argument he develops later, and showing the centrality of ecclesiastical issues in his mind at the time, he especially blames "Presbyterian" critics who took Calvinism to be a "petrifaction" and therefore opposed the Independents' sense of it as something to be "developed." He then quotes Robinson's farewell address to the Pilgrims at Leiden to the effect that God had still more to reveal to His people out of the Word. Finally, Kuyper praises François Guizot, *Histoire de la république d'Angleterre et de Cromwell* (Paris, 1854); Jean Henri Merle d'Aubigne, *Le protecteur, ou la république d'Angleterre aux jours de Cromwell* (Paris, 1848); Thomas Babington Macaulay, *Critical and Historical Essays* (London, 1862), vol. I, pp. 1-26 (on Milton); and "above all" Herman Weingarten, *Die Revolutionskirchen Englands* (Leipzig, 1868), for duly restoring the Independents' historical reputation.

result has left its stamp till today, for there is still a "Presbyterian Church" in England but of insignificant proportions, little spiritual power, small and languishing. It was not English and could not flourish on English soil in its French form!

This the Independents understood. They did not consider rejecting Calvinism. They left even the Presbyterians far behind in their attachment to the central doctrine of election. But they wanted their own form of church government — English, but at the same time authentically Calvinistic. They demanded separation of church and state, autonomy for the local churches, a voluntary, not coerced, relationship with the synod, voting rights for the laity, and open church meetings — almost the same system that is now gaining ground everywhere in Scotland and America, France and Switzerland, and, we may add, in our country. The Presbyterians suffered defeat. Once Milton appeared they were scattered as chaff in the wind, and after an artificial existence of nearly two centuries they have fully exhausted their vitality. . . .

But more important still was the second issue for which the Independents fought. *Would freedom of conscience remain a dead letter in the Calvinistic program?* The Inquisition refused to tolerate any deviance from the Roman confession. By comparison Calvin's declaration in his *Institutes* — "provided the main truths of Christianity are confessed," differences of opinion may be tolerated[20] — was the first expression of a glorious principle. As Servetus's execution showed, this was still tightly wrapped in the swathes of the old mother church. In Germany "cuius regio, eius religio" had pushed freedom of conscience aside. In France also it was far from pure. Elsewhere it only met abuse. To the honor of our fathers it may be said that the Union of our seven provinces was the most advanced on this point. Robinson, exiled from London, found refuge in Amsterdam; the Jews, driven from Portugal and Spain, found shelter in Holland's capital; there was even freedom of worship for deviating sects, albeit in private, clandestine churches.

But this owed more to practice than to theory. Our Dutch placards against Rome were far from tender. The state church ruled supreme. People with other opinions might be tolerated, but the principle of religious freedom was not done justice. The situation was even worse in England, where the growth of the Episcopal Church was identified with national honor, the gates of the Tower were opened for Catholics and Presbyterians in turn, and followers of Rome and Geneva sometimes

20. Kuyper (note 38) cites the *Institutes* at IV/1/12, then adds a quotation from Calvin's *Fidelis expositio errorum M. Serveti* in the Schipper's edition of Calvin's works, *Opera Omnia* (Amsterdam, 1667), vol. VIII, p. 516a.

climbed the scaffold together. Above all, the popular Reformation of the seventeenth century made this untenable. Thousands could be oppressed, but when these thousands grew into millions and then to half of the population, the whip fell from the torturer's hand.

This opened a new phase in the matter of freedom of conscience. Quite unexpectedly a practical issue had to be faced: How does your principle apply when not just exiles seek your protection or small sects ask for tolerance but when half your population despises the state church? The response of the Presbyterians to this question did not help but caused even sharper bitterness and became the spiritual cause of King Charles' death. For they said, "Simply abandon Episcopacy and let our church be the state church, as it is in Scotland, Holland, and Geneva!" This merely shifted the problem, for then the Episcopalians would feel wronged and freedom of conscience would remain just as far off. No, not the Presbyterians but their zealous opponents, the Independents, found the answer that saved the day. Their motto was "separation of church and state" and, linked with this, "the absolute freedom to serve God according to the dictates of one's heart." The Barebones Parliament has been accused of many evil things, but what you do think of this declaration, recorded in its minutes: "As for the truth and power of religion, it being a matter intrinsical between God and the soul, we conceive there is no power of coercion thereunto!" Freedom of conscience "to all that profess Christ, without exception," the Yorkshire farmer had already exclaimed. Milton made one exception: the followers of Rome, because of their allegiance to a foreign ruler. But Godwin went so far as to demand "a full liberty of conscience to all sects, even Turks, Jews and Papists." . . .[21]

Not that I excuse the Independents. In the heat of battle they often tolerated "Levelers" within their ranks, and in their pamphlets their glorious ideals were often marred by a mixture of Leveler-theories. In the worst of their distress the enthusiasts among them turned to a fanatical spiritualism that became a danger to the state. Indeed, the left wing of the Quaker movement which issued from them degenerated into the kind of radicalism that mocked the practical demands of faith and life and threatened to turn all society and Christianity upside down. Cromwell's idea to convene the "saints" in a parliament was an unforgivable political

21. Kuyper (notes 40-42) takes these quotations from Weingarten, *Die Revolutionskirchen Englands,* pp. 110-11. The Barebones Parliament (July-December 1653) was nominated by Puritan congregations to succeed the Rump Parliament. Falling into discord, it gave way to the Protectorate of Oliver Cromwell. The "Yorkshire Farmer" and John Goodwin were radical pamphleteers during the Commonwealth. The material deleted from the text gives more quotations and data to the same effect.

mistake. But on the other hand, never was England more secure than during their rule. Cromwell's army is probably the only one in history where soldiers did not swear but prayed, did not rob but gave, did not violate the honor of women but ran a bayonet through the rapist. The sinful desire to plunder and the lust of the flesh never lurked behind their pious façades to cast suspicion on the sincerity of their conviction. Therefore, I see no reason why the excesses of some enthusiastic members of their party should lead us to belittle their manly struggle for the most beautiful ideal of freedom. I would think we could make some allowances for a group of heroes who were the first to grasp the deepest principle and the farthest consequence of freedom of conscience.

It goes without saying that the constitution was to be altered. Theocracy remained, but in a different form. No longer was there a church in the state nor a state bound to the church. The church of Christ was the point of departure. She was to make sure that the principles of justice and truth held sway in the hearts of the citizens, but the citizens in their everyday life found free organization in the state to be indispensable. Once the ideal of freedom had established itself in the bosom of the church, it inevitably sought civil rights in the domain of the state. The development of political liberty grew inescapably from the ideal of freedom of conscience, once grasped at its deepest root. Of course, there could be no question of popular sovereignty in the minds of men who, as church members and citizens alike, worshiped Christ as their King. But if you are looking for the first and best defense of, say, the freedom of the press, you will find it with Milton; for public assembly, read about it in Godwin; for the holy and yet civil contract of marriage, look in the acts of the Barebones Parliament. Hard to believe, but true: the first report on the state's responsibility for scientific enquiry was published by a Committee appointed by that same parliament. They first introduced our modern concept of one treasury for all state income. The introduction of a public registry [of all citizens] dates from their rule. The Independents simplified the judicial system, seriously curtailed state spending, and were the first to plead for the mitigation of corporal punishment.[22]

Yet, they inevitably faced defeat in Britain. The politicians on which England could rely were and remained Episcopalian, and even the most sacred enthusiasm cannot instantly change the ordinary industrious citizen into a competent politician. Their ideas were excellent, but they lacked the education and force to reform English rule in accordance with

22. Kuyper (notes 45-47) cites Milton's *Areopagetica;* Weingarten, *Die Revolutionskirchen Englands,* pp. 127, 129; and Leopold von Ranke, *Englische Geschichte,* 2nd ed. (1872), vol. IV, pp. 82ff.

these noble insights. This and not their eccentricity, Guizot aptly states, brought their downfall. The principle would first show its viability in America, on a smaller scale. The *Memoirs* of Mrs. Hutchinson relate this first germination in a way that will delight and thrill you.[23] Thrown as exiles on America's coast, they bore along to the new world the spiritual fruit of their struggle and suffering. Their spirit nurtured whatever great and glorious was accomplished in America through a liberty subject to God.

But America was not the only place to benefit from that fruit. England, the Reformed Church, indeed, all the nations of Europe owe a glittering jewel to the spiritual power thus developed.

You know that England regained political peace only through the accession to the throne of our Stadtholder William III. This "Glorious Revolution" opened England's splendid era of influence and power. This change in dynasty has absolutely nothing in common with the French Revolution, for it did not directly affect the English people nor did it destroy the mechanism of the state. It did not result from abstract new theories but was an act of practical necessity, prompted by the theory of history that was generally accepted at the time. The Stuarts wanted to return to the past and to see England creep forward as if there had been no spiritual stir in the nation during the Cromwell period. This was an anachronism, an attempt — doomed from the start — to return the stream to its bed. It threatened Great Britain with political death. The nation had been plowed; precious seed had been sown in her wide-open furrows. The nation would not be robbed of the harvest of this spiritual labor. William of Orange, the courageous king, the bold strategist, the brave statesman, was privileged to attach that harvest to his noble name. And the Toleration Act, the emancipation of the Reformed Church in Scotland, the institution of an annual budget, the extension of parliamentary rights, and the abolition of secret courts offered the English nation the spiritual fruit of those same Independents whose utopia they had ridiculed while imbibing their spirit. The false theory of the misunderstood "Droit divin" was no more; the Whig party could freely introduce the ideal of the Independents in our constitutional system. . . . [The thorough opposition by this free England to the French Revolution proves how different were their respective animating spirits.]

But I also mentioned the *Reformed Church* as having been saved

23. Lucy Apsley Hutchinson's *Memoirs* were published as part of Guizot's 26-volume *Collection des mémoires relatifs à la Révolution d'Angleterre* (Paris & Rouen, 1823).

through the Independents' struggle. She was in danger of becoming a fossil by her desire to enjoy the fruit of the Reformers rather than to continue working in their spirit. In Holland the church emitted its last sign of life at the Synod of Dordt by including the need for continued reformation in her *post acta,* but this remained a dead letter.[24] In England, even in Scotland, the church fell asleep; in Switzerland she rested on her laurels; in France she succumbed to the crafty wiles of the court, supported by the sword of dragoons. And now? Look how impressive the church is in America; is she not the spiritual fruit of the Independents? Look at the mighty party of Dissenters in England, which gathers almost half the nation in its churches; is she not Wesley's trophy, and is not Wesley a spiritual child of the Robinsons and Godwins? Look at the free Scots church, delivered from its yoke by Chalmers's faith and courage, realizing in a flourishing ecclesiastical life the ideals for which the Puritans hungered with all their heart.[25] I will skip the free churches in Switzerland, France, and our own country; they are smaller and thus provide less evidence. But today the Reformed people in these countries extol lay suffrage and call for separation of church and state. They are tired of the synodical yoke and demand that church meetings be public. What else are they doing but copying Robinson to the letter? What else is the Calvinism of the free churches but the principle the Independents already stood for?

Finally, all of Europe shared in that blessing, even though it had to be extended at the hand of the most horrible revolution. For ever since the French Revolution political freedom has gained ground in Europe, and as a result much good has come about. Be not amazed to hear this from me. We are Antirevolutionaries not because we reject the fruits of the revolutionary era but because, history book in hand, we dare contest the paternity of these good things. With much evil the revolution also brought Europe much good, but this was stolen fruit, ripened on the stem of Calvinism under the nurturing warmth of our martyrs' faith, first

24. The Synod of Dordrecht (1618-19) was an international council of Reformed churches called to advise the Dutch on the Arminian controversy. It found against the pro-Arminian Remonstrants but after this conclusion ("post acta") also issued mandates for various reforms that were generally not carried out.

25. Kuyper's hostility to Arminianism did not preclude his linking of Wesley to Puritan roots! But see also Sydney E. Ahlstrom, *A Religious History of the American People* (Garden City: Doubleday, 1975), vol. I, p. 398. Thomas Chalmers (1780-1847) was a Scots Presbyterian pastor and professor of moral philosophy who helped lead the formation of the Free Church of Scotland (1843) in protest over civil control of church appointments. Kuyper often took this as a model for his own church reforms and quite resembled Chalmers in theology, charisma, scope of interests, and personality.

in our own land, then in England, and subsequently in America. I will provide the evidence for this statement later. Suffice it here to say that the beautiful morning sun which now lights our free Europe did not rise from the September massacres but from the bloodbath of our cities as they dared to challenge Spain; not from the guillotine but from the stakes of the Backers and De Breses;[26] not from the study carrels of the Encyclopedists but from the prayer rooms of the Independents; or, if you prefer, not from the furious Sans-culottes but from those bizarre Pilgrim fathers!

III

We now go back a century in time, from 1650 to 1550, from the Calvinist troubles in England to the struggle of the Huguenots in France. We must find out how Independents and Huguenots were kindred spirits but also how they differed. Calvinism's course of development runs uninterrupted only if we can establish a link between the two.

. . . [Deleted here is a long disquisition by which Kuyper paints the Huguenots as similar to the Puritans in "colonization strategy, regard for freedom of conscience, and moral character and political philosophy."[27]] Yet, for all their similarity the Independents and the Huguenots do not occupy the same standpoint. Both represent Calvinism but in different phases of its development. Robinson's Calvinism had progressed further than that of Coligny and La Noue.[28] That is already apparent from the fierce and bitter struggle between the Independents and the Presbyterians, for the Presbyterians in England wanted exactly what the Huguenots were planning for France, in church as well as state.

What did they want in the church? Not the Independents' circle of free, autonomous congregations but a well-organized church complex in

26. Jan de Backer was one of the first martyrs of the Dutch Reformation; Guido de Bres (1522-67) was a Flemish Reformed preacher who wrote the Belgic Confession, one of the three doctrinal standards in the Dutch Reformed tradition, and an early martyr in the war with Spain.

27. Kuyper's chief sources on the French Reformation are Gottlob von Polenz, *Geschichte des Französischen Calvinismus,* 5 vols. (Gotha, 1857-69); and Gottfried V. Lechler, *Geschichte der Presbyterial- und Synodalvefassung seit der Reformation* (Leiden, 1854).

28. Gaspard de Coligny (1519-72) was a principal political and military leader of the Huguenot party until his death in the St. Bartholomew Night massacre. François La Noue (1531-91) was an important officer in the cause until his death from wounds; he wrote an important *Memoirs* in 1587.

which authority rested with the synod and the laity were excluded from church government. The fusion of free congregations into one central unit was accomplished in 1559, while the power to appoint church boards was abolished only in our century. Did Calvinistic principle require this? Certainly not. At the time, Switzerland did not yet have a synodical structure. During Calvin's lifetime Geneva never had more than a consistory. Calvin's congregation was fully autonomous. No, the motive for such tight organization had a totally different source — not ecclesiastical but political, not for a spiritual but for a military purpose. Note the year! In 1559, shortly before the Amboise conspiracy,[29] the conviction arose that passive resistance had done as much as it could, that the sword would have to decide the issue. The prelude to the civil war had begun, and people knew that waging and persevering in such a war required organization. Unity of action and leadership was indispensable. The idea of building "a state within the state" did not yet exist; the "Regulations for the Police and for War" date from [15]73.[30] This necessitated a closely knit church organization that would substitute for the political body still lacking. Waging war requires money. The local church boards raised that money from their congregations. Troops had to be assembled, ammunition and cannon bought, a cavalry hired, command centers set up — all this was done through the network of consistories spread out all over France. To strengthen resilience, the cords had to come together in just a few hands. So it was done in our country, and so in France. And so an auxiliary *political* purpose, a *military* interest, rather than a requirement of faith put the Reformed Church in shackles, wherein it has languished for more than two centuries.

But this was not all. Consistently applied, the Calvinistic principle necessarily leads to separation of church and state when there are *others besides* Calvinists in the state. In Geneva this principle could not prevail. The discord Calvin had to allay among the citizenry there resulted from shameful libertinism, not from any confessional differences. There were no Catholics left. But there were in France. Now what? Would Calvinism draw the consequences of separation and as a free church respect the autonomy of civil government? People hadn't come that far yet. At first they still hoped that the other half of the French nation would also

29. The Amboise conspiracy (March 1560) was a Huguenot conspiracy to kidnap the young king Francis II in order to break the power of his handlers, the leading Catholic house of Guise. The plot failed, with many Huguenot casualties in consequence.

30. "Réglement de Politie et de Guerre" was a political code of the Huguenot shadow government.

embrace the Reformation, in which case the problem would disappear of itself and all France would be a Reformed state. But when that hope was disappointed and when two faiths persisted side by side in the same state, then did they find the right track? No, not even then. First, they sought escape in colonization: France would be a Catholic country and its colony Reformed. When this plan failed, people swung to the other extreme. The premature slogan became: two states for two religions, "l'état dans l'état," a Huguenot and a Catholic government in the bosom of the same nation. The union of church and state would be preserved. The Huguenots aspired to be the state church, or at least a church with its own [political] nation within the state. The French did not yet recognize that emancipating the church is the prerequisite for continuous growth.

Finally, I would point out the difference between the *aristocratic* character of the French and the *democratic* character of the English movement. Simply put, the French nobility supported the Huguenots, while the English nobility opposed the Dissenters. At least this influence was predominant until the Massacre of St. Bartholomew. It maintained itself particularly, and forcefully, at the synod of Orléans in 1562 in the face of the demagogic tendencies of Morel and his supporters. But when on and after the night of August 24 the Reformed nobility of France was literally exterminated, it was inevitable that the democratic element would gain influence and open the flood-gates for the kind of demagogic fanaticism that disgraced the last phase of the Huguenot wars.[31] This was to be expected under French conditions. In Holland and England the common people might safely take the lead, but not in France. Perren's masterpiece *La démocratie en France au moyen âge* has once again so graphically portrayed the scene of the Jacquerie and the mutinies of Étienne Marcel and Robert le Coq that we immediately perceive how far the Dutch and English citizenry were advanced compared to the French burghers.[32]

31. The St. Bartholomew's Day Massacre (24 August 1572) was a panic killing of some five thousand Huguenots that claimed much of the movement's leadership. The Huguenots' national synod of 1562, held in their stronghold of Orléans, asserted a strong presbyterian connection with authority over local congregations. Ironically, the proposals of Jean Morely (Morelli de Villieurs [1524-94]) for local lay power were quite like Kuyper's own and matched those of Milton and the English Independents which he lauds above. Morely did, however, agitate for these in a style that can be negatively taken as "demagogic."

32. Kuyper (note 61) cites F. T. Perrens, *La Démocratie en France au Moyen Age* (Paris, 1873). The Jacquerie was a peasant uprising in northeastern France in 1358 in the wake of English victories there during the Hundred Years War. It joined forces with the rebellion underway in Paris since 1355, led by Étienne Marcel and Robert le Coq, bishop of Laon.

One could predict from the fascinating dialogue *Le réveil matin des Français,* published as an expression of these demagogic ideas, that the apostolate of popular sovereignty would arise from the French. For we read therein: "A people may well exist without a government, but a government cannot exist without a people. Therefore, the people have created the government by way of a social contract, when they saw the advantages of such an established order." Literally the sentiment of Rousseau! . . .[33] These bloodthirsty thoughts were not Calvinistic, but they were mingled with it. They were dominant in France before Calvinism made its entry. . . .[34] Let us be fair to history. I know that even Melanchthon and Béza approved of killing a tyrant. But if we find the same sentiments before the Reformation began, before the father of the Reformation was even born, we should blame neither Calvinism nor Romanism but trace the origin of such immoral ideas to a sinful tendency in the Renaissance. There, in the false adulation of the ancient Greeks and Romans, was nurtured this bitter fruit.

No, if you want to know Reformed constitutional law from a purer, though still far from perfect source, I would recommend the standard works of Hottoman and Languet. Although I have to admit that the same false vein of the Renaissance runs through Hottoman's *Franco Gallia,* and Languet's — or, to use his pseudonym: Junius Brutus's — *Vindiciae Contra Tyrannos,* nonetheless you find especially with the latter an extension of the Calvinistic system in which true constitutional law is rooted.[35] For this learned statesman and fine diplomat indeed offers a system. He sees all authority as derived from God. He supports the "Droit divin" but vests the sovereignty of the crown neither in the person nor even in the office of the king but in the organic union of this office with the "lesser

33. Kuyper (note 62) cites this from von Polenz, vol. III, pp. 229ff. In the material deleted Kuyper quotes the tract's justification of regicide.

34. Kuyper cites medieval tracts (mostly via von Polenz) by the English monk John of Salisbury (1115-80), the French scholar Jean de Gerson (1363-1429), the Spanish Jesuit Juan Marianna (1536-1624), and others to the effect that these advanced "definite revolutionary concepts of popular sovereignty."

35. These two texts have received considerable attention in the history of political theory. A fine edition that also includes the tract by Théodore Béza to which Kuyper will later turn is Julian H. Franklin, ed., *Constitutionalism and Resistance in the Sixteenth Century* (New York: Pegasus, 1969). This volume gives the corrected spelling of François Hotman (1524-90) and the reasons for preferring Philippe du Plessis-Mornay (1549-1623) over his older friend, Hubert Languet, as author of *Vindiciae Contra Tyrannos* (pp. 138-39). Kuyper notes (71-73) that he consulted rare copies in the royal library at The Hague and the university library at Utrecht; also Richard Treitzschke's 1846 study of the *Vindiciae,* attributed to Languet.

magistrates." By these he means not royally appointed functionaries but the princes who are members of diets or parliaments independent of the king's authority. They are "officials of the realm, not of the king." Civil servants report to the king, but not they. Therefore, "the task of the former is to protect the king, while that of the latter is to make sure that no harm befalls the republic."[36] These lesser magistrates have, like the king, received part of the state sovereignty from God. Together with the king they are responsible to the King of kings that rule will benefit the people. They are not relieved of their oath if the king fails to perform his duty. If the king is not vigilant, *they* will have to be, even if the oppressor is the king himself.

Here indeed lies the first germ of constitutional law, with its deepest root not in the people but in God. It is this doctrine of the lesser magistrate, already taught by Calvin and commended in the *Liber Magdeburgensis,* that Languet first promoted to a learned constitutional system of the highest order.[37] Though mingled with some impure elements, it was based on God's Word, Germanic common law, and natural law. To this system the English revolution owes its basic philosophy, and this system supported the right of our fathers in their brave resistance against Spanish tyranny. This same view of sphere sovereignty constitutes the line of demarcation between popular sovereignty and our constitutional public law. Indeed, as Tocqueville shrewdly perceived, precisely through the disappearance of these lesser magistrates our political liberty is once again seriously threatened.

IV

This removes the uncertainty that obscured the origin of our civil liberties. . . . [Kuyper recapitulates the argument to this point.] If all the evidence indicates that the pearl of great price which is offered to us in the constitutional law for the people's liberty was not fished up from the unholy stream of the French Revolution but was stolen by the Rousseaus and Montesquieus from the martyr's crown of the Huguenots, from the blood-covered diadem of our Nassaus and Oranges — then dogmatic prejudice must give way before so undeniable an array of facts and Calvinism should no longer be denied its title of origin.

36. Kuyper's quotations are in the original Latin.

37. The *Liber Magdeburgensis* was a Lutheran confession of 1550 by which the pastors of Magdeburg appealed to the rights of lesser magistrates to justify their resistance to Emperor Charles V.

This must be demanded, provided that the last link in the chain of evidence can be supplied — namely, that the course of development we have traced does indeed take its point of departure from Calvin and can be conclusively explained by the hallmarks of the Calvinist confession.

Béza of Vézelay, Calvin's "fidus Achates," is the bridge between the Calvinism of Geneva and the Calvinism of the Huguenots; for that reason a word about him.[38] Béza was still reluctant regarding freedom of worship: "That every one should worship God in whatever form he prefers is but a diabolical doctrine." But he had already come to the point of abhorring executions. "Of course, no one should be persecuted for the sake of religion by fire or sword; this I hold as a basic principle," Béza wrote the Hungarian baron Thelegd. "Take care, however, not to allow immoral practice to hide under the mask of conscience." He also supports submission to authorities and disapproves of Brutus's murder of Caesar. But he is constitutional nonetheless. "Finally, the power of the legitimate magistrate is not unrestricted."[39] Therefore he wants parliaments and estates, tribunes and lesser magistrates with their own sovereignty. These, not private persons, are to resist tyranny. He explicitly applauded our uprising against Spain. He recruited cavalry for Condé and presided over the diplomatic office that served as liaison between the French Huguenots and the Reformed princes in Germany.

Thus, Béza lacks not a single element that we saw further developed in the course of Calvinism. In Calvin we discover them even more sharply delineated, though at a less mature stage. With him too I begin with *freedom of conscience*. Not to get involved in the story of Servetus's trial. Whoever chides the reformer of Geneva for this reason simply proves his own backwardness in historical understanding. The spirit of the times, not Calvin, was to blame for Servetus's stake. That cannot be made clearer than from Servetus's own testimony, when he writes in his own hand of the "incorrigible and obstinate wickedness of heresy: this crime is simply worthy of death before God and man." We are not concerned with what Calvin did and said in accordance with his times but with the new principle he introduced distinct from the spirit of the times. It was his position that no heresy be tolerated on major points of the Christian confessions but that deviations on minor matters had to be tolerated,

38. Théodore Béza (1519-1605) was the chief successor to Calvin in Geneva and a close associate of the Huguenot leaders in the French wars of religion. Achates was Aeneas's loyal companion in Virgil's *Aeneid*.

39. Kuyper quotes the original Latin from Béza's collected works. The two most relevant pieces are *De haereticis a civili magistratu puniendis*, a 1554 defense of the execution of Servetus, and *Du Droit des Magistrats* (Right of Magistrates) (1574).

"for there is none whose mind is not darkened by some cloud of ignorance."[40] This is a fundamental principle. The Huguenots extended this to tolerating unarmed Catholics. Our Dutch republic went even further and tolerated deviating forms of worship in private homes. In England it developed further yet in the "Act of Toleration," until at last in America the logical conclusion is drawn of giving freedom to all forms of worship and each individual conscience.

Secondly: *Sovereignty.* Calvin too honors the "Droit divin." All supreme authority, whether in a monarchy or a commonwealth, rules "Dei gratia." But divine right attaches to the crown, not to the person. They are common creatures, as a rule more depraved than others. "At court we often find the highest positions occupied by the worst scoundrels, and kings these days themselves are often as brutal and irresponsible as the asses among the animals." "Moreover, when they command something that is against God's law, they lay aside their sovereign power over us because they rebel against God; indeed, they are then worth no more among men than was Nebuchadnezzar." "One ought to spit them in the face than obey them when they are so conceited to oppose God and to usurp his throne."[41] I would think this differs rather significantly from the "Droit divin" of Louis XIV! Though we disapprove of his passion, we surely do not find that Calvin was a creeping slave.

Calvin regarded the form of government as a product of history that was to be respected. In a monarchy one should honor the king, in a democracy the "ephori," in a commonwealth the "proceres."[42] God can entrust sovereignty as well to the one, the many, or to all. This does not affect the principle of authority. But given a free choice, Calvin certainly prefers the republic. He had read too much in the register of royal sins not to despise despotism. Entrusting authority to many decreases the temptations to tyranny.

What if the government oppresses the citizens? May a private person take up arms? Never, Calvin says. And if the government commands something contrary to God's honor? Not then either. You should refuse to obey and take the punishment. But if you ask Calvin whether there is no means of resistance at all, he hastens to add: "I always speak of private persons." "For if there are among a people secondary powers, which

40. Kuyper (notes 85 and 86) cites Servetus's *Christianismi Restitutio* (Vienne, 1553) and Calvin's *Institutes* at IV/1/12.

41. Kuyper (notes 89-91) cites Calvin's *Commentary on Daniel* 4:27 and 6:22.

42. Kuyper (note 92) cites Calvin's *Institutes* IV/20/8. Ephori were the five elected magistrates in ancient Sparta who supervised the king. Proceres were nobles or chiefs in ancient republican regimes.

derive their authority from the people — like the ephori in Sparta, the tribunes in Rome, and today the three estates of Parliament, far from encouraging them to remain passive I would accuse them of having broken their oath if they abandon the liberties of the people which they have sworn to defend."[43] Thus, with Calvin himself lies the origin of the system of secondary powers, of the banner under which Condé rose against Charles, our States against Philip, the English Parliament against the Stuarts, and America's colonies against the mother country — the glorious principle from which our constitutional system was born.

Finally, I would emphasize just as strongly Calvin's opposition to non-intervention. In his concept of international law Europe was not just an aggregate of independent states but one family of peoples. Therefore, a neighboring prince had the duty to intervene when a ruler abused his own people. We learn from the letters published by Bonnet that Calvin himself cooperated on the basis of this principle in the levy to pay the German troops who went to France. And in this sense sang our Silent One: "As Prince of Orange I am *free*," that is: I stand as a sovereign ruler in Europe's association of states.[44] On that basis he invaded our land.

Concerning the church I'll say only this. Here too the form was not Calvin's main concern. If necessary, he could tolerate episcopacy, as in England. But his church form was invariably rooted in the laity themselves and thus hovered between aristocracy and democracy. His congregation in Geneva was autonomous. He always resisted an ecclesiasticism that turned the congregation into impassive "membra." His synodical system was based on confederation through voluntary membership, and he despised every kind of coercion.[45] Finally, as to separation of church and state: he certainly linked those closely in Geneva, but it should not be forgotten that in Poland as well as in Hungary and France he established free churches that had no tie with the state whatsoever. With that he entrusted the seed to the earth from which, after the Puritan struggle, the concept of the free state would develop of itself.

. . . [Given the proof by historical descent,] can we demonstrate in which Calvinistic doctrine these liberties are rooted? For Calvinism was first of all a reformation of the faith and so could not create any civic liberty except in consequence of its confession, through the power of its faith.

43. Kuyper (notes 94-97) cites Calvin's *Institutes* at IV/20/8, 16, 25, 29, 31.

44. Jules Bonnet, *Lettres de Calvin* (Paris, 1854), vol. I, p. 185, vol. II, pp. 182, 474. The quotation is from the "Wilhelmus," the Dutch national anthem.

45. Kuyper (note 100) cites Calvin's *Institutes* at IV/9/1-4.

Aanblik van de Tweede Kamer,
nadat dr. Kuyper zitting zal hebben genomen.

In practice as well as theory, Kuyper saw a close relationship between religion and politics. A cartoonist in 1874 criticized the young parliamentary orator for thinking he was still in the pulpit.

Do not be too amazed, ladies and gentlemen, however contradictory it might seem, if I answer that question by pointing to the fundamental doctrine of Calvinism: its confession of the *absolute sovereignty of God.* For this confession implies that no authority or power on earth is inherent but is imposed. Thus there is no natural authority to speak of either on the part of the ruler or of the people. Only God is Sovereign; He regards all creatures, born in royal palace or beggar's hut, as nothing in comparison with Himself. One creature cannot have authority over another except as God gives it. And God does not relinquish that authority but allows it to be used to his glory. He is sovereign and gives that authority to whomever He will — sometimes to kings and princes, other times to nobles and patricians, but sometimes also to the people as a whole. For Him a democracy, as in America, is just as useful for showing his sovereign glory as is Russian absolutism. The question is not whether the people rule or a king but whether both, when they rule, do so in recognition of Him.

This implies a twofold judgment. First, upon popular sovereignty as championed by Hugo de Groot and Mirabeau.[46] The idea that each person, by virtue of being born of a woman, is entitled to a share in political authority and that the state owes its existence to the combination of all these small parts — this limits God's freedom, places the source of sovereignty in man as man rather than in God's mighty arm, and cannot but end in the destruction of all moral authority. But it also condemns the "Droit divin" as it was advanced by the friends of the Stuarts, French legitimists, and Prussian "Junkerdom." . . . Even for a prince there cannot and should not be any other kind of "Regnum Dei gratia" or "Droit divin" except that by which all of us exercise the authority with which we have been entrusted and, while respecting the rights of others, remain responsible to God.

Hence the confession of *this* "Droit divin" goes hand in hand with abhorrence for any form of king-worship and strongly condemns any cringing before the royal throne. If God alone is sovereign, and if each of us, including the king, is a creature that depends on Him, then all adoration of kings as individuals, any attempt to see a king as a higher form of being, is base robbery of the glory of his name. Calvinists, therefore, treat a king in his churchly capacity as an ordinary layman. When one of the princes of Condé gave orders to begin the battle of Drieux, the chaplain did not hesitate to ask in front of the troops how he dared to begin a battle without first having confessed the crime he had committed upon a daughter of one of his officers. Whereupon the prince, rather than lashing him with his horsewhip, called the offended father to him, dismounted, and did penance.[47]

But this principle of divine sovereignty opposes just as implacably the rising *State-supremacy* of our day. It makes no difference whether one gives a prince, a parliament, or the State as a whole that which belongs only to God. The State is just as much a creature as the prince; it owes Him its existence and may never usurp the rights of which He spoke in his majesty: "I will give my glory to no other" [Isa. 42:8]. The Calvinists

46. Hugo Grotius/Huig de Groot (1583-1645), the Dutch statesman and jurist especially known for his theory of international law, was no favorite among the orthodox Calvinists owing to his close association with the Remonstrant party, thus Arminian theology, and Johan van Oldenbarnevelt, thus urban regency, in the early seventeenth-century controversies. Gabriel Riqueti, Comte de Mirabeau (1749-91) was the ablest orator and political thinker in the early stages of the French Revolution. He tried to mediate between monarchy and revolutionary republicanism.

47. Kuyper gives no citation for this story, but Louis, Prince of Condé, notorious for his licentiousness, did lead his troops into battle at Drieux on 19 December 1562, where he was defeated and captured.

expressed this in the unshakable argument that we should not, *may* not yield to a government which commands a single thing contradictory to God and his Word. For the Calvinist creature-worship is the worst sin, and it makes no difference in the political domain whether the Persian despot called himself the Sun god or Divus Augustus demanded that the people lay sacrifices before his statue or modern opinion loses itself in the apotheosis of the State. A true Calvinist will never join this detestable endeavor.

But there is more. If all earthly government bears God's sovereignty, then He realizes his plan both in the heroic deeds and in the *sins* of princes and peoples. While condemning the sins as such, we should also recognize the consequences thereof. No doubt his barons wrested the Magna Carta from John Lackland in a despicable manner. But through the Magna Carta the English Parliament would get a power of which an English joke says: "It may do everything except make a man a woman." That is something He wanted, a right which He sanctified. Nebuchadnezzar sinned in making war against Israel, but it was nonetheless God's plan that Israel would go to Babylon, bearing fruit for Israel which it was to accept. Likewise the French Revolution. It was, in the none-too-strong words of Burke, "the most horrible of sins," but the downfall of the ancien régime was a divine judgment upon the princes, and the fruits of the revolution we accept as Antirevolutionaries with thanksgiving, not to the revolution but to the sovereign God. Just here we differ from the Contra-revolutionaries, from those who refuse to recognize the rights created by history and want only violent destruction of what history has brought forth.

This I merely mention in passing. I call your attention to a more serious consequence of the confession of God's sovereignty, to the central doctrine of Calvinism, its "cor Ecclesiae": the *doctrine of election.* Calvinist nations have confessed this in every age of resilience, heroism, and glory; only in days of spiritual weakness have they forgotten or denied this profound thought of moral life. Election is based on God's sovereignty. The Calvinists never intended the doctrine as self-aggrandizement but only as a confession that all honor, including that of spiritual greatness and courage of faith, belongs to God. We need no reminder that this was Calvin's source of strength. We know it of our fathers and the Huguenots from their testimony and petition. . . .[48]

Whoever believes in election knows that he has been chosen *for something,* that this is a spiritual calling, and that, as a divine calling, it

48. Kuyper cites Bancroft to this effect regarding New England (*History of the United States,* vol. I, pp. 461-62), and Frederick Denison Maurice in "his brilliant work," *Lectures on Social Morality* (London, 1872), pp. 310-11.

may require the dearest sacrifice. At the same time it is a calling that guarantees success. Since God is the sovereign who calls him, he does not hesitate, does not weigh the pros and cons, but takes hold of the job and perseveres. And note this. A church that confesses election as the "cor Ecclesiae" cannot be clerical but is bound to find its power in the elect, i.e., in the church members. Thus the democratic form of church government sprang from this confession. Transferred from the church to the state, it would soon give birth to the liberties of our Dutch folk, the liberties of the Whigs' England, and, not least, the liberties of America. Election creates a dynamic sense of public responsibility and undermines any idea of religious persecution. . . .

Calvin's profound sense of *sin,* which flows from the direct recognition of God's sovereignty, paints a similar picture. As we saw earlier, he is a republican since he knows that kings are sinners too. Being tempted more severely they will succumb even sooner than their subjects. But he also knows that the same sin pervades the masses and that, as a result, there will be no end to resistance and rebellion, mutiny and troubles, except for a just constitution that restrains abuse of authority, sets limits, and offers the people a natural protection against lust for power and arbitrariness. This is system. It is consistent. And it is quite different from the French Doctrinaires' demand for liberty on the basis of the "citoyen's" excellence. Soon disillusioned of this excellence by the abuse of power and broken promises, they warded off the misuse of liberty by coup d'état and deportation.

One final conclusion. From God's sovereignty follows the sovereign authority of his Word. It is astonishing how the study of the Old Testament in particular has inspired the development of our constitutional liberties. All authors on Calvinistic constitutional law, whether from Geneva or Scotland, from our Union or France, from England or America, have without exception defended the people's freedoms by appeal to Israel's legal system. Not that they wanted to restore the Mosaic law in their own time. Calvin says of this demand: "Others may show how dangerous and absurd that theory is; to me its falseness and foolishness have been amply demonstrated."[49] But in the spontaneous appearance of the prophets, in the rights of the popular assembly (the Kahâl), in the particular rights of the tribes and the heads of families, and, most of all, in the manner in which the first king was chosen there lay a basic civic freedom, a breath of fresh air that would wipe out all forms of despotic government. . . . Was it not inevitable, therefore, that Calvinist statesmen, who would not take a step without consulting Scripture, learned to see the concept of a people's constitution

49. Kuyper in note 109 cites Calvin's *Institutes* at IV/20/14.

solely in the light of divine approbation — a constitution which, while not destroying the right of inheritance to the throne, was to limit the power of the crown? Thus, both the history of popular opinion and writings on constitutional law prove that Saul and David's coronation meant much more for the progress of our constitutional ideas among *Christian people* than the most beautiful theories.

. . . Does this imply that I think everything remained dark until Calvin, and that the first light followed his appearance? Ladies and gentlemen, I reject so unhistorical a thought. Even the brightest genius remains a child of his time, and Calvin's majestic edifice was also undergirded by the past. No, the reformer from Geneva was not the first to mix the thirst for freedom, the distaste for tyranny, with the blood of the Germanic people! Arminius in the Teutenburg forest and Claudius Civilis on our own soil knew how to break the chains of slavery. Through all the ages our nation has been an enemy of oppression, and Catholic as well as Reformed nobles have defended our rights and liberties against the Alvas and the Vargas.[50] Likewise, when Calvin came on the scene the Christian church had existed for fifteen centuries; that she in her true spiritual offspring did not opt for tyranny had been clearly demonstrated by the hero of Tarsus to the Corinthians, by Ambrose in Milan to the Emperor Theodosius, by Wycliffe in his shackles, by Huss at the stake, and by Luther at the Diet of Worms. Add to this the influence of the Renaissance, which gave a new voice to the heroes of Marathon and restored the splendor of the glory of Greece and ancient Rome. You have in these three — the Germanic, the Christian, and the Renaissance element — the components that promised greater freedom for the people before Geneva was ever mentioned.

But those factors worked against each other instead of giving mutual support. In the war of the Guelphs and the Ghibillines the church fought against the Germanic spirit, the satire of the Humanists was directed against Obscurantism, while presently all Christianity had to confront the Renaissance.[51] Each of these controversies resembled what happened

50. Hermann/Arminius led German tribes to a smashing victory over three Roman legions in the Teutoburg forest, A.D. 9. Gaius Julius Civilis was a first-century chief of the Batavi who led a rebellion against Rome along the Rhine in A.D. 69-70. Fernando Alvarez de Toledo, third Duke of Alba (Alva), was governor of the Netherlands 1567-73 and led the forceful suppression of Protestantism there. Juan de Vargas, like Alba a Spanish soldier, was his chief collaborator.

51. The Ghibillines were an aristocratic faction favoring German imperial control of Italy during the Middle Ages; the Guelphs supported the papacy and Italian city-states. By "Obscurantism" Kuyper means scholasticism.

in Solomon's court: both parties claimed to be the mother of the child of freedom but, more cruelly than in Solomon's court, they cut the living child in two. As a result absolutism could survive. To be broken the Germans' passion had to be channeled, the church purified, the Renaissance sanctified, and the three rubies strung on one chain. This Calvin did! The *power* of the Germanic, the *freedom* of the Christian, and the *nobility* of the classical he smelted in the fire of his spirit into that precious metal from which Holland minted its patroness, with Scripture and liberty cap competing on its legend: "hac nitimur, hanc tuemur!" [by this we strive, this we guard].

Alas! most of Europe's peoples did not long for the fresh waters of freedom from his hand. The Reformation was warded off and as a result Italy declined, Spain sank, the Hapsburgs quarried deep into the hearts of their people, and France hailed in its great king a genuine Oriental despot. This introduced the horrors of oppression which, respecting neither Parliament nor Cortes, allowed nobility and court to crush the people and extinguish every spark of freedom in the hearts of the nation. This same spirit spread to the German courts, where the Germanic element was sacrificed for French money and mistresses and the children of the land were sold like slaves to foreign armies. Indeed, in the worst times even the councils of Swiss cantons and Holland's free states were contaminated by this same spirit of pride and contempt for the people, in the form of patrician nepotism.

This could not continue. Europe's proud spirit must rule Asia, but there is no place in Europe for the Asian despotism of Persian satraps. There had to be a change, a terrible disturbance. God's judgment upon the power-lust of the courts and the servility of the people used the ignominy of the French Revolution as the instrument of salvation. People wanted a breath of fresh air, they cried for freedom, and behold, there lay an ample supply in the Calvinistic countries. The *forms* of freedom people could imitate. But they lacked the moral element, the heroic faith of our fathers that gave Calvinism its stature; the lesser magistrates, who could lawfully initiate the struggle for freedom; the international law, which promised outside help against the tyranny of prince and noble.

Then the *Encyclopedists* arrived on the scene, the spiritual children of Hugo de Groot, an intellectual giant but also an irreconcilable enemy of Calvinism. Although our Gronovius[52] refuted his arguments from the Bible, it made no difference: de Groot deliberately sought the starting

52. Joannes Fredericus Gronovius (1611-71) was a classicist who also wrote a commentary critical of Grotius's philosophy (Amsterdam, 1712). Kuyper cites it via von Polenz, *Geschichte des Französischen Calvinismus,* vol. III, p. 424.

point for his revolutionary idea not in the Christian faith but in the "gregarious nature" of man. In this he was followed by the Deists, and soon by the Encyclopedists in France. Thus originated the dogma of the "Droits de l'homme," which attempted to graft Calvinistic liberties, torn from their natural root, onto the wild stem of self-sufficiency and human wisdom. Above ground the similarity was striking; the antithesis lay in the foundation. Calvinism emphasized God's sovereignty, man's sinful nature, and stringent moral demands. In the clubs of Paris's September heroes God's omnipotence was replaced by the doctrine of human sovereignty. Man was flattered for his excellence, while his basest passions were unleashed.

The movement ignited France, and soon all of Europe. The individual, the home, state, and society were turned upside-down. The mobs broke loose. And after the wild song of unchecked revenge was over, Robespierre's reign of terror and Napoleon's iron fist made the people feel what happens to the freedom of a people that has declared itself sovereign without faith and without lesser magistrates. But at last, under Pitt and Stein's inspiring leadership, Europe re-emerged from such abuse and humiliation. . . . The shout of deliverance was heard at Leipzig's battle of the nations.[53] Justice had been meted out to the princes and grandees of the earth, including our own patricians and rulers. The blood and tears of the downtrodden nations had found its "sera vindicta" in the French Revolution; the honor of liberty had been saved. Of course, those who cultivated the sinful principle of this revolution and its crimes remain guilty; God will judge them. But nonetheless, in spite of guilt and judgment Europe had received a blessing! What had been refused from the hand of Calvinism was eagerly accepted from the hands of the French heroes of freedom, and however Rome, Restoration, and Romantic reaction sought to restore the former situation, the nations of Europe tolerated it no more. Thus, after the revolutions of [18]30 and '48, part of the fruit of Calvinism was spared.

Of *Calvinism,* I say emphatically. What the French Revolution wrought where left to its own designs you may ask of poor France. Having exhausted itself for a false idea, having suffered fourteen revolutions, having worn out all possible forms of government, she continues to search for the freedom that ever eludes her. What the revolution has accom-

53. William Pitt the Younger (1759-1806) was prime minister of Britain all but three years during 1783-1806 and thus led its opposition to the French Revolution. Heinrich F. K. von Stein (1757-1831) was a Prussian leader after the kingdom's defeat by Napoleon. He executed wide-ranging domestic reforms and led in the formation of the coalition of Russian, Prussian, and Austrian forces that defeated Napoleon in the "battle of the nations" at Leipzig, October 1813.

plished in its own power ask of sadly battered Spain which has so fallen from the zenith of her glory that today she can hardly find compassion without a mixture of ridicule. If you want more testimony, just compare Mexico and Peru, Chile and Uruguay, all revolutionary republics of the purest kind — one of them even taking the Phrygian cap on dagger as its coat of arms — compare them with the United States and tell me that the contrast does not speak loudly!

But our Western states also face danger. Again, I do not deny the fruit of the French Revolution. By God's plan, even in its sinful appearance it has served to spread Calvinistic liberties. I do not complain about this but am grateful for it — on one condition: that the poisonous element it introduced into the organism of the European states not be overlooked. For it did more than just copy Calvinistic liberties. It also introduced a system, a catechism, a doctrine; and this system, running counter to God and his righteousness, destroys the bonds of law and order, undermines the foundations of society, gives free play to passion, and gives the lower material realm rule over the spirit.

That system and doctrine, not those liberties, we Antirevolutionaries reject. We know that the "perspectives du paradis" cannot be realized on earth, but even less will we be pushed back to the "supplices de l'enfer." . . . So far are we from disliking revolutions in the ordinary sense that the Greek uprising against Persia incites our admiration, the Swiss rebellion against the Hapsburgs our sympathy, our fathers' revolt against Spain our love, England's "Glorious Revolution" our affection, and America's liberation our unconditional approval. We simply object when these revolutions and the French insurrection are lumped together! . . .

We direct your attention to Burke, who was introduced to our country in Professor Opzoomer's 1857 rectorial address at Utrecht as a liberal statesman par excellence and a reliable guide for our political affairs.[54] But Edmund Burke was an Antirevolutionary through and through. He defended the American uprising since religion, "always a principle of energy, showed itself in this good people the main cause of a free spirit, the most adverse to all implicit submission of mind and opinion." When people would compare England's "Glorious Revolution" with the French, he answers: "Our revolution and that of France are just the reverse of each other in almost every particular and in the whole spirit of the transaction." Should you ask him why he is so fiercely

54. C. W. Opzoomer, *De Staatkunde van Edmund Burke* (Utrecht, 1852); N.B., not 1857. Kuyper also cites (note 114) J. C. Bluntschli, a German liberal, to the same effect. Burke's combination of Whig liberalism with antirevolutionary conviction was a model for Kuyper, who had been reading him closely in preparation for this piece.

opposed to the French Revolution, he will say: "Because the French Revolution is a total overturning of society, and its system is an anti-Christian doctrine." "We are at war not with a people but with a system, and that system by its essence is subversive of every government." . . . Or, to put the contrast even more succinctly: "We are fighting for the rights of Englishmen, not of men."[55]

We Dutch Calvinists want to be like Burke: *for* freedom but *against* the total overturning of all natural order. *For* freedom and therefore not the kind of Calvinists who seek salvation in a return to the past. Our Calvinism is alive, it has an inner power of development, so how could we long for a phase that we have long since left behind? No, we do *not* want a restoration of the state church, for we know how detrimental that is to our faith. We do not long for the church to be schoolmistress once again, for we know how this robs education of its vigor. We do not want the old privileges back, since we know how this breeds envy and resentment. We do not want the unity of the state to be broken upon into seven pieces, since we know that the hope for the future lies not in provincialism but in a united nation. We would be the fiercest opponents to any attempt to disregard our constitutional rights or to violate our constitutional monarchy.

No, what we want is equal rights for all, whatever their situation or religion. With all our might we will defend freedom of conscience, a free press, freedom of assembly, and freedom of opinion. We desire the liberation of the church by a fair and complete separation from the state, also in financial matters; the liberation of the school, not by giving it back to the church but to the parents under the rules and supervision of the state, since the impersonal state, we believe, cannot be a schoolmaster. We want to tighten the bond that holds us to the House of Orange, on the condition that the republican character of our people, of which Orange itself is symbol and seal, be maintained. We promote decentralization, an organic representation of the people, and an ethical colonial policy. We demand more freedom for higher education, more independence for our courts — if necessary by introducing the jury system. As to our defense system, I would only remark that Switzerland, England, and America, the preeminently Calvinistic countries, have spent the least on their armies, yet would seem to have the most secure independence.

If people would class us with the radicals on the left because of the free program and the flag of Christian liberalism that we raise, we would not object, at least in part. In formal social program Fourier and

55. Kuyper (notes 116-20) cites Burke's *Works* in the 8-volume Thomas McLean edition (London, 1823).

Aº. 1872. Nº. 1.

DE STANDAARD.

Maandag 1 April.

BUREEL: Nieuwendijk L 76, Amsterdam.

The inaugural issue of Kuyper's daily newspaper, *De Standaard* (1 April 1872), with its lead article of "Freedom!"

St. Simon often stand close to the prophet of Nazareth. Deramey caught it well: St. Paul is also the apostle of democracy.[56] But one thing we should never forget: nothing so much resembles the leaf on the true vine as the foliage of the wild creeper that never bears fruit. This holds here too. Even though our demands sometimes resemble those of the most active radicals, they grow from different roots. "Duo cum faciunt idem, non est idem." [When two do the same thing, it isn't the same thing.] We expect everything, and they nothing, from the faith! *From the faith!* That demand we cannot surrender. For we love freedom, and we know from a history of almost three centuries that only faith offers the vital power to guarantee this freedom for ourselves and our children for generations to come.

Does this seem strange? If so, let me conclude by putting this question to you. Recently we celebrated the silver jubilee of our constitution. It too has attracted much faith, and even more fierce criticism. But whatever the reproach, everyone agrees that by comparison to the

56. Charles Fourier (1772-1837) and Henri de Saint Simon (1760-1825) were utopian-socialist theorists renowned for their detailed schemes. J. P. Deramey was a French priest and author of *L'apôtre St. Paul, étude de Démocratie religieuse* (Paris, 1873).

old regime of the united provinces, the constitution to which we now swear allegiance offers a model of organization. If, nonetheless, our fathers were three times more effective with rusty flintlock, unwieldy battle-ax, and awkward cannon than we are with our superior weapons, must there not be a reason and should we not search for that reason?

And so, ladies and gentlemen, I have completed my assignment. I thank you for your kind attention. If someone among you was hurt by any of my words, forgive me for the sake of freedom of speech. And should I have any reward because of this study, I hope it will be this: that at least the young people of the Netherlands will not echo the old libel and continue to say that we, Dutch Calvinists, are a party of reaction!

The case Kuyper laid before the learned in *Calvinism and Our Constitutional Liberties* he put to more common readers in the following editorial, with which he launched his daily newspaper, *De Standaard*.

The substance and the occasion were perfectly matched. Kuyper raised *De Standaard* on 1 April 1872, the 300th anniversary of the Dutch rebels' seizure of the port of Brielle which, in turn, induced William ("the Silent") of Orange-Nassau to take up arms against the Spanish occupation and Inquisition. The events and personages in this account are all historically real, although projected through Kuyper's own lens. It serves to show his particular mix of religion and patriotism as well as the ideal he would always hold before his audience. Shabby but brave, obedient to God's law but prickly toward man's, his readers were to be the new Beggars, a faithful remnant who might redeem the entire nation.

Freedom

"First of all, since it concerns the *glory of God* and the peace of the poor believers in the Netherlands, let everyone put aside all personal ambition and self-interest." So read the godly decree issued by William of Orange to his Sea Beggars.[1] On this occasion of national rejoicing, may that princely word of the Father of our country also control the minds and hearts of our Christian people today!

1. Dutch: "Watergeuzen"; from the French *gueux:* beggar, tramp; *gueux de mer:* "Sea Beggars." An imperial councilor scorned the Dutch nobles who petitioned for relief from religious restrictions as "beggars." The name also applied to the pirates and "sea tramps" who plied the Dutch coast. The two parties were linked by this epithet and came to use it with pride.

It was a small, motley fleet of inland vessels that three centuries ago, on the first of April, dropped anchor outside the Brielle harbor. But on board that little fleet the Word of God was a power. The ships' order was "that all ship personnel and soldiers would be expected, morning and evening, before eating or drinking, to come up on deck to hear the Word of God on pain of forfeiting a sixpence, one half for the poor and one half for the provost." However unconsciously, that holy Book, read freely on board ship but violently denied them in the beloved Fatherland, was the program of the armed struggle for which the staunch and stubborn Sea Beggars had buckled on their swords. The issue in that struggle was *Freedom,* the most precious good, for which a man of character willingly sheds his blood. A thirst for a *new,* mighty freedom was present throughout the ranks, but above all born in the heart. What kind of freedom was their goal?

It was not *political* freedom! The thought of renouncing the King of Spain had not yet occurred to them. "Before God and his great host I swear that at no time have I despised the *king!*"[2] Nor was it *civic* freedom! If that is what you thought, let the Thijms and Nuyens set you straight: there never was a freer people than lived on Dutch soil under earls and dukes![3] No, the *new* freedom whose divine creative ferment was to establish a *new* nation in our beloved Holland was still an unknown thing, a freedom of an infinitely higher order: *the freedom of conscience.*

In the letter the Prince of Orange sent to the States [of Holland and Zeeland] shortly after the capture of Brielle, the first article solemnly intoned: "So I call God Almighty as my witness that I have the following motives, and no other, for engaging in this war: (1) that all decrees by which our *consciences* and laws are now violated be abolished, and that everyone who so desires have the

2. A verse from the "Wilhelmus" (for William the Silent), the old Dutch national anthem:

Voor Gid wil ik belijden
    en Zijne groote macht,
dat ik den geenen tijde
    den Koning heb veracht!

3. Willem J. F. F. Nuyens (1823-94) and Petrus P. M. Thijm (1827-1904) were the leading Roman Catholic historians in the Netherlands at the time, specializing in the medieval roots of Dutch liberty and civilization. Thijm's brother, J. A. Alberdingk Thijm (1820-89), advanced the same cause as poet and professor of art history in Amsterdam.

freedom to accept the teaching of the Prophets, of Christ and the Apostles; and (2) that the name of the Inquisition be wiped out forever. . . ."

It was not for Liberal slogans but for *freedom of conscience* that people risked their necks; it was to create a place of peace also for the church of God. "Aldegonde!" cried the great prince of Orange, "let them trample us to death if only we may offer help to God's church!"[4] Thus *freedom of conscience* was the name of that new power whose birthing hour struck when Brielle's gate was battered down and its doors finally yielded amidst the smoke of pitch and straw.

That freedom was a *gift* from God, first to the Netherlands and soon, via the Netherlands, to the rest of Europe.

That freedom did not yet exist. Though the Reformers may have had intimations of it, as yet they did not know it. Calvin still erected a stake for Servetus! Neither did the Sea Beggars know it. They were still quite capable of shedding blood, by which the sacred rights of conscience were denied. That freedom came from above. The God who is Love sent it to us. Let the facts stand, especially the fact of this act of God. In those rough-and-ready sea-dogs, their ears cut short and their noses cut off,[5] the Lord created a thirst for that as-yet-unknown freedom, not by a long course of philosophical development, nor by a refined civility, but by sheer *distress,* the *agony of death.*

They had not *read* the chronicles of the martyrs, as we have. But they had *heard* the screams of the tortured, the ghastly groanings of the strangled. Not a black print but the ugly scaffold, painted red with blood, had shown them the image of a martyr. There was a father whom they had loved dearly, a brother their soulmate, a son to whom they had been attached with all their heart; and they had to look on as an executioner's hand "hanged, pierced, or throttled them, after having villainously treated them, or tortured them with red-hot irons." A dear mother, a daughter who was their hope, a bride who was their delight — they had seen armed men drag them by their hair, seize them by their breasts, burn them under their armpits, abuse them with ropes and cords, indeed, rape, injure, and kill them.

It was then they became Beggars. "Death to the Beggars!"

4. Philip Marnix, Lord of St. Aldegonde (1540-98), was William's secretary, special emissary, and councilor.

5. As punishment for their earlier crimes of piracy, desertion, etc.

cried the Council of Blood.[6] But they banged their drums! "Long live the Beggars!" became their slogan. And when the drums grew silent, they wept and cried out: "Lord God! Deliver thou us!"

Then it came. Then the birthing hour of *freedom of conscience* struck.

Brielle would be taken by surprise. It was God's plan. What a prince of the House of Orange once wrote about the work of liberation as a whole was true especially now: "This cause and this work was not of man but of God!"

He did it. Not the Sea Beggars, for they set sail toward Texel, not to Brielle. Not the Prince of Orange, for he did not know of it and more disapproved than approved of it. Not the great mass of the citizenry, who were frightened at hearing of it and fearful of vengeance. Not Count Lumey,[7] for once the booty was on board he was all for heading back to the high seas.

No, it was *the Lord* who did it. And what instruments did he use? First of all, *Alva* himself, who had persuaded England's queen to drive the "Sea Beggars" away from her coasts. *Alva* himself, who had to move his military personnel from Brielle's fortress to reinforce the garrison at Utrecht. Next, the *Prince of Orange* who as a sovereign had the right to keep a fleet at sea. Then "the wind and the storms" which cut off the sea journey to Texel and forced the Beggars to anchor off of Brielle. Particularly also *Treslong*, who had just joined the fleet when it was about to sail from Dover and, as the only citizen of Brielle on board, decided its surprising fate. Finally also the "Syrian in his simplicity," *Coppelstock*, the wide-awake ferryman who, hoping for the best, rowed out to the fleet and soon dismayed the city fathers of Brielle with his cry: "Five thousand Beggars!"[8]

6. The "Council of Blood" was the epithet the Dutch gave to the special court the Duke of Alva established upon his arrival in Brussels, September 1567, to ferret out dissenters. Its Spanish composition and use of torture made it especially infamous to the local population. Some six thousand Dutch citizens were killed at its command or those of similar courts convened in other places; Kuyper is graphically alluding to these measures in the preceding paragraph.

7. Count Guillaume Lumey de la Marck (1542-78), a Flemish petite-aristocrat, was an especially avaricious privateer and "admiral" of the 25-ship squadron that took Brielle.

8. Willem Blois de Treslong, Lumey's second-in-command, was a son of the former royal governor of Brielle and so was well known to its inhabitants. He both persuaded Lumey to occupy the town and conducted the negotiations with its magistrates. Peter Coppelstock, who operated a ferry across the Maas, served as a messenger to that purpose. His report exaggerated the number of Beggars eightfold and effectively put the local authorities to flight.

Necopinata per Contraria is the gold-embossed motto engraved upon the splendid commemorative medal struck for our tricentennial celebration. *Necopinata:* against all expectation; *per Contraria:* through what seemed dead wrong. And so it was. All eyes were on Germany — and it came from the sea. People dreaded the "Sea Beggars" — and they came to the rescue.

> Flat-out against what was desired;
> and through the flat-out unadmired.

Since then three centuries have washed over our people and fatherland. You no longer hear the crackling of the stake, no Alva tramples any more on our breast. Today every child on our streets can still sing of the capture of Brielle. The fact was so amazing. The ditty about "Alva losing his glasses" has not yet died out.[9]

But what *has* died out among the masses is the memory of what the Prince of Orange wrote: "This work is not of man but of God." People celebrate Revolution; they fly their orange flags; they honor the Beggars; everyone knows of Roobol and of Coppelstock. But where is the acclaim and gratitude to our God? Where is our self-mortification before Him?

What indeed threatens to die out is that distinctive national spirit which the Lord once breathed into our heart and conscience. What is being threatened and violated again is precisely that sacred freedom of conscience: the freedom, in church and school, to serve the God of our fathers in the manner of our fathers. What has almost died out is that sense of our people's moral calling, the conviction that especially the Dutch nation has been chosen to be for itself and all the peoples of Europe the standard-bearer not just of freedom but of *freedom of conscience*.

Nevertheless, there still remain people who, in keeping with the demand of history, carry this precious legacy in their heart. It is my prayer that they will not lose heart, though their number is small and their strength is little. "Small, too, was the fleet of the Beggars!" May they not only fly the tricolor [the Dutch flag] from their homes but send up gratitude and prayer for what God has *given* and, especially, *forgiven* our beloved fatherland.

9. The Dutch word for glasses is "bril," a pun on Brielle, the city that was captured. The ditty went: "Den eersten dag van April/Verloos Duc d'Alva zijnene Bril."

Their calling is so beautiful! To fight not just for themselves and their children but for their fellow citizens, for the peoples of Europe, for all of humanity, so that justice remain *justice,* that *freedom* of conscience not be smothered, and that, as the Prince's motto put it, our primary goal again be "the *glory of our God.*"

And fight they will, provided they have the courage to assume the standard under which both Prince and Beggars fought: the standard of "the Word of God."

> For God's Word ever dear
> have I, free, undaunted,
> a hero without fear,
> risked my noble blood.[10]

Fight they will if, instructed by that Word, they do not despise the voice of history. And if these "children of history" are found mostly among "the people of little and average means," what of it! Three centuries back a prince of the House of Orange wrote: "Many rich people pretend they have suddenly become altogether poor, indeed many contributed only to get onto the roll, but *the people of little and average means* showed their generous heart and warm affection." Don't forget: As a result of the Word this country not only became *free* but, after being plundered and looted, also the richest nation on earth.

Fight they will if, in conformity to that Word, they do not haughtily scoff at the unfaithfulness of others but, as children of the people and in solidarity with them, ask their God for forgiveness for the sins of the nation.

May He, in whose hands lie also the threads of our national life, make our country's celebration foster that spirit. May He grant us the sacred honor of again raising up the standard of His Word for our Christian people. So then, may our beginning be His, and may our help in this labor, too, be in the name of the Lord who also created *our* nation and rescued *our* fatherland![11]

10. Another stanza from the "Wilhelmus."

11. A quotation from the opening of service in the Dutch Reformed liturgy: "Our help is in the name of the Lord, who created the heavens and earth."

The South African Crisis

Kuyper's Anglophilia in *Calvinism and Constitutional Liberties* was a fixed sentiment until the end of the nineteenth century. The Boer War changed that completely. Kuyper explained the reversal by principial analysis, arguing that the Christian convictions of William Gladstone had given way to the cynical materialism of Joseph Chamberlain in the councils of British government. Unfortunately for this account, Chamberlain had grown up in the dissenting Protestantism that Kuyper celebrated among the English, had risen through the ranks of Gladstone's Liberal Party, had been a fellow advocate of Home Rule for Ireland and social reform at home. His move into Tory ranks and ardent expansionism stemmed from personal ambition and his perception of national needs amid the renewed imperialism of the 1890s. These were not foreign to Kuyper. Indeed, the apologia that follows can read as a tract of Dutch nationalism confronted by British power and mixed with the common European racism of the time.

The piece has particular value on two counts. It shows the Boer mentality that would, as Kuyper predicted, exact vengeance upon Britain's triumph. Although Kuyper did not anticipate the racist forms of that revenge, the architects of apartheid could find justification in sentiments such as he expresses below. More telling for his own intentions is his portrait of Boer pioneer stock, an idealization (though hardly a complete manufacture) of the facts on the ground and a projection of Kuyper's values of Spartan republicanism and Calvinist patriarchy. In retrospect Kuyper was also prophetic in decrying the fateful auguries on which the nineteenth century was closing. The Boer War was indeed a fit prelude for a century in which peace and progress gave way to ruthless war, war that would return from the far reaches of empire to the European heartland, destroying all the swagger — British, Dutch, and French alike. If this fulfilled Kuyper's predictions as culture-critic, it confounded his assumptions about Europe's rightful political hegemony.

A short primer in white South African history to explain the events to which Kuyper refers, in his own manner: After a first attempt in 1795, the British captured the Cape in 1806, asserting political control over the descendants of the predominantly Dutch but also French, Scottish, and German immigrants who had settled there from the seventeenth century on. In 1834 the practice of slavery — which was hardly as tender as Kuyper alleges — was banned by British decree; the next year began the "Great Trek" by some twelve thousand Boers from Cape Colony into the interior. In 1847 Britain annexed the two territories thus established, the Transvaal and the Orange Free State. It signed treaties relinquishing the first in 1852, the second in 1854, then reasserted its claims in 1877 subsequent to the discovery of diamonds in Kimberley. Boer forces took up armed resistance to those claims in 1880-81, which were then modified by the 1884 Convention of London negotiated under Gladstone's auspices. The Boer republics retained sovereignty in domestic but not in international affairs.

The Transvaal gold rush of 1886 precipitated another influx of British immigrants and capital into the interior. Cecil Rhodes won Charter Company status for his enterprises in 1888 and, with the knowledge if not consent of British Colonial Secretary Joseph Chamberlain, sponsored the abortive Jameson raid of 1895. Taking this as a sign of things to come, the Boers launched all-out war in autumn 1899 and achieved some remarkable successes in the field. The British government responded by committing, eventually, half a million troops to the Cape, which precipitated an anti-war movement at home and abroad. Kuyper wrote his piece in January 1900, between the initial Boer victories and the (February) turning of the tide. It was published in English by the "Stop the War Committee" in May, just as England successfully reclaimed the Orange Free State.

Kuyper's article first appeared in French in the prestigious *Revue des Deux Mondes* (February 1900) and was translated into English by A. E. Fletcher under the title used here. The following represents about two-thirds of the whole: all of Sections I-IV and IX-XII and a short half of section V. Sections VI-VIII, of a technical nature, have been deleted. I have slightly altered Fletcher's original for purposes of stylistic consistency and have fleshed out Kuyper's very spare footnotes with full references and explanatory comments. The Latin translations are by Kenneth Bratt.

THE NINETEENTH CENTURY is drawing to its close. It opened with splendid promise for liberty and demands for the restitution of violated rights. At first its high hopes were realized by the successful initiation of reforms that made for freedom. Why, now that it is about to pass away, should it be disgraced almost at its last hour by a war of aggression which nothing can justify? What magnificent hopes for the future had not the Conference at The Hague disclosed to the heart of the nations bowed under the ever increasing burden of military charges![1] Instead of appeal to arms, arbitration was henceforth to settle international disputes. Yet England today, England which was one of the most zealous participants in the Hague Conference, at the first menace of war gives it the kick and knows it no more!

Once more the Yuletide has sent forth the angelic message, "Peace on earth," even to where the natives gather at the humble chapels of our missionaries. Yet shocking as it may seem, these savages are standing by while a murderous struggle is going on between Christian and Christian to see whether the Christians of Europe or the Christians of Africa will finally get the upper hand. England has ever won for herself the glory of being the champion of the independence of weak and oppressed peoples; yet yonder, in South Africa, there are old men of seventy with their grandsons of fourteen scrambling all over the rocks to lie in wait for English soldiers [who are] preparing to steal their country's freedom.

A cry of distress has gone up, a cry of the conscience of Europe aroused this time not against the Turk but against the country of Burke and of Pitt, against the country that once prided itself on its inborn love of justice. Is it not a sad spectacle? Has progress been arrested? Can it be that in the century about to be born we are going to slip backward?

I

If we wish to thoroughly understand the causes and to trace clearly the origin of this unfortunate war, we must go back in history.

On two occasions in the course of the seventeenth century Holland made an effort to colonize extensively beyond the sea — in America in 1628, at the Cape in 1650. Both these colonies fell into the hands of the English by an act of aggression. . . . [Kuyper attacks the "fabrication" that "the Prince of Orange had *sold* the Cape."] In the occupation of the Cape in 1806 England saw not a question of right but what it devolved

1. The first international Peace Conference met at The Hague, 18 May-29 July 1899. It established a permanent court to arbitrate disputes usually settled by war.

Kuyper protested signs of English imperialism already in the 1870s, when his esteem for that country was still high. This "three-star" editorial appeared on 4 April 1878, immediately after the conclusion of the Russo-Turkish War (1875-78).

Treaties

We cannot stress strongly enough, both as Netherlanders and as Antirevolutionaries, the importance of observing international treaties. In those treaties, next to God, the Netherlands finds its surest support. To value mountain and stream or the kinship of race and tribe more highly than the moral bonds of law is to become revolutionary, marrow and bone.

In every respect, therefore, the current phase of the Eastern Question deserves our closest attention. Let's just be on our guard against one easily explicable misconception. Think not that *England today defends the sanctity of treaties.*

At the London conference it was stipulated that the Treaty of Paris [1856, ending the Crimean War] could not be legally modified apart from the consent of the signatories. On that basis, accordingly, Russia declared its willingness to consult its

upon Mr. Chamberlain later to christen with the name of "paramountcy." As she had lost her rich American colonies, England felt the need of consolidating the conquests of the famous Hastings in India, and it seemed to her indispensable to secure a naval station at the Cape. Captain Robert Percival who — probably one of her agents — visited the Cape in 1803 on a voyage of observation did not hesitate to declare "that the mere possession of the harbors of the Cape would indeed be nearly sufficient to bring all enemies into our power."[2]

Meantime neither in America nor at the Cape had England known

2. Robert Percival, *Account of the Cape of Good Hope* (London, 1804), p. 390. Joseph Chamberlain (1836-1914) had been Colonial Secretary in the British government since 1895. An ardent imperial expansionist, he was particularly connected with the policies and intentions leading to British annexation of the Boer republics. Francis Rawdon Hastings (1754-1826) was governor general and military commander of the British consolidation of control over India, 1813-18.

co-signatories on all points *pertaining to this treaty.* The Czar had just one reservation. He reserved the right to exclude from discussion the points that do *not* pertain to this treaty or imply *no* modification of it.

England is now registering a protest against this proviso, at the very moment she herself — *in open defiance of the Treaty of Paris,* against the will of the *Sultan* [of the Ottoman Empire], and without the consent of its co-signatories — is sending her fleet through the Dardanelles. Alas, England is *not* standing by the treaties. It did not stand by the treaties when it sacrificed our rights to Belgium [1839]. Nor when it abandoned Denmark [1864]. Nor when it allowed Hanover to be swallowed up [1867]. Nor when it permitted Nassau to be annexed [1867]. Nor when all the Italian principalities disappeared [1860s]. Nor when, in violation of the treaty, the Turks muzzled and murdered Christians. Nor, recall, when it sent Shepstone to the Transvaal [1877].

Only now, now that England is "worried about India" and the rabble of London and the soldiers sing of nothing but "India," now it sanctimoniously puts on the mask of "international treaties."

Let's just tell it like it is. Nobody in Europe any longer stands by treaties. England no more than Russia.

Might, not *right,* calls the shots!

how to win the sympathies of her new subjects of Dutch extraction. Every effort at fusion between them and their new masters was defeated by the tenacity of the race from the Low Countries. Even today in America, after the lapse of two centuries, the animosity of the people of Dutch origin against England continues as lively as ever. At a dinner in the premier club in New York I have listened to remarks made against the injustice and the violent methods of England such as have never been made either in Natal or at Pretoria.[3] Although the Dutch in America have now almost lost the memory of their mother-tongue, they everywhere still associate in unions called *Holland Societies.* Their Dutch origin is to them a title of nobility of which they are proud, and during the great war of independence they sealed their aversion to everything English with their blood. The same kind of thing has happened at the Cape. Captain Percival himself testified in 1803:

3. Kuyper had been feted at any number of Knickerbocker clubs and meetings during his visit to the United States in 1898.

"An Englishman will be surprised at the aversion and even the hatred which the Dutch seem to entertain towards us."[4]

This was left over from the rivalry of the two great naval powers of the seventeenth century — the struggle in which Holland had succumbed. Resentment against "perfidious Albion" had nowhere penetrated the national spirit more profoundly than in the Netherlands, and England herself had made this resentment more bitter by the high-handed manner in which she never ceased to apply to Holland the principle of *Vae victis* [woe to the conquered]. "Dutch" and "double Dutch" are still invidious expressions among the English populace. Time has softened these racial antipathies; in Holland a few circles are even open to the charge of Anglomania. On the other hand a historian like Rogers in his *History of Holland* has frankly acknowledged that England was not only indebted to Holland for a large share of her civilization but had also repaid this valuable service very poorly.[5]

At the time when the Cape was annexed the relations between the two countries were still very strained, and Mr. Theal, the well-known historian of the Cape, is bold enough to say that the Dutch colonists regarded the English as "arrogant above all other mortals, insatiable in the pursuit of wealth, regardless of the rights of others and viewing everything with an eye jaundiced by national prejudice." Moreover, the aversion was reciprocal. Captain Percival tells us that to the English the colonists appeared an "unsociable, inhospitable and boorish race, and their actions entirely guided by mercenary and interested motives."[6] On both sides there was exaggeration, no doubt, but in any case there is ample proof that the two elements which were henceforth to be compelled to live together in South Africa took very badly to a more intimate fusion.

The national character of the English, in fact, differs fundamentally from that of the Dutch. Both have their qualities well defined, but between the two there is an absolute incompatibility. As regards outward display, prompt and energetic action, large conceptions and methodic organization, the English are superior beyond dispute; but the medal has a reverse side in their love of show, their inability to observe well, and their propensity to confound the idea of organization with the effort for Anglicizing everybody. The Dutchman on the contrary is less enamored of parade; he is too slow in the development of his projects; he leaves

4. Percival, *Account*, p. 305. Kuyper also references John Centlivres Chase, *History of the Colony of the Cape of Good Hope* (Capetown, 1869), p. 349.

5. James E. T. Rogers, *The History of Holland* (New York, 1895).

6. George M. Theal, *South Africa* (London, 1894), p. 116. Theal was perhaps the most influential of all South African historians. Percival, *Account*, p. 223.

things alone, submits to impressions, and contents himself too much with observing things with an attentive eye. But from the instant that his dormant energy is awakened, he has always shown himself to be endowed with a perseverance and a tenacity that nothing can shake. Neither the Spaniards in the sixteenth century nor the English at the Cape ever comprehended this character based upon latent energy. Because in winter they noticed only a tiny rivulet like a thread of frozen, harmless water, they were not prepared for the powerful torrent that at springtime would rush down to overflow its bed as soon as the melting of the snow set in.

Shortly after the occupation of the Cape in 1814 affairs between the colonists and their new masters began to be troubled. Especially the farmers on the northern frontier of the colony refused to accommodate themselves to the new conditions. One of them, a man named Bezuydenhout, resisted single-handed a company of soldiers. He was killed on the spot. His wife, gun in hand, vowed vengeance. A disturbance broke out. Brought to a stand by a military force three times superior, some of the rioters were taken and tried, and five of them were condemned to be hanged while the rest were compelled to assist at their execution. On March 9, 1815, the gallows was erected on the top of a hill in the presence of a crowd of colonists accompanied by their wives and children. Presently the five condemned men, strung up to the same beam, swung together from side to side. They had already lost consciousness when suddenly the beam came down with a crash. The five bodies lay upon the ground. The unhappy men revived. The crowd, seeing in this an act of divine clemency, implored the mercy of the English magistrate with heart-rending appeals. But he, a man of a severity which nothing could ruffle, remained inexorable. The condemned men were again hung up and delivered anew to the agonies of a still more frightful death. The onlookers gave this scene of execution the name of *Slachtersnek,* which may be translated Slaughter's Hill. As English authors themselves admit, never has the memory of that horrible execution been effaced from the minds of the Dutch farmers. "Remember Majuba!" has been the war cry of the Scotch guards. "Forget not Slachtersnek!" has remained for a century the vengeance cry of the outraged Boers.[7]

7. Frederick C. Bezuidenhout had died defying an official summons to answer charges of cruelty to his slaves. His brother organized a group of Boer farmers in response; sixty were arrested and five hanged. This incident of Slachter's Nek, 1815, did carry much of the symbolic value Kuyper attributes to it, not least, however, because of its racial overtones. I retain Kuyper's spelling of names in the text but use current standardized forms in the notes.

II

We must not identify the Boers with the Dutch too closely, however. In the month of January 1659 there disembarked at the Cape a group of French Huguenots numbering about three hundred persons, followed afterwards by seventeen Piedmontese families. In 1827 three hundred Germans established themselves in the Colony, and after the Crimean War two thousand German members of the foreign legion obtained extensive farms there.[8] The Scots themselves to a considerable number have mixed with the Boers by marriage. To ascertain approximately the proportion of these divers elements I asked Dr. Muller, envoy and Consul-general of the Orange Free State at The Hague, to examine the list of electors of his country. I have thus ascertained that 68 percent of the names were Dutch, 12 percent French, 12 percent Scottish, 3 percent German and 3 percent Scandinavian, Italian, etc. The two great Generals Joubert and Cronje are of French origin; President Kruger and Mr. Reitz, the Secretary of State, are of German extraction.[9] Hence it appears that although the Dutch element so far predominates as to absorb the others at least with respect to language, the direct influence of the other nationalities over this complex and varied assemblage is far from negligible. Those whom we call Africanders [*sic*] are distinguished among the Boers by that light shade of character that reveals their greater accessibility to English civilization, inducing them to invite English farmers to make common cause with them against the mother country as Dutch and English did in America. The Boers, on the contrary, fear that the infiltration of English habits would enfeeble their type. At the moment of danger, however, the claims of blood have never proved false and the Africanders have always pleaded the cause of their brothers beyond the Orange and the Vaal.

The name "Boer" means peasant, but we would be deceived in comparing the Boers with French peasants, English farmers, or even American settlers. It is for the most part a conquering race that has established itself among the Hottentots and the Bantus, as the Normans in the eleventh century planted themselves amongst the Anglo-Saxons. Abstaining from handicraft, they attend to their properties comprising

8. Kuyper cites Chase, *History,* p. 108, for the Huguenots; William F. Purvis, *South Africa: Its People, Progress, and Problems* (London, 1896), p. 65, for the Germans.

9. Piet J. Joubert (1831-1900) and Piet Cronje (1836-1911) were Boer commanders in the wars against England. S. J. Paul Kruger (1825-1904) attained early success as a military leader but was most renowned as President of the Transvaal Republic, 1883-1900.

sometimes from two thousand to three thousand hectares, and raise horses and cattle. Beyond this the great business of their life is the chase, including even deer-stalking. They are intrepid horsemen and exercise themselves unremittingly in the handling of arms. Without being cultured or refined, they display that natural sagacity which has always been the gift of pioneer nations at the beginning of their historical development. Hence their thirst for independence and their insatiable love of liberty, social and political. They have too tough a backbone to bow the head under anybody's yoke, whoever it may be. Nowhere is there a public life more developed or more widely scattered. The Boer is *par excellence* the politician and military man combined. They have their own journal which they not only read but study. Their organization is thoroughly democratic. They themselves choose their President, their magistrates, their judges, and even their military officers whom they call Field Cornets and Commandants. Although ignorant of all military discipline as it is understood by European armies, they fight in a perfectly homogeneous manner, each of them being an officer to himself and cooperating on his own initiative for the end which their cornet indicates.

Their religion, thoroughly Calvinistic, is the very soul of their chivalrous existence and completely harmonizes with it. The Old Testament, above all, has impressed them with the paramount value of fervent piety in the consolidation of national strength. This explains why they open their councils of war with prayer and march to battle singing the Psalms of David, reviving thus the traditions of the armies of Gustavus Adolphus, of the Huguenots, and of Cromwell. Their well-defined predilection for Protestantism is no matter for astonishment in the descendants of the Gueux and the Huguenots, but it is not true that Roman Catholics are excluded for their opinions from all service under the State. Dr. Leyds has given me the names of several avowed Catholic functionaries of the South African Republic. When the English in 1814 took possession of the Cape they found a Catholic curate whom the Boers were tolerating but whom the English took care to drive away.[10] Their morality is above all suspicion. *Liaisons* with Negro women, which have always been the disgrace and scourge of colonizing nations, are among the Boers absolutely unknown. Their married life is most pure, and alcoholism has never seduced them. Families of fifteen children are not a very rare exception, and to have as many as ten is about the average. Add to this their longevity — equal

10. The Gueux were the celebrated "Sea Beggars" of the sixteenth-century uprising against the Spanish. On the English action in 1814, Kuyper cites Theal, *South Africa*, p. 139.

to that of the Russians — and you will find the explanation for their truly surprising increase.

Captain Percival in 1804 found only 60,000 persons of their race. This number had increased by 1822 to 111,451. In 1866 the whites at the Cape alone numbered not less than 187,439 persons. At present the population of European origin, according to the census of 1891, is 376,957 souls in Cape Colony alone, 285,270 in the Transvaal, 77,716 in the Free State, and 44,415 in Natal, making a total of 784,358 souls.[11] We must add further the whites of Bechuanaland, of Griqualand West, of Humpata and take care to raise the number sufficiently to account for the continued increase since 1891. Calculating according to the proportions for the preceding decade, this increase would be at the rate of 2.60 percent per annum, quickly yielding a total of 900,000 souls. On this estimate the Boers may be put down at 520,000, the other nationalities together at 380,000. In any case the increase is without doubt extraordinary as regards the Boers, who since 1804 have climbed from 60,000 to more than half a million. More interesting still, the Boers consider fecundity a blessing of the Almighty, and the wife-mother rejoices without a shadow of *feminisme* in her unquestioned predominance in family life and social arrangements. Free from all desire of luxury, Boer women are almost exclusively devoted to their husbands and their children. They are strong and courageous. Without dishonoring their sex they handle the rifle and mount the horse like men. The enthusiasm of their national feeling often surpasses even that of their husbands. When war broke out in October, it was they who set the hearts of their fourteen- and even thirteen-year-old boys on fire with an irresistible desire to go to the front, when the father hesitated and even refused.

The English with some rare exceptions have always painted the Boers as "exhibiting a most lamentable picture of laziness and stupidity" and their women as "passing a lazy, dull, and inactive life"! But the Boers invariably met these reproaches with: "Sir, you don't know the Cape," and the sad experience of the English on the Modder River and at Colenso does not allow them to say that the Boers were wrong. After more than eighty years experience they do not yet know either the Cape or the Boers, as their defeats have well proved. The English comprehend only what has some likeness to themselves and for that reason they try to assimilate everybody to their type. But the Boers remain obstinate, refractory, resolutely and absolutely unassimilable.[12]

11. Kuyper cites Percival, *Account,* p. 273; Chase, *History,* Appendix I, p. 3; and assorted almanacs and reference books for these statistics.

12. Kuyper does not give sources for his quotations. Modder River and Colenso

III

That government is not well advised which, having installed itself in a conquered country, does not make every effort to respect the susceptibilities and customs of its new subjects as far as possible. To this end any reasonable government will avoid all sudden changes in political and social organization, will study to make its yoke scarcely felt, will strive to create the impression that everything is to go on as before. Above all it will inquire into the grievances of the people against the administration it has displaced and will do its best to win the hearts of the people by effectual remedies. England above any other nation should have learned that lesson of administrative wisdom, for she had to know that in dealing with colonists of a rival nationality she would face a difficult pass. She did nothing of the kind. Quite the contrary. With arrogant presumption, self-conscious of her then-undisputed power, she ruffled the Boers from the start, wounding them in their religion, in their sense of honor, and in their material interests, and all in the most mischievous manner. Purvis has frankly acknowledged that the history of "the British control of South Africa is full of blunders consequent on the ignorance and prejudice of the Home government." And Mr. Froude in his lectures does not hesitate to say: "We are merely reaping the harvest of seventy years of mismanagement."[13]

In their inability to observe well, the English turned to their inner consciousness and evolved the belief that by trying to Anglicize the old colonists as quickly as possible, they were becoming their benefactors to a high degree. On January 1, 1825, eleven years after their official occupation of the colony, an imperial decree was issued to deprive the colonists of the use of their mother tongue in the courts of justice and in the conduct of public affairs. It is scarcely possible to conceive of a measure more irritating. At one blow the Boers saw themselves excluded from juries and deprived of their seats in public councils. Henceforth they were ineligible as judges; they were compelled to have recourse to English advocates and to incur the heavy expense of translating evidence by employing interpreters. They felt exiled in their own country and ousted from all participation in public life. Even when Parliament was instituted

---

were the sites of British defeats during the "black week" of December (10-15) 1899; they lost over a thousand men in each engagement, against minuscule Boer casualties. As English voices that attest to Boer character, Kuyper lists ("outside the circle of Gladstone") some six names, quoting the eminent British historian James A. Froude, *Two Lectures on South Africa* (London, 1880), and past governor of Cape Colony Sir George Grey (in Purvis and Biggs, *South Africa,* pp. 55, 115).

13. Purvis, *South Africa,* p. 6; Froude, *Lectures,* p. 4.

in 1852 the same regime prevailed; the act of April 3rd stipulated "that all debates shall be conducted in the English language." It was only in 1882 that article 2 of the act of May 25 conceded to the colonists the use of Dutch. To the primary injustice was soon added an interminable list of other grievances. An English missionary, Dr. Van der Kemp, laid a charge at Downing Street that the Boers had ill treated their slaves — had tortured them and assassinated several.[14] A Boer woman, it was alleged, had even scalded a Negro to death in boiling water. The Secretary for the Colonies ordered an inquiry. A Court went on circuit through the whole country; more than a thousand witnesses were heard, and 58 Boers were summoned on the most dishonorable incriminations. After all this to-do, the judges were obliged on March 9, 1816, to acquit all those who were accused of murder or torture. As for the Negro said to have been boiled alive, it was proved that, upon his coming in one day with frozen feet, his mistress had put them in too hot a foot-bath simply to thaw them out. This general acquittal was certainly satisfactory for the Boers, but such humiliation before their slaves could not sweeten the cup of bitterness they had drunk.

We come now to the enfranchisement of the slaves in 1834. They numbered 40,000 and, at an average value of two thousand francs per head, constituted for most of the colonists the chief part of their small possessions. The Parliament in London, which had promised compensation, ought to have paid 80 million francs, but for the Cape it allowed only a million and a quarter pounds sterling and stipulated that it should be payable, not at the Cape, but in London, a stipulation that had the effect of compelling the Boers to sell their awards to English agents for a third of their value. Consequently a small farmer who owned, say, a dozen slaves received as compensation only 4,600 francs instead of 24,000. Destitute of the means to pay their workmen, the Boers were compelled to give up the greater part of their lands, while the liberated slaves, dying of famine, became vagabonds, stole the cattle of the colonists, and even attacked them in their homes. Widows especially suffered. Many of them abandoned all they possessed and went to seek refuge in their families. The police, too few in number, were powerless to repress the lawlessness, notably on the frontier, so that the state of affairs became intolerable. Besides, at the instigation of the missionaries of the Clapham sect in London the courts all took the part of the natives

14. Johannes Van der Kemp (1747-1811) arrived in the Cape in 1799 and became the leading agent of the London Missionary Society. Kuyper is doubtless reciting one of the allegations of slave abuse that turned out to be exaggerated. Many others were not.

against the Boers.[15] The *rôles* were reversed: the Negroes bullied the colonists while the latter, humiliated before their former slaves, scarcely dared lift up their heads.

But exasperation soon brought matters to a crisis. It culminated in 1835-38 in what is historically known as the Great Trek. The Boer families in their thousands resolved to fly from their Egypt and its Pharaonic terrors and take their chance in the wide wilderness. Better to die in the struggle against the fates and the savages than to be further disgraced by such ignominy! They yoked their cattle to their wagons, filled them with whatever they could carry, and with the Bible at their head, descended into Natal, reached the Orange plateau and even passed — some of them — beyond the Vaal. They were severely tried in their encounters with the Zulus of Schaka under Dingaan and Moselekatsi.[16] Moreover, behind these they found English missionaries as their enemies' councilors and leaders. But they were free, they fought with a spirit and a heroism worthy of an Iliad, and after unheard-of sacrifices they succeeded at last in founding their three small republics — in Natal, on the borders of the Orange River, and beyond the great Vaal.

Then England was guilty of the great wrong of reclaiming them as British subjects. We know the old English theory that the quality of being a subject of the Queen cannot be annulled. *"Nemo exuere potest patriam."* [No one can put aside his fatherland.] Troops were disembarked at Durban, others invaded the Orange plateau. In July 1847 the Boers were defeated near Durban, and on August 29, 1848 at Boomplaats on the Orange River. Despite their protestations the "Sovereignty of the Orange River" and Natal were incorporated by proclamation with the British Empire. Thus England drove these intrepid colonists to despair. . . . That state of affairs could not last for long. A native uprising threatened to harass the English even in Cape Colony. Other statesmen of more liberal views were installed at Downing Street. The Governor of the Cape, Sir Harry Smith, himself recognized the need to put an end to political

15. The Clapham Sect was a group of wealthy Anglican evangelicals who were the leaders of social reform activism in England, 1790-1830, and connected with the *Réveil* in the Netherlands. Their most notable crusade was to end slavery in British possessions. Kuyper cites Chase, *South Africa,* p. 335, with respect to their activities vis-à-vis South Africa.

16. Shaka (1787-1828) oversaw Zulu consolidation of power in the early nineteenth century. His half-brother Dingane (1795-1840) led the forces that met defeat against the Boer *Voortrekkers* at Blood River in 1838. Mzilikazi had earlier broken with Shaka and set up his own kingdom in the high veld, 1823-37. Kuyper captures well the Boer perception of the Great Trek and its definition of Afrikaner nationalism in biblical and classical categories.

aggression, and a new era began. Natal remained an English colony but England retired from the Orange River and from the Vaal. And so it was that the independence of the Transvaal was recognized by the Sand River convention January 17, 1852, and the independence of the Free State by the convention of Bloemfontein Febuary 22, 1854.

Why then have the ideas of justice and equity that inspired these two treaties not continued to guide the councils of Downing Street? Had they, England would have been safeguarded by sincere and grateful allies and everybody would have applauded her. The famous Boer President, Mr. Brandt, declared very plainly: "Your friends and your allies we are willing to be: but your subjects, never." Unhappily England has not wished for that. Both treaties have been violated: that of Bloemfontein by the judicial robbery of Kimberley, that of the Sand River by the arbitrary annexation of 1877.[17]

IV

It would only be right, however, to acknowledge that the motive driving the English in their early dealings with the Boers was still amenable to the moral code. Though not free from ambition it yet betrayed nothing of that brutal egoism and passionate materialism of which Mr. Chamberlain has since become the rabid apostle. Scarcely mindful of the real claims of their old colonists, the English prided themselves on being the defenders of the supposed rights of the natives. Deceived by reports from their missionaries, little worthy of belief, and led astray by a sentimental love for primitive man after the fashion of that time, most of them, Deists as well as Christians, were convinced that the Boers treated the blacks ill and that the English had received a divine mission to protect them. It was the time of the Aborigines Protection Societies so eloquently stigmatized by Edmund Burke. Little satisfied with the moral, social, and political condition of contemporary society, Liberalism at the end of the last century believed that it must seek its ideal not among civilized men but in the haunts of the "noble savage" whose simple and nomadic life had become the subject of idyllic interest. Robinson Crusoe's man Friday was the vogue, and every form of oppression of native races beyond the sea was regarded as high treason against humanity. Thus the Deists in the political world, through their Aborigines societies, posed as the black man's protectors, while in the religious sphere the Christians by their

17. John Frederick Brand was president of the Orange Free State, 1864-88. Kuyper cites him from Froude, *Lectures*, p. 43.

Missionary societies gave themselves out to be his benefactors. The occupation of the Cape offered them the first favorable occasion for realizing their ideals. The Hottentot was the veritable child of nature whom they had made their idol, and therefore the Boer who held him in bondage loomed in their heated imagination as the marked enemy of the human race.

That this opinion was without foundation is now admitted by Englishmen themselves. Mr. Theal tells us "the Aborigines of South Africa were savages of a very low type, to the eye of a European the most unattractive in any part of the world, living in idleness and filthiness indescribable." They pitilessly massacred the Bushmen to be massacred by them in their turn, and both alike were constantly exposed to the continual butcheries of the Bantus. As they were but a very small number in the midst of these savage tribes the Boers were compelled to take effective measures to safeguard their families, and they introduced a system of slavery copied, it is true, from the system the English used in their American colonies, but greatly modified: "The testimony of every one competent to form a correct opinion concurred, that in no other part of the world was bondage so light." "No slaves," writes Mr. Froude, "had less to complain of than those at the Cape." And Captain Percival himself, the great calumniator of the Boers, wrote in 1804: "It must be allowed that in general the slaves are well treated." "In London, however, we are in the habit" — it is still Mr. Froude who speaks — "of attributing all the virtues to the natives and every injustice to the Boers." Mr. Purvis is constantly compelled to declare "that the Government exaggerated their love for the slaves while they trampled underfoot the rights of the colonists." Dr. Colenso also, the great Bishop of Natal, when he had corrected his judgment on site in 1880, bore the following testimony on behalf of the Boers in a letter to Mr. F. W. Chesson. It is worth remembering: "My conviction is that the Boers have been most shamefully treated, that they have acted admirably, restrained by wise leaders, and have done their utmost to avoid bloodshed. And as to their treatment of the natives, have the Boers done anything so horrible, as we, killing hundreds of women and children by dynamite in the caves of Indomo?"[18]

I do not deny that the Boers have sometimes been too severe and have committed excesses. But the fact remains, as we have seen, that the

18. The quotations in this paragraph Kuyper cites from Theal, *South Africa*, pp. 1, 4, 181; Froude, *Lectures*, pp. 11, 15; Purvis, *South Africa*, p. 8; and *The Life of John William Colenso*, vol. II, pp. 533, 519. Interestingly, Colenso was one of the key theological Modernists Kuyper had identified and criticized in *Modernism, a Fata Morgana*.

famous official enquiry of 1816 resulted in their favor; and in any case whatever can be placed to the charge of the Boers has been surpassed by what the original English colonists have permitted in similar circumstances. The eloquent pleading of Mrs. Beecher Stowe for the American slaves under their original English masters has not yet been forgotten. In the wars which the English have continually provoked with the Kaffirs, Colenso reminds us that as many as ten thousand Zulus have been killed in a single battle.[19]

The manner in which they treated the envoys of Lobengula is a disgrace to the Chartered Company. The havoc created by the British bombs of lyddite and dumb-dumb [*sic*] bullets in the recent conquest of the Soudan staggers the imagination.[20] Official documents quoted in Colenso's biography show us that in the wars with the American Indians General Sir Geoffrey Armherst [*sic*] did not hesitate to order Colonel Bouquet to distribute smallpox blankets among them and to employ mastiffs to devour them. His own words were: "You will do well to try to inoculate the Indians by means of blankets, as well as by every other method, that can serve to extirpate their execrable race, even by hunting them down by dogs."[21]

Needless to say, I do not dream of imputing these monstrosities to the English character. I am convinced that there is not a humane man in London who would not condemn them as abominable. But I do venture that, with these somber pages in their own history, the English have not sufficiently meditated on the parable of the mote and the beam before setting themselves up, this late in the day, as accusers of the Boers. It is quite clear also that English missionaries like Dr. Van der Kemp, Dr. Philips, and Mr. Read, who were indefatigable instigators of the anti-Boer movement and in their Methodist zeal treated the Calvinism of the Boers as hypocrisy and incessantly excited the Cape government and the native chiefs against them, had never been honored much in their circles. The

19. Kuyper does not cite specifically from Colenso's biography but does note an account, by one Count Marillac in the *Wiesbadener Tageblatt,* of English army atrocities in the 1875-80 war against the Griqua. Kuyper probably read this report while on his annual resort to the baths in Wiesbaden.

20. Lobengula was king of the Ndebele and was induced by Rhodes's agents to grant land concessions in 1889. Lyddite was an explosive made from picric acid; dumdum bullets were made with a soft nose to expand on contact and thus leave a gaping wound. England had completed its move into the Egyptian Sudan in 1898.

21. Jeffrey Amherst and Henry Bouquet were officers in the French and Indian War. Kuyper cites this infamous story from the *Life of Colenso,* p. 690, noting its reference to "the original of these letters" in the Bouquet papers, British Museum, no. 21, 634.

missionaries in British settlements have too often constituted themselves political pioneers rather than ambassadors of Christ, and the system — the Glenelg system — which they tried to apply at the Cape miscarried deplorably. The Boers know too well that they have had no worse enemies than these gentlemen of the cloth and have tried to keep them at a distance.[22]

The Boers are not sentimental but men of practical genius. They understood that the Hottentots and the Bantus were an inferior race and that to put them on an equal footing with whites, in their families, in society, and in politics, would be simple folly. They have understood, further, the danger of mixed *liaisons,* and to save their sons from this scourge they have inculcated the idea that carnal intercourse with the Kaffir women is incest. On the other hand they have treated their slaves as good children. They have habituated them to work and have softened their manners. In South Africa you will find no one more skillful in dealing with the natives than a Boer patriarch. Neither in the Free State nor in the Transvaal has the presence of natives on Boer farms raised the slightest difficulty. The most conclusive proof of the excellent relations between the Boers and their black servants is found in the lack of the least sign of disturbance even now, with all the male population across the frontier and women and children left with the Kaffirs on widely scattered and isolated farms. The Boers regard with ill-favor not Missions but English Missions of which they have preserved too painful memories. A Swiss missionary reports from the Transvaal: "The Boers themselves ask for evangelists for the natives established among them." At Pretoria the Kaffirs have two churches with their own pastors. And a German missionary tells how General Joubert, returning from his expedition against the cruel chief Mpefo, visited the mission station and expressed his pleasure at finding among the Kaffirs Christians and worshipers of the same God whom his own people worshiped.[23]

I may add that the Boers have always faced squarely the difficulty of the color question which the English have persistently kept out of view. The blacks are increasing in South Africa to an extent that may well give cause for uneasiness. Of old they had massacres among them-

22. John Philip was the superintendent of the London Missionary Society's work in South Africa. He led the agitation in England (1826-28) that moved the House of Commons to end slavery in South Africa and was a strong advocate of the expansion of British power there. Lord Glenelg, Colonial Secretary, authorized the British occupation of Port Natal in 1838 to prevent Boer control of the province.

23. Kuyper cites unnamed articles in the *Bulletin de la mission romande,* May 1899, p. 371; and *Berliner Missionsberichte,* October 1899, p. 346. Mphephu was the Venda chief who led resistance to Joubert's conquest of Soutpansberg in 1898.

selves every autumn. But now they have ceased to be nomads, they multiply from year to year, and ere long their numbers will reach a figure that will become menacing for whites, whether Boers or English. A gradual extinction such as has almost destroyed the American Indians is not at all likely to take place in South Africa. In 1805 there were in Cape Colony 60,000 blacks, Javanese included; now they number 1,150,337. The Basutos number 250,000. In Bechuanaland the native population is estimated at 250,000. In the Transvaal they number 763,225. In the Free State there are 128,787. Finally in Natal there are 459,283, without counting 50,000 Indians. Thus we have a total of from three to four million blacks against 748,536 whites. The figures for 1891 are wanting, but we gather from some returns that the increase has gone on since then. Already these blacks, so far as they are Christianized, have entered into relations with their colored brethren of America. A colored Methodist bishop has been appointed president of a kind of Negro council in Africa.[24]

Do not believe that Christianizing these blacks has obliterated their racial passion. During my tour in America last year I had confidential conversations with men-of-color of all conditions, and I brought away the conviction that conquest over the white man does and always will remain their chimerical ideal. They believe that Abel was black and that the sign of the curse which God put upon Cain was that he certainly became white. Moreover the violent scene at Wilmington in 1898 afforded another proof that between blacks and whites there will never be lasting reconciliation.[25] And if, sooner or later, the struggle of extermination between whites and blacks breaks out afresh in South Africa, all the responsibility for it will fall upon Mr. Chamberlain and his Jingo journalists who quite impertinently and with a more than foolhardy presumption have stirred up between the rival races a hatred whose livid flame they will try too late and in vain to put out.

24. Kuyper cites these statistics from D. Aitton, *Geschiedenis van Zuid-Afrika* (Amsterdam, 1897), p. 196, and various almanacs and political handbooks. The Ethiopian Church, founded in 1892 out of a separatist movement protesting white control in the Methodist Church of South Africa, had created links with the African Methodist Episcopal Church in the United States. AME Bishop H. H. Turner visited South Africa in 1898 and ordained some of the independent church's clergy.

25. Kuyper's tour of the United States in 1898 included visits to Maryland and New Jersey, where he had some conversations, arranged and spontaneous, with African Americans. The more salient talks, doubtless, were with American whites. There was a riot the same year in Wilmington, Delaware, over the deepening oppression of the Jim Crow laws.

[In Section V Kuyper gives an astringent account of British greed and duplicity in precipitating the renewal of armed conflict. The substance and spirit of his argument are evident in the following excerpts.] . . .

Unhappily during that period [in the 20 years after the Sand River (1852) and Bloemfontein (1854) treaties] public spirit in England underwent a complete change. Every moral consideration was set aside. The promptings of a selfish and aggressive materialism became predominant, and although England was bound by solemn treaties that she could not transgress without open violation of good faith, she did not hesitate to do so. The diamonds of Kimberley sparkled in the Free State with too seductive a brilliancy, and the gold mines of the Rand became the misfortune of the Transvaal. . . .[26] Once more the fate of the natives served as pretext. But the game had its by-play. Two years later the English themselves had to go to war with them and massacred ten thousand men, women, and children.[27] . . .

[In 1884 it] was Mr. Gladstone who, himself of Calvinistic confession and therefore able to understand the Boers, poured the oil of his idealism over the troubled waters of the prejudged colonies, and once more, as in 1852-54, the sun of peace smiled over South Africa. But Jingoism was not disarmed and presently met with a trusty ally in the capitalism of the Rhodes, the Beits, and the Barnatos. The discovery of gold mines was announced. A band of adventurers squatted on the Rand, and Johannesburg became the center of opposition to the government of Pretoria. They formed themselves in 1892 into a revolutionary committee under the name of "The National Union." Later they assumed the title of the "South African League." To retire from a poor State, that was possible; but to leave to the Boers the unheard-of treasures of the Rand, that would be pure folly! Already Dr. Jameson was preparing his raid at Mafeking under the protection of the Minister of the Cape; in 1895 he carried out his operations. Mr. Chamberlain has never been able to clear himself of a certain complicity in this villainy.[28]

26. Kuyper cites Francis E. Younghusband, *South Africa of Today* (London, 1895), p. 161. This paragraph comes from p. 28 of the original text.

27. Kuyper cites *Life of Colenso,* p. 519; the Anglo-Zulu war occurred in 1879. This material comes from p. 29 in the original text.

28. Cecil Rhodes (1853-1902) was a mining entrepreneur-turned-politician and geopolitical visionary who symbolized capitalist imperialism at the end of the century. He had outmaneuvered his exact contemporaries and fellow financiers Alfred Beit and Barney Barnatos for control of DeBeers Consolidated Mines, and commissioned his friend, Leander S. Jameson (1853-1917), to invade the Transvaal at Mafeking, on its southern boundary, in hopes of overthrowing the Kruger government. The raid failed, Jameson was tried and jailed, and Rhodes had to quit his post as Prime Minister of

Although the Boers soon took satisfaction of their invaders and the German Emperor issued his famous dispatch and the whole world rang with praises of the clemency of the Boers towards their captured enemies, President Kruger was too experienced a man not to feel that the fate of the Transvaal was decided by the Jingoes in London. With the indemnity of two millions unpaid, the guilty parties set at liberty after a short detention, Rhodes retained as a member of the Privy Council, the Parliamentary enquiry suddenly stopped at the moment when decisive evidence ought to have been produced — all this left no doubt that a plot was being hatched that would not be abandoned. And while Mr. Kruger, as a far-seeing statesman, began to augment his artillery, to provide munitions of all kinds, and concluded on March 17, 1897, the treaty of alliance with the Free State, Mr. Chamberlain for his part deliberately opened the criminal negotiations that have resulted in the present war. . . .

. . . Unhappily for him [Chamberlain], his adversary [Kruger], whom — according to Bismarck — no statesman in Europe surpassed in sagacity and sound judgment, did not fall into this trap. He prolonged negotiations in order to thoroughly sound the projects of Mr. Chamberlain and to give proof before all Europe of his own conciliatory intentions. But from the moment he had in hand undeniable proofs that Mr. Chamberlain was decoying him and seeking to gain time in order to surprise him with a superior force, he flung at him the accusation of coveting Naboth's vineyard and sent an ultimatum to London. This ultimatum Mr. Chamberlain took as a trump card in his game. It would now be clear that he was the man of peace because Mr. Kruger had forced Great Britain into war! And then the English army set out *en route* for its military promenade to Pretoria. But outside Mr. Chamberlain's following no one was duped by this inversion of *rôles.* Everywhere on the continent public opinion and the Press well understood that for the Transvaal to have waited patiently until the aggressor had finished sharpening his weapons would have been tantamount to committing suicide, and when we saw the English soldiers enter Pretoria as captives and the best English generals beaten repeatedly by the much-despised Boers, the heart of the nations throbbed to the sentiment of justice. It was indeed to the God of justice that the Boers had appealed: They had not been confounded.[29] . . .

---

the Cape. British Colonial Secretary Joseph Chamberlain did know something of the raid in advance and took no action to prevent it. This paragraph and the next are on pp. 31-32 in the original text.

29. Kuyper's judgment was accurate as of the time of his writing, but the Boers were soon to meet fatal reverses. This paragraph comes on pp. 33-34 in the original text.

[In sections VI-VIII, omitted here, Kuyper contests the various British justifications for their cause. In VI he argues that Boer economic and legal policies have been legitimate, especially given their situation of being caught between new British arrivals and large native populations. In VII he defends Boer naturalization policies on the same count, offering besides detailed comparisons of various nations' laws and international standards on the matter. In VIII he argues by logic, treaty, and international law against British claims to South Africa as a protectorate.]

IX

Weary of these paltry shifts and diplomatic chicanery, the more enlightened circles of public opinion in England turned round and pleaded *the civilizing mission of Great Britain.* The Boer regime belonged to the worst period of the middle ages, and England was duty-bound to replace it with her up-to-date civilization! But here we must pause for a moment. Has civilization the right to propagate itself by war? Does another people's state of inferior civilization constitute a *justa perduellionis causa* [just cause of treason]? Besides, there is civilization and civilization. Doubtless the English of Johannesburg wear clothes of a superior cut. Their social customs are in some respects a servile imitation of *high-life.* They are more expert in the exact sciences. Their libraries are full of all sorts of bad novels. As a result, drinking bars have multiplied at Johannesburg. Prostitution is becoming a scandal. Free fights are the fashion. A ruffianly mob constantly menaces public security. All the rowdyism of the seaport reigns there. This is not, I think, the kind of civilization whose blessings the moralists of London wish to spread among a people whom Mr. Gibson Bowles described, even in the English Parliament, as "a sturdy, brave, simple, God-fearing people."[30]

Certainly the civilization that one meets in the better circles of London is very superior to that of the Boers, but in respect to national morals the Boers yield the palm to no European nation. Again, how can we disregard the invariable connection and influence between the form of civilization and the climate, nature of the country, and habitual occupations? What a difference there is between Montenegro and Italy, and even in Italy between the great cities and the valleys of the Alps! The Boers have already made astonishing progress and they will advance further. Who then has the right to impose upon them methods of *"lightning-express" development?* Hothouse plants do not thrive on mountain ranges. What would the Boers have gained

30. *Acts of Parliament,* 1899, p. 776.

if a forced process of evolution had endowed them with vices which their character would not have been strong enough to resist? I do not sense that their development has by any means been too slow: on the contrary, I fear it is proceeding too quickly.

But in any case, to win over a people to your civilization you must preach to them by example. That is precisely what England has not done, either in her diplomatic struggle at Pretoria and Bloemfontein or, I am grieved to say, on the field of battle. Without scrupulous respect for acquired rights and without sincerity above all suspicion every civilization breaks down. But England has violated the treaties of Bloemfontein and the Sand River and, by an unjustifiable interpretation, has tried to escape from the Convention of London.[31] . . . [As to incidents of egregious British military conduct,] I am convinced that the English War Office reproves these inhumanities and that every humane man in England loathes them; but I ask again, is it thus that the propaganda of superior civilization can be conducted? The prisoners at Pretoria, I understand from Mr. Churchill, have been unanimous in acknowledging that the Boers treated the wounded and prisoners in a manner beyond reproach, and the English generals have admitted that they [the Boers] conduct the war in a chivalrous spirit.[32]

Arbitration is the *mot d'ordre* of modern civilization. Well, Mr. Kruger and Mr. Steyn have always adhered to it. It was admitted in principle, though with restrictions, in the Convention of London. It was adopted in 1885 in the affair of the coolies. Mr. Kruger presented to Sir Alfred Milner during the Conference at Bloemfontein a scheme of arbitration elaborated in several articles.[33] It was England who declined it. "Suzerainty cannot admit of arbitration!" she contended. The interpretation of the Convention was to be binding on one side only and, if need be, laid down by force. As if, even under the Chamberlain system, arbitration between masters and workmen were not the rule! Here again, on which side is civilization most advanced?

31. Under the Gladstone government, a meeting of British and Boer emissaries in London, 1884, agreed to a new convention granting the Transvaal full autonomy over its own domestic (though not foreign) affairs. In the deleted material that follows, Kuyper accuses Joseph Chamberlain of deceitful diplomacy, then reviews reports of British military atrocities in South Africa.

32. Winston Churchill was South African correspondent for a London newspaper in 1899. Captured while taking part in a battle against the Boers, he escaped from prison and returned to England a military hero, thus launching his political career.

33. M. T. Steyn was president of the Orange Free State during the Boer War. Sir Alfred Milner was governor of the Cape and British High Commissioner during the hostilities.

Minister Kuyper's reis naar Engeland.
Derde Blad van de „AMSTERDAMSCHE COURANT" van Vrijdag 24 Januari 1902.

An Amsterdam newspaper sympathetically depicted Kuyper's 1902 mission to London on behalf of the Boer cause: *left:* the abject petitioner "as portrayed in the English papers"; *right:* "how it actually was: setting the bait."

I recall the scene in Trafalgar Square where a ministerial rabble assembled *en masse* and threatened the friends of peace with all sorts of menaces, pelted them with rotten eggs, and prevented them from speaking. Do you imagine the report of that scandal made a very edifying impression at Pretoria? Have not the Boers been told that freedom of speech is the most sacred privilege of modern civilization? The press has everywhere been considered the great motive force of the progressive movement, and in its best days the English press marched at the head of the whole journalistic phalanx. But what is to be said of it since the beginning of the last jingo campaign? *The Westminster Gazette* alone holds to its principles. The editor-in-chief of *The Daily Chronicle* had to submit his resignation because he could not side with the Jingos. No difference of opinion can be tolerated.

From the press to the telegraph is not a far cry. What use has the War Office made of the telegraph? All the dispatches have been mutilated and defeats changed into victories. The smallest advantages gained in insignificant skirmishes have been inflated into important victories, the losses of the enemy exaggerated, the losses of the English minimized, while the censorship at Aden[34] has isolated the South African Republics from their own agents if not from foreign governments and the whole world. I know a distinguished family in Amsterdam whose married daughter was dangerously ill at Pretoria. No message from her reached them, and the parents were left in the most heart-rending uncertainty.

But what the doctors of the Transvaal (they number 250) fear above all is an invasion of syphilitic maladies which prevail to a very alarming extent in the English army of India. Lord George Hamilton in the House of Commons, January 25, 1897, himself went so far as to say: "The total number of admissions to hospital of cases of venereal disease amongst the Indian troops rose in 1895 to 522 per 1000; and the number of men out of service, owing to these maladies, was 46 per thousand per day." The Transvaal doctors are aware of this and that is why, though they are indifferent to the pest at Lorenzo Marques, they dread above all the venereal infection that the troops from India carry about with them. What do the moralists of London think of this? Are the Boers so very wrong when they refuse to accept, otherwise than *sous bénéfice d'inventaire,* the civilization that England promises to South Africa?

X

How are we to solve the enigma of England's present position? Surely it is playing with words to charge the glorious nation which throughout the century has been liberal and progressive above all others with the crime of this absolutely iniquitous war — a war of rapine and conquest that can only have futile results. In several respects that nation, in my opinion, is not surpassed by any other. If I were not a Dutchman I should like to be one of her sons. As a rule her veracity is above all suspicion. She has an innate sense of duty and right. Her constitutional institutions have been imitated the world over. Nowhere will you find self-respect more finely developed. Her literature, though inferior from a merely artistic point of view, glows with a conception of life altogether serious, healthy, and profound. Even in the style of her fashions and in the care of the body she exhibits a character of dignity that compels respect. Her philanthropy knows no bounds, her morality is above the average, and in religious activity she marches at the head of all other

34. "Censorship at Aden" refers to British control of telegraph dispatches from Asia and Africa at its colonial outpost on the south of the Arabian Peninsula.

nations. How is it, then, that such a nation can have come to such a fall?

The solution of the enigma must be found in the magic charm of the word *Imperialism* taken in a national sense, quite different from the personal Imperialism of an Alexander the Great or a Napoleon. Only once until now has the phenomenon of national imperialism been observed in history, namely in the Caesarism of the Romans. The same phenomenon now reappears in the mania of Anglo-Saxon jingoism. The analogies between the two are quite striking. At Rome as in London there was the strictest regard for the rights of the citizen and at the same time a lack of respect amounting to disdain for the rights of other people. The aim of the iron will of Rome was to dominate all the known world by her land forces; the "Rule Britannia" people take as a political axiom that they are to dominate the whole globe by their fleet. The Roman proconsuls like the English High Commissioners granted to the conquered nations the fullest measure of self-government on the one condition formulated by Mr. Chamberlain on October 19: "that we shall have the right to use force to compel submission to our will."[35]

Then, as now, there were two sorts of colonies. At Rome they were called *Senatus* and *Imperatoris;* in London they are called Self-Governing and Crown. At Rome imperialism concentrated in the lofty idea of the *Civis Romanus* whom, were he the sorriest of adventurers, the whole power of the empire had to protect; in London Mr. Chamberlain makes his eloquent plea for the *British subject,* the idol before whom all the flags of the fleet and of the army must dip. The *Auri sacra fames* [love of sacred gold] drew all the gold of the world to Rome so that, even in the time of the Republic, an upstart Crassus could amass a capital of 85 millions, a Lucullus could display his magnificence at his four-thousand pound dinners and, in the time of the Caesars, the Emperor could spend 600,000 francs on roses. In England we have the unheard-of luxury of the upper ten thousand; the Beits, the Barnatos, and the Rhodes amass incalculable fortunes; and a minister of the Crown pays insane prices for his orchids. At Rome the air was rent with the cry "Vare, Vare, redde mihi legiones meas!" [Varus, Varus, give me back my legions!]; in her palace at Windsor the English Queen burst into tears over the losses that the descendants of the Teutoburgerwald heroes had inflicted on her guards.[36]

35. Kuyper cites the *Acts of Parliament,* pp. 263, 299, and invokes Tacitus on the Roman treatment of the ancient Batavians (*Annals,* v. 1, c. 725,3).

36. Kuyper is invoking the victory in A.D. 9 of Germanic tribes led by Hermann/Arminius over three Roman legions in the Teutoburg Forest. The quotation is Caesar Augustus's invocation of the Roman general Varus.

Yes, this Imperialism is an obsession. It worms itself into the heart of the nation from the moment that the last opponent who troubles it bends under its blows, thus opening every land road to the eagles of its army, as formerly for Rome, and every sea route to the flag of its fleet, as for England after Trafalgar. So long as the last opponent continues to resist he will remain, in spite of you, the ally of your conscience. But once the last rival is brought to his knees, your love of right alone remains and must suffice for itself without any external support. If at this psychological moment the conscience of the nation betrays itself, it is in danger of precipitating itself from the highest idealism into the most vulgar cynicism. Stronger by land or sea than any other nation, or all other nations combined, its unlimited power unconsciously suggests the dream of universal power. Then may be repeated the history of Tyre as when God addressed it by the voice of Ezekiel (27:4-9):

> With thy wisdom and with thine understanding thou hast gotten thee riches, and hast gotten gold and silver into thy treasures. By thy great wisdom and by thy traffic hast thou increased thy riches, and thine heart is lifted up because of thy riches. Therefore thus saith the Lord God: "Because thou hast set thine heart as the heart of God," behold, therefore I will bring strangers upon thee, the terrible of the nations, and they shall draw their swords against the beauty of thy wisdom, and they shall defile thy brightness. They shall bring thee down to the pit, and thou shalt die the deaths of them that are slain in the midst of the seas. Wilt thou say before him that slayeth thee, "I am God"? But thou shalt be a man, and no God, in the hand of him that slayeth thee.

This Imperialism submerges the national idea more and more under an ecumenical conception, and in return tries to assimilate the whole world to its national type. It permits, it even encourages, every social movement to the most distant point of the periphery, provided it remains the center of such movement. *Urbi et orbi* becomes the tacit title of its decisions, and every time its supremacy runs the risk of being disputed, the Machiavellian principle of *Salus reipublicae suprema lex esto* [Let the republic's welfare be the supreme law] stifles the holiest aspirations in the mass of the nation. Lord George Hamilton did not fear to vaunt the patriotism of those who aborted the Jameson inquiry, "because they had behaved as Englishmen always do when English interests are at stake."[37] In other words, because they had sacrificed right to the glory of their country! This Imperialism glides unperceived as a streptococcus into the blood of the crowd, poisons it, and overcomes its conscience. The first

37. Kuyper cites William T. Stead, *Are We in the Right?* (London, 1899), p. 66.

man you meet begins to feel important from the mere fact that he carries in his veins the blood of his nation. All feel themselves lifted up, exalted, glorified. The greatness, the power of their country must be turned to account for their own greatness, for the welfare of their family, for the increase of their fortune. Once the barrier of right is down in politics, there is no reason why the moral barrier should block their advance to the bait of the treasure. Then the fatal descent begins to show. The capitalists no longer conceal their arrogance. They put out the corrupting bait of their greed even in the ranks of the nobles, impoverished by the decline of rents or encumbered with gambling debts. The electoral machine falls under their influence. The Press gives way. Public opinion allows itself to be won over. Statesmen feel themselves led by the bridle. And the lamentable consequence is accentuated every time yet another robust conviction is seen to pass to the enemy. *Optimi corruptio pessima.* [The corruption of the best is the worst.]

That the English character in its essence is endowed with such noble potential would only render its decadence more deplorable. "The higher the seat," the proverb says, "the deeper the fall." By the fall of England, human progress would lose one of its finest instruments. We cannot do without this England which has been noble, proud, and Christian, and which may become so again. For this reason well-disposed people throughout Europe, the best minds throughout the world, are at one and the same time grieved and indignant at the wild and distressing spectacle that England persists in forcing upon us by this war of conquest, one of the most iniquitous in the history of the nineteenth century.

Fortunately, the future of England is not yet determined. All our prayers are that she will retrieve herself. Her reverses might become her salvation. Already one of her Archbishops has raised the voice of repentance and humiliation. A group of eminent men,[38] giving evidence of a moral courage inspired by the better traditions of Gladstone and commanding our sincerest admiration — the Morleys, the Harcourts, the Courtneys, the Steads, the Clarks, the Labouncheres, the Harrisons, and so many more — are vigilantly guarding the most sacred treasures of their nation and disputing every inch of the ground with the Jingoes, and they are raising their voices so loud that soon their *vox clamantis in deserto* [voice crying in the wilderness] will reach the Highlands of Scotland. All possibility of a resolution is not yet excluded. The fall of Mr. Chamberlain would give the signal of salvation. And if a Cabinet of more discretion, abandoning all ideas of vengeance and caring nothing for military sus-

38. Kuyper is referring to the considerable dissent raised in England against its prosecution of the Boer War.

ceptibilities, offered a confederated South Africa its full independence, reserving only the Eastern part of Cape Colony proper and some indispensable points on the coast, perhaps England might still change a formidable enemy into an unequalled ally. But let there be no delay. Now is the supreme moment. England must come to herself again and renounce her dream of Imperialism. Otherwise, Imperialism will eventually destroy her, as it destroyed ancient Rome.

XI

There must be no mistake, however: the fear that England will not draw back from the fatal descent is far from chimerical. The danger lies in the indifference to moral principles and in the inadequacy of the Christian movement. Mr. Fairfield put it well: "Without being a moralist, I nevertheless maintain that morality and Imperialism cannot go together." Three years back, Mr. Chamberlain himself acknowledged it: "To make war on the Boers in order to wrest from them the desired reforms would be unwise and immoral."[39] The cause of this incompatibility is evident. Morality imposes before everything unalterable respect for the rights of another, and Imperialism cannot do its dismal work without disregarding such rights. To save appearances, then, it needs a conception of right that takes away its stability, its objective character, and its inviolable holiness by rendering it so variable that it bends at your will. This is the very thing opinion today tends to do. So long as principles of morality and right sought their support in God and Revelation, they were clothed with an objective character and imposed upon us an authority before which nations as well as individuals had to bend. But everything changed from the moment when Schleiermacher, among the Protestants, placed all our theological knowledge, including that of morality, under the empire of subjectivism. The Danish Lutheran bishop Martensen drew thence the indisputable inference when he said that "what is permitted or prohibited in the point of view of morality can only be individually determined."[40]

It is well known how this theory has been strained to dispense statesmen of Bismarck's stamp from all obligation to "bourgeois" moral-

39. William Stead, *The Scandal of the South African Committee* (London, 1899), p. 26; (unspecified) Chamberlain speech of 8 May 1896.

40. Friedrich Schleiermacher (1768-1834) was a highly influential German theologian who countered Enlightened-rationalist critiques of Christianity by rooting religion in feeling and inward experience. Kuyper quotes Hans Martensen (1808-84) from his *Die Christliche Ethiek* (Gotha, 1871), vol. I, p. 580.

ity. Imperialism declares itself content with it. The moment that right ceases to be a barrier that compels you to stop and is changed into a stage prop that every actor moves about according to his needs, even the most extravagant Imperialism has a perfectly free hand. It then matters little how the stage is arranged. The practical statesman who likes to flout every theory will take what suits him where he finds it and will manage to carry out his projects without any care for the rights of others. An earnest theorist like Mr. McKinley explains to you in his celebrated speech on "Duty and Destiny" at Omaha that every powerful nation ought to foresee the mission that God has reserved for it and to order its duties according to the exigencies of the end to be attained. Others, docile adepts of transformism, will tell you that Utility is the only directive force that should guide us and that right evolves from one form into another without any fixed rule, as cellular tissue simply by chance utility changes from reptile to bird.[41]

I am aware that Mr. Spencer has severely censured the dubious dealings of Mr. Chamberlain. I praise him for it. Yet I do not hesitate to express the opinion I have formed on mature reflection, that he and his school, by applying the Darwinism of Nature to Psychology and Ethics along a theory that M. Th. Ribot has most ably expounded, have weakened the fixed character of right and so leveled the main obstacle Imperialism would encounter in its triumphal progress. A very well known and distinguished clergyman, Mr. R. S. de Couvey Laffan, has furnished us with indisputable proof by his letter of December 29, 1899, published in the *Indépendance Belge* of January 15 [1900]. The terms "individualist egoism" and "social egoism," which he is fond of using, yield superabundant proof that he adheres to the theory of Mr. Spencer's *Data.* Now, what is his reasoning? He leaves to one side the question of right; he admits that the cause of the Boers may be just; but even on that supposition he maintains "that neither on the part of the English people nor on the part of the British Empire is there a moral error." Quite the contrary, this frightful war has drowned individualist egoism in a sort of national egoism. And this, in his eyes, is moral progress. Whether "the English people be mistaken or not mistaken as to the causes of the war" is all the same to him. It is enough that awakened patriotism marks an advance towards the ideal and that the English people are penetrated "with belief in the mission that God has entrusted to their country." And it is by so eliminating all question of right and justice that this English

41. Kuyper was referring to U.S. President McKinley's justification of American imperialism in the Philippines. "Transformism" was the French term for Darwinian evolution.

clergyman speaks of "working for the accomplishment of the Master's prayer: Our Father, which art in Heaven, Thy Kingdom come!"[42] To my mind, this is an execrable blasphemy. But what ground for surprise remains?

Darwinism intentionally avoids every influence of a teleological principle, thus foreclosing in advance the very end and object essential to the conception of right. Given up to the arbitrariness of individualism, subordinated to utility, and a prey to the caprices of chance, it is vaporized into a fog that eludes the grasp. This school, moreover, discovers in the "struggle for life" the directing principle of its movement, and thence deduces the brutal conclusion that the weak are predestined by fate to succumb before the stronger. It will be difficult for you, then, to escape the logic of Nietzsche, which appeals to the stronger to put the quickest possible end to the futilities of the weak in order to accelerate humanity's march toward progress.[43] There is scarcely any perceptible distance between this and the equivocal expedients Imperialism employs to realize its projects. Who, then, would venture to deny that where evolutionism is cultivated, men's minds are easily disposed to bend? In the German "Golden Book," Dr. Rothnagel has clearly established this proposition: "In the sciences, in the domain of Nature, the progress of our century has been surprising; but, in the point of view of ethics, its beginning was superior to its end."[44]

England especially runs the risk of being drawn away from moral fixity by this disturbing element. Ethical weakening branches in two directions, along the double track of human sin: toward the more despotic empire of sensuality and the empire of pride. There can be no doubt which way the English character inclines. "To fight everybody and to take everything" is the vulgar expression of the arrogant feeling that wants to soar above all. In colonial affairs this tendency lays itself more open to notice by the indisputable preeminence of the English fleet, by the superiority of every white race, and by the presumption that the English, the colonizers *par excellence,* are the great benefactors of the countries beyond sea. But without wishing to deny that the settlements of Australia

42. Herbert Spencer (1820-1903) was the leading social Darwinist in the Anglo-American world, yet an opponent of imperial wars which he thought unnecessary to the achievement of social progress and the assertion of superiority. Théodule Ribot (1839-1916) was a prominent French psychologist who wrote, *inter alia, L'évolution des idées générales* (Paris, 1897).

43. For more on Kuyper in regard to Nietzsche, see the opening pages of *The Blurring of the Boundaries* below.

44. Kuyper cites Rothnagel, *Das goldne Buch des Deutschen Volks und des Jahrhunderts ende,* p. 63.

and New Zealand may be taken as models, M. Tilon's article in the *Revue des Deux Mondes* of November 15 and Mr. Robert Buchanan's article in the *Contemporary Review* raise well founded doubts as to the advantages of English supremacy in India.[45] The plague and the famine prevailing there appear to give substance to this apprehension. In any case, one sees that the respect for right runs special risk of weakening in a colonizing nation once the conception of evolutionary, thus variable, right is installed in the minds of those unscrupulous adventurers who pride themselves on hoisting the English flag in the remotest corners of Asia and Africa.

Unfortunately, the Christian movement in England puts no check on this tendency. On the contrary, it encourages it. The dogma of justification, that impassable rampart for the defense of every principle of right, is absorbed in sanctification. The lesson of the old Covenanter, "to be blind to the issue, but to have one's eye fixed on the commandment," is forgotten even in Scotland. More and more people are in the habit of identifying the British Empire with the Kingdom of God and of Anglicanizing Christ himself. "God has raised up and so widely extended the British Empire, and always with it British Christianism. Real Imperialism sees in every fresh territory an expansion of the glorious opportunities of spreading the gospel of England's Christ." At a recent Assembly of the Free Church of Scotland in Edinburgh, the audience did not refrain from warmly applauding a Minister of the Gospel who exclaimed: "What Africa needs is a Christian civilization. The present war is a part of the price that must be paid for the attainment of this end. Such, then, is the light in which this war must be regarded so as to have neither regrets nor any doubts as to its necessity and justice."[46] This is how a church that has strayed from the path lulls the conscience, and how a Methodism in its one-sided passion for salvation ends by sanctifying the most censurable means in view of the sacred end. Such language turns your stomach and rouses you to anger against those ministers of the Gospel who betray the God of justice. It enables you to understand how an iniquitous exaggeration has spoken of the three P's — Pecksniff, Pirate, Pharisee. Instead of yielding yourself to such excesses, be careful to remember that it was again and always the same Methodism of Dr. Philips that provoked the

45. Kuyper cites one M. Tilon in *Revue des Deux Mondes* (15 November 1899); Robert Buchanan, "Voice of the Hooligans," *Contemporary Review* 76 (December 1899): 774-89.

46. For the two quotations Kuyper cites the *Greater Britain Messenger*, July-August 1899, pp. 319, 323; and *La Foi et la Vie* (Paris), 19 December 1899, p. 383. Covenanters were seventeenth-century Scots Presbyterians who militantly opposed Stuart absolutism and state power over church affairs. The Scottish Free Church had earlier in the century been Kuyper's model for church reform.

great Exodus in 1835 and that now, after a whole century of miscarriages, spurs the Imperialism of Mr. Chamberlain, that covers with the name of Jesus Christ the most flagrant violation of right as well as the rapacity of the gold-bugs of the Chartered Company.

Indeed the worst danger lurks under this Christian show of Imperialism. It is these Methodists — with the best intentions in the world, I am satisfied, but unfortunately astray from the true path — who believe themselves charged by the grace of God to bring their Anglo-Christian civilization to the Boers of South Africa by the open violation of acquired rights and by all the atrocities of a war of extermination. The doctrine that prevails among the Boers — namely, Calvinism — is the doctrine that has been the glory and the greatness of the Scots. They hear the Boers again pray in the fervent tone that rendered the prayer of the Covenanter all-powerful, and sing the same psalms as were the war song of their ancestors in their struggle against absolutism. But for themselves, they prefer to stay at home. It is the Queen, with her nobility, who makes war, and the people fill the treasury to enable them to enroll mercenaries. Down there in South Africa it is a whole people — fathers, sons, and grandsons — who, in the name of God, pour out their blood for their country and display a moral force that holds the world in suspense. The Boers do not boast, they do not call their defeats victories, they treat their enemies well, they care for the English wounded like good Samaritans, and their generals, when they harangue these citizens, urge them never to place confidence in the infallibility of their rifles but always to put their trust in God alone. Churchill himself, an escaped prisoner, acknowledged that an "unseen power" protected their commandos.

Above all, consider well the frateral faithfulness of the men of the Free State under their eminent President, Mr. Steyn. They could have stood apart. The English quarrel with the Transvaal had nothing to do with them. Their non-intervention could have been justified from the world's point of view. But no, they declined to take up that position. They determined as good Christians to go to the aid of their threatened brethren, and the whole male population quitted their country to oppose the English invasion. Cain would have asked: "Am I my brother's keeper?" But for their brethren they risked their own lives and their children's. A unique example in our century, as a Swiss newspaper remarked, of disinterested faithfulness, of an unsurpassable sacrifice for the maintenance of justice! Take the scales: place in the right the completely Christian heroism of the Boers and in the left the intrigues of capitalism, the bragging of the imperialists, and the aberration of those Christian Methodists. Which way will the balance incline? To know that these English Christians are sincere and serious people and that this noble

English people would curse all these projects of iniquity if the bandage fell from their eyes, but to see how the Jingoes draw the bandage tighter and tighter — is it not a distressing reality that is turning into a frightful tragedy? A tragedy that we disinterested spectators witness with profound grief and profound humiliation.

XII

What will be the *dénouement* of this tragedy?

Here I scrupulously refrain from all conjecture as to the issue of the military operations in progress. No one could forecast it. It depends on occurrences so fortuitous, on eventualities so uncertain, that it eludes all prediction even by the most competent observer. One can only say that, if England does not recover herself, the struggle will be desperate, bloody, and prolonged. With their own forces alone, the two Republics could not measure themselves with the power of England, supported by her auxiliary troops from Canada and Australia. The Boers altogether would hardly fill one suburb of London. If the elephant puts out all his powers to corner the goat, trample him under foot, and toss him in the air, he will always have some chance of success; and if Great Britain shrinks from no sacrifice, in men, in reputation, or in interests, it is not impossible that she will succeed, after a long and costly war, in momentarily crushing her valiant opponents.

Still, the first auguries have not been favorable, and history addresses to her its warnings. Greece, small as she was, was not overpowered by the Persians. Switzerland managed to escape the deadly embrace of Austria. The "Beggars" of Holland succeeded in resisting the crushing power of Spain for eighty years, and the Boers have the blood of the "Beggars" in their veins. Besides, they are well armed. They fight on their own ground, ground that they know thoroughly and that is exceptionally advantageous for defense. They form an army of mounted infantry, mobile and alert, such as exists nowhere else. Their tactics and strategy call forth the admiration of the European staffs. Most of all, they risk their lives neither for the capitalists of a Chartered Company nor for a political force of paramountcy but for existence itself and for their country's independence.

Pro aris et focis! [For altar and hearth!] They know that the conscience of the whole of Europe is on their side and they feel inspired by the rightness of their cause. They are not mercenaries who curse and swear and bluster but fathers of families who pray, and with common accord they have lifted their buckler in the name of the God of justice. With such a moral force, cannon has rarely had the best of it.

The destabilization of international affairs, which Kuyper predicted from the Boer War, came to Europe in the Bosnian crisis of 1908-09, when Austria, with British support, annexed that territory, much to the anger of Serbia and the humiliation of Russia. Kuyper addressed this "three-star" to the situation on 20 March 1909, forecasting the exact process by which World War I began.

The Smoldering Fuse

Several days ago we pointed out that the international situation is becoming less reassuring for the small states of Europe. This has since become even more evident, and there is a growing expectation abroad that war is about to erupt against Serbia.

Serbia has little claim on our sympathies because of the regicide [of 1903], but this does not alter the fact that it is a small people showing the manly courage, for all its insufficient means, to take a stand if necessary against a major power like Austria.

The most painful prospect here is that, should the blaze at

But suppose that General Lord Roberts succeeds in forcing the passes of the Drakenberg and Spytfontein, that Bloemfontein is occupied, and that siege is laid to Pretoria.[47] Then, surely, the difficulties of the English, far from being ended, would only be commencing. They would require an army of at least 50,000 men merely to secure communication with their base of operations at Capetown, Port Elizabeth, and Durban. Their convoys would be constantly harassed, their army of investment would be subjected to alarm day and night by the Boers, buzzing in swarms about their camp. Soon, as at Ladysmith and Mod-

47. Lord Roberts took command of British forces in South Africa after the reverses of December 1899. His lieutenants did succeed in breaking through the Drakenberg Mountains, the major physical barrier between the Cape and the Boer territories, and went on to take Bloemfontein, capital of the Orange Free State, in March 1900. Pretoria and Johannesburg followed over the course of the summer, and the Transvaal was annexed on 1 September. This was the end of war as usual but only the beginning of two years of guerrilla combat that both reflected and redoubled the hostile sentiments Kuyper describes. England did prove capable of delivering the superior force required — 500,000 troops against some 60,000 Boers-in-arms — but at some cost in world opinion and their own confidence.

the Danube spread, no one can predict the limits in which the war can be contained. Russia can hardly stand idly by as Serbia and Montenegro are crushed. But if Russia intervenes in the conflict, Germany, as Austria's ally, may swiftly follow suit and bring the danger right to our backyard. Even more, if Russia were hard pressed, France would have to take sides. So all of Europe could be set aflame.

Everyone is instinctively asking: What is behind all this? What moved the old Emperor of Austria [Franz Joseph, reigned 1848-1916] all of a sudden to annex two provinces, thereby violating the treaty of Berlin [1878]? And following that violation, steadfastly to refuse to enter negotiations to regularize the new situation?

Who is behind all this? Who is the person who sought war and then skillfully managed to make it appear as if *he* had been forced into war?

Or is no one playing for high stakes? Is the dangerous game we see being played nothing but the insane work of reckless people who have no inkling of the danger to which they are exposing their own country and all of Europe?

der River, the besiegers, caught between two fires, would become the besieged. Although their cavalry might then render them excellent service in keeping the bands of guerrillas at a distance, they would experience the greatest embarrassment in preserving their horses from the diseases of the country and in finding fodder for them. Even the boldest tacticians avow that there are distances and elementary forces which defy all human strength. Napoleon experienced this in Russia, and even after the capture of Pretoria the Vaal could become for Lord Roberts what the Beresina was for the victorious Emperor. Remember the strenuous words of Mr. Kruger: "If they succeed in overthrowing us, the world will be astonished at the human blood which it will cost."

Further, the army of the English is yet to be formed. Their best regiments are already engaged. What they are transporting at present has a very inferior military value, and once the conquest is achieved, they will require an army of occupation much in excess of the troops now at their disposal. Hitherto, following the principle of Cromwell, the program of England has always been the largest fleet and the smallest army sufficient for this heavy task. She will therefore have to change her system, and then her home policy would be at stake. Already there are arising sharply defined divergencies of opinion in the constituencies. The old guard of Mr. Gladstone does not ground its arms; the Irish are in open opposition; the sympathies of Wales are very doubtful; soon the enormous cost will frighten the lower middle class, and when to all this is joined every Englishman's profound aversion to compulsory service, the ministerial majority might very quickly be scattered. The popularity of Mr. Chamberlain might well be eclipsed.

Add also the dangers of external complications, which are far from chimerical and which oblige England to go on increasing her fleet indefinitely so as not to be at the mercy of a combination of the Continental fleets. France, awakened by the sad affair of Fashoda,[48] is filling her dockyards with new vessels in course of construction, more and more persuaded that a political course that would place her indefinitely at the discretion of England would end in national bankruptcy. Russia is doubling her fleet. Germany is going to treble hers. The sympathies of Italy have been galled in China. In America the fall of Mr. McKinley and the rise of Mr. Bryan would bring down the whole scaffolding of the Anglo-Saxon alliance.[49] Would England then be able to face the whole world, deprived of every ally, reduced to the completest isolation? Lord Salisbury, certainly a farsighted statesman, before embarking on this great war wisely attempted to come to an arrangement with Russia in China, with Germany in Africa and Samoa, and with France in Northern Africa. He wished to make a clean slate of the pending questions that might embarrass him, and he knew besides that the next exhibition would trammel all immediate action on the part of France. Nevertheless, there is no lack of sensitive points. In Afghanistan, in Persia, in Egypt, everywhere there is conflict of interests. In every corner of the earth the combustibles are heaped up. The least spark may cause the outburst of the conflagration that has been threatening us since 1870. Hence those alliance projects that are in the air and that indisputably tend to converge against this insular power which, in its

48. Fashoda was a fort in the Sudan where French and British forces, and imperial designs, crossed in September 1898. To the dismay of many in the homeland, the French backed down short of armed hostilities in the interests of winning Britain's alliance against Germany, a goal achieved in 1904.

49. Kuyper's support for a Democrat (William Jennings Bryan) against a Republican (McKinley) in a U.S. presidential election was rare for him, a measure of how deeply his customary political attitudes were affected by the Boer War. Previously Kuyper had regarded the Democratic party as infected with the "revolutionary" principles of its founder Thomas Jefferson. The Republicans, by contrast, he thought carried on the tradition of New England Puritanism.

self-sufficiency, has galled the sympathies of all the nations without gaining over any of them.[50]

But suppose England surmounts all these difficulties, that her cool temper succeeds in avoiding all these rocks, that her moral conscience does not awake, and that the taxpayer does not become tired of throwing every time a more considerable part of his savings into the insatiable gulf of South Africa; even then England would not be at the end of her troubles. Behind her in Africa she would have sown the seeds of a deep rancor, of an unspeakable repugnance, of an indestructible race-hatred, and these seeds would shoot up. The determination of the Boers is unshakable. Never will they be voluntary subjects of England. Subdued by brutal force, every morning and every evening their prayers would rise to the God of their fathers to implore deliverance from the yoke which they would ever curse in their hearts. At the first opportunity they would resume the struggle. In the first war that should burst on England they would be the devoted allies of her enemy. Read and re-read their manifesto "A Century of Injustice," and each line will convince you that their tenacity will never be overcome.

There is the wound from which England, unless she repent, will bleed for a whole century. In order to put down the Boers by the brutal force of numbers, it would be necessary for her to extirpate them and sweep them off the face of the earth. Then, indeed, South Africa would belong to the English alone — *and to the Negroes.* But as the mere idea of such a crime would horrify them and does not for a moment enter into their projects, let them know that to persevere in the beaten track of violence would undoubtedly presage the beginning of the end of England's greatness in point of power. Perhaps she would succeed in disarming the people; she will never destroy the fecundity of the Boer woman. In less than a century, thanks to this marvelous fecundity the Boers have grown from their former numbers of 60,000 to half a million. In the coming century, they will reach three, four, five million, and South Africa will be theirs.

The wife of General Joubert, who accompanied him into the thick of battle, is the perfect type of this Boer woman whose fecundity passes all forecast and who will be able to inspire in all her children the national

50. Kuyper is referring to the diplomatic revolution of the 1890s by which age-old enemies France and Russia entered into a mutual-defense alliance against Germany and its partner of the same sort, the Austro-Hungarian Empire. Kuyper rightly sees these developments spelling isolation for Britain, which it ended by allying — against 200 years of history and continuing rival imperial interests — with France and Russia. The resulting system figured heavily in the onset of World War I, of which Kuyper here shows some premonitions.

spirit. So long as the lioness of the Transvaal, surrounded by her young cubs, shall roar against England from the heights of Drakenberg, the Boer will never be definitively subdued.

CULTURE AND EDUCATION

The Blurring of the Boundaries

As was customary in Europe at the time, the rectorship of the Free University rotated annually from one professor to another. The ceremonies marking the transfer included a speech in which the outgoing rector would address the state of the institution, a major question in (still) his discipline, or an issue of general public concern. Kuyper used the occasion in 1892 to evaluate the entire course of nineteenth-century European culture.

This was a massive task, and the "pantheist" label Kuyper used to organize his materials was stretched to the utmost. It had to cover Nietzsche and Hegel, Darwin and Schleiermacher, yogis and Gnostics, the cult of progress, and what we would call the demotion of "character" to "personality."[1] One might fault Kuyper for the very "blurring of the boundaries" that he criticized in pantheism, but it is more helpful to take the resemblance as a clue to how close Kuyper felt to the forces with which he was wrestling. German Idealism he took to be a marked improvement over the cold rationalism of the eighteenth century, and mystical closure with God more admirable than the calculated ethics of duty. Kuyper's problem was how to harvest the virtues of this impulse without falling into its dechristianizing logic.

Most of the address is given to unfolding that logic, but toward the end Kuyper's answer comes clear: he will be two-thirds a Hegel, halting with the antithesis between contrary agents and avoiding synthesis at all costs. This choice would have the practical consequence of chartering the pattern of "pillarization" that would mark Dutch society for much of the century to come. If Kuyper's audience could not foresee that future, they could enjoy the meta-

1. See the essays on the 1920s and 1930s in Warren Susman, *Culture as History* (New York: Pantheon, 1984), pp. 122-49, 184-210. An earlier treatment of the shift is David Riesman, *The Lonely Crowd* (New Haven: Yale University Press, 1950), with its contrast of "inner-" and "outer-directed" types.

phors with which he scored the other options available, those of the "defender," the "broker," and the "amphibian."

More evident at our distance is Kuyper's share in *fin de siècle* anxieties about torpor and decadence. Doubtless, the death of his youngest son Willy, age nine, just three months before, deepened that mood. His vigor belies his tone, however. Kuyper worked hard to stay current, and the opening pages of this speech were among the very first introductions of Nietzsche to a Dutch audience. That philosopher might have derided being (uniquely!) presented as the "German Multatuli," but he probably would have appreciated the stature Kuyper assigned him and the stakes this implied for the soul of what had once been Christendom. Kuyper's sense of those stakes is evident from his long quotation of St. Augustine, another philosopher who spoke at the turning of the ages. He himself did not limn two cities but offered two poles: against pantheism, *palingenesis*, the rebirth promised in the New Testament for person and cosmos alike.

This translation, by John Vriend, reproduces the original text (*De Verflauwing der Grenzen: Rede . . . op 20 October 1892* [Amsterdam: J. A. Wormser, 1892]) virtually entire. I have not imitated Kuyper's capitalization of Pantheism throughout, and I have reduced Kuyper's massive notations — 184 footnotes, over 35 pages, citing some 130 works with extensive commentary on many — to those showing his sources. An older translation, by John H. de Vries, is available as "Pantheism's Destruction of the Boundaries," *Methodist Review* 53 (July & September 1893): 520-35, 762-78.

LADIES AND GENTLEMEN:

Today our neighbors to the east have their own Multatuli in Friedrich Nietzsche,[2] a writer who need concede nothing to Douwes Dekker in the lure of his aphoristic style, in the audacity of his ideas, or in the reckless radicalism of his unbelief, while being far his superior in conceptual depth and systematic capacity. Their respective positions in life explain this: Multatuli was a civil servant in the Dutch East Indies;

2. "Multatuli" (Latin for "much have I suffered") was the pen-name of Eduard Douwes Dekker (1820-87), a Dutch author most famous for his novel *Max Havelaar* (1860), based on his experience as a colonial administrator in the Netherlands Indies.

Two sides of Kuyper. *Left:* "Abraham de Geweldige" ("the magnificent" or "terrible"): the most famous caricature of Kuyper, conveying his image of vast knowledge and authoritative judgment. *Above:* The student behind the orator: Kuyper at his desk with ten-gallon pipe, sketched in 1892, the year of *Blurring the Boundaries*.

Nietzsche a professor of philosophy in Basel. But for the rest they have achieved similar success, for Nietzsche too has become the rising sun to the up-and-coming generation of Germany, particularly since the publication of his work *Also sprach Zarathustra.* People devour him; they quote him; they fawn over him. Heine and Feuerbach are old hat; Schopenhauer is a bore; today everything revolves around Nietzsche.[3]

As you would expect, this German Multatuli, like his Dutch counterpart, is no friend of the present leadership in academic and political circles. Rather he ridicules Germany's professors and statesmen, its art devotees and its Mammon worshipers with equal chutzpah; nor does he spare the calotte of the priest or the braided belt of the ascetic. He discerns no signs of progress in our current era; in fact he loudly complains of retrogression. His none-too-tender judgment is "that modern civilization is decaying; it has become ever thinner, less robust, and more mediocre."[4]

But however scornfully he castigates Liberalism, he has reserved his *hatred* for the Christ. And not merely for the Christ of dogma so as to pay tribute, like Strauss and Renan, to the Christ of the Sermon on the Mount.[5] It is precisely that Sermon which sticks in his craw. To believe Nietzsche, in those ardent cries that resounded on the shores of Genesareth's sea — "blessed are the poor," "blessed are the meek," "blessed are those who mourn" — a "slave revolt in morality" was breaking forth. The rabbi of Nazareth only voiced "the pent-up thirst for vengeance" that prompted the Jews, amid their powerlessness and "with the fangs of the most abysmal hatred," to trample under foot all that was high and mighty on earth. Over against the Lamb that takes away the sin of the world Nietzsche therefore poses *his* animal symbols, predators all: "You should see *my* animals, my *eagle* and my *snake.*" Soon these mighty ones of earth are coarsely mocking the symbol of the lamb in the same vein: "We are not ill-disposed toward you, dear lambs; we are even fond of you, for nothing is tastier than tender lamb." And while he acknowledges that Christ has ruled for almost two thousand years, it only serves him to ridicule the decline of this power with demonic satire. He depicts a Christ who, abandoned by man, has fled to a lush pasture; there, surrounded by a herd of placid cows, he bellows out his maxim: "Unless

3. Kuyper (note 3) attests to having first encountered Nietzsche through an article in the Paris *Figaro,* then to have learned more via Hugo Kaatz, *Die Weltanschauung Nietzsche's* (Dresden, 1892).

4. Kuyper (note 4) cites Kaatz, *Nietzsche,* vol. I, p. 76.

5. David Friedrich Strauss (1808-74) and Ernest Renan (1823-92) were the foremost radicals among nineteenth-century Scripture critics, known for their debunking of orthodox doctrine about Christ but honoring his ethical teachings.

you repent and become as these cows, you will in no wise enter the kingdom of heaven."[6]

Nevertheless, this Christ-hater has his own messianic ideal. Only the Messiah he longs for is the *Antichrist,* a kind of *Superman* as he calls him, who will be in all things the polar opposite of Christ. "This Antichrist, this conqueror of God," who will restore to the earth its purpose and to humanity its hope — *"someday he will come."* Thus a personal Antichrist, one who triumphs over God and his Messiah in living flesh. The coming of this human monster is not invoked by prayer but summoned, indeed applauded afar off, like the dawn of the eternal morning. Is it not terrifying to pick up in this raw cry from the abyss an echo of what Scripture prophesies concerning the Antichrist? The parallel fails only in one respect. That which was *theistically* revealed by the apostle looms up *pantheistically,* by way of Evolution, to Nietzsche. According to Scripture, the Antichrist will be a *man,* "the man of sin," a fearsome tyrant on earth. But to Nietzsche this Antichrist becomes a *Super*man, evolved from the *common* man, who has himself sprouted up from a *brute* [*Unter*mensch, *sub*man]. His appearance will be the fruit of what has been opposing God for centuries. What people have called "the evil ones" are nothing but the "Cyclopean architects of humanity." Only God and his Christ have thus far blocked the evolution of this higher sort of being. But now that is over. "This God has died. To you, higher man, this God was the greatest danger. But since he now lies in his grave, now finally comes High Noon, now finally the higher human becomes — Master."[7]

Ladies and gentlemen, in a tragically prophetic moment Nietzsche once wrote down these words: "Think of yourself, Zarathustra! You yourself, yes, you too could well become an ass through a superabundance of wisdom."[8] And now — for three long years Nietzsche has been insane, incurably insane, and is languishing away body and soul in a *sub*human state. Is this God's judgment? I will not say, but I may point to Nietzsche's appearance as the necessary consequence of the pantheistic storm that has driven the flow of our century's life. A person who binds good and evil together genetically by Evolution, who crowns that which *became,* i.e., *power,* with a diadem of glory, who is intoxicated with an ever-continuing

6. Kuyper (notes 5-8) cites Kaatz, *Nietzsche,* vol. I, pp. 23, 29; and Nietzsche, *Die Genealogie der Moral* (Leipzig, 1892), p. 25; *Also sprach Zarathustra* (1891), vol. IV, pp. 50, 54.

7. Kuyper (notes 9-12) cites Kaatz, *Nietzsche,* vol. I, pp. 122-23, 127; Nietzsche, *Zarathustra,* vol. IV, pp. 77, 130ff; and *Die Fröhliche Wissenschaft* (Leipzig, 1887), pp. 137, 153.

8. Kuyper (note 13) cites personal correspondence with Kaatz, and the Nietzsche quotation from *Fröhliche Wissenschaft,* p. 115.

process — such a person simply has to come out where Nietzsche did. Not a single element surfaces in Nietzsche that does not stem, by legitimate descent, from the premises of Schelling and Hegel. Would it not be naive, then, if we who have undertaken to confess the name of the Lord ignored so alarming a sign of the times and failed to discern how things are coming to a head? Our battle today has to be fought on the basis of principle. Arrows shot from afar will not reach the target. The clash between the basic theme of the Christian religion and that of our century cuts too deep to be left to the playful sparring of the apologists. If the working of the pantheistic poison is not stopped, the flood will roll over us. Hence the calling of Christianity to fight this evil unsparingly, especially in the realm of higher thought. And though the speech I am about to deliver lacks scope for the full range of this argument, you will not take it amiss if I call your attention to one of this poison's many effects. I mean the clear tendency of all pantheism, and so also of the pantheistic mood of our time, *to increasingly blur the boundary lines* in every sphere of life and not to rest until, at least in our imagination, they have been expunged.

In Scripture God is called by the Hebrew word *Hammabdîl,* because He it was who drew lines, first between Himself and the created world, and then throughout the entire domain of the created world. Lines of design, lines of demarcation, lines of distinction, lines of separation, lines of contrast.[9] It is precisely these lines that pantheism attempts to blur. It still knows of distinction but no separation may ever be real. *En kai pan,* one and all, remains the magic phrase. And since to the Christian the most essential issues are at stake here, it seemed to me that this *blurring of boundaries* is well worth a deliberate discussion. In this connection I aim to demonstrate, first, *that* the spirit of our age in fact inclines in this direction; next, what *dangers* this tendency brings in its wake; finally, what *resistance* must be offered here.

I

I would not be classified with those who have nothing good to say about pantheism in any form. In fact, I *may* not because of the stark contrast between our century and the one that preceded it. That was an age of cold Deism, of a spirit-deadening Rationalism, of omnipresent artifice and conventionality. Its society resembled the waiting room of a morgue,

9. Kuyper (note 14) cites Gen. 1:4, 6, 14; Ex. 26:33; Lev. 11:47; 2 Sam. 19:35; Ezek. 22:26, 42:20, "etc."

uninspired and devoid of idealism. In its place has come a century full of enthusiasm and resilience. All elements of society are seething and in ferment, and its spirit tackles everything with a dynamism that boggles the mind. So if I had to choose between an icy Deism that finally freezes the blood in the arteries of your soul and a melting pantheism that conveys the delights of tropical abundance, I could not possibly hesitate. In India I would have been a Buddhist and probably praised the Vedanta. In China I would have preferred the system of Lao-tse over that of Confucius. And in Japan I would have turned from the official Shintoism in order to share the suffering of the oppressed Buddhist priests.[10]

We must not forget that pantheism's profoundest feature is a *misguided* love — a love that crosses set boundaries, but even in that illegitimate form, something born from *love* nonetheless. It does not repel but attracts, aims not to break up but to unite. Call it spiritual adultery if you will, but then an adultery born of affection, of nostalgia, of the pathos of a sympathetic heart. For all pantheism is born as *religious* pantheism; subsequently it crystallizes in a *philosophical* system; and only in its degenerative spread does it wreak its *practical* havoc in life. The soul searches for its God and when, lacking the light of revelation, it cannot find Him in the dusk of reason, it becomes impetuous with longing and indiscreet to the point of irreverence. It would draw nigh to God, get next to Him, penetrate His inner being, and not let up until it loses itself in Him or unconsciously absorbs Him in itself. That trait, that urge is the same the world over. Whether you hear the Hindu's heart-rending homesick cry for Nirvana or see the Gnostic delight himself in his "couplings" ("syzygies") or see Böhme theosophically, Madame de Guyon quietistically, and later Schelling philosophically paint their pantheism in Christian colors — it is all the same drive of the soul, impetuous and urgent, to lose itself in the depths of the divine being.[11]

10. For pantheism Kuyper cites Georg M. Schuler, *Der Pantheismus Gewurdigt durch Darlegung und Wiederlegung* (Würzburg, 1884), Eduard Schmidt, *Über das Absolute und das Bedingte* (Parchim, 1833). On Buddhism, Albert Bruining, *Bijdrage tot de kennis van de Vedanta* (Leiden, 1871); on Chinese religion, Jean P. A. Remusat, *Mémoire sur la vie et les opinions de Lao-tseu* (Paris, 1820); on Japanese religion, J. Rend, *Japan: Its History, Traditions, and Religion* (London, 1880); and on all three, the *South Place Institute Lectures* (London, 1890) (notes 16-19).

11. Kuyper (note 20) cites Henri Louis Charles Maret, *Der Pantheismus in der modernen Gesellschaft* (German tr., Schaffhausen, 1842; originally *Essai sur le panthéisme dans les sociétées modernes* [Paris, 1840]), for his typology. He relies quite heavily on this title throughout. Jacob Böhme (1575-1624) was a German Lutheran mystic who formed something of a bridge between the Reformation and Pietism. Friedrich Wilhelm Joseph von Schelling (1775-1854) was the successor to Fichte in the line of German Idealist philosophy. Significantly, Kuyper (note 22) attributes the contemporary influence of

Again, spiritual adultery, but glowing with a tragic passion that feels better than the cold egoism with which the matter-of-fact man grants the existence of God, perhaps, but never with more than a casual thought. It has been remarkable in our century how, in Schleiermacher, the revival of Christian religion kissed the hand of pantheism and, particularly with Schelling, allowed itself to be seduced into gulping down the cup of pantheism, provided only the name of theism be kept. The pious mind shuddered at the coldness of rationalism, shrank from the conventional mechanism of our supernaturalists, until with Schelling it regained its mysteries, its holy Trinity, its incarnation, and even its resurrection of the body.[12]

But if this pantheism sprang up lush as prairie grass, in that grass lurked a poisonous snake. In the homes of the pious it [pantheism] received its corrective from that piety itself, but not when it began to glitter from the lecterns of our philosophers. Philosophical pantheism very quickly repressed the religious element. Already in Hegel the religious motif was lost in dialectics, and after him the spirit of our age commandeered the magical formula so that, freed from God and every bond He established, it might melt down the existing world and recast it in new form, everyone following the desires of his own heart.[13]

Three motives simultaneously pushed our century in that direction: its enormous *sense of power,* its inflated sense of *human worth,* and its penetration into the riches *of nature.* Compared to the preceding age, this century feels like a Titan who will put his husky shoulders under anything, assail the heavens, and not rest until he has re-created everything in a new, i.e., modern form. From that overwhelming sense of power its sons derive their inflated sense of human worth. In its mind man is the alpha and omega. An anthropotheism, as some have dubbed it: a veneration first of the ideal human being; then of the human self, however deep that ego may have sunk into the subhuman. An Ego-theism down to its most revolting implications. That man then, with his superior power and overstimulated sense of self, has thrust himself upon a defenseless nature — and *has* mastered it, has led it in a victory procession behind the chariot of his science and sensibility. These three motives . . . account entirely

---

Madame Guyon (Jeanne Marie de la Motte, 1648-1717) to Robert Pearsall Smith, his erstwhile guide to perfectionism in the mid-1870s. The book he cites is A. Marston, *A Short Method of Prayer and Spiritual Torrents* (London, 1875). Madame Guyon was a French Quietist mystic who taught a perfectionism of the surrendered will.

12. Kuyper (notes 24-26) cites extensively from Schleiermacher's *Dialectiek* (Berlin, 1839) and histories of modern philosophy, including those by Theodore Überweg (Berlin, 1888) and Kuno Fischer (Heidelberg, 1891).

13. Kuyper (note 27) cites Maret, *Pantheismus,* p. 29.

for the pantheistic cast of our century. Thus, people were not being presumptuous when — depending on their sympathies — they praised pantheism as the "favorite system" of our century or cursed it as the "radical heresy" now raising its head, or when a British pantheist triumphantly crowed that *at least ninety* out of a hundred leading intellectuals in our day are declared or secret pantheists.[14]

Not that *philosophical* pantheism still holds dominion in the schools today. Except for Italy, the opposite is the case. Hegel has long been dethroned, and that ended the luxuriant growth of systematic pantheism. Philosophy sees its lecture halls deserted. On every hand people groan about its being decrepit, its deep decline, its intellectual impotence. Having ceased philosophizing, professors flood the market with "histories of philosophy." Spencer has made Agnosticism, i.e., the inability to achieve higher knowledge, into a system. The long-forgotten Herbart is now thought to have surpassed Hegel in wisdom. Neo-Kantians are returning to Kant, a few even to Leibnitz. And as if to prove that one may have a most *un*poetic name and still stare oneself blind on poetic genius, the Viennese professor *Knauer* has at great length proclaimed Robert Hamerling the greatest of all philosophers, the one who put the capstone on the palace.[15]

But this does not mean that the fangs of what Goethe calls the "ever-devouring, ever-ruminating monster" of pantheism have been drawn. When the Socialists recently held their electoral meeting, they posted over the entrance the saying of Opzoomer: *"Every citizen, as a member of the commonwealth, has a share in sovereignty."*[16] Call this a misuse of the professor's words, if you will, but recognize that so it *always* goes with a statement of principle. It is first announced from a professor's lectern, but long after it has been weighed and found wanting in the halls of philosophy it still floats about in lower spheres, exerts influence in the different disciplines, dominates the textbooks. It is in the fabric of our

14. Kuyper (note 33) cites the anonymously written *General Sketch of the History of Pantheism* (London, 1879).

15. Kuyper (notes 34-36) cites Herbert Spencer, *A System of Synthetic Philosophy* (1862-79); and Vincenz Knauer, *Die Hauptproblem der Philosophie von Thales bis Hamerling* (Vienna, 1892). He identifies Robert Hamerling (1830-89) as a "Herbartian Monadist," referring to Johann Friedrich Herbart (1776-1841), Kant's successor at Königsberg but more a Realist than he, as the Neo-Kantians' conduit back to the master. Hamerling was best known for his epic poems, written in theatrical Romantic style.

16. Kuyper (note 41) cites Goethe's *Die Leiden des jungen Werther*, Bk 1, letter of 18 August. Cornelis W. Opzoomer (1821-92) was the Netherlands's leading intellectual in the previous generation, a professor of philosophy at Utrecht, and a doctrinaire liberal in religion and politics.

novels, glitters like tinsel in the daily press, and adulterates the inspiration of our poets. Its slogans color our conversation, and in the circles of mediocrity, or what the Germans call "Philistine-dom," it completely churns up public opinion. To take but one example: at the prompting of Broca and Von Nägeli Darwin himself admitted in the last edition of his *Descent of Man* and *Origin of Species* the inadequacy of his theory of selection; but the second-hand science of textbooks and public schools goes on honoring this defective theory as the philosopher's stone.[17]

. . . Thus you get something Maret found far more dangerous [than academic speculation]: derivative theories and their applications, whose underpinnings are *unspoken,* if not *concealed* — what am I saying? — often not even vaguely *suspected* by the person handling them. By way of example, let me just mention the worship of *Progress.* However much people accelerate their pace, there is no respite, never a rest, only a life without a Sabbath. No time to survey what has been won, much less to possess and enjoy it. No sooner have we arrived at one point along the way than we hurry off to the next. Something like the saucy gallop of the Death-Rider in Bürger's "Lenore." The wandering Jew, driven now by an all-absorbing passion, not by a haunting fear. We are rushed forward relentlessly, caught up in an Excelsior that must never end. Am I being too bold to assert that of every thousand people who speed along in this parade, not even two have an inkling of the genetic connection between this fevered *Progress* with our pantheists' *process?* What was once stated as a proposition, viz. *panta rhei kai ouden menei* ["everything is in flux and nothing ever remains (the same)"] has now been adopted as a life motto until finally the lack of an eternal Sabbath is projected on God himself so that even He, as Schüler quipped, is magically changed into "a veritable progress-God."[18]

17. Kuyper (note 43) quotes Darwin, *Origin of Species,* 2nd ed. (London, 1878), p. 171, and *Descent of Man,* 2nd ed. (London, 1890), n.p. Paul Broca (1824-80) was a pioneering French brain physiologist. Karl von Nägeli (1817-91) was a Swiss botanist best known for his development of cell theory and work on hereditary transmission, which he thought to be inherent (not environmentally shaped) and teleological (rather than random).

18. Kuyper (notes 48-52) cites Gottfried August Bürger, "Lenore" (1773), a very important poem for him (see his *Modernism,* note 20). He remarks of Longfellow's "Excelsior" that the public had generally misconstrued the poem's condemnation of the quest referred to by its title, and that Schuler's (*Pantheismus,* p. 7) "progress-god" was a pun critical of pantheism's "becoming" God. Kuyper adds respecting "progress" more generally that it had changed from a life-motto to a cliché, no longer inspired pursuit of the ideal but condemned people to eternal unrest, generated no power but fed pessimism by banning satisfaction from the heart.

* * *

But enough of this. It is not my purpose to deal with pantheism in general, only with one of its effects. I will not even detain you with an attempt to define this elusive Proteus but will focus on this one point — that pantheism blurs all distinctions, obscures all boundary lines, and shows a tendency to wash out all contrasts. You can see this in *religious* pantheism, which is afraid of a "far-away" God nor finds peace with a God "at hand" but attempts to enter into God's being by the mystery of prayer and yearns some day in the hereafter to melt back into God's being until the distinction between God and the soul is entirely gone. You can trace it in *practical* pantheism which, by its ceaseless leveling, first pulls down all that stands out, then prunes and chops it off until at last all distinction between the cedar and the hyssop [1 Kings 4:33] is lost. But the tendency is most pronounced in *philosophical* pantheism which systematically fuses every thesis and antithesis into a *synthesis* and, being fascinated by the concept of identity, casts all that seem dissimilar as similar, indeed, finally, as being of the same substance.[19]

This happens because this philosophy does not deal with what really exists but with the *image* of existing reality which it has caught in its mental mirror or, more correctly, formed for itself. Kant set this ball rolling by proclaiming that real existence eludes us and that at least the shape and dimensions of what we perceive arise from within ourselves. Then came Fichte who thought it best not to deal with something that eluded us anyway and maintained that what appeared to be an image we have ourselves imagined and is therefore the only reality. Finally Hegel transmuted all that existed into a purely logical formula and, having destroyed the *thing* itself as well as its *image*, was left with only the *idea* of it. And so this philosophy ineluctably takes us out of the really existing world into an abstract world of thought, where it can do what it pleases with the distinctions and antitheses of life. For then I am no longer dealing with living persons but with models of my own making. And naturally, on those crayon portraits I can blur or spirit away all sorts of wrinkles and lines which will always be on a living face.

If pantheism thus creates the *possibility* of escaping the grip of real distinctions, the very *law of thought* forces it to use that possibility ever more prodigally. Your thinking prompts you to integrate the phenomena you perceive into a stable order. Thought by its very nature tends toward

19. Kuyper (notes 54-56) cites, among others, Schmidt, *Über das Absolute,* p. 62; and Maret, *Pantheismus,* p. 205.

system.[20] The thinker looks for the general in the particular to explain the particular from the rule of the general. All dualisms run directly counter to the demands of the thought process, for it can rest on its laurels only when everything, without exception, is subsumed under a single concept. Now if you study reality and honor the laws of its existence, then in your thinking you will again and again encounter that which stubbornly resists your generalization. But if, like the pantheist, you do not live in the real world but in a gallery of your own paintings, then of course there is no resistance. Then you tolerate no stubborn resistance from your brush but simply smudge all the lines that fail to fit into your system.

Please pardon this dry argumentation, ladies and gentlemen, but I could not avoid it if I would make plain the force of inner necessity by which pantheism is driven to erase all boundary lines. To use Spinoza's grammatical image: there may remain forms of declension and conjugation that differ in tense and mood, person and case, but all these forms are merely modifications of the one root-word which always stays the same. Or as a German philosopher put it: "All that appears to our eyes as difference and distinction, however much our consciousness insists upon *non*identity, is nevertheless in essence one and the same; it is but the appearance, the formation, the characterization, the development, alteration, expression, revelation, or form of the *one* substance which *alone* exists."[21]

This becomes clear immediately and in principle from the relation people construe between God and the world. Centuries ago the church of Christ raised an official barrier against every appearance of crypto-pantheism by solemnly stating in the opening line of the Apostles' Creed: "I believe in God the Father, Almighty, Creator of heaven and earth." In the third century it rightly rejected the first weakening of the creation-concept by declaring Origen a heretic. The most clearly defined boundary line lies between God and the world, and it is by eliminating *that* line that all other boundary lines are blurred. Every distinction in our consciousness, even our capacity to make distinctions, is finally rooted in this primordial difference. Eliminate it and day turns into night, a night in whose shadowy darkness everything in your field of vision turns to a dull grey.

Every pantheist *starts out* by denying precisely this root constrast, the mother of all creaturely difference. The moment he opens the Bible and reads the solemn opening of Genesis 1, the pantheist finds himself

20. This fundamental and recurrent axiom in Kuyper he cites here (note 59) from Maret, *Pantheismus*, p. 205.

21. Kuyper (notes 60-61) cites Schuler, *Pantheismus*, p. 12.

disagreeing with God's holy revelation. No: not "in the beginning," for there was no beginning; not "created," for the world is eternal; and not "heaven and earth," for your "Beyond" is an illusion.[22] In this way the three most deeply etched lines of distinction are erased or blurred at a single stroke. Indeed, every boundary line between God and the world, between time and eternity, between here and there, is removed. Still, pantheism *must* begin with the elimination of these differences. There is no alternative. Our thinking has free run over the whole course of history, but at the point where history began and at the point where it will some day end, it [our thinking] stops. There, both *before* and *behind,* it encounters a bottomless abyss over which no leap is to be dared, much less a bridge to be built. And so, at whatever cost, that beginning and that end *must* be negated. For the pantheist, God and the world cannot exist as two distinct entities.

I well understand the objection you wish to raise. You will remind me that a moment ago I said a very different wind is blowing in scholarly circles today and that at those elevations pantheism along with materialism has long since been sent packing. Having candidly pronounced the verdict "it is not clear" concerning the origin, ground, and purpose of things, scientists have been content to investigate more carefully the phenomena of the natural and spiritual world, and for the rest to let our hearts feed on poetry. All this is true. But does this mean that the *principle* of evolution, the *Descendenztheorie* as our Germans call it, has therefore ceased to be the *Credo* of present-day science? What else is the Evolution-theory but the application of the pantheistic process to the empirical investigation of the phenomena? Here too we are told that *nature takes no leaps*. Here too we encounter the explanation of all phenomena in terms of a preceding phenomenon. And here too — for me, the over-riding concern — the theory rejects all essential differences in kind, all independence in origin, all deeper distinctions of being both for spiritual and natural phenomena, *in* either sphere as well as *between* the two spheres.

And so every boundary line is deleted and every post leveled that divides one kingdom from another. Von Hartmann did not exaggerate when he said that "for our times the theory of natural descent is absolutely right and is gaining converts amidst the storms of controversy." Or, as an English scholar put it: "Science, amongst us, is at its highest

22. Kuyper (note 63) cites Alois Biedermann, *Die Freie Theologie* (Tübingen, 1844), p. 208; and David Friedrich Strauss, *Die Christliche Glaubenslehre* (Tübingen, 1841), p. 739.

when it interprets all orders of phenomena as differently conditioned modes of one kind of uniformity."[23] Though Darwin himself admitted that his theory of natural selection was inadequate to explain the morphological differences of species, the Evolution-theory did not for that reason collapse. What Darwin explained mechanically could also be conceived dynamically, or if necessary even teleologically, as a spontaneous process in the cosmos that derives its impulse from the first germ or takes its motive power from the final idea which controls the whole process. One can even be a Darwinist and still, like Darwin himself, reverently bow his knees before a certain "God."[24] God created the dynamic which potentially included the entire cosmos within itself; or, alternatively, it was God who prescribed the goal of its process of development. Indeed, the system is so pliable that more than one Herbartian, defying his own principle, is making common cause with Darwinism.

This would not be hard to understand if Darwin had succeeded, with the aid of fossil discoveries, in laying out the stages of transition from the plant to the human species in specimens that locked into each other like the links of a single chain. But, as you know, this is not the case. Not only does the search for the "missing link" continue, but even when scientists go back 300,000 years, a period in which they claim to find certain proof in the world of fossils, what do they find? They do find traces of species that are now extinct as well as deviant formations. But prehistoric skeletons of species that still exist today are strikingly similar to the skeletons of our animals. Being an honest man Darwin therefore

23. Kuyper (notes 66-67) cites Eduard von Hartmann, *Philosophie des Unbewusstes* (Leipzig, 1889), vol. III, p. 46; and *General Sketch of Pantheism,* vol. II, p. 263.

24. Kuyper (note 69) cites *Origin of Species,* pp. 421-22. He continues: "That Darwin himself still believes in a God and holds to creation in a certain sense says nothing. We may not overlook the fact that a number of Theists think they can uphold evolution-theory in the sense that God himself teleologically — that is, with the eye on the end-result — deposited in the original creature, or even in the ancient germ of all that would come into being, the potential for this whole rich organic development. This closely approaches the atheistic theory of Murphy and Owen, the only difference being that what Murphy calls *nature,* the Theists call God. See Murphy, *Habit and Intelligence in Their Connection with the Laws of Matter and Force* (London, 1869), vol. I, p. 348." But in note 68 Kuyper said: "Evolution-theory is only to be scientifically contested by emphasizing the insufficiency of its proof and by recognizing what the Christian side has never denied, that each previous formation in the scale of creation is indeed entirely a preformation for the following higher formation. Above all it must be gratefully acknowledged that the research on behalf of this theory has yielded vast gains for our knowledge and has restored what too often has been missing, the concept of the unity of nature. . . ." This dual attitude would be elaborated much further in his next rectorial address, *Evolution* (1899).

admits that proof for his theories is far from complete: still incomplete in the realm of nature and, let us add, utterly inadequate for the realm of culture. But, he repeatedly adds, this does not undermine *my faith* in the theory of evolution.[25] From this it follows that we are not dealing with a compelling, tightly argued proposition but with a hypothesis supported by a highly deficient process of induction whose general acclaim is rooted *not* in incontestable facts, still less in complete *proof,* but in a general cultural mood. For Darwin's theory offers our learned and cultivated public precisely the solution to the cosmic problem that suits its inmost sympathies. So if we know that the dominant tone of our age is pantheistic, and that in the theory of evolution one of the most fertile ideas of pantheism, that of never-ceasing process, appears in its most fascinating form, then is it too much to say that I find as the principal motif in the theory of natural descent the propulsive dynamic of pantheism?

To probe the real motive even more deeply: in the theory of evolution as in pantheism generally there lurks the desire of the human heart to rid itself of God. Despite his "practical reason" this impulse controlled even Immanuel Kant, of whom Baader rightly wrote: "The fundamental error of his philosophy is that it makes humanity autonomous, spontaneous; it derives reason from itself; by this procedure humanity makes itself God and becomes pantheistic." Feuerbach merely articulated a corollary of this system, and therein the basic idea of our century, when he said: "God was my first thought, reason my second, man my third and last. The subject of deity is reason but the subject of reason is *man*." Büchner, himself an avowed atheist, frankly admits that Darwin's theory even more than Lamarck's must be considered purely atheistic — a statement with which I completely concur. For what does it profit you if you can track the law of causality without a break to the first nebula, the first cell or the first germ, if you nevertheless have to acknowledge behind that cell or germ the unexplained act of a creating God, and so for all your thinking still run into the very rock your whole theory was devised to avoid?[26]

So, though it be true that neither the "Moses of modern freethinkers," as Feuerbach calls Spinoza, nor his epigones have brought

25. Kuyper (note 70) quotes at length from *Origin of Species* at pp. 252, 408, and 424.

26. Kuyper (notes 71-73) quotes Franz von Baader (1765-1841) from Julius Baumann, *Geschichte der Philosophie nach Ideengehalt und Beweisen* (Gotha, 1890), p. 342; Feuerbach from his collected works; and Ludwig Büchner, *Sechs Vorlesungen über die Darwinische Theorie,* 2nd ed. (Leipzig, 1868), p. 125. He cross-references Charles Hodge's *Systematic Theology* (London, 1878), p. 17.

us to the promised land of philosophic rest, and that the bankruptcy of pantheistic philosophy can no longer be hidden, its harmful influence still simmers most insidiously in the theory of evolution, since it directs all its energy at upholding the *non*-existence of boundaries in every field of human knowledge. Valentinus, the weightiest of the Gnostics, relegated evolution back to the ultimate depths [*Bythos*] behind the creation, but he at least had enough of an eye for the danger this move posed for the destruction of boundaries to conjure up from the *Autopator* [self-engendered Nature] a god in the form of Horos, i.e., a *boundary* by which to uphold the order of all existence. Indeed, this idea, however oddly framed, is completely correct as a poetic image. Faith in the living God stands or falls with the maintenance or elimination of boundaries. It is He who created the boundaries. He himself is the ultimate boundary for all his creation, and to erase boundaries is virtually the same as erasing the idea of God. Thus, however true it is that modern philosophy "began with doubt and has now ended in despair," the entire pantheistic stream has left behind on its shores a toxic slime, and it is precisely in Darwin's theory of evolution that this deposit manifests its power.

For all the remaining differences in approach, therefore, it is fair to say that this theory of evolution is the "form of unity" that currently unites all the priests of modern science in their secularized temple. A few duffers may grumble against it, but they are old men who, as Hartmann put it, "feel themselves incapable of a second education but who have for a long time been dying out and so cannot stop the victory march of the new truth." It has become a *fashion*, this theory of evolution, and not only the Darwins and Haeckels, the Spencers and Nägeli's but also our theologians, our psychologists, and our moralists are enraptured with it. Even a follower of Lotze, like my learned colleague Dr. De la Saussaye at the city university, wrote just recently: "Nowhere can a definite boundary be clearly drawn between the natural and the spiritual world, or a given phenomenon assigned exclusively to one of these spheres."[27]

But what causes the greatest practical concern is the ground that this dubious theory is steadily gaining among our jurists, the divinely appointed watchmen over the boundary marks of society. Let me dem-

27. Kuyper (notes 76-77) cites von Hartmann, *Philosophie*, vol. III, p. 46; and Daniel Chantepie de la Saussaye, Jr., *Lehrbuch der Religionsgeschichte* (Freiburg, 1887), vol. I, p. 9. Kuyper adds respecting the latter: "This holds for all boundaries: between warm and cold, light and darkness, white and black. But if we cannot give an exact point where the boundary runs, that in no sense means no boundary exists. . . . Our consciousness knows immediately that a contrast indeed exists between light and darkness, etc., and that it is quite real. The old Realists already rightly defended this against the Nominalists."

onstrate with the example of the brilliant and recently deceased Von Jhering as an *In Memoriam.* I will not take a back seat to anyone in my respect for Jhering's talents, but we must not cloak the fact that he too was an evolutionist in the most positive sense of the word. Not himself a natural scientist, he did not wish to venture an opinion on Darwinism, but he does affirm that the conclusions he reached in his legal studies "fully corroborate this theory in my own field." "The idea of law to him is a process of *eternal becoming,* for 'everything that comes into being also deserves to perish.'" This eternal process necessarily evolves, which evolution begins already in the animal world, for he writes: "by the same necessity by which, according to Darwin's theory, one species of animal evolves from another, so one judicial goal gives birth to another." And then he adds in an altogether pantheistic sense: "The development of law knows of leaps no more than does nature; the precedent must be there before (by evolution of course) the higher form can follow."[28]

He does not deny God. In his preface he even deduces the *Goal* [*Zweck*] that explains everything for him from a conscious God. But as with all evolutionary theists that God is no more than an X, an unknown quantity, from whose authority he exempts himself in every concrete case. According to Jhering a sense of justice is not innate but is only bred in us by the evolution of law. A Christian ethics that still adheres to *eternal principles* he reproves precisely because it upholds the absolute. And where he, rightly, protests the separation that wrenches law from its moral base and himself traces the genealogy of the moral life, that moral life is generated from within the Goal — here again, the process of infinite becoming. If you ask him who is the subject of this Goal, who determines and realizes it, then theism is in fact completely abandoned when he states: "God is *not* the teleological agent of morality; the teleological agent of morality is *society.*" Whether or not God is still spoken of in a Gnostic sense as "a final ground of morality," this interpretation has in fact left the basis of Christianity completely behind. The ideal of human fulfillment is found in "each person's being his own end," and so he despises all else the moment it dares to assail him in that holy temple. The author commends Michael Kohlhaas in von Kleist's audacious novella, who draws his sword against society. And whereas *we* are taught "Rather suffer

28. Kuyper focused on the eminent German jurist Rudolph von Jhering (1818-92), a social utilitarian, because of his merit as an original scholar who also took care to communicate with a more popular audience (note 78). His citations (notes 79-82) come from the preface to *Der Zweck im Recht* (Leipzig, 1877), vol. I, pp. 10-13, except for the double quotation ("Alles, was entsteht/Ist werth dass es zu Grunde geht") from *Die strijd om het recht* (Dutch tr. of *Der Kampf ums Recht*) (Leiden, 1874), p. 10.

wrong," and Christ in the Sermon on the Mount exclaims "if anyone wants your coat, give your cloak as well," Jhering criticizes this as apathy, as a dampening of our sense of justice. He challenges every citizen in private cases never to tolerate an injury at the hands of another. Indeed, if his theory prevails not only our Christian but even Herbart's system, which even more Christianly derives the right from the aesthetic *thirst for peace,* will be juridically taboo.[29] The motto will not be "Blessed are the peacemakers" but "Blessed is everyone who like a rooster flares up to fight for his rights." If a titan like Jhering promotes these ideas, guess what we may expect from lesser gods!

. . . [Rather than trying to demonstrate the pantheistic-evolutionary influence everywhere, it will be enough] if I briefly note the main lines that have been blurred and, because I speak as theologian, dwell a little longer on the blurring of boundaries that has occurred in that field.

All boundary-blurring begins in our *perceptions* and *concepts.* Real boundaries — such as exist, for example, between man and woman — cannot be erased. It is as true for philosophy as for the British Parliament that "it can do everything except make a man a woman." A brilliant scholar in this country, whose oratory has often enraptured me too, once boldly ventured to predict that, like the demonic eros that militates against Nature, so also the divinely increated eros between man and woman would some day cease to burn.[30] I beg his pardon, but neither among my own contemporaries nor among the younger generation that daily inspires my teaching at the university have I ever come across the slightest sign that this natural love is eroding. No, the boundaries that exist independently of our thought in real life do not yield to our attempts to change them. You will never reconcile water with fire. An erasure of boundaries can occur only in our imagination, our perceptions, our concepts. Accordingly, it is of those concepts that Thilo complains in none-too-strong language that the modern view "finally mixes all concepts in the one great tangle of the absolute ego." Yet this did not happen all at once. The majesty of logic, with its unalterable laws of thought, stood in the way of such amalgamation. So before the other boundaries could be successfully blurred, the boundaries of *logic* first had to be violated. There

29. Kuyper (notes 83-90) cites, with copious additional quotations, *Zweck im Recht,* vol. I, pp. 10-13; vol. II, pp. 91, 122, 137, 152; and *Strijd om recht,* pp. 53ff, 64 (commending Michael Kohlhaas), 65-66 (defending duelling), and 69.

30. Kuyper (note 92) cites the eminent Dutch theological modernist Allard Pierson, *Eene Levenbeschouwing* (Haarlem, 1875), vol. II, pp. 268-69.

the ill-fated process started. Hegel clearly perceived that his system of identity could not co-exist with standard logic. Accordingly, he did not shrink from assailing logic itself, specifically by cutting through the principle of the excluded middle.[31] Only so did he clear the road for his cavalcade of identity concepts. He proceeded to let them file past his intellect two by two, arm in arm: the "something" side-by-side with the "nothing," the "here" with "the beyond," the finite with the infinite, the ideal with the real, being with thought, object with subject, the different with the indifferent, freedom with necessity, imaginary light with imaginary darkness.

But of course he did not stop with abstractions. His goal and that of all his sympathizers was applying the identity principle to life. At that point matters took a serious turn. For then the boundary between God and the world collapsed into what the old Greeks called at most a distinction in thought, never in time or in essence. Thus God, in the pertinent words of Dr. Mayer, was "reduced to a cosmic potency"; even worse, his conscious life dissolved in our *human* life. So the boundary between God and man vanished, with the point of gravity now on the human side. The boundary between man and man could not be far behind. We rise and fall like the waves of the ocean. We bud like leaves on a tree, withering to soon make way for the new leaves in the spring. Homer's line: "Now the wind scatters the old leaves across the earth" [*Iliad* VI, l. 172] is now understood *essentially,* not chronologically. Next came the spiritual lines. Between our physical and psychic life every boundary had to disappear. Truth was wedded to error. Stirner even ventured to speak of the "heroism of the lie." Good and evil, sin and sanctity had to settle their ancient feud. What is good? "Each person is only what he can make of himself." Nero and Jesus are merely different manifestations of the same divine dynamic. The ancient Parsees were no fools when, next to Ormuzd, they gave divine honor also to Ahriman and his Devi, for surely what you call Satan is only another name for the Holy One of Israel. And if you find much in human society that is noble above but also much that is revolting below, then Böhme's old image is there to tell you that in your own organism as well there is much noble in your skull but also much that is disgusting in your intestines — and that without the intestines the brains would not be there.[32]

31. Kuyper (notes 93-94) cites Christfried A. Thilo, *Kurz pragmatische geschichte der neuern Philosophie,* 2nd ed. (Gotha, 1881), vol. II, p. 427; and logic textbooks by Theodore Überweg (Bonn, 1874), Hermann Ulrici (Leipzig, 1852), Johann H. Loewe (Vienna, 1881), and Wilhelm Wundt, *Erkenntnisslehre* (Stuttgart, 1880).

32. Kuyper does not identify which "Dr. Mayer" he is quoting. His notes to this

In that manner the blurring of boundaries restlessly goes on, not only in equating power with matter but also practically by equating might with right, by dissolving accountability into a pitiable atavism, by confusing private property with theft, by weakening the contrast between civil authorities and subjects, absorbing both in the single idea of the state. Into that all-providing state, as Rothe himself wishes, even the church of Christ must vanish.[33] There should no longer be a difference between city and village — only communities. The love of country must dim under the impact of cosmopolitanism. The demarcations of marriage should dissolve into a system of free love. Distinctions of class, lifestyle, or modes of national dress should be no more. *Uniformity* is the curse our modern life deliberately feeds on. In music Beethoven was the first to pick up the pantheistic tendency of our age and to drill it into thousands upon thousands by his C Minor [fifth] and ninth symphony. After him Wagner deliberately broke down the boundary between the world of sound and that of thought.[34] Certain stylists in our day are increasingly inclined to confuse their inkpot with their palette. There is a growing circle who would dearly love to abolish the boundary that separates one language from another, who would find the world ideal if it were populated by one-and-a-half billion people from North Pole to South, all speaking the one holy *Volapuk*.[35]

But enough of this. . . . I wish to pause a moment longer at the issue of religion where lies, of course, the strongest motive to blur the

---

paragraph (97-101) cite Max Stirner's (Johann Kaspar Schmidt) *Der Einzige und sein Eigentum* (Leipzig, 1845), Feuerbach's *Wesen des Christenthums*, Hodge's *Systematic Theology*, Spinoza's *Opera*, Hegel's *Werke*, Nietzsche via *Kaatz*, Spencer's *Data of Ethics*, and Cousin's *Cours de l'histoire de la philosophie moderne*.

33. Richard Rothe (1799-1867) was a German theologian strongly influenced by Hegel. Methodologically speculative and deductive, and monistic by inclination, he identified religion with morality, individual with social ethics, and so anticipated the church being absorbed into a Christianized state (i.e., government-society organism).

34. Kuyper (note 105) gives a lengthy disquisition on this point, beginning: "It might sound strange to hear Beethoven characterized as the musical apostle of Pantheism, since it is known that in his latter days he returned to a more positive Christianity. It is notable in this regard that his confession lacked an *absolute* quality." Kuyper quotes from Louis Nohl, *Beethoven's Brevier* (Leipzig, 1870), p. 56; Franz Brendal, *Geschichte der Musik* (Leipzig, 1852), pp. 348-49; and Richard Wagner, *Das Kunstwerk der Zukunft* (Leipzig, 1850), pp. 9, 85, and 183. Against Wagner's program he quotes, among others, Arthur Schopenhauer, *Die Welt als Wille und Vorstellung* (Leipzig, 1891), vol. II, pp. 512ff.

35. Volapuk was an artificial language devised by Johann Schleyer and quite popular in the 1880s; its complexity allowed Esperanto eventually to surpass it.

boundaries. Our Christian religion drew a new and very deep line between the sacred and profane, and precisely this the spirit of secularization opposed with virtual howls of scorn. Theology was denied a place as a distinct science: the metaphysical part of it was said to be the same as philosophy, and the rest could be absorbed by literary, historical, and ethnological studies. The boundary between God and the idols collapsed since animism and fetishism were subsumed with Christianity under a single heading. In that organic connection religion — as far as its origin, essence, and idea are concerned — could be known only from its phenomena. Thus arose the "science of religion" to displace theology, no longer attempting to obtain knowledge of the *object* of religion but only of the perceptions, representations, and expressions that religious feeling inspires in the *subject*. Consequently all basic religious distinctions have vanished, every boundary line between heresy and confession. Inevitably, the yeast of pliability at work in a society alienated from Christ found its way into the church as well.[36]

And then — had it only been different! — the otherwise most attractive mediating theologians in their ethical, theosophical, and apocalyptic variations followed Schleiermacher to take refuge in the disastrous kind of negotiation that hands the game to the opponent before it starts. I appreciate their frequently brilliant efforts, I understand their good intentions, and I have no desire to offend any of them personally, but *their position* was simply untenable. They were clay mixing with iron; naturally they did not win the spirit of the age for Christ but the spirit of the age increasingly weaned them away from confessional Christianity. Schleiermacher was simply a pantheist and subjectivist. He brought religious pantheism along with him from the Hernhutters and found philosophical pantheism at the German universities of the day. This came out at the very start in his proposition that God is not conceivable apart from the world.[37] As Professor Bavinck has shown in great detail, the same proposition was argued in our country by the late Groningen Professor De la Saussaye. Since then whatever the Martensens, the Rothes, the Keerls, and Hoffmanns have devised in Germany has been echoed by our pulpits and presses to shift the old landmarks around every-which-way in the domain of Christian

36. Kuyper (note 109) cites Feuerbach, *Grundriss der Philosophie der Zukunft*. In note 111 he remarks that the Synodical Commission's finding against him in 1886 had used the "yeast in the people must ferment in the church" line.

37. Kuyper (notes 112-13) cites Schleiermacher's *Dialektiek*, p. 328, and A. Kulerkamp's 1740 critique of the Moravians ("Hernhutters"), among whom Schleiermacher had his education.

religion.[38] By ethicizing truth the boundary that separates moral expression from the life of thought was obliterated, and soon the discipline of dogmatics had to surrender its birthright to the "description of moral life." A "united church" without confessional discipline became the ideal in our country too. Stifling the Calvinist and sympathizing with the Modernist was considered the superior thing to do.

And so, little by little, all sorts of strange doctrines crept in. Christ would have come into the world even without the fall, for Christ was the natural ideal by which the course of the human race was designed. In that Christ, God the Son had not himself become incarnate, but in him human nature attained a higher, divinely human nature. As a human being Jesus could not have been just male, so the legend of androgyny was revived. Soul and body were no longer two entities but were absorbed into a mixed "spiritual-corporeality." The mystery of the Trinity was acclaimed but as magically converted along the lines of recent philosophy. Atonement did not consist in the Lamb of God dying for our sins but in the appearance of the ideal shoot on the tree of our race. Scripture no longer came by intentional revelation but as fruit of Israel's organic development under higher inspiration, and further in conjunction with what had been accorded to other nations. Justification by faith was almost completely submerged in the cultivation of heavenly sanctity. Indeed, even the absolute boundary between this life and the life to come was abolished. Conversion could also occur after death, and some of these theologians even preached the continued existence of a sacramental church on the other side of the grave so as to complete *there* the process of sanctification that remained unfinished *here*.[39]

What else peeps through all this but what Schleiermacher spun and what Schelling, more dangerously, embroidered with his glittering threads of gold. It is the recasting of forms, the obliteration of lines of demarcation, clothing Christian essence in a modern-philosophical dress. In the process truth was lost: not only the objective truth which is engraved in the core of our confession, but also that inner truth which prompts us

38. Kuyper (note 114) cites Herman Bavinck (then professor at Kampen Theological Seminary and later Kuyper's successor as chief theologian at the Free University), *De Theologie van Professor Dr. Chantepie de la Saussaye . . .* (Leiden, 1884). Hans Martensen (1808-74) of Denmark and Johann C. K. von Hoffmann (1810-77) of Erlangen were mediating theologians of the preceding generation. Philipp F. Keerl was a Reformed preacher in Baden, of the mediating type, with important contacts among the Ethical school in Dutch Reformed circles in the 1860s.

39. Kuyper (notes 115-22) cites Hans Martensen, *Die Christliche Dogmatik* (Berlin, 1856), pp. 101-4, 224, 240, and 368; and Johannes H. Gunning, *Blikken in de Openbaring* (Amsterdam, 1868), vol. III, pp. 234, 273.

to respond to that confession with the Amen of our heart. Everything became a vast confusion of tongues, a chaos of free-floating ideas. Schelling completed in these men what Kant had begun with his "statutory religion," by inspiring in them (as Scholten put it) the art of peddling "new and strange notions under ancient ecclesiastical labels, notions that sounded like the pronouncements of the orthodox long ago."[40]

It could be, indeed I assume, that people were hereby leaping into the philosophical stream to rescue the drowning. But theirs was the tragic fate to be pulled down in the clutches of the drowning ones so that they too were lost. Truly, I am no enthusiast of Ritschl, but after the chaotic would-be theology that lies behind him, his clarity brings some relief. At least you know that he has broken with the old metaphysics. Yet with Ritschl we go still further astray: there is literally not a single boundary left in the domain of religion that clearly and firmly marks the ancient track.[41] Piety, yes, but it must above all be *free,* very free, a piety such as could also be found in animals. More than one scientist thinks he has discovered real traces of religion, the rudimentary beginnings of "piety," especially in our canine pets. So bizarre a claim almost prompts you to ask whether these are to be ranked among polytheists or monotheists. To that a scoffer might answer by analogy to their inferior love, for monogamy has affinities with monotheism (Islam excepted), but our poodles and mastiffs have not yet realized the evolution out of polygamy.

II

. . . We come now to our second question: *what dangers lurk for us in this blurring of boundaries?* Let us first of all listen to the lessons of history. After all, human society has evolved under these sorts of influences over many centuries and on an enormous scale on the banks of the Ganges River and in part of the Celestial Kingdom [China]. Later, gnosticism and mysticism have animated smaller groups with the same spirit. These give us a clear and powerful warning, for human *wreckage* is a fair image of what these examples show us.

In the fair realm of India lives one of the most richly gifted peoples

40. Kuyper (note 123) cites his Leiden professor, Johannes H. Scholten, *Geschiedenis der Godsdienst en Wijsbegeerte* (Leiden, 1859), p. 196.

41. Albrecht Ritschl (1822-89), professor of theology at Bonn and Göttingen, was the foremost Protestant systematician of the 1870s and '80s. He was a modernist in method and conclusions, and revived the Kantian mode of grounding and valorizing religion in and for its ethical import.

on earth, profound in spirit, mighty in number, surrounded by natural abundance; a people in no respect inferior to our Western nations but able perhaps to surpass us. Yet that people has been asleep and has long since ceased to have a history of its own. Though a regal people they have been conquered, first by Islam, then by the Mongols, and finally, with very little power, by England. . . . [Despite movements to the contrary,] the ideal man of the Hindu remains that of the Yogi, a disheveled hermit, staring motionless at the sun with a snake's skin around his middle, his naked body covered with coarse hair, wild shrubs growing up around him, and a songless bird building its somber nest on his sacred shoulders.[42]

And what became of Lao-tse's splendid fantasies in China? Sir Balfour, who got to know Taoism by personal observation, laments in his South Place Institute lecture that Taoism has degenerated into "a low and despicable superstition, the worst and lowest form of 'religion', a hocus-pocus and an imposture." Once in Kiang-si province he called on the Chang Fien Shi, high priest of this religion; his holiness directed him in his splendid palace to a room filled with earthen jars, carefully corked and sealed, in which he had magically bottled up hundreds of evil spirits.[43] To what depths of human self-degradation and hideous immorality the Valentinians and Ophites among the Gnostics descended needs no further demonstration. The moral devastation this same mystical pantheism brought about among the Beghards and associates, and in our own country among the nudist cults and antinomian sects, is known to you all from history.[44] It all ended in the "rehabilitation of the flesh," as Hundeshagen labels this fanaticism. All these systems hold that "God is the form of everything that is" — with which the boundary between good and evil collapses. "The will of God determines our disposition, and were a man to commit a thousand mortal sins under the sway of that disposition, he need not even wish that he had *not* committed them."[45] The

42. Kuyper (notes 125-26) cites Karl J. H. Windischmann, *Die Philosophie im Fortgang der Weltgeschichte* (Bonn, 1832), parts 2 and 3, "on the Indian situation in general."

43. Kuyper (notes 127-28) cites Balfour's contribution to the *South Place Institute Lectures*, pp. 55, 71.

44. Kuyper (notes 129-30) cites J. N. Gruber, *Die Ophiten* (Würzburg, 1864) on ancient Gnosticism, and recent Dutch academic literature on sixteenth- and seventeenth-century movements, particularly those associated with Spinozism. He also mentions Percy Bysshe Shelley as a classic case of pantheism's association with dubious morals.

45. Karl Bernard Hundeshagen (1810-72) was a Reformation historian from whose work Kuyper had also gotten acquainted with the *Vindiciae contra Tyrannos* (see *Calvinism and Constitutional Liberties*).

lesson of history is thus alarming enough. Feuerbach once wrote: "Death, eternal supersensual death, is God," and in fact it seems here that everything is slipping into death, both national and moral. Of course this specter calls for further analysis, at least in broad outline. Let me perform that in three gradations: *personal, ecclesiastical,* and *political.*

A thinker who had let himself drift along on the seductive currents of this stream prefaces his translation of one of Herbart's works with this telling testimony: "I allowed myself to be carried away by it," he wrote, "because it promised me peace of mind. But what did it give me? A feeling of powerlessness and lethargy. Then I turned to Herbart and recovered the resilience that I had begun to lose."[46] I understand this completely, for if the boundary between God and the world is removed and in the holy Trinity you can no longer adore the fullness of the richest personal life, the mainspring of your own personal life is bound to break. Only those who can relate to God as their holy Friend deepen the features of their own character. Herbart has put it beautifully: "No longer to feel the need of this friend is to be drawn into such loneliness as only egoism creates in the midst of society, turning the dwelling-place of man into a desert."[47] No firm character can be formed when the chisel is exchanged for a stub. Character calls for strength of conviction, coupled with an energetic will. It demands a sense of calling, along with the faith that you will succeed therein. Precisely these factors of our personality begin to misfunction when the fixed lines of our life-conception melt and you no longer believe in any familiar truth, in any law governing your will, in any God who calls you and levels all obstacles to that calling. Then the downpours and bubbling seepage reduce the well-graveled roadbed on which you're walking to a giant quagmire in which you stumble and slide. Hence the lament, never more general than in our day, about the lack of character, of impressive personalities, of men with wills of steel. One need not be a devotee of bygone days to be saddened by how flat, unexpressive, and impotent we look compared to the striking figures on Rembrandt's canvases.

No, I do not look down my nose at agnosticism. When I hear Tyndall reverently exclaim: "Standing before the power that impinges on me from within the universe, I only dare speak poetically of a *He,* a *Spirit,* or even of a *Cause.* Its mystery overshadows me, but it remains a mystery,"[48] this

46. Kuyper (note 132) cites D. Burger, translator of Jhering's *Kampf ums Recht,* in his foreword to same, p. 1.

47. Kuyper (note 133) cites Herbart, *Philosophische Geschriften* (Leipzig, 1842), vol. III, p. 169.

48. Kuyper (note 134) cites John Tyndall, *Fragments of Science* (London, 1879), p. 336.

agnostic reverence touches me more deeply than the Kantian refrain of God, virtue, and immortality. But don't forget: we are speaking about the clarity of our human consciousness, and the clarity of our thinking is becoming clouded. In England only what someone has measured, weighed, or counted is regarded as science. "He teaches well who distinguishes well" is the disciplinary rule to which our thinking must conform to be conclusive, but it's becoming "he teaches well who mixes all things well." As I mentioned earlier, Hegel had to invent a new logic for this amalgamationist thinking. Naturally, with our thinking clouded, our strength of conviction has to wane. We cloak as modesty that which is basically mere doubt and uncertainty, until finally the thirst for knowledge switches sides with a flirtatious wink in the direction of *not*-knowing. First Du Bois-Reymond proclaims his "ignorabimus" ["We shall not know"], then Spencer pronounces his agnostic axioms.[49] And so not only does philosophy languish and the horizons of science shrink, but in daily life skepticism again takes possession of the human heart, an ever-thickening fog beclouds the clarity of our insights, until finally the spark of holy enthusiasm that can thrive only in clear air and under bright skies is quenched.

Athletics are fine, ladies and gentlemen, and I too was delighted when our batters and bowlers recently returned from England showered with honors. But I would have greater joy to see in the rising generation of our young men enthusiasm for the honor of our history, for our country, and for all that is lovely, pure, and beautiful. Alas, here too the blurring of boundaries blocks the way, not least in the sphere of morality. The word "sin" is deemed too strong; "holy" has been replaced by "well-behaved," "well-behaved" by "decent," and "decent" by "neat," a word descriptive of your clothes, not of you. How could it be otherwise when the boldest thinkers of our age have reduced good and evil to mere difference in degree; when they allow the autonomous subject to legislate the rules of morality, thus robbing every moral concept of its absolute character; when the aesthetic is glorified at the expense of the ethical, and people proclaim from the housetops the theory that the claims of the sensual life must be honored too. Does the boundary between truth and falsehood stand firm? Can we still tell what honesty is? And what is right, if not the rights of the stronger? Who distinguishes between theft and property? Above all, where is the boundary clearly distinguishing guilt from fate, accountability from irresistible inclination? But, of course, Buckle has demonstrated statistically that every year there *must* be so

49. Kuyper (note 137) refers to a speech Eugene Heinrich DuBois-Reymond made at a Leibniz celebration in Berlin, 1872.

many divorces, so many stabbings, so many murders by dagger, so many others by pistol, and so many again by strangulation.[50] It is all one and the same process that restlessly turns the wheel of life from the real to the ideal. No wonder, then, that excise taxes of the less honorable sort are ever going up; that the venal woman is so shamelessly assertive; and that our once proverbial Dutch soundness has become fictitious in the markets of the world.

. . . Ladies and gentlemen, I do not despise our century. God has blessed it with indescribable riches. In many respects it surpasses its predecessor. There are still many *dear* people, *lovable* people, folk who no longer dress in velvet but constantly remind you of it. But I miss the forceful personalities, the great men, the stars of the first order. How these stars, specifically in Leiden, have died, one after the other. Who is Caprivi compared to Von Bismarck?[51] When Gladstone dies, who will succeed him? Alas, the ebb tide is no longer to be denied. Second-rate imitators have replaced the originals, and at their feet gathers the world-weary crowd whose lack of animation their lusterless eye conveys. See the blank stares of boredom, the constant allure of suicide, the ever mounting number of the mentally ill. If you consider how this century began by putting man on ever so high a pedestal and ends by leaving him in a state of utter weariness, then does it not strike you as a soap bubble which, though strikingly beautiful for a second or two, soon proved to be no more than a cloudy drop?

Twice before Europe has known such a period of spiritual atrophy — once under the Roman empire and again at the close of the Middle Ages. Both times the *Church of Christ* took the cripple by the hand and pulled him up so that he walked again, renewed in the strength of life. Hence the question inevitably arises: Will the Church of Christ be able to do this again? Is there not reason for mounting anxiety when you see that, owing to the blurring and eventual obliteration of the boundaries, it is precisely the Church of Christ that is decaying within while being ever more tightly bound without?

Certainly, if there is anyone who is a radical protest against the very idea of evolution, it is he who came down from the Father of lights to manifest himself as God in the flesh. Christ is *the* miracle. Bethlehem struck a breach in the line of human genealogy. The resurrection of Immanuel broke through the natural order. And soon after, when the

50. Kuyper (note 140) cites Henry T. Buckle, *History of the Civilization in England* (Leipzig, 1865).

51. Georg Leo Caprivi (1831-99) had risen through staff positions in the German armed forces to succeed Bismarck as chancellor of Germany, 1890-94.

Church of Christ embarked on its mission in the world, its characteristic imprint was "being *not* of that world." Hence the Church of Christ is *ipso facto* antithetical to the unity-dream of the pantheistic process and denies that salvation can ever be achieved by evolution for a world that is lost in sin. This is its essential character, its very nature. The abandonment of that antithesis entails the loss of its character. The church *has to* stand dualistically over against the unregenerate world. And the moment the boundary that separates her from that natural world vanishes, she ceases to be the Church of Christ.

It is precisely this which the pantheistic trend of our century, and no less sharply the principle of evolution, opposes. Unless the offense of the cross is removed, pantheism cannot triumph; unless the folly of Golgotha is eliminated, the theory of evolution cannot hold. Hence the assertion of the German philosopher that "where education breaks through, there can no longer be a church." Hence Hegel's statement that the state "as the divine will today" must make the church serve its ends until she is finally dissolved in the state. For this reason Rothe threw away his honor as a theologian and committed treason to the church, when he predicted the approaching dissolution of the church into the state. For the same reason the cool determination with which the leading jurists in Germany are forging the shackles by which the church must be chained. From a circle of almost thirty law professors, Jhering among them, came the cry that the Protestant church is "a purely worldly organization"; stronger still, that "the church as legally constituted in the sense of current church law" is nothing but "a part of the world." Thus you see where the erasure of boundaries is taking us, and you are no longer surprised when another jurist, Professor Zorn, dares to write that the church of Christ is nothing more than a religious association and that the current relationship between state and church "rests on the principle of state sovereignty, to which the church too is subordinate."[52]

Still, this would not mean anything if the watch were still at its post within the bosom of the church. But the opposite is true, as you well know. Precisely those who rise to defend the boundaries are driven out across them. All confessional bounds are wiped out by doctrinal liberty openly proclaimed. The church must resemble a secular society as much as possible. Though the bulk of the population has defected from Christ,

52. Kuyper (notes 144-47) cites Hegel's *Philosophie des Rechts* (Berlin, 1832), vol. VIII, pp. 346ff; Rothe, *Theologische Ethik* (Wittenberg, 1869), vol. II, p. 461; Rudolph Sohm, *Kirchenrecht* (1892), in a series *Systematischer Handbuch des Deutschen Rechtswissenschaft*, K. Binding, ed.; and Philipp Zorn, *Lehrbuch des Kirchenrechts* (Stuttgart, 1888), pp. 5, 7.

it still has to be called the "national" church. Even those who no longer believe in a Father in heaven may preach their philosophy as though it were gospel. And where you once hoped that "believing" theologians would oppose this offensive state of affairs, you find that *mediating* theologians of all stripes are rubbing out the confessional boundary and mixing an ever more generous dose of their philosophical wine with the real thing, as if bent on obliterating in the very heart of the Christian mysteries the boundary separating God's holy revelation from the operations of our clouded reason.

Therefore, we must not count on these quarters for any support in resisting what Hermann calls the "spiritual disintegration" of our age. So long as church leaders prize the ideal of *tohu wa bohu,* our people will not receive from their hands either unassailable moral principles, or profound spiritual convictions, or steadfast general concepts.[53] Yet the restoration of just such a fixed starting point, a religious and moral "place to stand," may be the only means of rescue still available to our generation, also in view of the coming social storms that our political meteorologists are predicting. To speak concretely: restore belief *in a final judgment.* As long as you hold on to this belief you may calmly behold the constant violation of right in the world — violation perpetrated by the criminal but also by the law and the judge — since your own sense of right can still rest in the justice of your God who will some day arise to avenge it. But if you accept the pantheistic half-truth that "the history of the world is the judgment of the world" [*die Weltgeschichte ist das Weltgerichte*], you must secularize your concept of right; that is, you recognize no other legality than that which the government creates and enforces, subject to constant modification. Established law being thus always in process, you destroy the majesty of right in the eyes of those who will live under it. And so it has happened. Von Stahl himself confines legality within the boundaries of our human household and fails to see how it arises primordially from religion, how all ethical right is rooted in God's rightful religious claim on his creation. All this follows from Kant's partially correct attempt to lift up legality as the shield of liberty, or from Fichte's attempt to assign its rise to the conflict between the two egos. Already Hegel degraded the right to a morality of a lower order. According to Jhering it originates in a "teleological impulse of society." Still others cobble it together in Darwinian fashion as a mechanical product of ex-

53. Kuyper does not give a precise citation of the "Hermann" he mentions. The Hebrew phrase is a quotation of Gen. 1:2: "[The earth was] formless and void. . . ."

ternal historical factors, while the later disciples of Herbart perceive it as the jar of oil which the sailor pours out upon the seething waves to ward off threats to ship and crew.[54]

However endless these variations, common to them all is the idea that absolute right is validated only by the state as the instrument of society. Unfortunately, to none of these figures, with the exception of Von Stahl, is the power of the state a constant. Party succeeds party in gaining the upper hand — Napoleon is replaced by Bourbon, Bourbon by Orleans, Orleans again by Napoleon III, seizing authority by turns because they are temporarily the *stronger.* Rule in the state thus in fact goes to those with *power,* and in this stronger party the right of the stronger celebrates its dubious triumph not only *de facto* but also *in theory.* With that falls the boundary that divides civil authority as the power ordained by God from the people, the society, subordinated by God to that authority. Both are swallowed up in the one all-sufficient state, and that state puts itself in the place of God. The state becomes the highest power and at the same time the source of all right. Government no longer exists because of sin, but the state exists as the supreme ideal of human society, a state before whose apotheosis every knee must bow, by whose grace everyone must live, to whose word everyone must be subject, . . . the one all-providing state in which all human energy is channeled and seeks to come into its own.[55]

In this process, ladies and gentlemen, lurks a double and most serious danger. However eloquently people have reasoned away the boundary between the power that rules and the people who must obey, that duality nevertheless exists. It is a duality that necessarily produces a twofold struggle: on the one hand, the struggle of the state ever to expand its power over the people; on the other, the struggle of the people to gain control over the state. On the one hand, a creeping absolutism; on the other, looming anarchy. Thus people are already raising the question whether constitutional law has not had its day and whether the parliamentary system has not outlived its usefulness. The next step would

54. Kuyper (notes 153-55) cites Friedrich Julius von Stahl, *Die Philosophie des Rechts* (Heidelberg, 1870), vol. II, p. 192. He adds copious quotation and argumentation as to where Calvinist theory must differ from this conservative Lutheran view which, in Kuyper's estimation, values Hegel's "material principle" too highly, however critical it is of his logic. He also cites works on jurisprudence of Hegel, Kant, Fichte, Schelling, and Jhering.

55. Kuyper (note 158) asserts that, over against this formulation, Calvinist jurisprudence rests on the maintenance of three boundaries: (1) between the people and political authority (he uses "Overheid," not "Staat"), (2) between that authority and God, (3) between God's law and that instituted by political authority.

be to raise on the ruins of our civil liberties a government of Schleiermacher's virtuosos, that is, of academics and geniuses — a reprise of our old miserable Regency, this time in scientific garb.

Of course, the people will balk at this. After all, the boundaries have been obliterated; why still honor the *high* and treat the *low* as minors? Is not rich and poor a contrast which, all distinctions having vanished, shocks your much lauded harmony? Why should I comply when authority finds no grounds in my conscience and the right is no longer rooted in eternal principles? Power arises from the state? Well, then, we are the people and we, millions of us, constitute the state. Ours, therefore, is the power to re-create the right, and we will legislate it for you in such a way that all our demands will be met.

What now, you mighty of the earth, you sweet singers of the state's apotheosis: what will you oppose to this raw nihilistic cry? Conscience? You have disabled it. Moral concepts? You have rendered them fluid. The fear of judgment? You yourselves laugh at it. The majesty of the law? You have desecrated it. The influence of the church? You have destroyed it. Finally nothing, nothing, is left to you but your power. The entire edifice you have built up rests on raw power. With that power you can for some time yet offer resistance, for your armies are more powerful than ever and fearful is the devastation they can inflict. But woe to you when the cancer finally reaches the vitals of your armies. Then it's all over. Before the sun has set on that day of wrath, the people you have armed will strike down your enthralling power at a single blow. Having utterly crushed you, they will then taunt you: there are no boundaries, it's all Evolution! What have we done but bring on an inevitable phase in your pantheistic process?

Some time ago Max Müller pictured the Nirvana of the yogi as an extinguished lamp.[56] It is to such a social Nirvana that I see the nations of Europe heading if nothing stops the ongoing erosion of boundaries. When the boundary between arteries and muscle tissue is disrupted in a human body, the decomposition of the corpse follows with an inevitability that nothing can stop.

III

Ladies and gentlemen, some twenty years ago France was not saved by indiscriminately arming the mob, nor by Gambetta's wild cry that not a square inch of ground or a stone of the fortress should be surrendered.

56. Kuyper (note 160) cites Max Muller, *Biographical Essays,* p. 242.

No escape was possible through the iron net that Von Moltke had stretched around France. Thus at Frankfurt, in the old imperial city, the French capitulated. Yet France was not finished. When it finally came to its senses it followed Prussia's example after the battle of Jena.[57] It forcibly restrained its chauvinism, applied itself to discipline and restoring its inner strength, and soon proved to possess such resilience that Germany's emperor began to feel uneasy and asked for an additional 90,000 men per year to protect his borders. Does not this offer a lesson for us as we come to my final question: *what resistance can we offer?*

For the present situation of believing Christianity is not unlike that of France after Sedan and Gravelotte. The assault we had to endure has been nowhere successfully repulsed. Fortress after fortress has been surrendered. Time after time there has been treason in our ranks. Drunk with delight, the enemy is already predicting the day of our total defeat. And I cannot fault him, for I too am ashamed of the cowardliness and lack of wisdom on the Christian side in its struggle against unbelief over the last hundred plus years. If there is anything that could strengthen my faith that One greater than we has fought for his people, it is the surprising fact that, despite so reprehensible a resistance, our strength has not diminished but has grown much stronger.

I will say nothing of the humbug. Thank God, the hollow phrases with which a smug stupidity imagined for a moment to demolish a Strauss, disarm a Darwin, or put a Kuenen out of action have died away to the last echo.[58] . . . As always happens with cowardly, ignorant pride, of ten people who once protested so shrilly, perhaps eight have now joined the movement of unbelief. No, when I speak of the resistance offered thus far, I'm not thinking of that ineffectual yapping but have in mind serious efforts put forth to rescue endangered positions by people flying the colors of the *defender*, the *broker*, or with the mark of the *amphibian* on their shields.

In the role of *defender* a series of men first tried *apologetics*. As often as a bulwark or outwork was under attack, the defenders rushed to the area to answer each shot from the enemy with a shot of their own. Wherever the enemy appeared the defenders followed; however often

57. Kuyper is referring to the Franco-Prussian War (1870-71), a definitive historical marker for him. Gravelotte (18 August 1870) was its opening battle; at Sedan (2 September) the French Emperor Napoleon III was surrounded along with his armies by a Prussian strategy devised by Helmuth von Moltke. This was a reversal of the French triumph under Napoleon I at Jena (1806). The French defeat gave rise to the revolutionary Paris Commune, led by Leon Gambetta.

58. Abraham Kuenen (1828-91) was a preeminent Dutch Modernist and professor of Old Testament at Leiden.

they came home bloodied, they remained unbowed; with awesome patience they crossed lance with lance, struck sword on sword, whetted dagger against dagger. But no matter how hard they struck back, they gained nothing; for on the heels of one host of objections — held back only for a moment — came another army of yet weightier grievances. All the while they had allowed the enemy to determine the plan of campaign, were of necessity reduced to hopeless confusion, and found themselves finally cut off from their own base of operation. You know the outcome of this kind of apologetic resistance. It was as if some rustic militia were fighting the Prussian guard. Hence the endless series of concessions, till at last even the bravest fighter, thoroughly demoralized, lost courage.

With this sad spectacle before them, small wonder that our *mediating* theologians felt more attracted to the role of the *broker*, or of the *middleman* as our German neighbors call him. All too innocently our apologists had ventured upon an unequal struggle. Men of deeper insight, a more lenient mindset, and more philosophical erudition saw the futility of such fumbling and, being irenic by nature, opted for spiritual *negotiation*. So they marched onto the field carrying the white flag before them and at the approach of the enemy ordered the trumpeter to blow a *pax vobiscum*. They promptly informed the men of the modern worldview that they felt so warm a sympathy for modern life and such contempt for the old school that they would count it an honor to march alongside the Modernists, provided the name of Christ might be stitched in their banner and the cross embellish the top of their standards. That condition having been met, the negotiations turned out to be eminently successful. "Modern-orthodox," a truly pantheistic combination, was to be the name of this new auxiliary corps. And so we saw the heroes who should rescue our faith performing sapper services for the *zeitgeist*, charged with removing "the obstacles of orthodoxy" from among the common people, first in the countryside and further among ladies of class.

The position of the middleman soon lost its appeal, however, so then we saw men marching to the front with the sign of the *amphibian* etched on their shields.[59] . . . Head and heart, thinking and willing, had to be separated. "Value judgment" was the magic formula that could save you from every dilemma. Thus emerged the race of spiritual amphibians who playfully dived into the depths of modern waters and then again nimbly scaled the riverbanks to graze along with others in the lush clover of pious Christianity. But, of course, this could hardly be called "resistance." A basic dualism yields no system. Besides, Christianity is

59. Kuyper (notes 164-66) cites Friedrich H. Jacobi (1743-1819), Herbart, and Rudolph Hermann Lotze (1817-81) as typical of this position.

unalterably a revealed historic religion that confronts us at every step of the way with *concepts* that call for analysis and with *facts* for which you must make room in your cosmos.

However highly I value the intent of these three kinds of fighters, however great a debt I owe to their specialized research, I could not let myself be incorporated in their ranks. Not with the *apologists* because no argument will avail where Reason is both a party to the dispute and its judge. Nor with the *middlemen* because they exhaust their energies in making a monstrous marriage, and hybrids tend not to reproduce themselves. But even less with our spiritual *dualists,* because logic and ethics together have only one mind at their disposal, and all such divisions of the estate end up in the hypertrophy of the head and the atrophy of the heart.

Consistently, where resistance has proven effective, another and much safer road has been taken. God called Abraham from Ur, separated Israel from the nations, and thus, *in the midst of life itself,* threw up a dam against the flood of paganism. Christ came and formed amidst Israel a *distinct community* which, by being separated from the world, was empowered to overcome the spirit of that world. Once again in the sixteenth century people retreated to a *terrain of their own making* to regain their strength in *that separate circle* and thus by a *fact of life* and by *living deeds,* not by theories or phrases, to fortify themselves for the coming struggle. To just this Von Stein summoned Prussia after Jena, and just this is restoring France today.[60] With a view to our own struggle, I mean that those who still have faith and discern the danger of blurring the boundaries must start by drawing a line around *their own circle,* must develop *a life of their own* within that circle, must *render account* for the life thus constituted, and so acquire the maturity needed for the struggle they must at some point accept.

This is the only method that has passed the crucial test as often as it was consistently followed. It is the method Rome never abandoned and will prove to be the only rational one today as well. For how did pantheism, how did evolution acquire such unprecedented power? Certainly not because of Kant or Hegel, Darwin or Haeckel, as if one man could ever transform the mind of his time without being himself a child of that time.[61] No: toward the end of the last century the general outlook, the

60. Heinrich F. K. von Stein (1757-1831) led Prussia's resurgence after its defeat by Napoleon at Jena (1806), effecting both domestic reforms and the international alliance that defeated Napoleon at Leipzig (1813).

61. Kuyper (note 171) adds: "Men who are ahead of their time, like Socrates, drink the poison; men who are products of their time, like Hegel, are apotheosized. The Cross of Golgotha and Hebrews 11 are definitive here. See, regarding the deification of Hegel, Goethe, *Satyros,* 4th Act."

psychic tone, the set of the human heart, *all of life* down to its innermost promptings had risen up in rebellion against the boundaries God has appointed. Pantheism was in the air people breathed. Hegel and Darwin as children of their age only fostered the birth of the monster that our age had long carried in its womb. Therefore even exhausting yourself in a battle of words will not avail. So powerful a *life*-movement can be successfully countered only by the movement of an antithetical *life.* Over against those who blur the boundaries in life and in consciousness you yourself must posit a life with sharply defined characteristics. Over against the slithering fluidities of pantheism, the clear statement of a sincerely held confession. Over against the elevation of the word of the world, the absolute authority of Scripture. Only thus can you regain your own base of operations and give rise to a *reality* which already as such exerts influence on your environment. Only thus can you fortify a line of defense that makes it possible for you to postpone the battle until a time when, after quiet maturation, you have sharpened your weapons and trained your troops. Finally, only in this way is revived the holy comradeship, the confidence in your own cause, and the enthusiasm for the colors of your own glorious flag which redoubles the strength of any army.

I do not hide the frightening sacrifices this approach requires. It forces you to break with much that is attractive. It cuts off frequently fascinating contact with some of the nobler pagans. You pay a heavy price for it. Much worse, if you are firm and act boldly, it will bring down on you all kinds of family grief and make it very hard to find a lifelong post for yourself and your children. But with Scriptures before me I say: this sacrifice *must* be made. "Whoever loves father or mother more than me is not worthy of me" [Matt. 10:37]. Christ did not come to bring peace in a pantheistic sense but to bring division, that is, *to draw a line that no one can expunge* between those who seize the hem of his garment and those who reject him. Thus you may never accuse this system of exclusivism. Those are so guilty who arrogantly draw a *false* boundary and so separate what belongs together. But the system I recommend is above this reproach precisely because when the boundary is determined by your deepest life conviction, the system of putting people in boxes is condemned and all false partitions collapse.[62] Nor has this system anything in common with self-isolation from fear of the outside world. Calvinists have never been enchanted with the Anabaptist ideal of living with "a

62. Kuyper (note 173) adds: "I stress this strongly. All sorts of false boundaries have been drawn that I would not defend in the least but would rejoice to see erased. In each case it should be "separate what does not belong together and bring together what is united by principle, both in Church and State."

book in a nook." Besides, living in a house of one's own by no means precludes going out onto the thoroughfares of life. And, to repeat, we would retreat behind our defenses so as to improve our weapons and be ready for battle.

There is but one claim that none of us can deny. You must bear with our being *believers*. Just as you sting us by casting yourselves as "the enlightened" and "civilized," demeaning us as the "non-*thinking* part of the nation," so you must bear the sting of our setting ourselves apart as "believers" from you as the "non-*believing* part of the nation." But, then, that is precisely the issue. To preserve that boundary we are prepared to risk the whole outcome of our life. You deny the fall into sin; for us that fall is real. Consequently you *cannot* acknowledge a boundary established by the entrance of grace, while for us it is nothing less than the passage from death into life.

I must add something here. We have been taught by the word of God that sin not only spoiled the will and misdirected the mind but also *darkened the intellect;* conversely that palingenesia not only converts the will and transforms the mind but also uniquely illumines our consciousness.[63] Those who believe receive not only another impression of *life* but are also reoriented in the world of *thought*. I cannot explain to you better than from a passage in Augustine's famous "interrogatory." Augustine had once been a pantheist himself, unable to conceive God other than as inherent in matter. But when the Spirit took hold of him and turned his inner eye away from the "sufferable Jesus" of the Manicheans and toward the Man of Sorrows, then, with the same ears with which he heard particles of light crackling in a plant's leaf and stem, he now heard the very different speech of creation. Then, he wrote in his *Confessions* [X, 6]:

> I again interrogated the earth, and it replied, *"I am not he,"* and everything that grew upon the earth echoed that confession. I interrogated the sea and the deeps and the living things that creep and they also replied: "*We are not your God;* look for him above us." I interrogated the winds that howled around me but all the sky with its armies of birds replied: "philosophy is in error: *we are not your God.*" I interrogated the sun, the moon, the twinkling stars, but they repeated: "Nor are we the God whom you are looking for." Then I spoke to all the creatures surrounding me: "You say: 'we are not your God'; then tell me *something* of my God." Thereupon, with a loud voice, they cried out in unison: *"It is he who made us."*

63. Kuyper (note 174) explains: "Palingenesia means rebirth [or regeneration]. I deliberately use the Greek word because in Scripture it covers both personal rebirth (Tit. 3:5) and the re-creation of heaven and earth (Matt. 19:28)."

Solemn and splendid, ladies and gentlemen. Augustine *was* now another person and so he both *heard* and *thought* differently. Now he heard the voice of God speaking to him in Scripture, and therein our people too know themselves of one mind with Monica's great son. We, too, bow our heads before that Word, and so too Scripture draws a boundary line between us who are encamped behind it and you who live on the other side of it. I have often been told: you cannot possibly mean that. A pious old lady, maybe, but not a man of learning. Someone who lost his manners once yelled at me: "You do not believe the things you say. You are a fraud." Naturally, those who are not stupid *have to* agree with you or else you will suspect our sincerity. To us this is an old song.[64]

But you will have to grant this: Faith in Scripture can never be the result of criticism. Otherwise no one could ever have believed, for criticism is still incomplete. And how could Scripture have ever awakened faith in the hearts of humble people who understand nothing of criticism? Though it is completely correct that all sorts of objections and difficulties confront us in Scripture, difficulties that so far as I am concerned are by no means resolved, still these questions do not hold me up or trouble me, because my stance is different. None less than Kant in 1794 chastised the "arrogance of geniuses" who imagined they had outgrown this norm of faith, and added these weighty words: "If ever the Scriptures as we now have them should lose their authority, a like authority could never again emerge, for a miracle like that of Scriptural authority cannot repeat itself, simply because the loss of confidence in the Scriptures which for so many centuries held firm would a priori deprive any newly emerging authority of credit."[65]

Long ago when I read that statement, I felt the deep truth of it. In Scripture we confront a cedar tree of spiritual authority that for eighteen centuries has pushed its roots into the soil of our human consciousness;

64. Kuyper (note 179) sympathetically quotes (from Kaatz, p. 81) Nietzsche's response to similar slurs; gives an extensive citation also from Alfred Boegner, *Quelques Réflexions sur l'autorité en matière de foi* (Paris, 1892); then adds this personal note: "When I recently returned with heart deeply stirred from the funeral of my youngest child [Willy, who died 27 July 1892], I found at home a letter from an old university acquaintance. It accused me as sharply and grossly as possible of being insincere, a swindler and deceiver who could not mean what I professed. Why did this letter make so deep an impression on me? Because, in that most serious moment at the grave, I had just asked myself again whether what I professed before God and man was really true. To the glory of God's grace I may say that my heart found complete rest in our glorious confession."

65. Kuyper (note 180) cites Kant's *Der Streit der Fakultäten,* in *Sammtliche Werke* (Leipzig, 1838), vol. X, p. 323.

in its shadow the religious and moral life of humanity has immeasurably increased in dignity and worth. Now chop that cedar down. For a little while some green shoots will still bud out from its trunk, but who will give us another tree, who will provide future generations with a shade like this? This is why — *not* as a consequence of erudition but with the naiveté of the little child — I have bowed my head in simple faith before that Scripture, have devoted my energies to its cause, and now rejoice inwardly and thank God when I see faith in that Scripture again increasing. You know that I am not conservative, but this indeed is *my* conservatism: I will attempt to save the abundant cover of that cedar for our people, so that in the future they will not sit down in a scorching desert without shade. Just as my Savior believed in Moses and the prophets, so and in no other way do I wish to believe in the Scriptures. For whoever charges Christ with error in the matter of the Scriptures by that token violates the very mystery on which the entire church of Christ is based — denying that he is our Lord but also *our God*.

You are clear, then, on the purport of the system I am arguing for. A *life-sphere* of our own on the foundation of *palingenesia,* and a *life-view* of our own thanks to the light that the Holy Spirit kindles on the candelabra of Scripture. Not in the least, then, a passive group of pious mystics, but our own principle for our own higher learning, deriving from that principle our own conviction, and seeking to apply that conviction to life in all its rich fullness. For that reason we could not sit still but had to propagate our conviction among our children and grandchildren. We therefore had to support our own Christian nurture in the home by means of our own Christian school. Nor could we stop there, for a group of people, however devout, is powerless and unarmed if from its own midst it does not also produce men who have penetrated the higher spheres of human consciousness and can participate with manly courage in the debate about the higher interests of humanity. Thus the Christian elementary school soon called for gymnasia of our own, and the circle of believers could not properly stop short of founding a university of their own. For human life is never fully developed as long as you have not explained that life to the satisfaction of your own *thinking,* that is, *scientifically*.

It is certainly true that not all believers have joined in a *common confession* and that where unity of confession is lacking, cooperation in realizing this system is precluded. But it follows from the system that not only we Calvinists should form a circle of our own but that every other group of believers in the nation do the same. Specifically, the fundamental line of demarcation which separates our confession from that of Rome may not be abandoned for a moment. But the main goal toward which our system aims cannot suffer on this account. For even granting that two or more circles may be formed, you nevertheless continue to occupy your position in *life itself.* You constitute a force in *reality,* and precisely in that *reality* your principle will find well-prepared soil from which it will draw the sap of life. Every other system of defense amounts to a conflict of *opinions,* a wrestling with abstract *concepts,* a battle decided in a clever *phrase.* Thereby people self-indulgently avoid a much more costly *life-struggle* by raising the deceptive pantheistic cry that "truth will take care of itself" or that "nothing is *made* but everything has to *grow.*" Fancy theories — as if by that false standard there would ever have arisen an Israel in Canaan, a Christ in Bethlehem, a Calvinism in the Netherlands.

If, on the other hand, you should succeed in forming two or more powerful circles in your country or nation, which would each eventually achieve its own scholarly development; circles in whose midst the firm belief that "God created heaven and earth" would banish every pantheistic proposition, and the confession "born of the virgin Mary" would exorcise the system of evolution; a circle in which the Word of God is the authority before which everyone bowed and in which, because of that Word, all divinely ordained authority, every sacred commandment and holy ordinance were respected — then, ladies and gentlemen, there *would* be resistance, a spontaneously working force that blessed the entire nation and made itself felt in church, state, and society by virtue of the reality of your conduct and the fact of your existence. To sum it all up: . . . there is only one kind of resistance worth offering, but one that the whole of past history gives the promise of victory. It is this: that you draw a sharp, clear line between the circle of your life and that of *Evolution* and within that circle, awed by the majesty of the Lord, respect every boundary He has established.

Ladies and gentlemen: "In isolation lies your strength" was the marvelous maxim, short and pithy, bequeathed to the spiritual descendants of Calvin by our beloved Groen van Prinsterer. In this past hour you have listened to his grateful pupil give the material argument for this pregnant motto. May you thereby better appreciate its meaning, its allure, and its persuasive power.

And if at times you fear that by this maxim, with this system, you are giving up all poetry to pantheism and cosmic unity to evolution, then listen to how from the homes of the righteous in all ends of the earth there arises one voice, one summons. It gathers up and fuses together the animate and inanimate, the thinking and the non-thinking in a single outpouring of delighted acclaim, as the ancient harpist leads them in singing of a God "who has established an order for his creatures, an order no creature will transgress" [Ps. 148:6]. To the accompaniment of cymbals, all may sing these inspired words:

> Praise the Lord, you heavens, and you waters above the heavens!
> Praise the Lord from the earth, sea monsters and all ocean depths.
> Praise him, hills and mountains,
> wild animals and all cattle,
> fruit trees and all cedars,
> You kings of the earth and all peoples,
> young men and young women, old and young together.
> Let them all praise the name of the Lord!
> For he has raised up a horn for his people,
> the praise of all his faithful, of the people who are close to him.
> Hallelujah! [Ps. 148:4-14]

Evolution

Kuyper delivered this rectorial address on 20 October 1899, under grave signs and portents. His wife had died in Switzerland just two months earlier; the Boer War, with its high stakes for his national sentiments, had commenced days before; and the recent headlines in Europe, which he evokes in his opening pages, were of imperialism, anti-Semitism, and the slaughter of the Armenians. The ebbing away of the century only reinforced a mood Kuyper had been carrying throughout the 1890s.

But if the speech starts out on a morbid note, it ends by invoking faith and creation; even Pantheism, which had looked so bad in 1892, now had some spiritual luster. Given the missteps the orthodox crusade against Evolution took so often, Kuyper's choice of focus is striking to see. He does not invoke literalistic readings of early Genesis, does not fantasize about Flood geology, and does not argue theology at all. He offers some tantalizing points of contact between evolutionary theory and Christian, especially Calvinist, convictions. He lets God be God and greets "affirmatively, without reservation," the possibility that Creation proceeded by evolution over extremely long time and by one species producing another. He takes the fight instead to the level of philosophical framework, where science as science relinquishes its authority and theologians might speak with at least as strong a warrant as such dogmatic naturalists as Herbert Spencer and Ernst Haeckel. Kuyper's satire on Spencer's formulation of evolutionary law is reminiscent of William James's, and has a similar target: the monistic mechanics that are reductive of human freedom and liable to a cult of power.

Yet Kuyper diverged from James on the ultimate question. If James would "Damn the Absolute!" Kuyper would praise it, so long as it was the God of

Notes appended with [Ed.] or parts of notes [in brackets] are the editor's addition; the rest are Kuyper's originals.

Scripture. Kuyper was hardly one to accuse others of monism, and the relish with which he pitted Christianity vs. Evolution as "system" vs. "system" could not always do justice to important nuances in the science or the faith. Kuyper also made the classic mistake of resting too much of his case on lacunae that science had not filled but soon would: in this case, on the problem of genetic transmission that Gregor Mendel had already solved, unbeknownst even to most scientists. Kuyper's continuing commitment to philosophical organicism could confuse the issue when carried over to technical science, as he did.[1]

Still, the breadth of his reading and command of the issues are remarkable and overshadow the efforts of a good many advocates on both sides of the debate in the twentieth century. Kuyper discerned what in Evolution is worldview masquerading as empirical fact, discerned its ethical import, and identified what remain for Christians the nonnegotiable points of difference.

The material here represents approximately 90 percent of Kuyper's original (*Evolutie: Rede . . . op 20 October 1899 gehouden door Abraham Kuyper* [Amsterdam: Höveker & Wormser, 1899]) as translated by George Kamp on the initiative of Clarence Menninga. Walter Lagerwey reviewed and revised that translation, and Menninga prepared it for publication in the *Calvin Theological Journal* 31/1 (April 1996): 11-50. The German passages in the piece were translated by Wallace Bratt; the Greek and Latin expressions by George Harris.

My thanks to John Bolt, the *Journal*'s editor, for permission to reprint the piece here. Besides deleting some technical material (which is available in the *Journal* text), I have made some stylistic changes consistent with other pieces in this volume. In particular, I have sometimes literally reproduced Kuyper's usage of "Evolution-system" or "-doctrine" rather than using Lagerwey's more mellifluous "system" or "teaching of evolution" so as to underscore a point Kuyper is trying to make.

Kuyper could not fully annotate his speech owing to his wife's death. He did include some forty-nine footnotes, indicated below, but his reading manuscript has markings for about seventy more. I have supplemented his notes with additional materials and commentary, some of which were provided by Clarence Menninga, who also fleshed out Kuyper's short bibliographical references.

1. As Clarence Menninga notes, Western science maintained a sharp distinction between living and non-living matter well into the nineteenth century, premised upon the "vital force" the former was thought to contain. Kuyper's "organic" vs. "inorganic" usage evokes that distinction, as does his frequent contrast between "mechanistic" and "organic principles." The professional scientific community — but not religious and philosophical commentators — had largely abandoned the notion of vital force by 1899. [Ed.]

I

Our nineteenth century is dying away under the hypnosis of the dogma of Evolution. To be sure, both in our country and elsewhere Christian action has developed greater resiliency than has seemed possible since the time of the Reformation, but while rapidly gaining ground, this action until now has been almost exclusively *practical* and *mystical* in character. At the center of the life of human consciousness, i.e., in science, in literature, and in the press, leadership has remained largely in the hands of intellectuals with a Christless perspective. Although there are some indications of a change in this respect, and our university too is trying to hasten this change, it cannot be denied that in the sphere of higher thinking Christian presuppositions serve only sporadically as the lodestar. What is more, the influence of the time-honored Christian mind has diminished rapidly in the thinking of this century, and for that the hypnosis of the Evolution-dogma is especially to blame.

Previously the higher learning that rejected Christ preferred to deal with the empirically observable and left the mystically incomprehensible to religion and mysticism, but there has been a decided change in this regard over the last quarter of this century. The dogma of evolution appeared with the pretension that, by means of its monistic mechanics, it could explain the entire cosmos, including all life processes within that cosmos, to the very earliest origins. The principle that the adherents of evolution profess is *absolute*. Not only is all research in the natural sciences forced to follow that principle, but from the same principle Herbert Spencer in his *Data* derived ethics and Haeckel of Jena in his *Monismus als Band zwischen Religion und Wissenschaft*[2] derived religion. It may be said without exaggeration that precisely this *absolute* character of Evolution

2. Ernst Haeckel, *Der Monismus als Band zwischen Religion und Wissenschaft*, 8e ausgabe (Bonn: E. Strauss, 1899). [Kuyper does not include the reference to Herbert Spencer, *The Data of Ethics* (London, 1879). Haeckel may have been particularly in Kuyper's sights because of his pretentious international bestseller of 1899, *Die Weltrathsel: Gemeinverstandliche Studien über monistische Philosophie* (E.T.: *The Riddle of the Universe at the Close of the Nineteenth Century*). The year also saw the publication of the racist Social Darwinian Houston Stuart Chamberlain, *The Foundations of the Nineteenth Century*, which would become a fascist scripture.]

A caricature and a momento of Kuyper's mood of mortality at century's end. *Above:* The 1890s fad of bicycle racing pits Kuyper against Death. *Facing page:* Kuyper's youngest son Willy, who died at age 9 in 1892.

explains the audacious questioning of the received truths of Christianity increasingly evident in modernist circles.

Until now we in our Christian circles had the inspiration of a faith that bound all things into a unity, giving us an advantage over our opponents. They languished spiritually in the diaspora of their Unknowable [*Ignorabimus*]. But thanks to the dogma of evolution they too now possess an all-encompassing system, a world-and-life view derived from a single principle. They too now have a ground-dogma, and they cling to that dogma with unshakeable faith. The human spirit cannot get by for long without an answer to questions concerning the origin, the essence, and the future of things. Until now having such an answer was our strength over against the unproven claims of the intelligentsia. But precisely *this* advantage is now lost to us. In the bright glow of the Evolu-

tion-dogma, our opponents are no longer embarrassed by any of these questions. Raving on about their new discovery, most of them look down pityingly, if not arrogantly, on anyone who still holds to the old ground-dogma of Christianity and swears by the faith of the fathers in Him who created heaven and earth.

Unfortunately, the high exultation at this newfound Monism comes into a painful and mounting conflict with bitter reality. The emergence of a new faith has usually gone hand in hand with a certain elevation, a certain ennobling of human life. So it was when Christianity appeared, and so also in the days of the Reformation. This time, however, the "new faith" is closely followed by the shadow of Decadence.

A century's cherished expectation of "liberty, equality, and fraternity" has proven increasingly to be of the sort of which Schiller sang:

On 25 August 1899, while vacationing in Switzerland, Johanna Schaay Kuyper died. The figure of death that Kuyper saw lowering in the theory of evolution and in the close of the century was therefore personally close as well. The next week he published this meditation in *De Heraut.*

When What Is Mortal Is Swallowed Up by Life

"For while we are in this tent, we groan and are burdened, because we do not wish to be unclothed but to be clothed with our heavenly dwelling, so that what is mortal may be swallowed up by life."
(2 Cor. 5:4, KJV)

Given what lies before your eyes at the time of death, you can only say that Death, the fearful enemy of God and man, finally succeeds in swallowing up a life so precious to you.

This was not the first assault. At least it is exceptional when someone dies who has not been ill before with the fear of death hanging in the sickroom. But those earlier assaults had been turned

"The ideals that once swelled our ecstatic hearts have dissipated." With the passing of this century, humanity gloomily stares at the rising supremacy of materialistic tendencies, of eagerness for sensual pleasures, of the passion of money-power, and of a violent passion for material *expansion.* The Peace Conference in The Hague[3] accomplished little more than to bring into sharp relief the gap between the high ideals of so many and hard, brutal reality. Bismarck's name remains linked with the slogan "might above right." Rudyard Kipling strewed the evil seed of Caesarism in the hearts of the English people and, unless God forbids, proud Transvaal threatens to become its prey. The English nation, once so keen for right, is increasingly charmed by the evil disposition "to fight everybody and to take everything." Three hundred thousand Armenian Christians have been slaughtered by Islam's fanaticism, and even our government has pigheadedly rejected the Armenian exiles. America, once a noble land, is now playing the crude, cruel game in the Philippines for which it

3. The first Peace Conference at The Hague met from 18 May through 29 July 1899. It failed in its main objective of reducing levels of armaments, but it did prohibit certain types of weapons and established a permanent court of arbitration. [Ed.]

away. After a night of weeping that made our hearts weak, joy came in the morning. Having reached its apex, the illness subsided again. What an inexpressible luxury, to get a loved one back from the brink of death.

But this time things turned out very differently. Nothing helped. Nothing was of any use. When that last bit of breath expired it was as if Death mocked you with all your unheard prayers and pointless anxieties. It whispered derisively: "I won; your morning of joy will *never* come."

And there you stood with broken heart by the deathbed. There lay your deceased, lifeless, inanimate, for all the world as if she had been *swallowed up* by death. Swallowed up — a hard word. Devoured, as if by a beast of prey. All at once, gone: the look of the eye, the sweet words, the warm handclasp, the facial expression. Everything clean gone: cold, withered, somber. Life swallowed up by death.

Those without a choice see it that way. Those who know only this world cannot see it any other way. And let's be honest: in that first hard moment when a shock passes through the heart, the child of God sees it that way too. It is a dreadfully gloomy thing to stare

attacked Spain in Cuba. Entire nations are garbed in military uniforms, and the fruit of their labors is consumed in formidable batteries of Maxims and heavily armored fortifications. Small nations like the Netherlands perceive how the guarantee of their national independence is shrinking. In Africa men control "spheres of influence" wide as the sky, a "hinterland" whose boundaries are not given on the best maps. In China entire provinces are being leased out as only house and field have been hitherto. Many a jurist refuses to acknowledge as Right anything but that which is defined by law. A trial in France, not unlike that of Jean Calas, has amazed the world by its violation of justice. Serbia has displayed a more brazen abuse yet.[4] Nearly everywhere people sense and say that parliamentary glory is on the wane to clear the way for a new autocracy, if not a new despotism. Increasingly, bullfights enchant the highly cultivated

4. The Dreyfus Affair in France had come to a peak in August-September 1899 with the captain's second trial. One of his principal accusers had committed suicide in August 1898 after being exposed for fraud. The Serbian reference is to its authoritarian government's use of an attempt on the life of army commander H. M. King Milan to persecute dissenters. [Ed.]

into the dark emptiness of the valley of the shadow of death as we watch a dearly loved one enter there. Death is there, hauling away its prey before our eyes; and we are there, compelled to watch it happen, overcome by pain and helplessness.

But *that* is reality — the bitter reality of death in the visible world. To deceive yourself by hiding that hard reality behind funeral wreaths and flowers, to imagine that you can comfort the bereaved with generalities about God's providential love is cowardice. You're not serious, you lack courage, if you use a blindfold to hide the harshness of death from yourself and others.

You prayed, but God did *not* hear your prayer. Despite your prayer, death won. But is not God almighty? Where is that providential love when He lets death have its way — worse, *sends* it to you and *abandons* your suffering one to it?

No. Say rather that death came on account of sin and by sin. Let your conscience be touched, and acknowledge that God's fearful wrath was at work in that process of dying. That way at least you can tremble before God's holiness. But to babble about providential love when God lets bitter death rob you of the dearest thing you had on earth, when

French people. The call for bread and circuses, the dissolution of the marriage bond, and so much more create the perception that the decline and fall of the Roman empire is being repeated on an even more terrible scale in our highly touted age. Withal, one encounters dwindling enthusiasm and coolness toward higher concerns, over against which neither the rise of asceticism in small circles nor the passion for sports is much consolation.

If only we could say that the Evolution-system took a stand, at least in principle, against this physical violence and usurpation of power — but just the opposite is true. The Evolution-theory, by virtue of its "struggle for life," encourages this usurpation. Its basic law is that by diversification and adaptation, the stronger evolves alongside the weaker, that the weaker and the stronger are involved in a life and death struggle, that in this struggle the stronger must triumph, and that the triumph of the stronger is the only road to higher development. One of its adherents in England dared, profanely, to call this "through suffering to glory" [Rom. 8:17-18]. Thus Nietzsche was entirely consistent when, as a matter of principle, he branded Christ's call for mercy toward the weak as bad ethics and summoned all "strong spirits" to unite in the common struggle

you see a precious life wither, disappear, swallowed up before your eyes — that's lying to yourself. That you cannot do with any sincerity. That is playing with words right up to the grave.

But now comes God's Word which, without in any way discounting the harshness of that reality, turns it around for you. Totally.

To your bodily eye death is what it is and nothing else. But you also have an eye in your soul — an eye that remains stone-blind and sees nothing, not a ray of light, until God turns you around and gives you spiritual eyesight. Then, to your soul's eye a *totally opposite* reality unfolds, a reality which shows you that death does not swallow up life but that in death *what is mortal is swallowed up by life.*

How can that be? No one can unravel that mystery for you. But it can be so and is so *in Jesus.* He, the Marvelous One, took hold of death, forced it to let Him pass into glory, and kept open the road behind Him so that death would also let all His children pass into glory, unhindered and undisturbed.

Life, true authentic life, is too powerful to remain enclosed

against the miasma of the weak. His "Übermensch" is nothing more than the logical consequence of the ascent from the Monera to the Protista, from the Protista to the completed nucleus, and phylogenetically thence to plant, animal, and man. For that very reason, however, the process cannot rest with that *low* man but, continuing in a new struggle for life, must rise from this low man to the superman and presently to a higher form of life still. That same struggle, when transmitted from social to national life, incites the stronger nations to put an end to the lower-level existence of nations which are smaller and therefore weaker. And since the theory of evolution will allow no higher goal to direct this process nor any organic law to have a voice in it, and since the impulse for all life development arises exclusively from chemical action, it cannot be otherwise but that the possession of *physical* force be decisive in the end. Thus in the minds of persons, of groups, and of nations all higher life is made subordinate to securing whatever enhances the chances of victory in this material struggle. Wallace and Darwin were the precursors of Kipling as storyteller and of Chamberlain as statesman.[5] "The individual

5. Alfred R. Wallace (1823-1913) had developed a theory of natural selection

within this earthly tent. In that enclosure it cannot unfurl its wings. Therefore life must finally slough off that which is earthly and mortal to push on to the higher reaches of its potential. It has to break free from that mortal body. And while it is awful to watch that process of detachment, in this way life gets to where it has to be. Then it unfolds into the fullness of its majesty. Then you realize that, to this end, life first had to swallow up that which is mortal.

Accordingly, to the eye that peers from your soul into eternity, the dead body does not lie in its coffin as a sign that death has finally triumphed but as a sign of life's victory. It is the broken shell — more precisely, it is the brokenness of the shell — which shows that life has now become free and breathes in a higher atmosphere.

The brokenness of the body, which is otherwise hard and cruel, is now the sign of liberation, tangible evidence that life has wrenched itself free from the bonds of mortality. That act of breaking away from what is mortal so as now to unfold in glory is something your deceased could not accomplish, nor is it something *you* can do when

is nothing, the species everything" is the harsh fallacy that finally must kill all respect for the right. The antithesis between the Christian religion and the theory of evolution is by no means to be found only in the alleged development of man from the chimpanzee, but more principially in the two questions that govern all of life. First, whether the stronger must have mercy on, or whether it *may* — indeed *must* — crush, the weaker. The other question, concerning *species* or *individual,* finds its sharpest expression in the contrast between the Selection of Evolution and the Election of Scripture. Selection aims at the preservation of species; Election is the choice of persons.

We can hardly be serious enough in warning all who worship Christ as their realized Ideal to be on guard against every trysting with Evolution. It is impossible to bridge the gulf between the dogma of the Trinity and the pseudo-dogma of Evolution. The Christian religion and the theory of evolution are two mutually exclusive systems. They are antipodes that

---

simultaneously with but independently of Darwin. Joseph Chamberlain (1836-1914) had been British secretary of state for colonial affairs since 1895 and was a key figure in the maneuverings leading to the Boer War (1899-1902). [Ed.]

some day you yourself die. It is something your Jesus, the prince of life, accomplished — at least *if* there is life in you and you have been incorporated in Him and His life.

So your deceased does not die here with Jesus standing afar off; your deceased does not now *go to* Jesus. No, He was present in the dying; in fact, He accomplished it. And when death taunted you as though it had won, in that moment your Savior smiled at you and showed you a crown, the palm of victory.

The person alien to this is in a bad way. He who does *not* believe perishes when he dies. Death keeps him in custody. Those who see death thus can speak of consolation and hope only with floral wreaths and empty phrases of self-deception. The recklessness of those who stop their ears to the voice of Jesus, who even try to break down the principle of faith in others is thus appalling. Their awakening on the other side will be lethally dreadful.

Thus, on ordinary days God's children have no idea whatsoever how great a grace has come to them. They may *believe*. They may know that the loved ones they see die have been incorporated into Jesus. Granted, that knowledge does not remove the anxiety of being

can be neither reconciled nor compared. Undoubtedly, negative biblical criticism already undermined belief in confessional certitudes among many, but the Modernist theologians at least remained idealists who respected the authority of Jesus' ethical utterances. Pantheism, which soon crept into their thought, broke down the transcendent battlements of the temple but nevertheless still tried to link up with the mystical immanence of the Christian faith. But the Evolution-theory respected, spared nothing. Even as the Israelite had to search for every crumb of leaven and discard it before the Passover, so it examines every Christian atom to replace it with the opposite. The Evolution-dogma not only cuts to the deepest core of things but delves beneath the deepest life-principle to spy out with Argus eye whether some imprint of that principle might remain at the bottom of things, to the end of rendering even this slightest impression unrecognizable. If the theory of evolution is true, then all that humanity has thus far imagined, thought, pondered, and believed is a lie. Then the tree of knowledge on whose fruits we have lived thus far must be eradicated root and branch. Then the most absolute nihilism must be leveled against the world-and-life view current till now. Then humanity has thus far been dreaming and only now is beginning to awaken. If the

ill, the harshness of death, the coldness of the grave. All that remains. The sense of loss and abandonment will certainly follow, and the heart's wound will inevitably bleed.

But over and above life in the visible world, with its pain and deep sorrows, stands that other reality which is even more certain than the things that make you weep here. From that reality shine out to you a holy joy and a heavenly peace. This perception can be so powerful that you may experience the very thing that prompted Paul to write: ". . . we would rather be away from the body and at home with the Lord" (2 Cor. 5:8).

Don't say there's something sickly about this language of faith, that a person so minded becomes unfit for his vocation here below. Yes, this charge is on the mark if you merely worship your God and your Jesus as holy beings who exist to help you, to save you, to lead you into eternal life — that is, if *you* want to be at the center of things and construe God's holy ordinances solely in your own interest. But the charge is *not* true if you, along with your dead and those remaining with you, know yourselves to exist only for God and for his holy Name, both in life and in death, here and in the

theory of evolution, however untrue in its monistic and mechanistic zeal, should triumph, then the days of freedom of conscience, of tolerance and forbearance, are numbered and there will be a return, as in Nero's days, to an unsparing, violent persecution of all that is called Christian. After all, the dogma of Evolution not only *excuses* the violent eradication of the weak but makes it a matter of principle, a *duty* of the strong. From our viewpoint, therefore, both ignoring evolution and dallying with it are naive and shortsighted, and preachers as well as authors who fancy gaining scientific approval by mixing a dose of evolution with their Christian profession indict themselves, to one who knows, of unpardonable naiveté or characterless cowardice.

We must also reject the delusion of some who are misled by the false sound of the word into regarding the Evolution-theory as nothing but the latest form of Pantheism. Evolution — that is, unfolding, *evolvere* — *is* a genuinely pantheistic notion, but the Evolution dogma knows nothing of evolving in the real sense of the word. It is parading under a false banner. Rather, this dogma in principle denies all pre-formation, that is, any governance-by-plan over the budding of life. Unfolding is an *organic* idea, but the dogma of evolution tolerates nothing but *mechanistic*

world to come. Surely, He is our Father and we are His children; He is our Master, and we are His servants.

For life is good only so long as we do *His work* here and labor at the task *He assigned us*. But then that is also our imperative calling. Then we are born to serve Him, and born again with no other object but to glorify Him in the Son of His love. He gave us faith not to beatify us but to make Himself great in our salvation. Then our life is the Lord's, whether we remain here or whether we enter eternity.

And then *our* death and the death of our loved ones never comes except at the moment, and never otherwise than under those circumstances, which He deemed best for the full realization of His counsel and for the praise of his Name. Then freely say that the weeping of the evening and the joy of the morning [Ps. 30:5] dwell in the same heart.

The inner life of those who want to live solely for their God is very mixed indeed. There is weeping over the acute pain felt by their wounded heart. But from that same heart also rises the sound of rejoicing and praise for what God prepared for the loved one who went away and for what He left in this life by way of consolation, love, and holy calling.

action from beginning to end. The ancient distinction between Epicurus and the Stoics also separates Pantheism from the theory of evolution. Like Epicurus, the theory of evolution would explain the origin, being, and existence of all life in an atomistic, and consequently purely mechanistic, manner. When Haeckel in his *Religion und Wissenschaft* nevertheless claimed to be a pantheist, he merely exposed the fuzziness in his own philosophical conception; and when he even posed as professing a God who should be honored as "the spirit of the good, the true, and the beautiful," he engaged in a deceptive play on words or else deceived himself with obscurities. After all, the dogma of evolution knows of no spirit which forms, drives, or rules. With it the natural event is the only conceivable motive, and all that we honor as spirit is nothing but a chance product or an arbitrary result.

Asceticism and social action are again in vogue, thanks in part to Pantheism and in part to the Christian tradition; these phenomena owe absolutely nothing to Evolution. And if one time and again encounters people who want to be Evolutionists on the broad plain of nature but Stoics in the field of ethics, then one is dealing with spiritual amphibians who are not even aware of their inner contradictions. . . . [Kuyper gives examples of jurists and historians *sine nomine*.] The idea of a guiding purpose [*Zweck-theorie*], an unconscious striving of all things toward the realization of a mystically determined *goal*, is out and out pantheistic but is diametrically opposed to the dogma of evolution. Anyone who imagines that there can be any thought of purpose or of a compelling and guiding principle at any point along the phylogenetic way simply does not know the dogma of evolution. Indeed, *"Die Mechanik des Weltalls"* (The Mechanics of the Universe), the title of the discerning study by Dr. Zehnder, is the only correct formula for the Evolution theory, as Dr. Haeckel did not hesitate to say in plain terms: "The history of the world must be a physical-chemical process."[6]

Must we therefore write off the studies of the Darwinistic school, most broadly conceived, from the balance sheet of our scientific gains? Let me reply by asking whether well-established facts can ever be amortized. Nay, rather, all who love the light exult in the wealth of facts revealed by these studies and in the impetus they gave to even deeper, more methodical research. Who of us still capable of enthusiasm would conceal the ecstasy so often provoked by the profound insight these studies gave into the essential structure of the world? But the knowledge of these unveiled facts may not be equated with the Evolution-dogma falsely distilled from them. The empirical and the theory built upon it must be sharply differentiated here; the facts and the conception of the facts are two different things. For that dogma, that theory, that system — in France usually introduced as transformation [*Transformisme*], in Germany as the theory of descent [*Descendenz-theorie*], and in this country, following England's example, as the *Evolution theory* — purports to be nothing less than a strictly monistic understanding of the cosmos, seeking to explain all *organic* life in the *inorganic*. Its adherents, even in Germany, constantly emphasize the fact that "a philosophical understanding" of the discovered facts "is a necessary precondition for the complete worldview of the theory of descent." We read elsewhere that "the unshakeable edifice of true monistic science" comes into existence only when "empiricism and philosophy intimately permeate one another."[7] A frank acknowledgment, this, but one that then gives us the right and charges us with the duty of sharply distinguishing between those *facts* and the philosophizing linked to them. Every sincere person immediately agrees with that which is logically deduced from established facts, but before accepting these intertwined deductions as a well-rounded system, you must test the philosophical principles underlying these opera-

6. Ernst Haeckel, *Natürliche Schöpfungsgeschichte* (Berlin, 1898), vol. I, p. 153; Ludwig Zehnder, *Die Entstehung des Lebens* (Freiburg, 1899).

7. Haeckel, *Natürliche Schöpfungsgeschichte,* vol. II, pp. 780, 782.

tions against the basic axioms of your own thinking. Otherwise there is no fit for you personally.

This watchfulness is all the more urgent since our adversaries are inclined not only to *establish* the facts but also to *construe* them philosophically. To limit my remarks to this one, surely weighty, so-called fact, which no less than Haeckel formulated as follows: "Therefore it is indubitably certain: man comes from the ape." Has this alleged fact really been established? Not so. Haeckel himself acknowledges: "the enormous gaps in our paleontological knowledge" make definite proof impossible. Nor is the gap filled by the skeleton of *Pithecanthropus erectus* which was excavated in Java in 1894 by our own Eugene Dubois and upon which the famous Congress in Leiden in 1895 dulled its acumen.[8] Therefore the experts are careful to add that neither gorilla nor chimpanzee qualify as our patriarch, but that the likely progenitor among the apes which could also be a progenitor of *Homo sapiens* is the tailless, narrow-nosed species of ape *Catarrhina lipocerca.* Proof for this supposition is sought especially in the morphological resemblance between these two. However, this search has been so fruitless that a scholar like Rudolph Virchow denies the consequences derived from the foregoing and emphasizes to the contrary that the oldest excavated human skeletons display "heads of such a large size that many a living person would consider himself fortunate to possess one like it."[9] Haeckel himself acknowledges that proof in this case can never be produced "merely through individual empirical observations" but must be derived from the "philosophical evaluation" of the incomplete data. When we ask what he means, he replies: "It lies herein, that the theory of evolution follows as a general law of induction from the comparative synthesis of all natural phenomena of living organisms." The "Pithecoid theory," therefore, is nothing more than "a special deductive conclusion which must follow with the same logical necessity from the general laws of induction of the evolution theory."[10] No sober thinker, he continues, can escape the conclusion: "If the theory of development is at all true," and the individual animal species are not "created miraculously, then man, too, cannot be an exception." And that's called logic — begging the question by circular reasoning! You infer from animal data. Your deduction would therefore hold good only if it were established that man and animal were of one species. Precisely that which

8. Quotations are from Haeckel, *Natürliche Schöpfungsgeschichte,* vol. II, pp. 800, 798. [Eugene F. T. DuBois (1858-1940) was a Dutch medical doctor in the Netherlands Indies and the discover of "Java man," announced in 1894.]

9. Rudolf Virchow, *Die Freiheit der Wissenschaft im modernen Staat* (Berlin, 1877), p. 30.

10. Haeckel, *Natürliche Schöpfungsgeschichte,* vol. II, p. 799. [The next quotation in Kuyper's text is unattributed.]

you must prove you have thus smuggled in (there is no milder word for it) by means of your induction, contrary to all good logic. And yet all of Spencer's ethics rests on such a proposition, and with such argumentation from second-hand science people popularize ideas that are calculated to undermine all Christian faith.

What then does Evolution-theory desire, envision, seek after? Nägeli, usually a much more levelheaded thinker than Haeckel, hinted at it clearly when he wrote of "spontaneous generation" [*Urzeugung*], which most scholars concede to be "pure hypothesis": "To deny spontaneous generation is equivalent to proclaiming miracle."[11] Yet we must not interpret this abhorrence of miracle in a general, atheistic sense. The motivation for science cannot rest in the knowledge of the singular phenomenon. All of science is consumed with passion for the general. Unity, and therefore the general law that governs the particular case, is the food she will eat by the sweat of her brow, and it must be acknowledged that the focus on empirical detail by the so-called *sciences exactes* is a starvation diet. The zoologist, the botanist, every natural scientist had his private hunting ground, each proceeding from the available data without any interest in a deeper unity that binds all phenomena together. Lamarck may have theorized and Goethe prophesied about a unity in nature, but our natural scientists paid no attention to it, and the prevailing view of the public was satisfied with a mystical, magical idea of the origin of things that lacked any deeper conception. Now this has been avenged. The knowledge of a few bricks and beams did not suffice in the end. Again, as with Empedocles in Greek philosophy, the question had to arise concerning the architectonic structure by means of which so magnificent a building was erected from these few bricks and beams. Add to this the increasing aversion in scientific circles to the superficial fallacy of rootless supernaturalism, add as well the irreligious predisposition that felt an emancipatory joy in escaping the restraints of divine action, and the impulses that gave rise to evolution and the goal at which it aimed both become transparent.

In these matters the theory of evolution proceeded from the rather too readily accepted hypothesis that the inorganic world, with the data present there and with the laws that govern those data, no longer presented insurmountable difficulties for scientific understanding. The mystery that it sought to unveil, it believed, lay hidden only in the organic realms of nature,

11. Karl Wilhelm Nägeli (1817-91) was a Swiss botanist and pioneer in cell biology. The quotation is unattributed. [Ed.]

and it considered the problem solved when and if it succeeded in explaining those *organic* realms by the data of the *in*organic. That accounts for its sworn enmity against every presupposition of a previously established goal toward which the development of living organisms would be impelled, either by means of an indwelling principle or through divine power working from without. Darwin himself and every well-informed evolutionist after him stated honestly: If such a previously planned working principle should turn up at only one point along the phylogenetic way, the entire dogma of evolution would collapse. George John Romanes of Christ Church, Oxford, said it plainly: "Our theory seeks to bring all phenomena in organic nature within the same theoretical structure as the facts of inorganic nature, and if it does not *completely* reach that aim it has served no purpose except to create a great stir in the world of thought."[12] Until now the non-living and the living world were considered to be two sharply distinguished spheres of existence, the first of a lower and the second of a higher order, but without a unity that would link them together in principle insofar as one did not find this unity in God as Creator. The intent was to eliminate this duality, to explain both spheres by unity of operation — in the sense that the sphere of the *higher* order was to be explained by the sphere of the *lower.* Now if the mark of the lower order were the Mechanistic and that of the higher order the Organic, Evolution could be summarized as the theory that permits the organic to be swallowed up by the mechanistic.[13] Mechanism is its magic word. Whatever has not been explained mechanistically is still hidden in the uncomprehended darkness. Insofar as Evolution-dogma might have pressed for new research in physics and chemistry, it wished less to gain a more thorough understanding of inorganic nature as such than to elicit richer, more exact information that could serve to establish the absolute dominance of the mechanistic over the organic sphere of life. Did not Du Bois-Reymond crassly state: "What cannot be grasped in *mechanistic* terms has not been understood *scientifically*"?[14]

12. George John Romanes, *Darwin und nach Darwin* (Leipzig, 1895), vol. I, p. 65. [Originally published in English as *Darwin and after Darwin* (Chicago: Open Court, 1892.] "Before his death, Romanes returned from his error. See his *Thoughts on Religion,* edited by Canon Gore (London, 1896)."

13. See Ludwig Zehnder, *Entstehung des Lebens* pp. 2, 204.

14. Joseph Epping, *Der Kreislauf im Kosmos* (Freiburg, 1882), p. 102; Tilmann Pesch, *Die grossen Welträtsel* (Freiburg, 1892), vol. I, p. 505; Schopenhauer, *Die Welt als Wille und Vorstellung* (Frankfurt, 1819), vol. II, p. 357; Jacob Henle, *Anthropologische Vorträge* (Braunschweig, 1880), vol. II, p. 128; and J. Diebolder, *Darwins Grundprincip der Abstammungslehre* (Freiburg, 1891). [Kuyper does not here cite Emil Heinrich DuBois-Reymond, whom he quotes in the text; later he will cite that author's *Über Neo-Vitalismus* (Brackwede i. W., 1894).]

Darwin was not the first to devote his energy to solving this problem. Lamarck and Goethe preceded him, and Wallace was his contemporary.[15] But Darwin is superior in this respect: that he was the first to attach more importance to empiricism than to speculation and to gather a wealth of botanical and especially zoological data that were in every way suitable to show, in an original manner, the extent of the field where that metamorphosis is undeniably prevalent. In so doing he initially avoided drawing man within the circle of transformation. Like all English writers before him, it was also in his favor that he was far from chauvinistic in matters of faith; rather, he never stopped paying his respects to the mystery of religion. The idea of evolution arose in his mind through careful observation of what can be accomplished by artificial breeding in the case of plants and animals. He was especially impressed by the far-reaching transformation to which the dove is susceptible. Now this artificial breeding proceeds according to a definite law . . . that anyone can duplicate and none will gainsay. But this does not mean that Darwin had the final answer. Even though one still might presume that new species had arisen in the same manner, by the perpetuation of certain variations, the question remained by what power the knowledge and selection of the nurseryman and animal breeder are replaced in untamed nature. To say that this was an organic principle which impelled things toward their perfect goal, or to acknowledge that God regulated this selection, was not possible. That would have meant reintroducing the notion of purpose, and the entire theory would collapse along with Mechanism. A mechanistic power had to be enlisted. This was Darwin's greatest discovery, that he did indeed point out such a purely mechanistic agency which made the perpetuation of a more richly endowed variation self-explanatory — or as it has been put, that he succeeded in having the highest *Zweckmässigkeit* [functionality] emanate automatically from complete *Zwecklosigkeit* [aimlessness].

In so doing he proceeded from Malthus's theory that the means of subsistence for organic life are totally disproportionate to the rate at which life is propagated. Geometric procreation finds only arithmetically increased provisions.[16] Now if a gnawing hunger in a besieged city more than once brought a mother to act against nature by preparing the flesh of her own child for food, or a shipwrecked sailor perishing with thirst

15. See Ernst Haeckel, *Die Naturanschauung von Darwin, Goethe und Lamarck* (Jena, 1882). Concerning Goethe, see especially Eduard Oscar Schmidt, *Descendenzlehre und Darwinismus* (Leipzig, 1884), pp. 95-109.

16. The geometric progression is: a, $a \times q$, $a \times q^2$, $a \times q^3$, etc.; the arithmetic progression is: a, $a + d$, $a + 2d$, $a + 3d$, etc.

kills his companion to drink his blood, then we can understand how this "struggle for life" embodies an agency so general and so overpowering that Darwin indeed laid his finger on a law that governs all living organisms. From that law he obtained his selection, his choice-of-nature. Every kind of breeding exhibited variations. Among those variations some are weaker and some stronger. The stronger eat, and the weaker perish with hunger. That stronger element was embodied in a membrane or in a developing claw, in something morphological or histological. This was bequeathed to the offspring, was increased in each new generation by the same law, and was strengthened by adaptation.[17] Thus there occurred, automatically, entirely by chance, a constant strengthening of the formation of organs. And so it seemed to be explained how richer and stronger forms continued to appear both in the plant and the animal kingdom, assuming an unlimited span of time, thanks to this selection which resulted from the struggle for life. Not only did the improved structure of the privileged variations already appear stronger at birth [*ex ovo*], but during the individual's lifetime it also underwent effective alterations by means of adaptation to its environment; the advantages thus obtained, it was said, were transmitted by heredity to the offspring, thus propagating themselves.

The seal of straightforward truth seemed to be engraved on this discovery. Transformation by artificial breeding is a fact. Another fact is the distorted balance between the almost boundless multiplication of eaters and the scantiness of available food. Fact, too, is the struggle for life and the many-sided adaptations to life. And finally, an equally undeniable fact is the inheritance of the distinguishing characteristics by subsequent generations. Combine all these facts and arrange them as common sense dictates, as Darwin did in his inimitably placid manner, and the riddle indeed seems to be solved. One need no longer be concerned with God's influence, with direction by a guiding principle, or with the imposition of control by any plan or purpose. The richest organism automatically develops itself from the most insignificant organism. In the individuals of each generation we constantly find something new, and that something strengthens itself by adaptation. That something is advantageous. It maintains itself through the utility of that advantage while others perish, and enriches itself while others are impoverished. And that enrichment goes on from generation to generation. There is an additive effect, an accumulation, and through that accumu-

17. That the "adaptation" here is not the cause but the effect, and also that it is not the main issue, was pointed out very correctly by Johann W. Spengel, *Zweckmässigkeit und Anpassung* (Jena, 1898), especially p. 18.

lation of profitable attributes which promise victory in the struggle for life, the entire marvelous structure of the organic realm is erected. A system as thrilling as it is transparent. Nothing is more easily understood than the unbelievably rapid acceptance this system received, as if with a *"veni, vidi, vici."* For a scientific world which, by its lack of faith, had witnessed the collapse of the grandeur of unity in the diversity of details, yet retained the nostalgia for unity in its heart, the discovery of Darwin was indeed, if not the "Eureka!" that brought deliverance, then at least the *Fata Morgana* that lent enchantment.

Moreover, it cannot be denied that an entire sequence of phenomena which until then had not received attention or been accounted for were found to fit quite naturally into the structure of this system. Especially in France, so-called appendicitis is the subject of the day and receives universal attention. After all, it is said, this appendix is of no use to man while it performs a necessary role among many non-flesh-eating animals. It only threatens us with unwelcome surgery. If only we did not have it! But the theory of descent thrives on it. It is, so they say, a newly unwelcome legacy from our speechless ancestors. Even apart from the appendix it is possible to point to other parts of the body, in both man and animal, that have ceased to serve any clearly demonstrable purpose. Besides, morphology with its studies of comparative anatomy agrees with the idea. Indeed, the structural similarity of the human skeleton to that of beings with totally different external form is so obvious that one can hardly explain the striking difference in external appearance except by the hereditary unity of the inner structure modified by different adaptations to life. The same tendency appears in the embryological or, if you will, ontogenetic studies, which have disclosed a more and more detailed account of development from a single nucleus and have demonstrated how new cells develop either by dividing or by the formation of buds. These cells then, grouping themselves ectodermically and endodermically, gradually produce by mechanistic action all histological and morphological phenomena that are required for the formation of the structure of the organism. The embryological phenomena seem to repeat in the individual what is visible to the eye phylogenetically in all of the systematic groupings of plant and animal organisms.

The so-called geographic distribution of plants and animals throughout the various parts of the world, whose importance Darwin perceived on the coastal islands of South America, and especially the paucity of both flora and fauna in Australia's gigantic island — all seem to point to one identical process. Comparative physiology, by paying more heed than before to the important factor of physical and chemical action, also discovered a uniform law in the preservation, growth, and functions of the several organs, which could be reduced to the double process of feeding and propagating. To mention no more, paleontology has revealed the parallel ordered sequences of plants and animals arising in successive strata on the earth, and likewise has acquainted us with various species of extinct organisms and with still-surviving species that had different morphological characteristics in a bygone age. Even psychology applied itself to establishing that there is a close connection between the functions of our will and thought and those of the animal world, relating these to the physical functions of the lower organisms and the latter in turn to chemical behavior, even to the undulations and vibrations of the ether.[18] Finally, authoritative writers have made mention of a "primordial soul" [*Protistenseele*], have created in their way a cellular psychology, and have even ascribed the function of memory to the plastidule.

Thus the Evolution-theory has shone its brilliant light on an ever more encompassing field. Time and again, new provinces of our cosmic life were brought under its scepter, and in each territory that it annexed it quickened a spirit of more profound investigation, elicited research that had not been previously considered, and wrought a unity in studies that earlier dealt only with details. Such splendid results bolstered the belief that in its inspired thought *the* true explanation of the universe had indeed been found. To explain all that exists — in its origin, being, transformation, and functions — from a single principle was the richest and most absolute Monism, in which our thinking spirit could at last find the rest it so passionately desired. And this rest would be granted to our spirit not, as formerly, through the mental gymnastics of speculation, which raised itself from the earth to enjoy a bird's-eye view of the panorama, but by the most accurate research into nature itself, digging ever deeper into the mine of real life.

Soon something followed in the triumphal procession of Evolution that Darwin, in his sober and down-to-earth naiveté, had not remotely anticipated. First, monistic psychology declared its intent to establish genetic connections between the radiation, undulation, and vibration in the plastidule and the creative genius with which a Plato or Thomas, a Calvin or Kant had astonished the thinking world. Then came the audacious attempt to explain the entire development of man's intellectual,

18. The prevailing nineteenth-century theory was that light waves were transmitted from distant objects by means of the "luminiferous ether," a weightless and transparent but still material substance thought to be necessary for transmission through a vacuum. The Michelson-Morley experiment published in 1887 cast doubt on this theory, but it was not until the early twentieth century that the concept of waves traveling through empty space began to be taught to and accepted by the general public. My thanks to Clarence Menninga for this explanation. [Ed.]

aesthetic, ethical, religious, and thus social and political life not only according to the analogy of nature but in association with her phenomenal existence and the origin of that existence in the inorganic world. The symbolic parallel of the visible and invisible long honored by thinkers and poets was now converted into a genetic coherence. . . . Thus there occurred, especially in England, that total change in the study of the mental sciences which, guided by the psychological and ethical research of Herbert Spencer, Bain, and George Lewes, attempted to apply the mechanics of Evolution to the life of the soul as well.[19] In a much more general sense than Darwin had done, Evolution is thus recommended to us by this formula: it is *an integration of matter coupled with an infusion of energy so that matter which was formerly indefinite, homogeneous, and incoherent is changed to a condition of heterogeneity that is definite and coherent, while the excess energy undergoes a similar transformation.*[20] However intricate this formula, we will not take offense — provided that these naturalistic scholars, who so readily cast the reproach of haziness upon the formulations of Christian dogma, do not claim the glory of lucidity for their own. Armed with that formula, they proceeded to the evolutionistic reformation of psychology, ethics, and sociology, with the further goal to found all jurisprudence upon a changed basis, to change history into an action of mechanistic factors, to fit the economy together like a mechanistic jig-saw puzzle. Finally, they would not only undergird political concepts with entirely new principles but construe religion as a sublimate which, provided it be dissociated entirely from the personal existence of a living God, rises of its own accord from the undulation and ferment of inorganic phenomena and is conducted into the retort that is called *man*.

II

And yet, despite the power with which the point of this hypothesis has pierced every branch of science, it has a much more fragile basis than would appear at first blush. I will not enter into the question whether Dr. Gustav Wolff — lecturer in Wurzburg, an expert in this matter, and the famous discoverer of the regeneration of the lens in the eye of the salamander — goes too far when he writes: "Doubtless, the realization

19. Alexander Bain (1818-1903) was an associate of John Stuart Mill and an eminent physiological psychologist. George Lewes (1817-78), long-time companion to novelist George Eliot, was a philosophical radical, publicist of Comte, and theorist of an empirical metaphysics. [Ed.]

20. See Théodule Ribot, *La psychologie anglaise contemporaine* (Paris, 1896), p. 176.

that Darwinism was a chimera is slowly dawning," and that "the end of Darwinistic domination" is not far away.[21] But it must be stated without hesitation that discord has already entered the ranks of the Evolutionists, that sound criticism is driving them farther and farther into a corner. Their assertion that "the highest purposiveness has arisen through absolutely purposeless mechanics," completely disclosing the mystery of life, has proved to be ever less tenable.

In this case the Achilles heel was concealed in the factor of heredity, which makes or breaks the entire system. According to the theory, the innate privilege of the better-equipped varieties, as well as the preference these stronger individuals gained by virtue of adaptation to life, becomes permanent working capital. The fortunate possessor bequeathes it to his posterity. . . . But of course, if the system is to remain valid, not only the adaptation but also the diversity and transmission will have to be explained mechanistically. For if these were left unexplained or were governed by an indwelling organic principle, then, as the experts admit unconditionally, the entire presentation of the cosmos as arising mechanistically from atoms would prove to have been a cruel illusion. Of course, we would not think of denying that changeableness does occur by diversification or by adaptation among individuals, nor that such characteristics are transmitted to succeeding generations. Even a mole on the arm will sometimes reveal the mother in the child. Both facts are undeniable. Whether changes obtained through adaptation cannot be lost again may be a dubious matter. Weismann denies it, and surely it cannot be maintained in the case of domestication.[22] But apart from this, it is certain that what is begotten is not identical with the begetter, nor are the progeny identical among themselves; nevertheless, they have primitive forms in common both with their begetter and with each other. The dispute, therefore, does not involve these *facts* but their *explanation,* and the decisive question in the case of the Evolution-dogma is whether it can explain both of these facts and explain them mechanistically. If so, it's home free. If not, its spell is broken once and for all.

I will not pursue the first fact, the diversification of individuals, for lack of time and even more because over the past years the conflict has concentrated on the other fact, the problem of transmission. In that conflict hypothesis after hypothesis has been presented, but to date there

21. Gustav Wolff, *Beiträge zur Kritik der Darwinschen Lehre* (Leipzig, 1898), foreword, p. 1.

22. August Weismann (1834-1914) was a German zoologist, an ardent supporter of Darwin and of Bismarck. He argued against the inheritance of acquired characteristics, and his "germ-plasm" theory of genetics anticipated later DNA discoveries. [Ed.]

has been no progress at all. Darwin himself was careful to call his idea, later discarded, a "provisional hypothesis," and Haeckel frankly admits that these and other hypotheses "rest on pure conjecture" and are nothing more than "metaphysical speculations."[23] . . .

I trust that your kind indulgence will pardon this somewhat detailed presentation. The subject under discussion is of such great importance

23. Kuyper references the quotations to Romanes, *Darwin und nach Darwin,* vol. I, p. 199; and Haeckel, *Natürliche Schöpfungsgeschichte,* I, p. 205. He next proceeds on an extensive review (four pages of text) of recent proposals in transmission theory put forward by Darwin, Haeckel, Nägeli, Weismann, and de Vries. For Darwin he cites *The variation of animals and plants under domestication,* in Francis Darwin, ed., *The Life and Letters of Charles Darwin* (New York, 1887), vol. II, pp. 369ff.; cf. *Life and Letters of Darwin,* vol. III, pp. 83ff. Regarding Haeckel he notes Louis Elsberg, *On the Plastidule-hypothesis* (Buffalo, 1876), as a forerunner, and Virchow, *Die Freiheit der Wissenschaft,* p. 27, and Otto Zacharias, *Über gelöste und ungelöste Problemen der Naturforschung* (Leipzig, 1887), p. 60, as critics. For Karl Nägeli, Kuyper references his *Idioplasma Theorie* (Munich, 1884), noting the criticism thereof by Gustav Eimer, *Die Entstehung der Arten* (Jena, 1888), p. 21, and Haeckel, *Natürliche Schöpfungsgeschichte,* vol. I, p. 203. On August Weismann Kuyper cites *Mechanisch-psychologische Theorie der Abstammungslehre* (Munich, 1884); *Das Keimplasma, Eine Theorie der Vererbung* (Jena, 1892), and *Aufsätze über Vererbung und verwandte Biologische Fragen* (Jena, 1892). He does not discuss Hugo de Vries in the text but adds this in his notes: "The theory of intracellular pangenesis, proposed in 1889 by Prof. Hugo de Vries in *Intracelluläre Pangenesis* (Jena, 1889), returned in principle to the pangenesis of Darwin, but with this important difference, that it did not allow the pangenes to wander through the entire body. Instead the protoplasm itself was viewed as consisting of a complete set of pangenes, whereby each individual hereditary property, whether somatic or psychological, was borne by a separate pangene. 'I take intracellular pangenesis to be the hypothesis that all living protoplasm is constructed out of pangenes.' And further, 'Every hereditary characteristic has its own particular kind of pangenes.' (p. 211). Undoubtedly a much more natural representation, but one which, as one arranges these pangenes in their interactive relationship to each other and does not get his thoughts confused, brings us partway back to the ancient theory of pre-formation, as was correctly observed by Dr. Haeckel." Kuyper gives the last word to theorists dealing with teleological issues: Max Kassowitz, *Allgemeine Biologie* (Vienna, 1899), vol. II, pp. 359 and 361; Paul Nikolaus Cossman, *Elemente der Empirische Teleologie* (Stuttgart, 1899), p. 121; Eduard Strasburger, *Über die Bedeutung phylogenetischer Methoden für die Erforschung lebender Wesen* (Jena, 1874); and Johannes Reinke, *Die Welt als That* (Berlin, 1899), p. 482.

Clarence Menninga notes on this point that Kuyper was obviously ignorant of the work of Gregor Mendel, which provides the basis for twentieth-century genetic theory. Mendel published the results of his experiments in the 1866 *Proceedings* of a meeting of the Brunn Natural Science Society and sent a copy of the paper to Nägeli, the leading authority on heredity at that time, but Nägeli did not consider those experiments to be especially important. It was only in 1900, after similar experiments had been done independently by Erich von Tschermak in Austria, Carl Correns in Germany, and Hugo de Vries in the Netherlands, that a search of the literature rediscovered what Mendel had done 35 years earlier. [Ed.]

for the future of Evolution-theory that I reproach myself with having been too brief rather than too lengthy. These studies of heredity bore much splendid fruit in making us aware of a much more complex existence in the most deeply hidden life of the cell than we had suspected thus far. At the same time they have shed so revealing a light on the absolute inability of evolution to give a mechanistic explanation of the fact of heredity that it is not too much to say that the monistic mechanism of the entire Evolution-theory has been fatally wounded in its Achilles' heel. It cannot do without the all-controlling fact of heredity in the erection of its cosmos, and upon that fact of heredity its monistic mechanism breaks like a soap-bubble. If governance by a *nonmaterial* principle, by a *World-Mechanic,* or by *formation according to an idea* has proven to be an undeniable necessity at this point, then an organic factor appears alongside of mechanism and absolute Mechanism as well as strict Monism prove to be a figment of the imagination.

There are other, no less serious criticisms. In connection with heredity I have already referred to the problem of the origin of variations regarding diversity among individuals. Whence come these variations which, in the Selection system, are thought to bring new gains to the privileged individuals? But there is more. As Dr. Gustav Wolff most aptly remarks, not only is the origin of these variations a riddle but the system demands that they appear *without* previous definition. *Complete lack of regulation* must characterize them.[24] Without "totally undirected variation" Mechanism falls. The idea of differentiation, aided by additive accumulation, must provide the architectural style for the universe, but then the building blocks supplied by this idea may not have been previously adapted for insertion or Mechanism will fall and the organizing idea regain supremacy. Exactly here the theory of evolution runs against the facts. Were not the vertebrata symmetrically constructed? If the pigment spot on the left is always accompanied by a pigment spot on the right and a nearly analogous eye develops out of the two pigment spots by an identical process, how is it to be explained that two entirely independent "incremental variations," in the right proportion and clearly symmetrical, produced similar results? Here the undirected action of mechanism *cannot* give the answer. Here we find no free variation but a variation that in both cases is subject to the same determinant, law, or rule, and mechanistic variation by Selection, of course, does not allow a pre-forming rule.

We must say the same thing of *utility* as the exclusive motive for

24. Wolff, *Beiträge zur Kritik* p. 4.

Selection. Surely it is clear that an individual armed with two wings, born of wingless parents and alongside of wingless brothers and sisters, would by that token be uncommonly preferred and have a chance of getting the best of his wingless competitors in the struggle for life. But this is not the way Evolution-theory presents it. Originally there are not two wings, nothing more than two almost invisible stumps from which the wings eventually must emerge, right and left. Of what utility to the candidate for wings is this pair of little stumps? How can this pair of stumplets give him an advantage in the struggle for life over the stumpless? We would say, rather, that these two unsightly stumps pushed him backward in the course of sexual selection. The answer of Darwin and his adherents to these questions is far from satisfactory. But grant that their assertion holds good in the case of the wing stumps, and that for other variations in which no utility can be established Darwin's *Correlation* hypothesis permits a way out. Even then some things have by no means been explained. Dr. Romanes, although an ardent Darwinist, acknowledges, e.g., that the electrical apparatus of the ray (not the torpedo or electric ray but the common variety *raja*) delivers a thrust which is much too weak to have been useful to the fish in defending itself against its enemies; therefore we are faced here with a very complex phenomenon that *cannot* be accounted for by selection.[25]

The evolutionists are also embarrassed by the fossil record. The harvest thus far is extremely scanty when compared with expectations. Before the first complete eagle's wing had developed from the first stump, thousands and thousands of years must have elapsed, while eagle candidates lived first with wing stumps, then with small rudiments of quills, then with expanding wings, until finally the royal wing was completed. It might be expected, therefore, that in the catacombs of the fossil world one might find a host of quarter- and half-grown eagle's wings as well as a multitude of transition forms in the world of plants and animals. Bear in mind that these transition forms did not pass by rapidly but, according to the hypothesis, endured thousands if not ten thousands of years. Millions of examples must have existed. But the outcome is bitterly disappointing. The Darwinists themselves are at a loss for words to mourn the "incompleteness" of the buried world of life. Nothing even faintly resembling a genealogy has come to light. And the painfulness of this sore spot is nowhere more clearly revealed than in the fuss they make with their repeated appeal to the discovered genealogical transition forms of the horse, at least as it refers to the development of the hoof from the middle toe.

25. Romanes, *Darwin und nach Darwin,* vol. I, p. 432.

Even worse is the appeal to selective breeding. This interesting practice is indeed successful in breeding variations *within the limits of the same species*, but it has never succeeded in transforming an animal from its own into a higher species or in calling a new sort of animal into being. It has long been known that every species possesses the faculty of developing a multitude of variations within certain limits, and this has been amply confirmed by artificial breeding. Therefore nothing prevents us from accepting the fact that nature, in the same manner, by utility-selection, has converted its original uniformity of species into pluriformity. Even in the world of bacteria, the most knowledgeable bacteriologists maintain that the derivation of all the species from one basic type is unthinkable. Precisely for that reason the theory of evolution cannot gather the least support from artificial breeding. For evolution does *not* say that the species is variegated *within its own limits* but that one species changes into another. For *this* kind of variation artificial breeding proves *nothing*. . . .[26]

The foregoing argumentation yields this conclusion. First, that Evolution is to be greeted thankfully as a bold reaction against the clumsy detail-empiricism and the despondent rule of the vast realm of the Unknowable [*Ignorabimus*] which too long exerted a depressing influence upon natural philosophy. Over against this, the theory of evolution has boldly reopened the question concerning the origin of the organic world and pressed for unity in our worldview. In the second place, the theory of evolution has stimulated such a careful observation of nature in its most deeply hidden workshops that the half-magical speculation of former years has been replaced by the riches of microscopic observation. While previously people at most marked the movement of the second hand on the clock, now the mechanism of the clock has been opened to view and the movement of gears and springs may be observed. In the third place, by giving an impetus to ontogenetic, morphological studies Evolution-theory has discovered a unity of design in all organic life, even an analogy and correspondence of the organic with the inorganic that had previously been

26. Deleted is one page in which Kuyper discusses the need for an organic — vs. mechanistic — explanation in Darwin's own theory and invokes the era's commonly held assumption of a barrier between organic and inorganic compounds. He gibes that the only successful breaching of that wall to date had been Friedrich Wöhler's (1828) synthesis of the organic chemical compound *urea* from the inorganic compound *ammonium cyanate*, implying that such barnyard materials represented the real worth of the theories he was criticizing. My thanks to Clarence Menninga for this information. [Ed.]

hidden from view. And finally, in the fourth place, by applying the law of Malthus to variations, it has pointed to a factor in the development of particular variations in species that cast a startling light on otherwise inexplicable phenomena.

However, it is in error when, intoxicated with the joy of this discovery, it fancies that it has found *the* solution to the riddle of the universe and suggests in popular writings that the architectonics of a "cosmos without blueprint" has been disclosed to us. There is no satisfactory proof that the cosmos is thus mechanistically self-formed, and the proof cannot be supplied, even experimentally, in step-by-step detail. The catacombs of the fossil world have refused to furnish what is required to support the system. Not one egg or one cytode has been produced without egg, and the attempt to breed the individual of one species with another species has failed thus far. To put it more forcefully, not only do we lack proof *that* it occurred thus but on the hypothesis that it *could* be so Evolution-theory has come to a fiasco. Its own adherents acknowledge that Selection explains only one portion of the phenomena and that other, not merely mechanistic, forces must be enlisted for assistance. For while it was first imagined that the dual law of change and heredity would be the answer, further research soon disclosed that neither of these laws could be deduced from purely mechanistic principles, and its most skillful researchers came again to organic principles and teleological motives. As a result the once beautiful harmony among Evolutionists has given place to bitter argumentation, and accusations of betraying the system are being hurled about. "No exact physicist," said one to another, "recognizes in your assertions anything but fanciful metaphysical speculations."[27] Mark well — *metaphysical* speculations, the harshest stigma for an Evolutionist.

So matters stand. Nevertheless we hear the adherents of Evolution, whatever their strain, assuredly declare "that every unbiased and unprejudiced scientist who possesses sound judgment and the sufficient biological understanding" *must* agree with them. That they can and must "assert their general theory with complete certainty." That it is impossible to conceive "how stronger and more valid proof for the theory of evolution" could be furnished. That "if their power of proof is not sufficient, we must do without a reasonable answer to the question of all questions." That "no natural scientist doubts that the causes here are grounded purely mechanistically in the nature of living matter itself." That the principial dissent even of men like Carl Vogt and Johannes Reinke must be attributed to their antiquated viewpoint and their limited range of studies, to their "lack of sound logic" and their imperfect philosophical develop-

27. Haeckel, *Natürliche Schöpfungsgeschichte,* vol. I, p. 203.

ment. That one who opposes them on religious grounds has forfeited every right to a hearing because all "blind belief in revelation and confession is no different from superstition."[28] Thus we are confronted not with a theory or a hypothesis but with a real *dogma* of Evolution. A dogma that I brand a *pseudo*-dogma, because the authority that can establish it is totally lacking on scientific grounds.

III

This will become increasingly clear as I now, finally, proceed with the critique of Evolution-theory from *a spiritual standpoint*. There is a hierarchy of phenomena in the cosmos; the lowest rung is to be found in the naturally forming crystal, the highest in the cross of Golgotha. To arrive at Monism, therefore, a double course is indispensable: first an ascent, then a descent along this cosmic ladder. Only when the results of the two agree will a holy monistic joy thrill our hearts. What is the cosmos? Precipitate of the spirit or sublimate of physical atoms? Must all higher organized life be pulled down to the spheres of lower inorganic life, or must the lower be subsumed under the higher? The foregoing argument bears my challenge to those who, in their spiritual bird's-eye view, have no eye for "the lilies of the field" and "the sand on the seashore." Instead of "counting no human alien to me," I would "count nothing in nature alien to us." But I reserve for the spiritual sphere an autonomous character and a distinct principle, and so the right not just to raise objections to every utterly mechanistic, i.e., atomistic system but to criticize such from its own standpoint. I shall proceed to do so with respect to the Evolution-system as it affects *aesthetic, ethical,* and *religious* life.

The *aesthetically beautiful* is a dangerous reef in the breakers for Evolution-theory because it cannot abandon utility as the exclusive Selection motive without also abandoning its mechanistic explanation of the universe. People have therefore attempted to explain the *beautiful* from the *useful,* notwithstanding that all aesthetic development since Kant — with his "that which pleases us, though without usefulness" — opposes this in principle. They would have it that, in the animal world, the female is attracted by a beautiful male physique so that the gracefully formed

28. The quotations are all from Haeckel, *Natürliche Schöpfungsgeschichte;* in order: vol. II, pp. 799, 798, 801; vol. I, p. 190; vol. II, pp. 783, 767. Karl Vogt (1817-95) was a German geologist and physiologist who had published his *Lectures on Man, His Place in Creation and in the History of the Earth* in Germany in 1863. Johannes Reinke (1849-1931) was a biologist with similarly pronounced philosophical concerns. [Ed.]

has a better chance to propagate its species. This hypothesis says something but not much. For in the first place it neglects to note that, according to the theory of evolution, the graceful form was not complete until thousands of years had passed; as beautiful as the full-grown wing may be, so ugly were the stumps from which it gradually grew. Secondly, this selection of the beautiful via sexual preference does not hold true in the lower animal world. Thirdly, it assumes an aesthetic sense in the female without being able to explain mechanistically how this feminine sense matures. And yet people have thought to detect this sexual aesthetic sense even in the plant kingdom. Beautiful and fragrant flowers attracted the insects necessary for fertilization better than the ugly and scentless. The strawberry rather than the medlar lured the bird that swallowed the seed along with the fruit, let it pass through its intestines, and entrusted it to the earth elsewhere.

Now if a beech or cedar seems beautiful to our eyes, it could hardly be explained on the basis of insect or bird attraction but would simply be what we are accustomed to, for we have never known anything but the ordinary tree with the forms of its trunk, branches, and leaves. The Evolutionists themselves realized that, whatever the element of truth hidden in all this, it could not come close to explaining the luxuriant beauty of the world. In their embarrassment they sought a way out in subjectivism. One may go into raptures while gazing at the Pleiades or the beautiful lines of the mountains, or enjoy the view of stream or cataract, yet all this is only a subjective perception; nothing guarantees a corresponding objective beauty. Then what about the world of sound, which comes to the ear from without and enters the soul through the ear? But why go on? The very flight into the tent of subjectivism has cut off the theory of evolution from itself. It must explain not only our outward but our inner life mechanistically, or its Monism will be dead. . . . [E]ither the theory of Evolution must refer the aesthetic to the realm of fancy, or, if it be true that beauty undeniably exists both subjectively and objectively, aesthetics most emphatically gives the lie to the evolution hypothesis.

It's no different with *Ethics*. Undoubtedly Spencer and the Scottish school are correct, by contrast with the Kantians, in demanding that in the ethical realm we deal not only with the adult but also with the budding person, even before the cradle. For us Reformed the admonition was unnecessary; rather, we were plagiarized. For our earliest theologians thought that an *ability* to believe was potentially present already in the mother's womb. But the problem the Evolutionists face in their study of Ethics is totally different. There too they must prove that ethical consciousness is not governed by a teleological tendency or norm but is bound up with the stirrings of life in the plant and animal kingdoms, arises from the physical and chemical action of inorganic elements, comes into and continues in existence purely mechanistically, and only accidentally achieves higher organization. From that viewpoint a self-standing good to which man would be conformed is a self-contradiction, for then the teleological idea would have been reintroduced. Therefore, in Spencer's view, the perfect moral good can only be an act that simultaneously produces maximum integration of life for the individual and for his fellow-individuals. In this system, as Spencer frankly acknowledges, the idea of duty can rest only upon well-timed and fortunate error, for one who acts from a sense of duty acknowledges a higher determinant and thereby denies the automatic properties of Mechanism. Therefore Spencer and his school break with all earlier psychology and boldly demand that mechanistic evolution, which has supposedly been proved by induction in astronomy, ontogeny, biology, etc., and which leads to a unified conception of all cosmic life, shall also prescribe the study methods that govern psychology and ethics.

Thus, in their opinion, ethics will obtain the right to declare itself a science only when it establishes itself as an analogous subdivision of the unified science of mechanistic evolution. There can be no talk of a soul as separate entity. There is nothing but the human "living organism" which develops in two directions, physiological and psychological. In its course of development it undergoes no changes but those resulting from tendencies inherited from plant, animal, and man, from association with other similar beings, and from the resistance of material nature. Neither ruling principle nor organic motive nor a pursued ideal give guidance in this respect. At any given moment man is nothing more than the product of internal and external circumstance. There can be no thought of sin or guilt except in his erring notion, and the only good that spurs him on spontaneously and persistently is *desire* [*de lust*]. Initially the desire of one individual will clash with that of the other, but gradually the cause of such clashes wears off. For the more man lives in association with others, the less egotistical desire can find its rightful place without also seeking the happiness of its fellow beings. This altruism — or rather, this *companionable* egoism — will continue its struggle with *isolated* egoism for a while because of faulty associations. But finally, when the association is perfected, sympathy will cause egoism and altruism to flow together into a higher unity, and all to which our desire urges us will of itself be perfectly good. The idea of moral freedom is thus shown the door, with derision. In the ethical sphere, too, nothing is to be acknowledged but one continuing, albeit accidental, dynamic process. Just as the train of evolution rumbles on relentlessly in nature, thanks to the tension between single-cell and multi-cell existence, so all development in the field of ethics is but a blind process, the fruit of the clash between *homo solus* and *homo associatus* and of both with brute nature. There is no ethical ideal that would draw us as with a magnet; there is and remains, always in the noble sense, the atomistic pleasure principle of *Epicurus redivivus*.

Could we not apply to this quasi-ethical cobweb what Carl Vogt wrote concerning Haeckel's plastidule hypothesis: "Thus you simply throw psyche out the door, and psyche ceases to be psyche"?[29] The names of psychology and ethics continue to appear as labels on the signboard, but all the drawers and closets in the shop where the ethical ingredients ought to be laid out ready for use are bare empty. There is no longer a soul, for "that which one usually calls 'soul' is only the sum of the activities of a great number of ganglion cells." A soul in distinction from the body would attack Monism in its vitals. Spirit does not exist without matter. There can be no more talk of the soul's continued existence after death since it lacks independent existence. Experimental physiology and psychiatry, and no less ontogeny, have once for all demolished the dogma of immortality. The species remains, the individual perishes. There is no connection with a life beyond death, "and it must be complete nonsense to continue to talk about the immortality of the human person." Even Hallier states that "a continuation of our spirit after death is an impossible thing."[30]

Accordingly, the moral ideal, the moral world order, the moral law that governs us, the sense of duty that binds us to that law, and the Holy One who gives us the law all fall away, and with these basic ideas we lose the correlate ideas of sin, guilt and repentence, redemption and atonement. Thus Evolution robs Ethics of its entire subject and substitutes a sociological apparatus in which the psychological phenomena appearing in the individual throw very little weight in the scale. Even the idea of "righteousness," to which Spencer gives nominal deference, is based on a play of words. For right and righteousness necessarily pre-

29. Kuyper does not give a citation for the Vogt statement but adds: "In Germany the same ethic is gaining ground. See Gustav Ratzenhofer, *Die Sociologische Erkenntniss* (Leipzig, 1898), who, over against the point of departure of theology and metaphysics, bases his system on positivistic understanding (pp. 368-69). See also Georg Johannes Unbehaun, *Versuch einer philosophischen Selectionstheorie* (Jena, 1896), p. 137; and Oscar Hertwig, *Die Lehre vom Organismus und ihre Beziehung auf Socialwissenschaft* (Jena, 1899), pp. 20ff. There is an interesting critique of this system by Victor Cathtrein, *Die Sittenlehre des Darwinismus* (Freiburg, 1885)."

30. The first two quotations are from Haeckel, *Natürliche Schöpfungsgeschichte*, vol. II, p. 808; vol. I, p. 297; the third from Ernst Hallier, *Naturwissenschaft, Religion und Erziehung* (Jena, 1875), p. 41. [Ed.]

suppose an authoritatively imposed order to which life must be conformed, but just this idea of preformative authority, being branded teleological, is in irreconcilable conflict with the basic idea of the Evolution-theory. An ethical development can never be deduced from the theory of Evolution except as an accidental result of uncontrolled adaptations. Therefore, although true Ethics does not refuse to pay its toll of gratitude for so many latent powers revealed by the theory of Evolution, yet it will resist tooth and nail a system that robs it of its most sacred treasures, its ideal motives, its very life. It is firmly determined to give no quarter in this most bitter "struggle for life." All we have gained thus far in the field of ethics we owe *not* to the ethics of the Evolution-system but precisely to the ethical powers that Evolution excludes. It holds out to us an ultimate perfection so distant that, in the absence of all teleology, none can guarantee it. And although its theory may give some support to ethical respectability in a limited circle of intellectuals, as soon as its ideas penetrate to the broad masses, humanity as such will sink back into horrible sensuality and unbridled barbarism.

I now come to my last point, the critique of *religion*.

In England the adherents of Evolution have never passed by the altar without half a genuflection. Most of them are still faithful attendants at worship in the polychromatic Church of England. They are moved thereto partly by the traditions of the religious past, partly to get their theory accepted by means of their respect for the national religion. In Germany on the other hand, the Evolutionist, insolent and condescending, likes to wound pious feelings. Or perhaps "insolent" is too weak when Dr. Haeckel objects that our "personal God" is nothing more than a "gaseous vertebrate" and when, asked what is meant by God, he replies: "the sum of all atomic powers and oscillations of the ether."[31] Yet the German evolutionists rather than the English have undoubtedly derived the correct consequences from their principle. For Monism as understood by this school fully assents to Goethe's thesis that "matter can never exist or be effective without spirit, nor spirit without matter." The theory of Evolution considers an independently existing spirit to be a piece of nonsense. Thus in principle it *must* oppose the existence of angels, the existence of the soul, but then too the existence of a God. A spiritual Being that exists independent of the material world is death to the theory of evolution. And if it continues to speak of "religion," it is playing with words. It declares that true religion, after deleting all its "mystical doctrines and supernatural revelations," finds its invaluable core only in a purified "ethical doctrine which is based on rational an-

31. Haeckel, *Monismus als Band*, p. 33.

thropology," an ethics that is then formulated as being the "equilibrium between egoism and altruism." The feeling thus created is labeled piety, and this "equilibrium," tied in with the "sum of all atomic powers and oscillations of the ether," is conjured up before the multitude as the real "trinitarian-monistic religion" of what is True and Good and Beautiful.[32]

Ladies and Gentlemen, I do not hesitate a moment to brand such reckless play with the holiest things as the most cowardly quasi-religious invention ever put into words. Why not be honest, have the courage of one's conviction, and frankly admit that Evolution is not only atheistic but anti-theistic and would ban all religion as human self-deceit. Then you would know that you're dealing with *men*, and both sides could prepare for the newly defined condition. But to declare boldly on the one hand that the soul does not exist, that life after death is nonsense, that therefore nothing remains of Christ after Golgotha, that spirit without matter is unthinkable, that the highest unity is to be thought of only as a sum of ether waves, and yet to speak of a trinitarian God and of religion is to deceive oneself or others, and dishonors the man of science. He who would assign a distinct sphere to Religion alongside of and distinguished from Ethics must also maintain this distinction in its elaboration and let religion be what it is logically and historically in accordance with the normal meaning of the word. Religion presents a duality: man who worships and a God worshiped by him. He who negates the latter and destroys the former forfeits the right, morally and logically, to take the word Religion upon his lips. It no longer exists for him. His very speaking of a "Spirit of the True, the Good, and the Beautiful" makes him unfaithful to his own theory. That Spirit means a transcendent or immanent power that reveals the True, Good, and Beautiful to the spirit of man and irresistably draws him to them. Just this spiritual drive, which adopts a goal toward which it is driven, presupposes purpose and plan and influence, and thus belongs entirely to the teleological domain which is forbidden ground for Evolution. In a universe that is constructed purely mechanistically, there is no room physiologically or psychologically for such a guiding, inspiring, and purposeful Spirit.

Of course, it is an entirely different question — and one much discusssed, especially in England — whether religion as such permits a spontaneous unfolding of the species in organic life from the cytode or the nuclear cell. This question must be answered affirmatively, without reservation. We will not force our style upon the Chief Architect of the universe. If He is to be the Architect not in name only but in reality, He will also be supreme in the choice of style. Had it thus pleased God not

32. Haeckel, *Monismus als Band*, pp. 28, 36.

to create the species but to have one species emerge from another by enabling a preceding species to produce a higher following species, Creation would still be no less miraculous. But this would never have been the Evolution of Darwinism, for then foreordained purpose [*Zweck*] would not have been banished but would have been all-controlling. Then the world would not have constructed itself mechanistically but God would have built it with elements He himself had prepared.[33] The contrast is most clearly shown in an example chosen by Haeckel. To eliminate the difficulty inhering in a mechanistic explanation of a constructed organism, he asks whether a Zulu who sees an English battleship put in to Lorenzo Marquez would not automatically look upon it as an organic monster, while *we* know very well that it is mechanically constructed. This everyone will concede, but Haeckel overlooked the fact that the iron plates did not automatically *come together* at the shipyards but *were fitted into place* by an able architect according to a previously prepared plan. The same difference would distinguish such an evolutionistic Creation of God from the system of the Darwinists. Evolutionistic creation presupposes a God who first prepares the plan and then omnipotently executes it; Darwinism teaches a mechanistic origin of things, which excludes all plan or specifications or purpose. Not Preformation but Epigenesis is the slogan of this system.[34]

To go further. The claim of this system that the puzzle of the world's existence is solved by the mechanistic production of the living from the non-living rests on delusion and misunderstanding. Without the ether-molecules and their waves, and the atoms with their action, and the cells with their capacity to divide, and variability with heredity, thus also without the disproportion between the number of eaters and the available food, the monistic mechanics of this system cannot advance one step. No matter that Nägeli exclaims: "To deny spontaneous generation means to

33. DuBois-Reymond in his most recent publication, *Über Neo-vitalismus,* has actually accepted this position. He posited that God "before conceivable time created by a creative act all matter in such a way that the simplest living beings came into existence according to the concomitant laws of matter, out of which, without further assistance, the natural world of today arose from an original micrococcus all the way up to Suleima's sweet gestures and Newton's brain." This, however, was completely in conflict with the theory of evolution, and Dr. Haeckel also hastened to censure it in a later work: *Die Welträthsel* (Bonn, 1899), p. 274. Suggesting such a notion, he said, exposes "in a striking way the shallowness and illogic of his monistic thought." Gerardus Johannes Mulder, in *Das streben der Materie nach Harmonie* (Braunschweig, 1844), p. 24, took the same position as DuBois-Reymond.

34. Cf. Oscar Hertwig, *Zeit- und Streitfragen der Biologie,* vol. I, *Präformation oder Epigenese?* (Jena, 1894).

acknowledge miracle." To get rid of miracle he must also first explain mechanistically the existence of the ether-molecules and atoms, for the omnipotence that can create one atom may be a lesser miracle in degree, but not in essence, than that required to call man into being. The presumptuous notion of having arrived and having explained everything apart from God can therefore be maintained only so long as one halts at the borderline between the living and non-living world and shuts his eyes to what lies behind. Thus, too, the explanation of world mechanics on the basis of variability and heredity, of the disproportion between procreation and food, and of the consequent "struggle for life" *is* no explanation so long as the mechanistic explanation for *those three mighty factors themselves* has not been formed.

From the nature of the case my address must refrain from comparing one theory with another. This cannot be done in a few sentences, and a superficial treatment in this case would lead to misunderstanding. However, it should be noted that the adherents of the new studies declare for monotheism over against polytheism; place the unity of the entire creation in the brightest light; affirm the origin of every species from one specimen; commend the origin of the entire human race from one blood; explain the representative status of Adam [*in lumbis Adami*] according to Weismann's theory; elevate "through suffering to glory" to a principle; make the regeneration of the dead body more comprehensible; find Pelagianism to be in error; maintain capital punishment; and, in agreement with Romans 9, reject the idea that the construction of the universe was directed entirely to the happiness of man. To this I may add that the Scriptural charter of Creation eliminates rather than commends the *dramatic* entry of new beings. Scripture states that "*the earth brought forth* herb yielding seed after its kind" and also that "*the earth brought forth* the cattle and everything that creepeth upon the earth" [Gen. 1:11, 24], not that they were *set down* upon the earth by God like pieces upon a chessboard.

These points of contact we may not neglect. Yet the principial contrast between theory and theory remains unimpaired and irreconcilable. Man is and remains created after God's image. Animal nature has not determined our humanity; just the opposite, the entire lower cosmos is paradigmatically determined by the central position of man. Not as Ranke asserted: "the animal kingdom is dissected man, and man is the paradigm of the whole animal kingdom."[35] That statement needlessly invites refutation. And yet conceptually it is the case that everything on a lower plane culminates in man and in that respect is the *image-bearer of*

35. Johannes Ranke, *Der mensch* (Leipzig, 1894), vol. I, foreword, p. 1.

man, even as man bears the *image of his God.* Since the Evolution-theory thus destroys the object and kills the subject among the two indispenable terms for all real Religion — God and man — Religion can do nothing other than, like Aesthetics and Ethics, irrevocably condemn the system of Evolution by virtue of the law governing its own life.

To hesitate here would betray one's own convictions. Evolution is a newly conceived system, a newly established theory, a newly formed dogma, a newly emerged faith. Embracing and dominating all of life, it is diametrically opposed to the Christian faith and can erect its temple only upon the ruins of our Christian Confession. No satisfaction with or appreciation of the beauty and riches cast into our laps by the studies that it stimulated may let us be at peace for even a moment with this system *as system.* That system remains evil, even though in many respects good has come out of evil. And therefore against that *system* of the aimlessly and mechanistically constructed cosmos we set our full-fledged resistance. We must not merely defend ourselves against it but attack it. The textbooks into which it found its way must be laid aside, and we may not entrust our children to any instructor who teaches it. Like a deadly bacteria that would destroy all spiritual life, it must be microscopically investigated and its every trace removed from the tissue of our life. Over against Nietzsche's Evolution-law that the stronger must tread upon the weaker we cling to the Christ of God who seeks the lost and has mercy on the weak. Over against the undirected mechanism of Evolution we present faith in that Eternal Being who "has worked and continues to work all things after the counsel of His will" [Eph. 1:11]. Over against the Selection that respects the species and neglects the individual, we cling to Election which speaks of the "white stone and on the stone a new name written which no man knoweth but he that receiveth it" [Rev. 2:17]. Over against the annihilation of the individual person in the grave we continue to testify of a coming judgment and of an eternal glory. And over against an altruism that is nothing more than a "transformed" and therefore disguised egoism we raise up the fire of eternal love that burns in God's Father-heart, a holy spark of which has leaped to our own.

Ladies and Gentlemen, the first time I handed over the rectorate I warned against the "Higher Criticism" of Scripture which threatened to rob us of the Revelation of our God. When I spoke of the "Blurring of the Boundaries" I cautioned against the destructive influence of Pantheism.[36] Today I felt myself called to speak out against the even deadlier

36. Kuyper is referring respectively to *De hedendaagsche Schriftcritiek in hare bedenkelijke strekking voor de Gemeente des levenden Gods* (Amsterdam: J. H. Kruyt, 1881); and *The Blurring of the Boundaries* (Amsterdam: J. A. Wormser, 1892). [Ed.]

danger of Evolution. On the two previous occasions and again today I have not pleaded narrowly for a specifically Reformed view but for the sacred treasure of our Christian religion most broadly conceived. And so I conclude by returning to what was, is now, and ever shall be the starting point of the Confession for the entire Christian church on earth, by maintaining over against Evolution the first of all articles of faith:

I BELIEVE IN GOD ALMIGHTY, CREATOR OF HEAVEN AND EARTH.

Common Grace in Science

Kuyper was a man of many paradoxes. He mounted a radical defense of tradition; he proposed modern innovations in Baroque prose. So too with his epistemology. If *The Blurring of the Boundaries* presents a critique of German Idealism, his reflections on *Common Grace in Science* go after empiricism and naturalism. His own positive position can only be called subjective Realism, premised on a Victorian — or pietistic — dualism between "higher" and "lower" realms but issuing in a call for pluralistic scholarship that sounds postmodern a hundred years ahead of its time. The how, what, and why of this position are spelled out in the articles that follow, written in the first year of the twentieth century.

Two remarks about their original context. First, by placing them at the end of his long series on common grace, Kuyper meant these articles to raise science's stature among his followers and to explain the virtue, even the possibility, of genuine work by unbelievers in this domain. He accomplished both purposes at once by entailing *all* achievements as the fruit of grace and by entailing all reality as an emanation of divine thought. If his statements on the latter point sound intellectualistic or "scholastic," they should also be read as part of a long-standing tradition of Christian Idealism. Indeed, Kuyper is a "Realist" only as concerns the human point of view; with God, it's all an Idea.

Second, Kuyper was writing in the midst of a stiff argument, continent-wide, over the status of what we would call the humanities and social sciences. Did these or did they not have "scientific" warrant? If so, on what grounds? If not, where was their worth? Kuyper is decidedly in the party of the "human" or "spiritual sciences" — i.e., among those who thought that disciplines which treated the non-material world or worked with non-experimental procedures were fully as "scientific" as, say, physics and chemistry. "Science" as he uses it below, therefore, must always be taken to include theology, philosophy, literature, and political economy. A more accurate translation in our own idiom might be "higher learning," "systematic study," or "academic discipline/s;" this translation leaves it as "science" because it seems best to register Kuyper's own usage within the controversies of the time. Whether to render *geest* as "mind" or "spirit" is still more problematic, since Kuyper's intention is not always clear. That these technical questions involve such substantive issues might challenge his distinction between "higher" and "lower," neutral and charged, fields of study; but his defense of *geestelijke wetenschap* is a challenge to our thinking as well as our tongue.

> The three-volume *De Gemeene Gratie* (1902-4) did not include the articles on science and art that originally concluded Kuyper's six-year series on the subject in *De Heraut*. They were bound and issued separately as *De Gemeene Gratie in Wetenschap en Kunst* (Amsterdam: Höveker & Wormser, 1905). Of the five articles on science, the first three and a half are reproduced here, with some minor excisions of repetitive and summary materials. This translation is a reworking of an original draft by Hans van de Hel commissioned by Wayne Bornholdt, and is included with their permission.

I

. . . The autonomy of science rests upon the creation of humanity in God's image. In the Lord our God resides an independent thinking that did not come into Him from created things but preceded the creation of all things. He does not think because He created but created after having thought. This is what we confess under the Decree [of election]. As the will of God lies expressed in the Decree, so the will of God is aimed at what His wisdom had thought out. There is no such thing as a decision not preceded by thought. And that divine thought which preceded His decision is not, as some conceive it, a looming up of random ideas from a mystic, unconscious background of His being but totally autonomous in full divine clarity of consciousness. God is not inspired by anyone outside Himself, as Scripture expresses in saying that no one taught Him, that nobody stood by His side as a counselor (Rom. 11:34). . . . [Kuyper additionally quotes 1 Cor. 2:16 and Isaiah 40:13.] Hence it must be firmly confessed that thinking was completely independent and original in God, that from this thinking the Decree came forth and from the Decree the

Kuyper the world-traveler of 1906, shortly after
Common Grace in Science appeared.

world, just as today, in the same manner, all the history of the world proceeds from it.

. . . [Kuyper supports this position from Prov. 8:22-31 and John 1, and commends the Reformed churches for having seen and upheld its full implications in their decretal theology.]

If thinking is first in God, and if everything created is considered to be only the outflowing of God's thought so that all things have come into existence by the Logos — i.e., by divine reason, or better, by the Word — yet still have their own being, then God's thinking must be contained in all things. There is nothing in the whole creation that is not the expression, the embodiment, the revelation of a thought of God. Not that the thinking of God attempts to shape an immeasurable amount of matter; rather, this thinking sits in every created thing. A thought of God forms the core of the essence of things; God's thinking prescribes their form of existence, their appearance, their law for life, their destiny, and their passing away. All creation is but a visible curtain behind which the exalted working of divine thought shines. As a child at play sees nothing of your watch but a golden case, the face, and the moving hands, so the unthinking person observes in nature and all creation nothing more than the outward appearance of things. But you know better. You know that behind the face lies the hidden work of springs and wheels and that this hidden functioning causes the hands to move. Likewise, whoever has been taught from the Word of God knows that behind nature, behind creation, occurs a hidden and mysterious operation of God's power and wisdom, and that only thereby do things work as they do. This is not an unconscious operation of power executed without will, but the operation of a *power* directed by *thinking*.

The divine thought that causes all things to function in their course is no working without aim or plan but an operation directed at a destiny and moving toward that goal within stringent rules. Everything indispensable for reaching that destiny has been placed in created things at their origin. Hence, everything has come forth from God's thinking, from God's consciousness, from God's Word. Thereby is everything carried and assured of reaching its goal. And so it can and must be unconditionally confessed that all creation in its origin, existence, and course is a rich, coherent revelation of what God has thought in eternity and determined in His Decree.

Now the question is whether we human beings are equipped with an ability to *rethink* this thinking of God. Surely not every creature has that ability. The lily, however more beautifully dressed than Solomon in all his glory, knows nothing of its own beauty and does not comprehend the least of the divine thoughts that are expressed in its existence. How wonderful the fish living in water! Yet it knows nothing of water's composition, of water's ability to carry a body, nor of the nourishing powers that water contains. It does not even seem that the animals equipped with a high form of instinct — the ant, the bee, the spider, etc. — understand a thing of what they do, much less of what God reveals in them, even though we must speak of animals with great care as we cannot penetrate their inner being. . . . Of man, on the other hand, this great truth is revealed to us: He is created in God's image. On this basis the Reformed churches confess that the original man in his nature — i.e., as the result of his place in creation, not by supernatural grace — received holiness, justice, and *wisdom*. This bespeaks an ability imparted to man to unwrap the thoughts of God that lie embodied in creation, . . . an ability not added to but based in human nature itself.

> . . . On these three points [God's thought in eternity, expressed in creation, with human ability to grasp this thought systematically] human science is based. Such wonderful ability has not been given for possession without use. Man must use this ability to the purpose for which it was given. Science arises as soon as man engages that ability to rethink God's thoughts from creation, and it gains greater stability and richer content as he pursues it more precisely and with more enthusiasm.

We must not conclude, however, that the scientific task was committed in its full extent to each person individually. That is impossible: the range is far too great and any person's ability far too limited. Our confession of man's creation in God's image goes much farther than acknowledging that we personally, one by one, are God's seed. It is done justice only when we extend it to our *whole* race in the course of centuries and in the combination of the talents granted to individual persons. No one brain, one genius, one talent is given the ability to understand the fullness of *the Word* in creation, but all people together have the task of making this comprehension possible. If it were meant otherwise, then each individual man or woman should have complete possession of all genius and talent. But this is not the case: genius and talent occur rarely, and only in a few. Even granting that many things are different in this respect than they would have been without sin, no one would assert that people would have been without differences or distinctions under the original creation ordinance. The starlit heaven does not show us innumerable identical stars but endless groups of stars all different from each other. Precisely in this multiform distinction the beauty of the firmament shines. So it may not be assumed that God meant to have uniformity in His human world and that pluriformity arose as the result of sin. In that case sin would have enriched life, not impoverished it. Moreover, the very fact that God created male and female proves conclusively that uniformity was *not* part of the creation plan. Therefore, we can conclude only that the rich differences in nature and talent among people came forth from creation itself and belong to the essence of human nature. If this be so, it follows that no one single person has this trait of God's Image in full but that it lies only in the combination of all talent and genius.

Thus science is not built up by what a single person discovers, ponders, and works into a system but by the fruit of reflection and cooperation among successive generations over the centuries. Of course, each person has some knowledge he has mastered, but God's creation is limitlessly large, and the richness of thoughts expressed therein is so fathomlessly deep that anyone's personal knowledge fades to nothing by

Kuyper's ambivalence toward science and technology is captured in this photo as his traditional funeral carriage passes by the new automobile of the twentieth century.

comparison. Naturally, that little bit of knowledge is science in the most general sense of the term, but not *the* Science which, as a distinct creation of God, arises with its own law to fulfill its own task. Science in this exalted sense originates only in the cooperation of many, moves forward slowly over successive generations, accepts only that stability and rich content which assure it an independent existence, and then begins to function in the more general sense as an influence in life. Therefore science could attain importance only over the course of ages and will unfold its fullest riches at the end of time. It is like a great temple that first needs a hole dug for the foundation, upon which the walls can then be erected and the battlements placed. The full beauty of its lines, colors, and shape will be manifest only when *the whole building* is complete. . . . This is why the history of the last centuries, especially the sixteenth and nineteenth, records such a flowering in this field and why we all feel that science stands only at the beginning of her great triumphs. Anyone familiar with scientific matters thus joyfully anticipates the progress expected in the twentieth century too.

. . . [The collaborative pattern also authenticates science's autonomous character.] Science did not arise after a first-rate architect, prior to the construction of the temple, had produced an elaborate blueprint that subsequent generations could calmly follow. The entire temple was built *without* human plan and *without* human agreement. It seemed to arise by itself. One person made a brick and laid it; another broke it loose, reshaped it, and laid it differently. Working together in this fashion, everyone moved about in his own way and built as he thought proper. And when through all this seeming confusion a temple arose over the centuries with a definite form and style that lets you guess how the completed building will look, then it *must* be acknowledged that all the labor was guided and directed by some Architect and Artisan whom no one saw. No one can say that the most beautiful result emerges by accident, without plan, on its own. Rather, it must be confessed that God Himself developed His plan for the construction of science, created the genius and talent for its execution, and so guided all the labor that what He wanted and still wants will come to pass. . . .

II

. . . [A summary recapitulation is omitted here.]

To prevent misunderstanding we must pay express attention to a peculiarity in Holy Scripture. For we often get the clear impression that it condemns instead of commends human science or wisdom. As it says in Isaiah: "Your wisdom and learning have made you perverse" [47:10]. The Preacher says: "He who increases in knowledge increases in woe" [Eccl. 1:18]. Or as Paul writes to those in Corinth: "The wisdom of the world is foolishness to God" [1 Cor. 3:19]. . . . Add in the mocking tone with which men of science almost systematically speak against Scripture and what we call holy, consider too the way that the so-called results of science have destroyed many people's faith, and the suspicion against science that has crept in among believers is easily explained. Not a few see in it an enemy that needs to be fought instead of cultivated, while many curse it and retreat to the safety of their own tents. We will say against this only that Scripture distinguishes between true and false science. On the one hand it professes that "the excellency of knowledge is that wisdom gives life to those who have it" (Eccl. 7:12). On the other hand, it warns us of science "falsely so called" (1 Tim. 6:20). Hence, a science called excellent is placed over against a science that falsely calls itself by this name. . . .

This distinction originates in sin. It is sin that tempts man to disconnect science from God, to steal it from God, and finally to turn it against God. The plant of true science has its roots, origin, motif, and point of departure in the fear of the Lord. If one by sin detaches himself from that root, then what he calls science is a false front, lacking its essence. Yet we must guard against misunderstanding. Some take this contradiction to mean that good science, the true science, the "science of the saints" as some call it, exists only in the knowledge of God's grace in Christ, and that false science means research into things of the world. Not so. There is a false science of holy as well as of worldly things; conversely, a true science of the holy revelation of Scripture and of life in the world. In both cases, the false and the true, the object of science is the whole of things, all that we as human beings can know. The distinction between true and false science lies not in the field but in the manner of investigation and in the principle to which one adheres in the process. Sin has not only ruined our moral life but has *darkened our mind* . . . and this darkening has brought science onto the wrong track. Further, this eclipse will continue so long as it is not balanced by the enlightenment of that mind by the Holy Spirit.

Without common grace the descent of science outside the enlightenment of the Spirit would have become absolute. Left to itself, sin goes from bad to worse. It makes you slide down a slope on which no one can remain standing. Those who do not reckon with common grace must conclude, therefore, that all science outside holy precincts is fraud and self-deception and will mislead anyone who listens to its voice. But the evidence shows this is not true. The Greeks, completely deprived of the light of Scripture, developed a science that surprises us still by the true and beautiful substance it has to offer. The names of Socrates, Plato, and Aristotle have constantly been honored by Christian thinkers. We do not exaggerate in saying that Aristotle's thinking was a most powerful means of bringing Christians to deeper reflection. And no one can deny that these days a rich science is blooming in the fields of astronomy, botany, zoology, physics, etc. Although conducted almost exclusively by people who are strangers to the fear of the Lord, this science has produced a treasure of knowledge that we as Christians admire and gratefully use.

Thus, we confront the fact that a science has arisen outside the Christian church which has produced true and essential knowledge on the one hand but which has led to a life-conception and a worldview utterly opposed to the truth of God's Word on the other. To put it differently, we confront a science that has arisen out of the world under the rule of sin and yet may boast of results from which sin's darkening is virtually absent. We can explain this only by saying that, while sin has continued to spread decay, common grace has entered in to bind and temper its operation. . . . That we may and must speak most positively of God's work in this regard is evident from the undeniable fact that in men like Plato and Aristotle, Kant and Darwin, shone stars of the first magnitude, geniuses of the highest degree, who uttered the most profound thoughts even though they were not confessing Christians. They had this genius not of themselves but received it from the God who created them and endowed them for this kind of thinking.

To fathom this we may not stop with the formula, "darkening by sin," but account for how this darkening works. Did sin disable us from thinking logically? Has it made us unable to observe what exists and occurs around us? Does sin blindfold us so that we cannot see or notice anything? Certainly not. Whenever you reason with others about anything, you assume an ability in yourself and in them to think logically. You do not hesitate for a moment, wondering if what you hear and see exists as you observe it. As a rule you go through life with a feeling of complete certainty. We have not ceased being reasonable creatures because of sin, and as we compare our existence with that of animals we are fully conscious of the superiority our reason has given us. The power we have gradually acquired over the animals and the whole world is so plain as to convince us that our research and thinking are sound. It cannot be denied that the darkening of sin is noticeable here. How many are not terribly weak in logical capacity? How many errors do we not constantly find in our reasoning? How often is our observation deceived by appearances? How slowly do our investigations plumb their full depths! How hard have we not studied for an exam or for a job without any inspiration of holy enthusiasm? All this, however, amounts to a partial break, not a complete obstruction.

No, the real darkening of sin is found in something completely different, in our having lost the gift to comprehend the true context, the proper coherence, the systematic unity of things. We now view things just outwardly, not in core and essence; hence also, each thing individually, not things together in their connection and origin in God. That connection, the coherence of things in their original relation with God, can be felt only in our spirit. It does not lie in things outside of us and therefore could be well considered only so long as our spirit stayed in vital connection with God and could trace the thought of God in that coherence. Precisely this characteristic our human mind possessed at its pure creation, and precisely this it lost when sin cut off the vital bond uniting us with God. As a dog or bird sees the bricks of a palace, the wood and plaster, maybe the colors, but comprehends nothing of the architecture, the style, the purpose of the rooms and windows, so we stand with darkened understanding before the temple of creation. We see the parts and pieces but no longer have an eye for the style of the temple, no longer can guess at its architect, and so can no longer understand the temple of creation in its unity, origin, and destiny. We are like an architect bereft of his senses who once could grasp the building as a whole but now, peeping from the window of his cell, stares fixedly at walls and peaks without comprehending the motif. . . .

[S]cience does not only consist of examining wood, stone, and metal but becomes essential science when it knows how to capture *the whole* as in a mirror. The darkening of sin thus does not concern the knowledge of details but science in its higher and more noble conception. As long as non-human creation is studied independently of God, then science still produces its miracles by a careful analysis of things and by a search for laws governing their movement. But you cannot reckon so with man. Instead, you will come to face spiritual questions that bring one into contact with the center of spiritual life, i.e., with God. Then all certainty disappears as school stands over against school, program against program, until full-blown despair at last overcomes the investigators. They will still make some progress in knowledge of the human body and of what comes forth from the mind in a material way, but as soon as they tread on real *spiritual* ground everything runs on guesses and assumptions, on the supersession of system by system, and finally on doubt and skepticism.

How this has all come about would be much clearer had we known the original situation of man, when he had come forth from the hand of the Creator but not yet been touched by sin. We don't know much about this, but there are a few data that may suffice to let us comprehend the difference introduced by sin. In our present state we can find out about things only by observation and analysis, but in paradise it was not so. For we read that God brought the animals to Adam and that Adam perceived their nature in such a way that he gave them names at first sight, right then and there. Naturally, this cannot mean that, as the animals went by him, he uttered a sound without thought or sense. Imagine that someone carried two or three hundred suitcases in front of you and that you randomly made a sound at the sight of each, one after the other. Before you reached the hundredth, you would have forgotten the name of the first. Besides, what purpose did Adam's naming the animals serve? Eve was not there. Nobody heard him. The passage makes sense only if it is understood that Adam, directly penetrating to the *essence* of each animal, expressed his *insight* in a *name* that corresponded to that essence.

Adam's ability with respect to the animal world no doubt applied just as much to vegetation, indeed, to all of nature. That faculty of immediate comprehension we no longer possess. If we want to learn more of a plant or animal, we have to study it closely and for a long time and draw conclusions about its nature [*aard*] from our observations; but we will never thus understand its essence [*wezen*]. Even its instincts remain an unsolved riddle. But Adam *had* this ability. Recognizing that, we grasp how Adam, without the entrance of sin, would have immediately come to a science of all Creation that would have led on to a direct understanding of all Creation with respect to its origin and destiny.

This too. Adam not only penetrated to the essence of things but *named* them as well. This naming is also lost to us. We can give a name to a strange thing but take it over from another people [Kuyper cites Hollanders using the English "rails, trams, and locomotive"] or make such a name with the help of Greek roots, as with telegraph, telephone, electricity, etc. But new names in our own tongue expressing the essence of things we can only form by composition or by taking over two words already in use. We can no longer create language. Adam, however, could. In him *concept* stood in organic coherence with *essence,* and *word* with *concept.* He never learned to speak from his mother but spoke automatically and as God already spoke to him, which in turn he must have understood. All this shows at how high a level his language and conceptual ability must have stood. We do not exaggerate in saying that Adam possessed a clarity and insight in his own world of thought, in his own consciousness, that is lost to us. Without sin science would have had a completely different course and would have been built with an immediacy that we can scarcely imagine. . . . To Adam, science was an immediate possession; for us it is bread we can eat only in the sweat of our minds, after hard and strenuous labor.

. . . [Kuyper spends several paragraphs discussing remnants of the capacity for immediate comprehension: animal instinct, the intuitive abilities of people who have little formal education or belong to what he regarded as lesser races. This material is closely paralleled in the first section of *Ons Instinctieve Leven.* Notably, there Kuyper valorized unlettered intuition; here he praises science's systematic investigation and understanding.]

III

The clarity of our human science has suffered appreciably from our sin-darkened understanding. This wouldn't be so bad if science were based exclusively on observation and experience, if consciousness were nothing but a mirror reflecting the world around us. For although a mirror without flaw would be preferable, we could make do with a cracked one if necessary. Along this line, then, we could postulate that the mirror of our consciousness has been cracked by sin but that even with those cracks the mirror gives us a not-too-distorted reflection of the world. Something would be wrong with the unity of the picture, but the parts could be well taken.

The problem is, something entirely different from a mirror is within us and the image cast on our consciousness is hardly the only thing that brings us to science. Our mind does have a photographic capacity, but this is only a servant to the essential operation of our scientific thinking. In the lens of our eye there is, if you will, a camera. It captures an image; another person can even see it there. But *seeing* is a much more complicated business. Just compare someone watching intently with someone staring thoughtlessly. The glance of each catches the same boat, the same house, whatever. The same image lies on the lens of each eye, but the one does and the other does not see it. Proof enough that all essential *seeing* is twofold: (1) the reflection of something on the lens of our eye; (2) our mind's engagement with what is reflected. So also with our intellectual knowledge. Manifold observation captures the image, but that hardly completes the action of our intellect; in fact, only then does the higher work of our mind begin.

. . . [To demote empiricism Kuyper compares the observation processes of a farm boy and a professionally trained scientist to the effect that the two "in essence lie along the same line."] Nonetheless, people over the last century have increasingly come to think that artificial observation is the only genuine science and to award the highest scientific credentials to that which busies itself with the observation *of nature*. The French have honored such with the name *sciences exactes* and the English simply called it "science," as if only these studies could lay claim to the honorable title of *Science* [*Wetenschap*].

This attitude may have been caused by the carelessness, even disregard, with which observation was treated in times past. But an error and a danger lurk here that demand a protest. They consist in the attempt to free science from our subjectivity or, if you please, our person. Science must be neutral and so must be disconnected from our personal being. Only that should qualify as science which *everyone* will assent to immediately or upon compelling proof. But the notion that science must be impartial, its only task being to find "truth," begs the question. Why would an investigator ever search for anything but the truth? In the realm of science this is inconceivable. Yes, one can have a further goal in view. The doctor checks the lung to cure it, the miner wants to find gold. But doctor and miner both search for the *truth*. How else would the lung be healed? Could a mine yield gold that wasn't there? Everyone will agree, then, that in the first phase of the scientific endeavor — that of *proper observation* — truth remains the chief goal. Since we do not produce the object to be observed but find it outside of ourselves, the very nature of the task requires us to aim for as great an objectivity in observation as possible, in which process our own ego should play as passive a role as it can.

This remark, proper in itself, has given rise to the proposition that we accept as science only that which is observed in this manner, by all alike, and by direct conclusion from the data. The subject of the scientist, his own ego, is allowed no voice, and the old concept that our mind is a *tabula rasa,* a blank sheet of paper, arises in new form. While this approach goes on in physics and chemistry, it went wrong when people carried it over to history, philosophy, or any other human science. Indeed, as soon as there was talk of a science of man, people were so kind as to deny these higher disciplines a genuinely scientific character and to reserve that for those fields which only measure, weigh, and count. This has pushed people in the spiritual sciences to base their work as much as possible on external observation; even what we call psychology has to be constructed entirely on outward appearances. It has led to the increasing materialization of *all* science, feeding the false notion that spiritual life arises from material causes. And this trend, generally speaking, has won the field as the ruling characteristic of modern science.

This we must oppose. The autonomous character of the spiritual in us may not be lost or we will shortly arrive at the denial of spirit in general and thus of God. . . . If the autonomy of the spiritual life, of the spirit, and so also of the Father of spirits is to remain unharmed, then science has to reckon with that independent factor of the mind — and do so as much in the researching subject as in the spiritual things researched. From this follows the absurdity of the statement, "that alone is scientific which can be proved to the consent of all." Were all subjects alike, the statement would be undoubtedly true. But since subjects are *not* alike, since different points of departure prevail from one consciousness to another, and since not only differences but contradictions arise time after time as a result, the illusion of a single science can no longer be maintained.

Our observation of the spiritual world must always begin with a consultation of our own spirit. Only from our own spirit do we come by comparison and association to some knowledge of other spiritual existence. Seeing and hearing, weighing and measuring can help in this, but no more. Whatever we see and hear of others would never have caused us to find out that there is a spirit in them did we not possess a spirit ourselves. Scripture says: "For what man knoweth the things of man, save the spirit of man that is in him?" [1 Cor. 2:11]. So it is indeed. By self-consciousness we come to know the human spirit in general. Nor is that all. If a spiritual world exists in distinction from a physical world, then communication with that world is possible only through our own spirit. What we sense about the working of God in nature or about the spirit of man in history, literature, and our surroundings no doubt helps enrich our knowledge, but experience teaches us every day that it does not lead to a correct knowledge of God or man unless we possess a spirit in ourselves that brings us into touch with the realm of spiritual life. We ought not to try relying as much as possible on outward observation and call on our own spirit for help only when we can go no further. That is cowardice. No, we must boldly maintain the twofold nature of the terrain. On the one hand, a field of external things where everything depends on seeing and hearing, weighing and measuring; on the other, a field of invisible spiritual things where our own spirit within deserves the right of first action and where the outwardly observable can never function but as a servant.

How deeply this cuts to the essence of science we will sense by considering that science without reflection is inconceivable, yet thinking itself is a spiritual occupation. The very instrument that serves as a trowel in the construction of science belongs to the invisible things, and the law governing this thinking can never be discovered by seeing, hearing, weighing, and measuring but manifests itself in the human spirit. The contradiction arises immediately that our thinking cannot help but ask about the origin, coherence, and destiny of things, whereas observation neither can nor does teach anything on this score. Observation cannot begin before something is there. Suppose you were present at creation: you would not have seen or heard anything before it was, and you could not say anything about the cause whereby it came into being. Likewise, it is impossible for us to come to a solid, all-encompassing conclusion about the system of things by way of observation or calculation. Through careful observation we may notice one thing and another: that many things are connected, how one triggers another. But here too our knowledge is so limited that even in our personal lives we continually confront enigmas that we cannot solve. We are not satisfied to determine a particular connection; our higher consciousness demands that this be explained as a *reasonable* connection so that we see how everything fits together and what purpose the system serves. We see that there is a connection between Gladstone's death, the collapse of the liberal party in England, the discovery of gold mines in the Rand, the Rhodes clique, and the war in Transvaal. That's not difficult, but it does not satisfy us. All Europe and America are deeply moved by this cruel course of events and resent the lack of authority to end it. We don't want to know just the causal connection; our spirit does not rest until we can comprehend the idea that caused this connection to develop. The sense of justice will not rest so long as we cannot clarify the connection of right in this connection of events.

Now this depends on our third point of reference, the *destiny* of things. Our mind finds no rest in the concept of an endless continuation of our life here on earth. Personally, we cannot imagine having taken part in all the ages the world has already lasted; even less that the carpenter should do nothing century after century but saw and plane his wood or that the sailor would drift, age upon age, from port to port. Everything must come to an end, and we cannot help but imagine that the world will come to an end too. Then what? Could all that was or still is have had no other destiny than mere continuation? Thus the idea arises of itself that a destiny, a final goal, has been determined for everything, and that all that is or was is aimed at reaching that goal. But a science that only sees, hears, weighs, and measures cannot tell us a thing about this, for it cannot see to the end. To the extent that science holds on to the visible and observable, it cannot even entertain the question of the origin, coherence, and destiny of things. The Evolution-theory imagines it can do this now with respect to origins, but this is no more than self-deception, for it goes back to the first atoms and the energy within them and of the origin of these atoms and energy it can tell us nothing. It thus relocates the question but cannot answer it. Nonetheless, our mind constantly and inescapably asks these three great and mighty questions: whence? how? whither? The mighty rise of Darwinism itself is in no small part to be explained from unreflective people imagining that here at least was sufficient answer to the first of these three questions.

. . . [Kuyper summarizes the argument thus far, and recalls the church's ancient teaching about God being revealed in creation.] Surely, from the beginning the invisible things of God are understood from creation, both His eternal power and divinity [Rom. 1:20]. But while the lion has an eye and the eagle an even better one than you, and both observe the creatures you see, they guess nothing of the eternal power and divinity of the Lord of lords simply because they lack a spirit and so do not know the very idea of God. You, on the contrary, observe the same creatures and understand from them the eternal power and divinity of the Lord.

This does not derive from those creatures but from your having been created with a human spirit which from the start included the idea, the awareness, the consciousness of God's existence.

You may point out that any number of people observe the same creatures yet are not moved to worship God's eternal power and divinity. To which we answer that seeing through a microscope depends upon its being properly set up and focused. Anybody who has ever worked with a high-power microscope knows how much trouble you have to go through to see what you would see. So also here, you may not consider man as he is now in his false position. The first man saw God through nature in His eternal power and divinity in a way that our eye cannot behold Him now. We have no right to complain that we see so little. If I focus the microscope for a student and he changes the lens or the adjustment so that he sees nothing, the fault is his, not mine. This is exactly what we did when we fell into sin. Having no right to complain, we should rather be grateful that it pleased God to help us in this helpless situation by readjusting the microscope through common grace so that we can at least see *something*, even if not with the old clarity. But we can sin against this grace too. If someone is so totally engrossed in the sensory that the idea of God grows ever dimmer in his soul, if someone locks himself up in his self-sufficient thinking so that God falls outside his field of vision, then it only stands to reason that he is like an eagle that sees more sharply than common folk but, for all his eagle eye, can no longer discern the living God in His creation. Yet this is no cause for self-congratulation. If you discern a glimmer of divine life in creatures, this is but *grace* imparted to you. A grace that makes you no better but, on the contrary, should cause you to thank Him more humbly who has condescended to reveal His divine presence in your spirit, thereby enriching your life immeasurably.

IV

Whoever neglects to maintain the autonomy of the spiritual over against the material in his point of departure will eventually come to the idolization of matter by way of the adoration of man. The application of the scientific method to the higher disciplines makes that autonomy impossible to preserve. A science taking this road will wander ever farther from God and deny Him totally in the end. Likewise, the investigator who takes his foundation in the world outside himself and stakes his honor on the concept of neutral objectivity is doomed by his method to see the autonomy of his own ego go under. That is why we insist so urgently that the subjective point of departure again be honored in science. Modern science is ruled by a distrust of our own deepest sense of life, and that distrust is no more than unbelief.

People try to make good on this loss by taking their standpoint in the consciousness of the leading [*toongevende*] majority. What is generally regarded as true in scientific circles people will dare accept for themselves. What is agreed to in this manner is called *the* truth, the truth that people profess to honor. But pressing a little further, people notice that common acceptance is no proof, so they propose that that alone is scientifically established which I can make so clear to another person of sound mind and sufficient education that he will finally understand and assent to it. The Germans have made a hobby of this under the term *allgemeingültig*. . . . The result is like an army moving under orders that the cavalry not advance any faster than the infantry, nor the infantry any faster than its slowest soldier. Even in this approach faith remained necessary for further advance — be it only a faith in one axiom. Yet the result was that those richer in faith had to wait upon the one with the least faith of all. From which it followed that Christian investigators who were pulled along in this direction had to place the rich contents of their own faith outside scientific limits or even deny their faith and drift toward apostasy.

For this reason Christian thinkers have become more and more convinced of the need to restore the subject of science to its proper place. Only thus could the autonomy of the spiritual be maintained over against the material, and so also the existence of God *in* science. This also seemed more and more the position of Scripture. Scripture knows nothing of *allgemeingültigkeit*, as if truth were only that to which all must agree. On the contrary, Scripture clearly declares that the wisdom and knowledge that the world derives from its own principles stand directly opposed to true science, and that the difference between the wisdom of the world, which is foolishness to God, and the science that holds true for Him comes from the difference in spirit in the investigating subject. There are two kinds of people. Scripture calls them "natural" and "spiritual," and says this of them in 1 Corinthians 2:11-15:

> For who knows the things of a man except the spirit of man that is within him? Even so, no one knows the things of God except the Spirit of God. We have not received the spirit of the world but the Spirit which is from God, that we may know the things God has freely given to us. These things we also speak, not in words taught us by human wisdom but in words taught by the Spirit, speaking spiritual truths in a spiritual sense. But the natural man does not grasp the things that are from the Spirit of God, for they are foolishness to him, and he cannot understand them because they are spiritually discerned. But he that is spiritual judges all things, yet he himself is judged of no man.

Of course, this does not mean that there is no *lower* level of science that stands outside this antithesis. So far as conclusions are governed by sensory observation and acquired by weighing, measuring, and counting, all investigators are alike. As soon as one climbs up from this lower level to higher science, the subject comes into play and, with that, the difference between "natural" and "spiritual" man — and not just in theology but in any spiritual science as well as in the philosophical framework of the natural sciences.

From this it must follow that investigators part into two camps on the level of higher science. What the one calls science, Scripture — and with it, every Christian — calls foolishness; conversely, the wisdom of the world laughs at what we call science and thinks foolishness too weak a word to express its contempt for it. Other than letting go of the antithesis put forth in Scripture, how can we hold from a Christian standpoint that our science and that of the world must be one? How can we escape the division of the scientific enterprise into two well-defined groups? And how can we avoid the proposition that the cause lies in the differing condition of the subjects, as one lives from the consciousness of the unregenerate world and the other from the renewing of our spirit which only radical conversion affords? It is clear that Scripture by its antithesis of "spiritual" and "natural" man does not only mean that this one does and the other does not reckon with Holy Writ. The pronouncement goes much further and distinguishes between having and not having received the Spirit of God. It says so emphatically: "We have received not the spirit of the world but the Spirit which is from God" [1 Cor. 2:12]. This is in complete harmony with what Jesus Himself said, that he who "is not born of the water and of the spirit cannot enter into the kingdom of God" [John 3:5]. If you agree that the Kingdom of God is not in the least limited to the institutional church but rules our entire world-and-life-view, then Jesus' saying means that only those who have received the inner enlightenment of the Holy Spirit are able to get a view of the whole that is in harmony with the truth and essence of things.

. . . [Thus] one basic distinction lies in whether the subject is or is not born again. A second, equally true, comes from reckoning or not reckoning with the Special Revelation of God as it is preserved and sealed for us in Scripture. We have put up front the work of the Holy Spirit in the subject only because any number of investigators have busied themselves with Scripture without the inner enlightenment of the Spirit. First, they water down the content of Scripture, then interpret it in conformity with the spirit of the world. When they finally see this doesn't work, they dispute the authority of the content of Scripture, unravel it, and bring it to nought. Scripture itself can then help us no further. Precisely because Scripture is not of the world but had its content brought into the world by God's grace, it can be neither understood nor taught unless the teacher has been personally touched and enlightened by the Spirit. The bare statement that "I take account of Scripture" never leads to a satisfactory conclusion unless account is also taken of what a proper understanding of Scripture requires. The action of God's Spirit in the investigating subject must cooperate with the objective action of the Spirit in Special Revelation. Just here Special Revelation lets its light shine on common grace to strengthen it.

It cannot be denied that common grace has been active throughout the ages among a number of more developed peoples, greatly promoting the spiritual development of the human race through ingenious thinkers and brilliant talents. Yet Special Revelation was the first to shed indispensable light on the most important issues, especially as concerns the origin, government, and destiny of things. Only the Revelation of Holy Scripture affords certainty on the cardinal questions that govern our entire view of life, and these questions cannot be said to belong to the field of special grace. Special grace is the grace that saves a sinner and therefore concerns only the elect. When Holy Scripture reveals to us the mystery of creation, God's providence in the covenant with Noah, and the movement of the world toward a final catastrophe, all this most definitely concerns not only the elect but all people, everything that lives. Even the animals are not excepted, just as they were purposely included in the covenant with Noah. . . . So even though it is entirely true that this revelation concerning the deepest questions of life has come to us by way of special revelation and would not have been given to us had there been no special grace, yet it's plain as day that these have no part whatever in special grace but strengthen the light of common grace that comes to us by way of Special Revelation.

It is of highest importance to bring this clearly front and center. If Special Revelation were limited to what belongs strictly to the salvation of sinners and passed everything else by, then we would lack the data for buiding a temple of science on a Christian foundation. We would encounter nothing but the doctrine, or what Egeling calls, "the road of salvation."[1] We couldn't even attain a complete theology. But this is *not* so with Scripture. It not only teaches us about the way of salvation but

1. Lukas Egeling (1764-1835) was a Leiden pastor prominent in *Réveil* circles (e.g., presiding at da Costa's baptism) but taking its irenic rather than dogmatic direction. He was renowned as a preacher and Bible expositor and published, *inter alia, De Nadenkende Christen* (Leiden, 1833).

sheds light on great world problems. Even more, it does not place these two, the way of salvation and natural life, next to each other as in two ticket-lines but intertwines them and offers us a view of the world, its origin, its historical course, and its destiny in which the entire work of redemption fits as in an invisible matrix. With these fixed points in front of us, we are afforded the possibility of constructing an entire Christian science that frees us from idle speculation and gives us knowledge of the real condition of things, as it was, and is, and shall be.

Sphere Sovereignty

The Free University was at the heart of Kuyper's dreams. Here he could fulfill all his callings at once: scholar, institution-builder, leader, liberator, and guide of the common people. It is fitting, then, that the speech he gave to inaugurate the school captures so well the heart of his vision, from title to tone, in its substance and its unspoken assumptions.

The setting of the speech, that 20th day of October, 1880, was apt as well. Kuyper spoke in the New Church (in fact, centuries old) on Amsterdam's principal square, next to the royal palace — thus at the symbolic center of national life. The crowd of officials, dignitaries, academics, and common folk who gathered there witnessed "an impressive ceremony. The dim light of the somber autumn day fell through the high windows in the gothic arches of the ancient cathedral. The light accentuated the deep tone of the choir's oak walls within which the marble mausoleum of Michiel De Ruyter recalled [the] national struggle for liberty. With his back to the elegant copper screen Dr. Kuyper stood on a graceful podium, at the height of his powers."[1]

The near-climax of Kuyper's speech comes at one of his most famous utterances: ". . . there is not a square inch in the whole domain of our human existence over which Christ, who is Sovereign over *all*, does not cry: 'Mine!' " The first half of that sentence sounds an equally vital conviction: "No single piece of our mental world is to be hermetically sealed off from the rest. . . ." In light of such holism, some dualities in the speech deserve special note. Kuyper's tone here is militant and combative, staking out turf for his own particular group. Yet throughout he invokes national icons and appeals to a shared "folk conscience" of biblical memory and republican virtue. The very title of the piece harbors another ambiguity. "Souvereiniteit in Eigen Kring" can mean sovereignty in *its* circle, referring to the pluralistic ontology Kuyper unfolds in the text. But it can

1. J. C. Rullman, *Kuyper-Bibliografie,* vol. II (Kampen: Kok, 1929), p. 31.

mean just as well sovereignty in *our* circle, spelling out a pluralistic sociology and epistemology which Kuyper also argues for but which does not have ontological warrant. The tension can be resolved by assigning (à la Heidegger's title) the first term to being, the second to time. Or as Kuyper himself would explain later in *Common Grace*, the spheres of existence are given to all in creation under common grace; the divergence of worldviews, and so of human association, emerges under the operations of redemption or particular grace.

Finally, we should note that Kuyper here was founding a *university*. Higher education and advanced research had enormous importance for him: religiously, for exploring and enhancing God's creation; strategically, for (re)shaping society and culture; socially, for raising the self-respect and life-chances of common people. His too was a "culture of aspiration," but at once broader and deeper than the bourgeois sort which the educational revolution of his time aimed to serve.[2]

Souvereiniteit in Eigen Kring might be the most difficult text in Kuyper's corpus; it is certainly the most challenging original for this anthology. I have followed a typescript translation by George Kamp available in the Calvin College and Seminary Archives. A more literal rendering, which differs substantively with the following at certain points, can be found in the appendices to Wayne A. Kobes, "Sphere Sovereignty and the university: Theological foundations of Abraham Kuyper's view of the university and its role in society" (unpublished Ph.D. dissertation, Florida State University, 1993). Greek terms and phrases have been translated by Kenneth Bratt.

Kuyper's speech was originally published (and ready by the day of its delivery!) as *Souvereiniteit in Eigen Kring: Rede ter inwijding van de Vrije Universiteit, den 20sten October 1880 gehouden, in het Koor der Nieuwe Kerk te Amsterdam* (Amsterdam: J. H. Kruyt, 1880). I have followed the definitive version of the text found in W. F. de Gaay Fortman, ed., *Architectonische critiek: Fragmenten uit de sociaal-politieke geshriften van Dr. A. Kuyper* (Amsterdam: H. J. Paris, 1956), pp. 40-73. The translation below does not include the lengthy (some 20 percent of the total) and ornate rhetoric by which Kuyper recognized the various agencies and dignitaries present on the occasion. (The Kobes translation does provide this.) It is otherwise complete except for two short paragraphs.

Throughout, I have translated *wetenschap* not only in its strict sense as "science" but also as "scholarship" and/or "learning," since these register the Anglo-American connotations that the Dutch original (like the German *Wissenschaft*) bears.

2. For the American context, see David O. Levine, *The American College and the Culture of Aspiration, 1915-1940* (Ithaca: Cornell University Press, 1986).

THE MEN WHO ARE IN CHARGE of this institution have assigned me the honor of inaugurating their school of higher education by introducing it to the authorities and to the public. For that task I ask your benevolent ear and generous judgment. You will recognize the earnestness of that request when you consider that I am not to deliver a professor's inaugural address nor that attending the transfer of a rectorship. No, the nature of my task bars me from the quiet retreat of scholarly research and drives me onto the treacherous terrain of public life where nettles and thorns wound at every step. We neither can nor would disguise it: we have not been driven to this work like Maecenases[3] out of love for detached learning. Rather, the urge to this risky, not to say presumptuous, endeavor comes from the deep sense of duty that what we are doing *must* be done — for Christ's sake, for the name of the Lord, out of its high and holy importance for our people and country. Thus our action is not in the least ingenuous. We are deeply convinced that the interest that has anticipated this institution's founding through fair report and foul and that now attends its opening is not related in the least to our persons but has proceeded exclusively from the public's impression that the Netherlands is witnessing an event that might well leave its mark on the future of the nation.

Would we have undertaken this task if a higher standard could have induced us to acquiesce in the status quo? To put it mildly, our undertaking bears a protest against the present environment and suggests that something better is possible. Yet the appearance of presumption follows it like a shadow and causes some embarrassment, some diffidence. This might cause offense, this might hurt. Therefore I hasten to assure you that — given the scholarly power, the influence, and the money that oppose us — the assuredness of our words reflects no lofty imagination but a quiet humility. We would have preferred to stay in the rear; it would have been much more comfortable to see others take the lead. But since this was *not* to be, since we *had* to act, we came to the fore, hardly indifferent to human favor or aversion but drawing our *line of conduct* exclusively from what is demanded by the honor of our God.

3. Gaius Maecenas (d. 8 B.C.E.) was a prominent deputy of Caesar Augustus, patron of Virgil and Horace, and something of a minister of cultural affairs in the early Roman empire.

You expect me, then, to tell you how the school we are introducing fits into the Dutch garden, why it brandishes the liberty cap on the tip of its lance, and why it peers so intently into the book of Reformed religion. Let me link the answers to all three questions to the one concept of "sphere sovereignty," pointing to *sphere sovereignty* as the hallmark of our institution in its *national* significance, its *scholarly* purposes, and its *Reformed* character.

I. Its National Significance

Ladies and gentlemen, in this awesome century our nation too is struggling through a crisis, a crisis it shares with many other nations, a crisis that pervades the whole world of thoughtful humanity. Now every crisis concerns a threatened way of life whose course of illness augurs either a rejuvenation or a fatal degeneration. So what is the "threatened way of life" *here?* What is at stake for our nation? Would anyone repeat the old answers: that the contest is between progress and preservation, between one-sidedness and complexity, between the real and ideal, the rich and the poor? The inadequacy, the distortion, and the shallowness of these diagnoses have been too clearly exposed for that. Then "clerical vs. liberal" became the watchword, as though the issue was the misuse or purification of religious influence. But this curtain too has been contemptuously pulled aside as the realization dawned, first upon the leading lights of our age, then in ever broadening circles, that the world crisis involves not inequality, self-interest, or justice but a *living person* — involves Him who once swore that he was a King and who for the sake of this royal claim gave up his life on the cross of Golgotha.

"The Nazarene — our holy inspiration, our inspiring ideal, our ideal of piety!" Long have people voiced these generous words. But history has challenged that praise as contradicting the Nazarene's own claims. His calm and crystal-clear divine-human consciousness asserted that he was nothing less than the *Messiah,* the Anointed, and thus the *King* of kings, possessing "*all* authority in heaven and on earth." Not hero of faith nor "martyr to honor" but *Melek, rex, Basileus ton Ioudaion,* King of the Jews — i.e., *Bearer of Sovereignty* — read the accusation on top of the cross, proclaiming the criminal presumption for which he had to die. Over *this* sovereignty, over the existence or nonexistence of the power of the One born of Mary, the thinking minds, the ruling powers, the engrossed nations are as troubled today as they were in the first three centuries. That *King of the Jews* is either the saving truth to which all peoples say Amen or the principial lie which all peoples should oppose. That is the

Left: Kuyper in 1880.
Below: At Keizersgracht 162, this was from 1885 through 1968 the main building of the university Kuyper founded.

problem of sovereignty as it was once encountered in the blood of the Nazarene and has now again rent apart the whole world of our intellectual, human, and national existence.

What is Sovereignty? Do you not agree when I define it as the authority that has the right, the duty, and the power to break and avenge all resistance to its will? Does not your indestructible folk-conscience tell you too that the original, absolute sovereignty cannot reside in any creature but *must* coincide with God's majesty? If you believe in Him as Deviser and Creator, as Founder and Director of all things, your soul must also proclaim the Triune God as the only absolute Sovereign. Provided — and this I would emphasize — we acknowledge at the same time that this supreme Sovereign once and still delegates his authority to human beings, so that on earth one never directly encounters God Himself in visible things but always sees his sovereign authority exercised in *human* office.

Whence arises the very important question: how does this delegation proceed? Is the all-encompassing sovereignty of God delegated undivided to a single person? Or does an earthly sovereign possess the power to compel obedience only in a limited sphere, a sphere bordered by other spheres in which another is sovereign and not he?

The answer to this question will vary depending on whether you stand within or without the orbit of Revelation. Those whose minds have no place for revelation have always answered: "*insofar as practical,* undivided, and also penetrating *all spheres.*" "Insofar as practical," because God's sovereignty over what is above falls beyond human reach; over nature, beyond human power; over fate, beyond human control. But for the rest, yes, *without* sphere sovereignty. Let the state have unlimited rule, disposing over persons their lives, their rights, their conscience, even their faith. Once when there were many gods, the *one* unlimited State — through the *vis unita fortior* [united force yields greater strength] — seemed more imposing, more majestic than the *divided* power of the gods. At last the State, embodied in Caesar, itself became God, the god-"State" that could tolerate no other states beside itself. Thus the passion for *world* domination. *Divus* Augustus, with Caesarism as its worship. A profoundly sinful notion that was first elaborated for thinking consciousness eighteen centuries later in Hegel's system of the State as "the immanent God."

In contrast Jehovah proclaims to Israel through the voices of Messianic prophecy: "Sovereignty must be delegated not 'insofar as practical' but *absolutely* undivided and unbroken." That man-Messiah did appear, with power in heaven and power over nature; claiming power over all nations and, *in* all nations, over conscience and faith. Even the bond between mother and child has to yield before his call to obedience. Here then is *absolute* Sovereignty, extending over all things visible and invisible, over the spiritual and the material, all placed in the hands of one *man*. Not one of the kingdoms but *the* absolute Kingdom. "To be king, for that I was born and for that I came into the world" [John 18:37]. "All authority in heaven and on earth is mine" [Matt. 28:18]. "One day all enemies will be subdued and every knee shall bow before me!" [Rom. 14:11]. That is the Sovereignty of the Messiah which the prophet once foretold, which the Nazarene claimed, which he first demonstrated with miracles, which was described by the apostles, and which the church of Christ confesses, on their authority, to be undivided but nonetheless delegated — or rather, taken over to be given back again. For perfect harmony will break through only when Sovereignty goes back from the Messiah to God himself, who will then be *ta panta en pasi,* that is, "all in all."

But here is the glorious principle of Freedom! This perfect Sovereignty of the *sinless* Messiah at the same time directly denies and challenges all absolute Sovereignty among *sinful* men on earth, and does so by dividing life into *separate spheres,* each with its own sovereignty.

Our human life, with its visible material foreground and invisible spiritual background, is neither simple nor uniform but constitutes an infinitely complex organism. It is so structured that the individual exists only in groups, and only in such groups can the whole become manifest. Call the parts of this one great machine "cogwheels," spring-driven on their own axles, or "spheres," each animated with its own spirit. The name or image is unimportant, so long as we recognize that there are in life as many spheres as there are constellations in the sky and that the circumference of each has been drawn on a fixed radius from the center of a unique principle, namely, the apostolic injunction *hekastos en toi idioi tagmati* ["each in its own order": 1 Cor. 15:23]. Just as we speak of a "moral world," a "scientific world," a "business world," the "world of art," so we can more properly speak of a "sphere" of morality, of the family, of social life, each with its own *domain.* And because each comprises its own domain, each has its own Sovereign within its bounds.

There is a domain of nature in which the Sovereign exerts power over matter according to fixed laws. There is also a domain of the personal, of the household, of science, of social and ecclesiastical life, each of which obeys its own laws of life, each subject to its own chief. A realm of thought where only the laws of logic may rule. A realm of conscience where none but the Holy One may give sovereign commands. Finally, a realm of faith where the person alone is sovereign who through that faith consecrates himself in the depths of his being.

The cogwheels of all these spheres engage each other, and precisely through that interaction emerges the rich, multifaceted multiformity of human life. Hence also rises the danger that one sphere in life may encroach on its neighbor like a sticky wheel that shears off one cog after another until the whole operation is disrupted. Hence also the raison d'être for the special sphere of authority that emerged in the State. It must provide for sound mutual interaction among the various spheres, insofar as they are externally manifest, and keep them within just limits. Furthermore, since personal life can be suppressed by the group in which one lives, the state must protect the individual from the tyranny of his own circle. This Sovereign, as Scripture tersely puts it, "gives stability to the land by justice" [Prov. 29:4], for *without* justice it destroys itself and falls. Thus the sovereignty of the State, as the power that protects the individual and defines the mutual relationships among the visible spheres, rises high *above* them by its right to command and compel. But *within* these spheres that does not obtain. There another authority rules, an authority that descends directly from God apart from the State. This authority the State does not *confer* but *acknowledges*. Even in defining laws for the mutual relationships among the spheres, the State may not set its own will as the standard but is *bound* by the choice of a Higher will, as expressed in the nature and purpose of these spheres. The State must see that the wheels operate as intended. Not to suppress life nor to shackle freedom but to make possible the free movement of life in and for every sphere: does not this ideal beckon every nobler head of state?

Thus, two credos stand squarely against each other. He who lives from, and consistently within, the orbit of Revelation confesses that all Sovereignty rests in God and can therefore proceed only from Him; that the Sovereignty of God has been conferred absolute and undivided upon the man-Messiah; and that therefore human freedom is safe under this Son of Man anointed as Sovereign because, along with the State, every other sphere of life recognizes an authority derived from Him — that is, possesses sovereignty in its own sphere.

On the other hand, those who deny special revelation insist on an absolute separation between the question of sovereignty and the question of faith. Consequently they assert that there is no other authority conceivable than that of the State; they strive to embody this high sovereignty ever more perfectly in the supreme State; and they cannot grant to the other spheres a more generous freedom than that which the State permits them out of its weakness or confers out of its supremacy.

I call these *credos* about Sovereignty — life convictions, not theories. For the gulf that separates them lies not in a different arrangement of ideas but in a *recognition* or *denial* of the *facts of life*. For us who live from Revelation, that Messiah lives, that Christ reigns, and as Sovereign He is seated on the throne of God's power more certainly than you are sitting here in this chancel. Conversely, those who do not *confess* this must *contest* it as a harmful self-delusion that stands in the way of national development, a worthless dogma, a senseless fantasy! These stand, therefore, as diametrically opposing confessions. Again and again, with cowardly half-heartedness they have been shoved behind a long row of hybrid systems, mixed from more of this and less of that or from equal portions of each. But at critical moments the principial *credos* which give even these ghosts some color break through this charade with a vengeance. Then with visors raised they once again challenge each other to combat as the only two mighty antagonists that plumb life down to the root. And so they are worth people risking their own lives for and disturbing the lives of others.

Sphere sovereignty defending itself against State sovereignty: that is the course of world history even back before the Messiah's sovereignty was proclaimed. For though the Royal Child of Bethlehem protects sphere sovereignty with His shield, He did not create it. It existed of old. It lay in the order of creation, in the structure of human life; it was there before State sovereignty arose. But once arisen State sovereignty recognized Sphere sovereignty as a permanent adversary, and within the spheres the power of resistance was weakened by the transgression of their own laws of being, that is, by sin. Thus the ancient history of all people replays a shameful spectacle. Despite stubborn, sometimes heroic struggle, the freedom of the spheres dies out and State power — become Caesarism — triumphs. Socrates drinking the poison cup, Brutus plunging the dagger into Caesar's heart, the Galileans whose blood Pilate mingled with their sacrifices — these are all the wild, heroic paroxysms of a free organic life that finally collapses under the iron hand of Caesarism. As antiquity drew toward its close there was no freedom left, no nations, no spheres. There was only one sphere, one world empire under one sovereign State. Only by intoxicating itself in an emasculating luxury could a humanity so sunk in self-contempt drive that pain from its heart.

Then Jesus the Nazarene, through the supernatural power of *faith,* once again created a free sphere with a free sovereignty within the iron ring of uniformity. With God in his heart, one with God, himself God, He withstood Caesar, broke down the iron gates, and posited the sovereignty of faith as the deepest piling upon which all sphere sovereignty rests. Neither Pharisee nor disciple understood that His cry "It is finished!" entailed, beyond the salvation of the elect, also a *soteria tou kosmou* [salvation of the cosmos], a liberation of the world, a world of freedoms. But Jesus discerned it. Hence the sign *Basileus* [King] upon His cross. He appeared as Sovereign. As its Sovereign He contended with the usurping "Prince of this World" for authority over that world. And barely had His followers formed their own circle than they also collided with State sovereignty. They succumbed. Their blood flowed. But Jesus' sovereign principle of faith was not thereby washed away. *Deus* Christus or *Divus* Augustus became the shibboleths that would determine the fate of the world. Christ won and Caesar was toppled. The liberated nations each emerged with its own king, and within those dominions separate spheres, and within those spheres distinct liberties. Then began that glorious life, crowned with nobility, exhibiting in the ever richer organism of guilds and orders and free communities all the energy and glory that sphere sovereignty implies.

This was more pronounced in our dear fatherland than elsewhere. It seemed that the country could defend sphere sovereignty more forcefully against State sovereignty when divided into separate polder districts than when all one. So Philip discovered when the singers of the Souterlied and the leaders of the hedge-preachers clashed, despite themselves, with State sovereignty.[4] So also the Stuarts and Bourbons learned in the following century when the immortal sea hero whose mausoleum we see before us, our glorious De Ruyter, withstood the rising royalism of the Charleses and Louises on every sea and broke it on every shore.[5] "Next to God I am captain of my ship!" was the dauntless passion for liberty that inspired our whole phalanx of sea heroes along with him. It carried in seamen's terms on all the waters of monarchical pretension something of what in legal language is called "sphere sovereignty."

Alas! before a century had passed even our country fell away. Our Holland too sank away in sin, and with our republic fell the last bulwark of freedom on Europe's shore. And so the tide of royalism rose. It began to tread upon the countries, trample the peoples, torment the nations. Finally, in the most inflammable of the nations the fire of vengeance was kindled. Passions flared, the principle of Revolution took off the head of the crowned sovereign to crown the people sovereign. A terrifying event,

4. King Philip II of Spain (1527-98) tried to suppress the Dutch Reformation and the movement for political independence associated with it. Hedge-preachers carried on the Protestant cause against this repression by holding meetings in fields and barns. There and elsewhere the Protestants sang the *Souter Liedekens*, a Flemish psalter composed by Jacobus Clemens in 1556.

5. The Bourbons and Stuarts were the royal houses of France and England, respectively, in the seventeenth century. Louis XIV of France (1643-1715) was the epitome of royal absolutism and mounted perennial invasions of the Rhineland, to which the House of Orange led the opposition. Charles II (1630-85) restored the monarchy to England after the protectorate of the Puritan Oliver Cromwell and prosecuted naval warfare against the Netherlands. In the second (1665-67) and third (1672-74) phases of the conflict Michiel Adriaanszoon de Ruyter (1607-76), admiral of the Dutch fleet, achieved famous and brilliant victories. De Ruyter's tomb is in the Nieuwe Kerk where Kuyper was speaking.

born from a thirst for freedom, born also from a hatred for the Messiah, that only put freedom in tighter straits! For the sovereign people of that one election day found itself, courtesy of the ballot box, under an absolute and unwilling guardianship the next. First it was the Jacobins, then the Napoleonic Caesar, a little later the nice-looking State ideal that was rushed into place in France and more leisurely advocated as just and "enlightened" in Germany.

So liberty once again lay in disgrace, and for a second time a single sovereignty threatened to swallow up all other sovereignties. What *then* saved the day? Not the restoration spirit of the Congress of Vienna. Not Haller's or De Maistre's idolization of princes. Not the historical school whose physiological views smothered any higher principle. Not even the pseudo-constitutional system with its *roi fainéant* and tyrannizing factions.[6] It was truly the Messiah, the Sovereign seated at God's right hand, Who poured out a spirit of grace, of prayer, of faith upon the peoples through the purest revival that ever awakened them.[7] That created again a separate sphere where another sovereign than an earthly power was worshiped. A circle which reckoned with the soul, which practiced mercy, which inspired the states "not as citizens but as confessors of the Gospel." Not by political manipulation but by moral power there was born from within the soul a hope for the nations. Not to rule but to serve there arose also in our fatherland a people who believed in the Messiah, a "Christian group," in spite of itself a national party. Not a faction, i.e., a contrived group; not a fraction, i.e., a splinter group; but a *people's* party, i.e., a part of the people, a segment of what constitutes the whole, so that, if possible, from this temporary division the whole, the majestic unity of the people might again be inspired by a higher ideal.

. . . [In a paragraph deleted here, Kuyper briefly reviews the previous thirty years of the Dutch Antirevolutionary movement.]

Thus we contended for the indivisibility of sovereign authority. For the States-General standing *beside* and *with,* not *in* or *under* the government. Thus we did not maintain a deterrence theory but God's sovereign

6. Karl Ludwig von Haller (1768-1854) was a Swiss-German statesman and political theorist who championed traditional monarchy and hierarchy in the Restoration period. Joseph de Maistre (1753-1821) was an arch-Catholic and royal absolutist during and after the French Revolution. The "historical school" was founded by Friedrich Karl von Savigny (1779-1861), professor of law at the University of Berlin, who held that the law is the product of a people's particular spirit *(volkgeist)* historically developed. By "pseudo-constitutional system" Kuyper means the "July" or "bourgeois" (he calls it the "lazy") monarchy of Louis Philippe in France, 1830-48, which was marked by intense factional discord in the Chamber of Deputies.

7. Kuyper means the *Réveil* of 1815-60.

vengeance on whoever dared to shed man's blood. Thus we protested against the compulsory inoculation of our children. Thus we prophesied the emancipation of the church. And thus, finally, we focused all our fight on the school struggle.[8] For there the sovereignty of conscience, and of the family, and of pedagogy, and of the spiritual circle were all equally threatened. And because a principle, sowing seed according to its kind, *cannot* rest until *all* its seeds are sprouting in a scientifically ordered coherence; and because a people, arising for such a principle, *may* not desist until it has raised the fruit of knowledge from the root of faith; and because so concentrated a knowledge can be cultivated only in a school with university aspirations — so it *had* to come. By the iron necessity of an inner life-impulse what we see today had to come: the launching of this vessel, small and unseaworthy to be sure, but chartered under the sovereignty of King Jesus and expecting to show in every port of knowledge the flag of "sphere sovereignty"!

II. Its Scholarly Aspirations

You may also expect "sphere sovereignty" to be the signature of our *academic work*. This too I take up from the practical side: it leads not to abstract, dry scholasticism but to firmness of principle, depth of insight, clarity of judgment — in a word, to sanctified intellectual power, a power to resist whatever superior force would limit freedom in and of our human life.

Do not forget that every State power tends to look upon all liberty with a suspicious eye. The various spheres of life cannot do without the State sphere, for just as one space can limit another, so one sphere can limit another unless the State fixes their boundaries by law. The State is the *sphere of spheres,* which encircles the whole extent of human life. Therefore, in a nobler sense, not for itself but on behalf of the other spheres, it seeks to strengthen its arm and with that outstretched arm to resist, to try to break, any sphere's drive to expand and dominate a wider domain. But now again, look at the signs of the times. Hasn't Mommsen himself, in the bold image that he painted of Caesar, returned to the imperialistic line drawn by that Caesar as the standard for political wisdom in our day? Does the chancellor of Germany strike you as a

8. Kuyper is here reciting some of the chief points of the Antirevolutionary Party's platform: maintenance of capital punishment, *voluntary* vaccination against disease, separation of church and state, and equitable funding of religious as well as "public" school systems.

liberty-lover? How about the man so profoundly humiliated by that chancellor at Sedan? "Freedom-loving" or "tyrannical": what is your impression of the people's tribune that has replaced the man of Sedan in popular influence at the French capital?[9]

It *had to be* so, as the discipline and the cure for the cowardly and emasculated nation whose atrophy of moral resilience made it possible for their freedoms to knuckle under. The State is now again the supreme power on earth. There is no earthly power above the State that can compel the Sovereign to do justice. So whether from a base lust for power or from a noble solicitude for the *common good,* every State by its very nature will draw the iron band as tightly around the staves as the crimp of those staves allows. Ultimately, therefore, it depends on the life-spheres themselves whether they will flourish in freedom or groan under State coercion. With moral tensile strength they *cannot* be pushed in, they will not *permit* themselves to be cramped. But servility, once it's become shackled, has lost even the right to complain.

Right here is the sore spot. *Sin* threatens freedom within each sphere just as strongly as *State-power* does at the boundary. To tighten the band around the staves, one lights a fire inside the barrel; that fire within causes them to shrink much more than hammer blows without. So it is with our liberties. At the heart of every sphere there smolders and smokes the flame of passion, whence the sparks of sin fly upward. That unholy blaze undermines the moral vitality of life, weakens resiliency, and finally bends the strongest stave. In any successful attack on freedom the state can only be an accomplice. The *chief* culprit is the citizen who forgets his duty, wastes away his strength in the sleep of sin and sensual pleasure, and so loses the power of his own initiative. Among a nation healthy at its core, whose people still live soundly in the various spheres, no state can subvert the principles of justice without meeting the people's strong moral resistance under God. Only when discipline weakened and affluence slipped in and sin became brazen could theory bend what was enfeebled and Napoleon kick in the decrepit. And if God had not time and again poured vigor into those lifeless spheres, sometimes under pressure —

9. Theodor Mommsen (1817-1903) was the preeminent German historian of Roman antiquity. His work, including *Römische Geschichte* (3 vols., 1854-56) and *Römische Staatsrecht* (3 vols., 1876-88), endorsed the early emperors despite their ruthlessness and his own liberal sympathies, perhaps because of Mommsen's stronger pan-German commitments. Otto von Bismarck had been chancellor of Prussia, then Germany, since 1862 and had woven the diplomatic-military web that trapped Napoleon III of France at the battle of Sedan (2 September 1870). This defeat ended the French Second Empire and prompted republican proposals, a radical version of which was put forward by the popular and charismatic Leon Gambetta (1838-82).

Kuyper expanded on his assertion of the importance of higher education some twenty years later, just before his own election as prime minister confirmed, perhaps, the thesis he laid out.

[In light of the conflict that inevitably arises in the scholarly realm,] believers may not withdraw to the precincts of the church, rest content with their own faith, and leave the construction of the temple of learning to unbelievers as if it is no concern of their own. They may not because scholarly research is not a matter of human pride but a God-given duty. The honor of God demands that the human mind penetrate the entire system of creation to discover His greatness and wisdom there and to translate these into human thought through human words. Since the knowledge of the unbelieving world cannot help but obscure God's greatness and wisdom, it is the Christian thinkers' calling to buckle down to this enormous task which they alone can accomplish, even if it did not yield benefit for their own life.

But the latter is not at all the case. On the contrary, thinking Christians can arrive at a conception of things that harmonizes with their faith, that supports and strengthens it instead of undermining it, only when Christian learning inducts us into a well-considered, clearly articulated world- and life-view. A confessing Christian who lives amid this world cannot be satisfied with a profession of faith but, like anyone, needs a firm understanding of the world in which he lives. Without the guidance of Christian scholarship, he cannot help but absorb the conclusions of unbelievers. Doing so, he will live with a world- and life-view that does not fit but comes into conflict with his confession on any number of points. His thinking will divide into two, the content of his confession and the frame of

changing atoms into dynamos, as the latest philosophy has it[10] — the last distinct sphere would long since have broken down and nothing would remain of our freedom but the "sic transit" on its grave.

10. Kuyper is probably invoking the German Idealist *Naturphilosophie* in which atoms were viewed first of all as centers of force rather than as material entities. Matter then became a state of dynamic equilibrium between opposing forces. My thanks to Arie Leegwater for this explanation.

his scholarly operations lying unreconciled next to each other. That shatters his unity of consciousness and so also his power. It has the inevitable result as well that his faith gradually makes room for his scientific views, and that he unnoticeably drifts over to the unbelieving point of view. In the nineteenth century this took the form of a mixed sensibility, like the Ethical school in this country, which tried to unite a few parts faith with a few parts unbelieving philosophy into one whole. It nonetheless remained a hybrid.

By contrast, it is our duty to take hold of scholarship as an instrument for propagating our convictions. We can often see how a Christian group that does not feel this obligation isolates itself from the general public, locks itself up in a corner, and maintains itself among the less educated parts of the population but loses all influence over the course of events and public opinion. Naturally, the learned give this habit their stamp of approval. The universities mark out the direction that the thinking of people of influence will take. From the universities it spreads out among politicians, lawyers, doctors, teachers, and writers, and from these into the press, the primary and secondary schools, the civil service. If university life and its broad influence remain exclusively in the hands of unbelievers, public opinion — also on moral and religious matters — will one day go wholesale in this direction and work to the great detriment of our Christian circles. There is only one way to parry this, and that is for Christian thinkers to found a university that will unfold another world of seeing and thinking; to transmit this among those who pursue higher education; and so to raise a circle of educated, influential people who can turn the public way of thinking. . . .

De Gemeene Gratie in Wetenschap en Kunst, pp. 36-37

Among the means that God has granted nobler peoples to defend their liberties, scholarship often stands at the forefront. Among the spokesmen of the Holy Spirit the man of Tarsus was the academically trained, and it was from that Pauline treasure chest, not from the mystical John nor from the practical James, that Luther drew the freedom of the Reformation. I well know that learning can betray liberty and has done so more than once, but this was despite and not by virtue of its sacred mission. In its authentic form God sent it to us as an angel of light.

For what robs the lunatic, the idiot, the drunkard of their human respect? Is it not precisely the absence of *clear consciousness?* To come to clearer knowledge not only of ourselves but also of that outside ourselves — is not that *the* science? Thinking after God what He has thought before and about and in us? The being- and life-consciousness not of a single person but of humanity through all the ages! To be able to think of something that is, and thus to be able to put together in our reason what is mirrored in our consciousness, is an honor bestowed by God on our human existence. To possess wisdom is a divine trait in our being. Indeed, the power of wisdom and knowledge extends so far that the course of things usually runs not according to reality but according to how people conceive of reality. Who would say that ideas are unimportant? Ideas shape public opinion; that opinion, the sense of justice; and that sense, the thawing or congealing of spiritual life. Therefore, whoever expects his principles to exert influence cannot simply float about in feelings, does not advance by fancy, and even with his [religious/theological] confession comes only halfway. He gains a hold on the public only if he has also attained power in the world of thought, if he can transfer his *inner* urge, the "Deus in nobis," from what he *senses* to what he *knows*.

Provided that — and I hold to this strongly — provided that scholarship remains "Sovereign in its own sphere" and does not degenerate under the guardianship of Church or State. Scholarship creates its *own* life sphere in which truth is sovereign. Under no circumstances may violation of its life-law be tolerated. That would not only dishonor scholarship but be sin before God. Our consciousness is like a mirror in us, reflecting images from three worlds: from the world *around* us, from the world of *our own being*, and from the invisible world of *the spirits*. Reason thus demands (1) that we let each of these worlds reflect those images according to its own nature, or *aisthesis* [sense perception]; (2) that we receive those images with a clear eye, or *noesis* [intelligent thought]; and (3) that we make a harmonious summary of what has been perceived, or *gnosis* [knowledge, wisdom]. Not contemplation, therefore, but a reflection in us. Knowledge that makes wise. From life for life. Ending in adoration of the only wise God!

Spinoza grasped the sovereignty of learning in its own sphere, and therefore, measured on a moral scale, our admiration for Spinoza's character is as great as our disapproval of the insipid Erasmus.[11] Both organ

11. Baruch Spinoza, the eminent seventeenth-century Dutch Jewish philosopher, accepted excommunication from his Amsterdam synagogue rather than retract his views. By contrast, in Kuyper's view, the sixteenth-century Dutch humanist Desiderius Erasmus had compromised his convictions rather than side with the Protestant Reformation.

and perception were faulty with Spinoza, so his conclusion had to be false as well. But seeing what he did and as he did, he steadfastly refused to lend himself to a violation of the sovereignty of learning in its own sphere. *That* a truly Reformed person does not censure but places high above the wavering hesitation which has tempted many who knew what Spinoza never knew into an unprincipled compromise. We must therefore resist tooth and nail any imposition upon learning by the church of Christ. At the real risk of suffering at its hands, the church must insist that learning never become a slave but maintain its due sovereignty upon its own ground and live by the grace of God. There is certainly the satanic danger that some among the learned will degenerate into devils of pride and tempt learning to arrogate unto itself things outside its sphere. But a tall steeple cannot be scaled without the constant danger of a great fall. Further, what we just said about the tyranny of the state also applies to the tyranny of learning: it cannot occur unless the church declines spiritually first, so that when it wakes up spiritually again, the church itself will urge the learning that chastised it in God's name back to its rightful place.

Not wholly but nearly the same may be said of the State. Not wholly, because the State — given the power to define its sphere of justice — still remains the master planner for the sphere of learning insofar as this assumes visible form in the schools. But before it crosses the boundary into the domain of scholarship, the State respectfully "takes the shoes off from its feet" and lays aside a sovereignty which would not be seemly on that terrain. To make learning the servant of the State as the Ghibellines did over against the Guelphs, as the French bureaucracy did to control its own people, as German reaction sought to do in the shame of Göttingen[12] — this is a self-demeaning prostitution that forfeits every valid claim to moral influence. But even if the State is inspired by a nobler aim, as is our own regime; even if, as in our country, learning is too proud to stoop; still, learning in our realm will flourish and attain honor if university life grows up again from its own root and into its own life and so outgrows the guardianship of the State. So once stood the schools of the prophets in Israel and the school of wisdom in Jerusalem: free in the

12. The Ghibellines and Guelphs were, respectively, pro-imperial and pro-papal factions in southern Germany and northern Italy during the thirteenth and fourteenth centuries. Their long and vicious rivalry compromised the integrity of many institutions, including the educational, under their successive eras in power. The French government had asserted control over the universities both before, during, and after the Revolution. The "shame of Göttingen" was the 1837 dismissal of seven professors from the university there over their protest against the king of Hanover's abrogation of the constitution.

midst of the people. So stood the schools of ancient philosophy in Greece and of their imitators in Rome. So, free, the schools of the first Christian scholars once appeared, as did the ancient universities of Bologna and Paris. Not as vessels within the structure of State into which knowledge was to be poured, but knowledge that had entered into life and there created its own form. In that free form the university could work in the liberation of the Reformation. Only late in the last century was this free band conjured into being a "branch of the civil service" as the new-model university let itself be attached as an organ of the State.

This came not by the arbitary work of one person but from the press of events and the enervation of the people. It would border on the absurd to demand that the State now suddenly relinquish its hold on the university world. At present the public shows too little desire for knowledge, the wealthy too little generosity, and the alumni too little energy to hazard the attempt. For the time being the State *must* continue its support, provided — we insist — that it works only for the liberation that would have scholarship again seize "sovereignty in its own sphere."

Is it foolish then that our School should take a first, timid step in this better direction? At the state-university the scale of equity is tilted by so many weights. It cannot be said often enough: money creates power *for* the one who gives *over* the one who receives. Hence, art (except for music) can never permanently elevate popular liberty, for it needs gold. Who can gauge the influence State funds have wrought upon the destiny of the nation and the course of scholarship by the single appointment of a Thorbecke, a Scholten, an Opzoomer?[13] Where is the spiritual criterion to guide the State in making so influential a choice for the higher, most decisive disciplines? Besides, when Jews and Roman Catholics are compelled to contribute to the support of a theological faculty that in fact is and must remain Protestant, is not the sense of justice offended? So when the law of the land recognizes our right to have our own institution, and the Sovereign of the land — as we have just heard — takes our free, unencumbered institution under the protection of justice, then does not a university supported by the people themselves offer a beautiful prophecy for learning and for national life?

Here is a group belittled as a "night school" not even thirty years

13. Johan Rudolph Thorbecke (1798-1872), as professor of law at the University of Leiden, published the work that inspired the new Dutch Constitution of 1848; a political liberal, he served three terms as prime minister. Johannes Henricus Scholten (1811-85) was Kuyper's most influential professor at Leiden and the father of theological modernism in the Netherlands. Cornelis Willem Opzoomer (1821-92) was professor of philosophy at the University of Utrecht and the flagbearer of liberal humanism in nineteenth-century Dutch letters, culture, and religion.

Kuyper also considered the proposal that a few chairs be reserved for Christian instructors at secular universities. He acknowledged that this would give a port of refuge to students whose faith was floundering.

But it would do nothing to direct scholarship, which would remain on an incorrect basis. Then everyone would get the impression that real science proceeds from the unbelieving world, that there it receives its power and urge, that there its temple is built, and that the Christian religion has no higher calling than to exercise some criticism here and there and, if possible, to offer a little correction. The tree would still be bad, still grow from a cankered root, and all we would do on our side is cut off some useless shoots, weed out some nettles, and here and there drape the branches with some plucked flowers that are destined to wither away before people notice them.

No, what we need is . . . a plant of scholarship growing from a Christian root. To satisfy ourselves with the role of sauntering around another garden, clipper in hand, is to throw away the dignity of the Christian religion.

De Gemeene Gratie in Wetenschap en Kunst, p. 41

ago now pouring its energies toward an academic goal! The least respected of the "non-thinking" part of the nation come running from the plow and the feed-trough to collect money to build a university.[14] Elsewhere people expect progress from *above;* learning is to be brought *to* the people. Is not there something better in a group that will sacrifice its pleasures so that learning may bloom? Is this not a practical solution to the problem of connecting learning to life? Must not scholars who are supported by the people's money grow closer to the people and more averse to all that is dry and abstract? Besides, is not *giving* itself a power and the ability to part with money a moral asset? Who then can assess the moral capital that will accrue to our people precisely through this costly institution?

14. Kuyper is here quoting epithets his movement received from its cultured despisers. The institutional roots of the Free University go back to a night school Kuyper and his associates ran for people of their own persuasion who were unable to pursue the ordinary university route. The "non-thinking part of the nation" was a particularly egregious description of stout Calvinists by (in Kuyper's retort) "smug liberals."

People complain about a lack of character, but what will better form character than such free initiative on the part of vigilant citizens? If elsewhere the wheels of the university run oh so smoothly by the compulsion of tax assessors and the allowance of paymasters, we shall not be envious. For with us precisely "the struggle for life" generates the power of glorious devotion. In the money entrusted to us lies something more, something higher than the intrinsic worth of the metal. In the gold that flows into our coffers there is prayer, there is love, and the sweat of the brow.

III. As a Reformed Principle

We have seen how "sphere sovereignty" is the stimulus that gave birth to our institution, and we have frankly stated that for us "sphere sovereignty" is also the royal stipulation for all scholarship that would flourish. It remains for me to plead a disputed case, that we be granted "sphere sovereignty" as our *principle* — a *Reformed* principle. . . . [Kuyper argues for the necessity of differentiating among traditions within Christianity and of assigning each the label duly accorded them in and by history. Within those parameters he uses "Reformed."] We do not thereby reject our Lutheran brethren. To look down on other Christians would be to our blame. We simply ask that we not be compelled to exchange something that we consider finer for something less excellent, and that we be permitted to rebuild on the ruins a Reformed temple in pure Reformed style.

For such I am contending in this discourse. And so, according to the demands of Scripture and the precedent of Calvin, I have placed in the foreground the *Sovereignty of God,* for it alone stimulates life down to the root and overcomes all fear of man, even of Satan himself. Should anyone ask whether "sphere sovereignty" is really derived from the heart of Scripture and the treasury of Reformed life, I would entreat him first of all to plumb the depths of the organic *faith principle* in Scripture, further to note Hebron's tribal law for David's coronation, to notice Elijah's resistance to Ahab's tyranny, the disciples' refusal to yield to Jerusalem's police regulations, and, not least, to listen to their Lord's maxim concerning what is God's and what is Caesar's. As to Reformed life, don't you know about Calvin's "lesser magistrates"?[15] Isn't sphere sovereignty the basis of the entire presbyterian church order? Did not almost all

15. Kuyper treats these at some length in *Calvinism: Source and Stronghold of Our Constitutional Liberties* (see above).

Reformed nations incline toward a confederative form of government? Are not civil liberties most luxuriantly developed in Reformed lands? Can it be denied that domestic peace, decentralization, and municipal autonomy are best guaranteed even today among the heirs of Calvin?

Thus it is entirely within the Reformed spirit that we now ask for the sovereignty of our principle in our own scholarly sphere. We may not make a pact of neutrality with learning that proceeds from another principle, or sit at the same university table. I do not deny that among non-Christian authorities there exists a fear of God and of his justice, a fear that Calvin honored even among pagan tyrants; yet such a pious trait is nothing more than a foundation with at most a partial wall but without a roof or windows. Or if you prefer a more exact image, of what use is a tower that lacks the spire and therefore the carillon, clock, and weathervane — in short, everything for which it is built! More acceptable is the proposal that advocates a large State academy for which the authorities would provide nothing but lecture halls with podiums as well as museums and laboratories, and in which every scholar had the right to appear and every group the right to place its own scholars. An academic Central Station, where all lines would converge but each with its own direction and administration. But even here the royal right of each principle to "sovereignty in its own sphere" would be violated on both sides. Does not history teach that scholarship takes a different shape among every circle with its own principle? There was once a Greek, an Arabic, a Scholastic learning which, though not speaking to us, was duly developed in its own place by giant intellects in whose shadow none of us could stand. Likewise, after the Middle Ages, learning showed a readily distinguishable face at Catholic and non-Catholic universities. The succession of philosophers who appeared with and after Kant established schools of thought that were mutually exclusive, in accordance with their stress on the subjective or objective. How would you wed a monist to an atomist? So compelling and dominating is the strength of a principle that Hegel's intellectual power, everyone concedes, could bring forth an entire distinctive system — for theology, jurisprudence, physics, in every domain — so that to learn criminal law in Hegel's school and civil law in Herbart's will utterly confuse one's sense of justice.[16]

If it is impossible to weave a single garment because of a difference in *thought*-principle, how glaring the necessity of sphere sovereignty in the case of *life*-principle! As Fichte's example shows, so long as only

16. Johann Friedrich Herbart (1776-1841) was a German philosopher and educational theorist who postulated a Realist theory of mind and ethics. He negatively reviewed Hegel's (Idealist) *Philosophy of Right* (i.e., law) upon its publication in 1821.

Toward the end of his career, Kuyper reflected on the wholesale emergence of separate Christian organizations in the Netherlands, of which the Free University had been an early signal. The mixture of biblical argumentation and pragmatic reflection is typical of his thinking, and his sketch of motives summarizes several decades of Dutch Reformed social history.

This excerpt is from *Pro Rege, of het Koningschap van Christus,* vol. III (Kampen: J. H. Kok, 1912), pp. 184-94, and was translated by John Vriend.

The third instrument [after church and Christian school] that Christ uses to maintain his Kingship over society is the system of Christian societies that those who confess Him have called into being in differentiation from other social organizations. . . . This separation of Christian people into their own organizations is already being pursued in the Netherlands, just as it came about from the Roman Catholic side in other countries as well. Still, the reality does not relieve us of the task of examining on principle the legitimacy or illegitimacy of this separation. We need to know whether we are on the right track in this matter and to what rule we must hold ourselves. . . .

[After a lengthy biblical justification from 1 Corinthians 6:1-16, Kuyper reflects on the social experience that animated and ensued from such organization.]

[Yet] it is still regularly asserted even among us that this [scriptural] rule no longer generally applies. We no longer live in a

thought-principle is involved, one can return to what was originally rejected.[17] But with a *life*-principle, that is impossible. That is rooted in *facts*. Or to put it more strongly, in a *living person*. In a person whose appearance precipitated a crisis in the middle of the world, at the midpoint of world history, also in the center of the world's thought. Ask that living

17. Johan Gottlieb Fichte (1762-1814) was a leading German philosopher and successor of Kant. In the first phase of his career he asserted the precedence of ethics or moral law over religion but later reversed that priority and developed a mystical philosophical theology.

pagan society, it is correctly pointed out, but in a society still based on Christian principles. Furthermore, there are common interests that one can defend and do justice to only in cooperation with other involved parties. We agree with this in the abstract. Indeed, in times past no one thought about the issue of separate organizations: people either did not organize or organized without regard to religious differences. The question is only whether that earlier situation has not gradually changed in a very unfavorable way. It can hardly be denied that the mind of the world has increasingly pushed in all directions to organize on a basis that, unfortunately, can never be ours. Especially in the social question a spirit of anarchism and socialism has progressively established itself, setting a tone that turns these organizations into propaganda organs for unholy revolutionary principles. Granted, alongside these anarchistic and socialistic organizations a number of more neutral ones have also surfaced, but these too are almost universally led by men who let it be clearly known how intensely they oppose the positive confession of our Christian faith. The influence that comes from these organizations is thus almost always destructive to our Christian confession. Their members reason and act on the basis of principles diametrically opposed to our own.

Now if people join such organizations and mix with those who think along very different lines, then what *they* think and believe becomes the starting-point for decisions. By their membership in these organizations people thus support things that, based on their Christian confession, they ought to oppose. . . . The leadership in such bodies is never in Christian hands but invariably and unalterably in our adversaries'. They stubbornly

person, that Christ, or his authoritative interpreters; what do you learn? Does the Rabbi of Nazareth declare that *his* knowledge is wedded to that of earthly sages? Do his apostles tell you that graduate studies at Jerusalem or Athens will naturally and gradually lead to his higher knowledge? No, just the opposite. That Rabbi insists that *his* treasure of wisdom has been hidden from the wise and learned and revealed to babes. And the academically trained Paul draws a gulf so wide, so deep, so impassable between his earlier, acquired knowledge and the life-principle now implanted that time and again he contrasts the *foolish* thought of the one with the *wise* life of the other.

promote their ideas, aims, and schemes, and those of us who embark on their vessels will inevitably end up where we never should. There our principle is rendered inoperative, loses its vigor, and is pushed into a corner. In some confederative setup a certain degree of cooperation may be conceivable to advance some common interests, but mingling with leaders of a different mindset in the same organization always results in a bitterly disappointing fiasco for Christian principle, yielding victory for them and defeat for us.

If one simply ignores these realities and joins such an organization anyway, the additional danger arises that "bad company corrupts good character" [1 Cor. 15:33]. In the case of the organizations we have in mind here, material interests invariably are primary. The purpose is to gain more power against employers and higher wages for one's labor. Now by itself there is nothing wrong in asserting one's own rights and attempting to improve one's material position. That is life's law of self-preservation which cannot be ignored in any sphere. But precisely for that reason there is a strong temptation in such organizations, also for Christians, to let the end justify the means, to give priority to material interests over spiritual ones, to drift along with others on a current which can and may never be ours. . . . [In such unions] one cannot defend himself spiritually and, before knowing it, absorbs views and ideas that cannot stand the test of the Christian confession. People then yield without wanting to yield. They go along without considering where it will end. . . .

This threat has been felt so deeply among Christian groups in every area of life that distinct Christian societies or organizations

Shall *we* then pretend to grow from the selfsame root that which, according to the express pronouncement of Jesus' divine self-consciousness, is rooted entirely differently? We shall *not* risk it, ladies and gentlemen! Rather, considering that something begins from principle [*met een beginsel iets begint*] and that a distinct entity takes rise from a distinct principle, we shall maintain a distinct sovereignty for our own principle and for that of our opponents across the whole sphere of thought. That is to say, as from their principle and by a method appropriate to it they erect a house of knowledge that glitters but does not entice us, so we too from our principle and by its corresponding method will let our own have sprung up almost spontaneously, and in great numbers. As a result we have our own Young Men's Societies, our Girls' and Women's Societies, our Boys' Clubs, our labor unions, our associations of clerks, our Civil Servants' Unions, our choral societies, our music societies, our students' associations. In short, virtually every social domain has given rise to confessional organizations and established separate societies.

These people had first tried to be members in mixed organizations but could not remain in them. Life itself forced separation. People clashed at every point. The conflict asserted itself in almost every discussion and decision. People felt they were too far apart to be able to work together. They almost got a sense of liberation when at last they met on their own ground, no longer had to wage the exhausting struggle against the other-minded, could strengthen each other in upholding their own principle, and could jointly invoke the blessing of the Lord upon their work. The principled separation that should have come from the church but, in large part, could no longer come into its own there sprang up with vigor and with correctly marked boundaries out of the free life of society, first in the area of education, then in the sphere of social organizations. The overall situation in society became healthy again. Christian principle could again make itself heard, could again find application, could again take a considered position over against the principle urged by the mind of the world. . . . The formerly silent could now stand up for their principle and witness to their faith. Life again became delightful. The application of faith in practice was studied on all sides . . . and through practice people again supported each other in their most holy faith.

trunk shoot up whose branches, leaves, and blossoms are nourished with its own sap. Once again we claim to value something as true that our opponents label as self-deception. So be it. It is necessary for us to be regarded as fools since we cannot refrain from saying with the poet of Proverbs that "the godless of our age do not understand wisdom" [Prov. 29:7].[18] Not that he is our inferior in knowledge; he is probably our

18. The text of Kuyper's Staten-Bijbel is markedly different from that of most modern versions: "The righteous take note of the case of the poor, but the godless do not understand/grasp knowledge."

superior. But because he takes to be *no* fact that which for us stands *fast* as fact in Christ. He declares *not* to have found in his soul what the consciousness of our soul has grasped. Faith in God's Word, objectively infallible in Scripture and subjectively offered to us by the Holy Spirit — there is the line of demarcation. Not as if the knowledge of others rests on intellectual certainty and ours only on faith. For all knowledge proceeds from faith of whatever kind. You lean on God, you proceed from your own ego, or you hold fast to your ideal. The person who does not believe does not exist. At the very least, one who had nothing standing immediately firm before him could not find a point for his thinking to even begin. And how could someone whose thinking lacked a starting point ever investigate something *scientifically?*

We propose therefore to build alongside of what others have built without anything in common except the yard outside, the view from the windows, and a press which, like the mail, maintains the exchange of thought. For we certainly acknowledge that a battle of ideas is possible and necessary, again and again, but never over anything but *starting point* and *direction.* Once these are defined, then, provided you draw straight, the design of your line is determined. Your stance to the left or right makes everything look different and deprives any argument raised against you of persuasive power. Any organic thinker rightly scoffs at the atomistic pretension that everyone, growing up, must think through all systems, search through every confession, and then choose the one he considers the best. No one can do this, and no one does. Neither the time nor the mental energy is available. Only some naif, who does not yet understand higher learning, can fancy that he or someone else has accomplished this. Such sampling of all systems merely fosters superficiality, destroys thinking, spoils character, and renders the brain unfit for more solid labor. Believe me, a firm understanding of architecture does not come from nosing about in the alleys behind the houses but from a careful examination of one well-built structure, basement to attic.

Our scholarship will be "free," therefore, not in the sense of "detached from its principle." That would be the freedom of the fish on dry land, of a flower uprooted from the soil, of a Drentse day-laborer taken out of his village and suddenly set down in Fleet Street or the Strand. We bind ourselves in our own house strictly and inexorably to a fixed regimen, convinced that every home runs best under definite rules. For the most generous freedom in the realm of learning is established when the door is open for whomever would leave, when no outsider may enter *your* house to lord it over you, but also when everyone can freely build on the foundation of *his own* principle, in the style of *his own* method, with the cornice being the results of *his own* research.

Finally, if you ask whether we want this separate development not only for theology but for all the disciplines, and if you can scarcely control a smile when someone scoffs at "Christian medicine" and "Christian logic," then listen to our reply to that objection. Do you think that we would confess God's revelation — reformed, after its deformation — as the starting point of our efforts and draw upon this source only as theologians, scorning it as artists, jurists, and students of letters? Can you think of a science worthy of the name whose knowledge is divided up into cubbyholes?

What do people mean by the *medical* faculty? It is not a sick mammal that medical science would help but a person created in the image of God. Judge for yourself, then. Depending upon whether you view that person to be or not to be a moral agent, with a higher destiny for body and soul, bound to God's Word, will you conceal or tell him of his approaching death? Recommend or advise against anesthesia for the woman in labor? Compel vaccination or leave it to free choice? Urge self-control or indulgence for passionate youth? Curse the mother's fertility with Malthus or bless it with Scripture? Counsel the psychologically distressed or drug them? Do you condone cremation? Unconditionally permit vivisection? Would you arrest the syphilis virus in our society at the cost of dishonoring authority and offending human dignity by means of the most detestable of all medical examinations?

What about the *law* school? Do you see the human being as a self-developing product of nature or as a condemned sinner? Is the law a functionally developing organ of nature or a jewel coming down to us from God himself, bound to His Word? [Depending on your answer] will not criminal law have another purpose and international law another guide? When, outside of academe, the Christian conscience finds itself opposing the prevailing political economy, current business practices, and the rapacious nature of social relationships; when, in civil life, all our Christian people urge a return to decentralization by way of "sphere sovereignty"; when, under constitutional law, separate Christian schools have appeared by a three-to-one margin [over against neutral schools][19] — then can you name one chair on the law faculty that would not be struck by this conflict of principles?

I readily grant that if our *natural sciences* strictly limited themselves to weighing and measuring, the wedge of principle would not be at the door. But who would do that? What natural scientist operates without a hypothesis? Does not everyone who practices science as a *man* and not

19. Kuyper is referring to the high rate at which Christian schools were founded in the Netherlands after the mobilization campaign of 1879.

as a *measuring stick* view things through a subjective lens and always fill in the unseen part of the circle according to subjective opinion? Can someone assess the higher value of the book you published, your pamphlet, your collection of songs, who reckons only the cost of the paper and the amount of ink used in the printing? Is the value of the finest piece of embroidery calculated by the cost of the canvas and a few strands of silk? Or if you prefer: if the whole of creation lies before the natural scientist's eyes as one enchanting painting, is the beauty of the work then to be appreciated by the gold frame around it, the yards of canvas under it, the pounds of paint upon it?

What shall I say about the faculty of *letters?* Of course, "learning to read" and the "declension" of words has nothing to do with being for or against the Messiah. But as I go on and open up Hellas's palace of art or enter Rome's world of power, does it not matter whether I recall the spirit of those peoples again to banish the spirit of Christ or to put them in subjection to the spirit of Christ, according to both human and divine estimation? Does not the study of Semitic languages change depending upon whether I regard Israel as *the* people of *absolute* revelation or merely as a people with a genius for piety? Does philosophy remain the same whether it pursues the "ideal being" or joins us in confessing Christ as the ideal "made flesh"? Will world history come to the same conclusion irrespective of identifying the Cross with Socrates' cup of poison or viewing it as the center point of all history? And, to say no more, will the history of our fatherland kindle the same fire in the heart of youth with Fruin or Nuyens as it was unfolded in all its heroic beauty by Groen van Prinsterer of late, lamented memory?[20]

How could it be otherwise? Man in his antithesis as fallen *sinner* or self-developing *natural creature* returns again as the "subject that thinks" or "the object that prompts thought" in every department, in every discipline, and with every investigator. Oh, no single piece of our mental world is to be hermetically sealed off from the rest, and there is not a square inch in the whole domain of our human existence over which Christ, who is Sovereign over *all,* does not cry: "Mine!"

That cry we have heard, and this work, far too great for our own strength, we have taken up only in reply to this call. We have heard

20. Robert J. Fruin (1823-99) was the nineteenth-century Netherlands' leading historian and a devotee of the liberalism behind the 1848 Constitution. He differed sharply and in print with Kuyper's hero Groen van Prinsterer on this point. Willem Jan Frans Nuyens (1823-94), the country's foremost Catholic historian, refuted the work of John R. Motley but favored the 1848 Constitution for its religious liberalization.

Kuyper met criticism from his own followers with humor. Upon being criticized for serving wine at the banquet attending the Free University's inaugural, he replied:

"*Uilenspiegel,* rarely proper, says of banqueting that the Reformed are not the sort to water down their wine. That's true. From the chocolate kettle and the milk and water bottle rises no race of bold Calvinists."

quoted in J. de Bruijn, *Abraham Kuyper: leven en werk in beeld* (Amsterdam: Passage, 1987).

the wails of tragic powerlessness from brethren whose knowledge did not fit their principle, leaving them defenseless despite all their learning because their principle could not contend with a power commensurate with its honor. We have listened to the sighs of our Christian people who, in the shame of their self-abasement, again learned to pray for leaders to command them, for shepherds to tend them, for prophets to inspire them. We realized that the honor of Christ *may* not remain thus trodden under scoffers' feet. As surely as we loved Him with our souls, we *must* build again in his name. And when it seemed of no avail, when we looked upon our meager power, the strength of the opposition, the preposterousness of so bold an undertaking, the fire still kept burning in our bones. There was One mightier than we who urged us and spurred us onward. We could not rest. In spite of ourselves we *had* to go forward. That some of our own brothers advised aginst building at this time and preferred to go on living with Humanism was a painful source of quiet shame. But it only made the inner drive more urgent, since the hesitation of such men seemed an increasing threat to the future of our life-principle.

And so our little School comes upon the scene, blushing with embarrassment at the name *university,* poor in money, most frugally endowed with scholarly might, more lacking than receiving human favor. What will be its course? How long will it live? Oh, the thousand questions that arise in connection with its future cannot crowd your doubting minds more than they have raged in *this* heart! Only by ever focusing on our sacred principle each time the waves crashed over us did our weary head raise itself bravely from the water. If this cause be not of the Mighty One of Jacob, how could it stand? For I do not exaggerate: it is contrary to all that is called great, contrary to a world of scholars, contrary to a whole century, a century of enormous charm, that we institute this School.

So look down as freely as your conscience permits upon our persons, our power, and our intellectual significance. The Calvinistic credo, "To esteem God as *everything* and man as *nothing*," gives you the full right to do so. I would ask only one thing of you: even if you are our fiercest opponent, do not withhold your respect for the *enthusiasm* that inspires us. For was not the confession that we have dusted off once the heart-cry of a downtrodden nation? Has not the Scripture before whose authority we bow comforted the sorrowing in your *own* generation as an infallible testimony of God? Was not the Christ whose name we honor in this institution the Inspirer, the Chosen One, the Adored One of your *own* fathers? Suppose that as already written in the carrel and echoed in the blast furnaces, suppose that in accord with your own credo it's all over with Scripture, and Christianity is a vanquished position. Even then I would ask: is not that Christianity even in your eyes too imposing, too majestic, too sacred a historical phenomenon to collapse and die without honor? Has *noblesse oblige* disappeared? Could we permit a banner that we carried off from Golgotha to fall into enemy hands so long as the most extreme measures had not been tried, so long as one arrow was left unspent, so long as there remained in this inheritance one bodyguard — no matter how small — of those who were crowned by Golgotha?

To that question — and with this I conclude, ladies and gentlemen — to that question a "By God, Never!" has resounded in our soul. Out of that "Never!" this institution has been born. And upon that "Never!," as an oath of allegiance to a higher principle, I ask for an echo — may it be an Amen — from every patriot heart!

Selected Bibliography

General Background

A great deal has been written about Kuyper, during his lifetime and since. The titles below represent but a beginning on this literature, yet a good place to start. The lists at the end are meant to help readers who wish to follow up on a particular selection in the anthology, but they have some general interest as well since their titles overlap little with those in the following paragraphs. I have cited English works whenever possible in keeping with the purposes of the anthology, but readers should be aware that there are shelves of Dutch-language monographs, articles, and collections on all aspects of Kuyper — his thought, his projects, his times, his legacy. The only thing lacking, strangely, is a recent comprehensive biography.

The classic life was written by a Roman Catholic: P. Kasteel, *Abraham Kuyper* (Kampen: Kok, 1938). Worthwhile but older studies from within his own movement are W. J. Aalders, *Dr. A. Kuyper* (Haarlem: F. Bohn, 1921), and H. Colijn (ghostwritten by F. C. Gerretson), *Levensbericht van Dr. A. Kuyper* (Kampen: Kok, 1923). The most insightful single essay came from a left historian, Jan Romein, "Abraham Kuyper, 1837-1920: De klokkenist der kleine luyden," in Jan and Annie Romein, *Erflaters van onze beschaving* (Amsterdam: Querido's, 1971), pp. 747-70. Insightful though somewhat contradictory recent profiles are George Puchinger, *Abraham Kuyper: De jonge Kuyper (1837-1867)* (Franeker: T. Wever, 1987), and Johannes Stellingwerff, *Dr. Abraham Kuyper en de Vrije Universiteit* (Kampen: Kok, 1987). Jan de Bruijn, ed., *Abraham Kuyper: Leven en werk in beeld* (Amsterdam: Passage, 1987), is an engaging photo essay. The only full biography in English, Frank Vandenberg, *Abraham Kuyper* (Grand Rapids: Eerdmans, 1960), is uncritical; Louis Praamsma, *Let Christ Be*

King: Reflections on the Life and Times of Abraham Kuyper (Jordan Station, ON: Paideia, 1985), takes a conservative slant with some useful insights. James D. Bratt, "In the Shadow of Mt. Kuyper: A Survey of the Field," *Calvin Theological Journal* 31/1 (April 1996): 51-66, reviews some of this and other literature.

A brief English-language summary of Kuyper's overall project is James D. Bratt, *Dutch Calvinism in Modern America* (Grand Rapids: Eerdmans, 1984), chapter 2. C. Augustijn, et al., eds., *Abraham Kuyper: zijn volksdeel, zijn invloed* (Delft: Meinema, 1987), is a fine anthology on the several aspects of that project. Peter S. Heslam, *Creating a Christian Worldview: Abraham Kuyper's "Lectures on Calvinism"* (Grand Rapids: Eerdmans, 1998), is the most comprehensive study of his thought. Two volumes edited by Jan de Bruijn, *Een land nog niet in kaart gebracht* (Amsterdam: Passage, 1987), and *Bepaald Gebied* (Baarn: Ten Have, 1989), have illuminating articles on Kuyper's movement and its development through 1940. Dirk Th. Kuiper, *De Voormannen: een sociaal-wetenschappelijke studie over ideologie, konflikt en kerngroepvorming binnen de Gereformeerde wereld in Nederland tussen 1820 en 1930* (Meppel: Boom, 1972), offers a wealth of information and interpretive guidance on Kuyper's precursors and followers, as well as his own career, in both religious and political affairs. Joris van Fijnatten, *God, Nederland en Oranje: Dutch Calvinism and the Search for the Social Centre* (Kampen: Kok, 1993), surveys a broader sweep still.

The best discussion of Kuyper's politics is Dirk Kuiper, *De Voormannen.* Readers restricted to English will need to consult doctoral dissertations: McKendree R. Langley, "Emancipation and Apologetics: The Formation of Abraham Kuyper's Anti-Revolutionary Party in the Netherlands, 1872-1880" (Westminster Theological Seminary, 1995); Steven E. Meyer, "Calvinism and the Rise of the Protestant Political Movement in the Netherlands" (Georgetown University, 1976); and Johan Westra, "Confessional Parties in the Netherlands, 1813-1946" (University of Michigan, 1972). R. Kuiper, *Zelfbeeld en wereldbeeld: antirevolutionairen en het buitenland, 1848-1905* (Kampen: Kok, 1992), shows how Kuyper's group viewed international affairs, while Arend Lijphart, *The Politics of Accommodation: Pluralism and Democracy in the Netherlands* (Berkeley: University of California Press, 1968), studies the long-term consequences of his movement.

On Kuyper's religious context, Michael J. Wintle, *Pillars of Piety: Religion in the Netherlands in the Nineteenth Century, 1813-1901* (Hull, England: Hull University Press, 1987), offers a compact survey; A. J. Rasker, *De Nederlandse Hervormde Kerk vanaf 1795* (Kampen: Kok, 1974), is the definitive account. Wayne A. Kobes's doctoral dissertation, "Sphere Sovereignty and the University: Theological Foundations of Abraham

Kuyper's View of the University and Its Role in Society" (Florida State University, 1993), presents a good survey of Kuyper's theological position. Parts of Kuyper's own summa are available in English as *Principles of Sacred Theology* (Grand Rapids: Eerdmans, 1954). Jan Veenhof, "A History of Theology and Spirituality in the Dutch Reformed Churches (Gereformeerde Kerken), 1892-1992," *Calvin Theological Journal* 28/2 (November 1992): 266-97, is a good English overview of Kuyper's theological trail; James D. Bratt, "Kuyper and Dutch Theological Education," in D. G. Hart and R. Albert Mohler, Jr., eds., *Theological Education in the Evangelical Tradition* (Grand Rapids: Baker, 1996), analyzes the subject in the context of the Free University's development. Closer detail is available in *In rapport met de tijd: 100 jaar theologie aan de Vrije Universiteit* (Kampen: Kok, 1980).

The best overview of Dutch history for these years is E. H. Kossmann, *The Low Countries, 1780-1940* (Oxford and New York: Clarendon Press, 1978). Izaak J. Brugmans, *Paardenkracht en Mensenmacht: Sociaal-economische geschiedenis van Nederland, 1795-1940* ('s Gravenhage: M. Nijhoff, 1961), is the standard social-economic history. T. van Tijn, *Twintig jaren Amsterdam: De maatschappelijke ontwikkeling van de hoofdstad van de jaren '50 der vorige eeuw to 1876* (Amsterdam: Vrije Universiteit, 1965); Jan A. de Jonge, *De industrialisatie in Nederland tussen 1850 en 1914* (Amsterdam: Scheltema & Holkema, 1968); and G. J. Schutte, ed., *Een arbeider is zijn loon waardig: . . . De ontwikkeling van het christelijk-sociale denken en handelen in Nederland, 1891-1914* ('s Gravenhage: Meinema, 1991), depict Kuyper's more immediate context on this score.

Studies of the North Atlantic cultural world that help set the context of Kuyper's thought include such classics as Walter E. Houghton, *The Victorian Frame of Mind, 1830-1870* (New Haven: Yale University Press, 1957); H. Stuart Hughes, *Consciousness and Society: The Reorientation of European Social Thought, 1890-1930* (rev. ed., New York: Vintage Books, 1977); and Gerhard Masur, *Prophets of Yesterday: Studies in European Culture, 1880-1914* (New York: Macmillan, 1961). Relevant recent studies include William R. Everdell, *The First Moderns: Profiles in the Origins of Twentieth-Century Thought* (Chicago: University of Chicago Press, 1997); Stephen Kern, *The Culture of Space and Time: 1880-1918* (Cambridge: Harvard University Press, 1983); T. J. Jackson Lears, *No Place of Grace: Antimodernism and the Transformation of American Culture, 1880-1920* (New York: Pantheon, 1981); James T. Kloppenberg, *Uncertain Victory: Social Democracy and Progressivism in European and American Thought, 1870-1920* (New York: Oxford University Press, 1986); and Carl Schorske, *Fin-de-siècle Vienna: Politics and Culture* (New York: Random House, 1980).

Suggested Readings per Selection

For *Uniformity: The Curse of Modern Life*

Marshall Berman. *All That Is Solid Melts into Air: The Experience of Modernity.* New York: Simon & Schuster, 1982.

T. J. Jackson Lears. *No Place of Grace: Antimodernism and the Transformation of American Culture, 1880-1920.* New York: Pantheon Books, 1981. Chapter 1.

For *Confidentially*

R. D. Henderson. "How Abraham Kuyper Became a Kuyperian." *Christian Scholar's Review* 22/1 (September 1992): 22-35.

Margaret Mare and Alicia C. Percival. *Victorian Best-seller: The World of Charlotte M. Yonge* (London: Harrap, 1948).

George Puchinger. *Abraham Kuyper: De Jonge Kuyper (1837-1867).* Franeker: T. Wever, 1987. Chapters 3, 6, 7.

Johannes Stellingwerff. *Dr. Abraham Kuyper en de Vrije Universiteit.* Kampen: Kok, 1987. Chapter 1.

For *Conservatism and Orthodoxy: False and True Preservation*

C. H. W. van den Berg. "Kerk en Wereld in de Theologie en Wereldbeschouwing van Abraham Kuyper." *In Rapport met de Tijd: 100 jaar theologie aan de Vrije Universiteit.* Kampen: Kok, 1980. 140-66.

Henry Zwaanstra. "Abraham Kuyper's Conception of the Church." *Calvin Theological Journal* 9/2 (November 1974): 149-81.

Dirk Th. Kuiper. *De Voormannen: . . . de Gereformeerde wereld in Nederland tussen 1820 en 1930* (Meppel: Boom, 1972). 67-74, 84-108, 118-29.

For *Modernism: A Fata Morgana in the Christian Domain*

Malcolm Bull. "Who was the first to make a pact with the devil?" *London Review of Books,* 14 May 1992: 22-23.

K. H. Roessingh. *Het Modernisme in Nederland.* Haarlem: F. Bohn, 1922.

Eldred Vanderlaan. *Protestant Modernism in Holland.* London: Oxford University Press, 1924.

For *"It Shall Not Be So Among You"*

W. Bakker, et al., eds. *De Doleantie van 1886 en haar geschiedenis.* Kampen: Kok, 1986.

Gerrit C. Berkouwer. "Dr. Kuyper als Polemist." *Gereformeerd Theologische Tijdschrift* 38/10 (1937): 464-83.

A. J. Rasker. *De Nederlandse Hervormde Kerk vanaf 1795.* Kampen: Kok, 1974. Chapter 13.

For *Perfectionism*

David Bundy. "Keswick and the Experience of Evangelical Piety." In *Modern Christian Revivals.* Eds. Edith L. Blumhofer and Randall Balmer. Urbana and Chicago: University of Illinois Press, 1993. 118-44.

Melvin E. Dieter. *The Holiness Revival of the Nineteenth Century.* Metuchen, N.J.: Scarecrow Press, 1980.

Hans Krabbendam. "Zielenverbrijzelaars en zondelozen: Reacties in de Nederlandse pers op Moody, Sankey en Pearsall Smith, 1874-1878." *Documentatieblad voor de Nederlandse Kerkgeschiedenis na 1800* 34 (May 1991): 39-55.

For *Common Grace*

William Masselink. *General Revelation and Common Grace: A Defense of the Historic Reformed Faith. . . .* Grand Rapids: William B. Eerdmans Publishing Co., 1953.

Simon Jan Ridderbos. *De Theologische Cultuurbeschouwing van Abraham Kuyper.* Kampen: Kok, 1947.

Cornelius Van Til. *Common Grace.* Philadelphia: Presbyterian and Reformed Publishing Company, 1947.

S. U. Zuidema. "Common Grace and Christian Action in Abraham Kuyper." In *Communication and Confrontation.* Assen/Kampen: Van Gorcum/Kok, 1972. 52-105.

For *Maranatha*

Hans Daalder. "The Netherlands: Opposition in a Segmented Society." In *Political Oppositions in Western Democracies.* Ed. Robert A. Dahl. New Haven: Yale University Press, 1966. 188-247.

Dirk Jellema. "Abraham Kuyper's Attack on Liberalism." *Review of Politics* 19/4 (October 1957): 472-85.

James W. Skillen, ed. *The Problem of Poverty.* English tr. of Abraham Kuyper, *Het Sociale Vraagstuk en de Christelijke Religie* (Amsterdam: J. A. Wormser, 1891). Grand Rapids: Baker Book House, 1991.

For *Manual Labor*

Erik Hansen and Peter A. Prosper, Jr. "Religion and the Development of the Dutch Trade Union Movement, 1872-1914." *Social History* 9/18 (1976): 357-83.

A. J. C. Rüter. *De Spoorwegstakingen van 1903: Een Spiegel der Arbeidersbeweging in Nederland.* Leiden: E. J. Brill, 1935.

G. J. Schutte, ed. *Een arbeider is zijn loon waardig: . . . De ontwikkeling van het christelijk-sociale denken en handelen in Nederland, 1891-1914.* 's Gravenhage: Meinema, 1991. Chapters 1, 4, 5, 10.

For *Our Instinctive Life*

Anne Anema, et al. *Leider en leiding in de Anti-Revolutionaire Partij.* Amsterdam: W. ten Have, 1915.

H. Stuart Hughes. *Consciousness and Society: The Reorientation of European Social Thought, 1890-1930.* Rev. ed. New York: Vintage Books, 1977.

Dirk Th. Kuiper. *De Voormannen: . . . de Gereformeerde wereld in Nederland tussen 1820 en 1930.* Meppel: Boom, 1972. 241-50.

For *Calvinism: Source and Stronghold of Our Constitutional Liberties*

James D. Bratt. "Abraham Kuyper, American History, and the Tensions of Neo-Calvinism." In *Sharing the Reformed Tradition: The Dutch–North American Exchange, 1846-1996.* Eds. George Harinck and Hans Krabbendam. Amsterdam: VU Uitgeverij, 1996. 95-114.

Julian H. Franklin, ed. *Constitutionalism and Resistance in the Sixteenth Century: Three Treatises by Hotman, Beza, and Mornay.* New York: Pegasus, 1969.

A. A. van Schelven. "Emendaties op Kuyper's Rede over de Oorsprong en Waarborg onzer Constitutioneele Vrijheden." In his *Uit den strijd der geesten: Historische nasporingen.* Amsterdam: W. ten Have, 1944. 161-91.

Michael Walzer. *The Revolution of the Saints.* Cambridge: Harvard University Press, 1965.

For *The South African Crisis*

T. Dunbar Moodie. *The Rise of Afrikanerdom*. Berkeley: University of California Press, 1975.

Andre Du Toit. "No Chosen People: The Myth of the Calvinist Origins of Afrikaner-Nationalism and Racial Ideology." *American Historical Review* 88/4 (October 1983): 920-52.

Chris A. J. van Koppen. *De Geuzen van de negentiende eeuw: Abraham Kuyper en Zuid-Afrika*. Wormer: Immerc, 1992.

Dirk Th. Kuiper. "Theory and Practice in Dutch Calvinism on the Racial Issue in the Nineteenth Century." *Calvin Theological Journal* 21/1 (April 1986): 51-78.

Thomas Pakenham. *The Boer War*. New York: Random House, 1979.

For *The Blurring of the Boundaries*

Art Berman. *Preface to Modernism*. Urbana and Chicago: University of Illinois Press, 1994. 3-37.

Edward E. Ericson, Jr. "Abraham Kuyper as Cultural Critic." *Calvin Theological Journal* 22/2 (November 1987): 210-17.

J. Vree. "Tegen de evolutie de palingenesie: Abraham Kuyper's rede over de *Verflauwing der Grenzen* (1892)." *Geschiedenis van de wijsbegeerte in Nederland* 6/1-2 (1995): 81-94.

For *Evolution*

Peter Bowler. *The Eclipse of Darwinism: Anti-Darwinian Evolution Theories in the Decades around 1900*. Baltimore: Johns Hopkins University Press, 1983.

Ilse Bulhof. "The Netherlands." In *The Comparative Reception of Darwinism*. Ed. Thomas F. Glick. Austin: University of Texas Press, 1972. 269-306.

David Livingstone. *Darwin's Forgotten Defenders: The Encounter between Evangelical Theology and Evolutionary Thought*. Grand Rapids/Edinburgh: William B. Eerdmans/Scottish Academic Press, 1987.

James R. Moore. *The Post-Darwinian Controversies: A study of the Protestant struggle to come to terms with Darwin in Great Britain and America, 1870-1900*. Cambridge and New York: Cambridge University Press, 1979.

For *Common Grace in Science*

Jacob Klapwijk. "Rationality in the Dutch Neo-Calvinist Tradition." In *Rationality in the Calvinian Tradition*. Ed. Hendrik Hart, et al. Lanham, MD: University Press of America, 1983.

Del Ratzsch. "Abraham Kuyper's Philosophy of Science." *Calvin Theological Journal* 27/2 (November 1992): 277-303.

John C. Vander Stelt. "Abraham Kuyper's Semi-Mystical Conception." *Philosophia Reformata* 38/1 (1973): 43-61.

For *Sphere Sovereignty*

J. D. Dengerink. *Critisch-historisch onderzoek naar de sociologische ontwikkeling van het beginsel der "souvereiniteit in eigen kring" in de 19e en 20e eeuw.* Kampen: Kok, 1948.

Bob Goudzwaard. "Christian Social Thought in the Dutch Neo-Calvinist Tradition." In *Religion, Economics, and Social Thought*. Eds. Walter Block and Irving Hexham. Vancouver: Fraser Institute, 1986. 251-79.

James W. Skillen and Rockne M. McCarthy, eds. *Political Order and the Plural Structure of Society.* Atlanta: Scholars Press, 1991.

Printed in the United States
84029LV00001B/40-42/A

9 780802 843210